AF894082

Borders, Migration and Globalization: An Interdisciplinary Perspective

Anna Rita Calabrò

Borders, Migration and Globalization: An Interdisciplinary Perspective

Routledge
Taylor & Francis Group
LONDON AND NEW YORK

G. Giappichelli Editore

First published 2022
by Routledge
4 Park Square, Milton Park, Abingdon, Oxon OX14 4RN

and by Routledge
605 Third Avenue, New York, NY 10017

Routledge is an imprint of the Taylor & Francis Group, an informa business

British Library Cataloguing-in-Publication Data
A catalogue record for this book is available from the British Library

Library of Congress Cataloging-in-Publication Data
A catalogue record for this book has been requested

ISBN: 978-0367-18237-3 (hbk-Routledge)
ISBN: 978-1003-10651-7 (ebk-Routledge)
ISBN: 978-0367-61774-5 (pbk-Routledge)
ISBN: 978-88-921-0183-8 (hbk-Giappichelli)

Typeset in Simoncini Garamond
by G. Giappichelli Editore, Turin, Italy

The manuscript has been subjected to a peer review process prior to publication.

Contents

List of figures

Introduction

Drawing, crossing, deleting the borders [1]

Anna Rita Calabrò

Nowadays the reality of migrations defines the policies both of host and origin countries, invades the everyday life of all of us, dominates the public language, builds new borders, and destroys others.

In 1909 Georg Simmel stressed how space in itself does not have any concreteness and is only a frame, a border that conforms to its content without creating it:

> *a great empire is not built by a geographical context of a certain number of square miles, but by the psychological forces that keep politically together the inhabitants of these areas from a dominating central point.*[2]

---

[1] In 2015 the issue of migration became one of the five strategic themes of the University of Pavia, and the following program of research, teaching and third mission. It involved 11 departments, and a significant number of professors, researchers and post-docs were persuaded that such complex phenomena as the ones determined by the current migrations need an interdisciplinary perspective to be fully understood and governed. The disciplinary sectors are three: Biomedical Sciences, for a personalised treatment of patients aiming at inclusion; Social Sciences, to project adequate inclusion policies; and Liberal Arts, because culture and memory are a common patrimony. This book is one of the results of this 3-year collective work: we chose a common word – Borders – suggestive and appealing enough in the multiplicity of its possible meanings, to try to describe it by using languages and skills typical of each of us, without worrying too much about defining from the start a logical thread able to link consistently and conclusively the different interventions. On the contrary, we did the opposite: everyone suggested a proposal according their own scientific interest, driven by the urgency to answer some of the questions, and left to the editor of the volume the burden and the honor to try to link the various pieces in a common narration.

The result of such an unusual procedure is this book (for whose editing and the work of coordination and communication between the several authors, I thank Dr Angelo Scotto). Obviously, there are many issues that we have overlooked, and as many are the ones that we could and should have analysed, but I believe that it should be appreciated that we have not been intimidated by the objective impossibility of providing an exhaustive overview of all the important questions related to the current reality of geopolitical and symbolic borders, and to immigration in general, in the first place. Secondly, there is an attempt to mix the cards among the various disciplines a little and offer the reader many questions, rather than some answers. This is quite an original purpose at a time when there is demand for quick answers, miraculous recipes, easy solutions, simplistic interpretations for issues that are not simple at all.

We dedicate this volume to Marina China and M. Antonietta (Ettina) Confalonieri, two colleagues and travel companions who made a fundamental contribution to the Strategic Theme with their studies, their reflections, and their enthusiasm. We miss them so much.

[2] Simmel, G. (1989) *Sociology: inquiries into the costruction of social forms*, Italian edition, Milan: Edizioni di Comunità, 524.

This is why borders are a multifaceted concept that adapts to different disciplinary languages, that includes and covers unlike realities… and for this reason represents a useful gimmick to deal with a theme, migrations, that in turn needs numerous perspectives of analysis to be adequately faced.

Borders can have the concreteness of geographical, political and bureaucratic barriers, or they may be metaphorical barriers: identity, prejudices, culture. Through territories and consciences, they mark a space that includes and excludes at the same time. They may be made of words and stones.

They can be drawn, crossed, and deleted.

1. *Drawing the borders*

This Part welcomes nine contributions that illustrate from different theoretical and disciplinary perspectives the borders that, currently, drawn and drawn again, mark separations and barriers.

The issue is introduced by Maria Antonietta Confalonieri's chapter, The borders of Schengen and their functions, that aims to reconstruct the process of border definition in the European Union, starting from the 1990s, resulting from global pressures and internal political dynamics, on the basis of a dialectic of Europeanisation on the one hand and defence of sovereignty on the other. The observed borders are internal (between member states) and external, with reference both to spatial borders as delimitations of the territory institutionally controlled through security apparatus, and to citizenship borders, mainly concerning social citizenship. The refugee crisis and the growing politicisation of migrations, the contrast between humanitarian and securitarian borders, clearly disclose the contradiction that crosses the entire history of the European Union, marked by centripetal and centrifugal pushes – a contradiction that is now seriously undermining the stability of the EU precisely on the refugee issue.

With Antonio M. Morone's Containment policies, human mobility and phantom borders. The case of Libya, we move to Libya, a strategically relevant country as far as migration trajectories and European policies are concerned. The chapter aims to discuss the concept of phantom borders – borders that emerge and vanish over time – in relation to the building of social and institutional space in Libya. The current fragility of the Libyan state can be explained and analysed in terms of a difficult settlement between different social and regional contexts, in a cyclical succession of imperial, regional, colonial, national and international borders. In the specific case of migration flows from and to Libya, the author highlights how they have been influenced by the relationships with Europe, particularly with Italy, and shows the link between the increase and exacerbation of the measures to control the borders implemented in Libya after Ghaddafi and the increase of illegal migration towards Europe. Finally, it is stressed that the policies for containing the flows implemented by Europe, and mainly by Italy, raise questions on these measures' legitimacy, both substantial and procedural.

Emanuela Dal Zotto addresses sea and land borders in Defining migrants, defining borders. Arrivals in Italy by sea in 2011 between illegality and right to protection, and explains how the changes in the Italian system of reception of asylum seekers from 2011 to the present have been affected by two factors: the ever-changing conceptualisation of the borders that define and grant the right of asylum, and the Italian policies for managing territorial borders. The humanitarian and securitarian dimensions characterise the narration of these events: an ambivalent narration insofar as these dimensions, even if contradictory, appear to be inextricably related. There would be nothing bad if this were not related to the social construction of an emergency frame that distorts the context in which reception and rejection policies are implemented by speciously using this double need (this is what is happening today when the NGO ships are rejected as a measure to contrast migrant trafficking).

With stones and words the walls marking the borders are built.

In the chapter Irrational walls. Lessons from the US–Mexico border, Fiammetta Corradi analyses how not only did the progressive militarisation process of the border between the two countries not increase its effectiveness, but it also produced a series of unexpected and undesired effects, such as an exponential increase in costs, death tolls, and violence. In this sense, the speech Donald Trump made on August 31, 2016, during his presidential campaign, to present his political manifesto aiming at dealing with irregular migration from Mexico, was significant: a wall 'impenetrable, physical, tall, powerful, beautiful'. He ends his speech with the promise of a test to select the 'right people': the ones who deserve to enter. A speech that, in Corradi's analysis, shows all the weakness and fallacy of the pro-wall propaganda.

Another way to draw borders that mark insiders and outsiders is provided by demographic data on migration. However, as shown by Valentina Fusari in Mobility and data. Dataset or data nightmare?, the interaction between national and international policies often generates classifications that are likley to make the analysis of the composition of migrant populations slippery. In addition, there is a strong imbalance in data collections. In host countries, even due to the proliferation of international agencies carrying out population estimates and making their databases available online, we are witnessing a kind of data hypertrophy which is unknown in origin countries, where national statistics offices are not able to provide reliable and up-to-date population data (not to mention the migrants' invisibility in transit countries). Thus, there is the risk of generating misleading and decontextualised interpretations, mainly when words and numbers to describe immigration are often intentionally misleading and untied from reality.

Beside the borders which delimit and define territorial units, there are internal borders within the units themselves: this may occur when the territorial distribution of the groups constituting the population is determined by their socio-economic and cultural differences. A consequence of these internal borders is the ghettoisation of migrant communities, both in the cities and in rural areas where the praxis of the illicit mediation to agricultural work (caporalato) is widespread. In his contribution, Migrants and internal borders. Rural ghettoisation in Southern Italy, Angelo Scotto, taking the province of Foggia as an example, discusses how ghettoisation is not, or not only, a spontaneous phenomenon, but the effect of social and economic policies of local administrations reluctant to fight caporalato in order not to hinder local economic interests, and how the borders of the ghettoes mark a physical and moral space where exploitation is the rule, and caporals are the rulers.

Federica Di Pietro also discusses ghettoes and exploitation, in Migrant workers and the sponsorship system, where she deals particularly with the explotation of migrant workers in the states of the Persian Gulf, where foreigners number 13 million of an overall population of 35 million. Migrants, coming mainly from African and Asian countries, are forced to work as 'slaves', except that they cannot be defined as such because of their willingness to do the requested work. The phenomenon involves millions of migrants – many of whom are women employed in domestic work – who leave their countries hoping to find better economic conditions in receiving states. On the contrary they lose all their rights, and sometimes their documents as well, and are forced to work in demeaning conditions without the possibility of leaving and going back home because of the debts incurred in paying for their journey to the recruitment agencies that control the market.

And furthermore, the borders of prisons. In The centers for identification and expulsion (CIE) and immigration management. Criticalities and possible improvements, Salvatore Tuccari discusses the migrants' living conditions in the CIEs, with a main focus on the preliminary procedure before their restraint in these spaces that are real detention centres. In this way, it is possible to reflect upon the constitutional legitimacy of these regulations with regard to several constitutionally granted rights – focusing mainly on features concerning personal freedom. The Centres for Identification and Expulsion – recently renamed Centres of Permanence for Repatriation – were born with the aim of favoring regular immigration and discouraging irregular migration, but over time they have actually contributed to making it so that immigration is managed by administrations and perceived by the public opinion mainly in its securitarian dimension. So the positive and essential contribution of migration in economic and demographic terms has been gradually overshadowed, and the policies for protecting the migrants' rights weakened. Moreover, the CIEs failed to accomplish their mission to repatriate migrants who receive an expulsion decree and, in spite of the most recent legislative interventions inspired to a new model of reception, the so-called refugee crisis intensified these contradictions.

Therefore, legal borders are as exclusionary and unavoidable as political and physical ones. In this regard, in Criminalization of irregular immigration. Between the domestic courts and the Court of Justice of the European Union, Zuzanna Brocka shows how the legal interventions redefine the boundaries between legality and illegality depending on political contigencies. Her contribution intends to investigate the evanescent borderline between regular and irregular migration delineated by the case law of the European Union Court of Justice concerning the so-called Return Directive (2008/115/EC). Irregular migrants are often recipients of restrictive measures, including the one that most limits personal freedoms: detention. The criminalisation of irregular immigration divides Europeans from non-Europeans; the latter being confined in detention centres. The protection of human rights and the respect for the rule of public order are still the main essence of the current debate on immigration, even in spite of the objective impossibility of keeping any promise of immediate repatriation for irregular migrants.

Finally, the cultural borders, drawn by tradition, ethnocentrism, and reciprocal prejudice. In this regard, the first part of the volume is concluded by Vanna Berlincioni, Cristina Catania, Francesca Acerbi, Arsenio Spinillo, Alessia Arossa, Nehir Edibe Kurtas, Edoardo Errichiello, and Orsetta Zuffardi, who examine immigrant couples who, due to consanguinity, have an increased risk of recessive genetic diseases in their offspring, in Boundaries and precision medicine in consaguineous migrant couples. Genetic counseling after the identification of fetal pathologies. In order to provide these couples with adequate counselling, it is essential to remove the double obstacle represented by the reciprocal cultural conditioning: on the one hand these young couples are frequently tightly bound to their cultural traditions, while, on the other hand, the people in a position of power, in the specific case the clinician, may find it difficult to find the right way to act in such delicate and personal situations. In many cases, foetal abnormalities, possibly serious, may already be indentified in the prenatal phase: genetic counselling for these couples is particularly complex because of reduced communication capacity and differing cultural approaches that can place the woman in a condition of limited decision-making autonomy. The grief caused by an objectively traumatic condition is exacerbated by separation from the family of origin and being in a new environment. It is therefore necessary to develop effective intervention protocols for counselling and prevention, taking into consideration every possible cultural, individual and relationship issue influencing their experiences by means of ethno-psychological interviews.

2. *Crossing the borders*

Borders may therefore be geographical, political, or cultural... But how is it possible to cross the borders, and what does this experience cause at the subjective level? Who crosses them? What happens when crossing or trying to cross a border? And after crossing the border, what if you want to go back?

The second Part, composed of nine contributions, tries to answer these questions.

It is known that, in Europe, the closure of regular migration channels (in spite of the need for migration for the labour market and to increase birthrates) has exponentially fostered human trafficking by criminal organisations. This blurs the difference between economic and forced migrants, since both end up using the same routes to cross borders. Luisa Frigeni, in The offense of facilitating illegal immigration. Current questions about the constraints of the Italian jurisdiction, analyses the Italian law on the measures against the aiding and abetting of illegal immigration and the working, economic and sexual exploitation of migrants when illegal entries and trafficking are often in a means-end relationship. The author deals, from the point of view of immigration criminal law, with one of the most debated issues in the jurisprudence. This issue is very relevant to public opinion because it is linked to stories at the center of recent news and debate, also because of the stances taken by Home Secretary Matteo Salvini: the entry into Italy of irregular migrants after being rescued in international waters by NGOs or Italian police agents. Leaving the migrants at sea on improvised ships is a precise strategy by those commanding the boats so they do not risk being caught. The migrants who paid the journey know this and have been assured that the rescue would be called before they are abandoned. In these conditions, the rescue (mandatory by international conventions) could prefigure the felony of aiding and abetting for the rescuers. Some extend this reasoning to a paradoxical conclusion by claiming that without the rescues there would be no trafficking.

Migrants usually travel through illegal and dangerous routes through sea and land, via which an increasing number of unaccompanied minors cross the borders into Europe. They are, or declare themselves to be, alone for several reasons: family reunification would be difficult to obtain without the presence of an unaccompanied minor; the families themselved sent them away because they know that minors, once they have arrived, may benefit from a better protection system than in their own country; in the worst case, minors lose their families during their journey. European instruments for dealing with this issue have proven to be inconsistent and often inadequate. Minors who have often been victims of abuse and sexual exploitation during their journeys have been put in detention centers together with adults. The EU's juridical framework formerly had so many gaps that, in 2016, a change of direction was implemented in an attempt to grant better protection to such particularly vulnerable individuals. Katarzyna Gromek-Broc's contribution, Unaccompanied children in the EU. Towards a higher standard of protection and support for "Children on the Move" – unaccompanied minors-immigrants in the EU, seeks to evaluate the new legislative actions and other efforts made at the communitarian and national level to increase the degree of protection for unaccompanied immigrant minors. Specifically: the new juridical tools to improve the evaluation process of minors in transit zones, the measures to reduce delays in appointing tutors, and the reception network that takes charge of the minors. In order to be effective, this system takes into consideration greater coordination among member states.

But removing the obstacles to the actual inclusion of those who choose to live in another country requires that they are granted free access to justice. Besides, this right, granted to every individual without exception, is one of the main pillars of the rule of law; a bastion for democracy and civilisation. It acquires primary relevance when considering – as Silvia Favalli does in The right to free legal aid for migrants. For effective access to justice – that crossing the border of a state with a legal system that differs greatly from their state of origin leaves migrants in a vulnerable condition, insofar as the host country's legal system – if not known or correctly respected – risks creating a barrier not only to integration but, even before that, to entry and permanence. From this perspective, access to free legal aid in the host state becomes fundamentally relevant, so much so that the General Assembly of the United Nations includes this right among the eight objectives it indicated to ease human mobility in the next 15 years. Also the bloc of reforms of the Common European Asylum System (CEAS) – which aims to reduce the member states' current discretion in the management of the asylum procedures – would extend legal assistance and representation to all the phases of the procedure for granting protection. In light of these considerations, the author examines the current situation of discipline and application praxis on the subject of the effective access to justice in the European area, with specific reference to migrants and their right to fair trial in the civil, criminal and administrative fields.

The adventure that is migration calls for the crossing of other borders as well, such as those related to identity. In Boundaries of identity and belonging in migration, Maria Assunta Zanetti and Gianluca Gualdi place the issue of borders at the core of the identity-building process for every individual, since it involves the necessity to take into account several registers, in the planning of the Self: family history, cultural traditions, social belongings, past experiences, future projects… This situation, marked by precarious equilibriums, is amplified by the migrants' conditions, mainly due to their traumatic experiences related to the feeling of being uprooted and to the loss of their own social and cultural roles, together with the fear of not being able to integrate and face the changes that are to be confronted and will necessarily modify their way of life. The topic of border/s in the migrant's process of identity construction, and particularly for refugees, manoeuvres on the complex dynamics between integration and disintegration of parts of the Self. In the examined case – migrant teenagers – the process is even more delicate and risky because they have to face two delicate transitions: as teenagers, the transition between childhood and adulthood, as migrants the one between the original cultural code and the host society's one. This makes them particularly exposed to stiffening, conflicts, uncertainty and disorientation when the borders may become barriers to a balanced development of their identity.

The borders of identity are not easily crossed, since our identity, the way we imagine ourselves and how we introduce ourselves to others, can be a suit of armour we wear in defence against the outside world. This happens even more frequently when we feel fragile and menaced. However, we forget that identity is vitally nurtured by meeting people, being contaminated, and by crossbreeding. Thus, both in the present and in the past, the experience of migration has always produced identity as well as material loss and gain, also for individuals whose choices are only apparently determined by external actors. In this analytical perspective, Arianna Arisi Rota intervenes with Gaining and losing. Space crossing, identity perception and reinvention in 19th-Century Mediterranean exile. She outlines, in the current mainstream international scholarly debate on these issues, the experiences of material loss linked to the sconfinamento and actual exile from the Italian peninsula and in the Mediterranean during the Risorgimento. A reading that highlights how, during the time, it is always the dynamics of identity destruction and reconstruction that characterise the existential condition of the political refugee. The interpretation of refugee testimonies from the Risorgimento given by the author stresses how the experience of fleeing, being exiled, losing family, social status and every certainty, hence the experience of an immeasurable loss, is compensated, for everyone, by an equally immeasurable gain: hope. So it happens that crossing the Alps or the Mediterranean Sea, borders are themselves care, in a dangerous journey where life is at risk, becomes for some an epic adventure towards freedom, for others a chance of hope and solace. An experience that bonds the present refugees and the past ones, as if the meaning of that journey, that geographic and existential border, stays the same in time and space, like the nostalgia and the hope, the regret and the estrangement, the will to start again and the awareness of being saved… all these feelings accompany their experience.

That is what has been told by boys who have fled from various parts of the world and who have arrived at the University of Pavia, whose testimonies appear in Anna Rita Calabrò's chapter, Time boundaries of identity. Because, while identity is a continuous process of definition, redefinition, identification and differentiation in a story of ourselves that keeps on changing according to circumstances and experiences, it is also true that, due to the same reasons, identity may be defined as the ability to acknowledge your own entirety and continuity in time. This means emphasising the ways with which the individual 'crosses' time (that is, it relates and represents in itself your own history and everyday and your future project) and the strategies to use in order to give meaning and consistency to this path, be it continuous or discontinuous. Of course, individuals, when defining their own biographies, articulated by everyday rhythms, must both refer to and take into account time frames that are not only subjective, but also social and collective. They must therefore adapt their own time frames to those of the other individuals with whom they interact, and to those of the social institutions whin which they have dealings. The author shows how, for asylum seekers and refugees, this relationship seems problematic and fragmentary: because they come from cultural and social contexts where the social organisation of time does not necessarily coincide with that of advanced industrialised societies; because their forced migration 'forcibly' disrupted their everyday life and plans; because, lastly, the Italian reception system collocated them for a significant length of time in a sort of limbo where the time frame and modalities of release were not at all clear, and it is difficult to reconnect the threads that make the present the place where the past experience becomes a future project. For the interviewed boys, the journey, 'that journey', becomes the shadowy line they need to cross to become adults.

Before them, many youngsters of the same age crossed borders to reach European universities, on a journey too similar to an escape: they came from colonial empires, fled from restrictions, prohibitions, actual persecutions. The forgotten history of those who arrived in Italy from 1900 to 1940 is told by Elisa Signori in Intellectual migrations and elites' formation beyond the boundaries. Foreign students, Jews and non-Jews, and Italian universities (1900–1940). This time arc can be divided into roughly two phases. The protagonists of the former are students attracted by the artistic and cultural tradition of Italy and the children of the Italian migration diaspora. But it is in the latter, between the two world wars, when the number of foreign students triples compared to the previous phase; many come from Eastern Europe because of political uncertainty and economic instability. The authoritarian drift, caused by the geopolitical rearrangement decided in Versailles, eliminated the old borders and drew new ones, thus favoring nationalist extremism and the radicalisation of preexisting praxes of intolerance, mainly against the Jewish part of the population. So mainly Jewish students found haven in the Italian universities that did not ask for the religious affiliation at the moment of enrollment. But for them the doors began to quickly close on September 13, 1938, when the legislation 'for the defense of the race' came into force.

But how to 'narrate' in literary terms your own migration story? How to narrate your own identity and experience? In the language of your land, your roots, your memory, your most intimate feelings, or the 'other', the one projected to the future, the most suited to go beyond the borders and spread the story? Barbara Berri's contribution, Narrating migrations, is about a little-investigated issue, that is the latent conditioning of the paradigms and the cultural reference categories that influence, by different degrees of awareness, choices of communication and expression. The field of literature proposes several perspectives in precarious equilibrium: on the one hand multilingualism, multiculturalism and different kinds of linguistic contaminations take hold in globalised contemporary society, on the other hand the defense of differences, localness, minorities (cultural and linguistic as well) and linguistic purism responds to needs that are partially complementary and partially opposed. In this context it is useful to stress the complexity of the communication process, which involves many verbal and non-verbal languages, each with its own statute, and each irretrievably affected by the cultural context of 'formation', whatever the subsequent path of linguistic and cultural contamination might be. While building awareness of this condition seems to be essential, it is also essential to acknowledge the need to understand how and to what extent these categories can change or 'adapt', over the years, in the meetings/clashes of different cultures that constitute the experience of the individual and of the group. The analysis of the so-called 'migrant literature', which crosses physical and symbolic borders, and narrates migrations and contamination, is now present in many national literary corpora, representing an extraordinary observatory to understand the present.

As far as identity and borders are concerned, there is an additional consequence related to the crossing of borders as a result of the migration of populations coming from their original country and permanently settling in a new one, and having children, over time, with partners from the local population. We are talking about genetic identity, which Cesare Danesino and Carla Oliveri address in their chapter, Crossing borders: genetic mutations. To the end of preventing and curing diseases, genetic analyses tell us the history of mutations following migrations either within the same country or, for instance, between neighbouring geographical regions, such as the mutations found in the border populations of Italy and France as an effect of migration from the former to the latter. In other cases, finding identical mutations in individuals from different countries is related to a definite biological significance. There are regions and countries where the prevalence of a particular disease is higher than in the general population: these differences 'migrate' with this population. But when a rare disease is diagnosed in a migrant patient coming from a country where clinical and molecular diagnoses would have not been possible, there could be a (positive) 'return migration' of the curing and diagnosing ability.

Finally, the stories of returns, of borders crossed and then crossed again, of journeys towards promised lands that often prove they are not, lands where it is not possible to arrive or from where people, once arrived, move again, as 'losers' or 'winners' depending on the situation. In the chapter Borders of identity. Return migration and failure in West Africa, Giulia Casentini reflects starting from the life stories of migrants returning to Ghana. Stories that tell the crossing of many geographic and symbolic borders. For those who made it, for those who 'got rich', the return means admiration, more status, and social prestige, both in the formal and informal reference contexts. For those who come back as poor as before, it means failure, to let down those who saw them leave. The return is often forced upon them: because there is no guarantee of safety, especially for migrants crossing Libya; because they do not have the economic means to continue with their journey and reach their resolved destination; because they have been victims of traumatic experiences during the journey. The price is the loss of self-esteem and, sometimes, self-isolation. These stories provide the opportunity to discuss critically the categories of transit, waiting spaces, and migrant identity, and to look upon borders not just as physical limits to cross, but as thresholds that determine a change of social status, of perception of self and of the world.

3. *Deleting the borders?*

So the world, now as then, is characterised by clear political borders, often marked by natural elements like rivers or mountains, or artificial fortifications, like the Great Wall of China or, more recently, the infamous wall between the United States and Mexico. Although these borders are always clearly indicated on physical and political maps, they revealed themselves to be actually drawn by the winners and endured by the losers, and therefore ephemeral; or removed by the need for unity and then, as it is currently happening in Europe, evoked again. The symbolic borders are even more aleatory:

language, culture, law, identity and, as we have already seen, genetics of people and populations. Thus, borders change, are drawn, are crossed, are deleted.

Genetic identities beyond conventional boundaries, by Alessandro Achilli and Ugo Perego, explains how intertemporal gene flows deriving from multiple demographic events (migrations, conquests and wars, trading routes, slavery, explorations, etc.) have led to genetic mixing in every region of the planet and, in fact, cloud single vestigial genetic identities. This is why it is nearly impossible to ascribe any individual to a single ancestral group, although geneticists have identified vestigial informative markers that are peculiar to specific ethnic or population groups: our genetic makeup derives from migrations and expansions that occurred all over the world, over thousands of years. We all are, to use an expression, neither elegant nor scientific, and yet eloquent, 'bastard siblings'.

The lack of precise genetic borders among individuals and the awareness that everyone's genetic identity is nothing if not the result of ancestral medleys and migrations introduces Part III. Its eight chapters focus on deleting borders, in the sense of going beyond them, from the ethical, juridical, humanitarian or merely economic points of view. Here they call for calling borders into question: borders of identity, cultural and political. The circumstances when this necessity materialises in specific actions are examined.

But which are the juridical prerequisites for actions going in this direction? First of all, there is a higher order reason that deletes, in a manner of speaking, the borders: the humanitarian one. In recent decades there have been circumstances in which the international community believed it was necessary to intervene and militarily cross the borders of a state when reasons like a threat to security or the clear violation of human rights were recognisable. Nowadays, as argued by Ernesto Bettinelli in Migrat.In.G. "Migrations: towards an interdisciplinary governance model". Some considerations on the contribution of legal scholars to the Strategic Project of the University of Pavia, the phenomenon of 'forced' migrations is so great as to induce us to reconsider the formal and traditional concept the sovereign state as an entity constituted by a territory, a population and a government authority, whatever its legitimation or self-legitimation. For a traditional conception of international relations it is enough to verify the ability of a government to manage the borders within which it claims to exercise its sovereignty in order to acknowledge the existence of a state. If we were to leave the cage of realist (and conservative) doctrines, it would be possible to question the legitimacy of the (self-)attribution of the definition of state in those situations in which a government authority cannot guarantee minimal living conditions to its inhabitants in territorial contexts that have already been originally acknowledged at the international level as constituents of a given state. Therefore, in such cases, the state institution should (could) be called into question, even for international law, by substituting this category with the more befitting one of geographically connoted 'factual power'. Removing the causes of unliveableness in the places where exoduses begin is universally and abstractly recognised as the most effective and structural solution, and it is commonly admitted that this should be the true and proper mission of the international community. But there are divergent stances concerning which subjects are authorised to act, consequently, often by force of arms, against territorial powers defined as 'terrorist' or 'criminal'. The most useful concept in dealing with this question is perhaps that of 'humanitarian interference', which is not fulfilled only with the use of force against territorial powers, but also in other forms: that of rescue operations (episodic by nature) and of international cooperation (whose features are more enduring and structural).

But who are those that cross the borders? Or rather, how are the ones who Bettinelli calls 'migrants', that is the ones that leave their origin country for a non-predetermined period, classified. Words, it is known, can be prisons, can bond people the instant they are uttered in one way rather than in another to a fate different to what would otherwise have been. Norms change; destiny changes. Moreover, words delete individuality, the tags delete stories and feelings, people become numbers, categories. What value should law then concede to distinctions marked by words; what is the difference, in terms of rights, between an expatriate and a forced migrant when the differentiating element concerns two kinds of will: that which is free and that which is forced. And on the basis of this distinction, it is decided, in a completely arbitrary way, that the former have more rights than the latter. Does not the expulsion of those considered irregular entail, under the juridical profile, also the formal negation of their identity as a recognizable person? But to which point may supranational, international, European and national regulations that frame the migrant's status (regardless of their reasons and aims) legitimise discriminatory policies? If the point of view that freedom of movement (and settlement) is a universal, unconditional right, is accepted, juridical research must point out all the normative sources, at different levels, that allow such a conclusion to be positively affirmed. The ambitious aim is the definition of a corpus juris humanitatis, that is, of the higher order of the human person as such, to whom the universal status of 'itinerant citizen', even in the case of statelessness, can be conferred in the face of the passiveness of individual states. And as a consequence, the deletion of borders.

In any case, a cultural change is necessary in an intercultural and interethnic reality born from migrations that are neither temporary nor caused by emergencies. As Carolina Simoncini argues in Freedom of movement and new immigration rights, the study of international conventions on migrants' rights shows that the most important asset that migrants seek is to belong to a community and enjoy relative social rights. Thus, it will be necessary to acknowledge that integration is a necessary precondition for a cosmopolitan law focused on migrants' needs. This implies an inversion of the 'cause-effect' connection between freedom of movement and freedom of residence in general international conventions. For migrants, in fact, residence is not only a simple consequence of movement, but the specific goal that justifies the choice of leaving their home country and enduring the consequent uprooting. Hence, movement and the crossing of borders become necessary means to a final end. For this reason, some jurists appeal for the recognition of a new right to hospitality, that is, to quote Fauss, the right of every person coming from abroad, with their culture, language and way of living, to be accepted and respected. This seems coherent with the process of 'humanisation of international law' that is leading to a reinterpretation of the idea of sovereignty as a 'protection responsibility' toward migrants rather than as a 'competence'. This responsibility may be considered the right to movement in order to achieve free residence.

After all, the most recent juridical leanings on the different systems of protection of the migrants' human rights made at the universal level (in the 1966 Pacts and the 1951 Convention of Geneve Relating to the Status of Refugees) and regional level (ECHR and the Charter of Fundamental Rights) highlight the irrelevance of states' geographical borders, the duty to extend the international standards of protection being addressed to all the organs of the State that have a jurisdiction (that is a 'direct and effective power') on migrants even outside their territory and before the border is crossed.

In this regard Cristina Campiglio and Carola Ricci, in International law as limit to States' discretion on migration and the urge for alternative legal pathways. Humanitarian corridors opened by private sponsors in Italy, deal, from a juridical point of view, with the issue of the conflicts that arise when the norms regulating behaviours contradict each other insofar as they refer to different cultural and ethical orientations. From this perspective, the authors argue that it is possible to reassert some internal values considered uninfringeable, and therefore attributed to the 'margin of appreciation' (reserved and questionable) of every sovereign state, next and parallel to the promotion of a minimum core of fundamental rights to be uniformly granted to each migrant, regardless of his or her citizenship, ethnic or religious origin, political opinions and social extraction. These values are also explicitly defended by recent ECHR findings. An example is the decision on January 10, 2017 in the Osmanoğlu and Kocabaş v. Switzerland case, where the European Court for Human Rights rejected the appeal filed by two Muslim parents, fined for impeding their daughters from attending the mandatory swimming classes of their primary school, because these classes were opposed to their religious beliefs. In this way, the 'right [for Switzerland] to put school rules and full integration first has been affirmed' for both male and female students even if in contrast with Islamic precepts that do not admit the simultaneous presence of both sexes in the swimming pool (it has to be noted that female students were given consent to wear the 'burkini').

Continuing on the topic of of rights, Giovanni Cordini and Andrea Iurato, in Emigrations and immigrations in South America. Legal aspects, review the different juridical profiles of migration flows concerning Latin America, both in the current situation of tendential balance between arrivals and departures and increasing development of common migration policies at the regional level and in the decades around the turn of the 20th century, when the region was one of the main destinations for European emigration. Now as then, Latin America is a lively juridical laboratory, where migrations show a strong influence on the evolution of existing principles, institutions and juridical concepts, and on the emergence of new ones. In this region there are the first (and, so far, the only) judicial systems that theorise the 'right to migrate' (recognised in the Ecuadorean Constitution itself) and implement, like in Argentina, innovative norms for the access to civil, social and naturalisation rights. In this sense, Latin American sets of rules represent an interesting observatory for redefining the juridical concepts of border, citizenship, and foreigner, and for going beyond the gap of protection between refugees and economic migrants.

If inclusion is the only weapon to tear borders down, what is better than music? In Experiencing and crossing borders through music, Fulvia Caruso describes an experience in participatory action study carried out with students and former students of Ethnomusicology at the Department of Musicology and Cultural Heritage of the University of Pavia, in two different contexts: a centre of reception in the Diocese of Cremona that hosts more than 150 asylum seekers and a CAS (Centre of Special Reception) in the province of Piacenza, that hosts about 20 asylum seekers. The study shows how music is a strong tool for finding a way to communicate, both inside and outside the reception centres. In Italy, asylum seekers waiting for their legalisation live in alienating conditions. During this period they live in a 'non lieu', in a suspended time, after a long journey of deprivation and suffering. This situation produces a loss of faith in themselves and in others; often they lose the capacity to think of their future. They are in a state of limbo where their identities or sense of belonging can weaken or multiply. Through music, barriers and borders inside and outside the individual can be broken down.

But can borders stop ideas, words, and music? Or do they cross them without obstacles? Or could they even tear them down? It is a rhetorical question, even more so in the current age of globalisation and the internet. A lot has been written, and much more should be. In this volume, Francesca Fiorani tells a little story in Free voices beyond the borders. The experience of Italian exiles in Radio Londra (1940–1945). War makes friends of yesterday's enemies, and closes the borders that were open until a little while ago. That is what happened to Italians in the United Kingdom after Italy declared war on June 10, 1940. That is what happened to those Italians who, together with other citizens from enemy countries, worked at the BBC as highly skilled journalists and speakers. The broadcaster, in spite of pressures from public opinion and most conservative circles, protected by whatever means possible its migrant workers. So, on December 22, 1939, the first show of what later became the BBC's Italian Service was aired, with a rich schedule: news, culture, politics, entertainment, and satire in which the attacks against fascism were not propaganda, but information.

Finally, the circle is closed by Flavio Ceravolo's chapter, The great migration game. Who wins and who loses?, which returns to the starting points by acknowledging the evidence of a basic contradiction. All the evolutionary dynamics of a knowledge society require people to be able to move, and therefore foster migration flows both of middle class and of less-skilled economic migrants. In this context, some countries attract flows because of their stock of material and intangible resources, while others are, by definition, donors of human capital, and yet others are gateways and temporary corridors.

Only the former has the ability to effectively select the migration flows to their own exclusive benefit, while the others actually endure an irreversible process of impoverishment that prefigures a dynamic of reproduction of inequalities between central and peripherical countries. Moreover, the rhetoric of open borders, is in fact, reciprocated by creeping protectionist policies that foster more and more pronounced international inequalities. Social tensions lead some countries toward overtly protectionist policies and the building of physical walls to block the passage of migrants. This new protectionism makes the idea of 'border' a truly modern concept, and yet one that clashes ever more stridently with the productive needs of a globalised world. The future scenario of border restoration will intensify international inequalities and could create new arenas of conflict.

Part I

Drawing the borders

Chapter 1

The borders of Schengen and their functions

Maria Antonietta Confalonieri

Borders, as physical boundaries of the territory of exercise of the sovereign authority of the state, are a definitional component of the modern, sovereign, post-Westphalian state: the "skin" of the state, according to a common metaphor. As Samuel Finer notes, "tell a man today to go and build a state, and he will try to establish a definite and defensible territorial boundary and compel those who live inside it to obey him. Having done this, he will have founded his State" (Finer 1974: 79). Similarly, Giddens (1987: 49, 120) suggested that – contrary to feudal states separated by frontiers, which were essentially zones – a nation-state is "a bordered power container" and has the administrative monopoly over a territory with demarcated boundaries. The structuring of territorial space into "territorialitally disjointed, mutually exclusive, functionally similar sovereign states" (Ruggie 1993: 151) is a distinctive feature of modernity in Europe. The "modern system of rule consists of the institutionalization of public authority within mutually exclusive jurisdictional domains" (Ruggie 1983: 275), the reciprocal recognition of sovereignity being the basis of the international order. Borders are inseparable from territory, as the sharp edges of the territorial state. Defending borders and administering border crossings require the deployment at the state's territorial borders of controlled resources of force; further, borders are conferred strong symbolic value.

The process of European integration, with the emergence of common supra-national authorities and modes of governance through the "pooling" of sovereignty and the transformation of European sovereign nation states into "EU member states", inevitably impacts on national borders and modes of border management. Social scientists have provided diverse accounts of the fate of territory and borders in the integrated Europe. Postmodernists describe Europe "as a space of flows rather than a space of places … where the lines between inside and outside are increasingly blurred" (Walters 2004: 676): borders lose the significance they had in the post-Westphalian order and identities become de-territorialized. Yet this account disregards the enduring (even increasing) political salience of borders and the extensive political mobilization in favor of walled communities to keep out varieties of undesired others (Axford and Huggins 2000: 177). Ruggie refers to the EU as the most advanced case of "unbundling" of territoriality: the institutional negation of exclusive territoriality, through functional regimes, communities and the like, "as the means of situating and dealing with those dimensions of collective existence that territorial rulers recognize to be irreducibly trans-territorial in character" (Ruggie 1993: 119). Overlapping authorities and competing competencies, and the extension (with the process of enlargement and the European Neighborhood Policy) of the reach of EU governance beyond the territorial borders of the Union, justify the proposal of the neo-medievalism metaphors (Zielonka 2006), that still dismiss the fundamental difference, in terms of scope and depth of governmental activities, between middle age and modernity. On the other hand, the thesis of the shift from territorially to networked forms of spatial organization omits that in the EU these forms tend to be co-existing and complementary rather than mutually exclusive (Agnew 2008: 182). Various disciplines and theoretical approaches elaborate on the nature of EU borders, and discussing this vast and diverse literature is well beyond the scope of this chapter. Rather, the focus here is on the distinctive mode of border management of the European Union since the Schengen Agreement of 1985 and the process that originated from it, with the removal of controls on movement of people at the internal borders between the signatory states, and the development of common policies of management of Schengenland's external borders.

The distinction of types of borders proposed by Walters (2002) represents a potentially promising starting point. With reference to historical trajectories of development of the notion of borders and of the institutional apparatus associated with border management, Walters distinguishes between geopolitical borders, national borders, and biopolitical borders. Geopolitical borders are borders intended as "a crucial factor of war and peace, a potential line of confrontation where armed forces are arrayed", associated with the idea of states as rigidly defined territorial units, defending the extension and integrity of territory against other states or trying to expand it at their expenses (Walters 2002: 563). National borders are the outcomes of processes of state and nation building, through administrative and cultural homogenization, and of democratization with extension of civil political and social rights within the same spatial area. The notion of biopolitical borders, derived from Focault's theorizing on governamentality (Walters 2011), tries "to capture the relationship of borders, understood as regulatory instruments, to populations, their movement, security, wealth, and health" (Walters 2002: 562). Here borders are "a privileged instrument in the systematic regulation of national and transnational populations, their movement, health, and security" (Walters 2002: 571). Biopolitical borders regard the "filtering" function of borders; what is at stake is the security of the population rather than the security of the territory.

Regarding geopolitical borders, the prerequisite of European integration has been the demilitarization of the political borders of Western European states (Walters 2002: 564) with the creation of NATO. National borders maintain relevance in the integrated Europe: member states do safeguard sovereignty in a number of crucial policy areas, namely those affecting political and social citizenship, although the policy autonomy of governments is constrained by market and monetary integration. Identities continue to be based on nations: the borders of identity, that Geddes (2005: 790) calls "conceptual borders", still coincide with the territorial borders of the nation state, with European identity complementing rather than substituting national identities. And European integration does not look like the processes of centralization, hierarchization and bureaucratization that characterized state and nation building in the trajectory of the modern state; rather, the EU has a hybrid regime characterized by fragmentation and a combination of supranational and intergovernmental aspects. The notion of biopolitical borders is of undeniable pertinence with reference to EU borders. The fact that Schengenland does not coincide with the European Union confirms the primarily biopolitical nature of its border: while the new regime attenuated the filtering function of internal borders, the concerted action in the area of immigration and security was transferred to the external borders. Nevertheless, EU internal borders still have the function of biopolitical borders for non-EU citizens, since member states maintain sovereignty in issues of legal migration, namely labour migration, and also for EU citizens every time member states have reintroduced border controls on individuals claiming "special security concerns" or situations of emergency (Pascouau 2013). The external border of the EU, and in some cases even internal borders, are eminently biopolitical, which justifies, when discussing EU borders, focusing on migration policy.

The distinction between geopolitical, national and biopolitical borders concerns the function of borders. Two more dimensions of border management have particular relevance when discussing the Schengen regime, as suggested by Berg and Ehin (2006): the mode of governance of borders and the degree of openness of borders.

1.1. *Mode of governance of EU borders*

The emergence of the distinctive mode of governance of EU borders is conventionally explained as the outcome of the spill-over effect (Haas 1958) from market integration. The relaunch of the single market project implied, according to the neo-functional account of European integration, the functional needs of removing barriers to the free movement of people and, conversely, reinforcing the common external border. Yet this theoretical framework does not account for the choices of the member state, nor for "the very reasons which gave birth to specific institutions and procedures" (Stetter 2000: 81). Approaches based on a principal-agent model, which explore the motives of member state governments (principals) to delegate authority, in the politically-salient policy area of migration, to common institutions, seem to provide a more convincing interpretation of the development of border and migration policies of the EU. Giraudon and Lahav (2000) argue that the denationalization of policy making on migrations shifted the locus of elaboration and implementation to common European institutions, local authorities, non-state actors or foreign states – "up, down, out" – and so it allowed national governments to elude the "control dilemmas" (Giraudon and Jopke 2001; Giraudon 2000): that is the constraints, coming from human rights norms as adjudicated by international and national courts and the pressure from pro-migration domestic actors, that may prevent the adoption of restrictive policies intended to appease the anxiety of public opinion on migration and maximize electoral support. One sector of the state, the bureaucrats of the interior ministries, found in the transnational fora for coordination in security issues "policy venues more amenable to their ends by exploring new instruments and seizing upon windows of opportunity to occupy political space" (Giraudon 2000: 258; 2003), thus enhancing, according to a logic of bureaucratic competition, their competences and resources.

Transgovernmental networks of national security officials, operating outside the European Community institutional framework, acted as "laboratories" of the EU policy of border management and migration (Monar 2001; Zaiotti 2011: 75–78): the Trevi group, installed in 1977 to coordinate the combat to transnational terrorism, which added immigration to its mandate; and the Schengen regime, responsible for the elaboration of the Schengen Implementation Convention (1995) and the "compensatory measures" intended to counterbalance the abolition of controls on internal borders. In this first phase of elaboration of the European policy of border management, the mode of governance was predominantly "intensive transgovernmentalism" (Wallace 2000: 33–35; Giraudon 2003): the sustained policy cooperation, under the aegis of the European Council and the Council of Ministers, among topnational officers, with a marginal role of the European Commission and none of the European Parliament and the European Court of Justice, in an institutional environment lacking transparency and accountability. The parallel development of initiatives inside the community framework, "the Brussels initiative" (Zaiotti 2011), remained faltering. Both the Schengen Agreement and the Dublin Convention of 1990 were in fact adopted outside the institutional framework of the European Community, and implemented only in the mid-1990s.

The Treaty of Maastricht assigned policies of internal security and migration [1] to the intergovernmental institutional framework of the Third Pillar (JHA), yet the treaty allowed the transfer of policy making, by unanimous agreement, to the Community Pillar. Despite the formal inclusion in the EU institutional framework, and given the highly fragmented structure of the Third Pillar, "an archipelago, with islands of cooperation loosely linked through the coordinating K4 committee" (Den Boer and Wallace 2000: 501), the transnational networks of official operations in the Schengen regime remained central in policy elaboration, in particular regarding asylum and visas (Giraudon et al. 2003).

The Treaty of Amsterdam explicitly recognized the link between the goal of building an area of freedom, security and justice and the adoption of measures regarding external border control, asylum and migration, and assigned migration policy to the First Pillar. However, provided for its very gradual communitarization: for a transition period of five years unanimity remained the voting rule in the Council, with mere consultation of the European Parliament and the right of initiative shared between the Commission and the member states; the shift, after five years, to the co-decision procedure, implying a

[1] Except for some aspects of visa policy assigned to the first Pillar, as in article 100 of the Treaty of European Community (TEC).

stronger role of the European Parliament and qualified majority rule in the Council of Ministers, was made conditional on an unanimous decision of the Council. Further, the compromise on communitarization could be reached only by granting "opt-outs" to Britain, Ireland and Denmark. The Treaty of Amsterdam also formalized the incorporation of the Schengen acquis, the collection of provisions elaborated in the Schengen regime, into the EU legal order. Given the modest policy output of the Third Pillar, the reforms introduced by the Treaty of Amsterdam can be considered a collective response of member states to regulatory failure, but introducing control mechanisms to avoid agency loss (Stetter 2000); the incorporation of the Schengen acquis was a "marriage of convenience" (Den Boer and Corrado 1999: 399), with Schengen gaining in legitimacy and the Third Pillar in operational capabilities. In the new institutional framework a number of directives on asylum were approved between 2001 and 2005, merely defining minimum standards well below the objective set at the Tampere European Council of 1999 of "a common procedure and uniform standards for those granted asylum valid throughout the Union" (European Council 1999).

Finally, the Treaty of Lisbon has fundamentally reshaped the institutional framework of policies of border management, abolishing the Third Pillar and extending the Community's method to most areas of justice and home affairs. The Treaty explicitly mentions "appropriate measures in respect of border control asylum and immigration" as a correlate of the establishment of an area of freedom, security and justice (art. 32), conferring on the European Commission the exclusive right of initiative on border checks, asylum, and immigration, recognizing full legislative powers to the European Parliament, and the jurisdiction of the European Court of Justice. The ordinary legislative procedure (former co-decision) is established (art. 77 (2) TFEU) for measures concerning: "(a) common policy on visas and other short-stay residence permits; (b) the checks to which persons crossing external borders are subject; (c) the conditions under which nationals of third countries shall have the freedom to travel within the Union for a short period; (d) any measure necessary for the gradual establishment of an integrated management system for external borders; (e) the absence of any controls on persons, whatever their nationality, when crossing internal borders." Further, the Treaty provides for the adoption of "solidarity measures" (art. 78 (3) TFEU) with member states confronted with exceptional flows of migrants, upon decision of the Council and consultation of the European Parliament, and proclaims solidarity and "burden sharing" between member states as a general principle in issues of border checks, asylum, and immigration.

However, the communitarization of JHA policies with the Treaty of Lisbon did not produce true supranational governance of border management. The role of intergovernmental institutions remains eminent. On issues of high political salience and in times of crisis, the European Council is the institution which "takes the initiative and sets the frames within which other institutions operate" (Fabbrini and Puetter 2016: 636); regarding the Council Minister, decisions tend to be taken by consensus, with a paramount role in consensus-building being the informal meetings of JHA Counselors

(Maricut 2016). Intergovernmental governance dominated EU policymaking during the refugee crisis of 2015–2016. During the crisis the European Council took up the role of crisis manager, meeting seven times between April 2015 and February 2016, with disagreement between member states impairing its problem-solving capability (ibidem, 546). The EU-Turkey "Statement" of March 2016, de facto an international agreement, was stipulated by the member state governments outside the legal framework of the Treaty (art. 218 TFEU), and bypassing the European Parliament (Den Heijer and Spiikenboer 2016). The resurgence of intergovernmentalism in border management is also illustrated by the rubber-stamping by the European institutions of the requests of several member states, since September 2015, to reintroduce internal border controls: the reintroduction was authorized on the basis of the formal compliance with the procedures laid down in the Schengen Borders Code, without thoughtful examination of the credibility of the motivations provided (Guild et al. 2016: 42–45).

If supranationalization did not occur at the decision-making level, at the operational level member states remain the actors in charge of border management, both regarding most individual decisions on the admission of migrants and asylum seekers, with very different percentages of positive decisions (Eurostat 2017), and regarding control and surveillance of external borders. Bodies at the European level, such as the intergovernmental Standing Committee on Internal Security (COSI) (art.71 TFEU), have a coordinating role rather than the mandate to direct the work of national security agencies. The role of the EU has rather been one of capacity building, whereby it "creates new European actors and assigns new powers to them, which are exercised in parallel to, in competition to, or even instead of corresponding national powers" (Genschel and Jachtenfuchs 2014: 11): this is the case of FRONTEX (2007/2004), the EASO (2010), the European Border and Coast Guard, and of the development of common technologies of border management, such as the Schengen Information System (1995) and EURODAC (2003). Despite the installment of such agencies resembling the construction of state-like force capabilities, border management is operated through horizontal and hierarchical networks, connecting European and domestic actors (Lavenex Wichmann 2009).

In summary, despite the developments of supranational elements, the EU border regime remains differentiated and fragmented, combining intergovernmentalism and supranationalism, and has not evolved in a federal-like form.

The other distinctive trait of the European mode of border governance is the shifting of border controls "down" (through devolution to local authorities of function of control of migration) (Lahav 1997) and "out", delegating tasks to non-state actors (such as air carriers) or enrolling in the control of migration flows countries of origin and transit. "Externalization" allows governments to pursue the shared goal of controlling a transnational problem, avoiding both "control dilemmas" at the domestic level and upgrading their common interests without sovereignty losses (Lavenex 2006). Remote control of migration flows (Giraudon and Lahav 2000) takes various forms: the definition, since the Dublin Convention, of "safe third countries" in which asylum seekers can be legitimately remitted; visas; carriers' sanctions; and multilateral and bilateral agreements with countries of origin and transit. Re-admission agreements between the Schengen countries and Poland were inaugurated in 1991, and are now in place with 17 countries. The Council of Tampere included cooperation in the management of migration flows through partnerships with countries of origins and transit among the priorities, hence externalization proceeded steadily, in sharp contrast with the slowness of the process of the harmonization of regulations (Lavenex 2006: 337)

The process of enlargement included, among the conditions for membership, the reception and implementation of the Schengen acquis on the part of candidate countries. Beginning in the 1990s with cooperation and association agreements with east and south neighboring countries, cooperation in the management of migration became a crucial aspect of the European Neighborhood Policy launched in 2003/2004. Since 2005 the GAMM (Global Approach to Migration and Mobility) has provided the general framework for cooperation with third countries; among its tools, the Mobility Partnerships, bilateral agreements offering venues for legal migration and cooperation on development in return for cooperation on border management, found greater receptivity in eastern rather than in southern partners (Weinar 2017).

Externalization of border control has a number of implications. First, the fuzziness of the EU biopolitical border, which does not coincide with the EU territorial border. Second, the blurring of the distinction between the EU's domestic and foreign policy, in clear discontinuity with the post-Westphalian state, should imply a greater role for actors responsible for foreign policy. Since the late 1990s a "comprehensive approach" to issues of asylum and migration has been proposed, aimed to target the situation in countries of origin and impact on the "root causes" of flows (van Selm 2002), and creating agencies (for example, the Council's High Level Working Group on Asylum and Migration) to assure cross-pillar policy coordination. These developments, nevertheless, did not put an end to the predominant role of the EU justice and home affairs officials in the external dimension of EU migration policy, with a marginalization of services responsible for foreign affairs or cooperation on development (Carrera, den Hertog and Parkin 2012).

Third, the externalization of border controls has exasperated the tension between effectiveness in border management and compliance with the EU human rights regime. Criticisms of the prioritizing by the EU of keeping undesired migrants at its periphery over respect for human rights by third countries has been formulated by NGOs and international organizations. Fourth, externalization of migration control raises problems of democratic accountability, since EU citizens are insulated from border-related violence used "in their name" by non-EU countries' authorities (Little and Vaugham-Williams 2017: 540).

1.2. *Closure/openness*

The predominance of the security paradigm (Hall 1993) is a persistent feature of the EU's migration policy. Since its inception, migration has been approached as a "security threat". This framing of migration has marginalized competitive frames focusing on human rights or the economic function of migrant labour (Bigo 2002; Huysmans 2000). The association of migration with other "security threats" implies the redefinition of the external threat of Europe: "after communism, immigration is perceived to be a destabilizing factor of potentially destructive proportions" (Den Boer, 1995: 94).

The pre-dominance of the security paradigm has been explained (Bigo 1996; Giraudon 2003; Huysmans 2000) with the nature of the institutional framework where the policy originated, the trans-governmental cooperation between law and order officials for the Schengen Agreement and its implementation, which managed to frame the issue of migrations in terms consonant with their mission and organizational culture and propose policy solutions that required their expertise. Measures of containment of migration were thus amalgamated with the "compensatory measures" intended to preserve the security of the member states from a number of transnational risks (such as transnational crime and terrorism) after the removal of controls at the internal borders. Since the Dublin Convention of 1990, issues of security also dominated in asylum policy: the principle of "country of first arrival" has a coercive nature, discouraging the choice of country of destination (Hathaway 1993; Den Heijer, Rijpma and Spijkerboer 2016: 609). Neither the empowerment of the European Parliament (Ripoll Servent and Trauner 2014) nor the inauguration of the "integrated approach", which should combine restriction with preventive measures (Boswell 2003), targeting the "root causes" of migration and the "migration-development nexus", has succeeded in weakening the predominance of the security paradigm (Lavenex and Kunz 2008).

The security paradigm dominates migration policy, yet the common metaphor of "fortress Europe" does not capture its complexity. It contrasts with policies of openness towards economically desirable, "scarce forms of labor" (van Houtum and Pijpers 2005): the metaphor of "the gated community", where gates open to let the "wanted migrants" (Geddes 2005) in, as illustrated by the Blue Card (2009/50/EC) and the Scientific Visa Directive (2005/71/EC), is more appropriate in describing the filtering function of the EU's biopolitical borders.

The deceptiveness of the simple distinction between open or closed (securitized) borders is illustrated also by the ample, multidisciplinary debate on the "humanitarian border" [2]. There are multiple indicators of the emerging function of border as a space of humanitarian government (Walters 2011: 138): first and foremost are institutional developments, with the incorporation of the European Charter of Human Rights in the EU's legal order, as well as the jurisprudence of the European Court of Justice and of the European Court of Human Rights (Kaunert and Léonard 2012); the amended Frontex Regulation (1168/2011), which makes explicit mention of its commitment to human rights (Pallister Williams 2015: 60); the growing focus in EU policy and political rhetoric of the goal of "saving lives"; the creation of "humanitarian corridors" for

[2] For a review, see Polly Pallister Williams (2015).

refugees; and the involvement of international agencies such as UNCHR and humanitarian NGOs in border management.

The relationship between the humanitarian and the securitized borders is complex and relates to the fundamental control/care dilemma of humanitarianism (Pallister Williams 2015: 56): migrants' lives are put at risk because of the closure of channels for legal migration. Humanitarianism is also the legitimizing discourse of practice of securitization; humanitarian agencies can be coopted in securitarian border management. Yet they can, and in fact do, play a role of monitoring and advocacy, thus representing a challenge to the dominant security paradigm. Courts have the role of monitoring, sanctioning, and influencing policies. Far from being taken for granted, the security approach is thus an object of institutional, political and moral disputes.

1.3. *Conclusions*

Bartolini clarifies how the difference "the European state and the EU boundary setting process lies in the different consolidation timing" (2005: 242). European states evolved in a context of continual warfare: the consolidation of the control of territory through coercion was therefore preliminary to the standardization of internal markets and building of national community. Conversely, European integration took place within the secured geopolitical borders of the Western Bloc, which reduced the salience of the coercion borders, thus allowing the precedence of regulatory standardization and creation of a common legal order. In the climate of anxiety over the perspective of uncontrolled migration flows and criminal threats after the fall of Communism, the removal of controls at the internal borders, as a consequence of market integration, created a common interest for the control of border-crossing at the external borders: this led to a level of integration of policies of border management that sets the EU apart from other cases of regional integration. Despite this comparatively remarkable level of integration, and despite the progress towards communitarization of policies of border management, the mode of governance remains a combination of supranationalism and intergovernamentalism, with the latter prevailing, in particular in times of crisis. The reluctance of member states to increase the level and scope of integration of policies of migration and border control can be explained by the increasing politicization of the issue of migration at the level of domestic politics (Hooghe and Marks 2005). Nevertheless, the modes of governance of border management of the EU exhibit a number of fundamental weaknesses. Just to mention a few: intergovernamentalism proved dramatically ineffective during the refugee crisis, with the de facto collapse of the Dublin system and the failure to burden share; securitization, the lack of humanitarian channels for refugees, and the absence of a common policy for legal labour migration all push refugees and economic migrants on ever more risky migration routes, producing permanent humanitarian emergencies at the EU borders; the externalization of border controls to third countries implies unacceptable shortcomings in terms of compliance with humanitarian international norms; further, it risks undermining the role of the EU as a "normative power" (Manners 2002) in the international arena, and in its relations with neighbor and candidate countries.

Bibliography

Agnew, J. (2008) 'Borders on the mind: Re-framing border thinking', *Ethics and Global Politics*, 1(4): 175–191.

Axford B. and Huggins R., (2000) 'Towards a Post-National Polity: The Emergence of the Network Society in Europe', The Sociological Review, 48(1): 177.

Bartolini, S. (2005) *Restructuring Europe*, Oxford and New York: Oxford University Press.

Berg, E. and Ehin, P. (2006) 'What kind of border regime is in the making? Towards differentiated and uneven border strategy', *Cooperation and Conflict*, 41(1): 53–71.

Bigo, D. (1996) *Police en Réseaux. L'Expérience Européenne*, Paris: Presses de Science Po.

Bigo, D. (2002) 'Security and migration: Towards a critique of the governamentality of unease', *Alternatives*, 27: 63–92.

Bigo, D. and Leveau, R. (1992) *L'Europe de la Sécurité Intérieure*, Paris: Institut des Hautes Etudes de Sécurité Intérieure.

Boswell, C. (2003) 'The "external dimension" of EU immigration and Asylum Policy', *International Affairs*, 30(3): 619–638.

Carrera, S., den Hertog, L. and Parkin, J. (2012) 'EU migration policy in the wake of the Arab Spring. What prospects for EU-Southern Mediterranean relations?', *MEDPERO Technical Report*, 15.

Den Boer, M. (1995) 'Moving Between Bogus and Bona Fide: The Policy of Inclusion and Exclusion in Europe', in R. Miles and D. Trănhardt (eds) *Migration and European Integrations: The Dynamics of Inclusion and Exclusion*, New Jersey: Fairleigh Dickinson University Press, 92–111.

Den Boer, M. and Corrado, L. (1999) 'For the record or off the record: Comments about the incorporation of Schengen in the EU', *European Journal of Migration and Law*, 1: 397–418.

Den Boer, M. and Wallace, W. (2000) 'Justice and Home Affairs. Integration Through Incrementalism?' in H. Wallace and W. Wallace (eds) *Policy Making in the European Union*, Oxford and New York: Oxford University Press, 494–519.

Den Heijer, M. and Spiikenboer, T. (2016) 'Is the EU-Turkey refugee and migration deal a treaty?', *EU Law Analysis*, http://eulawanalysis.blogspot.com/2016/04/is-eu-turkey-refugee-and-migration-deal.html (accessed on March 14th, 2019).

Den Heijer, M., Rijpma, J. and Spijkerboer, T. (2016) 'Coercition, prohibition and great expectations: The continuing failure of the common European asylum system', *Common Market Law Review*, 53(1): 607–642.

European Council (1999) Presidency Conclusions of the Tampere European Council.

Eurostat (2017) Asylum Statistics, http://ec.europa.eu/eurostat/statistics-explained/index.php/Asylum_statistics#Decisions_on_asylum_applications (accessed on March 14th, 2019).

Fabbrini, S. and Puetter U. (2016) 'Catalysts of integration – The role of core intergovernmental forums in EU politics', Journal of European Integration, 38(5): 636.

Finer, S. (1974) 'State-building, State-boundaries and border control: An essay on certain

aspects of the first phase of State-building in Western Europe considered in the lights of the Rokkan-Hirschmann model', Social Science Informator, 13(4): 76–126.
Geddes, A. (2005) 'Europe's borders relationship and international migration relations', *Journal of Common Market Studies*, 43(4): 787–806.
Genschel, P. and Jachtenfuchs, M. (2014) 'Introduction: Beyond Market Regulation-Analysing the European Integration of Core State Powers', in P. Genschel and M. Jachtenfuchs (eds), *Beyond the Regulatory Polity. The European Integration of Core State Powers*, Oxford: Oxford University Press, 1–23.
Giddens, A. (1983), *Social Theory and Modern Sociology*, Stanford University Press, 49, 120.
Giraudon, V. (2000) 'European integration and migration policy: Vertical policy-making as venue shopping', *Journal of Common Market Studies*, 38(2): 251–271.
Giraudon, V. (2003) 'The constitution of a European immigration policy domain: A political sociology approach', *Journal of European Public Policy*, 10(2): 263–282.
Giraudon, V. and Joppke, C. (2001) 'Controlling a New Migration World' in V. Giraudon and C. Joppke (eds.), *Controlling a New Migration World*, London and New York: Routledge, 1–27.
Giraudon, V. and Lahav, G. (2000) 'A reappraisal of the State sovereignty debate. The case of migration control', *Comparative Political Studies*, 33(2): 163–195.
Guild, E., Carrera, S., Vosyliute, L., Groenendijk, K., Brouwer, E., Bigo, D., Jeandesboz, J. and Martin-Mazé, M. (2016) *Internal Border Controls in the Schengen Area: Is Schengen Crisis-Proof-Study for the LIBE Committee*, Brussels: European Parliament, Directorate General for Internal Policies.
Haas, E. (1958) The Uniting of Europe. Political Social and Economic Forces, 1950–57, London: Stevens.
Hall, P.A. (1993) 'Policy paradigms, social learning and the State: The case of economic policymaking in Britain', *Comparative Politics*, 25(3): 275–296.
Hathaway, J.C. (1993) 'Harmonizing for whom: The devaluation of refugee protection in the era of European Economic Integration', *Cornell International Law Journal*, 26(3): 719–735.
Hooghe, L. and Marks, G. (2008) 'A postfunctionalist theory of European integration: From permissive consensus to costraining dissensus', *British Journal of Political Science*, 39: 1–39.
Huysmans, J. (2000) 'The European Union and the securitization of migration', *Journal of Common Market Studies*, 38(5): 751–777.
Kaunert, C. and Léonard, S. (2012) 'The development of the EU asylum policy: Venue shopping in perspective', *Journal of European Public Policy*, 19(9): 1396–1413.
Lahav, G. (1997) 'Immigration and the State: The devolution and privatization of immigration control in the EU', *Journal of Ethnic and Migration Studies*, 24(4): 675–694.
Lavenex, S. (2006) 'Shifting up and out: The foreign policy of European immigration control', *West European Politics*, 29(2): 329–350.
Lavenex, S. and Kunz, R. (2008) 'The migration-development nexus in the EU external relations', *European Integration*, 30(3): 439–457.
Lavenex, S. and Wichmann, N. (2009) 'The external governance of EU internal security', *European Integration*, 31(1): 83–102.
Little, A. and Vaugham-Williams, N. (2017) 'Stopping boats, saving lives, securing subjects: Humanitarian borders in Europe and Australia', *European Journal of International Relations*, 23(3): 533–556.

Manners, I. (2002) 'Normative power Europe: A contradiction in terms?', *Journal of Common Market Studies*, 40(2): 235–258.
Maricut, A. (2016) 'With and without supranationalisation: The post-Lisbon roles of the European Council and the Council of Justice and Home Affairs Governance', *Journal of European Integration*, 38(5): 541–555.
Monar, J. (2000) 'The dynamics of justice and home affairs: Laboratories, driving factors and costs', *Journal of Common Market Studies*, 39(4): 747–764.
Pallister Williams, P. (2015) 'The humanitarian politics of European border policing', *International Political Sociology*, 9: 53–69.
Pascouau, Y. (2013) The Schengen Governance Package: The Subtle Balance Between Community method and Integovernmental Approach, European Policy Centre, Discussion Paper.
Puetter, U. and Fabbrini, S. (2016) 'Catalysts of integration: The role of core intergovernmental forums in EU politics', *Journal of European Integration*, 38(5): 633–642.
Ripoll Servent, A. and Trauner, F. (2014) 'Do supranational EU institutions make a difference? EU asylum law befeore and after communitarization', *Journal of European Public Policy*, 21(8): 1142–1162.
Ruggie, J.G. (1983) 'Continuity and Transformation in the World Polity: Toward a Neorealist Synthesis', *World Politics*, 35(2): 275.
Ruggie, J.G. (1993) 'Territoriality and Beyond: Problematizing Modernity in International Relations', *International Organization*, 47(1): 119, 151.
Stetter, S. (2000) 'Regulating migration: Authority delegation in justice and home affairs', *Journal of European Public Policy*, 7(1): 80–103.
Van Houtum, H. and Pijpers, R. (2005) 'Towards a gated community', *Eurozine*, https://www.eurozine.com/towards-a-gated-community/ (accessed on March 14th, 2019).
Van Selm, J. (2002) 'Immigrants and Asylum or Foreign Policy: The EU's Approach to Migrants and their Countries of Origin' in S. Lavenex and E. Üçarer (eds) *Migration and the Externalities of EU integration*, Lanham: Lexington Books, 143–160.
Wallace, H. (2000) 'The Institutional Setting: Five Variations on a Theme' in H. Wallace and W. Wallace (eds) *Policy Making in the European Union*, Oxford and New York: Oxford University Press, 4–26.
Walters, W. (2002) 'Mapping Schengenland: Denaturalizing borders', *Environment and Planning: Society and Space*, 20: 561–580.
Walters, W. (2004) 'The Frontiers of the European Union: A Geostrategic Perspective', *Geopolitics*, 9(3): 676.
Walters, W. (2011) 'Foucault and Frontiers: Notes on the Birth of the Humanitarian Border' in U. Bröckling, S. Krasmann and T. Lemke (eds) *Governmentality: Current Issues and Future Challenges*, New York: Routledge, 138–164.
Weinar, A. (2017), 'Cooperation on Migration and the Revised European Neighborhood Policy' in D. Bouris and T. Schumacher (eds.) *The Revised European Neighborhood Policy*, London: Palgrave Macmillan, 263–283.
Zaiotti, R. (2011) Cultures of Border Control. Schengen and the Evolution of European Frontiers, Chicago and London: The University of Chicago Press.
Zielonka, J. (2001) 'How new enlarged borders will reshape the European Union', *Journal of Common Market Studies*, 39(3): 507–536.
Zielonka, J. (2006) *Europe As Empire: The Nature of Enlarged European Union*, Oxford: Oxford University Press.

Chapter 2

Containment policies, human mobility and phantom borders

The case of Libya

Antonio M. Morone

Since the late 1990s, Libya has become a privileged destination for important international migration flows from other Arab countries, from different countries in Africa to the south of the Sahara, and even from Asian countries such as Bangladesh, India and China. The human mobility from neighboring countries, and subsequently from sub-Saharan Africa toward Libya and beyond towards Italy or Europe, were not two distinct processes, but were interconnected, since often residence and work in Libya for a more or less lengthy period determines the basis of selection between a first migration towards Libya and a second one to Europe. Exception is made for those migrants determined to seek political asylum or humanitarian protection in Europe from the start of their migratory project, including for example Somalis and Eritreans. In these cases, migrants move along networks that are well-structured and well-financed by friends, relatives or simple fellow countrymen already resident in Europe, especially in Northern Europe, who invest in a relatively rapid journey of their loved ones or acquaintances by identifying in Libya the most favorable illegal passage for reaching Europe. In many other instances, surely the majority, migrants headed for Libya have neither a predetermined migration project nor even readily available resources, so that it is usually during their work period in Libya that they come to the decision of trying to cross the Mediterranean, based mainly on the resources and opportunities at their disposal. They may instead decide to extend their residence in Libya or undertake a successful return migration if they have succeeded in setting aside enough money to meet their prior expectations or, failing this, take stock of the failure of their migration project.

Because of this complex migratory situation, over the past three decades Libya has been a true laboratory for European, and especially Italian, migration policies. Since the 1990s there have been two conflicting tendencies in Libya: on the one hand, the policies of the Qadhdhafi regime characterized by an open-door policy towards the influx of low-cost labor from sub-Saharan Africa and the Arab countries; on the other hand, the containment policies put in place by Italy and Europe to halt illegal migratory flows through the Mediterranean Sea, which were however an infinitely small proportion of the total number of migrants in Libya. With the collapse of the regime in 2011 and the beginning of the civil war, Italy, and increasingly the rest of Europe, have continued to exert a series of direct and indirect pressures on the new Libyan authorities, with the aim of reaffirming the policies of migratory containment. However, political instability and the persistence of conflict have strongly compromised the effectiveness of this attempt, urging rather a further extension of migratory containment southwards to other African countries. Containment policies of migration flows combine border externalization and securitization with an increasing use of non-democratic methods of governance: the present contribution thus aims at analyzing the migration issue along these three keywords within the framework of Italian–Libyan relations and in light of the postcolonial structure of these relations.

2.1. *Cheap bargaining at the migrants' expense*

During the 1990s, Qadhdhafi's foreign policy progressively veered away from Pan-Arabism toward Pan-Africanism, with the idea of making Libya a regional power on the African continent, and especially in the process of reforming the Organization of African Unity (OAU), which culminated in the creation of the new African Union (AU) at the Durban Summit in South Africa in 2002. Libya was actually one of the countries most committed to promoting the reform of the continental African organization, supporting it with both a lavish international cooperation program, financed by Libya's oil revenues, and by opening up the Libyan labor market to cheap labor from abroad. Qadhdhafi had already opened Libya's borders to foreign workers in 1998 by promoting the creation of the Sahelo-Saharan States (Cen-Sad), which established among the participating countries (soon all the North African countries and those of Sahel-Saharan Africa, with the sole exceptions of Algeria and Ethiopia) a vast area of free trade and free movement of workers. In 2002, the same year as the new AU was founded, Qadhdhafi launched what was called Libya's development program through African labor, literally opening Libya's southern border to foreign workers, who could not only gain access to the country solely with passports and in some cases with a simple national identity document, but could also find work without being obliged to submit to formal contractual, trade union and insurance regulations. Obviously, this arrangement substantially prefigured the exploitation of foreign labor in the absence of minimal protection of workers' rights, but for many poor or very poor migrants the chance to easily find a relatively well-paid job in Libya became a very attractive factor, such as to stimulate considerable migratory flows. Over the new millennium the number of legal migrants grew rapidly in Libya, reaching 10.4% of the Libyan population in 2010, estimated at 6.5 million persons, while the number of illegal migrants ranged from 1.5 to 2 million (Migration Policy Centre 2013).

Libya's open door to international migrants was accompanied, as a reaction from the northern side of the Mediterranean, by the progressive creation of policies promoted by Italy to contain illegal migration across the sea. While the numbers of migrants directed towards Europe were relatively small in relation to the total number of those in Libya, the political need for Italy to control the flows of migrants transformed irregular migrants into a bargaining chip in Italian and European relations with Libya. The average annual irregular arrivals on the Italian coasts during the 2000s have amounted to about 26,000 people, including not only arrivals from Libya, but also those from other southern routes, such as the Tunisian and Egyptian ones (Papavero 2015: 6). Even in the last few years, the increased landings – from an average of 30,000 to 35,000 persons at the beginning of the 2010s to more than 180,000 in the first semester of 2016 (Ministero dell'Interno 2017) – are still a very small number in comparison with those present in Libya. At the end of the Qadhdhafi era, irregular migrants in Libya were estimated to number as many as 1.5 or 2 million (Migration Policy Centre 2013). Thus, the representation of Libya as a country of transit, or a corridor towards Italy and Europe, is definitely misleading. The realty was that "most migrants remained in Libya" (Paoletti and Pastore 2010) during the Qadhdhafi era and even after the fall of his regime in 2011 (Danish Refugee Council 2014; Hani al-Tarhouni 2016; Morone 2017). There is no doubt that the dynamics of the conflict have opened up unimaginable opportunities of maneuver for the criminal networks that manage the trans-Mediterranean migrations. However, the Libyan economy continued to grow up to 2014 (at a rate of 116% in 2012) and continued to attract cheap labor to Libya from both sub-Saharan countries and other Asian or Mediterranean Arab countries (St. John 2013: 106).

Despite the relatively limited extent of sea crossings, the irregular landings rapidly heightened political concern in Italy and contributed to Italy's commitment to prevent them at any cost. On December 13, 2000, Italy signed an agreement with Libya to cooperate against terrorism, drug trafficking and irregular migration. This agreement was the basis for the subsequent secret and never publicized 2003 agreement, on the basis of which Italian patrols could enter Libyan waters and Italian police were sent to Libyan ports, while Tripoli obtained military equipment to control its borders. According to this 2003 agreement Libya was also willing to readmit irregular migrants that arrived in Italy. In 2004 and 2005 Italy intensified its collective repatriation activities, which were actual deportations, despite the condemnations of the European Parliament and the European Court of Human Rights. In reality, Italian operations were not particularly contested: although the European Parliament's 2005 condemnation was indisputable, "the European Commission took refuge in its lack of jurisdiction over the matter" (Perrin 2011: 297). In 2007, a Memorandum of Understanding was signed between the Italian Minister of the Interior and his Libyan counterpart, which established, at least in theory, Italian Navy patrol units with mixed crews in Libyan territorial waters, with the intention of halting migrant sea craft. The 2007 agreement finally became operative in 2009, following ratification by the Italian Parliament of the Treaty of Friendship, Partnership and Cooperation between Italy and Libya, signed in 2008.

During the same period, Italian political pressure on Libya was also effective in provoking the revision, at least partially, of Qadhdhafi's open door policy towards sub-Saharan workers. A tighter regulation of entry visas, with the exception of Maghrebis, was introduced by the regime, and foreign workers were obliged to obtain compulsory insurance and work and residence permits in Libya. Furthermore, the offense of illegal immigration was introduced into law and was punishable by up to 3 years imprisonment. We can conclude about Libya what has already been said about the introduction of the crime of illegal immigration in Tunisia and Morocco, that this offense responds primarily to requirements associated "with illegal immigration into Europe" and produces a great tendency to criminalize migration (Perrin 2009: 251). The combined effect of these measures, in compliance with Italy's demands for a stricter legislative discipline regarding international migration (Drozdz and Pliez 2005: 69), was to transform over a short period of time a mass of foreign workers who had free access to the country into irregular migrants, with the result of increasing their vulnerability and likelihood of being exploited. The final and contradictory result was that the increased irregular status among foreign workers in Libya produced an increase in irregular migration towards Italy and Europe.

The Italian–Libyan Treaty of 2008 marked a historic page in the relations between the two countries, owing to Italy's reparations for its colonial crimes. Since the Revolution of 1969, Qadhdhafi had repeatedly asked for the Italian compensations, while the remaining Italian colonial community was expelled from the country in 1970. On the Italian side, the Italian–Libyan Treaty of 1956 had never seriously been called into question, and Qadhdhafi's requests had never been acknowledged until the migration issue arose. After 2008, Italy became Libya's main economic and political partner among the Western countries: the control of irregular migration and the enlargement of Italian economic interests in Libya were exchanged for the Italian commitment to support the end of the international embargo on Libya and its readmission to the international community (Paoletti 2011). It was Berlusconi who on his return from Benghazi – where the Treaty was signed – triumphantly announced to the Italian press that the treaty would soon mean "fewer illegal migrants and more gas and oil" (Di Carlo 2008). Qadhdhafi was thus able not only to internationally (re)legitimize his regime, but also to internally increase his consensus by presenting himself as the true liberator from (post)colonial grievances. The postcolonial arrangement of Italian–Libyan relations functioned "as a mutual cover for the two leaders in the face of their respective public opinion" for quite different interests (Labanca 2011: 42).

The 2008 Treaty paved the way for the further implementation of Italian containment polices. The Italian–Libyan joint patrol activities to halt migrants at sea, and the so-called push-back strategy to forcibly return them to Libya, was only the first stage of a containment cycle. Since 2004, under the Italian–Libyan cooperation framework, the Italian government made available the funds and technical means needed to build transit camps in Libya that were de facto internment centers, actual prisons where irregular immigrants were detained while waiting to be deported to their countries of origin or to third countries. The main camps for this purpose were built in Cufra and Sebha, and totaled 18 or 19 structures (Ceccorulli 2014: 196). The closing of the Mediterranean Sea to the transit of irregular migrants was thus combined with detention in Libya of those pushed-back migrants and other migrants who were reputedly about to leave the country for Italy. The final stage, after imprisonment, was, at least in theory, the migrants' repatriation to their countries of origin. The appropriateness of the term "repatriation" may justly be called into question, as it is often used in official documents since it presupposes a voluntary decision on the part of the returnee, which appears very hard to believe in a context of imprisonment, exploitation and violence. It would be more fitting to speak of deportation, in a situation of compulsion, rather than a voluntary decision. In any case, expulsion from Libya ended up as a much more ambiguous process than what the international policies intended: the repatriations were often very difficult to carry out because of the lack of agreements between Libya and the governments of those countries, and ultimately because of the lack of mutual political interest. Qadhdhafi's pan-African policy presupposed good relations with many of the governments of which the migrants were citizens. Recognizing their demands for political asylum or expelling them from Libya threatened to compromise these relations, because in the first case the legitimacy of the partner state's government would have been called into question, and in the second case such a strategic resource as the migrants' remittances to their states of origin would have been limited. There were also extreme cases where so-called repatriation was not possible because of the state of war and conflict of the country of origin, as in Somalia. In the absence of well-defined political agreements and political interests, many deportees simply ended up being taken over the southern Libyan border into Niger, where the vast majority found themselves in another foreign country and subjected to new forms of exploitation and violence.

The push-back, detention and deportation cycle revealed more than one limit in terms of human rights, especially from the southern side of the Mediterranean, but it was very effective in halting the irregular landings on Italy's shores. For this reason the cycle was and still is implemented in violation of the rights of the migrants concerned. The refoulement of those migrants, which in 2008 was presented by the Italian Ministry of the Interior as the most effective means of "international co-operation on illegal immigration and the traffic in human beings" (Ministero dell'Interno, no date: 17), actually undermined the rights of migrants in their ability to seek asylum or humanitarian protection in Italy, and constituted an exception to the rule of law, with the result that Italy was found guilty of such a push-back strategy on June 6, 2012 by the judges of the European Court of Human Rights. The judgment in that case referred to the fact that the refoulements at sea did not respect the principle of non-refoulement and prevented potential refugees from applying for asylum (Conseil de l'Europe 2012). The international ruling revealed all of Italy's hypocrisy in accusing Qadhdhafi of never having signed the 1951 United Nations Convention on the Status of Refugees and failing to respect the human rights of migrants, when it was really Italy that passed onto Libya the task of receiving, accepting and assessing any right to asylum or protection of those who were turned back at sea. On the other hand, Qadhdhafi himself left no room for doubt on this point when, shortly after signing the 2008 Treaty, he proceeded to shut down the offices in Tripoli of the United Nations High Commissioner for Refugees, which until that point had operated in his country without any official recognition, precisely because Libya was not a signatory to the 1951 Convention. Qadhdhafi left no alibi to his European partners over the fact that it was entirely up to them to address the question of protecting migrants' rights, since the very concept of human rights was not recognized by the theory of the Libyan Revolution, which "did not guarantee civil and political rights because it did not recognize the concept of citizenship" (Baldinetti 2009: 232).

The containment cycle was a process of externalizing and securitizing the southern Italian (and European) border onto Libyan soil. The contemporary history of Libya indicates that this process overlaps and, in a way, re-establishes old borders and spatial arrangements. During the colonial occupation of Libya, after the end of Italy's extended war against Arab resistance from 1911 to 1931, the colonial authorities decided to divide Libyan territory into two main parts: in 1939 the coastline and its hinterland were organized into four districts (Tripoli, Msrata, Benghazi, and Derna) and designated as an integral part of Italy's mainland territory. The most important resource that Italy was extracting from its colony was space and land to facilitate the process of settler colonialism that was intended to follow its colonial conquest. The Libyan territory became officially Italian, while Libyans themselves were still considered colonial subjects despite acknowledgement of their Special Italian Citizenship, which was really a diminution of their status rather than an upgrade (Calchi Novati 2011: 233). The Libyan territory was thus divided between useful Libya and its useless southern desert area, which remained under military administration. The present process of border externalization and securitization has reintroduced not only external interference in Libya (and a consequent limitation of its sovereignty), but also a geopolitical partition between the Libyan coastline and its hinterland, where migrants are pushed back, and its southern region, where detention and deportation police are planned to be concentrated with the intention of preventing migrants from reaching the coastline. The (re)shaping of Libya's divisions can be methodologically addressed in terms of "phantom borders", or "visibility of historical borders" which are no longer formal, that is conceptualized in the literature as mostly in relation to post-Soviet space in Central and Eastern Europe (Von Löwis 2015: 99). The phantom border is also the emotional and perceptual phenomenon of an external threat and an internal identity (Kolossov 2005: 619) that is very much analogous to the Libyan situation. A good example is the increasing public backlash to the massive immigration from sub-Saharan Africa that took place in Libya during the 2000s. A series of stereotypes similar to those that characterize certain attitudes about migration in Europe spread around the country, combining racist ideas with nationalist identity memes. Stereotypes about migrants range from suggestions that they are dangerous criminals and responsible for the spread of infectious diseases, to their hypothetical role played in the "Africanization" of a country such as Libya, centered on its identity as an Arab and Islamic nation. In this context, it is understandable that the policies in question did not give rise to popular Libyan opposition because they did not affect Libyans, but foreigners, while they found a certain favor in the layers of a public opinion often disoriented by, if not openly hostile to, such large numbers of migrants.

2.2. *Continuity and change in post-Qadhdhafi Libya*

The fall of the Qadhdhafi regime in 2011 and the onset of the civil war immediately caused the collapse of the control system of irregular flows. Since the very beginning of the Libyan crisis, Italy, and increasingly, the European Union, were committed to restoring the control of migratory flows, trying to both resurrect relations with Libya and deploy a military force at sea. Through Operation Mare Nostrum, the Italian Navy patrolled the waters of the Central Mediterranean from October 2013 to December 2014, escorting migrants from Libyan territorial waters to Italy. The supposed change in Italian policy from refoulement to rescue at sea was in actuality "more quantitative than qualitative" (Cuttitta 2015: 133): the final objective still remains that of repatriating migrants after having rescued them at sea, except for those recognized as political asylum seekers or in need of humanitarian protection. Since the fall of 2014, Italy's naval mission has been gradually replaced by a new naval operation called Triton and, since April 2015, by another called European Union Naval Force Mediterranean (EUNAVFOR Med) "Operation Sophia": both operations have been under the direction of the European Border Control Agency (FRONTEX). The effect has been to considerably reduce and, at least in 2017, prevent rescue operations at sea, while the containment policies in Libya were resumed and running. Furthermore, the turnover of naval operations clearly marked the increased involvement of the European Union's, and Italy's, successful Europeanization of its agenda on migration.

On the Libyan side, the Italian Minister of the Interior, Annamaria Cancellieri, on a visit to Tripoli on January 21, 2012, signed a Memorandum of Understanding with her Libyan counterpart, expressing the intention to renew cooperation for training the Libyan Police and Coast Guard, building infrastructures aimed at containing migrants, coordinating programs for repatriating migrants to their countries of origin, and bolstering joint border control (International Federation for Human Rights 2012: 36). The first result was that the Libyan authorities began working to resume "the control of migratory flows in the region", monitoring the camps and the various detention facilities,[1] and the deportation operation by Libyan authorities: from May 2012 to

[1] Author's anonymous interview with a Libyan Police officer, Khums, April 20, 2014. The officer was in charge of the operations of monitoring migrants' flows from Khums to Gasr Garabulli, along the Eastern Tripolitanian coastline.

April 2013, at least 25,000 people were taken to the southern border of Libya near Gatron, near the border with Niger (Amnesty International, 2013: 6). According to the Libyan Ministry of Internal Affairs, among the 100,000 refouled sub-Saharan migrants from 2013 to 2016 there were also several Eritreans who risked incarceration, forced labor or even capital punishment once they returned to their country. [2] Furthermore, in 2013, under international pressure, the Department for Combating Illegal Migration (DCIM) was set up within the Libyan Interior Ministry, which was able in a short time to bring under the control of Tripoli, at least nominally, a number of camps and prisons for more or less informal migrants, in addition to coordinating migration control and deportation activities. In a context such as Libya's, where the state and its institutions have been and are still going through a period of particular weakness and fragility, the DCIM contradicts the stereotype of a failed state and highlights the enormous influence that foreign players, such as that exerted by Italy, the EU and other international agencies, can have on the Libyan situation. It is obvious that the situation described presupposes a political trade-off very similar to the one Italy negotiated with Qadhdhafi: the willingness of Libya to participate in controlling migrant flows in exchange for international recognition, which for the new Libyan authorities promises to be even more important than it was for the Qadhdhafi regime.

Conflict, institutional fragility and political instability in Libya have, however, greatly reduced the effectiveness of containment policies. For this reason, on February 2, 2017 Italy promoted a second Italian–Libyan Memorandum of Understanding that opened the way to new refoulement operations at sea, though this time executed autonomously by the Libyan Coast Guard thanks to Italy's training and materiel. Thus, Italy guarded itself against a new condemnation by the European judges by ceasing to participate actively in refoulements, but in political substance the Italian involvement has not changed significantly. In addition, the agreement reaffirms the will to cooperate in managing "temporary hosting camps" in Libya, which are to serve for repatriating migrants (Uselli 2017). The Memorandum of 2017 marked a direct return to the past, despite the official commitment of the Mario Monti government, announced on June 20, 2012, to give up the push-back strategy as a possible means of flow control after the European judges imposed their unfavorable verdict on Italy (ANSAmed 2012).

Despite all the attempts to reactivate the containment cycle in Libya, the political and military instability of the country urged Italian and European decision makers to replicate and export the same policies to other African countries, especially the Sub-Saharan ones considered of strategic importance for containing migratory flows, such as Niger, Sudan, Ethiopia and Eritrea. A good example is the "Khartoum Process",

[2] Mohamed Karwad, *Itinéraires de l'immigration illégale vers la Libye*, paper presented at the Internationl Conference *Les dynamiques de l'immigration du Sahel vers la Libye et de la Libye vers l'Europe : itinéraires et devenir*, Centre Maghrébin d'études sur la Libye (Cmel), Tunis, April 26 and 27, 2016. Mohamed Karwad is a Libyan official representing the Home Affairs Ministry of the Government of National Accord.

officially the EU-Horn of Africa Migration Route Initiative, launched in the autumn of 2014 and aimed at "improving national capabilities" of transit countries in "migration control" as well as ultimately extending or strengthening the means of flow control that have already proved effective in the Mediterranean area (Rome Declaration 2014). Another example is the increasing orientation of European development policies and aid programs towards migration issues. The trend is thus to increasingly subordinate the international cooperation to conditions regarding migration, which have taken precedence over those related to respect for human rights. The actual risk glaringly contradicts the granting of strategic aid in the name of migration control to governments such as those of Sudan or Eritrea, to give just two examples, which, according to the parameters of conditioning cooperation to respect human rights, had been excluded in the past, or greatly reduced, from participating in development programs. It is a paradox to fund governments that are recognized internationally as guilty of serious violations of human rights and to ask them not only to halt migrants but also to protect their rights. In broader and more conceptual terms the Khartoum Process and new trends in international cooperation were indeed moving in the direction of further externalizing Europe's borders southwards and replicating policies and strategies implemented in Libya.

The non-democratic methods of such migration governance are thus detectable on both the European and African ends. With the exception of the Libyan–Italian Treaty of 2008, all the other agreements signed by Italy with Libya have not had any parliamentary approval, be it Italian, European or Libyan, because of their category of governmental acts. In this way they more easily avoided the criticisms of "preventive refoulement" expressed in relation to certain containment policies. The containment cycle described makes it possible to circumvent the prohibition of refoulement sanctioned by the 1951 Convention of Refugee Rights by returning asylum seekers or other migrants to transit countries or to their regions of origin before they reach the sovereign territory in which they could make their request (Hyndman and Mountz 2008: 250). Thus, the rhetoric of international humanitarian protection is acting in practice to hinder, and if possible to halt, a much more "normal" migration associated with the aspirations of individuals to social mobility, rather than to protect potential asylum seekers. Beyond the physical halt of migrants, these bordering policies prevent reciprocal knowledge and understanding and definitely produce isolation, ignorance, mistrust, and fear towards foreigners that are all functional elements to legitimize those same policies.

Bibliography

Amnesty International (2013) 'Scapegoats of fear. Rights of refugees, asylum-seekers and migrants abuses in Libya', http://www.amnesty.org/fr/library/info/MDE19/007/2013/en (accessed on March 15th, 2019).

ANSAmed (2012) 'Immigrazione: Libia; Terzi, respingimenti non in agenda governo', www.ansa.it/ansamed/it/notizie/stati/libia/2012/06/20/Immigrazione-Libia-Terzi-respingimenti-in-agenda-governo_7068589.html (accessed on March 15th, 2019).
Baldinetti, A. (2009) 'Le Istanze Amazigh in Libia: La Nascita di Una Società Civile?' in A. Baldinetti and A. Maneggia (eds) *Processi politici nel Mediterraneo: dinamiche e prospettive*, Perugia: Morlacchi.
Calchi Novati, G.P. (2011) *L'Africa d'Italia. Una storia coloniale e postcoloniale*, Rome: Carocci.
Ceccorulli, M. (2014) 'The Mediterranean as a Buffer. Confining Irregular Migrant in North Africa' in M. Ceccorulli and N. Labanca (eds) *The EU, Migration and the Politics of Administrative Detention*, London: Routledge.
Conseil de l'Europe (2012) *Secrétariat général, Plans d'action du Gouvernement Italien dans l'affaire Hirsi Jamaa et autres c. Italie, requête n° 27765/09, réunion 1150 DH*, 6 juillet.
Cuttitta, P. (2015) 'Mare Nostrum e la retorica umanitaria', *Rivista di Storia delle Idee*, 4(1): 128–140.
Danish Refugee Council (2014) '"We risk our lives for our daily bread". Finding of the Danish Refugee Council Study on mixed migration in Libya', https://drc.dk/ (accessed on March 15th, 2019).
Di Carlo, P. (2008) 'Berlusconi, patto con Gheddafi "Ora meno clandestini e più gas"', *Corriere della Sera*, August 31.
Drozdz, M. and Pliez, O. (2005) 'Entre Libye et Soudan: La fermeture d'une piste transsaharienne', *Autrepart*, 36(4): 63–80.
Hani al-Tarhouni (2016) دراسة ميدانية عن الهجرة غير النظامية في ليبيا, *Libyan Affairs*, 1: 36–46.
Hyndman, J. and Mountz, A. (2008) 'Another brick in the wall? Neo-refoulement and the externalization of asylum by Australia and Europe', *Government and Opposition*, 43(2): 249–269.
International Federation for Human Rights (2012) 'Libya. The Hounding of Migrants Must Stop', http://www.fidh.org/en/north-africa-middle-east/libya/Libya-The-hounding-of-migrants-12255 (accessed on March 15th, 2019).
Kolossov, V. (2005) 'Border studies: Changing perspectives and theoretical approaches', *Geopolitics*, 10(4): 606–632.
Labanca, N. (2011) 'La guerra di Libia nelle pubblicazioni e negli studi italiani degli ultimi venticinque anni', *I sentieri della ricerca*, 13: 19–54.
Migration Policy Centre (2013) *Migration Profile: Libya*, Fiesole: European University Institute.
Ministero dell'Interno (2017) *Statistiche del Ministero dell'Interno*, July 13 http://www.interno.gov.it/sites/default/files/cruscotto_statistico_giornaliero_del_13_luglio_2017_-.pdf (accessed on March 15th, 2019).
Ministero dell'Interno (no date), *Iniziative dell'Italia. Sicurezza, immigrazione e asilo*, www.interno.it/mininterno/export/sites/default/it/assets/files/19/0843_Opuscolo_ITA.pdf (accessed on March 15th, 2019).
Morone, A.M. (2017) 'Policies, Practices, and Representations Regarding Sub-Saharan Migrants in Libya: From the Partnership with Italy to the Post-Qadhafi Era' in P. Gaibazzi, S. Dünnwald and A. Bellagamba (eds) *EurAfrican Borders and Migration Management. Political Cultures, Contested Spaces, and Ordinary Lives*, New York: Palgrave Macmillan, 129–155.

Paoletti, E. (2011) *The Migration of Power and North-South Inequalities: The Case of Italy and Libya*, Basingstoke: Palgrave Macmillan.

Paoletti, E. and Pastore, F. (2010) 'Sharing the dirty job on the southern front? Italian-Libyan relations on migration and their impact on the European Union', *IMI Working Papers Series*, 29 http://www.imi.ox.ac.uk/pdf/ (accessed on March 15th, 2019).

Papavero, G. (2015) 'Sbarchi, richiedenti asilo e presenze irregolari', Milan: Fondazione Ismu.

Perrin, D. (2009) 'Immigration et Création Juridique au Maghreb. La Fragmentation des Mondes et des Droits' in A. Bensaad (ed.) *Le Maghreb à l'Épreuve des Migrations Sub-sahariennes. Immigration sur Émigration*, Paris: Karthala.

Perrin, D. (2011) 'Fin de régime et migrations en Libye. Les enseignements juridiques d'un pays en feu', *L'Année du Maghreb*, 7: 285–301.

Rome Declaration (2014) *Declaration of the Ministerial Conference of the Khartoum Process*, EU-Horn of Africa Migration Route Initiative, November 28 http://italia2014.eu/media/3785/declaration-of-the-ministerial-conference-of-the-khartoum-process.pdf (accessed on March 15th, 2019).

St. John, R.B. (2013) 'The Post-Qadhafi Economy' in J. Pack (ed.) *The 2011 Libyan Uprisings and the Struggle for the Post-Qadhafi Future*, New York: Palgrave Macmillan.

Uselli, S. (2017) 'Italy-Libya agreement, the Memorandum text', ASGI, February 7, www.asgi.it/english/italy-libya-agreement-the-memorandum-text/ (accessed on March 15th, 2019).

Von Löwis, S. (2015) 'Phantom borders in the political geography of East Central Europe: An introduction', *Erdkunde*, 69(2): 99–106.

Chapter 3

Defining migrants, defining borders

Arrivals in Italy by sea in 2011 between illegality and right to protection

Emanuela Dal Zotto

According to migration sociologist Douglas Massey, 'defining a movement requires to draw a line and agree that it has been crossed. Where this line is geographically and administratively drawn is essentially a social and political construction' (Massey 2002: 47). This statement effectively explains how not only the geographical borders but also the administrative ones – constituted, for example, by the categories used to define and organize the different features of migrations – are the result of processes of social construction, and therefore they change in space and time. This contribution focuses in particular on the definitions that have been given to migrants arrived by sea in Italy in 2011 (simultaneously with the so-called Arab Springs) and the resulting forms of reception, with the purpose to highlight how the borders of these definitions changed from time to time depending on the necessity to defend or make crossable other borders: the maritime and terrestrial ones of the Italian State. The data and the considerations presented in these pages are a part of what I produced during my doctoral research, conducted in Italy between 2011 and 2014: my research revisited the 2011 events through in-depth interviews with policymakers and actors of the reception system (at the national and local levels) and the analysis of official documents (mostly decrees and ordinances), and related the succeeding representations of the situation with the implemented practices for governing migrations.

The arrivals of migrants on Italian shores are not a recent phenomenon, they have been observed since the early 1990s, with phases of higher or lower intensity due both to the conditions of the originary and transit contexts of migrants and to the policies adopted at several levels for controlling the migration flows. Although irregular entries by sea are not the most relevant feature of immigration to Italy from the quantitative point of view, they have always been at the centre of the public agenda, and the object of spectacularizing and mythologizing (Cuttitta 2012; De Haas 2008). Moreover, although they are not news at all, arrivals by sea are still interpreted and managed as an emergency, as was the case in 2011 (Campesi 2011).

I would consider rewording to something like: In fact, a state of emergency was declared by decree of the Prime Minister from February 12 until December 31, although fewer than 5,000 people arrived on Italian shores.

The construction of the emergency insists on the quantitative dimension of a phenomenon that, according to the decree, 'in the last days reached particularly worrying dimensions because of the unceasing landings of boats loaded with thousands of citizens from Tunisia on the island of Lampedusa'. This perspective was stressed also by the declarations of national and local politicians, spread by the media, about 'biblical exodus' and 'apocalyptic scenarios'. The decree introduces also the two different faces of emergency: the humanitarian one and the securitarian one. It provides for 'extraordinary and urgent measures' aiming on the one hand to the 'arrangement of facilities suited for the essential forms of humanitarian assistance', and on the other hand 'to the effective contrast of irregular immigration and the identification of subjects dangerous for the national public order and safety'. In this sense, the concept of emergency is dual: in it the humanitarian and securitarian elements coexist and appear as two poles between which it is easy to move depending on the necessity, and the insistence that one never completely cancel the effect of the other. A definition of the situation like the one shaped starting from this decree allowed a different categorization of the migrants who arrived in 2011 from Tunisia and then from Libya, and the implementation of different reception measures for them.

Later, in March 2011, 14,390 migrants arriving from Tunisia on Italian shores were registered. This fact was not interpreted as a consequence of the turmoils shaking the country since December and waning by then, but rather as the failure of border controls after the removal of Ben Ali. In an interview, the former Home Secretary, Roberto Maroni, described the situation in these terms:

> *The Ben Ali government ceases, the system of control falls, the police does not account to anyone and therefore, mainly from the South of Tunisia, they start to leave. They were all young males, thus people coming from a country where there wasn't a civil war, Ben Ali had been removed but there was not a situation of tribal conflict as it happened later in Libya, so they were to be technically considered as illegal immigrants.*

As regards the arrivals of Tunisians, the current prevailing definition seems to be a securitarian one that, while it criminalizes migrants, reclaims the already mentioned issue of invasion, particularly recurring in the anti-immigration rhetoric by Maroni's party, the Northern League. The picture of a besieged Italy is strengthened by the overcrowded Lampedusa island, where there were still 2,629 Tunisians at the middle of March 2011 (Manconi and Anastasia 2012). When the operation to 'free' the island, as will be said, begins, the Tunisians are transferred from here to several regions in Southern Italy and restricted in improvised, temporary facilities, mostly tent cities, where first reception and detention practices merge (Garelli and Tazzioli 2013). Their irregular status prevents them from proceeding to other European countries, although they aim for this, as proven by many breaks and departures from these facilities, especially towards France, at whose border, in Ventimiglia, groups of Tunisians start to gather, while the French government impedes entry to the country by reinstating border controls against the risk of suffering the irregular immigrations of the ones arrived in the European space through Italy.

While the securitarian dimension of emergency has proven to be the most functional so far for the management of migration flows from Tunisia, both at the local and national level, the situation changes when the issue shifts to the supranational level. In this scenario, the use of extraordinary measures and their indeterminateness appear to be an attempt by the Italian government to take time and reflect on which representation of the situation can be more useful to resolve the situation at the European level. At this point, the bivalence of the emergency frame proves to be a precious resource to use towards the European Union as well.

Already a few days after declaring the state of emergency, on February 15 Secretary Maroni addressed the European Union to disclose the emergency situation and to ask for the distribution among the European countries of the people arriving in range of a humanitarian emergency, together with support in opposing irregular immigration. The former request was actually a request for implementing the European Directive 2001/55/EU, which calls for the Council of the Union to propose, exactly in the event of a humanitarian emergency, a distribution of refugees among the Member States.

The EU's reply to Italy, voiced by Commissioner for Home Affairs Cecilia Malström, [1] was an offer for support in strengthening the control of sea borders, [2] but it substantially refused the idea that the arrivals from Tunisia were an emergency, let alone a humanitarian one. This position was reiterated in the following months until April 11, when the Justice and Home Affairs Council of the EU rejected Italy's formal request to apply the 2011/55/EU Directive. [3]

The Italian government cannot do anything but act unilaterally: although the European Union does not agree with identifying the arrivals from Tunisia as an humanitarian emergency, Italy can still resort to it for executing article 20 of the Consolidated Act on Immigration, which calls for the implementation of 'measures for temporary protection to adopt, even notwithstanding the instructions in this Act, for relevant humanitarian needs, in case of conflicts, natural disasters or other particularly serious events in Countries not belonging to the European Union'. Among these measures there is the issuance of a temporary residency permit for humanitarian reasons that allows the Tunisians to cross the internal borders of the European Union, and the Italian government to loosen the pressure caused by their presence both on the national territory and at the border with France.

---

[1] Session of the European Parliament, February 15, 2011. Speech 11/106, February 15.

[2] One of the ways to actualize this support was the start, some days later, of the HERMES operation by FRONTEX, the European agency for the control of the EU's external borders.

[3] *Immigrati, l'Europa boccia l'Italia. Maroni: così non ha più senso restare*, in La Repubblica.it, April 12, 2011, http://ricerca.repubblica.it/repubblica/archivio/repubblica/2011/04/12/immigrati-europa-boccia-italia-maroni.html?ref=search

> *Therefore, in order to avoid damage to, our, the overall system, to international relations etc., etc ... we found this solution, that was a humanitarian permit for six months, plus another six ... The residency permit for humanitarian reasons was consented by the Schengen agreement, so the other countries could not oppose, they had only to check whether the Tunisian crossing the border with France, with Austria, with Germany, had this permit for humanitarian reasons. Then, he who had this permit, was allowed to travel through Europe for six months, then he should have to come back to Italy, unless he got an extension for another six months ... which I did in October 2011, then our government fell in November ... but in the meanwhile they already scattered and the problem of having great numbers gathered, which is what causes social alarm, was no more. Because if you dilute, if these numbers are diluted in a year ... there is the possibility of absorbing on the territory without serious reactions, but if you gather 30 thousand people at the border in a month you see a very strong reaction, don't you?*

The emergency invoked to elicit social alarms does not make it now possible to solve what has been presented as a problem (because of the humanitarian element); instead, it causes its fragmentation, its reduction to invisibility and the restoration of the ordinary state of things. But we already said that the two poles of emergency never cancel each other completely, and the invisibilization of the Tunisians already arrived in Italy is backed up, in the same days (early April 2011) by a technical agreement with Tunisia against irregular immigration that provides for the repatriation of whoever arrives in Italy after the stipulation of the agreement, together with the strengthening of the collaboration between the police forces. From this moment there are not any new arrivals from Tunisia on the record, while the previous ones (almost 23,000 overall) do not leave any traces in the Italian reception facilities.

Beside the decrease of arrivals from Tunisia, in March the ones from Libya begin. A new Decree by President Berlusconi, on April 7, declares the state of humanitarian emergency in the area of North Africa in order to consent to effectively contrast the extraordinary flow of non-EU citizens in the national territory. In this case also, before decreeing the state of emergency, there had been hyperbolic previsions by the Government, whose Home Secretary said on March 2:

> *in Libya there are between one million and a half and two million and a half irregular migrants, who got into the country because of the impossibility to control the Southern borders. The crisis is pushing these people to move towards East and West; no one is going South. I expect that when the situation allows it, they will take again the route to North. This – the secretary stressed – is the worst case scenario among the possible ones, that is the arrival of almost 200 thousand people fleeing from war. The closure of the Libya-Tunisia border accentuates this risk. The government is getting ready for the risk of an unprecedented impact on our shores.* [4]

Indeed, the overall number of people who left Libya during 2011 largely passed the

---

[4] *Maroni: in Libia quasi 2 milioni di clandestini pronti a riversarsi sulle nostre coste,* in ilsole24 ore.com 2 March 2011, http://www.ilsole24ore.com/art/notizie/2011-03-02/maroni-libia-quasi-milioni-093456.shtml?-refresh_ce=1

million, but only a very small part of them reached Europe and Italy: according to the estimate by the UNHCR the civil war led 660 thousand Libyan citizens to expatriation and caused 550 thousand internal evacuees. Beside them, we need to count almost 800 thousand of the two million and a half migrants that were in Libya at the beginning of the war. [5] Thus, not only Europe, and specifically Italy, has to face a situation that, from the numerical point of view, cannot be defined an emergency (the people arrived in Italy from Libya are no more than 23 thousand), but also the resort to such a representation causes a strong reduction of complexity. With respect to the arrivals from Tunisia, the ones from Libya are read mainly from the humanitarian point of view, according to an extremely simplified scheme, that is consented also in this case by the emergency frame:

> *The scheme was simple: if a boat leaves Tunisia, they are all irregular ... if you see them when they arrived, they were all young males who wanted to go to France. When a boat left Libya, they were all asylum seekers because the fact that they leave from Libya determined this feature. According to where they left from we were able to establish which kind of migrants they were, which category, let's say so. In the 23 thousand arrived from Libya there were of any kind, there were women, children, the elderly ... because they were fleeing from a place ... The boats arriving from Tunisia, they were all young, male, and this was the difference. Thus the boats coming from Libya, we knew they could have the status of refugee.*

The simplification of the reality of the arrivals from Libya under the label 'people fleeing from war', used for the planning of a new *ad hoc* reception system, [6] entrusted to the Civil Protection and called 'North Africa Emergency', ends up provoking the block of the system itself, to the point that the measure adopted against the claimed emergency will cause a situation of actual emergency. In fact, the arrivals from Libya that are channeled in the procedure for the acknowledgment of international protection cause an increase in the requests for protection by 208.1% and a prolongation of the times for their examination by months. This leads to having to extend again and again the state of emergency that will be declared over only two years later, on 28 February 2013. On that date there are still many pending situations, also because of the high number of appeals issued by those who have seen their request denied (almost the 60%). An 'exit strategy' is then decided, a humanitarian permit for everybody whose

[5] Data reported in M. Zupi 2012.

[6] At the time of receiving as asylum seekers the people arriving from Libya, the System of Protection for Asylum Seekers and Refugees (the SPRAR), that is the ordinary reception system in Italy, had just 3,000 spots. The SPRAR is based on a reception project lead by the local administrations, and that is implemented with support from nonprofit organizations. The SPRAR's model of reception is widespread (a small number of people hosted throughout the national territory) and integrated (it should go beyond the supply of board and lodging in order to help the recipients to gain back their autonomy by providing them psycho-social and legal support, training, and job orientation).

request has not still been examined by December 2012 or has been denied. Such a solution makes it meaningless to force the migrants to a two-year wait in the extraordinary reception system, as such characterisd by the presence of several kinds of facilities, actually very often isolated and with very heterogeneous levels of reception. A system that, once again, on the one hand welcomes, on the other hand confines and detains. This is a further effect of the emergency that leaves a great margin of uncertainty and room for discretion to the actors in the organization of the system of reception (Dal Zotto 2014).

The case of arrivals to Italy in 2011 shows how the emergency can be invoked in the public discourse with regard to migration movements in order to raise social alarm and, at the same time, be used (in its two dimensions: humanitarian and securitarian) as an instrument to repristinate the normal state of things in front of public opinion. The exceptionality of the situation represented by the emergency requires the implementation of extraordinary and urgent measures in a problem–solution perspective that is flattened to a 'now and here' approach that does not seem able to acknowledge the historical complexity and depth of these phenomena that appear sudden and unexpected rather than the result of the progressive deterioration of social or natural situations. In this sense, an emergency frame favours generalizations and the use of juridical definitions for the migrants that result more functional to an immediate reaction to arrivals rather than to the understanding of the subjective experiences of those who arrive on Italian shores and protect their rights. In particular, the 2011 events show how the definition of migrants used in different phases first of all answered the need for controlling the borders and mobility: in my opinion, the weakness of the borders of the categories and of the use made of them is exemplified by the issue of a permit for humanitarian reasons for Tunisians, defined at the beginning as irregular migrants, as the choice to host as asylum seekers migrants coming from Libya, even when the majority of them were not Libyan citizens but migrants with different nationalities living and working in Libya for a long time.

Finally, the case of arrivals from Libya in 2011 is to be considered relevant also because it started the praxis, established with the institution of the Mare Nostrum operation in October 2014, of hosting as asylum seekers the majority of migrants arrived by sea and brought to Italy during the rescue operations (Marchetti 2015). In a phase of more and more restrictions to regular immigration, the humanitarian channel has consequently become for many the only possible access to Italy and Europe, thus making the journey by sea and the following asylum request the most widespread way to enter for those who have reached Italy since 2014, and putting the issue of reception of forced migrants at the core of the Italian political debate and agenda in recent years. Once again, the choice to define the migrants arriving on the Italian shores and the consequent choice whether to welcome or reject them on the basis of the category in which they fall is very telling of the current migration policies because while, as Zetter (2007) suggests, in the contemporary scenario of international migrations the causes of migration movements are so interrelated that it is almost impossible, and often arbitrary, to definitely distinguish between forced and voluntary migrants, it is as true that such a distinction is now widely used to separate at the doors of Europe the potential assignees of international protection from economic migrants, accepting the former to the European space and rejecting the latter, with the primary aim of protecting the EU's borders. In fact, the introduction in 2015 of the hotspot approach, as one of the measures provided for by the European Agenda on Migration, is based on this mechanism. This approach consists of opening in Italy and Greece, in areas considered to be 'hot' (therefore hotspot) in terms of the number of arrivals, centres for the identification of migrants and indeed the distinction of the potential asylum seekers (who are directed to the procedure for the request of international protection or the outplacement in other European countries) and the so-called economic migrants (who are conversely rejected). The migrants' identification happens in the hours following their arrival and it is worked out by the Italian police forces together with the European teams of Frontex, Europol and Easo (European Asylum Support Office), with the support of NGOs and international organizations (particularly the International Organization for Migration and the United Nations High Commissioner for Refugees).[7] The field studies (Squire et al. 2017) and the reports from NGOs[8] highlight how the distinction between who is entitled to stay and who must leave the European territory happens after the migrants compile a sheet in situations that are not always ideal (e.g. because of the lack of interpreters) and in many cases on the basis of the nationality they declared, once again on the basis of a praxis that favours generalizations and risks to undermine the subjective right to protection.

Bibliography

Bartolucci, V. (2013) 'L'invasione dei migranti: La costruzione simbolica di un'emergenza umanitaria nel discorso politico italiano durante i rivolgimenti nel mondo arabo' in P. Parmiggiani and P. Musarò (eds.) *Oltre le Narrazioni dell'Umanitario. Beyond Humanitarian Narratives*, Milan: Franco Angeli, 60–81.

Campesi, G. (2011) 'La norma e l'eccezione nel governo delle migrazioni. Lampedusa, le rivolte arabe e la crisi del regime confinario europeo', Jura Gentium, https://www.juragentium.org/topics/migrant/it/campesi.htm (accessed on March 14th, 2019).

Cuttitta, P. (2012) *Lo Spettacolo del Confine. Lampedusa tra Produzione e Messa in Scena della Frontiera*, Milan-Udine: Mimesis.

Dal Zotto, E. (2014) 'Frame dell' emergenza e migrazioni forzate. Il caso dell'emergenza

[7] Ministero dell'Interno, Dipartimento delle Libertà Civili e Immigrazione, *Procedure Operative Standard (SOP) – Standard Operating Procedures (SOP).*

http://www.libertaciviliimmigrazione.dlci.interno.gov.it/sites/default/files/allegati/hotspots_sops_-_versione_italiana.pdf.

[8] Cfr. Amnesty International, Rapporto Hotspot Italia, 3 novembre 2016, https://www.amnesty.it/-rapporto-hotspot-italia/, last accessed on December 31st, 2017.

Nord Africa' in P. Musarò and P. Parmigliani (eds.) *Media e Migrazioni. Etica, Estetica e Politica del Discorso Umanitario*, Milan: FrancoAngeli, 125–137.
De Haas, H. (2008) 'The myth of invasion: The inconvenient realities of migration from Africa to the European Union', *Third World Quarterly*, 29(7): 1305–1322.
Fassin, D. and Pandolfi, M. (eds.) (2010) *Contemporary States Of Emergency. The Politics Of Military And Humanitarian Interventions*, New York: Zone Books.
Garelli, G. and Tazzioli M. (2013) 'Arab Springs making space: Territoriality and moral geographies for asylum seekers in Italy', *Environment and Planning. Society and Space*, 31(6): 1472–3433.
Harrel-Bond, B. (1986) *Imposing Aid: Emergency Assistance to Refugees*, Oxford: Oxford University Press.
Manconi, L. and Anastasia, S. (eds.) (2012) *Lampedusa non è un'Isola. Profughi e Migranti alle Porte dell'Italia*, Rome: A Buon Diritto Onlus.
Marchetti, C. (2015) 'In alto mare sono tutti rifugiati. La mutevolezza della protezione dal 2009 a oggi' in L. Ciabarri and B. Pinelli, (eds.) *Dopo l'Approdo. Un Racconto per Immagini e Parole sui Richiedenti Asili in Italia*, Florence: Editpress, 165–172.
Marras, S. (2009) 'Falsi rifugiati? Pratiche di etichettamento di richiedenti asilo alla frontiera', *Mondi Migranti*, 3: 79–97.
Massey, D.S. (2002) 'La ricerca sulle migrazioni nel XXI secolo' in A. Colombo and G. Sciortino (eds.) *Stranieri in Italia. Assimilati ed Esclusi*, Bologna: Il Mulino, 25–49.
Squire, V., Dimitriadi, A., Perkowsky, N., Pisani, M., Stevens, D. and Vaughan, W. (2017) *Crossing the Mediterranean Sea by Boat: Mapping and Documenting Migratory Journeys and Experiences*, final project report, www.warwick.ac.uk/crossingthemed (accessed on March 14th, 2019).
Zetter, R. (2007) 'More labels, fewer refugees: Remaking the refugee label in an era of globalization', *Journal of Refugees Studies*, 20(2): 172–192.
Zupi, M. (ed.) (2012) 'L'impatto delle primavere arabe sui flussi migratori regionali e verso l'Italia', *Osservatorio di Politica Internazionale*, 59.

Chapter 4

Irrational walls

Lessons from the US-Mexico border

Fiammetta Corradi

4.1. *Introduction*

Not more than thirty years ago, and not only in the DRR, people were rejoicing in the celebration of the epochal fall of the Berlin Wall, a divide whose overcoming bore promises of a politically borderless, peaceful New Era. Snapshots of that time would nonetheless appear especially anachronistic today, when part of that same generation is witnessing a revival, on both sides of the Atlantic Ocean, of the old wall-building strategy against unwanted immigrants, for (supposedly) different security purposes.

In Europe, where new walls and fences against refugees and economic migrants rise along the national borders of Bulgaria, Hungary, Greece, Serbia and other countries, right-wing politicians in addition to those belonging to the "Visegràd group", [1] repeatedly claim that patrolled walls are the only (or best) solution against the "new waves of invasion" produced by the Syrian war and the Arab Spring since 2011. In the United States of America, where a significant part of Donald Trump's electoral campaign was based on the militarization of the US–Mexican Border, the newly elected US-President constantly renovates his promises to build an "impassable physical barrier" along the Frontera, a new wall about 2000 miles long, (as he claims) at Mexico's expenses.

The current global resurgence of walls as tools at the disposal of the emerging security state – and the disputed problem of their actual effectiveness – could but ignite renovated interest and multidisciplinary efforts in the academic world. The production in the field is so wide and heterodox that any account would be beyond a paper purpose. Here it would suffice to notice that many different aspects of the wall-building practice have already been extensively analyzed, from the past uses of walls and fences for defensive purposes against migration waves, since Hadrian's Wall and the Great Wall of China. Studies focus on the evolution of the implemented technical devices, from stone walls to barbed-wire fences until the most recent virtual innovations, (often

---

[1] The anti-immigration stand shared by the four countries belonging to the group – Slovakia, Czech Republic, Poland and Hungary – has given a new, unsettling direction to an old alliance, originally signed in the town of Visegràd on February 15, 1991 for the purposes of fostering their European integration, as well as for advancing military, economic and energy cooperation.

with references to the Foucaultian study on surveilliance and punishment, see Razac 2009) and on the consequences of enforced borders on people's lives, welfare and social identities on both sides of the walls.[2] While scientific journals and magazines in the field of political and social sciences constantly promote new conferences, calls for papers and monographic issues on the topic,[3] in 2006 G.P. Cella had already developed an innovative sociological analysis, brilliantly studying the intertwine between metaphor and reality in the social process of tracing confines.

Notwithstanding these intellectual contributions, the ongoing public debate about walls against migrants in Europe, too often polarized between absolute refusal and unconditioned acceptance of migrants, tends to remain somehow lacking in substance, with a worrying, detrimental reduction of complexity and the forestall of articulated and well-informed arguments.

It can be that such debate might benefit from the experience of the Frontera, especially as the new walls in Europe share with it a crucially distinctive feature: differently from other militarized borders in the world – for instance the one separating North and South Korea, or the Line of Control that marks the boundary between India and Pakistan in the disputed territory of Kashmir – the US-Mexico Border became progressively militarized not in response to a military threat from another sovereign state (Mexico), but to prevent the movement of civilians and to stop illegal migration across countries: it is this purpose that the new walls in Europe wish to accomplish.

Consequently, this chapter first reconstructs and reports the militarization history of the Frontera – the most frequently crossed one, with approximately 350 million legal crossings per year – and then it critically examines its effects, as an example of an irrational strategy to face migration challenges. The qualification of irrationality is not generically interpreted here as an emotional response to collective security worries or unconscious fears (even though fear might have a role in wall-building practices). Rather, it is qualified as irrational on the basis of three complementary arguments: first, I show that the militarization of the Frontera is not an effective strategy, because it fails to achieve its openly declared aims; then, I collect evidence to prove that the strategy itself produces unintended and perverse effects, enhancing processes it did not mean to foster or even worsening some of the conditions it meant to improve; finally, building on a non-automated discourse analysis, I point out that the speeches meant to legitimize it politically as the only or best solution to migration challenges are

[2] Investigative journalism, literary production, music, figurative arts, and movies report moving stories of individuals or groups struggling to cross patrolled borders, or to adapt to live in the shade of uncrossable frontiers. A masterpiece in the music heritage, is the song "La Frontera" by Lhasa de Sela, https://youtu.be/DScfCw77Fio.

[3] Special mention should be made of the one fostered in France by l'*Espace politique* (2013: 20), containing, among others, a contribution contextualizing this practice within the political science tradition, at the crossroad of realism, liberalism and conventional constructivism (Beaulieu and Brossard) and a study showing that the new walls built in Europe have only managed – so far, to diverge the flux of migrants towards other countries, endangering solidarity and cooperation among national states in times of crisis.

argumentatively poor and sometimes even fallacious, so bearing witness that the reasoning behind them is not analytical. In the conclusion I briefly discuss the conditions of comparability between the Frontera experience and the present situation in Europe.

4.2. *The militarization of the Frontera*

After the Boundary Treaty between the USA and Mexico in 1970, which settled some pending confine disputes, the Frontera acquired its present length and configuration: it extends 3,145 kilometers (1,954 miles), from the Pacific Ocean to the Gulf of Mexico. Presently, it runs along four American states (California, Arizona, New Mexico and Texas) and six Mexican states (Baja California, Sonora, Chihuahua, Coahuila, Nuevo León, and Tamaulipas), affording 48 crossings, with 330 ports of entry (Hodge 2012). Geographically, its line crosses very varied landscapes, from the river borderlands watered by the Rio Grande between the Gulf of Mexico and Ciudad Juàrez-El-Paso to the desert borderlands in the West.

Since its original establishment in the 1840s at the end of the Mexican–American War, it has changed radically in aspect and scope, undergoing a massive militarization process in the last thirty years (Miller 2014). For almost fifty years, in fact, the Frontera was just a line on maps, with the first stones settled on the ground separating Upper and Lower California in the late 1890s.

The creation of a first, small (and underfunded) US Border Patrol agency with the mission "to detect and prevent the illegal entry of aliens into the United States … facilitating the flow of legal immigration and goods while preventing the illegal trafficking of people and contraband" (quotation from the official website of the Department of Homeland Security) dates back only to 1924. Until that time, the agency mainly patrolled the Canada border, where the Asian migrants, main targets of the restrictive immigration legislation of Congress, were more likely to cross (Hernandez 2010). In the 1990s, when the attention shifted to the Mexican border, the agency comprised about 3000 agents, who relied on the so-called "interdiction strategy" to try to contain the crossing of migrants from Mexico to the US.

The enforcement of patrolling and the systematic construction of fences along the order line began in the mid-1990s, with "Operation Gate Keeper" in San Diego and "Operation Hold the Line" in El Paso. Interestingly, as Jones reports (2016: 35): "in order to hire such a large number of agents quickly, the agency removed some previous requirements, such as passing a polygraph exam, and drew heavily on veterans returning from wars in Iraq and Afghanistan, who make up 28.8 percent of agents. The lower standards, combined with the influx of veterans, altered the atmosphere at the agency, bringing a military ethos to the policing job".

However, it was only after the terrorist attacks of September 11 that the militarization process of the Border witnessed a sharp acceleration, both with regard to the number of patrolling agents and to the amount of invested resources by the US government (the Border Patrol budget rose up to 3.5 billion dollars in 2011). Official data from the Department of Homeland Security show that by 2010 the number of agents reached more than 20,000 units, so enhancing the so-called "Green Wall" (named for the green colour of the border patrol agents' uniforms). By the same year, Customs and Border Protection (CBP), established in 2003, already had 60,000 employees. As Figure 4.1 shows, in only six years, between 2005 and 2011, there was an 87 percent increase in staffing, and the number of border-miles covered by fences rose from 136 before 2006 to 649 miles in 2011. Following the passage of the 2006 Secure Fence Act, the fence now covers 670 miles.

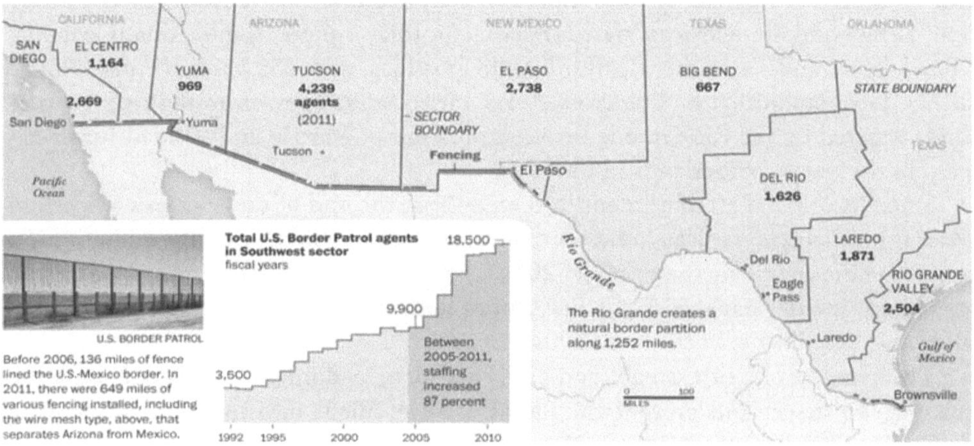

Figure 4.1. Fence-building and patrol agents' enforcement along the Frontera

Source: http://www.washingtonpost.com

In 2006, President G.W. Bush mobilized 6,000 National Guards troops for "Operation Jumpstart"; in 2010 and 2011 President B. Obama deployed 1,200 more for "Operation Phalanx" and more troops were mobilized by the Texas Governor in 2014 for Operation Strong Safety. Additional signs of the rise of a militarized zone are to be found in the implementation of new technologies for surveillance, such as drones, ground-monitoring radars (to detect tunnels) and other high-tech devices that monitor for movement, whose original purpose was military usage: a whole high-tech arsenal for surveillance at the disposal of the Green Wall.

Last but not least, the picture has been completed by a rise in deportations and deportation threats for illegal border-crossers. In the past, migrants were mainly considered desperate poor workers and peasants, in search of better economic and living conditions, sharing the perception that, if they managed to cross the Border, they could stay. In the past, those seized at crossing the border illegally were detained, quickly processed and repatriated to Mexico within a few hours. As the staffing and founding increased, illegal crossers were instead more often labelled as "criminals" and smugglers. Such criminalization process legitimized the establishment of new detention (and often private) facilities. The American Government "began to detain migrants, charge them with misdemeanours for their first offence and felonies for their second, and then formally deport them" (Jones 2016: 36). Detention facilities host a growing number of illegal migrants, from 85,000 in 1995, to more than 440,000 in 2013.

Presently, measuring the total flow of migrants is indeed a difficult task. Figures on border detentions are largely incomplete, because many migrants manage to evade capture. Since 2014, however, hundreds of thousands of Central American families fleeing misery and violence started to turn themselves in to the Border Patrol, asking for asylum because of the gang violence in their home countries. Such people were often allowed to live where they chose as they awaited a distant court date in the backlogged US immigration system. Notwithstanding this change, in 2017 President Trump publicly pledged to deport millions of illegal immigrants, a threat that has already produced some contradictory effects.

It would be incorrect, however, to think that the Frontera was militarized only on the American side. In fact, the Mexican Army too played a key role along the Border. It was called into action by the uprising, on January 1st 1994, of the EZLN, (the Zapatista Army of National Liberation), a revolutionary leftist political group that sided against the passing of NAFTA.[4] After the suppression of the insurrection, the Mexican army remained to patrol the borderlands, to forestall the importation of weapons on behalf of the EZLN and other militant groups, hence becoming "an ordinary presence" for the local people along the border. As reported by a Mexican journalist: "La gota que derramo el vaso fue el levantamiento armado del EZLN, el cual definitivamente convoco y justifico la presencia del ejercito en el area. Aparte del breve periodo de enfrentamiento armado en enero de 1994, el ejercito mexicano llego para quedarse, y su presencia y accionar en materia de control de la poblacion se convirtieron en un hecho cotidiano para la poblacion local".[5]

One could expect that such an impressive deployment of men, money, resources and other devices to enforce the Frontera has massively increased its effectiveness. This, however, does not seem to be the case.

---

[4] When the North American Free Trade Agreement (NAFTA) went into effect on January 1st, 1994, the Mexican ruling class greeted it as the opportunity they had long sought to intermingle with Corporate America. But for the Indian peasants and farmers, it promised to bear dramatic consequences. The Agreement in fact promoted corporate privatization, removed Mexico's right to review foreign investment proposals, banned subsidies to the indigenous farmers, fostered US imports and, most significantly, required Mexico to alter its constitution by abolishing Article 27 which provided land to those who worked it.

[5] Translation: "The last straw that broke the camel's back was the armed insurrection of EZLN, which definitively justified the presence of the army in the area. A part from the short military confrontation in January 1994, the Mexican army arrived to stay and its presence and action towards population control turned into a daily routine for the local people", "La Militarization de la Frontera", 13/11/2015. http://valladolid-y-oviedo.com/la-militarization-de-la-frontera/ (accessed on March 17th, 2019).

4.3. *The (in)effectiveness of a wall*

It is certainly true that the militarization process has been matched with a closer surveillance and more systematic monitoring of the events occurring along the US–Mexican borderlands. Controversies still linger, however, on the right criteria for assessing the Frontera's efficiency. While the American media coverage has been literally obsessed with the quantification of illegal crossings (and deportations), reporting almost daily apprehension numbers and death tolls, academics have developed a variety of more articulated criteria to evaluate the efficacy of the Border enforcement.

One example is the successful and debated work by Micheal Dear, Professor of City and Regional Planning, University of California-Berkeley, author of a book significantly titled Why Walls Won't Work, Repairing the US-Mexico Divide. Published in 2013 – before new calls for wall-building at the Frontera became politically fashionable – his work intended to prove that the wall strategy is totally ineffective against unwanted migration from Mexico. The product of a three-year journey along the borderlands, starting from Los Angeles, this book collects a range of evidence to support arguments against the wall. For example, he states: "As long as migrants hold onto an American Dream, and as long as Mexican labour is required in the US, people will cross the border with or without papers. Walls don't work simply because people are too inventive in circumventing them". Pointing at the mutually satisfying economic motivations pushing individuals to cross the US-Mexico border, Dear claims that people will always find ways over, under, through and around it. So, for instance, it is pointed out that the border has been growingly circumvented by people sailing in the waters off San Diego (where the number of sea-borne undocumented migrants has more than doubled in recent years). Tunnel-digging under the border, often matched with sophisticated drainage, lighting and ventilation systems, follows as the second most popular alternative: since 2008, almost 70 tunnels have been discovered, mostly in California and Arizona. The old method of climbing over the fence occurs with the implementation of new devices, like roof-ladders, extensible ramps, and even hand-held screwdrivers to scale steel-mesh barriers designed to forestall hand and toe-holds. The removal of panels from fences has produced more than 3,000 breaches, costing more than $4 million to repair. There are also other crossing techniques at the disposal of these border-crossers, including those who choose to bluff their way through official ports of entry. [6]

According to Dear, moreover, walls do not work also because government and private interests foster the opening of new "ports of entry" (POE) along the border. The main incentives for the establishment of such patrolled gates in the border are

---

[6] As Dear (2013) reports, some inventive smugglers hollowed out the seats in their SUVs and re-covered them with a migrant hidden inside. Others have crossed with a small child wrapped inside a piñata (a kind of large doll). Those with a professional interest in shepherding an illicit cargo through a checkpoint will employ spotters and corrupt inspection officers to schedule their delivery without interference.

connected with trade, tolls and fees collection, and the need to reduce congestion on the already existing POEs. Many other organizations and associations, like state-level Border Governors' Conference, the Border City Mayors' association, private business councils, joint economic development alliances, non-profit humanitarian aid agencies, law enforcement, cultural organizations, and tertiary education establishments, look with favour at the POEs as key communication portals. [7]

Finally, according to Dear, the Wall cannot work because the borderlands' inhabitants form a sort of "third nation", with a connecting tissue "that partition cannot compromise". Digging into the socio-economic history of the borderland population – about 12 million people – he notices that the Border has long been a permeable membrane, whereas inhabitants of these "in-between" territories thrive on cross border exchange and collaboration, sharing a deep sense of attachment and mutuality that has overcome and survived through past upheavals, local conflicts and tensions. As the following passage shows, he moves this argument a step further, rephrasing it in normative terms and claiming that the wall will fall because this is the destiny that any wall has undergone in history: [8]

> *The third nation is the place where bi-national lives and values are being created —organically, readily, and without artifice. The third nation will prevail, and is worth nurturing. It is the place of being and becoming in the spaces between two nations. What should be done about the Wall that so rudely interrupts the third nation? The Berlin Wall was torn down virtually overnight, its fragments sold as souvenirs of a calamitous Cold War; the Great Wall of China was transformed into a global tourist attraction. Left untended, the US-Mexico Wall would collapse under the combined assault of avid recyclers, souvenir hunters, and local residents offended by its mere presence. Nevertheless, we should preserve sections of the Wall to commemorate that fraught moment in history when the US lost its moral compass.* [9]

Some of Dear's arguments would hold in front of Trump's pleading for a further enforcement of the borderline and the construction of a 2,000-mile wall; the problem, however, is that his arguments tend to evaluate the effectiveness of the border-enforcement strategy in generalized, predictive and absolute terms.

I would rather suggest that the US-Mexico experience shows that the enforcement of segments of the border is locally effective, but only temporarily; moreover, it tends to re-direct illegal migration along other, still un-patrolled routes. A range of various

---

[7] "The most interesting (but little known) example is the International Boundary and Water Commission, United States and Mexico, (IBWC). The IBWC originated under Article V of the 1848 Treaty of Guadalupe Hidalgo and was established in 1889. In Mexico, the equivalent agency is the Comisión Internacional de Limites y Aguas (CILA). Both are charged with jointly implementing the international boundary and water treaties and settling disputes along the border".

[8] Please note that this argument is logically fallacious: from the fact that (almost) any wall was destroyed I the past, it does not follow necessarily that this will be the case for the Frontera as well.

[9] http://www.huffingtonpost.com/michael-dear/why-walls-wont-work-repai_b_2902953.html (accessed on March 17th, 2019).

evidence supports this surmise. For example, the immediate effect of the so-called "Operation Gate Keeper" in San Diego and the "Operation Hold the Line" in El Paso in the mid-1990s produced a short-term drop in illegal crossings: illegal border-crossers soon found different routes along less controlled or unpatrolled areas (Jones 2016: 54). More recently, a report in the Washington Post, [10] titled "The Trump effect has slowed illegal border crossings, but for how long?" (21/05/2017), piles up evidence against the durable effectiveness of the threat of illegal deportations. Data hint at a sudden drop in the number of apprehensions and detentions in 2017, after Trump's fierce declaration against illegal crossing. According to Kevin K. McAleenan, acting commissioner of US Customs and Border Protection, 3,400 people from the Northern Triangle countries (El Salvador, Honduras and Guatemala) were apprehended, while in the previous April, that figure was more than 16,000. In the first four months of the year, US authorities had detained about 98,000 would-be immigrants heading north, a 40 percent drop from the previous year. These data, however, seem only contingent. Interviews carried out by Washington Post journalist J. Paltrow with Border officials in El Salvador suggest that "The slowdown in migration could be temporary. Migrants and their families are watching closely to see whether the Trump administration moves ahead with mass deportations, or carries out its threat to prosecute parents for paying smugglers to bring their children to the United States. But the pressures pushing people north have not disappeared".

Finally, the evidence used to assess spikes and drops in the number of illegal crossings should be viewed with special caution. In fact, the data normally used – the sheer number of apprehensions – are often incomplete and to some extent unreliable (they do not reveal whether, say, the number 2 corresponds to the apprehension of two different people, or of the same person seized twice). Nonetheless, these are the data mostly quoted by the American Administrations. For example, in 2014, President Barak Obama proudly stated that "Overall, the number of people trying to cross our border illegally is the lowest it has been since the 1970s" (20/11/2014). Border Patrol data confirm Obama's claim: in 2013, about 420,000 illegal immigrants were apprehended at the border. The last time it was lower than that was 1972. After that year, apprehensions steadily rose throughout the 1970s, ending at just shy of 900,000 in 1979. Experts noted, however, that "Obama was creating an imperfect comparison, because the border situation was far different in 1970 than it is in more recent years, since at that time it was easier for people to make multiple attempts or excursions illegally across the border". [11] In addition, the economic conditions on both sides of the border have changed since the 1970s, improving in Mexico and deteriorating in the US after the 2008 financial crisis.

---

[10] https://www.washingtonpost.com/world/the_americas/the-trump-effect-has-slowed-illegal-us-_border-crossings-but-for-how-long/2017/05/21/dfa12a0a-39be-11e7-a59b-26e0451a96fd_story.html?-utm_term=.9754f5512556 (accessed on March 17th, 2019).

[11] http://www.politifact.com/florida/statements/2014/nov/25/barack-obama/obama-says-illegal-border-crossings-lowest-it-has-/ (accessed on March 17th, 2019).

The emphasis on border-enforcement effectiveness has somehow led to the underestimation of its non-intentional consequences, both at the macro and micro level. It is now time to turn our attention to these side effects and emergent processes.

4.4. *Un-intended processes and perverse effects*

Together with the exponential increase in border-patrolling investments and expenses (§ 4.3), the militarization of the Frontera has activated some un-intended processes with long-run negative effects, the most significant of which has probably been the blurring of the distinction between policing and militarization, which is generally considered an indicator of a lack of democracy.

Historically, as Weiss (2011) points out, the divide between police and military power is rooted in the national state and in its territorial sovereignty, with the police in charge of maintaining the internal social order and security and the military in charge of warranting the external security, defeating eventual enemies. Along the Frontera, the overlapping of these institutions' duties and tasks is certainly not new, but their merging has become more visible in the aftermath of September 11, with the rise of the security state.

The blurring of the distinction between police and military power – which in itself would deserve a dedicated (better if comparative) study – has been sustained and reinforced in the case of the Frontera by parallel and complementary processes, if we trust the existing literature on the topic. On the one hand, there is the already mentioned change in the composition of the border agency body, increasingly populated by war veterans. On the other hand, there is the flourishing of public legitimization strategies labelling the border-crossers as criminals or even as enemies (be they smugglers, drug-dealers, political criminals, felons, or merely homeless migrants crossing illegally). From a sociological perspective, this latter phenomenon is of special relevance, especially if we recall that the social construction and imputation of criminal identities – as the sociology of deviance teaches – can activate self-enforcing mechanisms, particularly in situations where the iteration of illegal actions is fairly common, like in border-crossing attempts. Moreover, while the criminalization process of migrants has already been deeply studied, highlighting different classificatory criteria and justificatory logics (Parking 2013; Brock et al. 2014; Ewig et al. 2015), additional analyses could profitably track and examine the progressive labelling-shift of border-crossers from criminals to public enemies.

Another perverse effect produced by the militarization of the border is the escalation of violence exhaustively documented by Correa (2013) with reference to Cameron County, Texas, and by Wright (2011), who focuses on "necro-politics" and gendered-violence on the US-Mexico Border. Along the same argumentation line, Jones (2016), makes explicit that the militarization of the Frontera itself causes additional deaths, re-directing migrants towards more hostile and risky routes:

The Border Patrol has recovered more than 6,000 bodies along the US-Mexico Border since the 1990s, deaths attributable to the construction of the border wall and the massive Border Patrol Presence. Migrants are funnelled to more dangerous and remote locations, just like migrants at the edges of the EU. Instead of crossing in a city, migrants are making the arduous journey through the deserts of Arizona, which requires hiking for fifty or more kilometres through arid and desolate terrain.

(Jones, 2016, p. 45)

Re-direction is actually one of the intended aims of the wall-building strategy, achievable (as I claim, only for a short time) by the wall builder; but detrimental for all the other shareholders and stakeholders. Significantly, pro-wall propaganda discourses carefully avoid making any reference to re-direction as an expectable effect of wall-building.

4.5. *Discursive legitimation*

On September 6, 2017, Trump announced his decision to "revisit" the DACA – the Deferred Action for Childhood Arrivals program – passed by the Obama Administration, so crushing the hopes and dreams of about 800,000 young undocumented immigrants (named "dreamers"), who benefited from protection from deportation under the Obama Administration. In this landscape, it is all the more interesting to re-read Trump's anti-immigration manifesto, delivered in Phoenix, Arizona, on August 31, 2016, during his presidential campaign. [12] On that occasion, talking to borderlands people, his declared intention was not to release a "rally speech", but rather to provide "a detailed policy address on the greatest challenge facing our country today: illegal immigration".

According to my analysis of the text – conducted through a non-automated structural and frame analysis, building on the model proposed by Stephen Toulmin (1955) for splitting arguments [13] – this discourse displays all the typical features of a populist

[12] Full transcripts of the speech available at http://www.latimes.com/politics/la-na-pol-donald-trump-immigration-speech-transcript-20160831-snap-htmlstory.html (accessed on March 17th, 2019).

[13] To study the anatomy and physiology of arguments (1955), Stephen Toulmin proposed a scheme for the identification of basic argumentative elements (claims, data and warrants) and additional ones (qualifiers, rebuttals, backings). Its systematic application allows a quantitative evaluation of the richness (or poorness) of an argumentative performance. At the same time, it helps in the search for eventual fallacious arguments (that seem sound, but are not), since logical or contextual fallacies most frequently hide in the warrants (the rules legitimizing the passage from data to claim). This methodology, extensively described and discussed elsewhere (Corradi 2016), is quite innovative within the landscape of the most recent analyses devoted to migration policies discourses. For interesting outcomes about interdiscursivity and intertextuality see Bennett (2018); for frame variation and frame repletion over time see Greussing and Boomgaarden (2017).

electoral speech, being rife with propagandistic factual and normative claims and with explicit, heavy charges to political adversaries. Moreover, the percentage of un-argued claims – claims with no data and no explicit warrant – is very high (more than 80 percent), an outcome that is all the more worrying given the overwhelming number of normative claims over factual ones (on how normative claims can be possibly argued for, see Corradi 2016). Stylistically, the speech is highly anaphoric: a feature that certainly shows the speaker's emotional participation to the issue in question, and his intention to enhance the speech persuasiveness (but it should be remembered that repetition of sentences does not necessarily add to the richness of arguments!).

Trump begins his speech by claiming that the American immigration system is "worse than anybody ever realized". The media and politicians, in fact, have "special (economic) interests" to cover it (a statement un-supported by any data or warrant, simply followed by a tautological sentence: "That's the way it is"). To "talk honestly and without fear about these important and very sensitive issues", requires instead to "listen to the concerns that working people, our forgotten working people, have over their record pace of immigration and its impact on their jobs, wages, housing, schools, tax bills and general living conditions: valid concerns expressed by decent and patriotic citizens from all backgrounds" (notice the unconditionally positive connotation of patriotism). On the presumed basis of such (un-detailed) concerns, Trump derives the (predictive) conclusion that "not anyone who seeks to join our country will be able to successfully assimilate". With a somewhat unexpected solution of argumentative continuity, he then advances, again without arguments, a very problematic normative claim: "It is our right, as a sovereign nation ..." (qualification containing an insufficient warrant) "to chose immigrants that we..." (who exactly?) "think are the likeliest..." (on what basis?) "to thrive and flourish and love us". As if this statement were self-evident, he jumps to another issue, security, claiming that "countless innocent American lives have been stolen because our politicians have failed in their duty to secure our borders and enforce our laws like they have to be enforced". This imputation of responsibility immediately becomes personalized: "countless American who have died in recent years would be alive today if not for the open border policies of this administration (Barack Obama) and the administration that causes this horrible, horrible thought process, called Hillary Clinton" (first open charges of a long series). Five victims' names and death stories follow (to be regarded as data), to support the claim about the security threat: the common denominator is the fact that all victims are "great" Americans, all criminal illegal immigrants.

After the security issue, there comes the economic argumentative frame. It is developed along two main lines: on the one hand, Trump hints at the public expenses for illegal immigration, that "costs our country more than $113 billion a year" (notice that no specification about what such "cost" accounts for is provided). On the other hand, there is the much abused and controversial argument about immigrants "stealing" jobs from American citizens ("most illegal immigrants are lower skilled workers with less education, who compete directly against vulnerable American workers"). Such argument would be dismissed by the media, according to Trump, that instead focus only on the "needs of the people living here illegally ..., who are, in many cases "treated better than our vets". The victimization frame on behalf of illegal immigrants is therefore shared and promoted by those "who have spent too much time in Washington" (elliptic sentence, though clear in its reference). There then comes a long imputation of pro-immigrant policies of the Obama Administration and Hillary Clinton in particular, who are charged to have pledged amnesty and to support "sanctuary cities", "catch and release" on the border, "visa overstays", the release of "dangerous, dangerous, dangerous criminals from detention" (notice the anaphoric emphatic repetition), not to mention the extension of Obamacare, Social Security and Medicare for illegal immigrants, and finally the plan to host 620,000 new refugees from Syria.

To fight against what is metaphorically named "a Trojan horse" – illegal immigration – Trump describes a normative policy plan in ten points. Most of the relative normative claims are stated, again, in an assertive way. Paradigmatic in this regard is the first and most important policy measure: "We will build a great wall along the southern border" (an action that, at the time of writing at the beginning of 2018, has not yet even been started, despite innumerable public re-statements of intention).

Such an "impenetrable, physical, tall, powerful, beautiful southern border wall will include above and below ground sensors". In addition, "Mexico will pay for the wall. One hundred percent. They don't know it yet, but they are going to pay for it". [14]

Together with the wall, "towers, aerial surveillance and manpower", the creation of a new deportation task force and 5,000 more Border Patrol agents will bring the militarization process a step even further. Other measures complete Trump's plan against illegal immigration: among them, the end of the catch-and-release era; zero tolerance for criminal aliens; block funding for sanctuary cities; the abrogation of amnesties and the enforcement of all immigration laws; and the suspension of the issuance of visas by any place where adequate screening cannot occur.

As for immigrants from Syria, Trump proposes "extreme vetting" ("I want extreme. It's going to be tough .... It's going to end badly folks"). This time Trump has an argument pertaining to the economic argumentative frame: "for the price of resettling one refugee in the United States, 12 could be resettled in a safe zone in their home region". The price of such resettlement, once again, will not be paid by the Americans, but instead by "the Gulf states".

---

[14] This statement saw an immediate reaction by the Mexican Government, which repeated, once again, that Mexico will not pay the $25 billion estimated to build the wall. Already on July 11, 2016, in fact, Enrique Peña Nieto had declared to CNN: "There is no way that Mexico can pay [for] a wall like that". However, as reported by *Townhall* columnist Katie Kieffer, "Every year, Mexicans working in the U.S. send at least $20 billion back to Mexico in the form of remittances, placing a huge drain on our economy. Through a combination of legal and procedural challenges, Trump could impound such remittances. ... Besides cracking down on remittances, 'visa fees', 'visa cancellations', and the enforcement or enactment of 'trade tariffs' are three additional ways in which Trump proposes to make Mexico pay for the wall". https://townhall.com/columnists/katiekieffer/2016/09/05/mexico-will-pay-for-the-wall-n2213934 (accessed on March 17th, 2019).

The most surprising proposal contained in the speech, however, comes close to its end. Trump ventilates the introduction of a test to get the "right people": "an ideological certification to make sure that those we are admitting to our country share our values and love our people" (sociologists could ask how he expects to overcome desirability biases).

4.6. *Conclusions*

Analyzing the militarization process that the US-Mexico Border has undergone in recent decades up until the latest enforcement call by President Donald Trump, this study has collected elements proving the irrationality of the wall-building strategy against illegal immigration. Such elements range from historical and factual data proving the ineffectiveness of the wall, to data showing the creation of unexpected and perverse effects, to the assertiveness and clumsiness of the argumentative performance displayed to support new border enforcement policies.

The Frontera certainly exhibits unique features that endanger any fast and easy exportation for comparative purposes. In any case, I believe it provides an instructive experience for Europe as well, right in a moment when the wall building strategy witnesses a worrying revival in some European countries. It could remind us that, like in an extended version of the prisoner's dilemma game, the wall-builder apparently wins the highest pay-off in the short-run by building the wall and redirecting immigrants elsewhere; this happens necessarily, however, at the other stakeholders' expenses (the other countries and most of all the border-crossers). The best choice for everybody (the Paretian optimum) would be instead to find a cooperative solution to the problem, one that does not lessen anybody's welfare. How and when it might be achieved is difficult to tell; but toward such an end, the wall building strategy is certainly one of the obstacles to be understood, and finally overcome.

Bibliography

Beaulieu-Brossard, P. and David, C.P. (2003) 'Le blindage des frontières selon les théories des Relations Internationales: Contribution et dialogue', *L'Espace politique*, 20(2).

Bennett, S. (2018) 'New "crises," old habits: Online interdiscursivity and intertextuality in UK migration policy discourses', *Journal of Immigrant & Refugee Studies*, 16(1–2): 140–160.

Brock, D., Glasbeek, A. and Murdocca, C. (2014) *Criminalization, representation, regulation. Thinking differently about Crime*, Toronto: University of Toronto University Press.

Cella, G.P. (2006) *Tracciare confini. Realtà e metafore della distinzione*, Bologna: Il Mulino.

Cimino, A. (2016) *Trump talking, The Donald, in his own words*, London: Robinson.

Corradi, F. (2016) 'The richness and quality of normative public argumentation: One method, two case studies', *Working Paper*, LPF No. 1-2016, pp. 1–36.
Correa, J.F. (2013) 'After 9/11 everything changed: Reformations of state violence in everyday lives on the US-Mexico Border', *Cultural Dynamics*, 25(1): 99–119.
Dear, M. (2013) *Why walls won't work. Repairing the US-Mexico divide*, Oxford: Oxford University Press.
Ewig, W., Martìnez, D.E. and Rumbaut, R.G. (2015) *The criminalization of immigration in the United States*, American Immigration Council, Special Report.
Greussing, E. and Boomgaarden, H. G (2017) 'Shifting the refugee narrative? An automated frame analysis of Europe's 2015 refugee crisis', *Journal of Ethnic and Migration Studies*, 43(11): 1749–1774.
Hernandez, K.L. (2010) *Migra! A history of the US border patrol*, Berkeley: University of California Press.
Hodge, R.D. (2012) 'Borderworld: How the U.S. is reengineering homeland security', *Popular Science*, 280(1): 56–81.
Jones, R. (2016) *Violent borders. Refugees and the right to move*, London-New York: Verso.
Miller, T. (2014) *Border patrol nation: Dispatches from the front lines of border security*, San Francisco: City Lights Books.
Parking, J. (2013) 'The criminalization of migration in Europe. A state-of-the-art of the academic literature and research', *CEPS Paper in Liberty and Security in Europe*, 61.
Razac, O. (2009) *Histoire politique du barbelé*, Paris: Flammarion.
Weiss, T. (2011) 'The blurring border between the police and the military: A debate without foundations', *Cooperation and Conflict*, 46: 396–405.
Wright, M.W. (2011) 'Necropolitics, narcopolitics and feminide: Gendered violence on the Mexico-U.S. border', *Signs*, 36(3): 707–731.

Chapter 5

Mobility and data

Dataset or data nightmare?

Valentina Fusari

5.1. *Introduction*

Population counting, its control and management, and border security, are issues in the contemporary political and social debate where demographics are used to justify different policies. The most widespread readings by media rarely take into account the demographics in the context of origin, hiding truths by using percentages or absolute values which have no meaning if they are not related with the population structure and migration patterns characterizing the context of departure. Moreover, freedom of movement is not equally distributed in the world, but it is subjected to unequal power relations: although means of transportation have shortened distances, borders, entry and exit visas, passports and residence permits regulate and prevent the concrete possibility of leaving one place and settling down in another. At the same time, these control systems provide sources for collecting data about specific movements because national statistics offices are interested in detecting exogenous socio-demographic groups.

The availability of suitable data will facilitate studies on mobility, generally defined as change in space, and on migration, that is, the movement of people across a specified boundary to establish a new residence. This chapter evaluates how over time the movement of people and sometimes borders have influenced the need to collect and produce demographics about migrants, in turn influenced by national and international policies generating classifications that make the analysis of such statistics slippery. Questions about human location and movement are of central importance in demography, but answers are limited by a frequent inability to observe and measure where people are and where they are going, failing to provide a dynamic picture. Census data tell about general patterns of human settlement and migration but very little about where and how they move. Interviews and surveys give more detail, but these are constrained by scale and self-reporting errors. New methods for gathering and analysing spatially rich demographic data using mobile phones or social networks are especially promising to record location and movement (Palmer et al. 2013; Zagheni et al. 2017), but they are still in the early stages of development.

The production process of demographics is affected by a strong imbalance towards the hosting countries due not only to the quality and expertise of their national statistics offices, but also to the proliferation of national and international agencies that provide estimates about population in open access databases. However, national statistics offices able to provide reliable information on population structure and dynamics in countries of origin, characterized by greater mobility, do not correspond with the "data hypertrophy" in hosting countries. Migration is the most volatile aspect of demographic behaviour, and studies have been conducted using different types of datasets, like vital statistics, repeated large-scale national surveys with limited retrospective information, and smaller-scale life history surveys, for gaining insight into the intersection between individual and historical time, and to determine appropriate methods for analysing them. Most states base their statistics on administrative data sources such as vital registers, foreign population registers or residence or work permit registers, or health or tax records, while others resort to speculative statistics.

The distance between these realities and the accessibility of demographic data, in the age of post-truth, generate a risk of misleading interpretations and suggest to intervene in helping final users in reading and understanding data.

This chapter, after reviewing the relationship between territory and population, will critically focus on sources to address the study of migration in demography. Further reflection will be dedicated to the limits of available data processing, with particular regard to the use made in the political arena and media as channels for disseminating misleading or biased information.

5.2. *Borders: territory and population*

The overlap of territory, culture, and people, was a strong and widespread ideal and political motivation for the birth and construction of the nation state, although it is a bundle of different groups, sometimes even in conflict with each other or more like an imagined than real community (Anderson 2009). Nevertheless, borders are frequently treated as empirical realities rather than a series of shifting, overlapping, and historically constructed concepts. Nation states – along with their juridical-legislative systems, bureaucratic apparatuses, economic entities, modes of governmentality, and war-making capabilities (Ong 1999: 15) – continue to define, discipline, control, and regulate population, whether in movement or in residence. In some languages, like Italian, French, German, the terms "border" and "boundary" are often used as synonyms to indicate a geographical and administrative limit. This analogy is the result of the slow process of formation of nation states. In the classical world, instead, the term "border" belonged to the dimension of the known space, of the known world and, therefore, of the populations and cultures that recognized each other. The boundary, however, represented the demarcation threshold that separated the known from the unknown, civilization from barbarism. Unlike the border, it was not a static and defined line, but a zone susceptible to mutation (Cassarino 2006). Currently, state boundaries are experienced as borders, and mark the nation state's authority even for statistical purposes, thus making it an analytical category like class, gender, age, and so on. However, where national statistics offices are not well reinforced and operational, estimates or guesstimates by international agencies, such as the United Nations, the World Bank, the International Labour Organization, and the International Organization for Migration, are available; or governments foster statistical cooperation through targeted projects and training.

Demography is concerned with the description, analysis and understanding of population behaviour. It is a descriptive and investigative analysis carried out mainly with a statistical method, and aimed at studying the structural and dynamic characteristics of human populations, both in their biological and social aspects, and in their relationship, in order to appreciate size, distribution, structure and population change over time. In fact, modern demography is the study of the determinants and consequences of population changes related to space including geographical or social borders; population is a group of individuals tied and identified by territorial, political, juridical, ethnic, cultural or religious characteristics (Buccianti and Fusari 2008: 9). However, any worthwhile interpretation of the causes and effects of population change must extend beyond formal statistical measurement of change determinants to draw on the theoretical framework of several disciplines, thus the broader aspect of the study of demography is known as "population studies".

Mobility has always been an inescapable character of all societies. Much of Western thought removed this reality for centuries, depicting humanity as naturally sedentary (Callari Galli 2004: 20). As a result, populations are often studied as closed and immobile (Capello et al. 2016), like the demographic transition theory that postulates a functional relation between birth and death rates, but does not posit a relation between them and migration (Fargues 2011: 590). Recently explored implications of the trends and projections of the ethnic or foreign-origin populations of selected European countries are an exception: if the composition of these European populations continues to change as projected, the resulting ethnic and social transformation should be regarded as a "third demographic transition" (Coleman 2006). Reversing the perspective and postulating that mobility does not represent the exceptionality, makes borders and identities the result of practices of contact and movement of different groups over time. Today, "new nomadisms" running contemporary society are a privileged object of research and debate, so much to disclose a feature of human beings as a new way of life. However, populations have always moved, but borders have not always existed nor they have always been the same, proving to be mobile and causing forced migration, like the 1923 population exchange between Greece and Turkey. With the establishment of borders, control and counting of the crossings have been introduced, and have become a new source of data for the study of human mobility. In fact, governments collect data for administrative purposes about population and their geographical distribution by various social, cultural and economic characteristics; population growth;

levels, trends and patterns of fertility and mortality; and patterns of movement and their redistribution over time. Moreover, sometimes borders have to be negotiated, and demographics become a primary strategic concern of governments, as it is in Israel and Palestine.

Since the 1980s, the "nomads of contemporaneity" (Callari Galli 2004) have been the focus of many studies dedicated to their life histories, numbers and agency. Classical sociology addressed migration from the side of the hosting societies, especially as immigration. Anthropology, instead, addressed migration from the side of the society of origin, as emigration, but there are still logistic and methodological difficulties in carrying out studies able to combine the impact on the sending and hosting countries without omitting transit countries. Demography, therefore, could be a bridge discipline between different geographical areas and approaches interested in mobility and migration (Buccianti and Fusari 2008).

5.3. *Sources: pride and prejudice*

Studying a processual phenomenon such as migration through a stock database sounds like a conceptual if not a methodological stretch, but it is actually a sign of the difficulty of statistics offices to follow migrants, causing a lack of adequate and reliable data. In fact, migration being the most volatile aspect of demographic behaviour, it can change over the course of an individual's life, and over history. Thus, attention should centre upon the intersections between individual time and historical time, and between individual micro-level experience and macro-level societal change. Analysing migrants' trajectories across time and space results in an in-depth notion of how migrants embodied mobility during different phases of their life projects and in different ages.

Although migration scholars have always focused on questions concerning human movement, their analytical principles have long been based on "sedentarist metaphysics" (Malkki 1992; Cresswell 2006). In other words, migration has mainly been studied from the position of fixed locations: the A and the B, the push and the pull, the place of origin and the destination. As a result, mobility processes have generally been reduced to residual in-between phases between two locations, and the migrants in question have been approached as moving from one state of fixity (in the place of origin) to another (in the destination). The transnational turn (Glick Schiller et al. 1995; Portes 1997), however, debunked this notion. By focusing on migrants' multiple relationships that cross geographical, cultural, and political boundaries, transnationalism positions migrants in two places simultaneously (the sending and the receiving country). Transnational migration studies have successfully debunked static notions of migration, but they have dealt only marginally with mobility processes stimulating a combined methodology of place-based and process-like research.

Population statistics are derived mainly from traditional sources (census, sample survey, vital registers, population registers), but not all of them are common in every country, for example developing countries have to rely on estimates or other non-traditional sources. Data from the below sources can be classified into two categories to show the state of the population in an area at a given point in time and the rate of change from this state. The two categories are referred to as the stock and the flow statistics. In particular, useful data to investigate migration flows derive from three sources: administrative sources such as population registers, visa applications, residence permits, work permits, etc.; border statistics due to checks made at the borders; and censuses and surveys whose household is the unit of measure. Obviously, to study international migrations, border statistics are the most useful, while internal migrations are studied on the basis of registers or surveys. However, censuses are not able to grasp temporary migration, and often they fail to detect even return migration; while sample surveys, although they are more flexible instruments, often only render a partial view, offering a misleading or incomplete portrayal.

Broadly, quantitative data to study mobility and migration in demography are derived from the following sources:

- Census is a procedure of systematically acquiring and recording information from all the members of a given population in a country or delineated territory, and it has all the limitations of a large-scale statistical investigation.
- Sample surveys provide reliable data on demographic and socio-economic characteristics of the population, collecting information only from a fraction of the population.
- Vital and civil registers include continuous registration of births, deaths, marriages, etc., and maintain a regularly updated list of people resident in a country with details of sex, date of birth, marital status, etc. Unfortunately, in many developing countries they do not exist because their maintenance demands a reasonably accurate address system and a literate population.
- Non-traditional sources usually without a primary demographic purpose.
- Population statistics collected and processed on a worldwide basis by different agencies such as the United Nations,[1] the World Bank, the International Labour Organization, the International Organization for Migration, and so on.

The value of stock data on migrants is the possibility of assessing the deterritorialization and reterritorialization of people, but they do not allow the analysis of flows, although transnationalism indicated a new direction to study migration, aiming to overcome the "bipolar" model of migration, which depicted the migrant only as "emigrant" or "immigrant".

---

[1] The United Nations try to fill the knowledge gap using census data of single countries to estimate the number of international migrants and publish the International Migrant Stock. However, for 19 out of 56 African countries there are currently no census data available or they have not conducted censuses since 1950 that include adequate questions to detect the phenomenon of migration, in a context in which part of the cross-border movements take place with minimal or no formalities (Dal Zotto and Fusari 2017).

In recent decades, the availability of longitudinal data in the Global North has grown significantly, offering broad opportunities for research in social sciences. It allows an accurate analysis of the behaviours, including their evolution and social dynamics underlying them. The diffusion of longitudinal surveys in social sciences depends on the development of life course research, an approach that emphasizes the processual and dynamic character of social phenomena and their rooting in a collective and historical dimension, by its nature institutional and path dependent. Therefore, moving from the use of stock data to that of routes and decision of the single unit makes it essential to use longitudinal data, which contain information on the same subjects over a longer period, collected prospectively or retrospectively (Scherer 2013).[2] Thus, the use of longitudinal data would be desirable in migration studies because, together with the ethnographic research that has brought the subject and its biographical dimension back to the centre, it is often overshadowed by methods and perspectives more prone to generalization and reification. As a consequence, multi-sited ethnography emerged (Marcus 1995), which reconstructs migration events following migrants' biographies and routes and attempts to provide an emic and not a purely quantitative vision of this phenomenon.

5.4. *Data: hypertrophy and limits*

In 2011, data being the lifeblood of decision-making, the Busan Action Plan for Statistics (BAPS) was adopted in order to have access to quality statistics for the definition of demographic policies, including migration and national development plans. Moreover, it states independence, impartiality, reliability, pertinence, timeliness and accessibility as principles behind official statistics.

In May 2013, in the report of the High-Level Panel of Eminent Persons on the post-2015 Development Agenda, "data revolution" was defined as an explosion in the volume of data, the speed with which data are produced, the number of producers of data, the dissemination of data, and the range of things on which there is data. Moreover, gaps in access and use of data should be closed because they are essential for decision making, accountability and solving development challenges. A growing demand for them from all parts of society drove this revolution, but at the same time it split the world. The volume of both traditional and new sources has been rising, and openness is increasing, but many people are excluded from the new world of data and information by language, poverty, lack of education, lack of technology infrastructure, remoteness or prejudice and discrimination. Too many countries still have poor data, they arrive too late, and too many issues are still barely covered by existing data

---

[2] Since migration is a dynamic process, having longitudinal data would allow a dynamic rather than static reconstruction of this phenomenon, with a potential distinction between "age effect", "cohort effect" and "period effect", and a more accurate estimate of causal effects.

(Independent Expert Advisory Group on a Data Revolution for Sustainable Development 2014).

National migration management capacities are also hampered by poor systems of data management, and a lack of capacity on the part of national institutions involved in it to organize, collect, process and disseminate statistical data on their activities. These shortcomings are aggravated by insufficiencies in financial, human and technological resources and other disturbing gaps: for example, entire groups of people and key issues remain invisible, and data are often insufficiently disaggregated at sub-national level. Too many countries still have data that are of insufficient quality to be useful in making decisions, holding governments to account or fostering innovation. Good data are relevant, accurate, timely, accessible, comparable and produced free of political interferences. Besides, one of the most fundamental inequalities is between those who are counted and those who are not. Millions of people of all ages in low- and middle-income countries are denied basic services and protection of their rights because they are absent from official records. The good news is that international partners and countries have recently agreed on a Global Civil Registration and Vital Statistics Scaling Up Investment Plan. It covers activities over a 10-year period (2015–2024), with the goal of universal civil registration of births, deaths, marriages, and other vital events, including cause of death, and access to legal proof of registration for all individuals by 2030.

National efforts and international cooperation are boosting the data revolution, taking into account basic principles to avoid unfair readings. First of all, poor quality data can mislead, so the entire process of data-design, collection, analysis and dissemination needs to be demonstrably of high quality and integrity. Secondly, to the possible extent and respecting individual privacy, data should be disaggregated across many dimensions, such as geography, wealth, disability, sex and age, because no one should be invisible. Thus, there is a global responsibility to ensure that all countries have an effective national statistics system, capable of producing high-quality statistics in line with global standards and expectations. Thirdly, standards should be tightened and technology leveraged to reduce the time between the design of data collection and their publication, since data delayed is data denied. Then, all data on public matters and/or funded by public funds, including those data produced by the private sector, should be made public and open access to guarantee transparency and openness, mainly because many national statistics offices lack sufficient capacity and funding, and remain vulnerable to political and interest group influence. Furthermore, data architecture should place great emphasis on user-centred design and user-friendly interfaces. Communities of "information intermediaries" should be fostered to develop new tools to translate raw data into information for non-technical potential users and enable citizens to offer feedback. As more disaggregated data are available and data-silos become more integrated, privacy issues are increasingly a concern about what data are collected and their use. Finally, human rights cut across many issues related to the data revolution, such as the right to be counted, the right to an identity, the right to privacy and to ownership of personal data, and so on, and they should be respected.

Despite efforts and principles, structural weaknesses remain and affect the statistical products that should be improved through technical and training assistance. Given that statistics play a strategic role in planning and defining policies, various efforts aimed at fostering statistical literacy are in place, like the Busan Action Plan for Statistics (2011); the Partnership in Statistics for Development in the 21st Century (2013); A World That Counts: Mobilising the Data Revolution for Sustainable Development (2014); Financing for Development (2015); and the Strategy for the Harmonisation of Statistics in Africa (2017).

5.5. *Demographics: use and misuse*

Two main factors can mislead: the first is the data quality as discussed in the previous paragraph; the second is the data use dealt with in this paragraph. The potential uses and misuses of data encourage further discussion and attention to the ways to collect and process field data. Researchers must consequently make a concerted effort to ensure that the limits of their data and analyses do not create the wrong impression or become highly problematic. Moreover, knowledge produced by scholars is sensitive to exploitation and manipulation when rooted in a highly politicized terrain such as that of contemporary migrations. Migration flows, apart from their actual number, are at the centre of political and media debate, and are the subject of security and humanitarian rhetoric, in line with migration policies (Brighenti 2009).

Governments, civil society, academia and the philanthropic sector work together to raise awareness of publicly available data, to strengthen them and the statistical literacy of citizens, the media, and other "infomediaries". People should be able to evaluate the quality of data, and use them to make decisions, and to participate in initiatives in the Information Age (Dörnemann et al. 2015).

It is not a case that the Oxford Dictionary's Word of the Year 2016 was "post-truth", that is circumstances in which objective facts are less influential in shaping public opinion than appeals to emotion and personal belief. Migration is an example of the use of demographics to influence and direct public opinion. An atmosphere of crisis surrounds quantitative and social representations of migration, although longitudinal studies on international mobility, both voluntary and forced, do not provide evidence of such vertiginous increase to justify the state of alarm spread widely in political discourse, in mass media and in everyday language. Nevertheless, accessibility, dissemination and political use of data does not limit the widespread discourse practice, aimed more at protecting the borders than the human beings that cross them, because in Europe, especially as regards migration policies, the nation state authorities still maintain absolute sovereignty over the decision-making process, which must be justified to the population.

When the same database drives different positions, it means that the difference lies in use and reading of data, so in a post-truth age, objective facts often hold less weight than emotional appeals and fake news when it comes to shaping public opinion. Nowhere has post-truth gained more currency than in debates around the so-called refugee crisis, but migrant and refugee arrivals in 2015 were a crisis relative only to what Europe had experienced before, and to its degree of unpreparedness. Countries like Turkey, Jordan, and Lebanon that had been absorbing large numbers of refugees for years certainly did not view Europe's predicament as a crisis. Nor did African countries like Uganda, Ethiopia, and Chad that have been hosting hundreds of thousands of refugees for years. The post-truth age is also paradoxically characterized by a desire for more reliable analysis to make sense of the world and an abundance of data, if only people can tap into and make sense of it. Agencies and scholars are constantly striving to produce better statistics to support decision makers, and they have ambitious plans to harness big data and exploit their potential to help policy makers understand the current socio-demographic behaviours. They must always look to understand current and future user needs and try to respond to them. Therefore, it is not just about producing better statistics, but there are challenges in explaining to a wide audience what the evidence says about any given issue when the matter at hand is complex, the evidence is not always clear, and the methodological limitations need to be made clear as well in the name of transparency (Langley 2017). The problem deals with a mass audience and a controversial issue, because a simple and clear message usually beats a complex one, but the risk of oversimplification or generalization is high. In fact, although dealing in complexity and nuance, researchers working on official statistics are committed to communicate better and in a way that is clear and accessible, which makes it tricky to get a message across where others may be peddling a simpler line and in a louder voice. Thus, statistics offices, civil society groups, media outlets, and ordinary citizens should work together to continue to build the case for evidence, and to challenge those who wilfully misuse or disregard it. Improving statistical literacy is valuable in order to understand the importance of evidence and challenge its misuse, because in the midst of growing digitalization and automation, the emotional and the instinctive have gained an upper hand over the rational. In fact, although the post-truth phenomenon is not entirely a new phenomenon, the speed, volume and reach of information flows in the current digital ecosystem have undeniably affected the scope and magnitude, creating the perfect conditions for fake news to thrive, and to condition public opinion and political choices (Langley 2017).

5.6. *Conclusions*

New international migrations, new communication systems, new financial flows and new political entities constitute relationships that cross, fluidize and shape borders, reshaping the model of the coincidence between territory and population. Migrants are defined with respect to borders: paradoxically, migrants would not exist if there were no borders, although few studies address the borders definition (Cagiano de Azevedo 2007). Borders have an impact upon people's movement because they may imply a seam or a split between two countries or territories. In the first hypothesis cross-border relations occur, in the second, walls or other legal instruments make the borders more and more rigid.

Addressing the question of methodology in migration studies means touching upon epistemological aspects ranging from the definition of the field of research to the relationship between powers and multiple knowledge. The field of research has always been delimited in space, but the inadequacy of traditional research tools has emerged in the face of social phenomena that characterize this era, leading some scholars to propose a multi-sited research, able to follow the subjects. This approach can take place moving along the routes travelled by migrants, or through the collection of narratives, memories and demographics, if the statistics offices have worked well. Currently, the majority of migration studies have been carried out exclusively in the countries of arrival, limiting the ability to restore the complexity of the social fields in which migrants' agency arises. The opportunity to study simultaneously people involved in migration in the places of departure, transit, and arrival would allow the reconciliation of extension and depth in research.

Nevertheless, mobility is a privilege that is unevenly distributed among human beings: citizens from developed countries may travel and settle down almost anywhere in the world, while their fellow human beings from less-developed countries depend upon the uncertain issuance of visas and residence permits to migrate. In this respect, citizenship is a birth right privilege that is difficult to justify, and together with border control, they play a role in inequalities. Although Art. 13-2 of the Universal Declaration of Human Rights states: "Everyone has the right to leave any country, including his own, and to return to his country" (United Nations 2015: 28), nothing is said about immigration. Emigration is a fundamental right, which raises the issue of the actual meaning of this right in the absence of immigration possibilities, and points to the necessity of envisaging a more comprehensive right to mobility. In today's world, most people are free to leave their country but only a minority of them have the right to enter another country of their choice because controlling immigration has become an important political issue. As a result, most receiving countries are strongly concerned with what they perceive as the porosity of their borders to flows of undocumented migration, and are developing new measures to police them (Pécoud and de Guchteneire 2007). However, overconfidence in formal demography to foresee the future can be misleading: although population changes take place slower than social, economic or political ones, migration flows have widely demonstrated that there are no closed populations, making projections unreliable.

Offering statistical training and literacy means to guarantee an adequate level of awareness about socio-demographic behaviours, avoiding the risk of prejudicial closures and introducing a more balanced account, overcoming disciplinary and methodological boundaries (Caldwell et al. 1987), in order to scale down the scaremongering of the media. In the post-truth age, it is important to know how to read words and numbers concerning migrations, understand how they are constructed, the information hidden in the grey zone, and increase data for those hidden populations that, physically present and visible, often escape official demographic survey. Although today population statistics are hypertrophic because international and national, governmental and non-governmental agencies are concerned with providing quantitative data, they hardly contextualize them, provide the most appropriate reading, or trace their genealogy by really explaining how estimates are done, what they detect, and what the difference is between various available data. In fact, it is not enough to make the data available, it is also necessary to help users in reading them adequately through data and statistical literacy.

Bibliography

Anderson, B. (2009) *Imagined communities: Reflections on the origin and spread of nationalism*, Italian edition, Roma: Manifesto Libri.

Brighenti, A (2009) *Territori migranti*, Verona: Ombre Corte.

Buccianti, C. and Fusari, V. (2008) *Lineamenti di etnodemografia*, Padova: Cedam.

Cagiano de Azevedo, R. (2007) *Le migrazioni internazionali*, Torino: Giappichelli.

Caldwell, J., Caldwell, P. and Caldwell, B. (1987) 'Anthropology and demography. The mutual reinforcement of speculation and research', *Current Anthropology*, 28(1): 25–43.

Callari Galli, M. (ed.) (2004) *Nomadismi contemporanei. Rapporti fra comunità locali, stati-nazione e "flussi culturali globali"*, Rimini: Guaraldi.

Capello, C., Cingolani, P. and Vietti, F. (2016) *Etnografia delle migrazioni. Temi e metodi di ricerca*, Roma: Carocci.

Cassarino, J.P. (2006) *Approaching borders and frontiers: Notions and implications*, Firenze: European University Institute.

Coleman, D. (2006) 'Immigration and ethnic change in low-fertility countries: A third demographic transition', *Population and Development Review*, 32(3): 401–446.

Cresswell, T. (2006) *On the move: Mobility in the modern Western world*, New York: Routledge.

Dal Zotto, E. and Fusari, V. (2017) 'Africa e Europa allo specchio: Contesti e pretesti della mobilità circolare', federalismi.it – *Focus Africa*, 1: 1–17.

Dörnemann, M., Overath, P. and Reinecke, C. (eds.) (2015) 'Competing numbers. Uses of population statistics in the nineteenth and twentieth centuries', *Contemporanea*, 18(3): 469–488.

Fargues, P. (2011) 'International migration and the demographic transition: A two-way interaction', *International Migration Review*, 45(3): 588–614.

Glick Schiller, N., Basch, L. and Szanton Blanc, C. (1995) 'From immigrant to transmigrant: Theorizing transnational migration', *Anthropological Quarterly*, 68(1): 48–63.

Independent Expert Advisory Group on a Data Revolution for Sustainable Development (2014) *A world that counts. Mobilising the data revolution for sustainable development*, http://www.undatarevolution.org/report/ (accessed 20 September 20th, 2017).

Langley, D. (2017) *Official statistics in a post-truth era, National Statistical. News and Insight from the Office of National Statistics*, https://blog.ons.gov.uk/2017/02/17/official-statistics-in-a-post-truth-era/ (accessed on December 27th, 2017).

Malkki, L. (1992) 'National geographic: The rooting of peoples and the territorialization of national identity among scholars and refugees', *Cultural Anthropology*, 7(1): 24–44.

Marcus, G.E. (1995) 'Ethnography in/of the world system: The emergence of multi-sited ethnography', *Annual Review of Anthropology*, 24: 95–117.

Ong, A. (1999) *Flexible citizenship: The cultural logics of transnationality*, Durham: Duke University Press.

Palmer, J.R.B., Espenshade, J., Bartumeus, F., Chung Chang, Y., Ozgencil, N.E. and Li, K. (2013) 'New approaches to human mobility: Using mobile phones for demographic research', *Demography*, 50(3): 1105–1128.

Pécoud, A. and de Guchteneire, P. (eds.) (2007) *Migration without borders: Essays on the free movement of people*, Oxford: Berghahn Books and Unesco.

Portes, A. (1997) *Globalization from below: The rise of transnational communities*, Oxford: Oxford University Press.

Scherer, S. (2013) *Analisi dei dati longitudinali*, Bologna: Il Mulino.

United Nations (2015) *Universal Declaration of Human Rights*, New York: United Nations.

Zagheni, E., Weber, I. and Gummadi, K. (2017) 'Leveraging Facebook's advertising platform to monitor stocks of migrants', *Population and Development Review*, 43(4): 721–734.

Chapter 6

Migrants and internal borders

Rural ghettoisation in Southern Italy

Angelo Scotto

6.1. *Internal vs external borders*

Borders, both in the academic and in the understanding, may be interpreted in several ways: merely from the physical point of view; as legal and institutional instruments; in a symbolic way. But they have a constant feature: they are elements that separate the reference community from the others. This is why the talk on borders usually implies that they are external. However, internal borders are not less relevant.

Such a distinction could seem a rhetorical gimmick, since the nature of a border depends on the level of analysis: e.g., the external borders between provinces are internal if the focus in on the national level. The same thing could be said also for levels of analysis closer to the individual, to the point that also the borders of city neighborhoods could be interpreted as external.

However, the distinction between internal and external borders has its own specific reason. When a social entity is studied, the level of analysis is not discretional, since it should be the one where the reference entity can be considered as one subject; once this level has been pointed out, if in the observed entity there are further relevant subdivisions, then it makes sense to talk about internal borders, which follow laws qualitatively different from the external ones.

In this chapter, we will deal with the ghettoisation of migrants at the local level in the province of Foggia, in Southern Italy, by using the tools of policy studies; therefore, the level of analysis should be the one where the policies are made, that is national and regional. As will be shown, these policies produce, together with structural features of the Apulian socio-economic system, cases of spatial segregation for specific groups of migrants, both in the rural and urban context. Although the borders of these segregation spaces are more social than physical, they should be considered as internal in the context of the analysis.

6.2. *Marginalisation, segregation, ghettoisation*

Ghettoisation, as will be meant in this chapter, is a peculiar form of spatial segregation, and it is the physical expression of social marginalisation.

In a social system, being marginal means having a lower level of integration in the system than the average one. This means that in any system with inequalities, be they economic, political or symbolic, there will be conditions for the existence of marginal people and groups. However, it is not always simple to define marginality and distinguish it from merely belonging to social groups with fewer resources. On the attempts of definition, Ranci notes that

> *Social sciences expressed altogether two different, yet not opposed, notions of social marginality. The first one defines marginality on the basis of exclusion from the access to the fundamental processes of a given social system – production, decision-making and distribution; it is thus a residual potion, functionally disconnected from the fundamental processes of social production and reproduction. Conversely, the second one defines marginality as a position of social eradication and uncertain status, caused by the transition from one belonging to another, by the emergence of new forms of social exclusion (on ethnic, territorial or other bases), or by the modern experience of social differentiation and 'pluri-belonging'.*
>
> *(Ranci 1996, translation mine)*

Thus, social marginality is not an unchangeable fact. On the contrary, it is a condition people can find themselves in, and they can get out of. Economic and/or political changes in a system may cause the shift to marginality for categories previously more integrated at the social level; finally, there are situations where this phenomenon is not an unintendend consequence of social changes, but it happens by explicit choice of power holders who want to distance some people or groups from the centre of the social system. In all these cases, we call marginalisation the process that produces social marginality.

Segregation can be considered as the most radical physical expression of social marginalisation: it happens when the social exclusion experienced by marginal people and groups matches the spatial separation from the community: e.g., the concentration of these groups in specific territorial units, dimensionally variable but generally separated from the surrounding social environment, and with explicit or implicit rules that make harder the passage from one area to another or the interaction subjects that do not belong to these units.

A classic historical example of segregation is the one of Jews in Europe, with the creation, within the cities, of designated districts they could not leave except for to work or move in other cities. These districts were called ghettoes, from which derives the term ghettoisation for similar phenomena. Therefore, ghettoisation is used to define segregation due to direct imposition or social changes, and with negative and limiting effects for the subjects.

6.3. *Urban ghettoisation in America and Europe*

While the term ghettoisation was born with reference to the segregation of Jewish people in Europe, nowadays it is commonly used to define neighborhoods in U.S. cities populated mostly by African-Americans. The physical separation of the black population is a direct consequence of the racial discrimination they endured for centuries that resulted both in racial laws still enforced in many Southern states even after the abolition of slavery and in discriminatory and segregationist measures in Northern areas as well (Lieberson 1980). Even after desegregation in the 1950s and 1960s, the disadvantaged socio-economic conditions of the African-American population caused the persistence of ghettoes, where the marginalisation matches with the claim of their own social and cultural identity.

Urban segregation can be observed as well if we shift the focus to other minorities in the U.S. population, that is the immigrants from the first decades of the 1800s, even when there was no racial discrimination or explicitly segregationist policies. The American migration policy had been rather open until the beginning of the 1900s, but the easy access to the country and, to a certain extent, the job market, did not translate to a quick social and political integration in the new context. The speed and effectiveness of integration varied from one national group to another; some of them reacted to the problems of inclusion in U.S. society by recreating their local and national communities; neighborhoods like Little Italy and Chinatown expressed both the migrants' desire to maintain their roots and have a protection network against the problems of life abroad, and the mistrust and hostility of the majority groups in American society which, while accepting the migration flows, promoted a system of separation or subordination that was produced not through ad hoc policies, but through informal mechanisms like the ones operating in the job and housing markets, where preferences influenced by ethnic or national belonging actually contributed to the persistance of socio-economic differences and to the spatial concentration of immigrants in separated enclaves, a factual ghettoisation.

Similar patterns can be found in the European immigration experiences. European countries adopted different approaches to deal both with ethnic, religious and national minorities and migration flows (Martiniello 2000). Whatever the prevailing approach, be it assimilationist, pluralist or multiculturalist, the current results on inclusion policies are not satisfactory, mainly for what concerns migrant groups. Migration flows to Europe, mainly the one started in the 1970s, are mostly directed to urban areas, and many cities experienced the gathering of migrants and citizens of foreign origin in separated neighborhoods; e.g. Paris, where the factual segregation in areas with high percentages of foreigners has not been resolved even with direct interventions for their requalification (Mahnig 2004).

Factual segregation in many European cities is an established fact, but there is no agreement as to whether it is correct to call them ghettoes. On the one hand there are not many ghettoes in the strictest sense in Europe (Droogleever Fortujin, Musterd and

Ostendorf 1998); on the other hand it is feared that the rise in social tensions and turmoils in neighborhoods with many migrants and socio-economic indicators far worse than the national average signal a process of ongoing ghettoisation (Peach 2007).

The analysis of this possible ghettoisation must take into account several elements: although it has been said that it happens because of spontaneous social dynamics, the presence of subjects campaigning for policies to promote the physical separation of migrant communities from the rest of the population cannot be ignored, be they political parties with anti-immigration manifestos or members of foreign communities with an interest in maintaining the separation (Glynn 2006). The existence of diverging interests in the community is related to the observation that residentially separated minority groups do not necessarily have a negative effect on their members, because they provide opportunities of community involvement that could be a relevant support in the process of social integration (Vaughan 2006).

Acknowledging the direct intervention of social actors in the development of ghettoisation is useful to orient the analysis of the phenomenon, but it does not change the essence of our definition; actually, it brings it back to the origin of the term. Instead, the chance of a positive effect of spatial separation on foreigners' integration requires a wider reflection on the nature of ghettoisation, that cannot be made in this context; however, if the potential effects are excluded from the discourse to focus on the present and actual ones, then spatial segregation definitely has a negative impact on social integration, and therefore, since migrants have a reduced ability to choose when it comes to their area of residence in urban contexts, it meets the criteria we pointed out to define ghettoisation.

6.4. *Urban and rural ghettoisation in Italy: the case of the province of Foggia*

In Italy, ghettoisation seems to be less widespread than in other European countries, because of factors like the smaller incidence of migrants in the overall population, and the later start of immigration flows. An exception is the management of the nomadic Romani and Sinti communities, some of which live in camps that have always been the object of debate and turmoil with the inhabitants of nearby towns. However, in political and journalistic language, the term ghetto is not used for the Rom camps, but for a peculiar kind of aggregation in rural areas of Southern Italy.

This fact could be surprising for several reasons: ghettoisation has been described so far as an urban phenomenon; moreover, this case is in Southern Italy, where the percentage of migrants is lower than the national average, while it would be reasonable to expect segregation to be related to higher numbers that could make the development of neighborhoods with a concentration of foreigners feasible. In light of these considerations, do these so-called ghettoes fulfill the above-described criteria for ghettoisation?

It is not possible to understand the rural ghettoes in Southern Italy without describing first a widespread work praxis: the so-called caporalato, or gang-master system.

In the political debate, the caporalato is almost exclusively linked to immigration in Southern Italy, but it has actually been present in Italy at least since the 1970s, and it concerns the whole country, although it is stronger in the South. It is a form of illicit mediation to work, and it was banned by law for the first time in 1970 and then with further acts that provide for sanctions both for mediators and employers who turn to them; the most recent law was in 2016.

The caporalato in Apulia originated from the differentiated development of the agricultural areas of the region: after the agrarian reform of 1950, some areas started modernisation processes while others stayed underdeveloped. The laborers from these areas become the workforce for the most developed ones, which did not lead to intraregional migration flows, but to commuting, that was organised by some workers who took on the task of selecting the workforce on behalf of the land owners, thanks to their experience and skills. In time, the mediators became more and more relevant, because of the increasing difficulty for the employers to find a workforce on their own; moreover, mediators also took on the role of transporting the laborers to the work fields, which made them similar to current caporals (Zaccaria 1998).

As a mediator, the caporal collects the requests for workforce from the employers, then he gathers with his own means the needed laborers and brings them to the workplace and back home at the end of the working day; tasks and wages are negotiated with the employers directly by the caporal, whose payment consists in a share of the laborers' wages. This system seems to totally favour the employers, who benefit from using irregular workers, and totally penalise the workers, who have to give part of their money to the caporals. The actual distribution of costs and benefits is more nuanced, for several reasons: first of all, in the past caporals used to be from the same geographical and socio-economic context as the laborers, and sometimes they still are; this belonging and the need to cultivate a network of relationships to perform their task prevented the caporals from misusing their privileged position; moreover, the normality of illegality makes it easier for the laborers to accept the caporal's role, which is considered a better option than the bureaucratic procedures of the official employment agencies. On the other hand, although the employers undoubtedly benefit from the presence of caporals, they end up becoming dependent on them, since the caporalato tends to monopolise the informal job market. Only the caporals themselves benefit from this situation, since they are an essential point of reference for employers and laborers, and they can use their centrality to organise their job to maximise their own benefits (Curci 2008).

The main features of caporalato is that its role of mediation focuses on the weaker segments of the workforce: in past decades, mostly women were employed through the caporals, while the migrants have increased since the 1980s. Immigrants brought change also to the organisation of the system, with the emergence of foreign caporals; some of them followed the same pattern of traditional caporals (workers become mediators after gaining the employers' trust), but the majority follow a different pattern that can be only partially assimilated to the one of classic caporalato.

Foreign caporals do not belong to the local agricultural communities, neither do the immigrant workers; therefore it is less important to keep good relationships with the workers. At the same time, foreign laborers are potentially harder to control than Italian ones, because they are more open to moving: they do not have family or economic ties with the territory, and since they are seasonal workers they can freely go where wages and conditions are expected to be better. The combination of these elements helps the emergence of violence as a means for caporals to control foreign workers, which leads to cases of forced work. This is what happened in the province of Foggia, where in 2006 a network to exploit and almost enslave Polish immigrants was discovered: their wages were very low, smaller than the promised ones and reduced by the requests for maney to pay for lodgings, it was impossible to leave the workplace and there was abuse by the caporals, with cases of murders and disappearances. The scandal enlightened the evolution of the caporalato and its peculiar internationalisation: Polish laborers were directly recruited in Poland, with the promise of hard but well-paid jobs – with respect to the local wages – and they left on buses of the recruiting organisation, that brought them to the province of Foggia and assigned them to the caporals, who were their compatriots (Leogrande 2008).

Beside the outstanding cases of enslavement, there is the problem of the awful living conditions of foreign laborers, who live in ruined buildings without sanitation and have to endure exhausting shifts in fields without resting or watering places. Such a demeaning situation has been denounced by NGOs such as Medici Senza Frontiere (2005, 2008), which did not have much effect; reporter Fabrizio Gatti (2007) was more effective by posing as an immigrant to work for a day in the field of the province of Foggia and providing documentary evidence of the caporals' selection methods and the laborers' living and working conditions; however, after a phase of stricter controls following the scandals, the situation went back to the usual: few inspections, sporadic controls and loosely implemented laws.

The caporalato has a role in the immigrants' precarious conditions: since they leave the selection of workforce to mediators, employers do not feel any responsibility in provinding services to laborers. But neither do caporals, because of the above-mentioned uselessness to keep good relationships with the workers: only cost avoidance and the maximisation of profits matter. The effects of caporalato on the workers' living condition also concern the development of another social phenomenon widespread in the province of Foggia: the rural ghettoes.

Ghettoes are usually isolated areas far from urban centres; they often grow in abandoned hamlets, where homeless migrants settle and build makeshift homes without water or sanitation. The biggest ghetto in the province is between the cities of San Severo and Rignano Garganico, and it has often been the focus of journalistic and academic discussion (Cristaldi 2014; Sardella 2016; Scotto 2016), but there are many smaller ghettoes widespred around the province.

Ghettoes are not born from the spontaneous gathering of migrants in one place; rather, once they are born they also develop through informal networks that bring foreigners who arrive in the province of Foggia for the first time to the same places used by the previous migrants, their original development is functional to the caporals' system: traditionally, caporals gathered the workforce in the main square of villages and towns and chose the daily laborers. The dispersion of migrants on the territory jeopardises their ability to organise and their wage requests, but if excessive it could make the gathering selection too slow and expensive. Ghettoes, where aspiring workers gather, are a solution.

The volunteers of NPOs that provide assistance in the ghettoes always state that, beside awful hygienic conditions, these places are dangerous because they favour the spread of prostitution and alcoholism. But beyond the ghettoes there are not any alternatives: the existing facilities are not enough and the local administrations in rural areas are often unresponsive to the issue. So the institutions are perceived to be missing – and actually, they often are; in such a void, caporals at least provide a place to stay and a job, no matter how exhausting or underpaid.

In this regard, it has to be specified that after the discovery of the exploitation of Polish laborers, the national and international outcry pushed the Apulian regional administration to intervene more actively against caporalato. The interventions from 2006 to the present included both measures to improve the laborers' living conditions (e.g. providing water in the fields or the creation of 'widespread hotels' as an alternative to facilities provided by the caporals) and regulations to obstruct the use of caporalato by the employers. The results are mixed: while the implemented interventions proved to be useful, they were still insufficient to get rid of both caporalato and ghettoes, that still exist nowadays in spite of several attempts, at the institutional level, to clear them once for all; moreover the new regional and national laws struggled to be actually implemented: the complete implementation has been held back by the scarce level of controls in the area, because of which the subject involved in the caporalato may feel safe enough, regardless of the hardness of the existing sanctions. The human and economic resources needed to increase the controls on agricultural activities are high, especially in light of the economic crisis that has affected Europe and Italy since 2008, but also from a political point of view.

Foreign laborers in the province of Foggia are seasonal workers that, during the harvest months, live in abandoned rural areas. The distance from the populated areas produces a physical invisibility that translates into social and, as a consequence, political invisibility as well, because the problem of ghettoes does not directly affect the interests of the citizens-electors, and therefore does not enter in the local political agenda and does nos receive any attention from the administrations. It is not surprising that the main institutional actors in the fight against caporalato are the regional administrations and the national government, because the NPOs' advocacy activity and the outcry caused by the reports on the seasonal workers' living conditions may create a stronger stir at those levels. Conversely, at the local level, promoting foreign laborers' rights is not perceived as a necessity or an urgency, and fighting the caporalato risks producing a negative reaction from the stakeholders who benefit from this system or think that its end would produce more risks than opportunities; in a socio-economic context where the agricultural sector produces a significant share of the local wealth, this is a disincentive to act.

This is why municipal administrations are usually the less committed institutional actors in the fight against caporalato; but since they are the nearest to the territory, their absence has a significant role in reducing the effectiveness of the measures decided at higher levels.

6.5. *Conclusions*

Strictly speaking, seasonal migrants who arrive in the province of Foggia are not forced to live in ghettoes. However, freedom of choice is severely limited by the scarcity of alternatives and by the role of ghettoes as a place of selection of workforce by the caporals. In other words, for many it is almost a necessary choice.

Does living in ghettoes have negative consequences? There cannot be a definitive answer: lacking other possibilities, ghettoes are still better than abandoned buildings in hamlets, in spite of bad hygeine and health conditions and the diffusion of alcoholism and prostitution, because they grant a minimum of community life and make it easier to receive assistance from voluntary organisations. But ghettoes themselves are functional to the persistence of the caporalato, because they simplify the mediators' activity and legitimise them as the provider of minimum levels of board and lodging; and it has been shown how the caporalato negatively impacts seasonal workers, by decreasing their wages, nullifying their bargaining power, and facilitating exploitation.

In light of these consideration, it is possible to say that rural ghettoes in the province of Foggia are a form of forced and damaging segregation; therefore, they are an actual case of ghettoisation on the basis of the above-mentioned criteria, aside from the definitions of journalists and nonprofit workers. They are peculiar with respect to traditional ghettoes, not only because of the rural context and the relative nature of the imposition and the damages: the main element of difference is the temporary permanence of their residents, who as seasonal workers experience a temporary segregation and then move to other harvest areas or go home. This element may be puzzling, especially for the laborers who every year come to work in the province of Foggia: is the choice of coming back knowing the living and working conditions in contrast with the idea of a forced segregation?

This doubt does not consider the fact that many seasonal migrants choose this job mainly because of economic need. The fine line between will and obligation creates a grey area of ambiguity where the ghettoisation of foreign workers can emerge. The same ambiguity is found in the internal borders of these rural ghettoes: the borders of the ghettoes do not exist from the administrative point of view, but they are built by the union of the social invisibility of the foreign laborers and the caporals' informal power.

Bibliography

Cristaldi, F. (2014) 'I nuovi schiavi: Gli immigrati del Gran Ghetto di San Severo', Rivista *Geografica Italiana*, 122(1): 119–142.

Curci, S. (2008) *Nero invisibile normale. Lavoro migrante e caporalato in Capitanata*, Foggia: Edizioni del Rosone.

Droogleever Fortujin, J., Musterd, S. and Ostendorf, W. (1998) 'International migration and ethnic segregation: Impact on urban areas – introduction', *Urban Studies*, 35(3): 367–370.

Gatti, F. (2007) *Bilal. Viaggiare e morire da clandestini*, Milan: Rizzoli.

Glynn, S. (2006) *Playing the Ethnic Card – Politics and Ghettoisation in London's East End*, working paper, Institute of Geography, University of Edimburgh.

Leogrande, A. (2008) *Uomini e caporali. Viaggio tra i nuovi schiavi nelle campagne del Sud*, Milan: Mondadori.

Lieberson, S. (1980) *A Piece of the Pie. Blacks and Immigrants since 1880*, Berkeley: California University Press.

Mahnig, H. (2004) 'The politics of minority-majority relations: How immigrant policies developed in Paris, Berlin and Zurich' in R. Penninx, K. Kraal, M. Martiniello and S. Vertovec (eds.) *Citizenship in European Cities: Immigrants, Local Politics, and Integration Policies*, Aldershot: Ashgate, 17–38.

Martiniello, M. (2000) *Le società multietniche: Diritti e doveri uguali per tutti?*, Bologna: il Mulino.

Medici Senza Frontiere (2005) *I frutti dell'ipocrisia: Storie di chi l'agricoltura la fa, di nascosto*, Rome: Sinnos.

Medici Senza Frontiere (2008) *Una stagione all'inferno. Rapporto sulle condizioni degli immigrati impiegati in agricoltura nelle regioni del Sud Italia*, online report: http://www.medicisenzafrontiere.it/sites/italy/files/allegati/Immagini/file/pubblicazioni/una_stagione_all_inferno.pdf (accessed on March 14th, 2019).

Peach, C. (2007) 'Sleepwalking into ghettoisation? The British debate over segregation' in K. Schönwälder (ed.) *Residential Segregation and the Integration of Immigrants: Britain, the Netherlands and Sweden*, Berlin: Social Science Research Center, 7–40.

Ranci, C. (1996) 'Marginalità sociale' in Vv.Aa. *Enciclopedia delle scienze sociali*, Roma: Treccani.

Sardella, R. (ed.) (2016) *Io ci sto fra i migranti*, Pisa: Istos.

Scotto, A. (2016) 'Focusing on the emergencies or on their roots? The role of nonprofit organisations in immigration policymaking in Italy', *Religion, State and Society*, 44(1): 51–64.

Vaughan, L. (2006) *Patterns of Immigrant Settlement and the Construction of Community*,

paper presented at the Conference "Ghettoised Perpeption versus Mainstream Construction of English Muslims", Birmingham.
Zaccaria, C. (1998) 'Lavoro nero oggi: Il fenomeno del caporalato agricolo in Puglia', *Critica Sociologica*, 127: 72–86.

Chapter 7
Migrant workers and the sponsorship system

Federica Di Pietro

7.1. *Introduction*

The kafalah system (guardianship or sponsorship) is the tool used by Arabian Peninsula countries to monitor the direct migratory flows within their own borders. [1] This system has its roots in a Bedouin tradition, [2] according to which foreigners who arrived in the Gulf Area countries were entrusted to the so-called kafil (or guardians) who were supposed to guarantee protection and safety to their guests. [3] During the years after the economic boom, which had characterized the economies of the Middle Eastern countries, the original meaning which had defined the kafalah system has changed. In fact, this institution has been sufficiently modified to justify migration policies aimed at the acquisition of cheap labour and only for the duration of the employment, with no guarantee of rights or possible stabilization for migrant workers. [4]

Among the countries that have mostly adopted this system are the Gulf Cooperation Council Countries (GCC), which are Saudi Arabia, Bahrain, Kuwait, Oman,

---

[1] The complaints lodged by the press and by the international organizations that have fought over the years against the system of *kafalah*, practised in the Gulf Area, are numerous. Among the many writings, we recall in particular the article by Richard Morin, 'Indentured Servitude in the Persian Gulf', in *The New York Times*, 2013, and 'The States of Forced Labour', in *The New York Times*, 2014, and the appeals of the Financial Times, see 'FT Seasonal Appeal: Vulnerable Migrants in the Gulf', in *Financial Times*, 2015, until arriving at the latest stories regarding the exploitation of migrant workers for the construction of the football plant that will host the World Cup to be held in Qatar in 2022.

[2] The term "Bedouin" refers to the nomadic tribes stationed in the Arabian Peninsula, mainly devoted to sheep farming and known to be extremely hospitable toward their guests.

[3] In this regard, the representative of the International Labor Organization (ILO) in Kuwait "is a custom, not a code. It is from the culture of the people", see *Walls At Every Turn: Abuse of Migrant Domestic Workers through Kuwait's Sponsorship System*, in Human Rights Watch, 2010. According to Heeg (2013) the system of kafalah derives from a Bedouin tradition of "temporarily granting strangers protection and even affiliation into the tribe for specific purposes", moreover, the author says that generosity is a distinctive sign of the Bedouin hospitality; see also the report by Asia Pacific Mission for Migrants, entitled *The Kafala: Impact and Relation to Migrant Labor Bondage in GCC Countries,* 2014, p. 27.

[4] See Khan and Harroff-Tavel 2011, and cf. ILO 2012: 1, in which it is stated that "the sponsorship system's economic objective rapidly brought into the county in economic boom and expelled during less affluent periods". For more detailed analysis about the socioeconomic effects of this phenomenon see Fargues and Shah 2014. Also read Baldwin Edwards 2013.

Qatar and the United Arab Emirates. Even Lebanon and Jordan benefit from this practice. [5]

Over the years, the phenomenon of migrant labour in the Gulf Area countries has achieved a remarkable impact, given it has led to these countries hosting 13 million foreigners out of a population of about 35 million people, and that migrant workers record a continued growth. [6] Despite the continuous exploitation of migrant workers, the countries of origin consider the migratory flow positive for the national economy, since the remittances sent by migrants to their families preserve the social order. [7]

Generally speaking, we could state that the kafalah system is applied to all foreign workers entering the Gulf areas, even if the categories worst affected by this phenomenon are in particular the female domestic workers, farmers and shepherds, who are forced to work in particularly arduous conditions in the desert. [8]

Among the various Gulf States, Qatar has recently attracted the attention of the world press due to the exploitation of migrant workers employed in the construction of the Khalifa Stadium which will host the 2022 FIFA World Cup. [9]

In this article it was decided to examine in particular the case of female domestic workers and migrant workers in Qatar, comparing and illustrating the connections between these two different categories of worker.

---

[5] For a deeper examination of the rules currently in force in the Member States affected by the phenomenon see Zahra 2015 and Rodrigues 2014.

[6] For a general framework of the foreign population present in the countries of the Gulf during the period 2010 to 2015 referring to Gulf Labour Markets and Migrations (Gulf Research Centre), GCC: Total population and percentage of nationals and non nationals in gcc countries (latest-national-statistics-2010-2015), www.gulfmigration.eu/total-population-and-percentage-of-nationals-and-non-nationals-in-gcc-countries-latest-national-statistics-2010-2015/ and to the UAE's website National Bureau of Statistics (NBS), www.fcsa.gov.ae/EnglishHome/ReportDetailsEnglish/tabid/121/Default.aspx.

[7] See Jeangey 2012: 398. The author states that "in the economies of the countries of origin, the result of emigrants' work represents a vital source for the national income. Almost always, those who choose to leave their own country to find jobs abroad, are forced by the need to maintain large families and to enable their children to receive medical treatment or an appropriate school education offering them a better future".

[8] See Jeangey 2012: 409 and Human Rights Watch 2014: 23–24. Farmers and shepherds are forced to spend most of their time in the desert, far away from civilization and without any access to essential services, such as hospitals.

[9] In this regard, see the article by Simeon Kerr, 'Qatar Under Fire over Treatment of World Cup Workers', in *Financial Times,* 2016 and the report by Amnesty International, *The Ugly Side Of The Beautiful Game: Exploitation Of Migrant Workers On A Qatar 2022 World Cup Site*, 2016, available at the webpage: www.amnesty.org/en/documents/mde22/3548/2016/en/, followed by a long exchange of correspondence with the Government of Qatar that even involved La Fédération Internationale de Football Association (better known as FIFA), see *Qatar: Letters Of Response – The Ugly Side Of The Beautiful Game: Exploitation Of Migrant Workers On A Qatar 2022 World Cup Site,* 2016, in www.amnesty.org/en/documents/mde22/3681/2016/en/.

7.2. The recruitment of migrants through temporary employment agencies

Retracing the origins of the functioning of the kafalah system, it emerges that the temporary work agencies [10] seem to play a central role in the recruitment of migrants, and they are the first point of contact between the migrants and their sponsors. [11] Female domestic workers and workers employed in the construction of the stadiums which will host the 2022 World Cup in Qatar are forced to pay a large amount of money in order to reach the Gulf Area countries.

In the past, the kafalah system was applied to domestic work which was intended almost exclusively for migrant women, [12] but recently in the lead up to the 2022 World Cup, even the workers employed in the renovation and construction of the stadiums are subject to this practice, as has been repeatedly denounced by various international organizations present in the area and involved in the defence of human rights. [13] Even if Qatar's laws forbid forcing migrants to pay for the costs of recruitment agencies, charging this expenditure on the employer, this practice is in force and shows no sign of diminishing. The Supreme Committee Workers' Welfare Standards (the Welfare Standards) requires companies to refer only to the placement agencies registered with the Ministry of Labour of Qatar. [14] Nevertheless, employment agencies continue to be

[10] Temporary work agencies are located in the countries where the phenomenon of domestic workers is more frequent, in particular in the Philippines, Sri Lanka and Ethiopia, while in the rest of the African countries brokers exploiting their contacts in the Gulf countries are more frequent.

[11] In many cases the recruitment of maids takes place in their villages of origin, where a person they know and trust acts as a liaison with the temporary work agencies which have their headquarters in large cities (Bajracharya and Sijapati 2012: 1). See also Fernandez 2013.

[12] In the 1960s and 1970s domestic work was a prerogative of Arab women, however during the 1980s the phenomenon was relegated to Asian workers because of the lower cost of their performance and because they could be subject to the system of kafalah. See The Journal of Developing Areas, Special Issue on Sydney Conference held in April 2015, vol. 49, n.6, 2015, 'Parental Styles and Closeness to the Domestic Servant as Perceived by the Children of Quatar', p.1 and Pande 2012. Furthermore, the fact that the domestic did not know the language and the Arab culture was perceived as an advantage for the house matrons, who could see the disadvantaged situation of the foreign workers as an opportunity to subdue them more easily (Juredini 2010).

[13] See in particular the report by Amnesty International. It is a dossier of 50 pages entitled The Ugly Side Of The Beautiful Game: Exploitation Of Migrant Workers On A Qatar 2022 World Cup Site, available at the website: https://www.amnesty.org/en/documents/mde22/3548/2016/en/ This dossier is the result of numerous discussions with workers, mainly from Nepal and India, employed in the restructuring of the Khalifa stadium. As described by the same Amnesty International report, "Migrant workers on Khalifa International Stadium and the surrounding Aspire Zone, one of the main venues for the 2022 World Cup, have been subjected to a range of exploitative practices. This includes high recruitment fees for which many took out loans; false promises about the pay and type of work on offer; passport confiscation; dirty and cramped accommodation; and threats for complaining about their conditions. Some were subjected to forced labour".

[14] Supreme Committee for Delivery and Legacy, 'Workers' Welfare Standards', Edition 1, February 2014, Articles 6.4, 8.6, 8.7 and Supreme Committee for Delivery and Legacy, 'Workers' Welfare Standards', Edition 2, February 2016, Article 6.4(a).

paid for their recruitment by migrant workers that fall into debt to find a job. [15] Moreover, once the employment contract is signed in their home country the terms and conditions of payments are modified and the workers often end up having a lower salary than was initially agreed. [16]

The female domestic workers, who originate mainly from the Philippines, Sri Lanka, Indonesia and Ethiopia, suffer the same fate. [17] A good level of education and an excellent knowledge of English or other foreign languages are considered an advantage for the female migrants, and also a source of pride for the sponsors who may choose their own collaborators according to their geographical origin: it is precisely for this reason that the country of origin and the level of education may greatly influence the remuneration of a domestic worker. [18]

Even the compensations required by temporary employment agencies may vary according to origin of the worker. Prices start from 1,000.00 dollars and often exceed 3,000.00 dollars, but agencies may alternatively also require the payment of the first three months' salary or in some cases both an upfront fee and a portion of the salary (Amrita 2013: 427).

An analysis of the expenditure incurred to become a domestic worker has underlined that there are costs that all migrant women must face in order to conclude an employment contract. These costs may include the commission to pay to the temporary employment agency, the outward flight to the country in which they will work and, depending on the country, the fee for their working visa. All of this leads to severe debt burdens suffered by migrant women, and means that because of their disadvantaged position and the need to pay back their creditors they can be exploited more easily by criminals. [19] Moreover, almost all domestic workers are poorly aware of what the phenomenon of kafalah (Kar 2009; Malit and Naufal 2014) is and how their life will be working under a sponsor. Most of the young women who emigrate to the countries of the Gulf Area come from remote areas where it is difficult to find job

[15] As reported in the dossier *The Ugly Side Of The Beautiful Game: Exploitation Of Migrant Workers On A Qatar 2022 World Cup Site* on page 19, "All of the 234 migrant workers interviewed by Amnesty International said that they had to pay recruitment agents in their home countries. The amount they paid ranged from US$500 to US$4,300 to obtain a job in Qatar".

[16] These practices are prohibited under Qatar law and the Workers' Welfare Standards. See Articles 45 and 65 of Law No. 14 of 2004 ("the Labour Law"), Articles 6.4, 8.6 and 8.7, Supreme Committee for Delivery and Legacy Workers' Welfare Standards. See also Article 2, Law No. 15 of 2011 Combating Trafficking in Human Beings.

[17] See Amrita 2013: 414 ff.

[18] Maids from Philippines, for example, are the most sought-after because they generally speak good English and may earn up to 250 dollars a month, while women from Africa are less remunerated and are paid between 100 and 200 dollars a month (Amrita 2013: 426).

[19] Note the article by Migrants – Rights.org, 'Recruiting "Maids" on Social Media Takes on Monopoly of Agencies in The Gulf; Workers More Vulnerable To Exploitation', March 2016, which points out a new trend and highlights the fact that temporary work agencies are giving way to recruitment systems through social networks.

opportunities, and in addition they often do not fully perceive what is going to happen to them. There is no doubt that the lack of information makes the migrant even more vulnerable to temporary employment agencies and sponsors (Bajracharya and Sijapati 2012: 9). For example, it is very common, as for the workers employed in the restructuring of the stadium in Qatar, that the domestic workers conclude a contract with the agency, which is then modified when it is translated into the Arabic language. The women are not aware that this takes place, as they do not know Arabic.

7.3. *The lives of migrant workers at the service of sponsors*

The primary objective of the countries in which the kafalah system is applied is to take advantage of the temporary nature of the migrant worker's presence in the country. This is confirmed by the fact that foreigners are never allowed to acquire the nationality of the state in which they work. [20] In order to be considered legal migrants, workers are forced to depend on the sponsors. In fact, if a maid or a worker employed in the construction of a stadium were to decide to quit their jobs without their employer's written consent they could be accused of clandestinity (ILO 2012: 1) and risk being repatriated or arrested. [21]

Because of the temporary nature of the work they do, migrant workers do not enjoy any benefit from the point of view of assistance and social security, which is normally free for citizens. Moreover, it is worth recalling that temporary migrants are generally not allowed to buy real estate or to take advantage of the national health service.

The workmen in Qatar and the domestic workers are all subjected to restrictions of various types, even on the possibility of traveling from one country to another and within the country to which they emigrate. The sponsors usually confiscate the passports of migrants on their arrival at the airport. A similar practice prevents workers from returning to their country of origin.

There are other restrictions which concern in particular domestic workers, given the condition of their greater vulnerability, who are forbidden to leave the house where they work without the consent of the lady of the house: the time outside the house granted to female workers can be as little as that which is necessary to perform work activities, such as taking the children that they care for to school. Domestic workers

---

[20] See Lori 2012.

[21] See Migrant Rights, 'Migrant Workers Under the "Kafalah" System in the GCC'. Available at http://www.migrantrights.org/2010/11/23/migrant-workers-underthe-%E2%80%9Ckafala%E2%80%9D-system-in-the-gcc. Migrant Rights, "Bahrain Further Restricts Migrant Rights while Publicly Expressing Concern for Migrants," 29 June. Available at http://www.migrantrights.org/2011/06/29/bahrain-further-restricts-migrant-rights-while-publicly-expressing-concern-formigrants, Amrita 2013: 430 and Jeangey 2012: 400.

are also forbidden to have children,[22] and the Madames are used to control how they spend their spare time.[23] Many women suffer from sexual abuse at the hands of the male members of the families where they work, and they often do not even have their own bedroom, instead living in crowded conditions together with all the domestic staff.[24]

Lastly, sponsors employ the practice of sequestering the cell phone of the maids so that, forced into a state of complete isolation from the outside world, they are totally dependent on their employers from both the financial and legal points of view.[25]

7.4. *The lack of legal protection for migrant workers*

Despite the abuses suffered by migrant workers, they have few resources to assert their rights; in fact, as mentioned above, those who decide to abandon their sponsors without permission are reported and become irregular migrants who may be deported at any time.[26]

As result of strong pressure exerted by the international press and by NGOS concerning the mistreatment of migrant workers involved in the restructuring of stadiums,[27] Qatar has emanated law No. 21 of 2015 abolishing the scheme of the

---

[22] For more on this issue, see De Genova and Peutz 2010.

[23] Among the many witnesses' accounts collected, see in particular Amrita 2013: 428–429. The author of this article writes: "Marie from Philippines explains her Madam's rationale for monitoring her leisure days. Her Madame would accompany her to church and pick her up as soon as the service ended: 'So she would say to me "you are a good Christian girl, you mix only with Filipino who go to church, no problem" ... And then if I get pregnant or something like that, she would get into trouble with the security (immigration officers). I understand why she is being like that with me on Sundays'".

[24] Among the numerous articles denouncing the domestic workers' conditions of exploitation, see R. Falconer, 'Qatar's Foreign Domestic Workers Subjected to Slave-Like Conditions', in The Guardian, February 2014, at: www.theguardian.com/global-development/2014/feb/26/qatar-foreign-workers-slaveconditions.

[25] See the report by Amnesty International entitled Qatar: Treat Us Like We Are Human: Migrant Workers in Qatar of November 2013, p. 13, www.amnesty.org/en/library/info/MDE22/011/2013/en.

[26] See ILO 2012: 4, which argues that "Migrant workers are often denied the right to justice for violation of their rights under the Kafalah system. Migrant workers are often faced with punishment should they report abuse, protest or question their terms and conditions of employment. Kafeels can retaliate in a plethora of ways including: lower wages, non renewal of the contract, abuse, accepting bribes in exchange for permission to leave, false accusations such as theft or having the worker deported. Kafeels can evade legal responsibility of charges under the Kafala system, as they can petition the authorities to cancel the workers residency leading to forcible deportation before a case can be filed or heard."

[27] Amnesty International, Dark Side of Migration, Spotlight on Qatar's Construction Sector Ahead of the World Cup, Amnesty special report, November 2013; Amnesty International, Promising Little, Delivering Less, Qatar and Migrant Labour Abuses Ahead of the 2022 Football World Cup, Amnesty special report, May 2015; Amnesty International, The Ugly Side Of The Beautiful Game: Exploitation Of Migrant Workers On A Qatar 2022 World Cup Site, Amnesty special report, January 2016; Hafsa

sponsorship system.[28] The new law establishes that the worker can remain in Qatar at the end of their contract, providing Articles 21 and 23 that migrant workers can change jobs before the expiry of the contract, after obtaining the consent of the employer the Ministry of Labour and Social Affairs (MOSA), and the Ministry of the Interior. In the case in which migrant workers have a permanent contract, they may be approved not earlier than five years after the beginning of the employment. Finally, migrant workers may be transferred to another sponsor with the approval of the Ministry of Labour and Social Affairs (MOSA) in case of death or ceased activity of the previous employer. Article 22 instead provides that workers can be temporarily transferred to another sponsor in case there is a pending legal dispute between the parties. The new law does not seem to resolve the problem of sponsorship system. Despite not openly mentioning the words "sponsor" and "sponsorship", the new law does not abolish the system of authorization to exit from Qatar and gives employers an excessive power of control over the people they employ. The law may make it easier for workers to return to Qatar after they have left the country, but at the same time it makes it easier for employers to confiscate their passports and hold them against their will. Finally, the powers of the "employer" in the new system are similar to those ones of the "sponsor" under the old one.[29]

As regards the domestic workers, their protections appear almost completely absent given the enormous amounts requested by temporary work agencies from migrants, and since the maids often send remittances to their families in their countries of origin the great majority of them decide not to lodge a complaint for the maltreatment suffered by local authorities.

On the other hand, the migrants who decide to go to court encounter many kinds of obstacles, such as the impossibility to lodge an appeal because of the prohibition of physically departing from the house of kafeel where they work in order to turn to the competent authorities, or the lack of access to mobile phones, which are often confiscated by Madames to maintain control over their employees.

Even if the maids were able to consult a lawyer, the lawyer's remuneration and the enormous cost of the process would represent an impediment not easily bypassed. In addition, the slowness of the legal process, the impossibility of being able to carry out another working activity throughout the duration of the process, and language barriers discourage women from taking judicial action against the employer.[30]

A., 'FIFA to Set Up Worker Welfare Body for Qatar 2022', Al Jazeera, 22 April 2016; Amnesty International, Treat Us Like Humans: Migrant Workers In Qatar, Amnesty special report, November 2013; Building a Better World Cup, Protecting Migrant Workers In Qatar Ahead Of FIFA 2022 – Human Rights Watch Report – June 2012.

[28] See Law No. 21 on the Entry, Exit and Residency of Foreign Nationals.

[29] The report by Amnesty International underlines the persistence of these problems. See in that regard: New Name, Old System: Qatar's New Employment Law and Abuse Of Migrant Workers, available at www.amnesty.org/en/documents/mde22/5242/2016/en/

[30] The different states of the Gulf Area are working to reform the system of *kafalah* and ensure the

7.5. *Conclusions*

After examining the characteristics of the system of kafalah we could question, based on the exploitation of migrant women, what are the means we can use in order to prevent such a phenomenon. The kafalah does not fall within the definition of slavery, reported by the Convention of the ILO n. 29 of 1930 on forced labour,[31] and even if all the Member States of the Gulf region have signed the main international conventions against slavery[32] none of them have adopted national laws preventing sponsors from using the system.

In addition, among the numerous treaties ratified by countries which largely use the kafalah, the most important conventions on protecting the rights of migrant workers are absent, namely the Migration for Employment Convention (Revised), 1949 (No. 97),[33] the Convention (No. 143) concerning migrations in abusive conditions, and the promotion of equality of opportunity and treatment of migrant workers[34] and the International Convention on the Protection of the

rights of migrant workers. See, for example, legislative reforms undertaken by Qatar with the approval of the new law on sponsorship, n. 21 of 2015. See in this regard, *The National*, 'Qatar Emir Approves Labour Law Reforms of October 2015', www.thenational.ae/world/middle-east/qatar-emir-approves-labour-law-reforms. However, many non-governmental organizations complain about the fact that the new reform is not sufficient to protect the rights of migrant workers, see Human Rights Watch, Qatar: New Reforms Won't Protect Migrant Workers, available at: www.hrw.org/news/2015/11/08/qatar-new-reforms-wont-protect-migrant-workers.

[31] The definition of slavery provided by the ILO Convention n. 29 of 1930 sets forth that: "all work or service which is exacted from any person under the menace of any penalty and for which the said person has not offered himself voluntarily". Also see the Financial Times article, 'Abeer Allam Arabie Saoudite, Le Code de l'Esclavage' of 28 June 2012, in which Waleed Abu Al-Khair, human rights lawyer, makes an explicit reference to the condition of slavery endured by domestic workers. "Every foreign worker, but also every foreign company is under protection, as a child. The 'kafalah' allows nationals to make profit from holdings opened on national soil (possessing the majority of the capital) or to exercise a power over immigrant workers. This system of medieval governance contains in itself all kinds of possible derives, including a sort of slavery of modern times for foreign workers who live in these countries. The existence of this system is aberrant and the silence especially by the competent bodies such as the UN Commission on Human Rights it's a scandal".

[32] In this regard, recall the above-mentioned Forced Labour Convention, 1930 (No. 29) Convention concerning Forced or Compulsory Labour, which came into force on 01 May 1932 and the Convention No 105 on the Abolition of Forced Labour. In addition to the Conventions mentioned above, all the GCC countries have adopted various international conventions to protect workers, including domestic workers, among which we recall in particular the International Convention on the Elimination of All Forms of Discrimination against Women (CEDAW), 1979; Convention on the Elimination of All Forms Racial Discrimination (ICERD), 1965; United Nations Convention Against Transnational Organised Crime (UNTOC) and the Protocols Thereto, 2000; ILO Convention N 100 on Equal Remuneration, 1951;56 and the ILO Convention N 111 on Discrimination (Employment and Occupation), 1958.

[33] The Convention came into force on 22 January 1952, is available at the webpage: www.ilo.org/dyn/normlex/en/f?p=NORMLEXPUB:12100:0::NO::P12100_INSTRUMENT_ID:312242

[34] The Convention adopted by General Conference of the International Labour Organisation in its sixth sessions on 24 June 1975 in Geneva, came into force on 09 December 1978. The Convention is available at the web page: www.ilo.org/dyn/normlex/en/f?p=NORMLEXPUB:12100:0::NO::P12100_ILO_CODE:C143.

Rights of All Migrant Workers and Members of Their Families (ICRMW). [35]

Aside from the ratification of the major international treaties for the protection of migrant workers, it would be desirable that the governments of the countries more affected by the phenomenon concluded bilateral agreements with domestic workers' countries of origin through a collaboration of the local authorities of the various countries in order to disclose the identity of migrants and their fates within host states. [36] It would be recommended to enact local laws aimed at making the whole system of kafalah and the consequent exploitation of migrants illegal by prohibiting even the existence of temporary employment agencies. Furthermore, the awareness of international public opinion could act as an incentive for the Gulf countries to work actively and quickly for the implementation of national laws aimed at discouraging the phenomenon. The whole process should be accompanied by information about what the system of kafalah [37] really is, and to which forms of exploitation it subjects migrant workers.

Bibliography

Amrita, P. (2013) '"The Paper that You Have in Your Hand is My Freedom": Migrant Domestic Work and the Sponsorship (Kafala) System In Lebanon', *The International Migration Review*, 47(2): 414–441.

Bajracharya, R. and Sijapati, B. (2012) 'The Kafala System and Its Implications for Nepali Domestic Workers', *Policy Brief*, 1.

Baldwin Edwards, M. (2013) *Labour Immigration and Labour Markets in the GCC Countries: National Patterns and Trends*, London: The London School of Economics and Political Science.

De Genova, N. and Peutz, N. (2010) *The Deportation Regime: Sovereignty, Space, and the Freedom of Movement*, Durham: Duke University Press.

Falconer, R. (2014) 'Qatar's Foreign Domestic Workers Subjected to Slave-Like Conditions', *The Guardian*, http:/www.theguardian.com/global-development/2014/feb/26/qatar-foreign-workers-slaveconditions

Fargues, P. and Shah, N. (2014) *Socio-economic Impacts of GCC Migration*, Gulf Research Centre, www.grm.grc.net/index.php?pgid=Njk=&wid=Mjc.

Fernandez, B. (2013) 'Traffickers, Brokers, Employment Agents, and Social Networks: The Regulation of Intermediaries in the Migration of Ethiopian Domestic Workers to the Middle East', *International Migration Review*, 47(4): 814–843.

Go, S.P. (2007) 'Asian labor migration: The role of bilateral labor and similar agreements',

[35] The International Convention on the Protection of the Rights of All Migrant Workers and Members of Their Families, has been adopted in the National General Assembly Resolution n. 45/158 of 18 December 1990 and it came in force on 01 July 2003. See webpage: www.ohchr.org/EN/ProfessionalInterest/Pages/CMW.aspx

[36] Concerning bilateral agreements among states, see Go 2007.

[37] Regarding this argument, see Malit and Naufal 2014, which analyzes in detail what the factors that prevent the domestic workers from having a clear overview of the *kafalah* system.

presented at the Regional Workshop on Labor Migration in Southeast Asia: "What Role for Parliaments", 21–23 September 2007, Manila, Philippines.

Heeg, J. (2013) 'Gender, international human trafficking norms and Gulf migration', presented at the annual meeting of the International Studies Association Annual Conference "Global Governance: Political Authority in Transition", Montreal.

Human Rights Watch (2014) *Shattered Dreams: Impact of Spain's Housing Crisis on Vulnerable Groups*, https://www.hrw.org/report/2014/05/27/shattered-dreams/impact-spains-housing-crisis-vulnerable-groups.

ILO (2012) 'Responding to Emerging and Critical Issues, Reform of the Kafala (Sponsorship System)', *Policy Brief*, Migrant Forum Asia, n. 2.

Jeangey, C. (2012) 'l sistema della kafala e la tutela dei lavoratori migranti nella penisola arabica', in L. Panella and E. Spatafora (eds.) *Studi in onore di Claudio Zanghì*, Rome: La Sapienza University.

Juredini, R. (2010) 'Irregular Workers in Egypt: Migrant and Refugee Domestic Workers', *International Journal on Minority and Group Rights*, 15(1): 81–115.

Kar, S. (2009) 'International Labor Migration, Asymmetric Information and Occupational Choice', *Trade and Development Review*, 2(1): 34–48.

Khan, A. and Harroff-Tavel, H. (2011) 'The implications of the sponsorship system: Challenges and opportunities', presented at "Strengthening Dialogue to Make Migration Work for Development in the ESCAP and ESCWA Regions", Beirut.

Lori, N. (2012) *Temporary Workers or Permanent Migrants? The Kafala System and Contestations over Residency in the Arab Gulf States*, Paris: IFRI – Center for Migrations and Citizenship.

Malit, F. and Naufal, G. (2014) 'Asymmetric Information under the Kafala Sponsorship System: Impacts on Foreign Domestic Workers' Income and Employment Status in the GCC Countries', working paper, Cornell University, www.digitalcommons.ilr.cornell.edu/cgi/viewcontent.cgi?article=1177&context=workingpapers

Pande, A. (2012) 'From "Balcony Talk" and "Practical Prayers" to Illegal Collectives: Migrant Domestic Workers and Meso-Level Resistances', Lebanon, *Gender and Society*, 26(3): 382–405.

Rodrigues, A. (2014) 'The Kafala System in the GCC', The Gazelle, www.thegazelle.org/issue/33/features/kefala-system.

Zahra, M. (2015) 'The Legal Framework of the Sponsorship Systems of the Gulf Cooperation Council Countries: A Comparative Examination', *Gulf Labour Markets and Migration*, 10.

Chapter 8

The Centers for Identification and Expulsion (CIE) and immigration management

Criticalities and possible improvements

Salvatore Tuccari

8.1. *Introduction*

The Centers for Identification and Expulsion (CIE) have for years been one of the most criticized aspects of the Italian management of immigration. Their history is dotted with numerous complaints about inhuman treatment, fatal accidents and high suicide rates.[1] The "guests" are for all purposes detained, deprived of personal freedom and forced to live in conditions of non-dignified life. Recently, however, we have returned to talk about the opening of new CIEs with the aim of achieving extraordinary plans of territorial control against irregular migrants.

In light of this, we intend to analyze the relevant discipline of the CIE (Campesi 2013),[2] focusing on both the preliminary procedure for the confinement of immigrants in these structures and the constitutional legitimacy of the entire discipline, also in light of the recent legislative decree 13/17 converted into law No. 46/17.

---

[1] It is easy to remember numerous episodes taken from ongoing trials and journalistic investigations, which show clear cases of mistreatment suffered by migrants. The mistreatment often remains unpunished for fear of retaliation. Ex multis, the journalist Fabrizio Gatti masquerading as an immigrant in the CPT of Lampedusa in 2004, told of the abuses, the humiliations and inhuman conditions that he was forced to suffer, in http://espresso.repubblica.it/palazzo/2005/10/07/news/io-clandestino-a-lampedusa-1.594 (accessed on March 16th, 2019). See also the "CIE deaths" investigation. Stories of ordinary administrative detention "through the work of scholars of immigration law issues in detail the cases of death within the CPT and CIE".

[2] The author points out that the ratio of the different structures devised by the legislator can be traced back to two macro-areas: on the one hand, the logic of risk management (CIE) and, on the other, the state of necessity (the other centers).

8.2. *The creation of CIE*

The CIE [3] derive from the Temporary Stay and Assistance Centers (CPTA) established to retain and identify immigrants and possibly expel them with the l. No. 40/1998 (Turco-Napolitano), the first organic law on immigration, then merged into the Testo Unico (T.U.) No. 286/1998 and the related implementing regulation (Presidential Decree No. 394/1999) which reorganized the relevant legislation. Compared to the previous fragmentary discipline (Law No. 39/1990), this law stands as legislation to overcome the emergency phase, with the aim of encouraging regular immigration and discouraging illegal immigration.[4] These rights have their foundation in human dignity that involves respect for an essential core of values that unites every human being regardless of diversity. They are recognized and guaranteed, according to art. 2 of the Constitution, which imposes on the State a general obligation to protect the inviolable human rights. As the Constitutional Court has affirmed, the exclusion of non-citizens from the enjoyment of certain fundamental freedoms is not reasonable. Such unreasonableness finds its raison d'être in the respect of the principle of equality as per article 3 of the Constitution which, although expressly referring only to citizens, "also applies to the foreigner when it comes to respecting fundamental rights". [5] In fact, foreigners do not enter the territory of the State "unwary of protection, or at least of the legal lining necessary even if they are given defense of fundamental rights". [6] However, this is not an equal position because the link between the individual and the State is different, with the consequence that the same principle can meet limitations with reference to legal situations connected to the diversity of relations existing between the State and the citizen and the State and the foreigner (Moschella 2016).

It must be stressed, in fact, that "if foreigners were by law in general and by the legal system equal to citizens, the legal category of citizens would cease to exist" (Esposito 1954: 24, No. 19).

With the Turco-Napolitano law the possibility of keeping irregular foreigners in the CPTAs was foreseen for the first time, without the necessary requirements to remain in Italy, as defined by the Schengen Treaty. The detention in these centers, regulated by administrative means, was scheduled for a maximum of 30 days, although over the years there was a preference to prolong in an increasingly sensitive manner this period, which – only in recent years – seems to have changed. [7]

---

[3] For a timely reconstruction of the institution of detention centers in Italy and in Europe see Mazza 2013: 21–40.

[4] See Rodotà 1994. The author highlights that the concept of citizenship as status, meant to exlude and separate people within a social organization, is obsolete.

[5] Constitutional Court, 120/67 and 62/94.

[6] See Berti 1997: 16.

[7] In fact, for the 30 days provided for by the Turco-Napolitano law, the 60 days of Bossi-Fini were followed in 2002 by the 180 days of the 2008 Safety Package and the 18 months of the legislative decree

A decisive change came, however, with the subsequent legislative intervention (c.d. Bossi-Fini law) having a strongly repressive scope as it was aimed at introducing stringent measures with the declared objective of combating irregular immigration. Among the various regulatory provisions in which this end appears more evident, it suffices to recall the provisions concerning the methods of entry into Italy – allowed only to those in possession of a work contract under which it is possible to deduct their financial support – as well as the procedure to be followed for obtaining the residence permit – granted only to those who are the holder of an employment contract, with a 2-year validity for permanent and 1-year contracts in other cases with the clarification that, if the person concerned had lost his job, he would have to return home. Furthermore, art. 14 of the legislative decree 25th July 1998 No. 286, as amended by l. 30 July 2002 No. 189 provides that "when it is not possible to carry out expulsion immediately by escorting" to the border, the commissioner "provides that the foreigner is kept for the time strictly necessary" at the CIE.

On the criminal law side, moreover, the so-called Bossi-Fini law introduced the crime of illegal immigration, subject to harsh criticism by doctrine and jurisprudence, as per art. 10 bis of Legislative Decree No. 286 of 1998. Although the decriminalization of the latter has been announced on several occasions, it is useful to report the views of the Cass. pen. 29 October 2014 (hearing on 19 September 2014), No. 44977 according to which "the contravention provided for by art. 10 bis of TU Immigration, which punishes illegal entry and stay in the territory of the State, cannot be considered repealed due to direct effect of Law. 67/2014, provided that this legislative act conferred on the Government a delegation, implying the necessity of its exercise, for the decriminalization of this case and that, therefore, the latter, until the issuance of the delegated decrees, can not be considered an administrative infringement".

Subsequently, the Legislator intervened again with the transposition of the community legislation (directives 2003/86 CE, 2003/109 CE, 2004/83 CE) which led to a first harmonization with the legislations of the other European States.

The so-called "security package" then made a new tightening of the legislation, which motivated the Constitutional Court to intervene repeatedly.[8] On this point, it

89 of 2011; subsequently, the deadline was reduced to 90 days following the amendment by Senators Manconi and Lo Giudice to the 2013 bis European law, and then expanded again, up to a maximum of 12 months, with the approval of the d. lgs. No. 142/2015, if the asylum seeker constitutes a danger to public order and safety and there is a risk of escape. In this regard, it should be noted that these are conditions assessed from time to time by the commissioner; as regards the assessment of dangerousness, it is also deduced from the existence of convictions for certain serious crimes and may even disregard a sentence of conviction. The risk of escape is also calculated "when the applicant has previously systematically used false declarations or statements on his personal details for the sole purpose of avoiding the adoption or enforcement of an expulsion order".

[8] The so-called "security package" consists of three main legislative instruments: l. No. 125/2008 which introduces new types of crimes for illegal immigrants and those who favor their illegal stay on Italian territory; the d. lgs. No. 160/2008 which limits the number of family members that can be reunited and raises the level of income necessary to access this right; the l. No. 94/2009 introducing the crime of illegal entry and stay, a further extension of the maximum detention periods of up to 6 months in the

is enough to recall sentence no. 359 of 2010 of the Constitutional Court that declared art. 14 c. 5 quater unconstitutional in the part in which it does not provide for the justification of the justified reason with reference to the crime of non-compliance with the removal order [9] and the pronunciation No. 249 of 2010 which established the constitutional illegitimacy of the aggravating circumstance of "clandestinity" (Article 61, No. 11 bis of the Penal Code) in contrast with the principle of equality and personal criminal liability, as well as in terms of compliance with the principle of reason. [10]

At the supranational level, even the Court of Justice of the European Union, with its ruling on El-Dridi of April 28, 2011, declared the incompatibility of art. 14 paragraph 5 ter with the Repatriation Directive 2008/115 / EC, as "Member States cannot introduce, in order to avoid the failure of the coercive measures taken to proceed with the forced removal in accordance with art. 8, No. 4 of the said directive, a custodial sentence, such as that provided for by art. 14, paragraph 5 ter, of the legislative decree No. 286/1998, only because a third-country national, after being notified of an order to leave the territory of a Member State and that the deadline set by that order has expired, remains irregular in the national territory". [11]

8.3. *CIE and administrative custody*

The CIE inaugurated in Italy the administrative custody that consists in the possibility to "limit the movements and to hold against their will the irregular foreigners in order to identify them and to allow their expulsion [...]. The detention is defined as administrative rather than criminal because it does not concern the ordinary penal system, it is not a punishment for having committed a crime, it is not established at the end of a trial, it does not require a sentence by a judge, but pertaining to administrative jurisdiction. In Italy, for example, it is ordered by the quaestor" (Colombo 2012).

Already from this preliminary definition there emerge some critical aspects of the administrative custody: the deprivation of personal freedom and the absence of a sentence by the judge at the time when the same is imposed. In fact, although we can find in doctrine an interpretative contrast between those who affirm the injury in the procedure of restriction in the C.I.E of personal freedom and those who, on the contrary, consider only the freedom of circulation to be affected (Gianfrancesco 2001: 2716 ff), the impact of the procedure on the good of personal freedom is now also recognized following sentence no. 105/2001 of the Constitutional Court; the Court in fact notes that the detention of the foreigner in the centers of temporary stay and assistance

CIE, the adoption of new economic standards for family reunification and the renewal of the residence permit.

[9] *Ex multis*, Leo 2010.

[10] *Ex multis*, Masera 2010.

[11] *Ex multis*, Viganò 2011; Corsi 2012.

constitutes an incident measure on personal freedom, which therefore requires the guarantees provided for by the provisions of art. 13 of the Constitution.

The Supreme Court also goes so far as to affirm that the measure in question affects the matter governed by Article 13 of the Constitution, as it possesses the characteristics of immediate coercion typical of the restrictions of personal freedom, different from measures only affecting freedom of movement. [12] The Court also considers that judicial review – necessary in light of the provisions of art. 13 of the Constitution – consisting of a validation of an act of the public security authority "does not entail any violation of the reserve of jurisdiction set by Article 13 of the Constitution". [13]

8.4. *Treatment in the CIEs and the absolute reservation of law*

The regular cohabitation within the CIE should be regulated in compliance with the principles established by art. 13 of the Constitution [14] which, as is known, introduces into the legal system a reserve of absolute law. [15] The Constituents, therefore, have established the need to regulate the matter under examination using only the law, with the consequence that the only secondary sources eligible are those of strict execution. [16]

With reference to the discipline under examination, however, it is the result of a primary legislation that devolves entirely to the administrative authority (prefect, after

---

[12] Statement of Constitutional Court strongly criticized both by Gianfrancesco 2001 and by Gaboardi A. in "*Difesa legitima e CIE. La vulnerabilità giuridica di una detenzione fuori legge*" in www.penalecontemporaneo.it.

[13] The Constitutional Court has not in fact endorsed the approach of the State Advocacy which states "that the minor physical bans would not seem to be detrimental to the provisions of Article 13 of the Constitution; in particular, the expulsion order would be in the order of the foreigner to abandon the national soil, while the coercive accompaniment would be an executive mode complementary to that order and, consisting in the identification and execution of a compulsory itinerary, would only affect the freedom of movement". Only in cases where it is not possible to immediately execute the provision for administrative expulsion, in fact, Article 14 of the same Legislative Decree no. 286 of 1998 provided that the commissioner would arrange the detention of the foreigner for the time strictly necessary at the center of temporary stay and nearest assistance, and then had to be sent to the court without delay and in any case within forty-eight hours from its adoption for its eventual validation "where the conditions are met and the interested party heard".

[14] *La libertà personale è inviolabile.*

Non è ammessa forma alcuna di detenzione, di ispezione o perquisizione personale, né qualsiasi altra restrizione della libertà personale, se non per atto motivato dell'autorità giudiziaria e nei soli casi e modi previsti dalla legge.

In casi eccezionali di necessità ed urgenza, indicati tassativamente dalla legge l'autorità di pubblica sicurezza può adottare provvedimenti provvisori, che devono essere comunicati entro quarantotto ore all'autorità giudiziaria e, se questa non li convalida nelle successive quarantotto ore, si intendono revocati e restano privi di ogni effetto.

È punita ogni violenza fisica e morale sulle persone comunque sottoposte a restrizioni di libertà.

La legge stabilisce i limiti massimi della carcerazione preventiva.

[15] On this point, the doctrine is vast; as an example, see Mainardis 2008: 102 ff; Pace 1974: 287 ff.

[16] *Enciclopedia Treccani*, voce Riserva di legge.

consulting the quaestor) the method by which the structures destined until now to become CIE are identified, the precise identification of the places to be used for them and the modalities with which to regulate the life within them. To this end, in 2014, the regulation setting out the criteria for the organization and management of the Centers for Identification and Expulsion provided for in Article 14 of the Legislative Decree of 25 July 1998, 286 and subsequent amendments was issued. However, although the regulation had the stated objective of ensuring uniform rules and reception levels for the organization and provision of services within the CIE, setting standards for linguistic and cultural assistance, health protection, freedom of correspondence and the right to receive visits did not achieve the desired results. In other words, compliance with the standards defined at the central level has not been achieved, and in fact strong inequalities have been perpetrated in the management of the various structures. It is then correct to note the careful doctrine (Pugiotto 2014: 573 ff) that, in detecting such inequalities, stops by way of example on the discipline pertaining to the freedom of telephone correspondence emphasizing how it was guaranteed in some centers and prohibited in others. It therefore seems difficult to retain that the CIE regulation can be considered to be respectful of the constitutional parameters set out in Article 13 of the Constitution, which provides for a reserve of absolute law that limits the use of regulatory sources only for the disciplines of strict execution and a reserve of jurisdiction as an additional protection for the individual deprived of personal liberty.

8.5. *The reserve of jurisdiction*

As already said, the Constitutional Court with the sentence No. 105/2001 has stated that the Legislator, to remove the impediments to the expulsion order, needs a period of time not exceeding 20 days, extendable for a further 10 days at the request of the commissioner under penalty of loss of effectiveness of the same. This period of time does not necessarily have to be consumed in its entirety as ex art. 14 c. 1 d.lgs 286/98 the foreigner must be kept "for the strictly necessary time". The Court also states that "the fact that the validation refers to the work of the public security authority and, together, constitutes a title for further detention up to the limit of twenty days, does not entail any violation of the jurisdiction reserve set by the Article 13 of the Constitution, since the validated detention is attributable, both for the limitation already suffered and for the remaining period within which it may be extended, to a motivated act of the judicial authority". The jurisprudence has therefore established that the mere validation of the work of the public security authority carried out by the judge is an appropriate instrument to consider the reserve of jurisdiction respected. Before verifying the correctness of this statement it is necessary, however, to dwell on the expression "reserve of jurisdiction". On this point, in fact, careful doctrine affirmed that the "concept of reserve of jurisdiction binds to the concept of inviolability and expresses two particular guarantees with respect to state interference in the law of the individual: on the one hand it identifies the specific subjective attribution of the restrictive power to the judicial authority (...) and, on the other hand, connotes the extent and the quality of the control that the same authority must be entitled to in the specific case on the legal requirements" (Marletta 2012). The purpose of guaranteeing the reserve in question, therefore, requires that the audit carried out by the judge is "full", having to cover all the cases and ways provided by law.

That said, it is necessary in light of the criticisms made by the doctrine and by virtue of the legislative changes introduced by the decree law 13/17 then converted into l. No. 46/17 to verify the effective respect of the jurisdiction reserve, understood in its meaning of "full" control by the judicial authority.

On this point, the judgment of the doctrine appears to be highly critical. The remarks focused in particular on the fact that, having the Legislator devolved to the judge of peace – therefore not to a member of the judiciary court – the task of validating the provisions of the public security authority and to rule on requests for extension from itself advanced, there is an unacceptable undermining of the reserve provided by the Constitution. The ratio that had led the Legislator to change with the d.l. 241/90 functional competence in favor of the judge of peace is no longer current; while when this provision had been introduced into the law coercion was envisaged as an ordinary form of expulsion and detention as the only possible measure, the current provision provides that the administrative detention must be the last resort. Therefore, the doctrinal orientation inclined to prefer a return of jurisdiction to a judge in court seems to be acceptable because they are considered the most suitable figure to guarantee the right to personal freedom. [17]

These shortcomings of the discipline appear, indeed, aggravated following the last legislative intervention. The latter, in fact, in addition to not bringing the discipline in question into the mainstream of ordinary jurisdiction has resulted in a further decrease with reference to judicial protection.

The l. 46/17, in fact, expressly established the elimination of the degree of appeal if the application for asylum presented by the migrant was rejected at first instance. The purpose of this provision is, obviously, to ensure a containment of the time trial even in order to obtain a saving of expenditure by the State. In doing so, however, there is an undeniable reduction in the procedural guarantees for migrants and, at the same time, the risk of determining an increase in the burden of pending proceedings before the Court of Cassation. The Legislator, therefore, far from resolving the criticalities already present in the previous legislation, seems to have exacerbated the situation by causing a further compression of the guarantees provided for in Article 13 of the Constitution.

---

[17] Marletta 2012 states clearly that "For ordinal position, instructing powers, technical skills and mental habitus (the judge togato) appears more suitable to know and protect the right to personal freedom"; the author shares the reasoning, strongly criticized, on the devolution of jurisdiction to the judge of peace. Reasoning that is present, among others, in Caputo and Pepino 2004: 13 ff; Bonetti 2009: 94.

8.6. *From the Centers of Identification and Expulsion to the Centers of Stay for Repatriation*

The CIEs have been modified by the recent legislative intervention under examination in repatriation centers. This terminological change, far from assuming purely linguistic significance, seems to confirm the approach underlying the entire regulatory intervention which, once abandoned, the strongly repressive imprint of the Bossi-Fini law makes a legislative choice addressed to not to close our doors but to increasingly transform migratory flows from irregular phenomenon to a regular phenomenon, in which life is put in risk and people can arrive safely and in a controlled way in our countries. [18]

In fact it has been argued that the choices to operate through the instrument of urgent legislation, introducing system changes that present extremely delicate profiles for the protection of constitutional and international principles (...), do not seem suitable to solve the current problems of the Italian international protection system. [19]

On this point, careful doctrine has affirmed that the Legislator, using definitions in which there are absent references to the discipline of prison law has in fact accomplished a real fraud of the labels (Pugiotto 2014). Such inaccurate, lexical choice assumes even more evident contours if compared with the discipline used by other European countries, such as France or the United Kingdom, where it has been preferred to resort to the more appropriate expression "Administrative detention centers" (Pepino 2000: 11).

In fact, the use of an expression such as the residence centers for repatriation continues to subtract the reality of the facts that is the assimilation of the stay at the Centers in question to a real administrative jail. [20] This assimilation would be obtained, first of all, from the material similarities of the different structures as actual containment sites. As was pointed out by careful doctrine, in fact, when we talk about CIE we "read first of all reinforced concrete, iron cages, barbed wire, video surveillance, armed surveillance" (Di Martino 2012). A fortiori it should be emphasized that the living conditions of the persons locked up in a CIE are, in many ways, worse than those of those who are obliged to stay in prison, [21] as evidenced by the high number of revolts within them.

---

[18] The expression refers to the Premier, Mr. Paolo Gentiloni, who expressed himself in these terms during the press conference to present the decree in question.

[19] Asgi-Associazione per gli studi giuridici sull'immigrazione, Magistratura democratica: d.l. 13/2017, sempre più distanza tra giudici e cittadini stranieri, February 2017.

[20] In these terms the sen. Carofiglio during the parliamentary work that then led to the approval of the so-called security package, subsequently resumed, among others, by Pugiotto 2014.

[21] On this point, several international organizations have reported this situation, among others: Amnesty international and Doctors Without Borders, the former with the report "Italia: presenza temporanea diritti permanenti. Il trattamento dei cittadini detenuti nei centri di permanenza temporanea", 2005 and the latter with the report entitled "Al di là del muro. Viaggio nei centri per migranti in Italia", February 2010.

This situation is determined, among other things, by the fact that "the immigrant interned in an identification and expulsion center does not have the status of detainee, missing a court that can monitor the methods of detention, as instead happens in the case of detention in prison" (Paleologo 2012).

8.7. *Conclusions*

The hypothesis of opening new CIE relaunches the old approach to the phenomenon of migration, which places the problem of security at the center of attention. This approach has shown all its limitations, and above all has shown that the administrative detention of irregular foreign citizens is ineffective to address and meet the needs underlying the containment of migratory flows.

The CIEs created mainly for the repatriation of irregular migrants did not actually work. Fifty percent of the people reached by an expulsion decree and "detained" in the CIE are in fact not repatriated: for the expulsion the collaboration of the State of origin is necessary, but the countries that have formalized the readmission agreements with the Italy are few. [22]

Currently, migrants who end up in CIE remain much longer than the limit set by law and often go underground. Welcoming migrants instead of rejecting them is essential for the implementation of fair migration policies. The recent legislative intervention, in an attempt to overcome that phenomenon of "bagatellarizzazione" personal freedom of the migrant (Caputo 2009: 10; Pelissero 2011: 266 ff), typical of the reforms of the last 20 years, seems to favor a new model of reception, the most widespread, which puts the network of local authorities at the center suitable to implement integrated reception projects.

As far as the identification of the areas destined to the new institution centers is concerned, the letter of the norm declares that this happens: "heard the president of the interested region, privileging the sites and areas outside the urban centers that are more easily accessible and in which there are structures of public property that may be, even through adaptation or restructuring, made suitable for the purpose, taking into account the need to create structures with limited capacity suitable to ensure conditions of detention that ensure absolute respect for the dignity of the person".

Migrants are expected to work in a free and voluntary way, engaging them with

---

[22] Egypt, Tunisia, Nigeria and Morocco, as well as countries like Sudan and the Gambia. With the latter two, however, Italy has not adopted readmission agreements but the so-called Memorandum of Understanding (MOU) which as noted by Paleologo F.V. *"Simplified espulsions to Nigeria continue, with the support of Frontex. Flurry of denials by the territorial commissions, but the judges overturn many decisions. Until there is the possibility of an effective appeal"* in rights and borders, "they are not subject to parliamentary ratification, even when they are political agreements and involve huge financial burdens, in open violation of art. 80 of the Italian Constitution".

public utility activities aimed at "filling the gap of waiting".[23] Incorporation of this element is very important because work is the main means of integration.

"[M]easures for the simplification and efficiency of procedures before the territorial commissions" are introduced, "for the recognition of international protection and integration of applicants as well as for the simplification and efficiency of judicial procedures for the recognition of the status of an internationally protected person and other judicial proceedings related to immigration phenomena".[24]

As evidence of the willingness to intervene in an incisive manner, the establishment of specialized sections on immigration, international protection and free movement of EU citizens in 14 courts and the introduction of provisions aimed at ensuring the effectiveness of expulsion measures must be highlighted. Moreover, the intervention of the Legislator is deserving of appreciation where it has established the assumption of figures of "professional pedagogical and legal officials, of professional social service officials and of cultural mediators (...) in order to support educational interventions, programs of work placement, measures to support the treatment activity and in order to fulfill the new functions and tasks assigned to the Department for Juvenile Justice and of the community in the area of external penal execution and testing "although the funding for this dedicated appear insufficient".

The legislative action where it was decided to regulate the matter using the instrument of the law by eliminating the possibility of parliamentary debate – not to mention the difficulties of identifying the requirements of necessity and urgency that, as is known , justify the use of this institute ex art. 77 of the Constitution, given the more than 30-year existence of the "immigration problem" – and when it established, for the first time in our legal system, a discipline for the so-called hotspots, is worthy of criticism.

The latter, indicated with the designation "crisis points" by art. 10 ter of Legislative Decree 286/98 as amended by art. 17 of the d.l. 13/17, as is well known, represent the places where migrants are taken in the phases immediately after their arrival in our country so that they are subjected to the necessary care and to photodactyloscopic and signaling operations. The Legislator, however, despite having provided for a primary legislation – which is also forced by the provisions of the Khlaifia judgement made by the Grand Chamber of the Court Edu December 15, 2016 which sanctioned the violation by Italy of Article 5 of the ECHR as these centers provide for a deprivation of the personal freedom of migrants even in the absence of any legal basis and without an effective possibility of resorting to the judicial authority – has, in fact, provided a regulation to say the least incomplete. The latter, in fact, is limited to referring to a decree law of 1995 that was called to regulate the flow of migrants from Albania but, in turn, simply stated the possibility for the Apulia region

[23] Another expression that can be attributed to the previously quoted Press Conference held by the Premier On. Paolo Gentiloni.

[24] Press release by Italian Cabinet, 10 February 2017.

to set up three centers for first assistance, saying nothing about the nature and organization of these centers.

The examination of l. 46/17 gives the impression that the Legislator has tried to address the doctrinal orientation that considers it important to intervene with a model of reception that points above all to integration because "integration policies increase safety much more than criminal law".[25]

For this approach to be successful, however, a rethinking of migration policies is necessary to identify more effective solutions. The need to guarantee the fundamental rights of the foreigner requires management of the migratory phenomenon at the European level, with a sharing of responsibilities.

In this sense, the judgment of the Court of Luxembourg appears to be very disappointing, which – with its ruling of 7 March 2017 (C-638/16) – states the principle that "Member States are not required, under EU law, to grant a humanitarian visa to refugees who intend to go to their territories to seek asylum, but remain free to do so on the basis of their national law". In doing so, the Luxembourg judges did not take the opportunity to provide a more relevant contribution to the process of European integration which, if it is true that the political institutions of the various member countries need to make choices, could have made use of a decision that was more "courageous" on the part of European jurisprudence.

Bibliography

Berti, G. (1997) 'Cittadinanza, cittadinanze e diritti fondamentali', *Rivista diritto costituzionale*, Torino: Giappichelli.

Bonetti, P. (2009) 'La proroga del trattenimento e i reati di ingresso o permanenza irregolare nel sistema del diritto degli stranieri: profili costituzionali e rapporti con la Direttiva comunitaria sui rimpatri', *Diritto, immigrazione e cittadinanza*, 4: 85–129.

Campesi, G. (2013) *La detenzione amministrativa degli stranieri. Storia, diritto, politica*, Rome: Carocci.

Caputo, A. (2009) 'I reati collegati all'espulsione: profili generali e principali questioni applicative', *Diritto penale e processo. Speciale immigrazione*, 9 ff.

Caputo, A. and Pepino, L. (2004) 'Giudice di pace e habeas corpus dopo le modifiche al testo unico sull'immigrazione', *Diritto, immigrazione e cittadinanza*, 3: 13–27.

Colombo, A. (2012) *Fuori controllo? Miti e realtà dell'immigrazione in Italia*, Bologna: Il Mulino.

Corsi, G. (2012) 'La direttiva rimpatri ed il caso El Dridi', www.diritto.it.

Di Martino, A. (2012) 'La disciplina dei CIE è incostituzionale. Un pamphlet', www.dirittopenalecontemporaneo.it.

Esposito, C. (1954) 'Eguaglianza e giustizia nell'art. 3 della Costituzione' in C. Esposito (ed.) *La Costituzione Italiana, Saggi*, Padua: CEDAM.

---

[25] Amato G., Intervention at the Conference State of the Union, Firenze 9 May 2013.

Gianfrancesco, E. (2001) 'La disciplina sul trattenimento e sull'espulsione degli stranieri extracomunitari al vaglio della Corte Costituzionale', Giur. Cost., 4: 2709 ff.
Leo, G. (2010) 'Parziale illegittimità costituzionale dell'art. 14, co. 5quater t.u. immigrazione', www.penalecontemporaneo.it
Mainardis, C. (2008), 'sub art. 13', in S. Bartole and R. Bin (eds.) Commentario breve alla Costituzione, Padua: CEDAM.
Marletta, A. (2012) 'Detenzione amministrativa dello straniero e riserva di giurisdizione in materia di libertà personale', *Criminalia*, 7: 603–618.
Masera, L. (2010) 'Costituzionale il reato di clandestinità, incostituzionale l'aggravante: le ragioni della Corte Costituzionale', *Diritto, immigrazione e cittadinanza*, 3: 59.
Mazza, C. (2013) *La prigione degli stranieri. I centri di identificazione e di espulsione*, Rome: Ediesse.
Moschella, G. (2016) 'Immigrazione e tutela costituzionale dei diritti fondamentali' in L. Buscema and G. Moschella (eds.) *Immigrazione e condizione giuridica dello straniero*, Rome: Aracne, 13–40.
Pace, A. (1974) 'voce Libertà personale (dir. cost.)' in *Enc. Dir.*, XXIV, Milan: Treccani.
Paleologo, F.V. (2012) 'I controlli giurisdizionali e le garanzie dello stato di diritto nei Centri di identificazione ed espulsione', www.asgi.it.
Pelissero, M. (2011) 'Il vagabondo oltre confine. Lo statuto penale dell'immigrato irregolare nello stato di prevenzione', *Politica del diritto*, 2: 239–286.
Pepino, L. (2000) 'Centri di identificazione ed espulsione. (Irrazionalità del sistema e alternative possibili)', *Diritto, immigrazione e cittadinanza*, 2: 11–24.
Pugiotto A. (2014) 'La Galera amministrativa degli stranieri e le sue incostituzionali metamorfosi', *Quaderni costituzionali*, 3: 573–604.
Rodotà, S. (1994) 'Cittadinanza: una postfazione' in D. Zolo (ed.) *La cittadinanza. Appartenenza, identità, diritti*, Bari: Laterza.
Viganò, F. (2011) 'Corte di giustizia dell'unione europea, sent. 28 aprile 2011, Hassen el Dridi, causa c-61/11 ppu (direttiva rimpatri e inosservanza dell'ordine di allontanamento dello straniero)', www.penalecontemporaneo.it.

Chapter 9

Criminalization of irregular migration Between the domestic courts and the Court of Justice of the European Union

Zuzanna Brocka

9.1. *Introduction*

S. Peers notes that "of all the groups of migrants in the European Union, irregular migrants are the least welcome" (Peers 2015). This proved to be particularly true following the Syrian crisis in 2011 that caused the substantial increase of the so-called mixed [1] migration flows towards the EU. In response to the unexpected intensification of fluxes the search for measures to combat illegal migration [2] became of paramount importance for the Member States most exposed to illegal fluxes. As Mr Marco Minniti, the former Italian Ministry of Internal Affairs, gloomily underlined, the inflow of irregular migrants towards the Italian seaports was endangering the "maintenance of social peace". [3] This statement, and the following EU decision to block migrants on their way towards the EU by "outsourcing" the management of fluxes to the neighbouring countries, testifies that the practical enforcement of measures on migration adopted under Chapter II of the the Treaty on the Functioning of the European Union ("TFEU") has been critical. The EU Commission ("Commission"), in a recent action plan on migration, [4] has observed that the effective removal of irregular third country nationals ("TCNs") is one of the most problematic aspects of EU migration law and policy. Indeed, according to available data, the Member States shall remove more than

---

[1] Fluxes composed of, among others, refugees, economic migrants, victims of trafficking, smuggled migrants, unaccompanied minors, migrants moving for environmental reasons, see also: https:// www.iom.int/jahia/webdav/shared/shared/mainsite/about_iom/en/council/96/Mixed_Migration_Flows_FINAL.pdf (accessed on March 12th, 2018).

[2] For statistics on illegal border-crossing see http://frontex.europa.eu/trends-and-routes/migratory-routes-map/ (accessed on December 3rd, 2017).

[3] http://www.ilgiornale.it/news/politica/migranti-minniti-laccordo-ue-ho-temuto-tenuta-dellitalia-1435291.html?mobile_detect=false (accessed on September 1st, 2017).

[4] "Action plan on measures to support Italy, reduce pressure along the Central Mediterranean route and increase solidarity", available at https://ec.europa.eu/home-affairs/sites/homeaffairs/files/what-we-do/policies/european-agenda-migration/20170704_action_plan_on_the_central_mediterranean_route_en.pdf (accessed on January 14th, 2018).

1 million irregular migrants.[5] The question is thus if the removal of such a large number of people is realistically possible, in particular, in light of the case law on the main EU instrument to combat irregular migration, i.e. Directive 2008/115/EC of the European Parliament and the Council of 16 December 2008 on common standards and procedures in Member States for returning illegally staying third-country national (known also as the "Return Directive").

This contribution argues that, in consideration of the above-mentioned dramatic data on irregular migrants, the case law of the CJEU on the interpretation of the Return Directive seems rather unbalanced in favour of the protection of human rights without dully considering the Member States' exigencies of ensuring public order and security. The analysis performed herein has no claim to completeness, but limits itself at attempting to grasp some instrumental aspects of judicial balancing of values underpinning public order vis-à-vis fundamental rights that characterize the dialogue (Jacobs, 2002) between the domestic courts and the CJEU in the context of the preliminary ruling mechanism under article 267 of the TFUE.

9.2. *Complexity of the Return Directive*

The essence of the Return Directive lies in establishing "an effective removal and repatriation policy, based on common standards, for persons to be returned in a humane manner and with full respect for their fundamental rights and dignity" (whereas (2)). The most important provisions regarding the return and removal of TCNs who have illegally immigrated or are residing without authorization confirm this ethical background. Yet, from the domestic case law on the enforcement of the Return Directive it seems to emerge that "effective removal" and "full respect of human rights" are ideologically opposed concepts in perennial conflict. This is particularly evident as regards detention, one of the measures that the Member States are entitled to use under article 15 of the Return Directive. The CJEU, in its ruling, moved from the assumption that this article must be interpreted narrowly as enforced detention constitutes an exception to the fundamental right to freedom.[6] In order to put the case law into a correct legal context, it is useful to review some of the most relevant provisions of the Return Directive.

---

[5] http://www.ilfattoquotidiano.it/2017/03/02/oltre-un-milione-di-migranti-da-rimpatriare-in-tutta-europa-il-piano-della-commissione-ue/3427594/ (accessed on September 1st, 2017).

[6] The European Court of Human Rights has ruled to the same effect regarding Article 5(1)(f) of the European Convention for the Protection of Human Rights and fundamental Freedoms, signed in Rome on 4 November 1950 ("the ECHR") (see, inter alia, ECtHR, *Quinnv.France*, 22 March 1995, § 42, Series A no. 311, and *Kaya v. Romania*, no. 33970/05, § 16, 12 October 2006).

9.3. *Return decision: voluntary departure or removal?*

The Return Directive sets out common standards and procedures for returning illegally staying third-country nationals, in accordance with fundamental rights and general principles of Community law, including refugee protection and human rights obligations (art. 1). Illegal stay is defined as "the presence on the territory of a Member State, of a third-country national who does not fulfil, or no longer fulfils the conditions of entry as set out in Article 5 of the Schengen Borders Code[7] or other conditions for entry, stay or residence in that Member State" (art. 3(2)). It does not mean that each migrant sans-papiers[8] shall be automatically considered as staying illegally: "no human is illegal". The illegality of stay must be stated or declared in an administrative or judicial decision or act defined as a "return decision". In such a decision, an obligation to return will be imposed or stated too (art. 3(4)). Return itself implies "the process of a third-country national going back – whether in voluntary compliance with an obligation to return, or enforced – to his or her country of origin, or a country of transit in accordance with Community or bilateral readmission agreements or other arrangements, or another third country, to which the third-country national concerned voluntarily decides to return and in which he or she will be accepted" (art. 3(3)). A return decision shall provide for an appropriate period for voluntary departure of between seven and thirty days (art. 7(1)).[9] Only if there is a risk of absconding, or if an application for a legal stay has been dismissed as manifestly unfounded or fraudulent, or if the person concerned poses a risk to public policy, public security or national security, Member States may refrain from granting a period for voluntary departure, or may grant a period shorter than seven days.

These introductory provisions clearly confirm that the EU law maker has been seeking to find a proper balance between protecting the rights of the TCN subject to return procedures and ensuring the effectiveness of returns by avoiding automatic or arbitrary procedures. But from the practical point of view, this procedure hides a material weakness linked to the terms set out for voluntary departure. With just a little stretch of the imagination, one can easily realize that no migrant, having devoted months or even years to entering the EU, will voluntarily leave it in such a short period. If the obligation to return has not been complied with within the period for voluntary departure, it is upon Member States to "take all necessary measures" to enforce the return decision (art. 8(1)) by removing the illegally staying TCN through physical transportation out of the Member State (art. 3(5)). In this phase, the Member States are entitled to use coercive measures as a "last resort" provided they are proportionate,

[7] Regulation (EU) 2006/399 of the European Parliament and the Council of 6 March 2006 on a Union Code on the rules governing the movement of persons across borders (Schengen Borders Code), as subsequently modified.

[8] Literally, a person without documentation. In more general terms, an irregular migrant.

[9] Without prejudice to the exceptions referred to in paragraphs 2 and 4 of art. 7.

do not exceed reasonable force, are in accordance with fundamental rights, and respect the dignity and physical integrity of the TCN concerned (art. 8(4)). A striking legal loophole between the obligation to take all necessary measures imposed upon Member States and the very vague wording of limits imposed on such a power-obligation (potere-dovere) emerges. This critical issue is acutely evident if the practical scope of measure of detention is concerned.

9.4. *Detention as a measure of last resort*

The use of detention is outlined under chapter IV of the Return Directive. It may be applied only as a measure of last resort and exclusively to prepare the return or carry out the removal process and shall be maintained only as long as removal arrangements are in progress. The Member States may only keep in detention a TCN who is the subject of return procedures in order to prepare the return and/or carry out the removal in two following cases: (i) there is a risk of absconding, or (ii) the TCN concerned avoids or hampers the preparation of return or the removal process (art. 15(1)). The detention shall be ordered by administrative or judicial authorities in writing, with reasons being given in fact and in law. When detention is ordered by administrative authorities it shall be subject to a speedy judicial review or the third-country national shall have the right to initiate the proceeding of judicial review. As a general rule, it shall cease if it is declared unlawful (art. 15(2)) or in case it appears that a reasonable prospect of removal no longer exists (art. 15(4)). In both the cases the TCN concerned shall be released immediately.

Thus, the detention shall be maintained for as long a period as the conditions laid down in paragraph 15(1) are fulfilled and it is necessary to ensure successful removal. Detention shall be maintained for a period which may not exceed six months (art. 15(6)). It may be extended for a limited period not exceeding a further twelve months in case the removal operation is likely to last longer due to: (a) a lack of cooperation by the third-country national, or (b) delays in obtaining the necessary documentation from third countries (art. 15(6)).

It emerges from the quoted articles, as is also clarified by the advocates general, that detention for removal purposes is neither punitive nor criminal and does not constitute a prison sentence.[10] While detention in the Return Directive ideally represents a measure of last resort, from a practical standpoint it is by far the most used measure to prepare the removal. Thus, the dividing line between detention understood as a punitive measure and as merely an administrative measure is rather blurred. This is reflected in the most representative referrals from the Italian courts for a preliminary ruling on the interpretation of the Return Directive.

---

[10] § 35 of the View of Advocate General Mazák in El Dridi (ECLI:EU:C:2011:205); § 54 of the View of Advocate General Wathelet in G. and R. (ECLI:EU:C:2013:553); and § 91 of the Opinion of Advocate General Bot in Beroand Bouzalmate (C-473/13 and C-514/13, ECLI:EU:C:2014:295).

9.5. *The CJEU interpretation*

The Member States were requested to transpose the Return Directive by 24 December 2010. The TFUE lifted the limitation on access to the CJEU by national courts in the field of borders, immigration and asylum (Guild, 2013). As of 2011 the domestic courts [11] started to file requests for preliminary ruling on the Return Directive. The CJEU was frequently required to rule on the so-called criminalization of illegal migration under the domestic laws in force before the entrance into force of the mentioned Directives and not yet amended at that time to enforce the same. Such laws were permitting, in certain cases, to apply the measure of criminal detention to combat the irregular migration. The Return Directive, on the contrary, considers the detention as a last resort, administrative, measure. The apparent contrast between the EU legal framework and those of some Member States brought about significant case law. Thus, the early cases were essentially concentrated on the interpretation of the meaning of the above quoted articles 15 and 16 on detention and on review of compliance of domestic laws with EU rules.

Among the most relevant judgments [12] in the field of criminalization of illegal migration, that paved the way for current understanding of the Return Directive, the following can be listed: C-61/11 PPU – El Dridi, [13] C-329/11 – Achugbabian, [14] C-430/11 – Sagor, [15] C-522/11 – Mbaye. [16] The CJEU, in these rulings, limited the right of Member States to detain the illegally staying TNC by enhancing the value of the universality of right to freedom of human beings.

9.6. *El Dridi – on undocumented migrants' rights*

The Court of Appeal of Trento in Italy requested the CJEU whether articles 15 and 16 of the Return Directive must be interpreted as precluding a Member State's legislation which provides for a sentence of imprisonment to be imposed on an illegally staying TCN on the sole ground that he remains, without valid grounds, on the territory of that State contrary to an order to leave that territory within a given period.

The request was made in proceedings brought against Mr. El Dridi, who was

---

[11] For a detailed list of requests for preliminary rulings filed in that period by the Italian courts see Raffaelli, 2013.

[12] For selected case law on the Return Directive see http://contention.eu/international-and-european-case-law/ (accessed on December 1st 2017).

[13] Judgment of the Court of 28 April 2011, ECLI:EU:C2011:268 ("El Dridi").

[14] Judgment of the Court of 6 Decembre 2011, ECLI:EU:C2011:807 ("Achugbabian").

[15] Judgment of the Court 6 December 2012, ECLI:EU:C:2012:777 ("Sagor").

[16] Order of the Court of 21 March 2013, ECLI:EU:C:2013:190 ("Mbaye").

sentenced to one year's imprisonment for the offence of having stayed illegally on Italian territory without valid grounds, contrary to a removal order made against him by the chief of police of Udine. Mr El Dridi was a TCN who entered Italy illegally and was not holding a residence permit. A deportation decree was issued against him by the Prefect of Turin in 2004. An order requiring his removal from the national territory was issued in May 2010 by the chief of police of Udine. The reasons for that removal order were that Mr El Dridi had no identification documents and that it was not possible for him to be accommodated at a detention facility as no places were available. During a check carried out later by the police it was found that he had not complied with such order.

Under the Italian immigration law in force at that time [17] it was provided that any foreign national who: (a) entered the territory of the State without going through border control and has not been returned and/or (b) has remained on the territory of the State without applying for a residence permit within the period imposed, was subject to the expulsion ordered by the chief of local government and carried out by the chief of police with deportation by the law enforcement authorities. If it was not possible to perform the expulsion by deportation or return, the chief of police had to order the detention of the foreign national for the length of time which is strictly necessary. If neither forcible removal nor detention were possible the chief of police had to order the TCN to leave the territory of the State within five days. A TCN who was remaining illegally and without valid grounds on the territory of the State, contrary to the order issued by the chief of police, were subject to a term of imprisonment of one to four years if the expulsion or the return has been ordered following an illegal entry into the national territory.

The CJEU stated that in a situation where previously adopted measures have not led to the removal of the TCN against whom they were issued the Member States remain free to adopt measures, including criminal law measures. Then, while constructing the arguments relating to the effectiveness of the EU law and so-called "effet utile", it deprived such measures of their dissuasive effects. In practice, the Member States may not apply rules, even criminal law rules, which are likely to jeopardize the achievement of the objectives pursued by the Return Directive. Indeed, "the Member States may not, in order to remedy the failure of coercive measures adopted in order to carry out forced removal pursuant to article 8(4) of Return Directive, provide for a custodial sentence, [...], on the sole ground that a [TCN] continues to stay illegally on the territory of a Member State after an order to leave the national territory was notified to him and the period granted in that order has expired; rather, they must pursue their efforts to enforce the return decision, which continues to produce its effects" (§58).

---

[17] Legislative Decree of 25 July 1998 no 286/1998 consolidating the provisions regulating immigration and the rules relating to the status of foreign national (Ordinary Supplement to GURI No 191 of 18 August 1998), as amended by Law No 94 of 15 July 2009 on public security (Ordinary Supplement to GURI No 170 of 24 July 2009) ("Legislative Decree No 286/1998").

Consequently, the CJEU interpreted articles 15 and 16 of the Return Directive as precluding a Member State's legislation, which provides for a sentence of imprisonment to be imposed on an illegally staying third-country national on the sole ground that he remains, without valid grounds, on the territory of that State contrary to an order to leave that territory within a given period. In so stating, the CJEU involuntarily opened a "Pandora's box" facilitating in practice the permanence of irregular TNCs within the territory of the Member States.

9.7. *Achughbabian – impossibility of a prison sentence?*

The Court of Appeal of Paris in France requested the CJEU to interpret the meaning of articles 15 and 16 of the Return Directive. The reference was made in the context of a dispute between Mr Achughbabian and the Prefect of Val-de-Marne concerning his illegal stay in French territory. He entered France at the beginning of 2008 and applied for a residence permit, but his application was rejected. The rejection was confirmed in 2009 by the Prefect of Val-d'Oise and accompanied by an order of the latter to leave the French territory within one month. Mr Achughbabian did not comply with such order. Indeed, during identity checks performed in June 2011, the police found that he was continuing to stay in France in breach of applicable law on the entrance and stay of foreigners. As a consequence, a deportation and an administrative detention order were adopted by the Prefect and served to him. In the same month, the competent judge ordered the extension of detention beyond 48 hours and dismissed the objections of invalidity raised by Mr Achughbabian against, inter alia, being held in police custody.

Under the French law on the entrance and stay of foreigners and asylum in force at the time, a foreign national who has entered or resided in France without complying with the provisions of articles requiring from any foreigner, to hold the documents and visas for entry and residence permit for stay, and who has remained in France beyond the period authorized by his visa, commits an offence punishable by one year's imprisonment and a fine.

The CJEU, by recalling El Dridi, confirmed that the Return Directive does not preclude national legislation that classifies an illegal stay by a third-country national as an offence and provides for penal sanctions, including a term of imprisonment, to prevent such a stay. Yet, the duty of loyalty of the Member States and the requirement to grant effectiveness to the Return Directive impose on the Member States the obligation to carry out the removal, which must be fullfilled as soon as possible. "That would clearly not be the case if, after establishing that a third-country national is staying illegally, the Member State were to preface the implementation of the return decision, or even the adoption of that decision, with a criminal prosecution followed, in appropriate cases, by a term of imprisonment. Such a step would delay the removal (El

Dridi, paragraph 59) and does not, moreover, appear amongst the justifications for a postponement of removal referred to in Article 9 of Directive 2008/115" (§45). In any case, the CJEU did not exclude the right of the Member States to adopt or maintain provisions which may be of a criminal nature in the situation in which coercive measures have not made it possible for the removal of an illegally staying third-country national to be effected. In this case, the CJEU seems to move cautiously away from the strict interpretation of provisions on detentions by permitting the use of detention if other coercive measures have failed.

9.8. *Sagor – fines to penalize illegal stay?*

In August 2009, an individual questioned by the police declared that his name was Mr Sagor and that he had been born in Bangladesh. Upon examination of Mr Sagor's situation, it became apparent that he had no fixed abode in Italy and was operating there as a street vendor with no residence permit. According to the report drawn up by the police, Mr Sagor declared that he had entered Italy in March 2009. In July 2010 Mr Sagor was summoned before the Tribunale di Rovigo for, inter alia, the offence of illegal entry or stay referred to in Article 10a of Legislative Decree No 286/1998. The Italian court found that illegal stay had been duly proven, but having some doubts as to the compatibly of national legislation with the EU law it requested the CJEU to state whether the Return Directive must be interpreted as precluding Legislative Decree No 268/1998, which penalizes illegal stays by TCNs by means of a fine which may be replaced by an order for expulsion or home detention.

The CJEU confirmed in a strong manner that the Return Directive does not preclude the law of a Member State from classifying an illegal stay as an offence and laying down criminal sanctions to deter and penalize such an infringement. It also stated that the possibility that criminal prosecution may lead to a fine is not liable to impede the return procedure. Indeed, "the imposition of a fine does not in any way prevent a return decision from being made and implemented in full compliance with the conditions set out in articles 6 to 8 of the Directive 2008/115, nor does it undermine the common standards relating to deprivation of liberty set out in Articles 15 and 16" of the same (§36). On the contrary, the home detention order was considered as potentially liable to delay – and thus to impede – the measures, such as deportation and forced return, which can be used to achieve removal. This interpretation of the CJEU does not represent a deviation from a narrow interpretation of provisions concerning detention. It states that fines are admissible to penalize the illegal stay, but it seems rather avulsed from reality if it is considered that the illegally staying TCNs are notoriously without sufficient financial means. Thus, in practice, neither the detention, including the home detention, nor the fines are practically feasible to combat illegal migration.

9.9. *Mbaye – a different approach?*

Mr Mbaye, a Senegalese citizen, was found during a police force check to have illegally entered the territory of Italy and that he was not in possession of a residence permit. Mr Mbaye was brought before the Justice of the Peace of Lecce to respond for the offence of irregular residence under Article 10-bis of Legislative Decree No. 286/1998. The Justice of the Peace asked the CJEU whether this article, in conjunction with article 16 that permits expulsion as sanction alternative to detention, rendered the common rules and procedures introduced by the Return Directive ineffective.

The CJEU recalled that the Return Directive does not prevent the right of a Member State to classify the illegal residence of third-country nationals as a criminal offense and provides for criminal sanctions to discourage this infringement. Along the same lines of El Dridi, the CJEU has also pointed out that a Member State cannot apply criminal legislation which is likely to jeopardize the application of the common rules and procedures provided for by the Return Directive, thus depriving it of its effectiveness.

The CJEU again stated that the Return Directive does not preclude legislation of a Member State which penalizes the illegal residence of TCNs with a fine which can be substituted with the punishment of expulsion; substitution may be exercised only if there is a risk of absconding, or if an application for a legal stay has been dismissed as manifestly unfounded or fraudulent, or if the person concerned poses a risk to public policy, public security or national security. This judgment appears less constructive as regards the margin of appreciation of domestic courts. The CJEU seems to have left the national judge free to take into account different factual elements while deciding on substitution of fines with expulsion. In this regard, the Court found, "on the one hand, that paragraph 4 of Article 7 allows Member States to refrain from granting a period for voluntary departure, in particular when there is a risk that the person concerned may flee in order to avoid the repatriation procedure, and, secondly, that any assessment must be based on an individual examination of the situation of the interested party" (§31).

9.10. *Conclusions*

It appears from the examined case law that the domestic courts avoid facing the delicate task of balancing values underpinning human rights against the necessity to enforce public order rules, and prefer to "delegate" the task to the CJEU. Even more than in other fields, it seems that there is "symbiotic relationship" (Weiler 2013) between domestic courts and the CJEU as regards the interpretation of the Return Directive. Whatever the question the domestic court may have "it does not have to grapple with hermeneutic uncertainty as to the correct interpretation of the treaty norm. It receives an authoritative interpretation from the Court" (Weiler 2013). Yet the CJEU also evades taking clear positions in its rulings. It prefers a strict interpretation of the Return Directive compliant with "effet utile". Thus, the rulings frequently do not provide sharp answers to the requests formulated by the domestic courts, but instead offer a general interpretation of the EU law that does not take into due account the actuality of migratory fluxes affecting the Member States. More in particular:

- in El Dridi an Italian court requested a ruling as to whether articles 15 and 16 of the Return Directive must be interpreted as precluding a Member State's legislation which provides for a sentence of imprisonment in case of illegal stay on an illegally staying TCN on the sole ground that he remains, without valid grounds, on the territory of that State, contrary to an order to leave that territory within a given period. The CJEU stated that the Member States remain free to adopt criminal law measures in a situation where previously adopted measures have not led to the removal of the TCN. The CJEU then, however, based on effet utile doctrine, stated that the Member States may not adopt custodial sentences, but rather "they must pursue their efforts to enforce the return decision, which continues to produce its effects";
- in Achughabian, following the request of Court of Appeal of Paris, the CJEU reiterated the right of Member States to adopt or maintain provisions, also of criminal nature, but limited the use of such provisions to a situation in which coercive measures have not made it possible for the removal of an illegally staying TCN;
- in Sagor the CJEU stated that the Return Directive does not preclude Member State legislation which penalizes illegal stays by TCNs by means of a fine, but it precludes laws which allow illegal stays by TCNs to be penalized by means of a home detention order without guaranteeing that the enforcement of that order must cease when the removal is possible;
- in Mbaye – the CJEU stated that the Return Directive does not preclude the legislation of a Member State which penalizes the illegal residence of TCNs with a fine which can be substituted with the punishment of expulsion, but substitution shall be substantially limited to cases in which there is a risk of absconding.

The jurisprudence of the CJEU and its consequent implementation into the domestic contexts has rendered it more difficult to remove an irregular TCN. Yet, paradoxically enough, this case law, which is strongly influenced by ethical principles, has not improved the level of observance of migrants' human rights. On the contrary, for example in Italy, it brought with the adoption of a law decree in February 2017 [18] under which one degree of judgment – appeal – was abolished as regards the procedures concerning

---

[18] Law decree of 17 February 2017 no 13, converted with modification in Law 13 April 2017, no 46 on urgent provisions for the speeding up of proceedings in the field of international protection, as well as for the fight against illegal immigration (Ordinary Supplement to GURI No 90 of 18 April 2017).

migrants requesting the recognition of asylum. It should be underlined that the Italian "government, denied a degree of judgment where 70% of the applicants saw international protection recognized". [19] In conclusion, the above analysis suggests that the case law, in particular that of the CJEU, shall take into account the reality of migratory fluxes affecting a member state. Otherwise, there is a tangible possibility that, in the final analysis, it might produce effects opposite to those that are expected. Still, in the EU which remains strongly divided on migration, judges might find themselves in a better position than legislators to mitigate increasing intolerance toward irregular migrants. This would however request that the courts, both on the EU and domestic levels, balance values in a sharper way.

Bibliography

Guild, E. (2013) 'EU Immigration and the New EU Treaty Framework', in S.S. Juss (ed.) The Ashgate Reserach Companion to Migration Law, *Theory and Policy*, Farnham: Ashgate, 43.

Jacobs, F.G. (2002) *Judicial Dialogue and the Cross-Fertilization of Legal Systems: The European Court of Justice*, presentation at a conference on Judicial Dialogue and the Cross-Fertilization of Legal Systems, University of Texas School of Law, http:// www.tilj.org/content/journal/38/num3/Jacobs547.pdf (accessed on May 3rd, 2017).

Peers, S. (2015) 'Irregular migrants: Can humane treatment be balanced against efficient removal?', *European Journal of Migration and Law*, 17: 289–304.

Raffaelli, R. (2011) *Case note: An analysis of the El Dridi judgment*, http://briguglio.asgi.it/immigrazione-e-asilo/2011/maggio/raffaelli-cgue-c-61-2011.pdf (accessed on January 12th, 2018).

Weiler, J.H.H. (2013) *Revisiting Van Gend en Loos: Subjectifying and Objectifying the Individual*, presentation at a conference at the 50th anniversary of the judgment in Van Gend en Loos 1963-2013, Luxembourg, https://curia.europa.eu/VGL/book/files/assets/basic-html/index.html#3 (accessed on September 1st, 2017).

[19] https://altreconomia.it/diritto-asilo-appello/ (accessed on January 10th, 2018).

Chapter 10

Boundaries and precision medicine in consanguineous migrant couples

Genetic counseling after the identification of fetal pathologies

Vanna Berlincioni, Cristina Catania, Francesca Acerbi, Arsenio Spinillo, Alessia Arossa, Nehir Edibe Kurtas, Edoardo Errichiello and Orsetta Zuffardi

10.1. *Consanguinity and genetic disorders*

The current migratory phenomenon brings numerous consanguineous couples to Italy and Europe, mostly with first degree consanguinity. The risk of genetic disorders in the conception products of these couples is significantly greater than in non-consanguineous couples. Indeed, while most people with rare genetic variants show no clinical signs because of a second non-mutated copy of the gene, a subject who inherits two copies (alleles) of the same rare variant will most likely express the disease related to the functional or quantitative alteration of the protein encoded by that gene. Two healthy carriers of a recessive gene have a 25 percent probability in each pregnancy to have a child with both mutated copies of that gene, and thus be affected. Recessive genetic disorders can lead to the alteration of physiological embryogenesis with fetal malformations detectable through routine ultrasound scanning during pregnancy or to morphological and/or functional abnormalities detected immediately after birth. A premise for possible "precision" therapies is the identification of the causative genetic variant, which is carried out through the analysis of the coding sequences of the genome (the so-called "exome") in the affected subject and parents (i.e. trio). It should be emphasized that, due to the numerous DNA variants detected in the healthy human population, investigations aimed at identifying the molecular bases of the disease assume diagnostic significance only if they are related to the clinical features of the subject under investigation, with the further complication that fetal alterations highlighted by imaging in the prenatal age might not be representative of the entire "pathological picture" observed during the postnatal life. Although the identification of the genetic basis of the disease may be irrelevant for parental decisions regarding the progression or interruption of the current pregnancy, it is however necessary for (a) the prognosis and management of the unborn and/or newborn (also by considering the current developments in precision medicine approaches for diseases considered incurable until a few years ago); and (b) the appropriate planning of following pregnancies.

10.2. *Genetic counseling in consanguineous couples of migrants*

From a practical point of view, the output of a genetic analysis is delivered to the parents in the context of a genetic counseling process that aims to explain the molecular basis of the disease and the possible medical, psychological and familial implications of these findings. The counseling can be particularly complex in the case of DNA variants not reported in the medical/scientific literature, as frequently occurs for fetal and/or postnatal diseases in consanguineous couples, largely due to extremely rare genetic mutations and almost never immediately referable to a known disease. Moreover, in prenatal diagnostics, any decision to continue pregnancy, despite the awareness that the unborn child will present a series of medical complications, must take into account the fact that prolonged hospitalization or possible surgical interventions may require parent closeness and economic efforts.

10.3. *Genetic analysis, genetic counseling and psychiatric support in the MIGRAT.IN.G project*

Over the past two years we have followed the pregnancies of 21 consanguineous migrant couples, in which the ultrasound examination, performed between the first and third trimesters of pregnancy, had also highlighted multiple malformations affecting various fetal districts. The whole exome analysis in the trios allowed us to identify the probably causative genetic variant in 19 cases.

In all cases, the genetic counseling was made complicated not only by the language barrier but also by the general unawareness of the couple about the risk of fetal malformations related to consanguinity, a practice that in the cultural context of their country of origin is habitual, and thus not considered "risky". Seven couples were also followed by a team of psychiatrists through more focused interviews following the administration of genetic counseling and the decision to interrupt the pregnancy and, in one case, the subsequent death of two infants. These analyses (see Table 10.1) highlighted the social isolation of most pregnant women due to the fact that often only the male partner is still in touch with the population of origin, leaving the woman in a condition of extreme loneliness and melancholy for her relatives. However, elaboration of mourning was shown to benifit from both genetic counseling and psychiatric support, with the acceptance of the situation and the desire of both partners to undertake further pregnancies, regardless of the number of previous healthy children, as long as appropriate genetic monitoring had been provided.

10.4. *General conclusions*

The situation that we depicted in Pavia is generalizable to many areas of Italy and Europe, and points to an international emergency of newborns with malformations that need prolonged assistance and appropriate medical interventions. Thus, the creation of centers with a team of gynecologists, medical geneticists and neuropsychiatrists is mandatory not only for effective social integration of migrants but also for implementing primary prevention strategies through information for parents concerning their reproductive risk and identification of the DNA causative variants.

10.5. *Results of the talks with the seven migrant couples subjected to ethno-psychological evaluations and the administration of specific questionnaire by psychiatrists*

Couples were subjected to administration of a specific questionnaire and interviews aimed at evaluating the ethno-psychological context, together with two self-administered tests, namely the Hamilton Depression Rating Scale (HAM-D:http://www.assessmentpsychology.com/HAM-D.pdf)) and the Decisional Conflict Scale (DCS). These questionnaires were compared with those of other non-consanguineous couples. Importantly, it was not possible to identify Italian consanguineous couples; therefore, the different approach to genetic diagnosis has been evaluated regardless of consanguinity in control subjects. However, the number of control pairs is small compared to the examined couples. Until now, we have interviewed seven consanguineous couples and three control couples. The couples were selected at the Department of Gynecology and Obstetrics at the Policlinico San Matteo of Pavia, where the interviews were administered.

10.6. *Interviews and statistical evaluations*

The consanguineous couples were all married and Muslim; the average age of males was 41, and 33 for females. The average scholarization was 12 years for males and 11 for women; only one woman had a university degree, and none of the men. While men all had an external job the women were housewives, except for one who was temporarily unemployed. All affirmed that in their countries of origin consanguineity is a common occurrence. In some countries (e.g. Turkey and Tunisia) pre-conception blood tests to assess the risk of beta-thalessemia are highly recommended; however, genetic tests for the screening of specific diseases related to consanguinity are not recommended in any of the countries.

The first couple, composed of first cousins, comes from Bizerta, Tunisia. A. has lived in Italy since 1990, and B. since 2001 after their marriage in 2000 in Tunisia. A. is a driver and B. is a housewife. They are satisfied with life in Italy, however they do not exclude returning to Tunisia at some point; the wife seems to think about this possibility very often, despite having good friendships in Italy, in order to rejoin her relatives who remain in her country of origin. The couple has three children: the first-born is healthy, the second-born is affected by a severe form of congenital ichthyosis caused by a novel variant in the TGM1 gene, which was identified by the analysis of the exome in the trio. Chorionic villi DNA testing detected the presence of the mutation at the recessive state in the third pregnancy, which led to the voluntary interruption of the pregnancy. On the contrary, the genetic test in the fourth pregnancy detected the mutation at the heterozygous state with the subsequent birth of a healthy daughter. The fifth pregnancy was again voluntarily interrupted since the fetus was a homozygous carrier of the mutation. The couple reports that a brother of A., married to a first cousin, also has a child affected by ichthyosis. Although there were no obvious language limitations, they appeared reluctant to deepen their own emotional experiences.

C. and D. come from El Fayoum, Egypt. They are first cousins, married since 2004. Only the wife, D., was present at the appointment. D. had a considerable language barrier, while showing herself available to the interview. D. arrived in Italy in 2007 to reach C., who has been a bricklayer in Pavia since 2000. She is satisfied with her life in Italy and does not think of returning to her country of origin, even though she still has many relatives there. She is a housewife and mother of four children: unfortunately, the third child died at one month of age due to severe respiratory distress. The clinical picture prompted physicians to carry out genetic investigations, which showed the presence of a novel homozygous mutation in a gene associated with dysfunctions of the pulmonary surfactant, which resulted at the heterozygous state in both parents. During the interview, it seems that D. did not fully understand the correlation between consanguinity and reproductive risk. In fact, she feels herself responsible and guilty for the death of her son by attributing the cause of health conditions during pregnancy (hypercholesterolemia, dyspnoea) to the "will of Allah". The couple, very much distressed by the mourning, returned to Egypt for a certain period due to extreme sadness and anguish in both of them, as also emerged during the interview. It was not possible to complete data collection for the HAM-D test because of the resistance of D., although depressed mood, feelings of guilt, psychic anxiety and somatic symptomatology were well documented.

The third couple comes from Casablanca, Morocco. A cultural mediator was present during the interview because they do not speak Italian. In 1999 E. came to Italy looking for a job; he lived for a few years in Naples, then he moved to Pavia where he worked as a carpenter. F., a housewife, arrived in Italy in 2008 after getting married in 2005, to be rejoined with her husband's second cousin. Despite the parents and many family members remaining in the country of origin, they are satisfied with their current life in Italy. They have a good economic position and a good network of friends. The children were born in Italy. The request for information on their degree of relationship gave rise to laughter: they do not believe themselves to be relatives, or at least only distantly related. They have known each other since childhood, they were playmates and neighbors: they claim to be in love and "predestined" forever. The sister of E. is also married to a cousin and has had no sick children. E. and F. have two healthy children, one eight years old and one four years. However, the third child was born with a congenital malformation and he died shortly after birth. Ultrasounds showed an important cardiac malformation and reduced fetal growth during the third pregnancy, but the husband forced his wife to complete the pregnancy. Unfortunately, the newborn died a few months after birth. Genetic analysis did not show any causative genetic alteration. The couple, although aware that the death of the child was a consequence of a genetic disease, strongly denied the hypothesis that the latter might be somehow linked to consanguinity. Although they are very frightened by possible complications, they do not exclude other pregnancies in the future. After the death of his son, E. suspended his work for several months and returned to Morocco. His wife remained alone with the children during that period, with whom she had to handle the difficult mourning process: the older child reacted in a more adequate way by understanding the complex situation, while the younger child suffered for a long time. The couple did not mention the possibility of genetic risk even with their closest relatives, fearing their judgment. During the interview they still appeared confused, unable to face the situation, and very lonely in the management of this event. HAM-D revealed a mild pattern in the wife, with psychic anxiety, insomnia and feelings of guilt (Score 11); the HAM-D of the husband turned out to be negative (score 2). Therefore, psychological support for the wife was suggested. The DCS (score 59.4) revealed a high conflict of decisions.

A cultural mediator was present at the interview with the fourth couple. M. and N. are Turkish first cousins, married since 2005. M. emigrated to Bari in 2007, subsequently moving to Pavia where he worked for a fast food restaurant; the wife, N., a housewife, only reached her husband in 2013. They left parents and some other relatives in their country of origin, while many brothers and sisters of both M. and N. have moved to Europe. While the husband found a good job in Italy, N. would like to leave Italy, having not created a good network of friends. In Turkey they underwent pre-conception blood tests to assess if they were carriers of the trait thalassaemic, which gave negative results. In 2014 they had their first child, who died shortly after due to prematurity. In 2016 their second son died when he was one month of age due to serious heart malformations. The genetic investigations revealed the presence in both parents of an autosomal recessive mutation within a gene associated with abnormal development of the heart. This couple, supportive and well-knit, supported by family members, friends and clinicians who have them in charge, appeared fully aware of the reproductive risk associated with consanguinity. HAM-D showed mild depressive symptoms, insomnia, and loss of interests in both parents. By virtue of their high degree of awareness, the decisional conflict was low at the DCS testing (score 15.6): the couple was determined to try other pregnancies in the future, after first processing the current mourning. A psychological support was also proposed during the counseling.

The fifth pair was from Menzel Temime, Tunisia. They were second-degree cousins, while their grandparents were brothers. G. came to Italy in 1998 at the age of 15; H. joined him in 2010 after their marriage in Tunisia. The husband had poor education and he is currently a mason; the wife, graduated in foreign languages, was an English teacher in Tunisia. Before coming to Italy she asked for a five-year work expectancy on the assumption that they could repatriate in the future and she would resume the work. They have known each other since they were children, "always in love". They describe their love as an extremely natural event; their marriage was not arranged, a custom that in their opinion no longer exists in Tunisia, but a free choice. Both considered themselves well integrated in our country, they spoke fluent Italian and have social contacts with Italian people. The couple has a six year old girl and a three year old girl. A few months ago H., during the third pregnancy, had to face a pregnancy interruption, an extremely painful but inevitable decision: at the second trimester ultrasound check, a serious spinal malformation was discovered in the fetus, which would have resulted in a severe disability. They decided to face this critical moment alone, without talking to other family members. They said they had overcome many difficulties with mutual support and thought that it was not necessary to involve their own families. Genetic diagnosis was performed on the fetus, whose results were explained to the couple during the interview. Before knowing the outcome of the genetic survey, H. became pregnant again. Until now, the couple thought that the malformation was due to the chicken pox she contracted during pregnancy. They discovered that they were both carriers of a mutation at the heterozygous state, in a gene involved in the development of the spine, present at the homozygous state in the fetus. Their second-born was also a carrier, while the first daughter is healthy. They claimed that if they had known before of a genetic risk they would not have faced a new pregnancy, so now they showed themselves rightly worried, but ready to face any complications and, if necessary, a new pregnancy interruption. The analysis of the new fetus was normal and the couple declared that after birth they will use contraceptive methods to avoid risky pregnancies. The woman's HAM-D score was 11, corresponding to a state of mild depression; in the husband there were no depressive symptoms (score 3). The DCS test revealed an extremely low decisional conflict with a high degree of awareness (score 3.2).

The sixth couple came from Lebanon. The husband, L., from Al Kossiebh; his wife, M., from Jebchit. They were first degree cousins. Married since 2015, they spoke Arabic, Italian and German. L. studied for 14 years, interrupting his studies at the first year of university; he initially moved to Germany with his brother to work in a car dealership and in 2011 he moved to Italy. M., after 9 years of study, moved to Italy in 2013; she currently is a housewife. In Italy they live with L.'s brother while his parents and other brothers remained in Lebanon; they think that one day they will return to their country of origin. In their families there were other marriages between cousins. At the first pregnancy, during an ultrasound screening, fetal malformations were found, which led the couple to decide to carry out a pregnancy termination. The genetic investigations detected a homozygous variant in the fetus and a heterozygous one in both parents. The affected gene, TCTN1, is involved in different crucial processes during embryonic development. At the second and last pregnancy they refused to perform prenatal tests, relying on "fate". They claimed to have had clear and comprehensive information on the genetic risks and to be aware of them. However, they denied that more information on consanguinity risks might be useful, since they did not believe that prenatal diagnosis/contraceptive methods are necessary. In their HAM-D scores there was evidence of negativity for L. (score 3) and a framework of slight deflection for M. (score 8). A slight decisional conflict emerged at the DCS scale (score 21.9).

The last couple that we evaluated came from Morocco (Casablanca); P. was 37 years old, and Q. 31. They were first cousins. They came to Italy in 2002 to rejoin their families of origin. Married since 2009, they were satisfied with their life in Italy, and they did not think of returning to their country of origin. In 2012 they had a daughter who died during the neonatal period, reporting multiple malformations, but no genetic investigations were performed at that time. In 2013 a healthy son was born, while in 2015 a sick daughter was born, in whom a syndromic disease was found at the ultrasound screening during gestation; despite this, the couple refused to perform genetic tests before birth. Postnatal genetic analysis resulted in a very rare condition, the type 1 tricoepatoenteric syndrome, due to a genetic mutation present at the heterozygous state in both parents and the homozygous state in the last newborn. The clinical phenotype perfectly overlapped with the first daughter, in whose DNA, collected post-mortem, the same mutation at the homozygous state was shown. The second healthy child, on the other hand, did not carry this mutation. Once they realized that this situation was a consequence of genetic factors related to consanguinity, both recognized the urgent need for more information about risks related to marriage between relatives. While expressing trust in doctors, P. – unlike his wife – claimed that prenatal diagnosis is not helpful. Q. appeared to be the most stressed by the diagnosis: P. said that nothing has changed in his life, except for greater sadness and fear of the future; Q. on the other hand, reported that he has lost his social contacts. They described themselves as a very close couple, stating that their feeling is strengthened by overcoming difficulties together. They were aware that their daughter may not have a "normal life" and this generated the fear that others will judge their daughter as a "different child". The HAM-D test revealed a picture of mild depression (score 9) in the mother, while the DCS showed a slight conflict in decision-making (score 20.3).

10.7. *Control subjects*

The first control pair is Italian; A. is a 40-year-old cook, B. is a 27-year-old bartender. They were married in 2015, and now live near Pavia; they are not religious. They are both affected by beta minor thalassemia (asymptomatic, mutation in heterozygosity). They always knew about being affected, therefore they underwent prenatal diagnosis at the first pregnancy, from which was born a healthy daughter (mutation absent). They intend to have new pregnancies, so they will submit to the required genetic tests, with the intention, in the case of homozygosity involving the beta thalassemia major gene, to terminate the pregnancy. They reported that because their condition was already known to both of them, they have always been prepared for such an eventuality, and they have lived guilt-free until now, having had a healthy daughter.

The second control pair is also Italian: C. is a 24-year-old warehouse owner, and D. is 20 and is a hairdresser. They both have a middle school diploma; they are non-practicing Catholics. They are not married, have lived together since 2015, and the woman is 5 months pregnant. Like the previous couple, they are both affected by beta thalassemia minor. Although they know about the disease, in the first hospital they were not adequately and comprehensively informed about the risks of genetic transmission and the severity of the condition of the disease in homozygosity. They asked for a second consultation in Pavia when the pregnancy was already in progress; D. underwent amniocentesis in the prospect that, if the fetus had mutations in homozygosity, they would have carried out a therapeutic abortion. The couple mentioned their different ways of facing this waiting period: the mother with anxiety and worry, praying and seeking the help of the neighbors, with the father being more fatalistic, trying not to consider the worst situation. From the test that was carried out it finally emerged that the expectant baby is heterozygous for beta thalassemia, as are parents. The couple intended to have other pregnancies in the future, and declared that they will certainly undergo diagnostic tests to avoid a late pregnancy interruption.

The third control pair is from Albania (Valona). E. is 32 years old, F. is 35, and both are atheists. She moved to Italy (in the area of Pavia) at the age of 13 together with her family, to rejoin her father who came to Italy looking for work. She worked, and continues to work, as a goldsmith. She feels more Italian than Albanian. Her husband has been in Italy since 2001 and works as a plumber. They met in Italy and got married in 2012. They are not consanguineous, and they are amazed that marriages can occur between relatives, as such marriages are illegal in Albania. They are very satisfied with their life in Italy: they have a good income, a house (which they own), a good friendship network, F.'s parents and numerous relatives. In 2013, during the pregnancy of the eldest daughter, they discovered that they were both affected by beta-thalassemia minor. Fortunately, at the time of villocentesis, the daughter was shown to be affected at the heterozygous level. Learning about the genetic risk, they tried a new pregnancy in 2016, undergoing villocentesis: the fetus was affected by beta-thalassemia major, therefore they performed a pregnancy interruption. The mother is currently pregnant. At the time of our meeting she was waiting for the villocentesis. The level of awareness was high, the degree of decisional conflictuality was null and there were no anxiety-depressive symptoms. They reported only a moderate stress level. The husband and wife supported each other, and there was no lack of support from relatives. Together with friends they decided to be more reserved in their choice. No depressive symptoms were detected in the three control couples. In the first two couples the DCS test was not administered, as the possibility of a decision-making conflict was completely absent; in the third pair, the DCS was negative (score 0).

10.8. *Conclusions of the interviews conducted by the psychiatric team*

We compared a sample of seven consanguineous couples of Muslim faith with a sample of threee non-consanguineous Italian couples, not having Italian couples bound by ties of kinship. Therefore, we cannot evaluate any cultural difference regarding this type of union on the basis of the collected data. In fact, the custom of "consanguineous unions" is currently extremely rare in Italy. What emerged from the experience of the interviewed couples is that the marriage between cousins in the Muslim population is considered a tradition, and therefore a natural event; they said that it was not only maintained to ensure economic and power interests, but above all to consolidate emotional and trustworthy ties within the extended family. Despite some communication problems related to the language barrier, and thanks to the help of a cultural mediator in two cases, it was possible to carry out all the interviews. All the couples collaborated in the data collection, despite the delicacy of the faced themes: in some foreign couples a certain degree of understandable distrust has emerged in their experiences. In particular, in one couple the woman showed an attitude of greater withdrawal towards the interviewer, entrusting to her husband the function of spokesperson for them both. The wives in our couples were all housewives, with the exception of one teacher who is currently unemployed, while all the men have a permanent job in the secondary and tertiary sectors. This aspect creates a strong bond of dependence on the spouse for the partners, not only from the economic side, but above all concerning the link with the external society. Here a greater sense of isolation is generated for the woman with the consequence of feelings of loneliness and nostalgia for the homeland. In our samples, for equal schooling, women also had some sort of work activity and therefore greater integration at the social level. We have been able to ascertain that in countries where consortium marriages are the practice, information about genetic risks is very lacking, or even non-existent. As a consequence, these couples minimize this risk, considering it to be an extremely rare event. Because of this belief, the subjects would not seem conditioned by the procreative risk in choosing to marry a first- or second-degree cousin. Furthermore, it emerged that the reception of genetic diagnosis elicits different kinds of reactions, not always in keeping with the communication of the unfortunate event. Indeed, some couples showed an attitude of negation of the procreative risk linked to consanguinity; other couples reacted in a fatalistic way, others with greater awareness, and this led them to resort to contraceptive precautions and to undergo genetic control tests. A mild depressive symptomatology appeared in all women and in one man following the experience of the mourning. For the subjects with positive HAM-D testing results, psychological support was strongly suggested. Despite the prejudice concerning the poor power of the woman's decision within Muslim couples we have not grasped this kind of disqualification between spouses in our sample, consistent with apparent solidarity between the couples sampled. On the contrary, all but one of the Italian couples were aware of the genetic risk. Thus, the Italian couples showed a rational and confident attitude towards the attending institution and greater acceptance of the biological data, which generated less guilt.

In conclusion, the most striking fact is the misinformation of migrant couples with regard to the consequences of consanguinity. Hence, there is a need for operators involved in this type of investigation to implement an approach to these subjects that is sensitive and respectful of the cultural diversity and to achieve a more effective and incisive communication not oriented by prejudices.

Part II

Crossing the borders

Chapter 11

The offense of facilitating illegal immigration

Current questions about the constraints of the Italian jurisdiction

Luisa Frigeni

Among the tragedies that upset modern society, the facilitation of illegal immigration is one of the most alarming. The political instability that the North African countries are facing and the geographical position of Italy have led to the increase of landings. Over the past year it is estimated that over 80,000 migrants have arrived on the Italian coast, including illegal migrants and asylum seekers. [1] These are significant figures that show how the management of migratory flows and the trafficking of human beings have become a social emergency that has required, and still requires, many measures. From the legal point of view, an interest arises for the analysis of the Italian law against the facilitation of illegal immigration and the labor, sexual and economic exploitation of migrants. In this regard, an important role for the repression of the facilitation of illegal immigration is attributed to art. 12 of the Consolidated Law on immigration ("Testo unico dell'immigrazione" T.U. imm.).

11.1. *The offense of facilitating illegal immigration*

First, it is important to examine the structure and the constraints on implementation of the crime provided by art. 12 T.U. imm, as well as the relationship of the same with other crimes and, specifically, with the trafficking in human beings to which the crime of facilitation is often connected by a means-to-an-end relationship. Recent events show that the activity of facilitation is sometimes one of the means to fuel a criminal activity of a real commodification of illegal migrants. Moreover, the facilitation of illegal entry and trafficking in human beings constitute two distinct events. In fact, it was considered necessary to distinguish the two phenomena. [2] The facilitation of illegal immigration implies an agreement between the illegal migrant and the one facilitating

---

[1] Official data of the Ministry of the Interior from 1 January 2017 to 30 June 2017 at www.ansa.it

[2] See the "Protocol to Prevent, Suppress and Punish Trafficking in Persons Especially Women and Children" adopted by the UN on 2000 in Palermo.

the illegal entry into the State for a payment generally consisting of a large sum of money: this entry concludes the "contractual" relationship between the illegal immigrant and the facilitator. By contrast, trafficking does not imply any agreement: the illegal migrant is exploited, in his condition of irregularity, by coercive, violent and blackmailing means.

The regulation of the facilitation of illegal immigration in art. 12 T.U. imm. is articulated and is the result of many legislative changes aimed at strengthening against any form of conduct intended at facilitating not only the entry, but also the illegal permanence of migrants in the State.[3]

In the current provision, the first paragraph of art. 12 T.U. imm., punishes, with imprisonment from one to five years,[4] the conduct of those who "promote, direct, organize, finance, transport foreigners into the territory of the State, or perform other acts aimed at obtaining the illegal entry into the territory of the State". As can be read in the accompanying report to the article, the main objective that was intended to be pursued was to "enhance the action to fight illegal immigration by means of more stringent and articulated penalties both on the administrative and criminal side".[5]

The rules of art. 12 T.U. imm. have undergone many legislative changes, most recently in 2017.[6] Specifically, the rule was first amended by law No. 189/2002 (called the "Bossi-Fini law") which replaced the original expression: "activities aimed at facilitating the entry" with the current one "acts aimed at causing", trying to make the rule more compliant with the principle of offensività.[7] This change, which is not merely lexical, has led to important effects on the substantive level, strengthening, according to some, the theory of the not necessarily commissive nature of the case and confirming its nature of delitto di attentato.[8] Therefore, having preferred the term "acts" has allowed the extension of criminal relevance also to conduct with omissive nature, thus making the case structurally homogeneous to the attempt (Forlenza, 2003, contra Caputo 2004[9]).

---

[3] Art.12, paragraph 5 T.U. imm. punishes the conduct of those who "in order to gain an unfair profit from the conditions of illegality of the foreigner (…) favors the permanence of this subject in the territory of the state".

[4] In addition to imprisonment, a fine of 15,000 euros is added for each person whose entry is facilitated.

[5] Government bill, No. 3240 on "Regulation of immigration and rules on the condition of the foreigner".

[6] The law No. 46/2017 introduces paragraph 9 which governs the procedures for managing and monitoring administrative procedures for entry in the State.

[7] Principle under Italian law requiring an offense to have been committed against a protected legal asset.

[8] Delitti di attentato is a type of crime in the Italian law and implies that the fulfillment of suitable and unequivocal acts aimed at the realization of the event constitutes, according to the preferable opinion, already consummation of the crime.

[9] According to Caputo the change was limited to reinforcing the nature of crime that is not necessarily multi-existent, given that also the original formulation of art. 12 T.U. conferred criminal relevance to atypical contributions of participation in the activity of facilitation.

With the Bossi-Fini law, the legislator has also replaced the purpose of "facilitating" the illegal entry of the foreigner with the more incisive purpose of "causing" this entry. Even this change has a notable innovative potential: the verb "cause" refers to the necessary existence of a causal link between the trafficker's conduct and illegal entry into the State, with the effect of shifting the punishment threshold to fulfillment of acts suitable for illegal entry (Gizzi 2003). [10] According to some decisions of the case law of the Court of Cassation, the replacement of the verb "facilitate" with "cause" has determined and reduced the scope of application of the law. Since the term "cause" has a more circumscribed scope of application compared to the one that can be hypothesized in relation to the notion of "facilitate", it is claimed that through the new rule a significant number of conducts that were punishable [11] have been subtracted from the criminal area, that is those consisting of the simple facilitation, but not those providing illegal entry of the immigrant.

As for the legal nature of the facilitation of illegal immigration, the offense falls into the category of delitti di attentato and, specifically, that of the case of strict liability for whose perpetration is sufficient the requirement of unambiguousness. However, the prevailing orientation interprets the rule requiring both the requirement of unambiguousness, as well as that of suitability [12] (Gallo 1966), in order to avoid an excessive anticipation of criminal protection and an unjustified extension of the area of criminal law also to acts that are merely preparatory (Grasso 1986 [13]). Such an approach has been suggested also by the jurisprudence of the Court of Cassation, according to which "in order to complete the crime of facilitation of illegal entry it is sufficient to carry out activities aimed at favoring the entry of foreigners into Italy in violation of the law, subject to the necessity, implicit in all the cases of the so-called 'delitti di attentato' or 'with strict liability', of the suitability of the activity carried out with respect to the end". [14]

---

[10] Reference is also made to the judgment of the Cassation, of 29 February 2012, which states that "the ratio legis of this substitution can be easily identified with the intention to avoid, after the significant worsening of the sanctions introduced by the new provisions, interpretations of application that extended the penal rule even to cases of little importance on the concrete level of the negative value and the offense to the interest protected by the rule".

[11] See Judgement of the Cassation, of 29 February 2012, according to which if the conduct of the agent has been limited only to facilitate and not to cause, the same must be absolved, since the "fact is no longer a crime".

[12] The inclusion of the suitability among the constituent elements of the crimes of the attack determines the structural identity of the delitti di attentato.

[13] Quoting the words of Grasso, "the threshold of the punishment is retreated to the fulfillment of a fact directed to the realization of the indicated result, without the actual verification of it to be necessary".

[14] Judgement of the Cassation, of 8 May 2002. In jurisprudence, for example, it was considered that the activities managing the transport are included in this case, even if the journey is interrupted before entering the limit of national waters, and the provision of accommodation for the future illegal stay of immigrants in the State. On the other hand, see Court of Genoa, Judgment of 31 January 2003,

As a strict liability crime, therefore, it is sufficient for the immigrant trafficker to conduct immigrants in international waters, regardless of whether they reach the coast or not. According to a part of the legal literature, moreover, the crime of facilitation of illegal immigration is a crime with concrete danger, and it takes place if concretely suitable and unequivocally directed acts are performed to facilitate the illegal entry of the immigrant, regardless of the actual occurrence of the latter (Grasso 1966; Lanza 2011).

In legal literature and in jurisprudence, the identification of the legal asset protected by art. 12 T.U. imm. is controversial: in respect of a theory that indicates the management and control of migratory flows, as a legal asset that is aimed to the protection of the final asset of public order, a different opinion that contrasts it and gives to this case a pluri-offensive nature, as it is aimed at protecting not only public order, but also of the security and dignity of migrants (Caputo 2006). According to the latter approach, therefore, not only the public protection of public order and security is being detected, but also that of the personal interests of migrants. This reconstruction would confirm the provision contained in the Protocol of Palermo for the fight against the trafficking of migrants, based on which no relevance must be attributed to the consent given by the irregular migrant to his exploitation.

Equally discussed is the identification of possible authors of the conduct of facilitation of illegal entry. This is a question connected with the role to be attributed, on the one hand, to the traffickers, often themselves irregular migrants, and on the other, to the subjects who deal with the rescue in international waters of the immigrants who are victims of trafficking. In relation to the first profile, according to the jurisprudence, "the literal and logical interpretation of the rule concerns the punishment even of those who are illegal immigrants and perform acts aimed at encouraging illegal immigration". [15] This theory is not unanimously supported. The debatable nature of the jurisprudential approach, firstly, was supported by referring to the Protocol of the UN Convention against Transnational Crime, according to which migrants cannot be authors because they themselves are the subject of trafficking in migrants. Also, the risk related to the extensive theory of self-facilitation advocated by the jurisprudence produces an unjustified enlargement of the criminally relevant conduct that can consequently cause problems of systematic coordination with other incriminating cases provided for by the Consolidated Law, such as the offense of illegal entry and stay in the State. [16]

---

in which it was considered that there is no crime, due to lack of unambiguousness, in relation to the recruitment activity, in a non-EU country, of persons to be exploited in the work, after illegal entry into the State.

[15] Verbatim, Court of Cassation, judgement of 28 November 2002.

[16] Refer to Court of Cassation, judgment No. 23872/2010, which states that "the offense is characterized by the necessary requirement of detached status of the agent with respect to the immigrant or to immigrants and it must be excluded that it may concern 'self-facilitation'. The fact that the conduct (...) should be typified as a different and further activity compared to that carried out by those who enter illegally (...) derives directly from interpretation in accordance with international instruments".

As for the role to be attributed to rescuers at sea, referring to the following paragraph we anticipate that there are judgments in the jurisprudence that qualify such subjects as "intermediary authors" who contribute to the realization of the crime. In this regard, it is noted that the use of the theory of the intermediary author constitutes an expedient to consider the Italian jurisdiction subsistent with respect to conduct that is carried out in international waters.

With the reform implemented by law No. 94/2009, [17] the legislator once again changed the crime of facilitation of illegal immigration, by introducing a specific reference to the conduct of promotion, management, organization, financing for the transport of illegal migrants.

The specification of the different conducts included in the legislative reform of 2009 is justified more by the need to satisfy a requirement of greater incisiveness of the rule rather than by the need for greater specificity of the case. [18] The rule takes into consideration the activities of promotion, management, organization, financing and carrying out of the transportation of foreigners in the State: these types of conduct evoke the associative crimes. A consequence is to believe that the legislator affirmed the necessary existence of a structure for the existence of the crime of facilitation. This consideration cannot be founded: the types of conduct described, indeed, are autonomous and do not depend on the existence of an associative structure, since they are able to realize, more simply, a hypothesis of participation of persons in the crime.

At the beginning of this examination we mentioned the means-to-an-end relationship which, sometimes, is found between the facilitation of illegal immigration and the crime of trafficking in persons. According to estimates by international organizations, the victims of trafficking exceed two and a half millions (mainly women and children). It is an activity that generates large profits for organized crime groups, for both small associations or large criminal "empires". Basically, the former is dedicated to the mere illegal transport of people from one country to another; the latter directly exploits the trafficked persons and controls their employment in various activities, profiting on their suffering. Indeed, it is noted that the more the criminal groups are branched into the territory of the destination country of trafficked immigrants, the greater the possibility that the immigrants, once they arrive in the destination country, are subject to the same organization of exploitation in various illegal activities.

A large part of the illegal migration flows, therefore, are organized and guided by transnational criminal organizations that manage this activity through the collaboration of other organizations. Indeed, surveys in recent years have shown that, in general, the promoters and "bridgeheads" of smuggling of migrants tend to be foreigners already resident in the national territory for various reasons, or temporarily detained in an

---

[17] Law of 15 July 2009 No. 94, called "*Primo Pacchetto Sicurezza*".

[18] The scope of the clarification, however, should not be overestimated: although it has the merit of explicitly extending the criminal relevance to the forms of illegal facilitation organized, it does not introduce new elements since such conducts have been considered previously subsumable in the notion of "acts directed to facilitate illegal entry into the state".

Identification and Deportation Centre that exploit their presence within national borders to facilitate the exploiters' criminal activity.

In general, the regulatory actions of the European Union and of the United Nations concerning the fight against the facilitation of migrants and the trafficking in persons have been oriented in two directions. On the one hand, that of defining the conduct of "facilitation" and "trafficking in persons" in a complete manner; on the other hand, that of trying to harmonize the different legislations of the Member States by providing suitable instruments for investigative and judicial cooperation. The Protocol of the Palermo Convention is based on the formulation of the first international definition of trafficking in persons "such as recruitment, transportation, transfer, harbouring or receipt of people, by means of threat or use of force or other forms of coercion, kidnapping, fraud, deception, abuse of power or of a position of vulnerability or by giving or receiving sums of money or benefits in order to obtain the consent of a person who has authority over another for the purpose of exploitation". This is a non-exhaustive list which does not exclude other forms of exploitation, such as begging. The Protocol of the Palermo Convention requires States to introduce criminal provisions aimed at criminalizing the conduct described in the definition of trafficking in persons. This is a particularly extensive criminalization obligation that requires the attribution of criminal relevance to the mere attempt of trafficking in persons, as well as to any form of participation in trafficking and any conduct that aims to exploit immigrant victims.

In the Italian criminal system, through the law No. 228/2003, the legislator wanted to implement the Framework Decision 2002/629/JHA, reformulating the provisions of articles 600, 601 and 602 of the Italian Criminal Code. The reform wanted, "to strengthen the action to combat the trafficking in persons and the enslavement of illegal migrants, on the assumption that the instruments of the old Rocco Code were now inadequate to contrast these new criminal offenses in their occurring and incomprehensible in an exclusively national repressive perspective". However, the legislator, instead of creating a single rule capable of attributing criminal relevance by itself to the conduct of "trafficking in persons", has preferred to articulate the incriminating conducts in the different hypotheses of reduction to or maintenance in a state of slavery or bondage of the trafficking in persons and of the sale of slaves, all sanctioned with the same maximum and minimum penalty limit.

As for the relationship that can be established between trafficking in persons and art. 12 T.U. imm., the prevailing orientation maintains that there can be involvement because they are cases that protect different legal assets, the former protecting freedom and personal dignity (Peccioli 2005; contra Resta 2008 [19]), while the latter the internal security. Another theory, however, amounts to the relationship between the two rules in terms of incompatibility: art. 601 of the Italian Criminal Code in fact implies the

---

[19] According to the author, the involvement between the two crimes is not admissible due to the presence in art. 12 T.U. imm. of the subsidiarity clause "unless the fact constitutes a more serious offense".

constriction and the induction by means of deceit of the trafficked subject, elements that are not necessary for the existence of the crime of facilitation. Therefore, it is stated that, given the difference between the two crimes essentially by the different condition of the trafficked person and his relationship with the agent, the two cases are in a relationship of incompatibility (Pavarani 2006).

11.2. *The extension of the Italian jurisdiction to facilitation of illegal immigration*

As anticipated, in the application of the facilitation of illegal immigration, one of the issues most debated in legal literature and jurisprudence concerns the prevalence of the Italian jurisdiction if the illegal migrant's entry into the State occurs because of intervention of rescuers at sea in international waters, interrupting the traffickers' transport activity.

The sadly known case is that of the "traffickers" who, starting from the African coast, transport migrants to Italy on boats that do not allow safe arrival [20]; the traffickers of migrants prefer to make use of real fleets of small ships and boats that make necessary the intervention in support of the "mother ship" in carrying out the embarkation operations from the State of departure and disembarkation on the coast of the country of arrival. Generally, the mother ship flies the flag of none of the States or, in any case, a State flag different from that of the State of the future landing of migrants. A request for assistance is sent by the mother ship to the authorities of the State of destination which, in accordance with the principles of international law and the protection of the rights of the survivors, intervene when the mother ship is still in international waters to rescue the migrants off the Italian coast. Therefore, the rescue on the high seas of the port State control authorities constitutes, in the strategy of the criminal organizations that manage the trafficking in human beings, an indispensable contribution to carry out their criminal project. So this modus operandi gives rise to important issues in terms of prevention and the fight against migrant smuggling. [21] In particular, a question arose about the responsibility of rescuers at sea as accomplices in the crimes of facilitation of illegal immigration and the prevalence of the Italian jurisdiction (Reverso 2011).

In this regard, one theory maintains that, since the rescue of ships flying the Italian flag has occurred in international waters, the crime cannot be considered perpetrated,

---

[20] In this regard, Judge for Preliminary Hearings of Trapani, judgement of 9 November 2016, stated that "it is a fact of experience that the arrival in Europe because of international rescue operations is the expected and wanted outcome of 'hope trips' organized for profit, by unscrupulous subjects and faced by migrants who risk losing their life".

[21] See the Operative Proposals of the National Anti-Mafia Directorate for the solution of the problems of national criminal jurisdiction of the criminal association dedicated to the facilitation of illegal immigration.

even partially, in the national territory with the consequence of excluding the prevalence of Italian jurisdiction.

A different part of the legal literature and jurisprudence, however, believes that the Italian jurisdiction prevails also in relation to the conducts of traffickers carried out in international waters on the basis of art. 111 of the Montego Bay Convention, according to which "the pursuit of a foreign ship is allowed when the authorities of the coastal State have reasonable grounds to believe that it has violated the laws and regulations of the State itself".[22] These reasons can certainly be identified in the facilitation of illegal immigration.

Moreover, the most recent orientation of the jurisprudence affirms the prevalence of the jurisdiction of Italy in cases of rescue in international waters according to art. 6 of Italian Criminal Code,[23] according to which the Italian criminal law applies to crimes committed even partially in the territory of the State.

As evidenced by the Court of Cassation, the intervention of rescuers cannot be considered an action that interrupts the conduct of facilitation. It must be noted that the rescue, in fact, "cannot be considered only" with respect to the action of abandonment at sea of migrants, but "is linked to a direct casual derivation".[24] Specifically, according to the Court of Cassation, the smugglers view the rescue operation in extra-territorial waters, undertaken according to international rules on the law of the sea (in particular, the Hamburg Convention of 1979, the London Convention of 1974 and Article 98 of the Montego Bay Convention) as a forseen and intended fact to achieve the result of the landing and thus guarantee impunity. Therefore, even if the last part of the criminal action is enacted by rescuers, the same however is in continuity with that of the smugglers without interruption, giving rise to a single conduct of facilitation of the illegal entry into the Italian territory. In this way, the jurisprudence comes to believe that "the conduct of traffickers cannot be assessed in its unitality without fragmentations and must be considered aimed at a result that is achieved by the provocation and exploitation of the state of necessity".[25]

Indeed, according to the jurisprudence of the Court of Cassation, rescuers at sea are involved as intermediary authors[26] of the offense of facilitation of illegal entry, even

---

[22] Articles 110 and 111 of the Montego Bay Convention are sometimes considered limits to the possibility of recognizing Italian jurisdiction to illegal conduct committed in international waters.

[23] Art. 6 of Italian Criminal Code establishes that "anyone who commits a crime in the territory of the state is punished according to Italian law. The offense is considered committed in the territory of the State, when the action or omission, which constitutes it, has occurred there fully or in part".

[24] Court of Cassation, judgement No. 14510/2014.

[25] Court of Cassation, judgement No. 3345/2015 according to which "the last part of the conduct is nothing but an essential and planned piece of a concatenation of acts that can not be interrupted or broken".

[26] Court of Cassation, judgement No. 3345/2015. The theory of the intermediary author has been elaborated in the German law to punish the hypotheses not referable to the typical forms of involvement provided by the German code. With the expression of "intermediary author" reference is made to the subject who commits a crime exploiting the action of an innocent performer.

if they are not punishable as their conduct is marked by the "status of necessity caused and exploited by traffickers". [27] The responsibility of facilitation, therefore, "must in any case be, pursuant to Articles 54 and 111 of the Criminal Code, of those that have determined said situation and said intervention". [28]

Moreover, some have observed that the use of the theory of the intermediary author displaces the crime perpetration at the moment of entry into the State and the transformation of the case from a crime of conduct into one of event, the latter identified precisely in the crossing of the borders (Trapasso 2017). However, as already noted, the rule is constructed as a strict liability crime (considering sufficient the performance of preparatory actions aimed at obtaining entry into the State) and not as a crime of event. Furthermore, it has been observed that the reference to art. 54, paragraph 3 of the Italian Criminal Code is criticizable, as the last provision is based on the absence of a rescue obligation, instead, expressly regulated by numerous international conventions in relation to the rescue at sea of people who are in a dangerous situation. According to these authors, the existence of such obligation makes the conduct of the rescuers not punishable pursuant to art. 51 of the Italian Criminal Code (Trapasso 2017): rescue at sea constitutes, in fact, the fulfillment of the duty imposed by various legal regulations – including art. 98 of the Montego Bay Convention (Scovazzi 2016) – so that "the assessment of the necessity of the rescue is entrusted not to the initiative of the active subject, but by making an assessment in terms of obligation" (Trapasso 2017). [29] Furthermore, it is noted that the typical content of the conduct of rescue appears to be linked to art. 51 of the Criminal Code and not to art. 54 of the Criminal Code: in this second case, in fact, the content of the conduct is not predetermined (as in the case of the fulfillment of a duty), but is left "to the determination of who exercises the compulsion"(Trapasso 2017).

Recently, the Court of Cassation also confirmed the theory of the prevalence of Italian jurisdiction in relation to the conducts of facilitation of illegal immigration that have been interrupted by the intervention of rescue in international waters "since parts of the actions that constitute the offense are committed in Italy, both directly and through the interposition of the subjects that have to give assistance and that have determined said intervention". [30] Therefore, a theory is becoming consolidated in jurisprudence which recognizes the prevalence of Italian jurisdiction pursuant to art. 6 of the Criminal Code in the cases of rescue in international waters of vessels also

---

[27] See Court of Cassation, judgement No. 14510/2014, Court of Cassation, judgement No. 18354/2014, Court of Cassation, judgement No. 36052/2014, and the Court of Catania, judgement of 4 May 2015.

[28] Verbatim, Court of Cassation, judgement No. 17625/2016.

[29] According to the author, "the reference to art. 51 of Criminal Code can only be applied to the event in which the definition of the content of the obligation is entrusted to a person who is determined by it for the commission of a crime".

[30] Court of Cassation, judgement No. 25613/2016; similarly, Court of Cassation, judgement No. 17625/2016.

without flag (and, therefore, not belonging to any State) considering that part of the conduct was carried out in Italy both directly and through the intervention of subjects who have aided migrants. If this extensive interpretation of art. 6 of the Italian Criminal Code, on the one hand, has allowed and allows the repression of a serious phenomenon such as the facilitation of illegal immigration (often instrumental to phenomena as serious as that of trafficking in persons), avoiding the risk that human traffickers would remain unpunished, on the other hand, requires a reflection on the need to provide for new provisions that allow effective repression of the smuggling of migrants and that, above all, involve all European States.

Finally, the recent orientation of the Court of Cassation tends to extend the Italian jurisdiction, recognized about the crime of art. 12 T.U. imm. also to "all crimes committed at the same time, by virtue of their close connection with that of facilitation of illegal immigration which is considered committed in Italy, even though the intervention of rescuers".[31] In fact, the conducts of criminal organizations and immigrant traffickers, in consideration of the treatment of the latter, could integrate the crimes of beatings, personal injuries and kidnapping, and in the most tragic – and unfortunately, frequent – cases, of negligent shipwreck or homicide. However, the theory that recognizes Italian jurisdiction also in relation to crimes committed in international waters on the occasion or in connection with the offense of facilitation can be criticized for constituting, on the one hand, an unacceptable derogation to the principle of territoriality – extending the Italian jurisdiction outside the territory of the State – and, on the other, for not taking into account the existence of specific rules (Articles 7 to 10 of the Criminal Code) that provide alternative criteria for the attribution of Italian jurisdiction. Precisely the application of such alternative criteria would prevent the establishment of a lack of protection in relation to crimes, even those that are serious and damaging to the life and physical safety of migrants, committed on the occasion or relating to the facilitation, without having to resort to art. 6 of the Criminal Code.[32]

Furthermore, the theory of the recognition of the Italian jurisdiction of the crimes committed on the conduct of facilitation on the analogical application of Articles 1135 and 1136 of the Navigation Code which, pursuant to art. 12 of the Italian Criminal Procedure Code, gives the Italian court jurisdiction over crimes related to piracy, as it is an exceptional discipline.

Considering the positions taken by the Italian jurisprudence it is important to question the effectiveness of the rules governing the management of migratory flows, and, above all, the protection of victims of trafficking in human beings. These are issues that involve the formulation of the rule regarding the facilitation of illegal immigration, which should be reformed in the respect of an extension of the scope of application and of a broader protection of the life and physical safety of migrants.

---

[31] See Court of Cassation, judgement No. 3345/2015 and judgement No. 25613/2016.

[32] Specifically, for crimes committed outside the States by foreigners and to the detriment of foreigners, the prevalence of the Italian jurisdiction is submitted to the evaluation of opportunity of the Minister of Justice.

Bibliography

Caputo, A. (2004) 'I delitti di favoreggiamento delle migrazioni illegali', *Diritto e Formazione*, 4(1): 56–65.

Forlenza, O. (2003) 'Per configurare il reato di favoreggiamento non è necessaria la violenza fisica o psichica', *Guida al Diritto*, 7: 80.

Gallo, E. (1966) *Il delitto di attentato nella teoria generale del reato*, Milan: Giuffrè.

Gizzi, L. (2003) 'Sulla natura giuridica del delitto di agevolazione dell'immigrazione clandestina', *Giurisprudenza italiana*, 5: 1012 ss.

Grasso, G. (1986) 'L'anticipazione della tutela penale: i reati di pericolo e i reati di attentato', *Rivista italiana di diritto e procedura penale*, 2: 707.

Lanza, E. (2011), Diritto penale degli stranieri, Padua: Cedam.

Pavarani, C. (2006) 'sub. Art. 601' in A. Cadoppi (ed.) *Commentario delle norme contro la violenza sessuale e contro la pedofilia*, Padua: Cedam.

Peccioli, A. (2005) *Unione europea e criminalità transnazionale*, Turin: Giappichelli.

Peccioli, A. (2009) *Il favoreggiamento dell'immigrazione clandestina nella giurisprudenza e la riforma del 2009*, in Diritto Penale e Processo, 1s.

Resta, F. (2008) *Vecchie e nuove schiavitù*, Milan: Giuffrè.

Reverso (2011) 'Osservazioni sull'istituzione della zona contigua', *Rivista del diritto della navigazione*, 2: 596–600.

Scovazzi, T. (2016) 'Il respingimento di un dramma umano collettivo e le sue conseguenze', in T. Scovazzi (ed.) *L'immigrazione irregolare via mare nella giurisprudenza italiana e nell'esperienza europea*, Turin: Giappichelli.

Trapasso, M.T. (2017) 'Il richiamo giurisprudenziale all'"autoria mediata" in materia di favoreggiamento dell'immigrazione clandestina: tra necessità e opportunità', *Archivio penale*, 2: 583–602.

Chapter 12

Unaccompanied children in the EU

Towards a higher standard of protection and support for "Children on the Move" – unaccompanied minors-immigrants in the EU

Katarzyna Gromek-Broc

12.1. *Structural inconsistencies in a fragmented legal framework*

At the EU level, the issue of unaccompanied children was initially considered sporadically, mainly in relation to free movement of workers with reference to family reunification, but only with the creation of the Common European Asylum System, it has become, an increasingly relevant problem (Stalford and Drywood 2009).

Unaccompanied minors were defined in a Council Resolution in 1997 as "third country nationals or stateless persons below the age of eighteen, who arrive at the territory of the Member States unaccompanied by an adult responsible for them". [1] Other definitions coexist but all have three elements in common: the children are third country nationals, they are underage, and they are not accompanied. Hence, there are a number of difficulties from the EU Law perspective; they are third country nationals (Zschirnt 2011), generally outside of the scope of application of the Treaty; for whom the EU has some but not clearly discernible responsibility. Given its primarily economic objectives the EU has neglected children's interests since its origins, and although something in the policies has changed, it did not sufficiently inform legislation within the CEAS system. On one hand, the initiatives to protect children multiply and legislation is increasingly centred on children, following the 2011 Commission's Agenda on the Rights of the Child [2] – there are many recent directives to oppose trafficking, child pornography, cyber crimes. On the other hand, there are few steps on the issues of children coming from outside the EU. Thus, unaccompanied minors fall in "a grey zone" where the legal framework becomes weak, stepping in a politically

---

[1] Council Resolution of 26 June 1997 on unaccompanied minors who are nationals of third countries (97/C 221/03), 19.7.97 EN, Official Journal of the European Communities No C 221 /23.

[2] 'An EU Agenda for the Rights of the Child', Brussels, 15.2.2011 COM(2011) 60 final, http://eur-lex.europa.eu/legal-content/EN/TXT/PDF/?uri=CELEX:52011DC0060&from=EN (accessed on March 1st, 2018).

sensitive domain of immigration and asylum laws. Flowing from this artificial division between child EU nationals and child asylum seekers, the efforts to make children's interests paramount have been uneven. As a result, we are confronted with a double standard, despite the EU's constant commitment and reaffirmation that "all children must benefit from the same rights as children without discrimination".[3]

12.2. *Unaccompanied minors in the CEAS system*

The CEAS in operation has brought to the fore a series of backdrops in the procedure and its implementation that in fact were detrimental to children. Age assessment is one of the best-known flaws in the system. A very recent UK case, R (on the application of AA (Sudan)) v Secretary of the State,[4] again demonstrates disproportionate and heavy handling of a child by the UK Authorities. An unaccompanied minor, but in appearance an adult, was detained despite the age assessment procedure. Yet, the Commission Action Plan 2010–14[5] states clearly that "a presumed child should be considered as a child". However, this time a High Court Judge, Silber, held "that the claimant had been unlawfully detained for an identified period and ordered the Secretary of State to pay damages caused by the wrongful detention".[6] There is a vast array of procedures in Europe, and some are very invasive and often unreliable. Dorling suggests that the most consistent approach towards age assessment is provided by specialist centres, where the staff are appropriately trained to conduct age assessment in coordination with social workers and paediatricians (Dorling 2008). A 2017 Council of Europe report on age assessment recommends a series of precautions while assessing the child's age (Wenke 2017), "including the presumption of a minor age, care and protection prior to and during age assessment, age assessment methods should be child-sensitive and adapted to gender and cultural sensitivities, age assessment should not take place without the child's and their guardian's informed consent. [...] Age assessment interviews should uphold the dignity of the child. Physical and medical examinations

---

[3] 'Save the Children, Briefing Note on the Stockholm Programme', Brussels 2009, https://www.savethechildren.net/sites/default/files/libraries/Briefing_Document_Stockholm_Programme_FINAL_2.pdf (accessed on February 25th, 2018).

[4] *UK – R (on the application of AA (Sudan)) v Secretary of State for the Home Department*, 9 March 2017, http://www.asylumlawdatabase.eu/en/case-law-search?f[0]=field_keywords%3A88 (accessed on 4th February 2018).

[5] 'Communication from the Commission to the European Parliament and the Council – Action Plan on Unaccompanied Minors 2010 – 2014 (6/5/2010 – COM (2010) 213 final)', https://ec.europa.eu/anti-trafficking/eu-policy/action-plan-unaccompanied-minors-2010-2014_en (accessed on February 5th, 2018).

[6] *UK – R (on the application of AA (Sudan)) v Secretary of State for the Home Department*, 9 March 2017, http://www.asylumlawdatabase.eu/en/case-law-search?f[0]=field_keywords%3A88 (accessed on February 4th, 2018).

should be measures of last resort" (ibidem). The EU SCEP position paper showed that[7] Europe is lacking a "common approach" on age assessment, that rights and procedural safeguards are not upheld consistently, the practice of age assessment is not monitored, and the quality of standards is often questioned. Some methods are too invasive and are detrimental to the child's physical and mental health. The results are often unreliable. What then is the relevance of age for the investigations?[8] In many cases the outcome brings nothing or very little to the handling of the case.[9] The new Italian law could be quoted here as an example for the rest of Europe, providing that "a social and medical age assessment procedure may be ordered by the judicial authority, when there are well-founded doubts about the age declared by a presumed unaccompanied minor and it is impossible to establish his or her age through documentary evidence."[10]

Another noteworthy concern is that unaccompanied minors are exposed to a risk of exploitation and trafficking. A UNICEF and IOM report, based upon interviews with 22,000 migrants and refugees, including 11,000 children (aged 14–17) and youths (aged 18–24) who came to Europe through the Mediterranean routes in 2016 and 2017 (UNICEF and IOM 2017), revealed that children and young adults under the age of 25 are subjected to abuse, trafficking and sexual exploitation. Among those coming through the Central Mediterranean route, 78 percent of the children and 77 percent of the young adults have reported abuse, exploitation and/or trafficking, compared to 69 percent of the individuals aged 25 or over."[11] Often they take clandestine, undetected routes where it is almost impossible to intervene. Yet, the problem needs to be taken seriously in the reception centres and transit zones, and the existing rules on monitoring and supervision should be toughened. Moreover, there are many viable proposals on awareness-raising in the form of templates and booklets that should

[7] 'Position Paper on Age Assessment in the Context of Separated Children in Europe 2012', http://www.scepnetwork.org/images/16/163.pdf (accessed on February 20th, 2018).

[8] 'UNHCR Guidelines on Child Asylum Claims', 2009, par. 7 and 75. Lansdown, Gerison, *The Evolving Capacities of the Child, Innocenti Insight*, United Nations Children's Fund Innocenti Research Centre, Save the Children Sweden, 2005, p. 49; United Nations Children's Fund, 'Age Assessment Practices: A Literature Review and Annotated Bibliography', 2011, pp. 7, 9. 'Separated Children in Europe Programme, Position Paper on Age Assessment in the Context of Separated Children inEurope', 2012, p. 6. Also quoted in the Position Paper, 2017 COE Report. http://www.separated-children-europe-programme.org/p/1/229/council-of-europe-publishes-report-on-age-assessment (accessed on February 20th, 2018).

[9] 'Separated Children in Europe Programme, Position Paper on Age Assessment in the Context of Separated Children in Europe', 2012, http://www.separated-children-europe-programme.org/p/1/229/council-of-europe-publishes-report-on-age-assessment (accessed on February 20th, 2018).

[10] Italian Law 47/17; Rozzi Elena, 'The New Italian Law on Unaccompanied Minors: A Model for the EU?', http://eumigrationlawblog.eu/the-new-italian-law-on-unaccompanied-minors-a-model-for-the-eu/ (accessed on February 15th, 2018).

[11] http://www.separated-children-europe-programme.org/p/1/228/unicef-and-iom-publish-report-on-children-and-youth-on-the-move-at-risk-of-trafficking-and-exploitation (accessed on February 18th, 2018).

rigorously be delivered to children in all centres. The tighter rules on the appointment of the guardian in the 2016 proposal ensure more information, clarification delivered in child friendly language, as well as more vigilance to detect if a child was targeted as to exploitation or trafficking. More importantly, the time in the reception centres should be reduced to a minimum, with some other solutions to accommodate children, such as the use of family-based care/foster care, seen as preferable. [12] The EU Commission also proposes "closely supervised open reception centres designed to ensure the protection of children, or small-scale independent living arrangements for older children." [13]

The third identified problem is the detention of children. However, the SCEP advocates that despite legislative efforts children are still frequently detained, referring to "the increasing reliance upon the immigration detention even it is not essential." [14] The European Committee on Legal Co-operation has reaffirmed that immigration detention is never acceptable for those who are in situations of vulnerability, such as children. This includes matters related to their immigration status or illegal entry, but also "temporary or otherwise, detention at the border or in international zones, in detention centres, in police cells, in prisons or in any other special detention centres for young people." [15] An alarming number of unaccompanied children have been detained in Greece in police cells, detention centres called "protective custody", where "unaccompanied children are often detained in overcrowded and unsanitary conditions", and placed in small cells with adults of no relation to them where they have little access to information and basic care services. "The camps in Athens dispose of two Safe Zones of 24 shelters providing 600 places for unaccompanied children. The Safe Zones offer poor conditions where the safety of the children is in stake." [16] Many unaccompanied children are under the protective custody of the police, meaning that in the absence of an alternative they are detained in cells (Defence for Children 2017). The detention

---

[12] 'UNHCR Global Strategy: Beyond Detention 2014–19, Option Paper 2, Options for Governments on Open Reception and Alternatives to Detention', http://www.unhcr.org/protection/detention/5538e53d9/unhcr-options-paper-2-options-governments-open-reception-alternatives-detention.html (accessed on February 20th, 2018).

[13] Communication from the Commission to European Parliament and the Council, 'The Protection of Children in Migration', Brussels, 12.4.2017 COM(2017) 211 final, https://ec.europa.eu/home-affairs/sites/homeaffairs/files/what-we-do/policies/european-agenda-migration/20170412_communication_on_the_protection_of_children_in_migration_en.pdf (accessed on February 20th, 2018).

[14] A Fundamentally Different Approach is Needed, Joint Statement to the European Committee on Legal Cooperation on the Council of Europe on the Codification of European Rules for the Conditions of Administrative Detention of Migrants, https://idcoalition.org/wp-content/uploads/2017/06/Joint-Statement_COE-administrative-detention-of-migrants_FINAL-1-1.pdf, (accessed on March 1st, 2018).

[15] http://www.scepnetwork.org/p/1/222/scep-signs-joint-statement-on-immigration-detention (accessed on March 1st, 2018).

[16] Montero Alfonso, 'Thousands of unaccompanied children in Greek island camps need help', *The Guardian*, 25 October 2017, https://www.theguardian.com/social-care-network/2017/oct/25/thousands-unaccompanied-children-greek-island-camps-need-help (accessed on February 10th, 2018).

of children could be improved by a functional relocation mechanism, but again the Member States do not always want to cooperate.

In April 2017 "all 568 unaccompanied minors have been registered for relocation and 341 have been relocated [...] mainly by Finland (130 relocated). Member States with large allocations do not accept unaccompanied minors (e.g. France), or only a few (e.g., Belgium or Spain) or impose requirements regarding family links in the Member State of relocation [...] leaving some separated minors and their relatives in a legal limbo, being rejected both under the Dublin Regulation and under the relocation procedure (e.g., Germany)." [17]

A subsequent hurdle unaccompanied children are facing, are hotspots and the transit zones. The 2016 report on hotspots in Italy brought to light the use of coercive methods and physical force, and prolonged detention in case of persons refusing to be fingerprinted. Unaccompanied minors are placed in hotspots although "Italian Law prohibits it, detention is frequent and there is no access to effective remedy against such a decision". [18]

The SCEP recommends the codification of EU rules on the conditions of detention of immigrants, which would provide greater transparency, greater fairness and equal treatment. Any decision in relation to detention of minors should be based on an individual assessment. [19] If the child is, however, detained, a system of thorough monitoring and supervision should be in operation. [20] The current Commission's Proposal on detention of children maintains the status quo, allowing children's detention as a last resort. It is regrettable that the detention of children has not been completely outlawed. [21]

The "hotspot" approach introduced in 2015 provided an immediate solution to the mass influx of asylum seekers into Italy and Greece. [22] The hotspots played a positive role in the procedural tasks, but the reception conditions did not meet the necessary standard. [23] At the end of 2016 the reception facilities were extremely poor: "unaccompanied children [were] living in squalid conditions with poor infrastructure lacking of basic services and being exposed to exploitation". [24] Children in hotspots were

---

[17] 'Eleventh Report on Relocation and Resettlement', https://ec.europa.eu/home-affairs/sites/homeaffairs/files/what-we-do/policies/european-agenda-migration/20170412_eleventh_report_on_relocation_and__resettlement_en.pdf (accessed on February 1st, 2018).

[18] 'The Implementing of the Hotspots in Italy and Greece', https://www.ecre.org/wp-content/uploads/2016/12/HOTSPOTS-Report-5.12.2016.pdf (accessed on February 15th, 2018).

[19] *Ibidem.*

[20] *Ibidem.*

[21] *Ibidem.*

[22] Special report no 06/2017: 'EU Response to the Refugee Crisis: The "Hotspot" Approach', https://www.eca.europa.eu/en/Pages/DocItem.aspx?did=41222 (accessed on February 25th, 2018).

[23] *Ibidem.*

[24] *Ibidem.*

"registered, identified and finger printed" but did not receive the treatment due to vulnerable groups, consideration for their young age or dignified accommodation conditions. [25] "As of September 2017, only 32 unaccompanied children had been relocated from Italy and 420 from Greece." [26] In May 2016, "Save the Children" reported 50 cases of unaccompanied children being held alongside adults in Pozzallo for over a month. [27] The children were exposed to crime and violence and did not have access to basic information. In sum, the hotspots approach did not convince the children's rights defenders, and apart from being convenient for administrative purpose, this approach failed to meet the most basic standards. [28]

The situation is also difficult in the transit zones, such as airports, harbours and other border premises. Frontex elaborated a comprehensive handbook (Vega Handbook) for border guards, making some very useful recommendations such as that "border guards have to take care of a child at risk until a trained person arrives", he/she should be interacting with a child, ensure that the child is not hungry, thirsty or has other needs or requires medical assistance; the guard needs to check for injuries. Vega Handbook also suggests the questions that could be asked in the first and second line of control. [29] The initiative is important, but the Vega Handbook concerns only recommendations and cannot replace what the law does not prescribe. Both hotspots and the transit zones are more concerned with formalities, identification assessment, registration, and human rights or a right of the child to socio-psychological well-being come second. In addition, there is certainly a problem with a fluctuating number of unaccompanied children, and in case of a massive influx, the situation gets out of control. Under the Estonian presidency a three-track approach was proposed, establishing a hierarchy between normal circumstances, challenging circumstances, and severe crisis circumstances. [30] This

---

[25] *Ibidem.*

[26] 'Keeping Children at the Centre', https://www.savethechildren.net/sites/default/files/libraries/KEEPING%20CHILDREN%20AT%20THE%20CENTRE%202017_%20DEF_%20LOW_%202__.pdf (accessed on March 1st 2018); http://www.libertaciviliimmigrazione.dlci.interno.gov.it/sites/default/files/allegati/cruscotto_statistico_giornaliero_11_settembre_2017.pdf (accessed on March 1st, 2018); 'Fifteenth Report on Relocation and Resettlement', https://ec.europa.eu/home-affairs/sites/homeaffairs/files/what-we-do/policies/european-agenda-migration/20170906_fifteenth_report_on_relocation_and_resettlement_en.pdf (accessed on March 1st, 2018).

[27] 'Keeping Children at the Centre', https://www.savethechildren.net/sites/default/files/libraries/KEEPING%20CHILDREN%20AT%20THE%20CENTRE%202017_%20DEF_%20LOW_%202__.pdf (accessed on March 1st, 2018).

[28] 'Children in Crisis: Unaccompanied Migrant Children in the EU' at https://publications.parliament.uk/pa/ld201617/ldselect/ldeucom/34/34.pdf (accessed on February 2nd, 2018); also 'EMN Focussed Study 2014, The Use of Detention and Alternatives to Detention in the Context of Immigration Policies', http://emn.ypes.gr/images/docs/EMN_FOCUSED_STUDIES/EMN_STUDIES_2014/12a_greece_emn_national_report_detention_alternatives_en.pdf (accessed on February 15th, 2018).

[29] 'VEGA Handbook: Children at Airports', 2015, http://frontex.europa.eu/assets/Publications/Training/VEGA_Children_Handbook.pdf (accessed on February 10th, 2018).

[30] 'Legislative Train Schedule', http://www.europarl.europa.eu/legislative-train/theme-towards-a-new-policy-on-migration/file-revision-of-the-dublin-regulation (accessed on February 18th, 2018); also 'Migra

strategy envisages different types of measures depending on the gravity of the situation.[31] Such a tailored approach would provide more organised and functional response to crises and unpredictable events.

12.3. *The 2016 Proposal for Reform of the CEAS system regarding unaccompanied minors*

The CEAS legal framework acknowledged from the beginning that unaccompanied children deserved special attention. But a simple acknowledgment was not enough: the system simply failed to make children visible and assist them in a meaningful way.[32]

In May and June 2016 the Commission put forward two packages of proposals for a reform of the CEAS, the biggest revamp of the system since its creation. The proposals intend to amend the Dublin III Regulation, to replace the EASO with the European Union Agency for Asylum, to modify EURODAC and the Reception Conditions Directive, and finally to replace the Procedures and Qualifications Directives with regulations and to adopt a new regulation on resettlement. The shift from the directives to regulations is particularly important for the standardisation of procedure and uniformity of practices across the EU. From the very beginning the system has been very complex, and the provisions on unaccompanied minors have been dispersed in the different texts. Although their basic needs were identified, the texts did not provide any guidance as to how they could be secured.

First, the Temporary Protection Directive (Beirens et al. 2016) identified the need for appropriate representation and accommodation, but the lack of the definition as to what should be considered as such weakened this provision (Zschirnt 2011: 45). The Directive provided the possibility of accommodating an unaccompanied minor with adult relatives, foster families, and in reception centres, but also with a person who "looked after the child while fleeing". This was an important provision, offering to an unaccompanied child some emotional support in case other options were unavailable (ibidem), but the subsequent directives dropped this possibility (ibidem). The

tion; a Common Challenge' at http://www.europarl.europa.eu/news/en/headlines/priorities/20150831TS T91035 (accessed on February 18th, 2018).

[31] 'CEAS Reform: State of Play of Negotiations on the Dublin IV Regulation' at http://www.asylum ineurope.org/news/30-11-2017/ceas-reform-state-play-negotiations-dublin-iv-regulation (accessed on February 20th, 2018).

[32] The system comprises the Procedure Directive, Qualification Directive and Reception Conditions Directive, Dublin III Regulation and EURODAC, two more decisions were added in 2015 on the relocation of asylum seekers from Greece and Italy to other Member States, Council Decision (EU) 2015/1601 of 22 September 2015 establishing provisional measures in the area of international protection for the benefit of Italy and Greece;

Council Decision (EU) 2015/1523 of 14 September 2015 establishing provisional measures in the area of international protection for the benefit of Italy and of Greece; also https://www.ceps.eu/system/files/pe%20583%20132%20en_All%281%29.pdf (accessed on March 1st, 2018).

Temporary Protection Directive also has some incontestable strengths: it envisaged "a solidarity mechanism" upon its activation, i.e. financial solidarity via the AMIF and solidarity in terms of physical reception based on the rule of "double voluntarism". Regrettably, the poor engagement on behalf of the Member States made this provision ineffective (ibidem; Beirens et al. 2016).

The 2003 Reception Conditions Directive lies at the heart of the political and social dilemma regarding unaccompanied children.[33] It set up the basic framework and raised many questions, only partially resolved by subsequent reforms. For example, what competencies should a child guardian have? Once appointed, is the guardian suitable for this particular child? What are the alternatives to detention? Could children be placed with adults if they are 16 years old or over? Article 18.2 of the Directive 2003 provided access to rehabilitation services for minors who have suffered traumatic experiences.[34] Article 19 established a regular assessment of whether a child received an appropriate representation, raising the issue of suitability of a guardian for that particular child or relevance of his/her competence to assist the child in the best possible way. Unfortunately, the methods for evaluating the guardians were absent in the 2003 text, depriving this provision of any meaningful content.

Another weakness of the Directive 2003[35] concerned considerable discretion left to Member States to restrict or withdraw assistance provided. According to Article 16.2 Member States could "refuse reception conditions where an asylum seeker has failed to demonstrate that the asylum claim was made as soon as reasonably practicable after arrival in that Member State".[36] Nonetheless, "Member States shall under all circumstances ensure access to emergency health care". Hence, Member States in practice did apply this provision in a restrictive way. Carrera's report in 2010 showed that the majority of unaccompanied children have had access only to emergency health care, and that access to education was widely limited (Carrera and Merlino 2010).

Smyth noticed that in light of Article 16.4 "minors and unaccompanied minors were not exempted from having their health care under the directive reduced or withdrawn". In fact, this Article has done very little to look after the child's well-being (Smyth 2013: 230). A further point weakly defined in the directive was the right to family unity and family tracing, in practice leading to a lengthy process not sustained by cooperation between the Member States. The Reception Condition Directive (Recast) enhances the standard, making a few important improvements: unaccompanied minors are automatically classed as vulnerable, therefore further identification is not necessary. Article 22(1) imposed an obligation on the Member States of "adequate

---

[33] Council Directive 2003/9/EC of 27 January 2003 laying down minimum standards for the reception of asylum seekers. L 31/18, http://eur-lex.europa.eu/LexUriServ/LexUriServ.do?uri=OJ:L:2003:031:0018:0025:En:PDF (accessed on March 1st, 2018).

[34] *Ibidem;* Zschirnt 2011: 46.

[35] Council Directive 2003/9/EC of 27 January 2003.

[36] *Ibidem.*

support for persons with special reception needs throughout the duration of the asylum procedure [as well as] appropriate monitoring of their situation." There is also a new Article 11 that guarantees access to health for vulnerable people, and detention in their case is only permitted if there is no threat to their health (ibidem; Smyth 2013: 230). In addition, Member States are obliged to conduct an individual assessment in order to identify "special reception needs of vulnerable persons and to ensure that vulnerable asylum seekers can access medical and psychological support". Finally, there is a mention regarding the fundamental rights of asylum seekers in detention.

In short, the current Reception Conditions Directive displays the common features shared with other CEAS instruments: a considerable degree of discretion left to the Member States regarding "What is an adequate standard of living and how should it be achieved?" Thus, reception conditions vary considerably between Member States as to the methods and forms under which the system is organised, which negatively impacts on the standard provided.

The European Agenda on Migration pointed out the need for "a clear, consistent and harmonised system for the reception of asylum seekers that should be operational in times of crisis". [37] For the time being the 2016 (EASO) guidance on reception conditions brings some examples of possible common standards and indicators.

"The guidance describes specific common standards which are applicable to national reception systems across all EU Member States and the indicators with which such standards should be measured against. The standards included in the document reflect already existing practice in EU Member States." The new 2016 Proposal for the Recast Reception Conditions Directive aims at harmonisation of standards and more equal treatment for asylum seekers, which would dissuade them from asylum shopping. [38] The new proposal should provide some solutions to the overcrowded temporary centres. Article 17a stipulates that an asylum seeker has no right to receive material assistance if he/she lodged the claim in another Member State. This solution was seen as too drastic by the European Social and Economic Committee, so the final text of the directive should allow some exceptions to this provision. [39] Similarly, other provisions "excluding, reducing and withdrawing" the entitlements have been condemned by the Committee and heavily criticised by the NGOs.

The 2016 proposed reform of the reception conditions directive retains the possibility of detention of children as a last resort, which has been heavily panned by the EU Parliament considering that "detention or any confinement of children, whether unaccompanied or with families, should be prohibited." Also, COREPER advocated for a higher protection for unaccompanied children in relation to the

---

[37] European Agenda on Migration COM (2015) 240 final.

[38] Radjenowic Anja, European Parliamentary Research Service, 10 July 2017, http://www.europarl.europa.eu/RegData/etudes/BRIE/2016/593520/EPRS_BRI(2016)593520_EN.pdf (accessed on February 15th, 2018).

[39] *Ibidem.*

right to education or a right to a legal representative.[40]

The original Qualification Directive laid down minimum standards for third country nationals to qualify for international protection.[41] Article 6c recognised non-state actors as actors of persecution, and article 9.2.f distinguished acts of a gender-specific and child-specific nature (child conscription, infanticide or child sale).[42]

The Directive is considerably wider in scope than the Geneva Convention 1951, enlarging the grounds on which protection could be granted.[43] Hence, unaccompanied minors, even if their refugee status has been refused, might be granted subsidiary protection until they reach the age of maturity.[44] The (Recast) Directive 2011 addressed a few issues in favour of unaccompanied children: it equalises beneficiaries of subsidiary protection with refugees regarding right to family unity (Art 23), issuance of travelling documents, and access to healthcare and integration facilities (Smyth 2013: 63). In contrast, Article 23 is weak, allowing Member States to determine who are the members of the family who would benefit from subsidiary protection and who would be excluded (Bauloz and Ruiz 2016: 245). Although the definition has been extended to the parents of a minor, it is limited to the existing family or family present in the host state at the time when the application was made.

The Directive grants a differentiated treatment of vulnerable groups such as minors and victims of torture (Article 20.3). Article 31 makes it clear that children's accommodation should be appropriate for their age and that the child's view should be taken into account (ibidem; Smyth 2013: 63, 238). Appropriate training should be provided for those who deal with children, but there is still no precision as to what such training should entail.

The Procedures Directive[45] regulates the process of claiming asylum, including the methods and the effects of the application. The guardianship and legal aid assistance are crucial in cases of unaccompanied minors. They need to receive appropriate support, information, and be assisted without a delay. The Recast Procedures Directive[46] takes a holistic stance: "In assessing the best interest of the child, Member States should in particular take due account of the minor's well-being and social development, including his or her background" (recital 33).

---

[40] 'Legislative Train Schedule, Towards a New Policy on Migration' http://www.europarl.europa.eu/legislative-train/theme-towards-a-new-policy-on-migration/file-reform-of-the-reception-conditions-directive (accessed on February 15th, 2018).

[41] Council Directive 2004/83/EC of 29 April 2004.

[42] *Ibidem,* Zschirnt 2011: 45.

[43] *Ibidem,* Zschirnt 2011: 48.

[44] *Ibidem,* Zschirnt 2011: 48.

[45] Directive 2013/32/EU of the European Parliament and the Council of 26 June 2013 on Common Procedures for Granting and Withdrawing International Protection (recast), L 180/60 Official Journal of the European Union 29.6.2013.

[46] *Ibidem.*

The first Procedure Directive 2005 was particularly harsh towards unaccompanied children. Article 17(2) allowed an option for a Member State to refrain from appointing a legal guardian, making this provision conditional.[47] Derogations in the form of even lower standard were allowed for married minors or those close to the age of maturity.[48] Overall, the vagueness of the article indicated a multiple standard detrimental to many children.[49] The (Recast) Asylum Procedures Directive 2013[50] is clearer and grants a greater protection of the minor's rights. It provides specific arrangements at the borders, processing of applications within 6 months, better training for the decision makers, and more help in the early stage of completing the application: an "unaccompanied minor should be assisted by a qualified representative while preparing his/her application" (Article 25). There are some additional guarantees for children who have suffered abuse, which are applied during the interview proceedings, medical examination, and age assessment (Article 25.5). The new Proposal for Regulation replacing Procedures Directive would help to impose a uniform application of the law across the EU[51] (Guild and Moreno-Lax 2013; Chetail et al. 2016: 550 at 4).

The proposal underlines the importance of determining the needs of unaccompanied minors in the early stage in order to provide them with adequate support and guidance throughout all stages of the procedure (Article 20(1)). Children are entitled to a personal interview unless it is manifestly not in their best interests (Article 21(1) and (2)). Finally, there is a long awaited provision imposing a time limit to appoint a guardian: Member States must appoint a guardian "as soon as possible and not later than 5 working days from the moment when an unaccompanied minor makes an application (Article 22(1))" (ibidem: 14). The proposal is seeking "to standardise guardianship practices to make sure that guardianship becomes prompt and effective across the EU" (ibidem).

The proposed Dublin IV Regulation fuels the current debate. For unaccompanied minors, there are clear provisions on guardianship and transfers, setting very tight time limit (Gualco 2016). The transfers "must always be preceded by individual guarantees from the receiving Member State, confirming that it will fulfil its specific obligations – including the appointment of a guardian before the transfer takes place" (ibidem). Article 10(4) of the proposal is under attack for disregarding the decision of the CJEU

[47] *Ibidem*, Zschirnt 2011: 45.

[48] *Ibidem*, Zschirnt 2011: 45.

[49] *Ibidem.*

[50] Directive 2013/32/EU of the European Parliament and of the Council of 26 June 2013 on Common Procedures for Granting and Withdrawing International Protection (recast) (applicable from 21 July 2015.

[51] Proposal for a Regulation of the European Parliament and of the Council establishing a common procedure for international protection in the Union and repealing Directive 2013/32/EU, COM(2016) 467 final 2016/0224 (COD).

in MA and others v Secretary of State regarding the "first lodged rule" in relation to unaccompanied children.[52] The Court held that the wording of Article 6(2) of the Dublin II Regulation refers to the state "where the minor has lodged his or her application for asylum" cannot be construed as meaning "the first Member State where the minor has lodged his or her application for asylum". The Court concluded that "according to Article 24(2) of the Charter of Fundamental Rights, the best interest of the child needs to be taken into consideration in all actions relating to children. Article 6(2) shall not disregard this fundamental right". Thus, the CJEU obviates the "first lodged rule" and decides that "the Member State in which that minor is present after having lodged an asylum application there is to be designated the 'Member State responsible'."[53] Nevertheless "if an unaccompanied child has no family members or relatives, and where no other criteria apply, he or she will be subject to the allocation mechanism."[54]

Further, the EURODAC Regulation created in 2003 and its Recast in 2013 comes in the Commission's 2016 package.[55] The initial Regulation did not provide the possibility of data comparison by the law enforcement authorities, but the 2013 Recast did, becoming a very useful instrument for the comparison of fingerprints in the hands of Europol. The EURODAC practice was often a traumatising experience for unaccompanied minors. Member States used different techniques in conformity with the EURODAC Regulation[56]: some countries used X-rays of the wrist and hand bones or other more invasive physical examinations. The current proposal is not encouraging, intending to add a facial image with the prospect of introducing at a later stage facial recognition software assisting the Entry/Exit System (EU-LISA).[57] The Fundamental Rights Agency expressed serious concerns considering excessive the procedure of

[52] Ibidem, Case C-648/11, MA, BT and DA v Secretary of State of the Home Department, 6 June 2013.

[53] *Ibidem.*

[54] Proposal for a Regulation of the European Parliament and of the Council establishing the criteria and mechanisms for determining the Member State responsible for examining an application for international protection lodged in one of the Member States by a third-country national or a stateless person, (Brussels, 4.5.2016 COM (2016) 270 final 2016/0133 (COD) EN; also C-648/11, *The Queen, on the Application of MA and Others v Secretary of State for the Home Department*, 6 June 2013, ECLI:EU:C:2013:367, para. 66.; European Council on Refugees and Exiles, ECRE, Comments on the proposal for an Asylum Procedures Regulation, cit. supra note 66, pp. 49–51.

[55] Brussels, 4.5.2016 COM (2016) 272 final 2016/0132 (COD) a Proposal for a Regulation of the European Parliament and of the Council (EURODAC).

[56] European Agenda for Migration 2015 two packages (2016 repealing Directive 2013/32/EU), COM (2016) 0467, http://www.europarl.europa.eu/atyourservice/en/displayFtu.html?ftuId=FTU_4.2.2.html (accessed on February 3rd, 2018).

[57] https://ec.europa.eu/home-affairs/sites/homeaffairs/files/what-we-do/policies/european-agenda-migration/proposal-implementation-package/docs/20160504/eurodac_proposal_en.pdf (accessed on February 3rd, 2018).

"keeping the fingerprints for a period of five years of those people who do not apply for international protection and the processing of biometric data from children starting from the age of 6" (Zlătescu 2015; 2016). The FRA's position was that "minors, suspects to be victims of torture, sexual abuse and gender-based violence, or victims of other serious crimes, [...] and traumatized [children], should not be constrained to undergo the procedure of fingerprinting" (Zlătescu 2016). Thomas believes that "the social and moral significance of fingerprinting children has been overlooked, children are being inducted into the world of the 'surveillance society' without really knowing what it means" (Thomas 2008: 22).

The age assessment under the EURODAC was severely condemned by NGOs and human rights organisations: children were subjected to invasive examination although the procedure was often unnecessary and frequently unreliable; children were often wrongly identified as adults and deprived of the basic rights that should be available to children. The recent Italian Law (the so-called Zampa Law) introduced in 2017 provides much better guarantees and an exemplary procedure (ibidem).

The 2016 Proposals to reform the CEAS raised many objections in relation to children. JRS Europe warned about the retrograding effects of the compulsory status reviews and their impact on families,[58] and advocates that these reviews introduce "the instability, uncertainty and anxiety" running a high risk of undermining the ability of "children to make plans for their future, to make choices about whether to further their education or enter the workforce, to set long-term goals for themselves, and be motivated to continue their education and language instruction."[59] JRS Europe observes that without a permanent and secured residence, children will be hampered in achieving the best in their education and future lives.[60] In addition, unaccompanied children who changed the country of their first entry are denied reception conditions, and consequently also access to education and healthcare; this measure is supposed to deter secondary movements, but instead[61] it removes the previous entitlements with the exception of emergency health care.[62] Furthermore, collecting facial images and fingerprinting from 6 years of age seem to be unnecessary steps and invasive for children,[63] "as the collection of such data is not per se efficient, proportionate, or useful for the better functioning of the system".[64]

[58] The CEAS reform package: the death of asylum by a thousand cuts?, https://jrseurope.org/assets/Regions/EUR/media/files/JRS-Europe-CEASreformWorkingPaper6.pdf (accessed on March 1st, 2018).

[59] *Ibidem.*

[60] *Ibidem.*

[61] https://jrseurope.org/assets/Regions/EUR/media/files/JRS-EuropeCEASreformWorkingPaper6.pdf) (accessed on March 1st, 2018).

[62] Case C-179/11 *Cimade & Gisti*, Judgment, 27 September 2012.

[63] Explanatory Memorandum, proposed Eurodac Regulation, p. 4. Brussels, 4.5.2016 COM (2016) 272 final 2016/0132 (COD) Proposal for a Regulation of the European Parliament and of the Council.

[64] ECRE (2016), "ECRE Comments on Dublin IV", https://www.ecre.org/wp-content/uploads/2016/10/ECRE-Comments-Dublin-IV.pdf (accessed on February 20th, 2018).

12.4. *Conclusions*

There are many findings that we can draw from this research, some of which are long term objectives, and other are recommendations that need to be put in place with the shortest possible delay if we want to safeguard unaccompanied minors.

From the start, the EU law, primarily not designed to protect children, offered only a fragmented and incomplete legal framework, unable to provide responses to the most challenging situations. Similarly, the CJEU and the ECtHR did not step in to fill the gaps on the content of the best interests or child rights approach in a more rights-authoritative way.

Unsurprisingly, the CEAS system, arising within the EU context, was tainted by the same shortcomings. Apart from a few express provisions addressing children's issues, the system was lacking child visibility and unable to protect unaccompanied minors.

The role of European Parliament as a co-legislator in the CEAS legislation might become crucial in renegotiating regressive provisions. However, the biggest weakness in the design of the CEAS system was the discretion left to Member States that the latter used favouring protectionism and national interests without making the best interests of unaccompanied children paramount (Nascimbene 2016: 101).

Moreover, the solidarity principle has not been followed in the CEAS where the Member States are the relevant actors (ibidem). Bonino pointed out that the Member States did not want to give full competence to the EU in the area of immigration. [65] Thus, they bear responsibility for the malfunctioning of the system since they have impeded its further development by hanging on too much to national interests. It is time for a stronger cooperation between Member States, since it is in their hands today to make the system work. Many lacunae have been closed and others might disappear with time through consistent good practice. Solidarity, mutual trust and determination in achieving a common goal should prevail over national interests (Mitsilegas 2014). This cooperation is particularly important in the case of unaccompanied children, where the exchange of good practice, exchange of information, collection of data, exchange of findings and communication between institutions could make the system more effective and avoid causing additional trauma to children.

Solidarity should become a guiding rule, a principle that involves sharing responsibility effectively in the entire process, sharing the burden of the new arrivals, relocations, hotspots and the transit zones, as well as in "a follow up" of these children once they have been relocated.

Secondly, as a long-term objective it is vital to provide a context for successful integration of unaccompanied minors. There is not a viable programme yet on how to provide durable solutions, a healthy environment in which children can grow and

[65] Bonino Emma, https://www.youtube.com/watch?v=7mkyDe5sptU (accessed on March 1st, 2018).

develop. Hence, policy documents and legislative initiatives should prioritise a holistic approach and ensure proper monitoring and supervision, as well as a frequent assessment of children's needs and their adaptability to the new living conditions. Schooling, accommodation and access to health services should be monitored in the long term in order to promote smooth integration.

So far, the EU framework and the proposals are concentrating on regulating entry to the EU territory, offering some solutions in the short term.

Thirdly, replacing the CEAS qualification directive and procedure directive with two new regulations is of particular importance to standardise the system given the discrepancies and inconsistencies depending on the country of entry in the current procedures to which unaccompanied minors are subjected.

Fourthly, the current proposals do not promote enough family unity or set up the vehicles for family reunification. Transfer procedures would need to ensure child visibility, and again the Member States' cooperation is desperately needed in this process. The reception conditions in hotspots and transit zones are often not appropriate for children – the centres are overcrowded with only basic facilities. Member States need to improve the bureaucratic profiles regarding identification and registration of minors, otherwise the invasive and traumatising practices will continue for children. At this point the new Italian Law 7/2017 regarding protection of unaccompanied minors provides some exemplary provisions on how to carry out the age assessment procedures in the least invasive manner. In addition, unaccompanied children might be adversely affected by the new time limits imposed under the proposed Dublin IV Regulation.[66]

Incontestably, the Commission's efforts to strengthen the protection of unaccompanied minors must be acknowledged. The Proposal for a Recast Reception Conditions Directive[67] is a big step forward in relation to children's access to information about their situation. Further, the Proposal for Asylum Procedure Regulation gives a child the right to a personal interview unless it is not in his/her best interests. The most important novelty in the proposal concerns the 5-day time limit on the appointment of guardians.

Chetail effectively compares the above described system to a puzzle where some of the pieces are still missing. The success of the revamped CEAS depends very much on the seriousness of implementation by the Member States. The CJEU's decisions are fundamental to shaping the road ahead and putting the puzzle together by giving meaning to different instruments and connecting them together[68] (Chetail et al. 2016:

---

[66] ECRE, ECRE Comments on Dublin IV, https://www.ecre.org/wp-content/uploads/2016/10/ECRE-Comments-Dublin-IV.pdf (accessed on February 20th, 2018).

[67] Proposal for a Directive of European Parliament and of the Council laying down standards for the reception of applicants for International Protection (recast), 13, July 2016, COM (2016) 465 final.

[68] *Ibidem.*

550 at 4). The CJEU itself could also attribute more content to best interest of the child.

Chetail argues that there is a need to develop EU Protected Entry Procedures and Humanitarian Visas, and for this solidarity between Member States needs to increase (ibidem).

In any case, the child's best interest should prevail over administrative convenience, and child visibility should transpire through all provisions in the CEAS legal framework.

Bibliography

Bauloz, C. and Ruiz, G. (2016) 'Refugee Status and Subsidiary Protection. Towards a Uniform Content of International Protection?' in V. Chetail, P. De Bruycker, F. Maiani (eds.) *Reforming the Common European Asylum System: The New European Refugee Law*, Leiden: Brill.

Beirens, H., Maas, S., Petronella, S. and van der Velden, M. (2016) *Study on the Temporary Protection Directive Executive Summary*, Brussels: European Commission.

Carrera, S. and Merlino, M. (2010) *Assessing EU Policy on Irregular Immigration Under the Stockholm Programme*, Brussels: Centre for European Policy Studies.

Chetail, V., De Bruycker, P. and Maiani, F. (eds.) (2016) *Reforming the Common European Asylum System: The New European Refugee Law*, Leiden: Brill.

Defence for Children (2017) *Athens, The Reflection of a Broken Protection System for Refugee Children*, Leiden: Defence for Children.

Dorling, K. (2008) 'Seeking change. Reforms to the protection of unaccompanied asylum seeking children', *ChildRight*, 245: 14–17.

Gualco, E. (2016) 'Unaccompanied Minors Seeking for Protection in the European Union: Will a Fair and Adequate Asylum System Ever See the Light?' in G.C. Bruno, F.M. Palombino, D. Amoroso (eds.) *Migration and Development: Some Reflections on Current Legal Questions*, Rome: Cnr, 175–195.

Guild, E. and Moreno-Lax, V. (2013) *Current Challenges Regarding the International Refugee Law with Focus on EU Policies and EU Cooperation with UNHCR*, Brussels: Centre for European Policy Studies.

Mitsilegas, V. (2014) 'Solidarity and trust in the common European asylum system', *Comparative Migration Studies*, 2(2): 181–202.

Nascimbene, B. (2016) 'Refugees, the European Union and the "Dublin System". The reasons for a crisis', *European Papers*, 1: 101–113.

Ruxton, S. (2000) *Separated Children Seeking Asylum in Europe: A Programme for Action*, London: Save the Children.

Smyth, C.M. (2013) *The common European asylum system and the rights of the child: An exploration of meaning and compliance*, Leiden, thesis, https://openaccess.leidenuniv.nl/handle/1887/20462 (accessed on January 20th, 2018).

Stalford, H. and Drywood, E. (2009) 'Coming of age? Children's rights in the European Union', *Common Market Law Review*, 46: 143–172.

Thomas, T. (2008) 'Children and fingerprinting: sleepwalking into a surveillance society', *ChildRight*, 245: 22–24.

UNICEF and IOM (2017) *Harrowing Journeys: Children and Youth on the Move Across the Mediterranean Sea, at Risk of Trafficking and Exploitation*, New York: Unicef.

Wenke, D. (2017) *Age Assessment: Council of Europe Member States' Policies, Procedures and Practices Respectful of Children's Rights in the Context of Migration*, Strasbourg: Council of Europe.

Zlătescu, I.M. (2015) *Human Rights A Dynamic and Evolving Process*, Bucharest: Pro Universitaria.

Zlătescu, I.M. (2016) 'Aspects of the protection of migrant children's rights in the EU Law', *Law Review*, 6: 117–123.

Zschirnt, E. (2011) 'Does migration status trump the best interests of the child? Unaccompanied minors in the EU asylum system', *Journal of Immigration and Nationality Law*, 36: 34–55.

Chapter 13

The right to free legal aid for migrants

For effective access to justice

Silvia Favalli

13.1. *Effective access to justice for all: the role of legal aid*

The unprecedented number of undocumented cross-border movements resulting in deaths, violence and abuses at borders over the past few years have demonstrated that the status quo in the approaches of States to border control and migration is no longer sustainable (Busatta 2017).

Within this context, on 19 September 2016, the UN General Assembly, through the adoption of the New York Declaration for Refugees and Migrants (UNGA 2016), has established a two-year process leading to the adoption of two global compacts, one on refugees on 13 July 2018 and the other for safe, orderly and regular migration on 17 December 2018 (Guild and Grant 2017). On 28 April 2017, the Special Rapporteur on the human rights of migrants submitted a report proposing the development of a 2015 Agenda for Facilitating Human Mobility. This Agenda – to be developed alongside the 2030 Agenda for Sustainable Development – would encompass eight human mobility goals, aimed at facilitating human mobility in the next fifteen years, while ensuring respect for the human rights of all migrants. In particular, Goal No. 5 points out the necessity to provide effective access to justice for all migrants, in the awareness that effective and accessible justice systems can be tools to overcome exclusion, discrimination and marginalisation faced by migrants. While affirming that one of the major obstacles in accessing justice for migrants is the cost of legal advice and representation, it highlights the need to ensure equal access for all migrants to effective legal aid. The report stresses the importance to ensure equal access for all migrants to "reliable legal information, effective legal aid, competent and affordable legal representation and competent interpretation and translation services" (target No. 5.5), recognising the right to legal aid as a central component of strategies to enhance access to justice.

In the same vein, at the European level the Council of Bars and Law Societies of Europe (CCBE) has called on the European institutions to "deal with legal aid as a fundamental right" and, in particular, to implement the right to legal aid for migrants (CCBE 2010) and asylum seekers (CCBE 2017) within the EU legal and policy framework. On the one hand, the current global economic crisis, which is affecting all aspects of life in the EU society, strongly impacted on legal aid policies by means of the reduction of the budget provided (Aliverti 2017). In a context of legal aid cuts, migrants are among the first victims of the crisis, as are their working conditions, both social and economic, which were already precarious (Eurostat 2017). They are more subject to discrimination and exploitation in the workplace, forced labour, and extortion as a result of exorbitant recruitment fees. Nonetheless, they often do not seek redress for the violation of their rights because of their limited knowledge of the local language, laws and systems, also facing cultural barriers and fear of detection, detention and deportation (UNGA 2017). On the other hand, the so-called "migrants and refugees crisis" has determined the adoption of the 2015 European Agenda on Migration (European Commission 2015) and the presentation of several draft Regulations to reform the common European asylum system (CEAS). In these legislative proposals, the right to benefit from the free assistance of a lawyer at the various stages of the asylum procedure is guaranteed, in the awareness that the right to effectively access asylum procedures is the necessary corollary to the principle of non-refoulement (Giuffrè 2016). However, something is still missing in the EU asylum policy, where the use of immigration detention as a border management and deterrence tool against migrants has become a widespread trend (Grange and Majcher 2017), as well as a means to prevent their access to justice. In this context, the right to access free legal aid for migrants plays a key role in overcoming systemic barriers to their integration in the host country's society.

Against this background, this manuscript examines free legal aid as a central component to enhance the right to access to justice for all, including vulnerable groups – i.e., women, children, persons with disabilities, migrants, etc. (Lelkes, Platt and Ward 2009; Ippolito and Iglesias Sánchez 2015) – and as a primary goal of human rights law. It focuses on the analysis of legal aid as a (human rights) tool to overcome systemic barriers experienced by migrants to effective access to justice, social inclusion and equality, while adopting a specific European perspective.

13.2. *Legal aid in the human rights background: nature and content*

In the human rights context, legal aid is regarded as central in providing the right to access to justice, which is nowadays guaranteed as a fundamental right in all the relevant universal and regional human rights instruments (Francioni 2007; Cappelletti and Garth 1977; Cappelletti, Garth and Trocker 1982; Francioni 2008; Trinidade 2011, 2015; FRA and Council of Europe 2016; Cornford 2016; Gerards and Glas 2017).

However, to date, the juridical nature of legal aid among human rights remains controversial. In the most recent legal scholarship, where a dual attitude emerges, the main point of discussion is the qualification of legal aid as an autonomous (substantive) human right or merely a (procedural) aspect of existing human rights. On the one hand, it is argued that legal aid is a human right, because the establishment of an obligation to provide free legal aid is essential to guarantee the fundamental human right to access to justice (Jüriloo 2015). Such a statement lays its foundations on the position of the former UN Rapporteur on the Independence of Judges and Lawyers, Gabriela Knaul, who affirmed that "legal aid is both a right in itself and an essential precondition for the exercise and enjoyment of a number of human rights, including the rights to a fair trial and to an effective remedy" (OHCHR 2013). On the other hand, the reasoning upon which the affirmation of legal aid as a human right places its foundations is proposed in a rhetorical manner, rather than in a conceptual one (Rice 2017). One of the main points of criticism is the qualification of legal aid as a substantive right on its own, rather than "an aspect of substantive procedural human rights" (Rice 2017: 210), such as the right to a fair trial (Flynn et al. 2016) or to access to an effective remedy. It is thus assumed that the right to legal aid is an aspect of existing human rights – and, in this capacity, an integral part of the human rights system – but not an autonomous human right in itself. Namely, "the nature of legal aid is such that it is not obviously amenable to being a new, substantive human right" (Flynn et al. 2016: 211).

Nevertheless, as has also been argued, some hints of the affirmation of a human right to legal aid implicitly emerge from Article 13 of the 2006 UN Convention on the Rights of Persons with Disabilities (CRPD) (Flynn 2016) and Article 5 of the Convention of the Elimination of all Forms of Racial Discrimination (CERD). Such provisions have been interpreted as indirectly providing a right to legal aid for disabled people (Gibson 2010) and persons facing racial discrimination (Rice 2017). Whilst not directly recognising an autonomous right (or maybe human right) to legal aid, these norms may pave the way for a wider affirmation of legal aid in the human rights background. Hence, it would be illogical to guarantee the right to legal aid to persons with disabilities and persons facing racial discrimination, while not to all human beings.

Further, the content of the right to legal aid in international human rights law remains uncertain. Legal aid is generally understood as the provision of assistance to people otherwise unable to afford legal representation and access to the court system, with the aim to contribute to the elimination of obstacles and barriers that impair or restrict their access to justice. However, not one of the existing human rights treaties provides a precise definition of legal aid. In such an absence, the discourse about legal aid has been developed differently in relation to criminal and non-criminal matters (including civil law, administrative law and regulatory enforcement).

In particular, in international human rights law the standard conception of legal aid is well established in the criminal limb as an integral part of the right to a fair hearing (Flynn et al. 2016: 199), while it remains less developed in non-criminal matters. Meaningfully, the only internationally agreed definition of legal aid is that contained in the 2012 United Nations Principles and Guidelines on Access to Legal Aid in Criminal Justice Systems (UNGA 2012) – the world's first international instrument dedicated to the provision of legal aid – and refers only to the criminal limb. Such an international instrument, alongside Article 14(3)(d) of the 1966 International Covenant on Civil and Political Rights (ICCPR) (Nowak 2005), lays the foundations of legal aid as a "precondition" to guarantee the right to a fair trial and to an effective remedy for persons charged with a criminal offence.

By contrast, the regional human rights system developed in Europe provides a broader interpretation of legal aid, encompassing both criminal and non-criminal matters. Article 6(3)(c) of the European Convention on Human Rights (ECHR) guarantees the right of a person "charged of a criminal offence" to be given free legal assistance under determined conditions. However, after the cornerstone ruling Airey v. Ireland [1] of the European Court of Human Rights, Article 6(1) ECHR has been interpreted as implicitly providing a right to necessary legal aid as part of the right to access to courts (Mowbray 2005). In this sense, the EU Charter of Fundamental Rights (EU Charter) does not provide such a distinction (Gruodytė and Kirchner 2014; Peers 2016), whereas Article 47 guarantees legal aid "to those who lack sufficient resources in so far as such aid is necessary to ensure effective access to justice" (EU Network of independent experts on fundamental rights 2006).

Against this legislative background, the human rights jurisprudence (Rice 2017) has gradually developed a sort of standard conception of legal aid, referring to three core elements: free legal advice, free legal assistance, and free legal representation. Starting from this baseline, legal aid can also extend to "legal education, access to legal information and other services provided for persons through alternative dispute resolution mechanisms and restorative justice processes" (UNGA 2012). In particular, special attention has to be paid to the promotion of legal aid services to vulnerable groups (Kyiv Declaration on the Right to Legal Aid 2007). In this vein, according to the UNHCR (UNHCR 2001) among others (Council of Europe Commissioner for Human Rights 2001), legal aid for migrants must also involve the free assistance of an interpreter during the asylum seeker's interview with the authorities.

13.3. *Free legal aid for migrants: a European perspective*

To date, in the human rights framework developed in Europe there is no legal instrument specifically addressing the right to legal aid as a central component of strategies to overcome the systemic barriers experienced by migrants to effective access to justice, social inclusion, and equality. The related provisions are spread in a (fragmented) set of international and European instruments, which will be briefly analysed below in order to set the scene of the relevant legal framework.

For the sake of completeness, the personal scope of the subsequent analysis will be

---

[1] European Court of Human Rights 1979, *Airey v. Ireland*, Application No. 6289/73.

far-reaching. In this vein, the term "migrants" will be used in its broader and most general sense, encompassing a wide variety of different human situations – i.e. migrant workers, asylum seekers, refugees, irregular migrants, nationals of States parties to a convention residing in other Contracting Parties, EU citizens moving throughout Europe, stateless persons, etc. – in the awareness that in migration and asylum law these categories become all relevant insofar as they are recognised in specific international instruments or their circumstances require particular attention (McBride 2009; Long 2013; Goodwin-Gill and McAdam 2007; Campiglio 2010; Ricci 2017).

Relevant international standards

As mentioned above, in international human rights law legal aid is mainly considered an essential element of a fair, humane and efficient criminal justice system (Chetail 2014). In this sense, the UN legal instruments providing access to free legal assistance and representation for migrants refer exclusively to the criminal context. The 1990 International Convention on the Protection of the Rights of All Migrant Workers and Members of Their Families (CMW), similarly to the ICCPR, points out the right of migrant workers and members of their families facing criminal charges to consult with a counsel of their own choosing, to be informed of their rights, as well as to access legal aid if they do not have sufficient means to pay (Article 18 CMW). In the same way, the 2012 UN Principles and Guidelines on Access to Legal Aid in Criminal Justice Systems (Willems 2014) stress the importance of affording free legal aid for migrants, in compliance with the CMW. Principle No. 10 states that special measures should be taken to ensure meaningful access to legal aid for groups with special need, such as, among others, "stateless persons, asylum-seekers, foreign citizens, migrants and migrant workers, refugees and internally displaced persons".

Conversely, outside the human rights context, the 1980 Hague Convention on International Access to Justice (Hague Conference on Private International Law 1980) addresses legal aid in civil and commercial proceedings. It requires migrants who are nationals and residents of Contracting Parties to be granted legal aid in other Contracting Parties under the same conditions as if they resided there, with the purpose to ensure that the mere status as an alien or the absence of residence or domicile in a State are not grounds for discrimination with regard to access to justice in that State.

In this context, the issue of granting legal aid to applicants of international protection – which Mikolajczyk (2016) evocatively defines as "Cinderella of international protection" – deserves separate mention. According to Article 16 of the 1951 Refugee Convention, refugees shall enjoy the same treatment as nationals of the State in which they have habitual residence pertaining to access to courts and to legal aid (Hathaway 2005, p. 908). As noted by McBride (2009), this provision does not provide any explicit guarantees concerning access to legal aid as regards the determination by national authorities of the refugee status. The absence of such a guarantee, according to this author, reflects the fact that the Refugee Convention is concerned only with the position of persons having that status. Nonetheless, it would be illogical – and in breach of the international obligation undertaken in ratifying the Refugee Convention itself – if an asylum seeker actually fulfilled the relevant criteria for the refugee status was not accorded the right of access to legal aid because his or her entitlement had not yet been recognised by the relevant national authorities. In this vein, the provision must be interpreted as referring to the factual situation of a refugee, which does not require the recognition of refugee status. However, as noted by Mikolajczyk (2016), the scope of this provision is very narrow. It provides only a terse reference to access to courts in judicial proceedings, without considering procedure before administrative bodies, while asylum procedures are usually administrative procedures. In addition, there is no mention of access to legal information, assistance and representation provided at the (crucial) moment of the refugee's first clash with the authorities of the foreign country.

Relevant European standards

a) Council of Europe

The Council of Europe has long recognised and promoted the right to access to justice and to legal aid in several soft law measures (Committee of Ministers of the Council of Europe 1976, 1978, 2005).

Furthermore, both the European Convention on Human Rights (ECHR) and the European Social Charter (ESC) expressly provide the right to access to legal aid – which, having a financial dimension, is considered both a civil and political right (like the right to access to court and to a fair trial) and a social and economic right (Gruodytė and Kirchner 2014). However, only the Charter (ESC) pays specific attention to the peculiar situation of migrants, more precisely migrant workers who are nationals of a State party of the Council of Europe and their families (Article 19 of both the ESC of 1961 and the Revised ESC of 1996).

Likewise, the European Agreement on the Transmission of Applications for Legal Aid – which is concerned with the provision of assistance in transmitting applications for legal aid in civil, commercial or administrative matters in a State party other than the one in which the potential applicant has his or her habitual residence – refers specifically to nationals of a State party of the Council of Europe residing in another State party.

Separate mention must be made of the Council of Europe Convention on Action against Trafficking in Human Beings, which purports to protect the victims of trafficking and to safeguard their rights, as well as to prevent trafficking and prosecute traffickers. This convention focuses on the peculiar situation of migrant victims of trafficking, providing to them free legal assistance in order to be able to claim their rights before national courts (Article 15).

However, not one of the existing Council of Europe's legal instruments refers to the situation of applicants for international protections and to their right to make an effective asylum claim in a Council of Europe Member State. The most recent ECtHR case law has filled this gap, finally affirming that a fair asylum procedure requires that the applicant have access to free legal aid and to an interpreter. In line with the Committee of Ministers' guidelines on procedural guarantees in asylum (Committee of Ministers of the Council of Europe 2009) and return procedures (Committee of Ministers of the Council of Europe 2005), on several occasions the European Court pointed out the resistant State's failure to provide access to legal assistance and to an interpreter for applicants for international protection. Accordingly, in historical rulings such as M.S.S. v. Belgium and Greece,[2] I.M. v. France[3] and Sharifi and Others v Italy and Greece,[4] the Court highlighted that Article 13 requires that a remedy should be sufficiently accessible in theory and practice. In this vein, practical access to a remedy lies in the consideration of linguistic barriers, as well as free access to legal information and advice. Accordingly, in Hirsi Jamaa and Others v. Italy,[5] the Court specified that – in the "maritime environment" – whereas on the military ships onto which the asylum seekers were made to embark there were neither interpreters nor legal advisers among the personnel on board, the applicants had no access to a procedure to identify them and to assess their personal circumstances before they were returned. In Abdolkhani and Karimnia v. Turkey,[6] the Court also considered the denial of free legal assistance to two asylum seekers as a relevant element for the violation of both Articles 13 and 5 ECHR, whereas the applicants had no effective opportunity to challenge the lawfulness of their conviction for illegal entry.

b) European Union

Within the EU legal order, the individual asylum seeker's right to free legal assistance and representation is directly enshrined in the EU Charter of Fundamental Rights and in the Treaty on the Functioning of the EU. It arises from the combination of Article 18, which sets out the right to asylum in EU law, and Article 47, which provides the procedural guarantees necessary for the protection of that right – i.e. the right to an effective remedy and to legal aid (Guild 2017). Article 78 TFEU requires the EU to develop a common policy on asylum, thus establishing the legal basis for the so-called Common European Asylum System (CEAS) (UNHCR 2010; FRA 2010a, 2010b; ECRE/ELENA 2010). On these bases, EU secondary legislation sets forth specific provisions addressing legal aid for

---

[2] European Court of Human Rights 2011, *M.S.S. v. Belgium and Greece*, Application No. 30696/09.

[3] European Court of Human Rights 2012, *I.M. v. France*, Application No. 9152/09.

[4] European Court of Human Rights 2014, *Sharifi and Others v. Italy and Greece*, Application No.16643/09.

[5] European Court of Human Rights 2012, *Hirsi Jamaa and Others v. Italy*, Application No. 27765/09.

[6] European Court of Human Rights 2009, *Abdolkhani and Karimnia v. Turkey*, Application No. 30471/08.

long-term residents, irregular migrants and asylum seekers.

The Long-Term Residence Directive (Directive 2003/109/EC)[7] and the Return Directive (Directive 2008/115/EC)[8] refer respectively to long-term residents and irregular migrants (illegally staying third-country nationals), and guarantee access to free legal aid in the context of the so-called return or expulsion procedure. In particular, Article 12 of the Long-Term Residence Directive sets forth the procedural obligations of the national authority deciding for the expulsion of long-term residents. It provides that a judicial redress procedure shall be available to the long-term resident in the Member State concerned and, in the context of the proceedings, "legal aid shall be given to long-term residents lacking adequate resources, on the same terms as apply to nationals of the State where they reside". Similarly, Article 13 of the Return Directive states that irregular migrants shall be accorded an effective remedy to appeal against decisions related to return, with the possibility to obtain legal advice, representation and, where necessary, linguistic assistance. However, the same limitations provided in the Asylum Procedure Directive (Directive 2005/85/EC)[9] – which has been recast in 2013 – are applicable (Acosta 2009).

Hence, the Recast Asylum Procedure Directive (Directive 2013/32(EU)[10] ensures legal information at first instance (Article 19), and free legal assistance and representation only at the appeal stage (Article 20) (Costello and Hancox 2016), while leaving Member States considerable discretion in introducing their own modalities, exemptions and limits to legal aid (Mikolajczyk 2016). Article 8 allows Member States to restrict access to free legal information for applicants already at the border. Member States may impose limits to providing information and counsel to persons held in detention facilities or present at border crossing points "where, by virtue of national law, they are objectively necessary for the security, public order or administrative management of the crossing points concerned". In the same vein, Member States may also restrict the applicant's legal advisor access to information, "where disclosure of information or sources would jeopardise national security, the security of the organisations or person(s) providing the information or the security of the person(s) to whom the information relates or where the investigative interests relating to the examination of applications for international protection by the competent authorities of the Member States or the international relations of the Member States would be compromised"

[7] Council Directive 2003/109/EC of 25 November 2003 concerning the status of third-country nationals who are long-term residents, OJ L 16, 23.1.2004, pp. 44–53.

[8] Directive 2008/115/EC of the European Parliament and of the Council of 16 December 2008 on common standards and procedures in Member States for returning illegally staying third-country nationals, OJ L 348, 24.12.2008, pp. 98–107.

[9] Directive 2005/85/EC on minimum standards on procedures in Member States for granting and withdrawing refugee status, OJ L 326, 13.12.2005, pp. 13–34.

[10] Directive 2013/32/EU of the European Parliament and of the Council of 26 June 2013 on common procedures for granting and withdrawing international protection, OJ L 180, 29.6.2013, pp. 60–95.

(Article 23). However, in such cases, Member States shall secure the applicant's right to defence establishing in national law appropriate procedural guarantees. In addition, at the appeal stage, legal assistance and representation may be limited by numerous conditions. Accordingly, Member States may decide on granting free legal aid only "to those who lack sufficient resources", and only once in the appeal procedure before the court of the first instance. They may impose monetary and time limits, "provided that such limits do not arbitrarily restrict access to the provision of legal and procedural information and legal assistance and representation" (Article 21). They may also restrict access to free legal assistance and representation to applicants who are no longer present on their territory (Article 41(2)(c)). Likewise, Member States have the possibility not to grant legal aid in cases with "no tangible prospect of success" (Article 20).

In addition, the Recast Reception Condition Directive (Directive 2013/33/EU) [11] guarantees access to legal information to applicants, also establishing that Member States shall ensure "information on organisations or groups of persons that provide specific legal assistance" (Article 5), and legal assistance and representation in case of appeal (Article 26). Article 9 extends the reception conditions to detained applicants, and guarantees to them legal aid under the same conditions provided in the Recast Asylum Procedure Directive analysed above.

The Regulation Dublin III (Regulation (EU) No 604/2013) [12] has also provided meaningful changes in terms of access to legal information and legal aid. While former Regulation Dublin II did not contain any reference to legal aid, Regulation Dublin III ensures the right to access free legal assistance and representation in case of appeal or revision of a decision to transfer (Article 27). It also provides the right to information in a language that the applicant understands or is reasonably supposed to understand (Article 4), as well as the obligation of the Member State to conduct a personal interview with the applicant and to provide the summary of the interview to the applicant themselves or their legal advisor (Article 5).

Finally, separate mention should be made of Directive 2002/8/EC, [13] which secures to EU citizens resident in another Member State access to legal aid in cross border disputes in civil and commercial matters. Although these individuals are included in the general understanding of the term migrants, under EU law they are properly considered as EU citizens exercising their right to freedom of movement, rather than migrants. Accordingly, the Directive purports to advance judicial cooperation in civil matters and to implement the functioning of the internal market.

---

[11] Directive 2013/33/EU of the European Parliament and of the Council of 26 June 2013 laying down standards for the reception of applicants for international protection, OJ L 180, 29.6.2013, pp. 96–116.

[12] Regulation (EU) No 604/2013 of the European Parliament and of the Council of 26 June 2013 establishing the criteria and mechanisms for determining the Member State responsible for examining an application for international protection lodged in one of the Member States by a third-country national or a stateless person, OJ L 180, 29.6.2013, pp. 31–59.

[13] Council Directive 2002/8/EC of 27 January 2003 to improve access to justice in cross-border disputes by establishing minimum common rules relating to legal aid for such disputes, OJ L 26, 31.1.2003, pp. 41–47.

13.4. *Legal aid in the prospective CEAS reform: one step forward and two steps back?*

Under the pressure of the so-called "migrants and refugee crisis", the European Commission launched on 4 May and 13 July 2016 seven legislative proposals aimed at reforming the Common European Asylum System. This package includes the recast of the Dublin Regulation and of the Eurodac Regulation, a proposal for a Regulation on the establishment of the European Union Agency for Asylum (EUAA), a proposal for a Regulation establishing a common asylum procedure in the EU, a proposal for a Qualification Regulation, the recast of the Reception Conditions Directive, and a proposal for a Regulation establishing a Union Resettlement Framework. Despite harsh criticism from legal scholars (Bendel 2017; Hruschka 2016; Thym 2017; Maiani 2016), this reform provides some improvements in relation to the rights of people with special needs (Ferri 2017) and unaccompanied minors (Baldin and Zago 2017), as well as to access to free legal assistance of applicants for international protection. However, as the subsequent analysis purports to highlight, the prospective reform still fails in taking all the necessary steps for effectively ensuring access to legal aid to asylum seekers.

The reform package – which aims at reducing the current discretion of Member States in the implementation of the asylum procedure and the relevant procedural guarantees – replaces the existing directives on recognition of refugee status (Qualification Directive) and on common procedures for international protection (Recast Asylum Procedures Directive) with regulations.

While the Recast Asylum Procedures Directive in force guarantees access to free legal aid only at the appeal stage, the draft Regulation [14] provides for free legal assistance and representation of a legal adviser or other counsellor to asylum seekers at all stages of the asylum procedure (Article 14). It also provides for the right of the applicant to request free legal aid in administrative procedures, subject to some exceptions. Accordingly, Member States may decide not to provide free legal assistance and representation when the applicant has sufficient resources, where the application or appeal are considered as having no tangible prospect of success, and in case of subsequent applications or with regard to a second level of appeal or higher (Article 15). In this vein, they may impose monetary limits or time limits on the provision of free legal assistance and representation (Article 17).

As noted by the CCBE (2017), however, such exceptions – which mostly repeat the discipline of the Recast Asylum Procedures Directive – may disproportionally reduce the common guarantees for applicants to international protection. This is particularly the case when "the applicant is considered as not having any tangible prospect of success". Having regard that the draft Regulation provides a time-limit of ten

[14] Proposal for a Regulation of the European Parliament and of the Council establishing a common procedure for international protection in the Union and repealing Directive 2013/32/EU, COM/2016/0467 final, 2016/0224 (COD).

working days for lodging an application (Article 28), which is new compared to the Recast Asylum Procedures Directive, the CCBE is of the opinion that the specific case of exclusion referred to above should be deleted. The CCBE also points out that asylum seekers should be able to benefit from the free assistance of an interpreter when meeting with their lawyers during the administrative and litigation phases, whereas the draft Regulation only provides for the presence of a free interpreter during the applicant's interview with the authorities (Article 12).

Furthermore, the reform package introduces some relevant changes in access to legal information of applicants. With the purpose of reducing reception-related incentives for secondary movements within the EU, the proposal repealing the Recast Reception Condition Directive [15] requires Member States to inform applicants of any benefits and obligations, which applicants must comply with in relation to reception conditions, including the circumstances under which the granting of material reception conditions may be restricted. This information shall be given in written form, using a standard template developed by the European Union Agency for Asylum (Article 5).

Similarly, the Dublin IV Regulation proposal [16] guarantees the right to information to asylum seekers, including both benefits and obligations (Article 6), as well as the obligation of the Member State to conduct a personal interview with the applicant and to provide the summary of the interview to the applicant itself or his or her legal advisor (Article 7).

Nonetheless, as noted by ECRE (2016), the Dublin IV Regulation reduces the guarantees set out by its predecessor relating to the individual's right to a personal interview. In both the Dublin III and Dublin IV Regulations, the interview may be omitted where the applicant has absconded or where the information provided is sufficient for the determination of the responsible Member State. While, in the latter case, the Dublin III Regulation requires Member States to allow the person to present information at a later stage in order to correctly identify the responsible country, the Dublin IV Regulation proposal has deleted such a guarantee, ostensibly with a view to avoiding delays in the procedure. Hence, such provisions reflect the general (and criticized) approach of the prospective Regulation, which "pursues efficiency through sanctions and reduction of rights" (Maiani 2016). On the assumption that "changes added under the 2013 Dublin III reform resulted in increased rights for applicants which could be misused to frustrate the entire system" (Dublin IV Regulation proposal p. 13), the Dublin IV Regulation increases the obligations and sanctions imposed on

[15] Proposal for a Directive of the European Parliament and of the Council laying down standards for the reception of applicants for international protection (recast), Brussels, 13.7.2016, COM(2016) 465 final, 2016/0222 (COD).

[16] Proposal for a Regulation of the European Parliament and of the Council establishing the criteria and mechanisms for determining the Member State responsible for examining an application for international protection lodged in one of the Member States by a third-country national or a stateless person (recast), Brussels, 4.5.2016, COM(2016) 270 final, 2016/0133 (COD).

asylum seekers in order to stop them from secondary movement from one Member State to another.

From the analysis above it emerges that the European legal framework addressing the right to legal aid for migrants is highly fragmented. The relevant provisions are spread over a set of international and European rules, referring to very different human and legal situations. In such a disjointed and incomplete legal context, every country provides legal aid in different ways – i.e. contracting private lawyers, funding their own practitioners, providing grants to specialised non-governmental organisations or exemptions from court fees – and in different conditions. However, under the pressure of the recent large-scale migration flows, the necessity to overcome exclusion, discrimination and marginalisation faced by migrants throughout the provision of effective access to justice systems in Europe strongly emerges. In this vein, several focused policy interventions – awareness-raising activities for timely and proper legal information, provision of ad hoc funding, initiatives in training and capacity building, including support for networks of courts and legal practitioners – are currently under the analysis of the EU institutions (Rass-Masson and Rouas 2017).

Against this background, the prospective reform of the CEAS plays a crucial role for the future development of the EU migration policy and legal framework. It represents the possibility to move toward more effective and accessible justice systems for migrants who are in an exceptionally difficult situation, i.e. asylum seekers. Nonetheless, alongside some promising improvements, the reform package still reduces the guarantees for applicants for international protection – frustrating their right to legal aid and to access to justice – in order to implement the efficiency of procedures. In this respect, a change of approach in the current EU migration policy is crucial. As long as the reform package addresses the management of migration flows through externalisation and restriction, rather than through the improvement of solidarity, the quality of protection for forced migrants, and the respect for international protection obligations, there is still a long way to go before the fulfilment of effective access to justice, social inclusion and equality for migrants in Europe.

Bibliography

Acosta, D. (2009) 'The good, the bad and the ugly in EU migration law: Is the European Parliament becoming bad and ugly? (The adoption of Directive 2008/15: The Returns Directive)', *European Journal of Migration and Law*, 11(1): 19–39.

African Commission on Human and Peoples' Rights (2003) Principles and Guidelines on the Right to a Fair Trial and Legal Assistance in Africa, DOC/OS(XXX)247.

Aliverti, A. (2017) 'Austerity and Justice in the Age of Migration' in A. Flynn and J. Hodgson (eds.) *Access to Justice and Legal Aid: Comparative Perspectives on Unmet Legal Need*, Oxford-Portland: Hart, 287–304.

Baldin, S. and Zago, M. (2017) 'The Common European Asylum System and the Social

Emergency of Unaccompanied Foreign Minors', in S. Baldin and M. Zago (eds.) *Europe of Migrations: Policies, Legal Issues and Experiences*, Trieste: EUT, 63–88.
Bendel, P. (2017) EU Refugee Policy in Crisis. Blockades, Decisions, Solutions, Bonn: Friedrich-Ebert-Stiftung.
Busatta, L. (2017) 'L'effettività del diritto d'accesso alla giustizia per gli stranieri' in F. Cortese and G. Pelacani (eds.) *Il diritto in migrazione. Studi sull'integrazione giuridica degli stranieri, Quaderni della Facoltà di Giurisprudenza*, 30: 447–467.
Campiglio, C. (2010) 'Disciplina delle migrazioni: limiti internazionali', in G. Cordini and V. Gasparini Casari (eds.) *Il diritto dell'immigrazione*, Modena: Mucchi.
Cappelletti, M. and Garth, B. (1977) 'Access to justice: The newest wave in the worldwide movement to make rights effective', *Buffalo Law Review*, 27: 181–292.
Cappelletti, M., Garth, B. and Trocker, N. (1982) 'Access to justice, variations and continuity of a world-wide movement', *The Rabel Journal of Comparative and International Private Law*, 46(4): 664–707.
CCBE (2010) *CCBE Recommendations on legal aid*, http://www.ccbe.eu/ (accessed on January 14th, 2018).
CCBE (2017) Comments of the Council of Bars and Law Societies of Europe (CCBE) on the draft Regulation presented on July 13, 2016 by the European Commission establishing a common asylum procedure for international protection and repealing Directive 2013/32/EU relating to minimal standards concerning the procedures for the granting and withdrawal of international protection, http://www.ccbe.eu/ (accessed on January 14th, 2018).
Chetail, V. (2014) 'Are Refugee Rights Human Rights? An Unorthodox Questioning of the Relations between Refugee Law and Human Rights Law' in R. Rubio-Marin (ed.) *Human Rights and Immigration, Collected Courses of the Academy of European Law*, Oxford: Oxford University Press, 19–72.
Committee of Ministers of the Council of Europe (1976) Resolution (76) 5 on legal aid in civil, commercial and administrative matters.
Committee of Ministers of the Council of Europe (1978) *Resolution (78) 8 on legal aid and advice*.
Committee of Ministers of the Council of Europe (2005) Recommendation (2005) 12 containing an application form for legal aid abroad for use under the European Agreement on the transmission of applications for legal aid (CETS No. 092) and its Additional Protocol (CETS No. 179).
Committee of Ministers of the Council of Europe (2005) *Twenty guidelines on forced return*.
Committee of Ministers of the Council of Europe (2009) Guidelines on human rights protection in the context of accelerated asylum procedures.
Cornford, T. (2016) 'The Meaning of Access to Justice', in E. Palmer *et al.* (eds.) *Access to Justice: Beyond the Policies and Politics of Austerity*, Oxford-Portland: Hart.
Costello, C. and Hancox, E. (2016) 'The Recast Asylum Procedures Directive 2013/32/EU: Caught between the Stereotypes of the Abusive Asylum Seeker and the Vulnerable Refugee', in V. Chetail, P. De Bruycker and F. Maiani (eds.) *Reforming the Common European Asylum System – The New European Refugee Law*, Leiden-Boston: Brill Nijhoff.
Council of Europe Commissioner for Human Rights (2001) Recommendation concerning

the rights of aliens wishing to enter a Council of Europe member State and the enforcement of expulsion orders (CommDH(2001)19).

ECRE (2016) *ECRE Comments on the Commission Proposal for a Dublin IV Regulation COM(2016) 270*, https://www.ecre.org/wp-content/uploads/2016/10/ECRE-Comments-Dublin-IV.pdf (accessed on January 14th, 2018).

ECRE/ELENA (2010) *Survey on Legal Aid for Asylum Seekers in Europe*, October 2010, https://www.ecre.org/wp-content/uploads/2016/07/ECRE-ELENA-Survey-on-Legal-Aid-for-Asylum-Seekers-in-Europe_October-2010.pdf (accessed on January 14th, 2018).

EU Network of Independent Experts on Fundamental Rights (2006) *Commentary of the Charter of Fundamental Rights of the European Union*, http://ec.europa.eu/justice/fundamental-rights/files/networkcommentaryfinal_en.pdf (accessed on January 14th, 2018).

European Commission (2015) Communication from the Commission to the European Parliament, the Council, the European Economic and Social Committee and the Committee of the Regions A European Agenda on Migration, COM/2015/0240 final.

Eurostat (2017) *Migration integration statistic – At risk of poverty and social exclusion*, http://ec.europa.eu/eurostat/statistics-explained/index.php/Main_Page (accessed on January 14th, 2018).

Ferri, D. (2017) 'The Role of the European Union in Protecting the Rights of Asylum Seekers with Disabilities' in S. Baldin and M. Zago (eds.) *Europe of Migrations: Policies, Legal Issues and Experiences*, Trieste: EUT, 89–106.

Flynn, A., Hodgson, J., Mcculloch, J. and Naylor, B. (2016) 'Legal aid and access to legal representation: Re-defining the right to a fair trial', Melbourne University Law Review, 40(1): 207–220.

Flynn, E. (2016) Disabled Justice? Access to Justice and the UN Convention on the Rights of Persons with Disabilities, London-New York: Routledge.

FRA and Council of Europe (2016) *Handbook on European Law Relating to Access to Justice*, Luxembourg: Publications Office of the European Union.

FRA (2010a) *The duty to inform applicants about asylum procedures: The asylum-seeker perspective*, http://fra.europa.eu/en/publication/2010/duty-inform-applicants-about-asylum-procedures-asylum-seeker-perspective (accessed on January 14th, 2018).

FRA (2010b) *Access to effective remedies: The asylum-seeker perspective*, http://fra.europa.eu/en/publication/2010/access-effective-remedies-asylum-seeker-perspective (accessed on January 14th, 2018).

Francioni, F. (ed.) (2007) *Access to Justice as a Human Right*, Oxford: Oxford University Press.

Francioni, F. (ed.) (2008) Accesso alla giustizia dell'individuo nel diritto internazionale e dell'Unione europea, Milan: Giuffrè.

Gerards, J.H. and Glas, L.R. (2017) 'Access to justice in the European Convention on Human Rights system', *Netherlands Quarterly of Human Rights*, 35(1): 11–30.

Gibson, F. (2010) 'Article 13 of the CRPD: A right to legal aid?', *Australian Journal of Human Rights*, 15(2): 123–142.

Giuffrè, M. (2016) 'Access to Asylum at Sea? Non-Refoulement and a Comprehensive Approach to Extraterritorial Human Rights Obligations' in V. Moreno-Lax and E. Papastavridis (eds.) *'Boat Refugees' and Migrants at Sea: A Comprehensive Approach*, Leiden-Boston: Brill Nijhoff, 248–275.

Goodwin-Gill, G.S. and McAdam, J. (2007) *The Refugee in International Law*, Oxford: Oxford University Press.

Grange, M. and Majcher, I. (2017) 'When Is Immigration Detention Lawful? The Monitoring Practices of UN Human Rights Mechanisms', Global Detention Project, Working Paper No. 21, https://www.globaldetentionproject.org/category/publications/working-papers (accessed on March 16th, 2019).

Gruodytė, E. and Kirchner, S. (2014) 'The Contribution of the European Charter of Human Rights to the Right to Legal Aid' in T. Kerikmäe (ed.) *Protecting Human Rights in the EU*, Berlin-Heidelberg: Springer, 71–90.

Guild, E. and Grant, S. (2017) *CEPS Research Report No. 2017/05: What role for the EU in the UN negotiations on a Global Compact on Migration?* http://aei.pitt.edu/85023/1/COMPACTS_RRpt_No_2017-05.pdf (accessed on January 14th, 2018).

Hathaway, J.C. (2005) *The Rights of Refugees Under International Law*, Cambridge: Cambridge University Press.

Hruschka, C. (2016) 'Dublin is dead! Long live Dublin! The 4 May 2016 proposal of the European Commission', *EU Immigration and Asylum Law and Policy*, blog post, http://eumigrationlawblog.eu/ (accessed on January 14th, 2018).

Ippolito, F. and Iglesias Sánchez, S. (2015) *Protecting Vulnerable Groups: The European Human Rights Framework*, Oxfort-Portland: Hart.

Jüriloo, K. (2015) 'Free legal aid – a human right', *Nordic Journal of Human Rights*, 33(3): 203–219.

Kyiv Declaration on the Right to Legal Aid (2007) Conference on the Protection and Promotion of Human Rights through Provision of Legal Services, Best Practices from Africa, Asia and Eastern Europe, Kyiv, 27–30 March.

Lelkes, O., Platt, L. and Ward, T. (2009) 'Vulnerable Groups: The Situation of People With Migrant Backgrounds' in T. Ward *et al.* (eds.) *European Inequalities: Social Inclusion and Income Distribution in the European Union*, Budapest: TÁRKI Social Research Institute Inc., 69–103.

Long, K. (2013) 'When refugees stopped being migrants: Movement, labour and humanitarian protection', *Migration Studies*, 1(1): 4–26.

Maiani, F. (2016) 'The Reform of Dublin III Regulation', Study for the European Parliament, PE 571, http://www.europarl.europa.eu/RegData/etudes/STUD/2016/571360/IPOL_STU%282016%29571360_EN.pdf (accessed on January 14th, 2018).

McBride, J. (2009) *Access to justice for migrants and asylum seekers in Europe*, European Committee on Legal Cooperation (CDCJ), https://rm.coe.int/1680597b1a (accessed on January 14th, 2018).

Mikolajczyk, B. (2016) 'Legal Aid for Applicants for International Protection', in V. Chetail, P. De Bruycker and F. Maiani (eds.) *Reforming the Common European Asylum System – The New European Refugee Law*, Leiden-Boston: Brill Nijhoff, 446–470.

Mowbray, A. (2005) 'The creativity of the European Court of Human Rights', *Human Rights Law Review*, 5(1): 57–79.

Nowak, M. (2005) *UN Covenant on Civil and Political Rights: CCPR Commentary*, Second edition, Kehl-Strasbourg-Arlington: Engel.

OHCHR (2013) Report of the Special Rapporteur on the independence of judges and lawyers, Gabriela Knaul, A/HRC/23/43, para 20.

Peers, S. (2016) 'Europe to the Rescue? EU Law, the ECHR and Legal Aid' in E. Palmer *et al.* (eds.) *Access to Justice Beyond the Policies and Politics of Austerity*, Oxford-Portland: Hart, 53–68.

Rass-Masson, N. and Rouas, V. (2017) *Effective access to justice*, Study commissioned by the European Parliament Policy Department for Citizens' Rights and Constitutional Affairs, PE 596.818, http://www.europarl.europa.eu/supporting-analyses (accessed on January 14th, 2018).

Ricci, C. (2017) 'I diritti "essenziali" della convivenza universale' in E Bettinelli (ed.) *Umanità e sovranità. I diritti negati ai migranti (1986–2015)*, Pavia: Pavia University Press.

Rice, S. (2017) 'Reasoning a Human Right to Legal Aid' in A. Flynn and J. Hodgson (eds.) *Access to Justice and Legal Aid: Comparative Perspectives on Unmet Legal Need*, Oxford-Portland: Hart, 195–220.

Thym, D. (2016) 'The "refugee crisis" as a challenge of legal design and institutional legitimacy', *Common Market Law Review*, 53(6): 1545–1574.

Thym, D. (2017) 'Pitfalls of the Law, Politics and Administrative Practices in the Reform of the Common European Asylum System', *EU Immigration and Asylum Law and Policy*, blog post, http://eumigrationlawblog.eu/ (accessed on January 14th, 2018).

Trinidade, A.A.C. (2011) *The Access of Individuals to International Justice*, Oxford: Oxford University Press.

Trinidade, A.A.C. (2015) 'Some Reflections on Access to Justice in its Worldwide Dimension' in R. Wolfrum, M. Seršić and T. Šošić (eds.) *Contemporary Developments in International Law. Essays in Honour of Budislav Vuka*, Leiden-Boston: Brill Nijihoff.

UNGA (2012) United Nations Principles and Guidelines on Access to Legal Aid in Criminal Justice Systems, 20 December 2012, A/67/458.

UNGA (2016) New York Declaration for Refugees and Migrants, 19 September 2016, A/RES/71/1.

UNGA (2017) Report of the Special Rapporteur on the human rights of migrants on a 2035 agenda for facilitating human mobility, A/HRC/35/25, 28 April 2017.

UNHCR (2001) Asylum processes. Fair and efficient asylum procedures, EC/GC/01/12.

UNHCR (2007) General Comment No. 32, Article 14: Right to equality before courts and tribunals and to a fair trial, CCPR/C/GC/32 23, par. 10.

UNHCR (2010) Improving asylum procedures: comparative analysis and recommendations for law and practice – Key findings and recommendations, http://www.unhcr.org/protection/operations/4ba9d99d9/improving-asylum-procedures-comparative-analysis-recommendations-law-practice.html (accessed on January 14th, 2018).

Willems, A. (2014) 'The United Nations principles and guidelines on access to legal aid in criminal justice systems', *New Criminal Law Review: An International and Interdisciplinary Journal*, 17(2): 184–219.

Chapter 14
Boundaries of identity and belonging in migration

Maria Assunta Zanetti and Gianluca Gualdi

14.1. *Introduction*

Identity is a complex concept which refers to a plurality of definitions, its treatment requiring an interdisciplinary approach. Indeed, identity is a term which is situated in an uncertain analytical zone, at the crossroads of different disciplines: cultural anthropology, developmental and social psychology, sociology, political science, and history.

Analysis of the dynamics which form the identity base and which sustain its development is social science's purpose. Identity can be understood as the dynamic outcome of a process of subjective self-awareness which results in a self-constructed resource which satisfies one's need to belong and integrate in the attempt to give life meaning. But if identity can be defined as the capacity to recognise one's wholeness and continuity through time, this means putting emphasis on the way in which the individual "goes through" time (that is, connects and represents their history, everyday life, and their future plan in themselves) and the strategies to which they turn to give significance and meaning to this continuous or discontinuous path. Naturally the subject, in designing their biography, punctuated by daily rhythms, makes reference and must take into account a time which is not just subjective, but is social and collective. They must, then, adapt their times to those of other subjects with whom they interact and to those social institutions with which they relate. We know: every social phenomenon has a time and develops over time. Time has both an internal-subjective element (in the relationship that the individual draws between past, present, and future), and an external-social element, the interaction of many time segments expressed by various social sectors. Construction of identity cannot be separated from either its relationship with the social environment or the particular relationships which the subject has in the course of their life.

14.2. *In search of identity: a balancing act*

It is possible to identify interdisciplinary points of convergence around the concept of identity which can be specified as such:

a. identity recalls, at once, the idea of equality and that of difference;
b. identity is not a given entity forever, fixed and unchanging, but rather an ever-changing reality, which continually evolves and is subject to social and cultural influences and transformations;
c. the process of constructing identity does not happen within the individual in isolated conditions, but rather has a social nature, that is, it is defined in the interaction with other members of society and in the cultural context in which everyone lives;
d. identity is constructed in the dialectic between equality and otherness. This answers the need to identify oneself, "to feel similar to" and, on the other hand, to affirm one's uniqueness, "to distinguish from".

When the protagonists of this event are adolescents, it becomes important to understand its scope in terms of psychological experiences, trying to identify protective factors and probable risk agents linked to the migratory experience and the process of adaptation to the receiving society.

Adolescence is already a very delicate phase in itself in an individual's development, since it entails not just physical and psychological changes, but transition from childhood to adulthood. Generally, the society and culture of origin ensure adolescents a sense of stability, support which is lacking for immigrant adolescents, who, caught between different cultures, have many obstacles in maintaining their emotional stability (Schimmenti 2001).

Necessarily, the process of constructing identity involves establishing boundaries between the self and the other, this process is born from a progressive distinction between the primary attachment figures and the subsequent internalising of parts of the world that are culturally defined by the social contexts of life, all this requires a delicate balancing act between cognitive, emotional, and value aspects. In a sense, identity structuring requires each person to establish, for their own stability, permeable boundaries that can be passed. Yet it therefore means to differentiate oneself, while recognising and finding oneself reflected in the other because they have the same dimension of values. Differentiation involves the ability to organise past and present experiences in a future dimension that is able to find meaning in the context of life since others also recognise the same experiences in themselves.

Identity formation in immigrants is a more complex task since they must reconcile different identity options: ethnic, personal, and cultural, which are often in conflict.

This path can therefore become even more difficult and risky for those who lack anchorage regarding both place and experience. In particular, the preadolescent and adolescent migrant must deal with the "migratory check" in which often value and cultural references are not easily traceable in the context of real life but only in a family narrative dimension which often obstructs the physiological process of differentiation-separation which allows them to arrive at an identity redefinition as it is difficult for them to identify the cultural and value dimension from which they must differentiate.

The central element on which we must focus our attention is the relationship between the individual, culture of origin, and culture of reception. It is between these polarities that the adolescent development of young migrants plays out, who, compared to their peers in the receiving country, are forced to follow a surely more tiring growth since they must confront a "double transition", that is the passage towards adulthood, as well as that towards the receiving society. This phenomenon involves the combination of psychological, cognitive, and social changes which happen during the adolescent period and provokes what Erikson (1968) has called the "identity crisis" which influences the immigrant's interior world, influencing their sense of self and their process of identity formation (Schwartz et al. 2006; Schwartz 2005; Phinney et al. 2001). These young people face conflicting social contexts in which they try to incorporate "here" and "there" into a meaningful sense of self (Zhou 1997; Rumbaut 1994) through community, familial, and ethnic models of socialisation in which the language, values, and customs of the origin country have been adopted, but at the same time they have been educated in the host educational system, assimilating habits, linguistic competences, and cultural models (Bernal and Knight 1993; Berry 1997, 2001; Berry et al. 2006; Rumbaut 1994). This duality of contexts makes the process of identity formation significantly different for immigrant adolescents from that of their first-generation parents. Amongst immigrants' children, this process is very complex, and often entails a delicate balance of competing alliances and attachments. Situated within the two cultural worlds, they must define themselves in relation to multiple reference groups (sometimes in two countries and in two languages) and classifications in which they are placed by their native peers, schools, ethnic community, and by society at large (Rumbaut 2005).

The migratory phenomenon makes the process of co-identification – that is the physiological distance between generations – and the search for their own identity even more difficult for immigrant adolescents. To confront the double transition, the immigrant minor can draw on various resources, including linguistic competency, a fundamental skill during the cross-cultural adaptation process. Indeed, this reduces social difficulties, allowing for greater interaction/integration with the residents of a place (Ward et al. 1999).

14.3. *Boundaries or barriers?*

The boundary, in an etymological sense, indicates the end, the extreme limit which separates a property of any kind, territorial, linguistic, or social, from another. In biology this becomes the membrane of passage between the inside and outside, the regulator of the body's homeostasis. This function can be found in identity structuring when we come to identify the edge of our identity, separating "what's inside" from "what's outside" but perceived in continuity and only in this way can we experience stability. This stability, in the case of adolescent immigrants, becomes more difficult to identify as they must learn, in the majority of cases, to manage dissonant cultural contexts. Due to the complicated identity development process amongst these young people, they become aware of the national and ethnic boundaries which surround them (Rumbaut 1994, 2005) and therefore, they are required to incorporate more rules, values, and expectations. All this causes a situation of greater instability which provokes and intensifies the conflicts which the adolescent is called to experience and which often are not so much attributable to fundamental questions such as moral, political, or religious ones, but rather to questions of lesser significance and more linked to the everyday. Cicognani's research (2012) shows that the principal reasons for conflict involve house rules (who must handle domestic work, when bedtime is), some personal questions like doing homework, management of free time, and above all, life outside the home (if and with who you can go out, what time you must come home, use of money), an area of conflict in which children register dispute while parents seem sure of their decisions.

In the psychological sense, the concept of the boundary plays a fundamental function in the construction and production of identity, for which I must, however, find correspondence in the context of life. In the case of immigrants, establishing borders of one's identity becomes much more complex as it is a process of reconciliation between two value systems and cultural beliefs (new context and family context of origin) in a precarious balancing act. This produces that phenomenon defined as acculturation stress which can manifest with behavioural symptoms which can have negative consequences for both self-esteem and level of satisfaction with one's life, thereby creating barriers (Madsen 2003).

In this context, foreign minors not only find themselves faced with changes linked to growth, typical of every evolutionary condition, but also with those regarding their location and their insertion into a social organisation and cultural tradition that are very different from those of their family's origin and sometimes theirs, with specific requirements which they must know how to respond to in the quickest and most coherent way possible. And amongst the different challenges posed by this condition, the "multi-belonging", or rather the "combination" of different belongings, seems to be one of the fields to which new generations are most committed, born from migratory movements which have characterised and changed the face of Italian society in recent years, projecting them towards a search for integration that is able to guarantee balance between the different cultures in which they find themselves living (Valtolina 2006).

All of this is reflected in the process of identity redefinition that can go from a low level of cultural identity with their culture of origin or the culture of their parents' origin and low level of cultural identity with the new context "neither here nor there" or low level of cultural identity with their culture of origin or the culture of their parents' origin with the new context's values "here and not there". As we have observed, the process of identity formation in immigrant adolescents is much more complex since they most move in multiple scenarios.

From this point of view, identity formation is a dynamic process in which boundaries are continually being defined.

Identity formation between immigrants' children can thus be described as a continual process in which the host country, the country of origin, both or neither, create dynamic models of identity. The risk of all this is the possibility that these adolescents can have different, even contradictory, identities with loose boundaries.

The collision of two different cultures causes significant cultural transformations which, on the one hand, bring new knowledge and experiences, but, on the other, could cause stiffness, conflicts, uncertainties, and disorientation. In this case, one speaks, in particular, of the cultural discomfort referenced to the problematic and often conflictual reality that follows the collision of two cultures due to migration phenomena or even cultural disturbance if the situation of discomfort, more or less strong, is connected to a situation considered to be negative by the individual or group they're part of because it is contrary to their expectations/aspirations (work, interpersonal relationships, social relationships, etc.).

It is therefore important to allow the process of cultural mixing in which immigrants adopt aspects of the host culture, integrating them and re-elaborating them with the rules and values of the new context, so they are equipped to face the "double transition".

14.4. *Identity or culture problems?*

There are many studies in psychology which focus on themes of identity and culture; particularly, there has, in recent years, been talk of ethnopsychiatry, understood as the study and classification of psychiatric disorders and syndromes, but taking into account the specific cultural context in which they manifest and the ethnic group the person comes from. These stories therefore provide understanding of behaviour based on the cultural origins of the person enacting it. For example, if we think of populations that practice and believe in Voodoo, they are considered "normal" in countries in which this religion is practiced, while they may appear "disturbed" in western cultures or ones with different religions. The risk, therefore, is labelling these behaviours as pathologies, when they are shown in one culture compared to another and to provide a diagnostic label which can influence identity's development, particularly during an adolescent's growth (Losi 2000).

From this perspective, the most recent version of the Diagnostic and Statistical Manual of Mental Disorders – DSM-5 (American Psychiatric Association 2013) also underlines, to those seeking to understand the individual's personality and identity, the need to know and/or try to understand the cultural context of the person compared to the problem they report or others report for them (when thinking of adolescents, usually the problems are in fact referred by parents or teachers). Indeed, frequently migrants or second-generation children come to care services for deviant or extreme situations, instead revealing problems of a different kind, which were not previously recognised. It is therefore fundamental that in the processes of care and taking responsibility for a person, we seek to understand their language, religion and spiritual world, as well as family structure, and stage in life cycle, rituals, and ceremonies. These aspects are also important in school and educational contexts, in which the moral and legal systems of a person are quickly made evident, often appearing deviant within the host context, but which are in line with the country of origin. If these aspects are not integrated with each other they risk influencing self-understanding and awareness, and therefore the possibility of understanding one's identity in a clear and defined framework. Different cultures are at the base of one's identity formation and help a person give their experiences meaning (Bateson and Ruesch 1976). A child of a couple born and raised in the same country will have less difficulty integrating amongst the three different cultures of belonging: father's culture, mother's culture, country's culture. In cases of migration, international adoption, relocation, etc., this integration becomes more complex, since one or more of the three cultures is different and more time and resources are required to be integrated among them.

14.5. *Family boundaries*

Adolescence has always been considered the crisis moment in a family, with the idea that it is a complex evolutionary stage for the individual experiencing it, as well as for all those around them. Often with the term family, we consider the mother-father-offspring triad, but in reality it is a broader system that "is that specific and unique social group which deals with and keeps together the originary human differences, those between gender (the masculine and feminine genders), those between generations (parents and children) and those between ancestry (that is, the maternal and paternal family tree) and for which generativity is an intrinsic objective" (Scabini and Iafrate 2003: 45). In adolescence, we observe, however, the need for the child to single themselves out from their parents and broader family system. At this time, the individual finds themselves confronting new experiences with semi-autonomy, for example, studying, first jobs and emotional relationships which impose a progressive physical and/or emotional distancing from the family. This process happens when all the parties are truly involved and in agreement with allowing the individual to become autonomous, including on the emotional and cognitive plane, with, therefore, the development of an increasingly clear and defined identity, until personality structuring is defined (Pietropolli Charmet 2005; Andolfi and Miscellani 2010). We observe, however, that the individual tends to lead this process but that this is not observed in all families. Indeed, there are theories which refer to the existence of different types of families (Olson et al. 1979; Olson 2000); such models underline how some families struggle in the negotiation of the adolescent's distancing, for example, so-called entangled families experience the adolescent's separation as a betrayal, while in the disengaged, this detachment is not calm since relatives are not experienced as significant on an emotional level (Olson et al. 2007).

We observe that this process is complex for all, but even more so for the migrant family, which finds itself having to confront and manage the cultural differences between their home country and the host one.

The structure and representation of family, in immigrants, can be different compared to that of the host society. In western society, family has a nuclear structure and is composed of parental couples and children, while, in other countries, the family is larger, and composed of different degrees and levels of parenting: father, mother, brothers, sisters, uncles, aunts, and cousins.

Moreover, the family is a complex and collective entity in which there is an exchange between its components, and an exchange with the environment. These are all interactions which produce beliefs, representations, and a behavioural and value system that underlies identity construction.

Sluzki (1979) suggests some stages of the immigration process involve the family on different planes. The preparatory stage is that of consultation which leads family members to decide to emigrate, with a process of assigning the final decision to some members of the nucleus. This choice can fall to a child or young adult, in a direct way (the child asks to leave) or indirect (the parents want the best for the child and decide to move, but giving them the responsibility). The second stage is the act of migrations: a strong influence is whether the family moves together or at different times, since time is spent apart, maintaining, however, mental representations of the other or imagining the other in a context of luck and privilege. Moreover, some acts are transitory, while others are permanent; in the first case, the melancholy and desire to return the country of origin as soon as possible remains while with the permanent act, much depends on how the family adapts to the new context. It is a different matter for refugees or those expelled from their own country, who find themselves confronting a deeply traumatic separation and reconciliation since it is unwanted and uncontrollable. Once the migratory act is over, the balancing stage arises in which the family inserts itself into the new social reality and is characterised by the necessity of meeting primary needs. It surfaces as at this stage the family appears very united in facing situations and tries to best integrate itself into the environment. Discomforts and conflicts that are not usually expressed are therefore placated. There is, therefore, a decompensation stage (crisis) in which the family inserts itself into the social context, trying to maintain a balance between its identity and the new culture. Conflicts in the parental couple or amongst them and children often surface because the internal roles and rules of the system must be reviewed and renegotiated. The final stage is that of the trans-generational phenomena in which cultural conflicts between the second generation and parents arise.

Specifically, the fourth stage of decompensation is fundamental, it being the moment of crisis and of putting one's identity into play. In particular, an adolescent at this stage faces many crises: family identity against culture, individual identity against the family. It is in this moment that identity boundaries are therefore put into play, modified and changed (Belhadj Kouider et al. 2015).

The tasks of the immigrant family's development are therefore the care of the culture of origin and the host culture, the integration of differences, and the construction of a new family identity. This final aspect depends on the possibility of constructing a psychic and relational space that integrates experiences, cultures, and differences, in a meaningful model, with respect to ethical values and acceptable behaviours.

The adolescent immigrant finds themselves constantly having to "renegotiate" their identity between the inside (the family) and the outside (the social reality). Like their peers, they must move between the sense of belonging to the family and the autonomy or individuation from the nucleus, but those who are foreign must also continually renegotiate their identity between two different cultural contexts (Molcho et al. 2010).

The adolescent can adopt different strategies in adjusting to the differences between the family value system and that of the social context. We can observe a process of separation, in which the adolescent remains connected to the culture of origin, avoiding contact with the host culture (reduces the possibility of building a social network). In other cases, the adolescent assimilates the new culture, adhering to the values and behaviours, refusing all or part of the culture of origin. Another possibility is the strategy of marginalisation, in which the young person doesn't maintain links with anyone of the two reference cultures; this process is that which most negatively influences the individual's psychological wellbeing. Finally, we observe a process of integration, in which the adolescent maintains their family's culture but shows openness to that of the host. A good integration allows differences to be combined with a consequent construction of identity which is integrated at the level of thoughts and emotions.

Research shows that the solidity of the sense of belonging to the ethnic group of family origin is a major protective factor for the adolescent. Indeed, from this foundation, the young person can discover and know the social context of life, integrating and fostering a rich and complex identity.

Models of resilience (Masten 2011; Ungar 2013) highlight the stressors of a migrant family which, should they transform into insurmountable obstacles, become risk factors for the integration of cultures in the process of identity construction. The principle factors are: economic deprivation, separation in families and loss of some members, changes social roles and loss of esteem, witnessed or suffered psychic and psychological violence, ethnic persecution, loss of home, country, family members, and friends, type of welcome upon arrival in the new country, potential insertions into collective centres or private houses, and uncertainty regarding the future.

Relationships are therefore fundamental and protective factors within the family or in the social context. Starting from the assumption that man is a social creature (Bateson 1977, 1984), we observe how the relational aspect is fundamental in the construction of a solid identity, since it is within relationships that one learns to modulate behaviours and learnings. It is therefore important to work on several systems to allow for good integration: families, schools, afternoon spaces for adolescents, etc. (Bronfenbrenner 1986).

As well as individual resilience, resilience at a family level also surfaces, with a foundation of relationship patterns which establish cohesion, flexibility, open communication, problem solving abilities, and to support one's belief system (Walsh 1998). From this point of view, family resilience does not predict surviving a crisis in an unchanging manner, but the possibility of structuring potential to grow despite adversity. A "sufficiently good" family thus pushes the adolescent immigrant towards a process of integration of their identity with the country of residence, not towards processes of separation or assimilation. The work of the family in such situations is therefore to provide for the implementation of a dynamic process, so that in the course of events one or more protective factors can arise: connection of the members, commitment of family members, respect, support, division of tasks, organisational stability, socioeconomic status, communication, openness towards the outside, and having support networks. All these factors have been observed as universal, but culturally connoted: in some countries, for example, the division of labour requires that parents take care of children, in other cultures, that older siblings raise younger ones. A "better or worse" is not observed, rather how the second behaviour is less integratable with the first or vice versa.

14.6. *Conclusions*

The concept of identity has a complex and difficult explanation, even more so when linked to the theme of migration. Identity is a continuous search for balance and stability between different values, rules, and messages, which, however, originate from a common and shared foundation, which is that of the culture. When we witness the influence on a culture by other cultures in the migration process, we observe a greater resource need to integrate them with each other. Identity's shell, which ensures coherence and wellbeing, becomes more permeable and sensitive to changes and external and internal influences during the migration; this weakness of the self's boundaries risks creating disorientation, with possible repercussions on self-perception and the individual's wellbeing. The family plays a fundamental role in redefining the individual's identity boundaries, in particular if they're an adolescent; it is therefore necessary that this stage in life is increasingly characterised by interventions to support parenting and the adoption process. The challenge of integration can be played out in the context of the redefinition of family boundaries by implementing social policies of support and intervention for parents when the entire value and behavioural system of origin is in crisis.

The process of identity construction is not exclusive to a single person and their family system, but being dependent on relationships, is also strongly influenced by educational contexts, such as school, youth centres, sports groups, etc. It is also necessary to reflect, therefore, on specific learning strategies and methods for child and adolescent migrants, so as to guarantee them the best possible level of wellbeing.

Bibliography

American Psychiatric Association (2013) *DSM-5. Manuale diagnostico e statistico dei disturbi mentali*, Milan: Raffaello Cortina.

Andolfi, M. and Miscellani, A. (2010) *Storie di Adolescenza: esperienze di terapia familiare*, Milan: Raffaello Cortina.

Bateson, G. (1977) *Verso un'ecologia della mente*, Milan: Adelphi.

Bateson, G. (1984) *Mente e natura, un'unità necessaria*, Milan: Adelphi.

Bateson, G. and Ruesch, J. (1976) *La matrice sociale della psichiatria*, Bologna: Il Mulino.

Belhadj Kouider, E., Koglin, U. and Petermann, F. (2015) 'Emotional and behavioral problems in migrant children and adolescents in American countries: A systematic review', *Journal of Immigrant Minority Health*, 17: 1240–1258.

Bernal, M.E. and Knight, G.P. (eds.) (1993) *Ethnic Identity: Formation and Transmission Among Hispanics and Other Minorities*, New York: State University of New York Press.

Berry, J. (1997) 'Immigration, acculturation, and adaptation', *Applied Psychology International Review*, 46: 5–34.

Berry, J. (2001) 'A psychology of immigration', *Journal of Social Issues*, 57: 615–631.

Berry, J.W., Phinney, J.S., Sam, D.L. and Vedder, P. (2006) *Immigrant Youth in Cultural Transition: Acculturation, Identity and Adaptation Across National Contexts*, Mahwah: Lawrence Erlbaum Associates.

Bolaffi, G., Gindro, S. and Tentori, T. (1998) *Dizionario della diversità*, Firenze: LibriLiberal.

Bronfrenbrenner, U. (1986) Ecologia dello sviluppo umano, Bologna: Il Mulino.

Chiodi, F. and Benadusi, M. (2006) *Seconde generazioni e località. Giovani volti della migrazione cinese, marocchina e romena in Italia*, Rome: Labos.

Cicognani, E. (2012) 'Comportamenti a rischio per la salute, benessere e processi psicosociali. Uno sguardo agli adolescenti immigrati', in P. Marmocchi (ed.) *Nuove generazioni. Genere, sessualità e rischio tra gli adolescenti di origine straniera*, Milan: FrancoAngeli, 41–58.

Di Vita, A.M. and Granatella, V. (2009) *Famiglie in viaggio*, Rome: Edizioni Magi.

Erikson, E. (1968) *Identity, Youth and Crisis*, New York: Norton and Co.

Gambini, P. (2007) *Psicologia della famiglia*, Milan: FrancoAngeli.

Gozzoli, C. and Regalia, C. (2005) *Migrazioni e famiglie*, Bologna: Il Mulino.

Lévi-Strauss, C. (1986) *L'identità*, Palermo: Sellerio.

Losi, N. (2000) *Vite altrove – Migrazione e disagio psichico*, Milan: Feltrinelli.

Madsen, K.D. (2003) 'Migration, identity, and belonging', *Journal of Borderlands Studies*, 18(1): 61–75.

Masten, A.S. (2011) 'Resilience in children threatened by extreme adversity: frameworks for research, practice, and translational synergy', *Development and Psychipathology*, 23(2): 493–506.

Molcho, M., Cristini, F., Gabhainn, S.N., Santinello, M., Moreno, C., Gaspar de Matos, M., Bjarnason, T., Baldassarri, D. and Due, P. (2010) 'Health and well-being among child immigrants in Europe', *Eurohealth*, 16: 20–23.

Olson, D.H. (2000) 'Circumplex model of family systems', *Journal of Family Therapy*, 22(2): 144–167.

Olson, D.H., Gorall, D.M. and Tiesel, J.W. (2007) *FACES IV Manual*, Minneapolis: Life Innovations.

Olson, D.H., Sprenkle, D.H. and Russell, C. (1979) 'Circumplex model of marital and family systems: I. Cohesion and adaptability dimensions, family types, and clinical applications', *Family Process*, 18: 3–28.

Phinney, J.S. (1991) 'Ethnic identity and self-esteem: A review and integration', *Hispanic Journal of Behavioral Sciences*, 13(2): 193–208.

Phinney, J.S., Horenczyk, G., Liebkind, K. and Vedder, P. (2001) 'Ethnic identity, immigration, and well-being: An interactional perspective', *Journal of Social Issues*, 57(3): 493–510.

Phinney, J.S., Romero, I., Nava, M. and Huang, D. (2001) 'The role of language, parents, and peers in ethnic identity among adolescents in immigrant families', *Journal of Youth and Adolescence*, 30(2): 135–153.

Pietropolli Charmet, G. (2005) Adolescenza. Istruzioni per l'uso, Milan: Fabbri.

Rumbaut, R.G. (1994) 'The crucible within: Ethnic identity, self-esteem, and segmented assimilation among children of immigrants', *International Migration Review*, 28(4): 748–794.

Rumbaut, R.G. (2005) 'Assimilation, dissimilation, and ethnic identities', in M. Rutter and M. Tienda (eds.) *Ethnicity and Causal Mechanisms*, Cambridge: Cambridge University Press, 301–335.

Scabini, E. and Iafrate, S. (2003) *Psicologia dei legami familiari*, Bologna: Il Mulino.

Scabini, E. and Rossi, G. (2008) *La migrazione come evento familiare*, Milan: Vita e Pensiero.

Schimmenti, V. (2001) *Identità e differenze etniche*, Milan: FrancoAngeli.

Schwartz, S.J. (2005) 'A new identity for identity research', *Journal of Adolescent Research*, 20(3): 293–308.

Schwartz, S.J., Montgomery, M.J. and Briones, E. (2006) 'The role of identity in acculturation among immigrant people: Theoretical propositions, empirical questions, and applied recommendations', *Human Development*, 49: 1–30.

Sluzki, C. (1979) 'Migration and family conflict', *Family Process*, 18(4): 379–390.

Ungar, M. (2013) 'The impact of youth-adult relationships on resilience', International Journal of Child, *Youth and Family Studies*, 4(3): 328–336.

Valtolina, G.G., Marazzi A. (eds.) (2006) *Appartenenze multiple. L'esperienza dell'immigrazione nelle nuove generazioni*, Milan: FrancoAngeli.

Walsh, F. (1995) *Stili di funzionamento familiare*, Milan: Franco Angeli.

Walsh, F. (1998). *Strengthening family resilience*, New York: Guilford Press.

Walsh, F. (2008) *La resilienza familiare*, Milan: Raffaello Cortina.

Ward, R.-D. (1999) 'Acculturation and adaptation revisited', *Journal of Cross-Cultural Psychology*, 30: 422–442.

Zanetti, M.A. (2011) 'Identità migranti' in A. Passerini and M. Talamoni (eds.) *Migranti: transculturalità ed esperienza immaginativa*, Milan: Alpes, 1–18.

Zanetti, M.A. and Peruselli, S. (2010) 'Immigrazione: una prospettiva verso l'integrazione' in A. Passerini, M.A. Zanetti and M. De Palma (eds.) *Strategie a confronto nell'integrazione delle culture diverse*, Milan: Alpes, 1–10.

Zhou, M. (1997) 'Growing Up American: The Challenge Confronting Immigrant Children and Children of Immigrants', *Annual Review of Sociology*, 23: 63–95.

Chapter 15

Gaining and losing

Space crossing, identity perception and reinvention in 19th-Century Mediterranean exile

Arianna Arisi Rota

> Gaining freedom we lost many enjoyments of freedom. I remember when we used to cross over the border between Austrian Lombardy and the Piedmontese territory beyond the river Po. The very moment of the passage was a moment of anxiety and silence. Yet as soon as the bar on the bridge changed from yellow to white-red and green colors our hearts gave a start and a cry came to our lips. It seemed as if we had emerged from a deadly sultriness. It seemed as if we could already breath the purest, the cristal clearest air [...]. The "crossing of the border" will be one of my beloved memories forever! [1]

In his memoirs of his years spent as a teenager in Pavia during the Austrian rule, Carlo Dossi – a versatile writer and a diplomat in the final decades of 19th-Century Italy – recalled the pleasure experienced when crossing the border marked by the Ticino river which divided the university town, belonging to the Kingdom of Lombardy-Venetia, from the surrounding territories of the Kingdom of Piedmont and Sardinia. The national colors adopted by the Piedmontese Kingdom after the constitutional change of 1848 were on the bar at the police station, embodying the change of political atmosphere travelers would breathe as soon as their coach had overcome the Austrian sentry box.

What Dossi, now a citizen of the unified Italy, seemed to be regretting was his juvenile emotion of breathing freedom when entering the Piedmontese territory: actually, what he was really missing was the feeling of brotherhood that the political divisions of the peninsula had inspired in its inhabitants. Almost a paradox, "nowadays borders have disappeared. – And so much did we Italians love each other when the

---

[1] "Acquistando la libertà abbiamo perduto molti dei godimenti della libertà. Io mi ricordo quando si passava il confine che stava tra la Lombardia austriaca e l'Oltrepò piemontese. Il momento del passaggio era un momento di ansia e di silenzio. Ma appena la sbarra del ponte da giallo diventava bianco-rosso e verde i nostri cuori balzavano, e un grido ci erompeva dalle labbra. Ci pareva di essere usciti da un'afa mortale. Ci pareva di respirare già la più pura, la più cristallina delle arie [...]. Il "passaggio del confine" sarà sempre una delle mie più care memorie!" (Dossi 2010: 283–284, my translation). At that time University students were forbidden to walk to the border area, the so-called *Gravellone*, and even to swim in the river Ticino being it a way to cross the frontier with the Piedmontese State.

Germans were guarding us. All brothers. One enemy". [2]

Yet, during the Risorgimento decades, the passage of that same border, especially at night and with the help of patriotic boatmen, had for many meant putting their lives at risk and, perhaps even more, becoming political refugees. Exiles.

What kind of feelings arose when crossing land, river or sea borders, leaving homeland, the beloved ones and, last but not least, professional status and family assets?

> Now we are sure we won't be taken to Alger; we are free; a passport can't be refused to us; I personally don't care to be in Switzerland or in France; the only part of Europe where I want to live is Italy, if it is denied to me, any other country doesn't matter. [3]

This is how one Cesare Rosa, an exile from the 1831 revolution in Modena who had left Ancona on board of the boat Isotta, [4] described his emotions as a newcomer entering the refugees' environment in Toulon, France, on July 5, 1831. That wave of middle class exiles scattered from one shore of the Mediterranean to another, as many other waves from the Mediterranean diasporas of that century (Isabella and Zanou 2016; Isabella 2006, 2009, 2011), helps us to approach the experience of gaining and losing in a sample of famous and obscure Risorgimento exiles. Though recent scholarly literature revisiting the Italian nation-making process has paid new attention to the emotional dimension of political engagement and militancy (Banti and Ginsborg 2007; Patriarca and Riall 2012), the dynamics of material loss and status loss in the case of exiles have not yet received the attention they deserve. [5] The obsession with economic support and the challenge of existential reinvention playing a great role in daily life in a foreign environment, the awareness of what is left behind and the disorientation for what is awaiting ahead create a powerful mixture worthy of being approached. Caught physically and mentally when "on the border", in the rift between their previous lives and the uncertain new ones, these men (and women)'s emotions do not seem much different from those of all displaced people entering an existential condition ruled by absolute arbitrariness and contingency. [6]

---

[2] "oggidì sono spariti i confini. – E come ci s voleva bene tra noi Italiani quando i Tedeschi ci facevano la guardia. Tutti fratelli. Uno solo il nemico" (*ibidem*, my translation).

[3] Quoted in Sorbelli (1931: 204–205), my translation.

[4] The boat had been blocked by the Austrian Navy soon after its departure and the nearly one hundred people onboard had been imprisoned in Venice.

[5] Useful remarks on this subject are to be found in P. Audenino, *Esuli risorgimentali: esploratori della libertà o naufraghi della rivoluzione ?* in *Archivio storico dell'emigrazione italiana*, 9/2013, p. 19, while the first outcomes of a promising team research coordinated by Catherine Brice and devoted to confiscation and seizure policy of the assets of political refugees are presented in the *Mélanges de l'École Française de Rome Italie Méditerranée* online series, No. 129-2/2017. See also Audenino and Bechelloni (2009: 343-348).

[6] Pasquinelli (2009: 44). Useful remarks on the deep feeling of uncertainty experienced by the exile in the making are to be found in Zanini (1997: 70–71).

15.1. *Beyond the Alps*

In the visual narrative of Italian exile, probably no image has better served the patriotic cause than the picture showing Giuseppe Mazzini crossing the Italian border on the Alps. A double version is known, one by Edoardo Matania, dating from late 1880s[7] (Figure 15.1), and another by Mantegazza and Barberis (Figure 15.2).

Figure 15.1. Edoardo Matania: *Giuseppe Mazzini on the road to exile*

[7] One copy in the collections of the Museo Centrale del Risorgimento in Rome (MCRR Ved3(88)), which I wish to thank for the permission to reproduce the image. A similar iconic representation is to be found in Antonio Ciseri's *L'Esule* (1860–1870 ca), located at Museo d'Arte in Lugano. https://commons.wikimedia.org/wiki/File:L%27Esule_by_Antonio_Ciseri_(1821-1891).jpg .

Figure 15.2. G. Mantegazza and Barberis: *Mazzini on the road to exile, arrived at the border of Italy, says farewell to his homeland from the Alps* (from J. White Mario, *Della vita di Giuseppe Mazzini*, Milano: Astra, 1986: 105)

The two still-frames, though not coeval to the event, are nevertheless extremely meaningful as iconic representations of the exile identity in the making. While Matania chose to focus on a Mazzini dressed all in black and isolated from ordinary travelers (shown at some distance walking or sitting in a stage coach heavy with luggage and belongings), standing on the rocky edge of the road and sorrowfully looking at the Italian landscape below, Mantegazza's Mazzini is caught in a more dynamic attitude, showing with his hand the Italian valley he is leaving behind to a friend and the driver of a gig waiting for him close to the at that time improbable road sign "Confine d'Italia". No wonder that, after the failure of the Italian 1848 revolution, Mazzini, back on his way to exile, committed his feelings to a lacerating poem whose title was L'addio dalle Alpi (The farewell from the Alps) (De Marco 1996: 41).

The passage of the Alps – together with the surrounding Mediterranean sea, the physical border nature had assigned to the Italian peninsula – had a long symbolic and epic tradition as the land-gate crossed by invaders and conquerors in a sublime but also hostile environment (from Hannibal caught by a snowstorm with his elephants to Napoleon Bonaparte's enterprise iconized in David's painting). During the Risorgimento it acquired new meaning as one of the most immediate and dynamic experiences of exile, being Switzerland and France were the closest destinations especially for political refugees from Lombardy and Piedmont-Liguria. [8] Yet, in spite of their already established vocation as lands offering political asylum, [9] both countries were entered with mixed feelings: intimate sources confirm that the crossing and later on the sight of the Alps "from the other side" proved to be the most effective visual evidence of the new existential condition. "I left the Canton of Berne and I took shelter in this half desert", Agostino Ruffini, a close friend of Mazzini's, wrote from the Swiss village of Boujan in July 1834:

> How many times I do sit sadly by my window and I gaze at these Alps, my arms folded across my chest [...]. Here you are, and behind you the beautiful, the charming, the magnificent Italy, the Eden where angels should live and where devils live. Oh my homeland, will I ever see you again? And you, powerless Alps which offer no dangers to the foreigner, will you open yourselves to the refugee who sighs at the balsamic breath coming from his homeland [10]

The "powerless Alps" are a clear projection of the powerlessness of the exile himself, which recalls the perennial perception of exile being the place of powerlessness stressed by contemporary exiles such as the Chinese poet Yang Lian. Even more significantly, the natural barrier which hampered the sight of Italy to the 1834 refugee testifies the dimension of the migrant-exile as an "in between" identity experience matching with an "in between" memory experience. As Maria Neagu and Olivier Côté have recently pointed out, "partant d'un 'ailleurs' vers un 'ici', d'un 'là-bas' vers un 'au-delà', le personnage migrant ne cesse de vivre dans un 'entre-deux', sur un pont imaginaire qu'il bâtit lui-même de souvenirs et de découvertes" (Neagu and Côté 2013).

It is thus when the homeland is still in sight, or can still be imagined as laying behind a visual obstacle, that the exercise of mentally entering the domestic space takes

---

[8] The tradition of the passage beyond the Alps in Italian migration history has been recently focused at the international conference *Oltrepassando le Alpi, prima e dopo Schengen. Giornata di studi italo-francesi sulle migrazioni italiane in Francia nel XX secolo/Franchir les Alpes, avant et après Schengen. Journée d'études italo-françiases sur les migrations italiennes en France au cours du XX siècle*, Turin, Centro Altreitalie, May 6, 2017.

[9] A recent important research on the French case distinguishes the experiences of different waves of exiles according to the changes in the receiving policies adopted by the French government in the Restoration (Diaz 2014).

On the French long-term case, also very useful and inspiring Aprile (2010). As to the Swiss case, still useful Martinola (1980, 1994).

[10] "Ho lasciato il cantone di Berna e mi sono rifugiato in questo mezzo deserto [...]. Quante volte mi seggo tristemente presso la mia finestra e contemplo queste Alpi, le braccia incrociate sul petto. [...] Eccovi, e dietro a voi la bella, la ridente, la magnifica Italia, l'Eden dove gli angeli dovrebbero abitare e dove soggiornano i demoni. O patria mia, ti rivedrò? E voi Alpi impotenti che non avete pericoli per lo straniero, vi aprirete al proscritto che sospira al soffio balsamico della terra natale?" (Agostino Ruffini to his mother, Boujan, July 6, 1834, quoted in Cavassa 1931: 205, my translation).

place: "Thought by thought I come to the place where I was born, I enter the house where I gave my first cry. I see a woman in a room [...], it's you, my tender friend, my mother, my sister, my Guardian Angel". [11] The virtual trip from Switzerland to the hometown Genoa is therefore but one of the possible emotional strategies meant to nurture the feeling of absence and loneliness suffered from the moment the mountain border had been crossed. Even more profoundly, it enables the refugee to fight the present feeling of estrangement – the feeling of being "another person" – with the memory of his coming to life as an individual.

If the experience of crossing the land border and spotting the homeland from a distance contributes to the shaping of an early awareness of a new identity – a kind of no man's land citizenship – it is with the following search for material support and economic sufficiency that the new condition is established. The poverty of the Risorgimento exiles, forced to reinvent themselves as teachers of Italian, of music, or as fencing masters (this was the case of many veterans from the Napoleonic army), in the early stages contributed to the building of their narrative and myth. "Ici on meurt de faim, de froid et de désespoir", Carlo Botta, an Italian exile in the 1799 wave, wrote from France a few months after his departure from the peninsula (Rao 1992: 20). "Without the conquibus one dies like a dog", Luigi Tinelli, a leader in the conspiracy network founded by Mazzini and a deportee to the United States in 1836, would write later in his life (Sioli 2004).

In the light scattered by recent scholarly research, it is thus worth stressing how much financial support and professional status did indeed matter as soon as the host or the transit country was entered. Obsessed by material need, even in spite of local personal networks (the exile chains acting as migration chains), refugees from the peninsula States depended on family support and on benefits granted by hosting governments, as happened in the French case masterfully investigated by Delphine Diaz. [12] As Diaz has pointed out, trajectories from being a beneficiary to entering the labour market were not easy ones – due also to the linguistic barrier – and they deserve further investigation. [13] Barriers other than the physical and administrative ones represented by borders were therefore added in the 19th-Century decades as they are nowadays to the political refugee/migrant trying to reinvent their own future while keeping their memory and emotional roots in the past. Material need and holy memories prove to

[11] "Di pensiero in pensiero arrivo al luogo dove sono nato, entro nella casa dove ho emesso il gemito che annunciava la mia nascita. Vedo in una stanza una donna: [...] siete voi, mia tenera amica, mia madre, mia sorella, mio Angelo protettore" (Agostino Ruffini to his mother, Boujan July 6, 1834, quoted in Cavassa 1931: 205, my translation).

[12] Actually the nearly one thousand liberals migration wave entering France after the 1820–1821 crisis did not receive benefits. Their final destinations were mainly Spain, Portugal and England (see Bistarelli 2011: 72 and Diaz 2014: 48–49).

[13] A recent fruitful approach to 19th-Century political migration from the innovation and knowledge transfer perspective is offered by the monographic issue of *Revue d'histoire du XIXe siècle, Mobilités, savoir-faire et innovations*, edited by C. Brice and D. Diaz, No. 53-2016/2 and by the special issue of *Diasporas. Circulations, migrations, histoire*, No. 2/2017 edited by C. Brice and devoted to *Mobilités créatrices*.

be inextricably interlaced in the mind-set of the Risorgimento exile: "Is the olive harvesting coming? Or has it already gone? And if it has not gone yet, will you have one year, half year, a quarter of a year harvest or nothing?", Giovanni Ruffini, Agostino's brother, asked his mother who was depending on family owned olive plantations to financially support her children's exile, [14] while a few months later it would be Agostino's turn to give way to the memory of home at Christmas time: "Two years ago I was celebrating Christmas around my father's table; I was happily eating my bit of sweet bread [...]. Two years! What a change, so empty is my father's table! So empty is my heart!". [15] In two years' time no progress had been made from the moment he had crossed the border, from the physical and the emotional moment of the sconfinamento. [16]

15.2. *Sailing off and landing in the Mediterranean*

Is there what we might call a typical Italian 19th-Century experience of sailing off on political exile?

What were the emotions on the eve and on the departure day? What kind of Italy did these refugees carry in their baggage? [17]

Thinking of departure as "the border between [...] those who leave and those who stay, between hope and absence" (Grinberg and Grinberg 2004, quoted in Bistarelli 2011: 28), an insight into the Spielberg prisoners to be deported by Austria to the United States in 1836 [18] offers a good emotional case. While waiting to sail off on board of the brick Ussaro, a group of men from different generations and conspiracy seasons faced their new condition: having accepted to change their sentence to long imprisonment in the fortress with deportation for life to America, their fears and worries revealed different awareness of their forthcoming fate. Fifty-one-year-old Count

[14] "Siamo vicini alla raccolta delle olive? O è già passata? E se non è passata avrete un'annata, una mezza, un quarto o niente?" (quoted in Cavassa 1931: 207, my translation).

[15] "Or sono due anni i festeggiava il Natale alla tavola paterna; mangiavo il mio pezzo di pane dolce [...] con delizia...Due anni! Quale cambiamento, quale vuoto alla tavola paterna! Quale vuoto nel mio cuore!" (*ibidem*, my translation).

[16] As Iveković (2005: 220) has remarked: "The *sconfinamento*, the repositioning of oneself with respect of thinking as a vital need and in a non-self-centred universe requires, indeed, time, it requires the *longue durée* of political processes, education, negotiation, confidence building, disarmament, yielding power, building-up of secularism".

[17] *L'Italie pour bagage. Migration, circulations et Italianité XIXe-XXe siècles* is the title of an international conference organized by the Italian Cultural Institute and the National Museum for the History of Immigration in Paris, June 16–17, 2017 (www.sciencespo.fr/departement-histoire/sites/sciencespo.fr.departement-histoire/files/3-programme-italiepourbagage-BD.pdf).

[18] The following year political prisoners were deported form the Papal States to Brasil. An earlier flux of some 300 prisoners had been deported in 1820 from Naples to Lisboa and then to Brasil. See Lodolini 1978.

Federico Confalonieri, belonging to the 1821 Milanese opposition to the restored Austrian rule, morally and physically worn out by imprisonment, at that time described his existential horizon as a space located "between a painful past and a discouraged future" (Arisi Rota 2012): efforts from his family and friends networks to negotiate with Vienna a destiny for him within Europe having failed, he felt he was about to cross the border between the space of civilization and that of barbarism – in which he included America. [19]

On the contrary, Luigi Tinelli, a 37-year-old nobleman engaged in business activities who played a role as Mazzini's conspiracy leader in 1830s Lombardy spent the weeks before the so many times postponed departure arranging with his brother the future of his assets, with special attention for the beloved porcelain factory he had expanded in Milan. Nevertheless, the letter he wrote to his wife the day before the at last fixed departure proves a more predictable emotional split: "Goodbye, my dear and beloved Hannah, the pain of this farewell smoothens the pain of the farewell to the country where I was born and that I won't probably see anymore". [20]

An even more different story can be seen in the experience of Cesare Benzoni, a 25-year-old passenger on board sailing off in the Northern Adriatic Sea to start a long trip across the Mediterranean, to Gibraltar and then across the Atlantic to the final destination, New York. A rank-and-file member of Mazzini's network, a naïve young man from Cremona with neither connections nor linguistic skills in view of his American adventure, his future was a gloomy one both in the eyes of the brick's captain and in those of his fellow travelers (Arisi Rota 2010: 180). The fragile man in the group, his fate seemed precociously marked, as often happens in the silent predictions shared by refugees and exiles setting out on their journeys.

Gaining freedom for the exile and for the former prisoner, now a deported man, did not compensate the loss of identity (nurtured with family affection and professional status): in fact, crossing borders was often experienced as a disruptive entering a nowhere space. Losing their own existential center (Pasquinelli 2009: 44), the Risorgimento exiles in the making soon became "on edge", people with "broken lives": [21] "Women and men struck by an adverse, sometimes merciless fate, even more cruel for those without family assets and incomes or professional status protecting them from the painful ghost of poverty in a foreign country" (Bernardello 2008: 256). This is why political refugees endowed with professional skills and background could soon figure out clearer trajectories in their sea and land crossing: the cases of veterans – mainly officers – from the Napoleonic Army engaged in the independence wars from the Mediterranean to Latin America (Bruyère-Ostells 2009), and of deserters from the

[19] See for the perception of America in the Italian Risorgimento Körner (2017: 79) on Count Confalonieri.

[20] "Adieu, chère et adorée Hannah, la douleur de cet adieu me rend moins cruel celui, que je vais faire à mon pays que m'a vu naître et que, peut-êre, je ne verrai à jamais", quoted from Luigi Tinelli's private papers in Arisi Rota 2010: 179 (my translation).

[21] See for the post-1848 Venetian case Bernardello 2008.

Piedmontese Army after the 1821 revolution, offer a meaningful evidence of identity continuity in spite of displacement. Or, even better, of displacement in view of identity continuity.

As Ersilio Michel's seminal studies on Italian exile in Algeria pointed out, most of the 1830s exiles from the peninsula who reached the Northern shores of Africa – often via France on board State steamers – were already enlisted in the Foreign Legion. According to the Sardinian Ambassador in Paris, "as soon as they arrive on the French soil, they find themselves in an awful poverty and they are absolutely compelled to enlist in the Foreign Legion and to leave and suffer in Africa, where the burning climate, illnesses and war take a heavy toll of those unhappy people". [22] As soon as they arrive on the French soil...: the diplomat's words offer a clear instance of need as the true master of many exiles from the very moment they entered France or the colonial space of Algeria, where some, urged by material poverty and endowed with technical skills, did not think twice and offered their services to the "enemy". This was the case of a young refugee from Milan, one Vincenzo Luigi Albergoni, an expert of mechanics, who was hired by the Emir for a 6000 francs a year pay and free accommodation to work at gun carriages. After the exclusion order he was re-embarked to Marseille to join the French exiles-dépôt of Allier, but he refused and sailed off to Mexico (Michel 1935: 73). Needless to say, the French government had a tough time in managing political refugee fluxes: the newly created colony of Algeria – in need of agricultural and commercial expansion as well as of military defense – seemed a good dislocation space for exiles in poverty.

Receiving, dislocating and controlling new refugees was a big challenge indeed for France as host (ibidem: 133; Diaz 2014: part II), whose government soon met the discontent of Prince Metternich: displacing refugees in Algeria meant to lose control over them, since from there they could easily plan expeditions and landings on the peninsula shore. In short, they would be able to cross borders again, this time on the way back to revolution in their home country. That same scenario was feared by the head of the Neapolitan Police, who on November 8, 1823, wrote to the Neapolitan consul in Tunis that once entered into the dominions of the Bey, refugees from the Two Sicilies – significantly indicated as "gli eliminati", the eliminated – could sail off again and go where they liked, with the exception of the King of Two Sicilies' territories and Malta (Michel 1941: 35). Malta and Corfou were in fact the most popular stopovers on the way to exile and back, forming two powerful hubs for conspiracy networks and arms gathering.

Nevertheless, the idea of crossing borders moving towards the Southern shore of the Mediterranean as a safer and most promising space for a relatively free and decent life soon met with practical pessimism: "For Heaven sake, do not create illusions for

[22] "Appena essi sono giunti sul suolo francese, si trovano in preda ad una miseria spaventosa e nella assoluta necessità di arruolarsi nella Legione Straniera e di andare a soffrire in Affrica, ove il clima ardente, le malattie e la guerra mietono larga messe di quegli infelici" (quoted in Michel 1935: 48, n. (22), letter of May, 1, 1835, my translation).

exiles about coming to Tunis: they would find only hunger and despair and the impossibility to find any job", count Corrado Politi, from the Roman Republic 1849 refugees flux, wrote a few weeks after his arrival in Summer 1854. "To me only Egypt can offer a temporary shelter, but to reach Alexandria from here one needs to go back to Malta".[23]

In the end, in the difficult 1850s not even Egypt proved to be a paradise land at all, if there Piedmontese consular protection to refugees from the Kingdom of Lombardy-Venetia had to be reduced, and if some exiles from Naples, such as the Vollaro brothers, could write home: "We live a tranquil life, if the one who is far from his homecountry and from his beloved can call himself a tranquil man".[24]

15.3. *Dead men (and women) walking?*

One of the most inspiring visual sources of 19th-Century Mediterranean exile – the painting Francesco Hayez dedicated in 1831 to the refugees escaping from Parga, an iconic episode in the Greek–Turkish war[25] – , catches the exiles to be on the physical and emotional border between land and sea, between their village set on fire and the crowded beach where men and women carrying children in their arms are awaiting for sailing off. The double simultaneous tale is about despair and dejection, but also about pride in the very moment of forced departure. A woman is embracing and kissing an olive tree, another is picking up a handful of earth to symbolize the material loss and the effort to preserve physical and touchable memories of their homeland, while people confusedly gathering on the beach below are fixing their eyes on the land and the village. The emotional maieutic condition of this unexpected and massive exile was not much different from the one experienced by single refugees when crossing borders, clandestinely or with official expulsion documents: they all knew they were entering

---

[23] "Per carità che alcuno non illuda degli esuli a recarsi qua: non troveranno che fame e disperazione e l'impossibilità di lavorare in qualunque mestiere […]. Per me non c'è che l'Egitto che offra momentaneamente un rifugio, ma per andare di qua in Alessandria è necessario ritornare a Malta" (Michel 1941: 312, my translation).

[24] "Viviamo tranquilli se colui che è lontano dalla patria e dai suoi può dirsi tranquillo" (Michel 1958: 178, my translation). As Maurizio Isabella (in Isabella and Zanou 2016: 79) has clearly pointed out, patriots had to face many political (and, I would add, existential) dilemmas "during decades marked by uncertain political circumstances, not to mention sudden changes in borders and governments […] in a period of great flux".

[25] www.lombardiabeniculturali.it/opere-arte/schede/D0090-0037/. In his work Hayez was mainly inspired by Giovanni Berchet's 1823 ode *I profughi di Parga*. The poem would become a powerful message for patriotic engagement in the sense it alluded to the condition of the Italian people under foreign rule. It widely circulated hand-copied in the underground network of Giuseppe Mazzini's *Giovine Italia* in the early 1830s. Another interesting painting allusive to Italian exile is Carlo Arienti's *I profughi di Tortona* (1843–1854 ca), exhibited in Turin Galleria di Arte Moderna: https://commons.wikimedia.org/wiki/File:I_profughi_di_Tortona_by_Carlo_Arienti.JPG

the space of eradication and of civil death. As Sylvie Aprile has remarked, departure is a trauma and civil death is a veritable obsession for the exile in the making (Aprile 2010: 113-116).

It is no surprise then if, once the decision to cross borders was taken, patriots committed themselves to provide safety for their family and family assets. This is the case of some leading personalities in the Milanese revolution of 1848 who at the end of July, with General Radetzky and the Austrian army approaching to reconquer the town, chose to reach the close border with Italian Switzerland. According to what Mazzini wrote to his mother from Lugano, the whole of Milan was there, the local newspaper Il repubblicano counting not less than 20,000 Italian refugees (Audenino and Bechelloni 2009: 345). And yet, this time a hosting State for the nearly 75,000 refugees from Milan could be found also inside the Italian peninsula: the constitutional Kingdom of Piedmont became a receiving country for the fluxes of 1848–1849 exiles (many accompanied by family members) whose difficult recording can nevertheless be based on the figures given by some contemporary observers and those offered by archive papers, ranging roughly from 30,000 to 50,000 units. [26]

We can imagine, and private letters and journals prove, that these sorrowful men and women – long or short their trip had been in order to cross the border and reach safety from restored dominators and their reprisals – had their hearts heavy with feelings not so different from those of the migrants leaving Italy for the Americas some decades later. And they were probably staring as sleepwalkers at the landscape they were leaving behind, just like their followers on the way to displacement for economic reasons. As Emilio Franzina has pointed out, transatlantic migrants used to add rhythm to their trip and the crossing of sea-space singing popular songs, almost litanies, which told about passages and loss, and of passages as loss: "Dear Rita I must leave you/ I'm going to look for borders/ I entrust my beloved children to your care/since I am shattered by having to leave them". [27]

15.4. *Conclusions*

The double dimension of gain (the gain of freedom and the safety for life) and of loss (leaving behind the beloved ones but also a professional identity and family assets) is a perennial feature of exile for political reasons. According to a refreshed historical study and to the new questions asked of old sources, historians of the Long 19th Century are casting light on some less investigated aspects of political exile in the Mediterranean space. In this frame, the transnational Risorgimento offers a good deal of cases where single individuals or members of fluxes produced by the insurgency crises in the

[26] Useful figures in De Fort (2003).

[27] "Cara Rita ti devo lasciare/*me ne vado a cercare i confini*/Ti raccomando i miei cari bambini/che mi distrugge doverli lasciar", quoted in Franzina (2005), my translation, italic by Franzina.

peninsula experienced the crossing of borders as an existential turning point, opening the way to the "possible futures" for the political refugee meant as a migrant. This article has tried to catch fears and expectations of exiles in the making, just before or just after they had passed the physical barriers marking the separation from their homeland. Land and sea journeys were thus maieutic adventures putting at stake both identity and memory, and urging to work out possible strategies for reinventing oneself after the sconfinamento had occurred. With the exile's existential dimension ruled by arbitrariness and contingency, crossing borders during the post-Napoleonic crises meant to enter a nowhere space where the time of planned family life or political underground militancy were to leave space to uncertainty and financial need and dependence. And where receiving countries could change their attitude towards political refugees, who often experienced expulsion or, if sailing, refusal for landing. Current geopolitical and social challenges urge the historian to approach the 19th-Century political exile – even its less investigated dimensions, such as the deportation to the United States – as the experience of emotionally shipwrecked people, rather than of heroes, whose more intense need, once the "transit threshold" had been crossed, was to look for a new existential anchorage.

Bibliography

Aprile, S. (2010) *Le siècles des exilés. Bannis et proscrits de 1789 à la Commune*, Paris: CNRS.

Arisi Rota, A. (2010) *I piccoli cospiratori. Politica ed emozioni nei primi mazziniani*, Bologna: il Mulino.

Arisi Rota, A. (2012) '"Fra un addolorante passato e uno sconfortato avvenire". Rileggendo l'esilio nel lungo Ottocento', *Bollettino della Società Pavese di Storia Patria*, 112: 159–164.

Audenino, P. (2013) 'Esuli risorgimentali: esploratori della libertà o naufraghi della rivoluzione?', *Archivio storico dell'emigrazione italiana*, 9: 15–23.

Audenino, P. and Bechelloni, A. (2009) 'L'esilio politico fra Otto e Novecento' in M. Sanfilippo and P. Corti (eds.) *Storia d'Italia. Annali 24. Migrazioni*, Turin: Einaudi, 343–369.

Banti, A.M., Ginsborg, P. (eds.) (2007) *Storia d'Italia. Annali 22. Il Risorgimento*, Turin: Einaudi.

Bernardello, A. (2008) 'Vite spezzate e contrasti ideali. Esuli veneziani negli stati italiani ed europei (1849–1859)', *Società e storia*, 120: 253–278.

Bistarelli, A. (2011) *Gli esuli del Risorgimento*, Bologna: il Mulino.

Bruyère-Ostells, W. (2009) *La Grande Armée de la Liberté*, Paris: Tallandier.

Cavassa, U.V. (1931) 'Lettere dall'esilio' in Vv.Aa. *Giovanni Ruffini e i suoi tempi. Studi e ricerche*, Genoa: Comitato regionale ligure della Società nazionale per la storia del Risorgimento.

De Fort, E. (2003) 'Esuli in Piemonte nel Risorgimento. Riflessioni su una fonte', *Rivista storica italiana*, 115(2): 654–655.

De Marco, G. (1996) *Mitografia dell'esule. Da Dante al Novecento*, Neaples: Edizioni Scientifiche Italiane.

Diaz, D. (2014) *Un asile pour tout les peuples? Exilés er réfugiés étrangers en France au cours du premier XXe siècle*, Paris: Armand Colin.

Dossi, C. (2010) *Note azzurre*, Milan: Adelphi.

Franzina, E. (2005) "Varcare i confini": viaggi e paesaggi degli emigranti. Il caso italiano e le teorie transnazionali, in S. Salvatici (ed.) *Confini. Costruzioni, attraversamenti, rappresentazioni*, Soveria Mannelli: Rubbettino, 120–121.

Grinberg, L. and Grinberg, R. (2004) *Psychoanalitic Perspectives on Migration and Exile*, New Haven: Yale University Press.

Isabella, M. (2006) 'Exile and nationalism: The case of the Risorgimento', *European History Quarterly*, 36: 493–520.

Isabella, M. (2009) *Risorgimento in Exile. Italian Émigrés and the Liberal International in the Post-Napoleonic Era*, Oxford: Oxford Scholarship Online.

Isabella, M. (2011) 'Esilio' in A.M. Banti, A. Chavistelli, L. Mannori and M. Meriggi (eds.) *Atlante culturale del Risorgimento. Lessico del linguaggio politico dal Settecento all'Unità*, Rome-Bari: Laterza, 65–74

Isabella, M. and Zanou, K. (eds.) (2016) *Mediterranean Diasporas. Politics and Ideas in the Long 19th Century*, London: Bloomsbury.

Iveković, R. (2005) 'Some thoughts on borders and partitions as exception' in S. Salvatici (ed.) *Confini. Costruzioni, attraversamenti, rappresentazioni*, Soveria Mannelli: Rubbettino, 219–232.

Körner, A. (2017) *America in Italy. The United States in the Political Thought and Imagination of the Risorgimento, 1763–1865*, Princeton-Oxford: Princeton University Press.

Lodolini, E. (1978) 'L'esilio in Brasile dei detenuti politici romani (1837)', *Rassegna storica del Risorgimento*, 65: 131–171.

Martinola, G. (1980) *Gli esuli italiani nel Ticino, 1791–1847*, Lugano: Fondazione Ticino Nostro.

Martinola, G. (1994) *Gli esuli italiani nel Ticino, 1848–1870*, Lugano: Fondazione Ticino Nostro.

Michel, E. (1935) *Esuli italiani in Algeria 1815–1861*, Bologna: Cappelli.

Michel, E. (1941) *Esuli italiani in Tunisia, 1815–1861*, Milan: Ispi.

Michel, E. (1958) *Esuli italiani in Egitto 1815–1861*, Pisa: Domus Mazziniana.

Neagu, M. and Côté, O. (2013) 'Frontières, barrières, horizons. Réinterroger l'histoire et les mémoires de la migration', *Consevreries mémorielles*, 13, http://cm.revus.org/1306 (accessed on May 23rd, 2017).

Pasquinelli, C. (2009) 'Il tempo dell'esilio', *Parolechiave*, 21: 59–72.

Patriarca, S. and Riall, L. (eds.) (2012) *The Risorgimento Revisited. Nationalism and Culture in Nineteenth-Century Italy*, Basingstoke: Palgrave Macmillan.

Rao, A.M. (1992) *Esuli. L'emigrazione politica italiana in Francia (1792-1802)*, Neaples: Guida.

Sioli, M. (2004) 'Se non c'è il conquibus si muore come cani: Luigi Tinelli a New York (1851-1873)' in D. Fiorentino and M. Sanfilippo (eds.) *Gli Stati Uniti e l'Unità d'Italia*, Rome: Gangemi, 141–150.

Sorbelli, A. (1931) *L'epilogo della rivoluzione del 1931. Da Rimini a Venezia*, Modena: Società Tipografica Modenese.
Zanini, P. (1997) *Significati del confine. I limiti naturali, storici, mentali*, Milan: Mondadori.

Chapter 16

Time boundaries of identity

Anna Rita Calabrò

Identity is understood as the capacity each one of us has to recognise our continuity over time. It includes telling ourselves and others our story, believing and making people believe in the project that is giving sense and coherence to that which we have been, we are now, and we reasonably think we may be in the future. The project we have for ourselves determines our choices and testifies the continuity between past, present, and future, and therefore represents our identity, a project that includes experiences from the past and changes in relation to what happens in the present and what we want to achieve or preserve in the future. A life story that, continually written and rewritten by the subject and dictated by circumstances and encounters, unravels over time and only in time does it find concreteness and meaning.

Indeed, as is well illustrated by Erikson (1968, 1980), identity is a process that does not end with adolescent crises and the start of adult life but continues throughout life because the experiences that the individual has in the course of his existence often represent a challenge to our own self-image. Hence the effort to reduce dissonant elements or a surrender to the need to reconsider and modify such images. [1]

Every social phenomenon has a duration and develops over time. Time check is both an internal-subjective element (in the relationship that the individual draws between past, present, and future), and an external-social element (the interaction of many time segments expressed by various social sectors).

The particular ways in which the individual positions himself in relation to temporality determine the characteristics of his identity, while the dynamics of the relationship between social time and individual time outline his degree of integration (understood as adhesion to social institutions and participation in social processes). Defining identity as the capacity to recognise our wholeness and our continuity over time means

---

[1] In this regard a longitudinal study by Carisson, Wängqvist, Frisén (2015) is very interesting. The authors, by referring to James Marcia's model of identity (1966), show how arriving at the adolescent crisis leads to personalities – identity achievement, floreclosure, identity diffusion – that present themselves in a different way with respect to the ability to elaborate new experiences, create new meanings and renegotiate their own identity status. After repeating the survey on the same subjects years later, it was recorded that, even when it stays within these models, the process of identity development does not stop. I am quoting this work to stress that a significant, if not traumatic, experience such as migration is a challenge for the identity, and even when it does not lead to actual states of suspension, it still produces significant changes even in less flexible personalities.

emphasising the ways in which an individual "experiences" time (that is, how he connects and represents his history, his everyday life, and his future plans) and the strategies to which he turns to give significance and meaning to this continuous or discontinuous path.

Naturally the subject, in designing his biography, punctuated by daily rhythms, makes reference to and takes into account a time period that is not just subjective, but is social and collective. He must, then, adapt his rhythm to those of the subjects with whom he interacts and to those of the social institutions with which he relates. This network of temporal interconnections represents the structure of social relationships, reveals the characteristics of each person's relationship with the social fabric of belonging, and defines its own nature. The relationship between individual time and social time can, depending on the circumstances, be conflictual, the object of negotiation, harmonious, or simply dictated by conformism. However, we need to take into account how fractures and discontinuities are not exclusively attributable to an individual dimension but are generally the outcome of ongoing social processes (just think of how the current precariousness of youth employment prospects affects both daily life and life plans).

It seems evident that, in general, such a relationship is problematic and fragmentary in the case of asylum seekers and refugees. This is because they come from cultural and social contexts where the social organisation of time does not necessarily coincide with that of advanced industrial societies. Furthermore, forced migration has "forcibly" upset daily life and plans. And finally, the current receptions system in Italy[2] places them for a significant amount of time in a sort of limbo in which the duration and means of exit are by no means clear, that is to say, for as long as the request for asylum remains unevaluated by the appropriate Commission.

In these pages, I will take inspiration from the life stories of some young people who have obtained refugee status and who currently attend the University of Pavia, as part of a host project offered by the university for the duration of their university career. In this sense, it seems plausible to hypothesise (and evaluate at an empirical level) that they may have suffered from a "general syndrome of temporal destructuring" (Cavalli 1985). This syndrome presents as historic memory fragmentation, temporal frailty of future plans involving personal identity definition, and an absence of relatively constant criteria in the allocation time in daily life. At the moment, during their stay at the University of Pavia, a different organisation of time is reallocating the threads of their identity in a particular stage of life – youth – in which the task of identity is particularly arduous because they are entering adult life.

In this article, I will limit myself to the analysis of two temporal dimensions: historic time and biographic time. The representation of historic time indicates the subject's capacity to link his life story to a vaster dimension that precedes him and will

[2] See E. Dal Zotto, in this volume.

certainly surpass him. Biographic time, or lifetime, is made of a past of preserved memories, a present that gives us awareness of who we are, and a future of hopes and fears which outlines the characteristics of identity. [3]

16.1. *Yesterday: an ordinary normality*

Memory is selective. It is in the present that we remember what has happened in the past and memory adapts to the image that we have of ourselves. It's about what we are today, not what we were yesterday. We want coherence between our past, present, and future. We tend to overshadow contradictions in the attempt to eliminate any cognitive dissonance (Festinger 1957). But this is not easy when there is a fracture between the past and present that must be put back together; a wound that must be healed. When finding a reason for why our life has changed is complicated; or when reconciling the image of who we have been with who we are is challenging.

That said, among the many ideas that these life stories offer is an initial consideration. Most of the stories recount a serene childhood, an adolescence like many others with the intemperances and conflicts of that age such as university life. Only a few details hint towards distant places, a different culture: the perfume of a Middle Eastern orange garden, the close relationships in an African village, circumcision as a rite of passage, etc. It is understandable that nostalgia softens the memory of the past – childhood, adolescence, siblings, friends – but it is in their ordinary normality that greatly resembles our ordinary normality that the unexpected breaks through. Of course, there are some exceptions – dramatic tales of a violated childhood or a difficult adolescence, but for the most part this is not our normality. From a certain point of view, it seems even more worrying to us because it is easier to identify and consider how what has happened to them can happen to us.

> But then I hadn't truly understood the reason why the civil war really started from one day to the next. Let's say there's one person with petrol and another with a lighter in their hand. For the moment they are far apart from each other but there's danger because as soon as they get close, the fire is ignited.
>
> (B. Syria)

> When I was in Syria I had a very precise picture of my future, I thought that everything would be peaceful, that I would become a graphic designer, that I would have my own family... My future was completely organised. I had a job as a shopkeeper, a newly bought

---

[3] The analysis of the collected life stories is still ongoing. In these pages the first reflections are provided. The conceptual apparatus that links time and identity is in A. Cavalli (1985).

car, a girlfriend, I was at university... I was happy. Then havoc: the war. The future is extinguished, I can't see anything anymore. I lost everything.

(F. Syria)

In May of 2014 I graduated in law, after the holidays I intended to work in prosecution. In July we went on holiday to my grandmother's house in the countryside. The moment when I started to really understand what was happening was during that trip, when we left the city: in the opposite direction there was a line of tanks heading towards Donetsk. I had never seen such military power... they scared me, but we didn't think that...

(A. Ukraine)

16.2. *History and destiny*

None of the interviewees place themselves in the story: as protagonist or victim. This is surprising if one considers that they are all young people with a university level education and that all of them have had to flee their country because of war or their political activity. Yet for all, without distinction, the historic, collective dimension is not perceived, told or claimed. It is not history that has determined the events which led them to brave their journey, but destiny, and this difference is substantial. Substantial because if history leads to a collective, common dimension, in which causes and effects have their own – albeit perverse – reason for being and compared to which there is even a minimal possibility of action, destiny is such because it is inscrutable, immutable, and inescapable. A fatal inevitability that strikes blindly and, if you are its victim, leaves you lonely and vulnerable.

The story of a war that forces you to flee your country – whether it is Syria or Ukraine makes no difference – is the story of an event that, in its horror, has no logical explication, no precedent that can give it reason, no sign that can provide warning. War, in their story, is like an earthquake that strikes blindly, destroys all of a sudden, kills without leaving any possibility of defence. It bursts into your life and surprises you in the tranquillity and banality of your daily habits.

When the civil war broke out, we always thought it would be over straight away and instead, six years passed and it still wasn't over... in Syria, it is also an evil war because it is a civil war for which the reasons are not understood... Since before, Syria wasn't bad, everyone lived in peace, there weren't economic problems in Syria, there wasn't a huge divide between rich and poor, it was all normal and everyone lived normally... Then the first demonstrations against the government started. Things got worse with time, instead of extinguishing, the flames grew bigger than ever. At the time we thought it was a small war, one of those that finishes straight away but no, after some years it reached the capital, it reached my city, and it reached the whole country. Then came ISIS... they weren't there before and

> then they were... Their mouths are full of words of God and religion but they know neither God nor the Prophet... they are people who don't have a political conscience or an education, many of them never went to school and they dare to speak in the name of God.
>
> (B. Syria)

But this way of attributing history to a personal destiny does not occur because you are unaware; it happens because when tragic events in history affect you directly and the distance between you and history is removed, the gaze of the general narrows to the particular, it moves from the world to your small world. Rationality gives way to fear, astonishment, pain. It gives way to a story that, in its most dramatic moments, breaks through into the present, almost reliving what happened.

> I could still run away, but inside myself I can't let go of my family, because what is going on happens right here, here in my city, where I am, where my mother and brothers are. The war is not distant, it's not something I see on the news, or read in the papers, the war is here, I feel it and I see it with my own eyes... And I'm afraid.
>
> (B. Syria)

And this astonishment remains after being rescued, even if, prompted by questions, you are able to put the sequence of events in the right order and analyse the responsibility of what has happened. It remains even, if afterwards, destiny assumes history's rational features.

> I consider myself lucky… Something was guiding my choice, my life… I don't know, destiny maybe. Because, even if these three years have been difficult, even if we have made sacrifices and even if now we're not home and we have lost everything there, it could have been worse, much worse. I want to think like that. Destiny, I don't know, maybe God... I believe. A God who lets us decide and then protects us... I think it is so. These things are too abstract, but I believe in fate, destiny, the fact that what should have happened is what happened... Yes, yes. People make their choices, but there are things that aren't up to us. We chose but then there are external conditions that don't allow us to do what we chose to do… You say that this is history and not destiny? Destiny is a personal thing. History is the destiny of a country. It is history that determines people's destiny. I think that the history of a person doesn't exist, history exists, history as destiny and what has been couldn't have been any other way
>
> (A. Ukraine)

Others haven't fled from a war, but from prison, torture, authoritarian regimes. They fled because of persecution and terror. And also in these cases, in their story, they don't appear as people who have tried to change history which left them as victims, but as actors unaware of the parts they were playing. It is true, none of them were militant political opponents, they were just young university students who, like many, in many other parts of the world, formed assemblies, took part in demonstrations, wrote flyers against the regime, but nevertheless they did it in countries where doing that is enough to risk your life.

> Torture is a normal practice in Turkish prisons. It's physical and also psychological violence. It starts as soon as you enter, it's not methodical, there isn't a rule. They can beat you, or give you electric shocks. Or they can put you in a completely white cell where there is nothing, nothing that you can look at. Or where there's a loudspeaker which plays deafening music without interruption, day and night. Or, to the contrary, you go into a cell that is silent and you can't hear a thing, except your voice and this is what scares you the most. Because you are alone, you don't hear anything, only your voice if you speak.... I was tortured many times.... No, no, they didn't want information from me, they didn't want names. No, no, nothing. They knew full well that I wasn't involved in any terrorist groups. They just wanted to scare me. They wanted to make me leave politics. What they want is that when you leave and go home you don't go out anymore.
>
> (I. Turkey)

> Then once I was in Lomé, with my mother's family, there was a demonstration... when these things are here, you don't have a choice, you have to go. That is, you have a choice, but you think: "If something changes, it changes for all of us", therefore you have to go. Maybe not shouting, not doing anything, only showing that we want change, we don't want this situation of poverty, corruption, violence, lack of liberty anymore, because maybe, maybe... one day things could change. So everyone goes out, all the young people, you hear that there is a demonstration, you go out and you go to the square even if you're not a part of any organisation... So we are all there and then they started to arrest people, to beat them up, to release gas, and these things here. I escaped and thought: "Okay, this always happens, tomorrow it will all be over and nothing will happen, right?" Then the next day and the day after that they started going to houses to take all the young people...
>
> (R. Togo).

Still, whether in Turkey or Togo or Afghanistan, they use almost the same words to tell their story. History has nothing to do with it, political protest represents a phase of life, a sort of rite of passage from adolescence to young adulthood. A phase before growing up and becoming adults. Torture, prison, a test of courage necessary to be part of the peer group. And at the moment in which they realise that to save themselves they must escape, there is only disbelief caused by the unexpected and unpredictable. Only in that moment they realise the risks and stakes at play.

> And then in Turkey it's like this: all the young people, when they are at university, are involved in politics... Then they graduate, they stop, they start a family, and they don't mention anything anymore, or talk about it, or do anything. I don't know, in Turkey it's

tradition... Young people are involved in politics and they just do it at university. I know, now things have changed because with Erdogan, being against the government has become a war… But before, until ten years ago, it was like a cultural event, a sort of obligatory rite of passage for young people who went to university. They are involved in politics, then they forget it, then they stop.

(I. Turkey)

Of course I was afraid, police and prison meant blows and torture for me. I wanted to stop myself, but with my friends we were a group, we were a community, we studied together, fought together… Maybe, if what happened the last time – they arrested me – hadn't happened, maybe I would have finished university, maybe I wouldn't have been involved in politics any longer… To be in politics, to oppose the regime, to risk is a young person's thing, so once you become an adult you don't do it anymore. Because there is energy when you are young, it makes you decide more with your heart than your head. When we grow up we become more mature and we seek to decide more with our head than our heart… As young people we don't worry about the consequences of what we do, as young people we are reckless. Maybe if I'd known how it would end... maybe I wouldn't have done what I did. If I hadn't risked conviction, once I had finished university, I would probably have... changed paths... I would have got married, I would have carried on playing football – that is my profession – and then, after a few years, I would have become a coach. If I had foreseen my situation today, I would have left politics. I would have preferred to live like all the others, with my family… Of course, someone has to fight to change things... But everyone says: "Why me?"

(D. Iran)

16.3. *The journey*

There are many ways to define, describe and experience a journey of initiation, discovery and knowledge. The journey can be, for example, a dream of freedom, a goal, the realisation of a project or a means to realise a project, it can be an escape and the escape can be an act of cowardice or a bid for safety. The meanings are numerous, innumerable stories, limitless literature and essay writing. The journey represents an archetype of the human condition. This can be seen in Ulysses's journey beyond Hercules's columns, Orpheus's into the underworld, Ahab's across the oceans, Moses's towards the promised land. These journeys make up a part of our imagination and those who have completed them, become companions in our personal journey of initiation.

It is certain that, in each case, the journey indicates the border between a before and after and this is even truer in the case of migrants, whose journey takes them far from their country with an uncertain prospect of return. Those whose stories I am taking inspiration from for this reflection are all young, come from places very different from one another, and have different reasons for having left. However, they have all faced a journey. A long journey. Even for those who arrived at their destination after a few hours, by plane, it is a long journey because such is the distance between life before the journey, and life now, after the journey. Quite unexpectedly they arrive in the same place, Pavia, after having requested and obtained political asylum once they arrived in our country.

The peculiarity of their situation is the fact that their stay in Italy is legitimate due to the very impossibility of their return and because, for all, the journey was in fact an escape and that on arrival they found themselves in an unknown country, one in which they could not count on anyone and that they considered to be just a country to pass through. They are young people for whom the journey represented a real point of no return. They can never go back because there isn't anywhere to go back to.

> You can't ever go back. ...There are dreams, you don't know where the dreams disappear to but maybe one day something happens close to you and the dreams are no more... this is the uncertainty...
>
> (A. Ukraine)

> I often think back to when I ran away seeing my city destroyed... houses burning, blood on the ground. It doesn't seem real that I spent my childhood there, the beautiful moments spent in my city with my friends are so unreal... . I left it running away and all I have of it is a picture of death... I don't know anyone anymore because I'm not able to contact anyone, not even friends... some are dead, some have been taken, others have escaped... but even today I don't know where to find them. There are still people in there... there are friends who I still don't know whether they're dead or alive...
>
> (B. Syria)

The story that each one tells of the journey undertaken obviously changes according to his origin. It is now known to be particularly dramatic for those who come from Africa following the route which leads to Niger and across the desert into Libya and from there, on the "rubber boats", it crosses the Mediterranean. Less dramatic, but just as tiring and dangerous, is the Balkan route. And then there are those who, taking advantage of particularly fortunate circumstances, were able to take a plane.

But beyond the different circumstances, different characters, different origins, and different routes, all the stories (invaluable because they are sincere, circumstantial, and rich in memories, pictures, and feelings) share the same plot and unravel in the same way. At the age of twenty, whatever the circumstances may be, the journey, "that journey", represents the shadowy line that must be crossed if they want to become adults. Even though the story of the journey seems to cause only dismay – the creeping paralysis of a hopeless future – to use Conrad's words, sometimes the same story unexpectedly changes tone and becomes the epic tale of an unrepeatable adventure in a world which reveals its horror and wonder in everything.

> By constantly paying I had ended up with no money, so I said to him: "Do you want to shoot me? Shoot me if you want, but I'm not paying anything, I'm sick and tired of paying and of your rules, which force us to do this. I can't do it: shoot me if you want!". My friends said to me: "Quiet, he has a gun." "I know he has a gun, but I've had it!" In the end he let me go.
>
> (L. Gambia)

> I wasn't scared when I was in Niger, I was very excited. Of course, I thought about who I was in Gambia, in my town and who I was in that moment: sleeping on the street, without anything. But it still seemed to me… a kind of education, because you don't stay the same person forever. And so, where would I end up? What would I become? These thoughts moved me, but I wasn't scared. I didn't think of the future… . Because I had learned so much since I had left. It seemed to me I had grown, I had become a man. During the journey, I had seen so many things I never imagined I would see, I had seen people eating rubbish, living in terrible conditions… . I know there is poverty where I'm from, but I had never seen poverty like this. So in that moment, in Niger, I was too focused on observing what was happening around me to be angry or afraid. Of course, when I found myself desperate on the street, with no food, no bed, in the rain… but also in that moment excitement prevailed over fear… . Only in Libya did I really begin to feel scared… . One day, after a week of us being in Tripoli, my friend and I were on the street and there was someone shouting in Arabic from the third floor. "Go away!" But we didn't understand what he said. Then he started to shoot us. We started to run… . He hit my friend here, in the neck. He fell to the ground. It was the first time I saw someone die in front of me. They had hit him, everyone had run away but I was there, standing up. He said to me: "Go, go, otherwise he'll shoot you too" and I said: "No, no, quiet". I stayed with him until he died.
>
> (L. Gambia)

> For me the journey was like an adventure. Yes, it's true, I felt that way. It's not that I wasn't scared, I was scared because I had seen things that are probably bad, like the car accidents which happened during the journey, the traffickers who sold people to make money. I saw all this. The whole journey, everything I've been through … it was all an adventure.
>
> I met many young African people from different countries, from all over West Africa, they told me how they suffered, what happened with the military, police, traffickers, or bandits. I lived and heard it. And those things are ugly, right? But everything aside, the journey was a great adventure for me because I saw things I didn't know, that I never imagined… like Senegal, I saw life in Senega … I also saw how people live in Mali, I passed through Bamako. Country by country I arrived in Burkina Faso and there I saw a different life again ... I was just learning during the journey, I was just learning! It opened my mind so much! I crossed

> the desert from Niger to Sebha in Libya, and from there to Tripoli … and then the sea. I saw many things and they opened my mind!
>
> (T. Gambia)

And all of them, in the most dangerous moments, say they weren't afraid. Maybe it's just a young person's quip, or maybe it really happened that way, in those journeys, in those moments, at that age. Maybe a challenge. Maybe being fatalist is the only way to keep pushing onward.

> I was very afraid in the first 10 minutes, but after I said: "I can't change anything now, if we must die, we die here." Because, from the moment you board the ship, you already know that you either die or you save yourself, and everyone has this thought… When the rubber boat began to set sail on the water I was calm, I remember laughing with a friend of mine at those who were screaming. I wasn't scared. I was waiting for the trip to end, I didn't think I could die.
>
> (L. Gambia)

> The best moment of the journey? … Crossing the borders because I left my country looking to arrive at a destination … Even when the rubber boat broke, it started to fill with water and everyone was screaming and we had to turn back … I could also have died there but I knew it wouldn't happen because the journey I was making was destiny, a destiny that God had designed for me …
>
> (F. Nigeria)

16.4. *Waiting period*

And then the arrival. The first days, the first months pass in a sort of suspended time, spent tracing the map of unknown territory in which you find yourself not living but surviving.

> My father was ill, my sister shut herself off, my mum, who even at home spoke very little, was silent. That period was truly terrible because we didn't know what to do, we had to start again from zero and none of us seemed to have the strength to do it.
>
> (B. Lebanon)

The attempt to reconnect the threads of one's own identity, where the journey represents a clear boundary between the before, prior to the journey, and the now, after the journey, only happens at a later stage. It is disorientating and discomforting for everyone but obviously different characters and temperaments cause different reactions, which are strongly related to the life plan that characterised the before. That is to say, the more the life plan was self-determined and well established in an identity representation in which biographic time is strongly connected to past experience, organisation of time in daily life, and future plans, paradoxically, the stronger the disorientation, sense of powerlessness, and the discomfort with respect to confronting an unprecedented reality. There is a different perception of what is happening on the part of the younger ones for whom the life plan, at the moment of departure, was still vague or less promising. There is a kind of optimistic recklessness in them as they face the unknown again with the idea of living an adventure.

For all of them, however, the route in unclear, there are only a few directions, in fact, only one. The first step, depending on information collected during the journey, must be the closest police station to which they go immediately for help. Some documents have long since been disposed of before arriving in Niger for those who followed the African route, or before arriving at the Italian border or airport of arrival for the others. This is to avoid immediate repatriation. Here, each person completely and passively trusts an authority which often, in his own country and during the journey, represented an enemy, torturer, the one who had to be corrupted, to cross the borders. And from that moment onwards, from when they enter any police station, the wait in suspended time begins.

> I stayed outside the police station for a while not knowing what to do … It's not easy to be afraid of the police the week before and trust them the week after. And so, with my bag, first I approached a little and then I went back a bit… and they knew: "This man here is coming to us". Then they looked at me and when they looked at me I pretended not to need them. Then they gestured to me like this, I went forward afraid, even they saw I was scared. They told me it was now too late, that I had to come back the next day. I said: "Where do I go? Will I be back tomorrow?" And so I did not move from there, when it was time to sleep, I slept outside there … somewhere on the street.
>
> I was outside there for three days without moving because I didn't know where to go. Then eventually they met me. But it wasn't over yet. All of October passed and I only got the place at the end of November. I spent all that time at the station, in a train left there, or outside because when the police were there they sent us away. For a month I went on like this… I was desperate yes. I went back to the police station every day to ask. By then they all knew me. Then finally one day they said to me: "It's your turn now and we're sending you to the reception centre and there are professionals there who will look after you".
>
> (R. Togo)

In the end, all the protagonists of this story were lucky, reasonably lucky compared to many others, as they themselves recognise without exception. Some go to the reception centre immediately, while others will arrive within a few weeks. The centres are often crowded, not very comfortable, but nevertheless they have guaranteed medical assistance, a bed, and food. Some weeks pass, a few months for the least fortunate, just the time needed for verification and they are transferred to accommodation within the national SPRAR network waiting for their asylum application to be evaluated by the designated committee.

But the subjective perception of time, we know, does not follow the mathematical rhythm of a clock but a more emotional one: fear, uncertainty, anxiety can infinitely slow down the hands of the clock and make the wait endless and unbearable. Especially when the waiting time, in the immigration centres, is not an organised schedule, but a rhythm marked exclusively by meal and sleep times.

> I didn't know what to do, I didn't know what Italy was like, I didn't know its cities, its culture. Nor could I know it. I never left the camp. We communicated little among us. Few spoke Turkish. They spoke a hundred languages in this camp. Some spoke French, others English, some spoke many languages… but nobody spoke Italian. Every now and then there were rows. Because if you put seven hundred people in a line every day to eat, seven hundred people who waited on their feet for an hour twice a day just to eat. They made a line, waited … if one person came and put himself in the middle of the line, a fight would break out …
>
> It was a very bad time. The worst thing that happened to me? Waiting. Waiting on my feet for an hour for dinner and an hour for lunch. Waiting for them to call you, waiting, waiting. But the worst thing was waiting without doing anything. We did nothing. Nothing.
>
> (I. Turkey)

16.5. *Resilience*

> Once in the SPRAR, things changed. I knew that it would be so. I'm Muslim. They teach us that there isn't anything that comes and stays the same forever, it's always a passage. Surely it is only a passage: you can't live in difficult situation for ever. It comes and you have to be able to show you are strong enough to bear it, then when it goes away it won't come back. So, in the most dramatic moments, I always thought this way and thus I was able to restrain the anxiety and fear.
>
> (R. Togo)

Entering a SPRAR project signals a real turning point and the start of a new life in which it is possible to begin to reconstruct an image of one's identity in the present. An image that is as coherent as possible with what it was in the past. A place in which time starts to move again, slowly at first and then increasingly more quickly, letting you see the possibility of a future. Daily rhythm is no longer passive waiting time, but it becomes active, organised into meaningful activities (Italian and professional training courses, working internships etc.). Obviously, professionals play a fundamental role in organising time spent within such structures in order to offer resources – material and symbolic – that are useful for bringing this task to an end. But beyond this, the capacity for resilience that each individual is able to put into action is significant. That is to say, to process the trauma immediately, to put a positive attitude in place even in adverse circumstances, to give meaning to and process the dramatic experience of fleeing, of the journey, of abandonment to the point of finding the strength in themselves to make such an experience an identity resource (Luthar and Cicchetti 2000).

Overcoming the journey was proof of their ability to overcome obstacles; because now, unlike before, one needs to count only on themselves and is free to make their own decisions (family is far away or if it is there, has more urgent problems to face). The present can also be the start of a new life, the moment to turn a page or reclaim the thread of their own life plan with more knowledge; now they don't feel like children, but men.

16.6. *The present and the future*

The future starts in Pavia with the opportunities that the university offers them. An unexpected change once again, but this time it's really a beginning, an event that offers the possibility of a positive self-image. The response to the question "Who am I?" becomes easy: a student at a prestigious Italian university who belongs to a community and is building his future.

Of course, compared to their peers, with whom they share daily Pavian life, the effort of study, uncertainty of that age, and past experiences make a substantial difference. It is not so much about cultural differences or linguistic difficulties (the capacity of these young people to adapt and learn is surprising) as much as it is about having seen prison, death, and war up close. And it is this fact which makes them very fragile and very strong at the same time, but still different.

> If I can play in a football team, work a part-time job, and study to graduate? Well, this is what I have to do! When we speak with young Italian people about work, they say: "But come on, who can work and study?" and these words come from Italians studying in their own language! But, even if we study twice as much because we have language problems, we must keep ourselves busy, accept that this is our situation and that we can only count on ourselves, not like the Italians who have family …
>
> (D. Iran)

And knowledge of their own strength allows them to regain possession of their past and their story in a less dramatic and painful way. And the story of what they have experienced, becomes not only a way for some to process their grief and to start again, but also to free themselves from an image of themselves as a fugitive, an aimless outcast.

> In these last months, what is the most important thing that has happened to me? I went to some schools to tell my story and read my poetry. Something that made me feel not only happy, but also proud, because many times I feel that I'm not worth anything and instead I saw that when I read my poetry, people listened to me and were emotional. For me, writing poetry is very important. For me, writing poetry means knowing myself. There are so many people who have a lot inside themselves, but don't know how to express it.
>
> (L. Togo)

Reconnecting the threads between past and present means starting to repair an identity fracture that has inevitably been created. It means considering the present as the privileged temporal dimension because the past is still an open wound and the future is uncertain. It means making the present the place in which you hinge your identity.

> There is a Persian saying which says: "If you are depressed you are thinking of the past, if you are nervous you are thinking of the future, if you are calm you are living in the present". In my opinion, someone who is thinking of the past and what they haven't done has failed.
>
> (D. Iran)

The present isn't a nostalgic time for those who have been war victims, and nor is it a time of repentance or regret for those whose youthful recklessness gambled their life by demonstrating hope for the future in public squares or in university classrooms.

> No, no, we never talked about it among ourselves. We never talked about the war, our fears, our country, we stopped talking about it as soon as we arrived here. We tried to leave everything behind. Even when we spoke with our family, our friends, we tried not to open this door … We ask: "How are you?" We don't ask: "How's the situation?"
>
> (B. Syria)

> No, I never regretted what I did. I had a girlfriend when I was in prison. Of course, sometimes I thought that instead of being in jail because I was involved in politics I could be out with her and go to the cinema … Yes, yes, I thought it but … I wanted to have both together.
>
> (I. Turkey)

The present is the time in which one can start to think about the future. It's true, we look to the future very carefully with a kind of superstitious attitude. For those who have seen their lives turned upside-down, this is even more understandable. These young people show real courage and faith if we then consider the uncertainties faced by the majority of young people who have much more security regarding their working future. These plans are therefore short-term plans. One proceeds in stages with the optimism of someone who has fled a storm and found a safe place.

> If I think about the future? The distant future no. I think of what I have to do, I take things like this, like today, I do what I have to do, then this evening I think of what there will be to do tomorrow and tomorrow I will do it. Even when I was in Ghana, before leaving I only thought about the journey, I didn't think about what I would do once I arrived. I always thought about the next stage, because I didn't want to project myself into the distant future, so I wouldn't be disappointed later.
>
> (R. Ghana)

> I don't know where I'll live in the future. I can't say I will return to my country after I graduate. I can make my plans but I had also made my plans in Gambia and then in the end they didn't go how I wanted. I can say: "I'm going back tomorrow." Then I meet a girl, we marry and I never go back … Anything can happen ... I don't know, but it's the same for me here or in Gambia, because I built something in Gambia, and now I'm building something here, maybe it doesn't make sense to go back and build something different again …
>
> (L. Gambia)

> Thinking of me, of my future, the thing that scares me is the uncertainty. Even if you study and you choose a course there is always uncertainty, a kind of uncertainty … and the uncertainty scares you. Of course, uncertainty is a common thing for all young people of my age, yes but for me it's greater. For those like me it's greater!
>
> (A. Ukraine)

But even in the uncertainty of the future, it seems evident that identity, the image these young people have of themselves, regains its coherence little by little. The outline is recomposed through new relationships and new experiences, in the memory of who they have been and who they hope to be.

Bibliography

Carisson, J., Wängqvist, M. and Frisén, A. (2015) 'Identity development in the late twenties: a never ending story', *Development Psychology*, 51(3): 334–345.
Cavalli, A. (ed.) (1985) *Il tempo dei giovani*, Bologna: il Mulino.
Erikson, E.H. (1968) *Identity, Youth and Crisis*, New York: W.W. Norton Company.

Erikson, E.H. (1980) *Identity and the Life Cycle*, New York: N.Y. Norton.
Festinger, L. (1957) *A Theory of Cognitive Dissonance*, Palo Alto: Stanford University Press California.
Luthar, S.S. and Cicchetti, D. (2000) 'The construct of resilience: Implications for interventions and social policies', *Development and Psychopathology*, 12: 857–885.
Marcia, J. (1966) 'Development and validation of ego-identity status', *Journal of Personality and Social Psychology*, 3: 551–558.
Pastore, F., Salis, E., Villosio, C. (2013) 'L'Italia e l'immigrazione low cost: fine di un ciclo', *Mondi Migranti*, 1.
Pogliano, A. (2014) 'Immigrazione, media, opinione pubblica: crisi dell'umanitario?' in P. Musaro, P. Parmiggiani (eds.), *Media e migrazioni. Etica, estetica e politica del discorso umanitario*, Milan: Franco Angeli.
Portes, A. and Rumbaut, R.G. (2011) 'Immigration, diversity and social capital', presented at the Norface Migration Conference "Migration: Economic Change", Social Challenge, University College, London, 6-9 April.
Zanfrini, L. (2007) *Cittadinanze. Appartenenze e diritti nella società dell'immigrazione*, Rome-Bari: Laterza.

Chapter 17

Intellectual migrations and elites' formation beyond the boundaries

Foreign students, Jews and non-Jews, and Italian universities (1900-1940)

Elisa Signori

The history of intellectual migrations, scientific exchange and international cooperation is a key issue that, since the Middle Ages embodied the process of elites' formation of Western Europe. This field of research has only recently been recognized as a potentially rich subject in new perspectives also for contemporary Italy (Rudiger and Tikhonov 2003; Karady and Nagi 2012).

Of course, it was well known that the ancient Italian universities were transnational communities of students and scholars. They were accustomed to the experience of peregrinatio academica operating in a sort of European academic circuit for several centuries. But the phenomenon of foreign students' presence – enrolment and graduation – is now verified also in contemporary Italian universities, particularly between the end of the 19th century and the Second World War, and represents a peculiar case-study of a historical European dynamic. Although Italy was a latecomer both in the process of state-building, either in economic modernization and technological development, Italian universities became a hospitable environment for a variegated typology of foreign students and scholars.

Initial research results reconstructing this experience suggest interesting considerations, which illuminate basic aspects of Italian universities during the first forty years of the 20th century, but also help to understand the deep interrelation and cogent links with the political establishment between liberalism and fascism, with the evolution of Italian foreign policy and with the main changes in balance of power and cultural climate in Europe.

This chapter has two main aims: the first is to outline the trends of different waves which led foreign students to Italy, drawing the map of their countries of origin, following their curricula in Italian universities and faculties, and eliciting the different reasons why they were attracted to Italy, by adopting the push/pull scheme used by historians of the Great Emigration.

The second aim focuses on the different kinds of official sources and archives concerning this subject and presents the bibliography available.

All this documentation helps us to reconstruct a deeply contradictory dynamic. Liberal Italy opened universities' doors to foreign students and tried to emulate the most celebrated German, British and French institutions of high learning. Early Fascism first used facilities and scholarships as ways of extending its political influence abroad, but ten years later this hospitable attitude and promotion of cultural exchange was converted into a system of increasing political control, which culminated in selective, but conspicuous expulsions from universities in 1938-1940. Italian universities ceased to be open, zealously followed racial laws and, in the name of a vaunted primacy of "Italian Science", expelled about 400 Italian lecturers and a difficult to calculate number of Italian and foreign students, who were recognized as Jewish. Hence a new intellectual migration began from Italy to different foreign contexts. However, only some of these exiles could find new opportunities for scientific work and study and could integrate to the local academic community.

17.1. *A 'hidden' mobility phenomenon*

In Italy, as in other European countries, towards the end of the 19th and the beginning of the 20th centuries awareness increased that the opening of international horizons was a crucial and strategic policy for the modernization of university structures and the development of scientific activity. This was not a change in perspective in terms of the "nationalization" of Italian universities which started in the mid 19th century. Of course, while state infrastructures in the newly founded kingdom were being established, the university system was also redesigned with the adoption of a rigidly centralized administrative system inspired by the French example under Napoleon's rule. The priority shared by political elites after unification was to establish a secular and rational higher education system freeing it from those local, religious and corporative aspects characterizing previous centuries and placing it firmly under the control of the national government.

Nonetheless the trend towards the creation of a coherent national system had in academic communities, as among politicians responsible for university policy, been associated with the widespread awareness of the internationality of culture, research and learning. This orientation consolidated strongly in the 1870s and 1880s and gained concreteness in two different trends: one towards institutional and organizational emulation and the other in terms of intellectual mobility.

On the one hand, comparative study of foreign models of university organization in the light of their efficacy as educational institutions as well as in terms of scientific research has highlighted to many observers, scientists, lecturers and politicians, the gap which separated the Italian universities from the most advanced foreign examples, particularly the German system which had become a world pioneer in scientific innovation. This comparison helped to focus on structural bottlenecks of the university system and motivated reforms emulating this most prestigious of foreign models, grafting onto the Italian context some key ideas from the Humboldt university system and its adaptation to the special integrated organization of institutions, seminars, libraries and laboratories which had made the German system so scientifically dynamic and productive.

On the other hand, interaction with foreign university models created the phenomenon of intellectual migration which led students, and particularly young Italian graduates to study at foreign university institutions. "Scientific method and German method became equivalent terms in current usage and training in Germany was for years considered an indispensable start to any serious study" (Romeo 1978: 122).

This tendency was concretely promoted by individual universities, by private foundations institutions, and by the Ministry of Public Education which distributed scholarships and prizes.

It is this widespread admiration for foreign university models and the equally widespread criticism and self-criticism of the Italian university system, which for a long time probably obscured perception of the phenomenon of intellectual mobility in the other direction and which drew from abroad students of different nationalities who enrolled, attended and graduated in Italian universities. This phenomenon had peculiar characteristics and occurred in a wide variety of different situations and experiences regarding which we find limited but significant traces in documentation. The first estimate of the phenomenon was made in 1913 with the publication of all the data regarding the six-year period 1905-1910, and dealing more analytically with those regarding the academic year 1910-1911.

In those years a new focus on the flow of students from abroad which had hitherto been ignored, but was all but negligible, opened the way towards a new approach to the problem. Not only did this intellectual ability become recognized as a worthy phenomenon for study but for the first time its positive characteristics were highlighted by the desire to give it value and to encourage it. "By profiting from the great attraction that our country already has on foreigners for its natural and artistic beauties" – wrote Carlo Francesco Ferraris in 1913, the editor of the cited volume of university statistics and rector of the University of Padua – "we have brought many of our universities and higher institutes up to the level of foreign universities and from this aspect draw our advantages in cooperating with the international organisation of science towards which mankind tends irresistibly and with vigour" (Ferraris 1913: LVII). In Ferraris's words the evocation of the cosmopolitan and universalistic ethos of knowledge was strongly connected to the implicit singling out of benefits in economic terms and motivated some proposals for university reform: regulations needed to be simplified to help foreign students enroll, ad hoc academic qualifications could be devised for them and specific courses created based on their needs.

From this initial change in the perception of the phenomenon until the Second World War, statistical interest in student flows from abroad would always be prominent despite its limits and gaps. This attention would be interrelated with the launching of specific initiatives having the objective of promoting, sometimes guiding and selecting foreign students: particularly, in the period between the two wars, the promotion of universities' internationalization was transformed into a precise objective of cultural policy.

17.2. *A general overview: trends and phases*

If we leave aside the years 1860 to 1905 for which we only have disaggregated data gathered from a variety of universities, the chronology of the following 36 years for which there still persist serious gaps in official statistics (1906 to 1940) shows that the presence of foreign students was documented for a total of 31504 enrolments with a yearly average of 1086. This is a greatly underestimated evaluation because we do not have all the data for seven academic years: 1912-1913, 1919-1920, 1923-24, 1924-1925,1925-1926, 1927-1928, 1928-1929, and also because only in some years were the "out-of-course" students counted (in the Italian university system students can continue to enroll until the completion of their degree even beyond the officially prescribed time limit). If we integrate this data with "estimated theoretical data" we come to a total of 37000 cases for the whole period.

Even more underestimated is the data regarding the qualifications conferred for which we have a discontinuous series between 1905 to 1906 as well as 1910-1911, 1926-1927, 1929-1932, and 1940-1941. If we add these together we obtain a total of 5563 degrees and diplomas, distributed over 19 academic years at an annual average of 309. Beyond the statistics it is important to note the impact that this intellectual migration had on the total student population in universities and higher institutes of Italy: over the whole period foreign enrolments oscillated between the minimal percentage of 0.4% in the years 1918-1919 to a maximum of 5.3% for the years 1933-1934, while the qualifications given out went from a minimum of 0.8% in the years 1905-1906 up to 5.3% for the years 1937-1938 out of the total of those conferred in Italy.

The overall trend which we have outlined briefly presents a dynamic with at least two different phases corresponding not only to the changes in numbers and intensity of student flows but also reflecting transformations which were traumatic in the historical context of Europe and Italy. The first period went from the beginning of the century to the First World War, the second from the 1920s to the Second World War. The watershed was the new geopolitical situation created in Europe by the Versailles treaties and the inception of fascism on a political and institutional level, which was destined to influence both foreign and university policies not to mention the cultural climate and the legal system of the Italian kingdom.

17.3. *In liberal Italy*

The first phase from 1906 to 1919 showed a student flow of less intensity, enrollments of foreigners were around 3500 with an annual average of 270 and a peak of 497 cases in 1913-1914 when their incidence on the total of enrollments was 1.1%. Their places of origin and their choices in curriculum and universities (see Figures 17.1, 17.2, 17.3) reveals a very complex picture of motivations and expectations.

We can elicit the overall reasons for this mobility, in particular political conflict and ferment by minorities within the two largest continental empires: the Russian Empire and the Austro-Hungarian Empire. Groups of students sympathizing with or belonging to revolutionary movements and/or in favor of the emancipation of "oppressed nationalities" chose Italy on the basis of a cost/benefit calculation because the university system in Italy was cheaper compared to others which had more scientific prestige. Within this flow there is also significant participation by Italian subjects of the Hapsburg Empire, which after being frustrated in their request to obtain an Italian language university from the Imperial government, deserted the universities of Innsbruck and Vienna to come to Padua, Turin and Milan.

Amongst other aspects making Italian universities attractive were two important beliefs: one, more traditional, was that of Italy as a "museum territory" to use an expression coined by Gramsci, whose archaeological, artistic and historic cultural heritage drew scholars of antiquity from Europe and abroad, not to mention historians of art and culture interested in Rome and in the Renaissance (Gramsci 1955: 56); the other was the affection and historical cultural affinity, which brought foreign students to Italy from those countries witnessing the Italian migratory diaspora as well as Italians by language and culture living abroad or their sons. In those years there was no ad hoc assistance for students from abroad and procedures for the recognition of previous qualifications depended on the individual universities which in the case of people of "worthy fame and particular abilities" could be substituted by a Royal decree of admission. However, the Italian option was certainly favored by economic factors and the traditions of student hospitality typical of cities with old universities such as Padua, Bologna or Pavia. (see Figures 17.1 and 17.2 [1]).

---

1 These graphs and the following are my elaborations starting from the official statistical data.

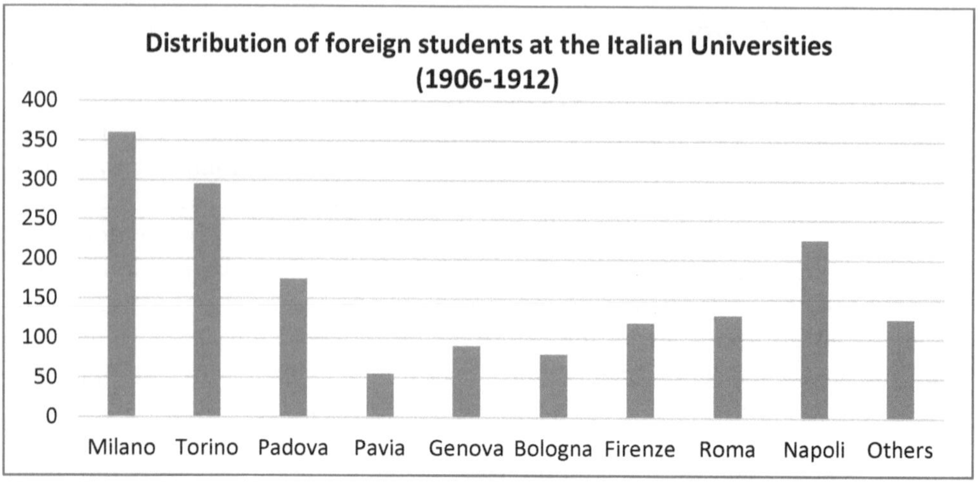

Figure 17.1. Distribution of foreign students at the Italian Universities (1906-1912)

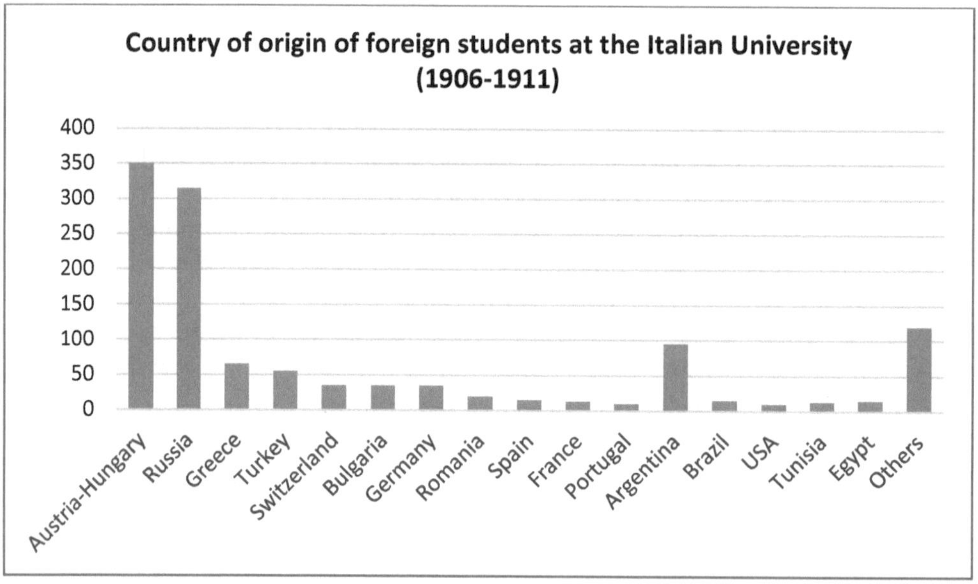

Figure 17.2. Country of origin of foreign students at the Italian Universities (1906-1911)

There are also particular cases regarding those flows from nearby areas like Switzerland, and particular, on the basis of ties of language and culture, from the Italian speaking Canton-Ticino (Castro 2004). Finally, there were cases of enrollments in specific schools and universities which had international scientific prestige. Activating these dynamics were student networks, which starting from the first positive experiences, acted as catalysts capable of consolidating and orienting the flows of specific groups of intellectual migrants.

17.4. *Contradictory internationalization in the fascist era*

The second phase, 1922-1939 was characterized by an increase in the rate of internationalization of universities in Italy, which for example in 1926-1927 already witnessed the tripling of foreigners across the whole of the student population (5.1% compared to the highest values of the previous year). Nearly 90% of foreign enrolments documented for the whole period considered (1905 to 1939) were concentrated in the 20 years between the two world wars (see Figures 17.3 and 17.4).

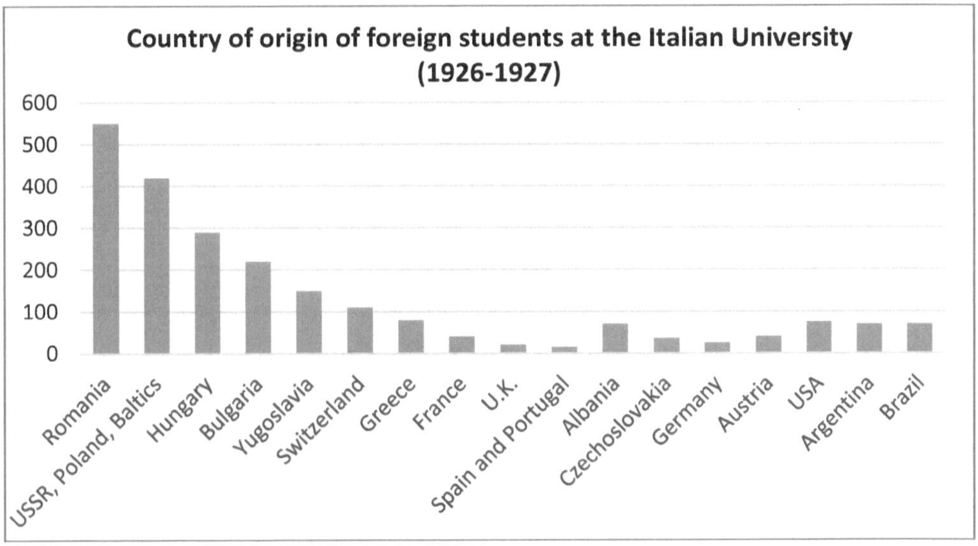

Figure 17.3. Country of origin of foreign students at the Italian Universities (1926-1927)

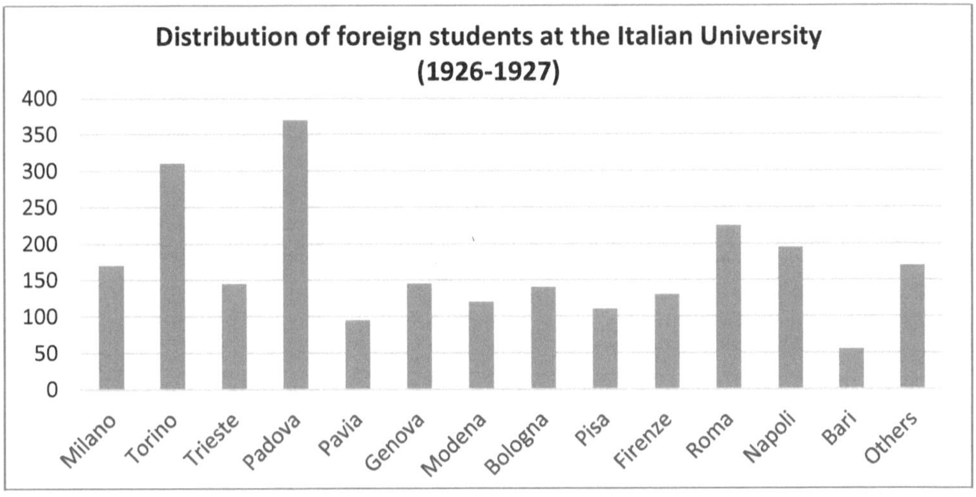

Figure 17.4. Distribution of foreign students at the Italian Universities (1926-1927)

We do not have overall data regarding the origin of students from abroad except for a few years where there are more complete series in regard to curriculum choice and student distribution in the different universities. On the basis of these incomplete data it is possible however to recognize the persistence of certain migration flows which had already consolidated in the previous period: Italians or their children resident in the Americas, in the Orient and in some European countries; scholars of historical, artistic archaeological and historical studies regarding ancient or Renaissance Italy; consolidation of exchange between Switzerland and Italy; and the rapid affirmation of new flows from Eastern Europe, which were destined to become the true protagonists of this mobility during the 1930s (see Figure 17.5).

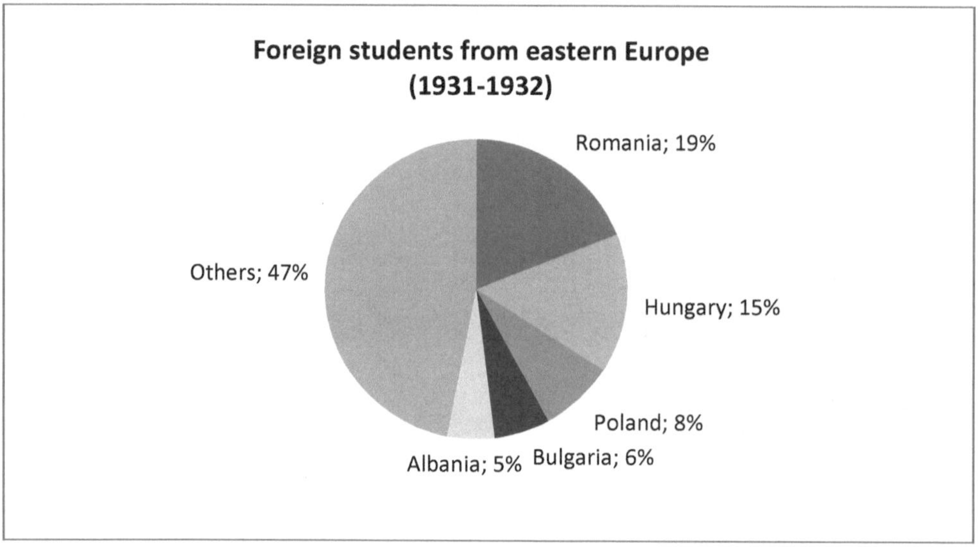

Figure 17.5. Foreign students from Eastern Europe

If we also include in this context the push-pull paradigm, this highly visible phenomenon of students from Romania, Hungary, Bulgaria and Poland should mainly be ascribed to expulsions in those countries after geopolitical changes due to the Versailles treaties. Economic difficulties in the post-war period, problems of integration of minorities included or excluded by the new borders, and political instability and authoritarian trends of governments favored nationalist extremism and the radicalization of pre-existing practices of intolerance, especially with regard to the Jewish members of the population.

The defining characteristic of these groups from Eastern Europe is that its members were mostly enrolled at the Faculty of Medicine and secondarily at the Faculty of Sciences (see Figures 17.6 and 17.7).

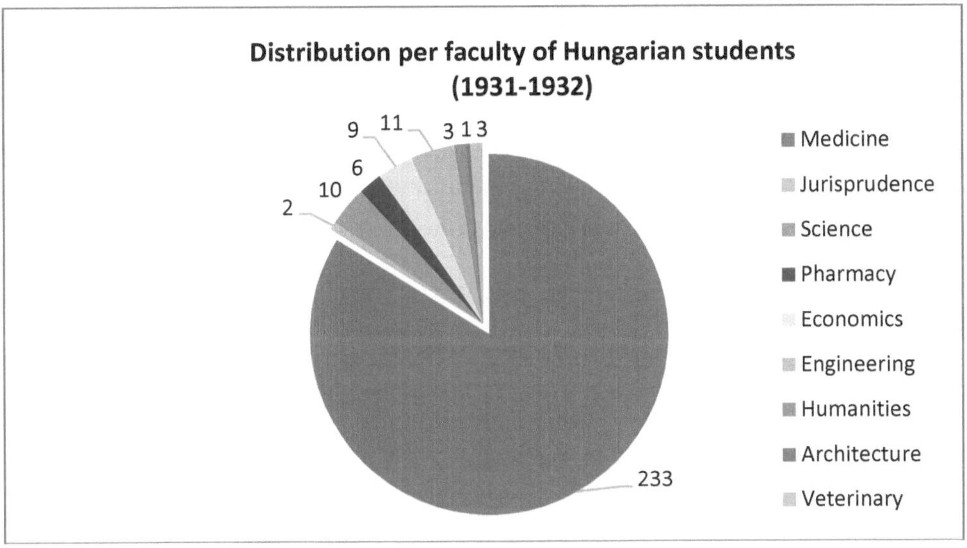

Figure 17.6. Distribution per faculty of Hungarian students (1931-1932)

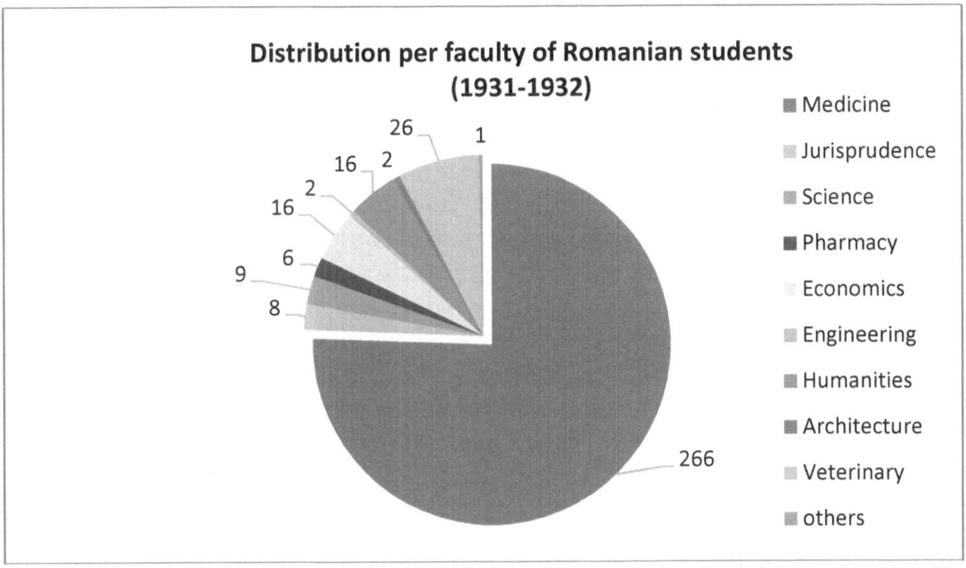

Figure 17.7. Distribution per faculty of Romanian students (1931-1932)

A particular aspect of this history of exchange was the unique expansion of the university for foreigners of Perugia founded in the 1920s as part of initiatives promoting culture and tourism which, in the years of the fascist regime, became an important attraction for foreign students and for the spread of Italian language and culture. Growing from 208 enrolments in 1929 to 600 in 1934, this university did not confer degrees and diplomas, but instead issued a qualification of linguistic and cultural competence which it attempted to have recognized in the countries where its students came from as a prerequisite for access to the teaching of the Italian language. Hence, it was a singular aspect in the Italian university system, and with its innovative offer it was successful in terms of the propaganda objectives of fascism abroad (Gheda 2004).

17.5. *Jewish students: 'unwanted' guests*

Even before specific anti-Jewish legislation was adopted, restrictions on access to higher education and professional careers, together with the increase in anti-Semitic prejudice acted persuasively in stimulating students to look for more hospitable university environments and social cultural contexts elsewhere.

The Jewish proportion in this intellectual mobility was difficult to establish until, in 1938, specific data was gathered ad hoc indicating geographic origin and religion (Voigt 1993; Signori 2000: 139-162). Of course, not all student flows from Eastern Europe were concerned with this type of motivation. There were also other reasons and an important role was played by funding introduced by the Italian fascist government. In that complex interactive system which was the European arena of higher education, the simultaneous activation in 1926 of new appealing factors, and particularly the halving of student fees for foreigners and the simplification of enrollment procedures were incentives initiating and consolidating direct student flows towards Italian universities from abroad. To these stimuli one should also add those incentives such as scholarships and agreements which fascism stipulated with various countries from Eastern Europe and in the Balkans: this was an innovative policy of openness with the objective of cultural and propaganda expansionism on a political level. These initiatives were carried forward in parallel with a foreign policy of convergence and friendship in ideological terms with similarly authoritarian regimes, particularly in Hungary and in Albania, where policy had the final objective of annexation. In the flow of students from Eastern Europe, the Baltic countries, the Balkans, and after 1933-1934 from Nazi Germany, student migration to Italy mingled and mixed two components: the non-Jewish students attracted by the opportunities to study offered by fascist cultural policy, and Jewish students, who were certainly more numerous, looking for inexpensive and accessible universities.

The premises for the disappearance of the Jewish student group occurred when, on the 13th September 1938, the Italian government passed legislation titled "For the defence of the race" followed by other laws in the autumn: enrollment of an Italian or foreign student of Jewish origin was prohibited and only allowed to those university students already enrolled in the previous years, who had passed all their examinations – but specifically excluding German and Austrian Jews – to conclude their studies, without the possibility of repeating any examination in case of failure (Sarfatti 1994).

The exclusion from enrollment was a heavy blow to equality in the right of access to higher education, but the exemption, provided for students already enrolled, also meant precariousness and revocability: the beneficiaries became, within the scientific community of which they were part, a new type of students – at the same time "in extinction" and "in danger".

Moreover, some other exclusion measures built insurmountable walls of a new invisible ghetto inside the university. First of all, the decree with which all Jewish students were expelled from the University Fascist Group (GUF): this caused not only a marginalization with a political and symbolic meaning, which cut relational networks and habits, but also the loss of the possibility of using the services organized for students, such as handouts, canteens, sports facilities and student homes. For these "tolerated" students these measures had the effect not only of psychological isolation, but also had an impact on their living conditions.

Finally, a particularly odious measure completed the discriminatory framework: the ministerial circular of 11th February 1939 established that "students of Jewish race, even being authorized to continue their university studies until they graduate, cannot continue to enjoy further benefits such as scholarships". [2]

It is not a coincidence that the peak number of academic qualifications conferred on foreigners was reached in 1937-1938, with 625 qualifications. The brusque contraction of foreigners to 462 in the following year and the steep drop to 206 in 1939-1940, illustrate how this particular student population in the 1930s was significant and its forced exit was because of state anti-Semitism adopted by fascism. With increasing tension on the international level and looming priorities in economic issues for fascist Italy, the policies of cultural promotion hitherto enacted were reduced and the presence of foreigners in universities diminished greatly.

17.6. *Sources and archives*

A Department of Statistics was founded in 1861 in the United Kingdom of Italy with the task of monitoring and statistically analyzing various aspects of the new state's life, but only several years later did a careful system of tracking, collection and transmission of the data including university education begin. Even so, during this initial period (1880-1898) the presence of foreign students was not identified as an important phenomenon and we do not find any trace of it (Cammelli 2000: 9–32). [3]

In particular the foreign students' situation continued to be "hidden" until 1911. After this year, some series of data were collected and published, but they were fragmentary and heterogeneous. Sometimes, as in the years 1905-1910, the data for the six years

[2] Ordinance to Universities' rectors, 11 February 1939, No. 7025.

[3] For an overview on official statistic sources about foreign students see Signori (2000).

are collected together and not year by year, sometimes the collection was suspended, creating wide gaps, as in the years 1912-1913, 1919-1920, 1923-1924, 1924-1925, 1925-1926, 1927-1928 and 1928-1929. Also, when collection was done it did not comply with uniform criteria: for instance, the counting of degrees and diplomas which were conferred on foreigners was omitted in the years 1913-1918, for which we have only the number of enrollments. The fundamental datum of the foreign students' distribution according to country of origin is available only for a few years (1906-1910, 1910-1911, 1925-1926, 1931-1932, 1932-1933); more ample information concerns their enrollment, the different universities or Royal Institutes they attended, their allotment by faculty and school and the gender balance. The reliability of these quantitative series is also called into question by numerous mistakes and inaccuracies. Finally, data about the payment of university fees (total or reduced), student grants, and the participation of foreigners in "state exam" sessions for admission to practice are all totally lacking.

In addition to the "Gazzetta ufficiale del Regno d'Italia", official legislative gazette of the Kingdom of Italy, the main source focusing on the evolution of the university legislation system is the above mentioned "Bollettino Ufficiale del Ministero della Pubblica Istruzione", where all laws, regulations and administrative measures on universities are published.

In 1931 the Ministry (Ministero della Pubblica Istruzione) took on the title of Ministry of National Education and under this name published complete collections of current laws, but a specific collection of regulations directly or indirectly connected to student mobility from abroad does not exist.

The Italian university archives are deposited in each university and preserve the documentation on the basis of many different standards: normally there is a specific section of the archive for individual students' dossiers (Fondo Studenti), where their curricula studiorum are registered, from enrollment to their thesis. These dossiers can contain basic information and administrative documents concerning the payment of university fees and their social-economic family conditions, petitions and students' letters to academic authorities, their curriculum indicating examinations, results, the name of the lecturers, papers and essays presented during their studies and for the final examination, files relating to transfers and validation of higher education diplomas and possibly previous university courses, and any correspondence with the administration after the end of their studies. In the dossiers of the foreign students in the 1930s we can also find birth certificates and residency permits in their original language with a translation approved by embassies abroad. Jewish rites celebrated at birth are sometimes mentioned in these documents, which focused on the religious attributes of a great number of Eastern European students, allowing them to be selected and eventually expelled from Italian universities. These students' dossiers constitute a potentially very rich corpus of documents, but sometimes they are not preserved in excellent condition and sometimes they are incomplete and damaged.

In addition to the student section, useful consultable documents are the "Minutes of the Academic Council", which later became the "Academic Senate", which were responsible for settling doubtful cases of enrollment and recognizing the qualifications of the foreign students.

In reality, the most significant source focusing on the foreign presence are by yearbooks that the royal universities and the royal superior institutes published starting from 1860. One circular of Minister Perez on October 1st 1879 imposed a uniform scheme on universities to organize a yearbook. He required the university to publish the lists of enrolled students and graduates. Even if such lists are often incomplete and contain some mistakes, they constitute a precious point of departure for every investigation into foreign students' mobility. Already in the early years of the 1900s, the data concerning foreign students and its distribution according to origin appear in a few yearbooks. Only from 1935 another circular of February 12th, sent by the Ministry of National Education, force the universities to include in every volume ten statistical tables. They concerned a lot of institutional aspects, scientific and administrative information about academic life and also a specific table, dedicated to foreign enrollments, separated according to area of origin and gender, and completed by data regarding qualifications acquired. This initiative inaugurated the collection of homogeneous and comparable series of data on the academic community and made attention towards these aspects of academic life systematic. During the 1930s these spreadsheets often contain the definition of "statelessness", referring to foreign students deprived of citizenship rights by the countries in which they were born.

In addition to bulletins published by the Ministry, a rich specialized periodical press follows the evolution of Italian university history. Among the several journals published at the time, such as "Vita universitaria" or "Levana", one in particular stands out: "L'Università italiana", founded in Bologna in 1904 by Domenico Barduzzi and directed by Pietro Albertoni and Raffaele Gurrieri between 1923 and 1940. This magazine, to which lecturers and rectors from all over Italy contributed, was an open forum on university policy, attentively commented on legislative initiatives, promoted debate within the Italian academic community and offered a wide view of scientific life in the different universities of the kingdom. By contrast, "Gli Annali dell'Università italiana", a magazine published in 1939-1943 and edited by Giuseppe Giustini, was a mouthpiece for the fascist government about Italian university policy.

The student press was mostly discontinuous until the 1920s, distributed only within the context of each university. An interesting case-study concerns intellectual migration from Switzerland, and especially from Canton Ticino. Swiss students, who were enrolled in Italian universities organized themselves into a federation and published a university journal between 1919 and 1925.

When fascism seized power all free student organizations were broken up and made silent, with the exception of the Italian Catholic university federation (Fuci). Instead, the organization of the fascist university groups (GUF) monopolized student communities: the GUF were disciplined under a hierarchical order and became a fundamental organization within the Fascist National Party (PNF). In many universities the GUF constituted "foreign student sections", already envisaged by the special statute of 1927. Obviously they were, however, involved in political and cultural activities of the groups and were subjected to intensive indoctrination. This propaganda effort was pursued for instance with the "Courses of Fascist Culture", organized expressly for foreigners in Bologna in 1934 and Rome in 1935. The aim of this involvement was twofold: on the one hand, foreign students were seen as a tool for spreading Italian culture and a positive, winning image of fascism abroad. On the other hand, Italian fascism was presented to foreign students as a new political and institutional model which they could import into their countries, creating ideological links and friendly international relations. For all these reasons the press published by the GUF is another interesting source focusing on the foreign presence in the Italian universities. Among the most important newspapers one should mention "Roma Fascista" of the University of Rome, "La Nuova Guardia" of Bologna (Salustri 2009), which was published in 1935-1936 in several languages, "Il Bo" of Padua and "Libro e moschetto" of Milan. Finally, the local periodical press of university towns can be usefully consulted.

The public records of the Ministero della Pubblica Istruzione (MPI, 1860-1931) and the Ministero della Educazione Nazionale (MEN, 1931-1943) are both deposited in Rome in the Central State Archive (ACS). The richest section for research is Direzione generale dell'istruzione superiore (DGIS), divided according to years and subjects. For connections between foreign students, one should consult the GUF dossiers in the National Fascist Party Collection (PNF) also available at the ACS.

The foreign students' presence was also perceived as a problem of public order, political control and vigilance, in view of the prevention and repression of possible ferments of opposition. The political police, the provincial offices of Pubblica Sicurezza (PS) and the prefectures were all mobilized to carefully monitor the activity of these young people, who could become vehicles of antifascist propaganda, and particularly communist propaganda, and constitute dangerous, subversive or revolutionary groups. The documentation produced by these offices and institutions, through reports and correspondence, sometimes of considerable interest, is available in the papers of the Ministero dell'interno (MI), Pubblica Sicurezza (PS).

Starting from Klaus Voigt's innovative study about German Jews in fascist Italy, this work in progress of historical research has analyzed different contexts of this intellectual migration, such as Pavia, Bologna, Pisa, Padova (Signori 2000, 2009; Brizzi 2002; Pelini and Pavan 2009; Simone 2014), and has focused specific aspects – such as the experiences of Hungarian students (Kelemen 2015), foreshadowing a forthcoming approach to a full understanding of this forgotten chapter of Italian and European history.

Bibliography

Brizzi, G.P. (2002) *Silence and remembering. The racial laws and the foreign Jewish students at the University of Bologna*, Bologna: Clueb.

Brizzi, G.P. (2014) *Tehijà. Un gruppo universitario sionista all'Università di Bologna negli anni del fascismo in Per continuare il dialogo ... Gli amici ad Angelo Varni*, Bologna: Bononia University Press.

Brizzi, G.P. (ed.) (2015) *Diaspore. L'Università di Bologna davanti alle leggi razziali*, Bologna: Clueb.

Cammelli, A. (2000) *'Contare gli studenti. Statistica e popolazione studentesca dall'Unità ad oggi'*, Annali di Storia delle Università italiane, 4: 9–32.

Castro, S. (2004) *Tra Italia e Svizzera: la presenza degli studenti svizzeri nell'Università di Pavia, 1860-1945*, Milan: Cisalpino.

Ferraris, C.F. in Ministero di agricoltura, industria e commercio (MAIC) (1913), *Annali di statistica*, Statistica delle Università e degli Istituti superiori, V(6).

Gheda, P. (2004) *La promozione dell'Italia nel mondo: l'Università per stranieri di Perugia dalle origini alla statizzazione*, Bologna: Il Mulino.

Gramsci, A. (1955) *Gli intellettuali e l'organizzazione della cultura*, Turin: Einaudi.

Karady, V. and Nagy, P.T. (eds.) (2012) *The Numerus clausus in Hungary: Studies on the First Anti-Jewish Law and Academic Anti-Semitism in Modern Central Europe*, Budapest: Pasts Inc. Centre for Historical Research.

Kelemen, A.K. (2015) *'The Semaphore of Mobility: Hungarian Jewish Press and Peregrination to Fascist Italy'*, Annali di storia delle Università italiane, 2, 41–54.

Pelini, F. and Pavan, I. (2009) *La doppia epurazione. L'Università di Pisa e le leggi razziali tra guerra e dopoguerra*, Bologna: Il Mulino.

Romeo, R. (1978) *L'Italia unita e la prima guerra mondiale*, Bari: Laterza.

Rudiger, H.P. and Tikhonov, N. (eds.) (2003) *Universitaten als Brucken in Europa: studien zur Geschichte der studentischen Migration*, Frankfurt: Lang.

Salustri, S. (2009) *La Nuova Guardia. Gli universitari bolognesi tra le due guerre (1919-1943)*, Bologna: Clueb.

Sarfatti, M. (1994 1st edn., 2017) *Mussolini contro gli ebrei. Cronaca dell'elaborazione delle leggi del 1938*, Turin: Zamorani.

Signori, E. (2000) *'Una peregrinatio academica in età contemporanea. Gli studenti ebrei stranieri nelle università italiane tra le due guerre', Annali di Storia delle Università italiane*, 4: 139–162.

Signori, E. (2009) 'Contro gli studenti: la persecuzione antiebraica negli atenei italiani e le comunità studentesche' in G. Procacci and V. Galimi (eds.) *"Per la difesa della razza." L'applicazione delle leggi antiebraiche nelle università italiane*, Milan: Unicopli, 173–210.

Simone, G. (2014) 'Studenti e docenti ebrei espulsi dall'Università di Padova', *Quaderni per la storia dell'Università di Padova*, 47: 165–181.

Voigt, K. (1993) *Il rifugio precario. Gli esuli in Italia dal 1933 al 1945*, I, Firenze: La Nuova Italia.

Chapter 18

Narrating migration

Barbara Berri

> There was a wall. [...] As any other wall, it was ambiguous, two-sided. All that was hidden behind and all that was left outside depended on the side you were looking at it from.
>
> (Le Guin 1974)

> Conscience is a wonderful symphony. The conscious mind has different levels of the self: the primordial self, which we share with several animals, allows us to feel, for instance, pleasure or pain, but it does not allow reflection on these feelings, which is something that only human beings can do. We are also reflective, that is, we are able to meditate on what happens to us, also taking into account our history and our memories. Everything happening to us is the echo of our past and takes on a meaning in that which happens later. We can therefore state that, as human beings, we grow out of a symphony, which later turns into a script as soon as we become able to speak. This is what we do, we write everything, every single time [...] the more we understand how we are, the more we can understand how we work.
>
> (Damasio 2012)

Stories, defined as narration, through various means and codes, related to different contents, intertwine with the daily life of individuals, groups and societies in such a recurring and pervasive way so as to often turn, in this routine, into a production and reception process that is so ordinary and apparently banal so as to remain at the border of awareness. Actually, the conscience itself, identity, [1] the building and presenting of the self are structured through stories in the broad sense (narrative, scripts) (Randall 1995; Whitebrook 2001; Cosso 2013) that, consciously or not, the individual tells himself and others. The study of such stories, their interpretation, the revealing of their underlying linguistic, rhetorical, stylistic and, ultimately, conceptual and speculative

---

[1] In particular, contemporary culture in a broad sense, characterized by an increase in perspectives, reference systems, data and information exchange, the movement of people and ideas, is particularly sensitive towards issues related to identity and imposes the inescapable need for a (re)definition of concepts (see Derek Parfit's concept of "glass tunnel" in Lyotard 2008). Identity and otherness, as a fluid and interdependent concept, divided and connected by a mobile and partially permeable boundary both need to be analysed taking into account social and cultural dynamism, as well as environmental and personal features. Culture is the "result of interactions, exchanges and influences from elsewhere" (Fabietti 1995: 21; Remotti 1996).

mechanisms and expedients opens up a wide epistemological perspective, where stories become the enjoy privilege as an object of study for different purposes, through various methods and in different disciplines. In this narration, some areas are more dense and interesting, as they constitute an enlarged variety. The issues typical of all communicative and narration processes, including those intra-cultural, [2] are even more resounding in settings where the reference culture is very different and, sometimes, also in open (or intended) opposition to the other, because of significant differences in values or ideological clashes, often fomented by media interest or other various interests. Each act of communication, as the pragmatic use of a skill (Akmajian et al. 1984), depends on the setting, intentions, alleged and shared opinions and other contingent factors. If difficulties based on having different reference cultures, different educations and different skills are added to these objective, universal difficulties, communication can easily become a trying experience, which can potentially raise uncertainty or misunderstandings. Along these lines, for example, there is the case of the so-called "high context cultures" and "low context cultures" (McKay et al. 2009), the combination of which can lead to remarkable difficulties in understanding each other correctly due to the different values each attributed to verbal and non-verbal codes, to paralinguistic elements and meta-messages.

On the one hand, if communication should connect distinct and separate worlds, be they spatially, culturally or individually so, instead, what happens is that, like any other aspect of interrelation, that communication inevitably undergoes multifaceted changes imposed by the individuals involved, interpreting and building themselves, others and the world according to their own sensibilities and experiences, [3] especially in virtue of the connective nature of illocution.

If each speaker constantly questions the other's aims and ways of communication in addition to analysing the methods and the codes used to evaluate analogies and differences, such awareness (and good will) would facilitate the exposure of some of the most common, deep causes of intercultural misunderstanding. The majority of the time, such processes, and their consequences, are simply ascribable to a myriad of concepts in terms of the cultural basis that the individual is only partially aware of and responsible for. The latent conditioning of paradigms and referent cultural categories affect the communicative and expressive choices of the individual, with different degrees of awareness. Each intercultural narrative process can be analysed from different perspectives, often maintaining a fragile balance. On the one hand, multilingualism, multiculturalism, and linguistic contaminations of various types are gaining so much ground in the globalized contemporary society, that, for instance, in the field of contemporary (socio)linguistics, the writing and analysis of linguistic autobiographies has

---

[2] It is clear that none can be defined in a univocal or linear way but each is divided into several group of subcultures and cultures up to the extreme case of the individual micro culture.

[3] It is of course a matter of sensitivity and individual and group experiences, of education and culture. In this context, it is emblematic of the philosophy of representing life within life, both at the theatre and in books (McKay *et al.* 2009).

become extremely relevant, even in a comparative sense. It is also true that the safeguard of differences, localism, minorities (linguistic, cultural, national or gender) and linguistic diversity meets needs that are, in part, complementary and, in part, opposed. Furthermore, communication generally resorts to different types of codes, both verbal and non-verbal, each with its own rules and encoding and decoding processes, each shaped by the "educational" cultural context, regardless of the linguistic and cultural contamination process to follow, and adapted (and/or mitigated, where necessary) by the specific illocution, in terms of time, space, context, status, and means.

Along those lines, we can therefore assume that, if the presentation and the representation of one's conscience, the telling of one's life experience and even the idea of a future is developed through a series of stories addressed to the teller or to other people and according to different points of view, then the particular context of intercultural communication and communication in the context of the cultural hybridization process (and, in this specific case, of migration) is where the diachronic redefinition of narrative (and, as a consequence, of the building of the self, the script narration) is more subject to a radical need for adaptation: the awareness and the direct experimentation of different models of culture and values provokes culture shock[4] that affects both the individual and the group at different levels, modifying their perception, representation and, as a consequence, narration. Considering countless different possible reactions to that process, from acceptance to refusal, with a range of forms of and formulas for compromise that may change over time and that are identified according to taxonomic superstructures with different labels,[5] some criteria categorize and steer the study of the phenomenon. First, it is to be considered that in every openly intercultural setting, each part of the system is influenced by the power inequalities in effect, which differ based on background (for instance, migration, colonialism or postcolonialism). As widely proven by the colonialism and postcolonialism of the nineteenth century, communication and narration are managed through various means, like many other relational and non-relational dynamics, by the dominant group, even if they are a minority in terms of number of members. In this sense, choices concerning language use are particularly explanatory (Palusci and Bertacco 2008), as they offer a wide range of possibilities that, among others, directly influence the evolution of the language according to a mass of possible combinations, and indirectly influence[6] the reference culture(s) and the system(s). This could range from the identification and recognition of an official language (the one of those in power), existing alongside different forms of native language(s) or pidgins and Creole variations, according to the various related modus operandi and the political choices of the conquerors, to the extreme case of the

---

[4] The term *culture shock* was first used by the American anthropologist Cora Du Boisnel in 1951 to refer to the feeling of confusion and disorientation experienced by anthropologists themselves. The term later started to be widely used and, in particular, its meaning and field of application were widened by the Canadian anthropologist Kalervo Oberg.

[5] Such as "salad bowl" and "melting pot".

[6] See study by M. Heidegger.

rule of slavery, which stated that slaves would be gathered in groups who did not speak the same language(s). From a literary point of view, Marlene Nourbese Philip, a migrant and writer, creates an interesting transposition of the concept and the law in a single short text, "Mother Tongue," in which versatile concepts of "language" and "mother tongue," and related lemmas, emerge from both in graphic transposition and the variability of (sub)genre.[7] In migratory phenomena, instead, power relations are reversed and newcomers learn the language of the country of destination, adjusting themselves, to some extent, to local customs and practices.

Even though, insomuch as being narration, stories, broadly considered holistic experiences, they may be recounted through a combination of different possible channels and codes and by means of media, transparent or not, and the role of spoken language therein still tends to be predominant, though complementary. In the different forms of the self-narration, language choice is one of the most highly problematic issues to face. Again, there can be two perspectives: when the author has been educated in a post-colonial or neo-colonial setting (often later experiencing disorientation due to migration) and finds himself having to choose between either salvaging native language,[8] inevitably, significantly reducing the ability to spread and use of the tale beyond local borders, and therefore also the ability to spread the stories and cultural heritage one wishes to transmit, or, the second option, which is using the "language of the conqueror", scorned but effective to cross geographical or non-geographical boundaries.

At the same time, the migrants that decide to share themselves, their identity and experience must take into account their love for their country and perhaps their feeling of homesickness, as well as their roots and therefore their own language, which, in this sense, may be the favoured means of expression and in line with a significant part of contents and images of their narration; on the other hand, choosing to use the language of the destination country instead, or, in any case, a European language, would lead, also in this case, to easier, broader spreading of the message in the area that migrant wants to reach and "inform" others about themselves. Furthermore, at least at the beginning, that migrant must acquire a suitable knowledge of the new language (L2) and this ever-changing process (which will be a resource to a bilingual or trilingual migrant in the future) can be a limitation[9] or, at least, a difficulty when communication starts and, in fact, to remedy this, co-authorship is often resorted to. The issue of the

---

[7] The particular sensitivity towards this topic is also shown, among the others, by the celebration of the International Mother Language Day (SS2, 21st February). The contemporary spirit of many (post-colonial) countries is characterized by the search for one's roots, by the attempt to recover (lost) traditions and myths.

[8] The idea of recovering and/or reconstructing the native language is strongly felt in view of the preservation/re-founding of local culture. The lack of "voice" is often a central topic, both in terms of the related cultural decentralization and the absence of a native or shared language, which is missing or irrecoverable (Palusci and Bertacco 2008).

[9] The use of L2 can obviously be a choice or, finally, an opportunity, as was the use of French for the literary production of Samuel Beckett (intra-European migrant) (Chini and Andorno 2018).

language is managed and solved in different ways but also becomes a literary topos: the Nobel Prize winner, John Maxwell Coetzee, an emigrated South African writer, uses the recurring theme of mutilation to metaphorically convey the idea of being forced to silence. With his sensitivity and experience as a translator and linguist, Coetzee chooses the approach of "rewriting", widely used in this type of narrative, aimed at revising the traditional and consolidated European cultural and literary models to reveal their relativism and arbitrariness and, at the same time, proposes various possible alternatives. In this process, authors usually set out and sometimes mix the patterns and demands of minorities, be they linguistic, cultural, national or gender, in a sort of mutual acknowledgement of a weak or subordinate (Spivak 1987) condition which may be contrasted through various means: for instance, instead of a binary identity/alterity structure, often generally based on stereotypes, the hybridity model could be used, inspired by a more comprehensive and mature idea of "cultural difference" (Bhabha 1994), in which it is acknowledged that different cultures, "fluid, constantly criss-crossing borders and changing directions" (ibidem), are – today more than in the past – in a continual relationship of mutual influence.

In the specific case of Coetzee's novel, the traditional book of relevance is Robinson Crusoe by Daniel Defoe. In the book inspired by that novel, Foe (1986) (a title of significance), Coetzee introduces Foe (Defoe), an author that becomes a character, thus creating a setting that allows the development of another topic dear to this type of literature, which is meta-narrative reflection. [10] There are several recurring literary structures and themes within, from the epistolary style to the reflection on the meaning and future of literature (plausibility, immortalization, etc.). In addition, there are technical aspects of the latter, and above all, at the centre, there is the need or lack of need to narrate. The protagonist, (significantly a female character, with a number of repercussions, and linked to the topic of authorship) Susan Barton is victim of a shipwreck on a desert island where she meets Cruso and Friday, who are completely different than the ones in the original novel, both in their individual features and mutual relationship. What is mainly of interest is Friday's condition, deprived of his own language and, at the same time, of his tongue, with reference to linguistic and cultural means (once again, the Mother Tongue) and the possibility of free expression. Along these lines, it is appropriate to underline how in our culture, values and emotions are deeply correlated with linguistic structures [11] and how the narration of the self is deeply intertwined with the narration of the culture of origin, especially in multicultural contexts. In Coetzee's novel, Friday – who cannot narrate – emigrates, travelling to Europe with Susan Barton.

With Coetzee's work, we can analyse the particular case of the narration of the self

---

[10] In this sense, particularly explanatory are the narrative and philosophical parables of J. Barth (1967, 1972, 1984).

[11] Even here, you may think about M. Heidegger or the famous quote by L.J.J. Wittgenstein: "The borders of my language are the borders of my world".

in a literary form, with different levels of interference and transposition of real life (with all the paradigmatic and epistemological limits of an (auto)biography that are well known among the narrative disciplines) in contexts of fiction. This kind of narrative often resorts to a structure that first brings together, then creates clashes and moments of discussion between different cultures in various settings, from the country of origin to the country of destination and in the context of travelling. [12] Equally attentive to the safeguarding of cultural petitions from minorities is Sylvia Wynter, a Jamaican author and intellectual who has studied and lived in various countries. Her studies particularly focus on the representation of human beings in relation to their culture of origin, gender, skin colour, intercultural and migration experiences. In the form of a paper, the author analyses, for instance, another classic of English literature, re-discussing themes and models. In "Beyond Miranda's Meanings" (Wynter 1990), the lack of an indigenous female character in The Tempest by William Shakespeare is denounced, as it may have partially balanced the structure of the work, already strongly imbalanced in favour of patriarchal and Western components. The native figure is a man and is attracted by the only female model present, belonging to the dominant group, "the metaphysical invested and 'idealized' object of desire for all classes (Stephano and Trinculo) and all population groups (Caliban)" (ibidem: 127). Wynter expands her analysis up to imagination, space and time, in the attempt to give reason to the variety and variability of the narration of the self. On the one hand, language and communication identify and illustrate several macro factors that influence the development, transformation and adaptation of language and culture and that are in their turn influenced and shaped by them, such as the concept of time and space, the concept of destiny and personal responsibility, and the safeguarding of self-image and non-verbal communication. On the other hand, each need and contingency of code switching implies confrontation between different cultural reference systems, of imagery and of structures of the style of the language. In particular, recent studies have shown that multilingualism itself, moreover, affects the perception of time (Athanasopoulos and Bylund 2017). To set the duration of time, several languages resort to various mental representations based, depending on the case, on distance, volume or other reference parameters that the speaker is not aware of until facing multilingualism.

> The study confirms the importance of language also from a cognitive point of view and its ability to shape our mind [...] Being constantly exposed to two systems leads a bilingual to develop a more sophisticated sensitivity towards the structures of the language, on the one hand, and to continuously inhibit the language they are not using at a certain time, on the other [...] Bilingualism is a valuable experience able to modify the structure of our mind, the way we think about and react to incentives, switching from one task to the other, thus being less affected by irrelevant stimuli [...] This cognitive flexibility seems to provide a

[12] Among the most significant authors, Marsha Meharan, Malala, Azhar Abidi, Waheed Rabbani, Kahlil Gibran, Basmael-Khatib, Rania Ibrahim, Fayza Ismail, Benyamin Somay.

greater ability to focus only on relevant incentives, as well as higher efficiency when switching from one task to the other.

(ibidem: 912)

Of course, as a cultural occurrence and product, narration acquires different shapes based on purposes, points of view, context, codes, means and many other variables. It is therefore useful, as well as interesting – even though it is not the right time or place – to create a taxonomic table that takes into account the range of options and, for each one, defines and explains the strengths and weaknesses, potential and limitations, both in terms of usefulness in the general system and in terms of intracultural and intercultural communicative effectiveness. In particular, in the context of borders, both literary and metaphorical, geographical and cultural, the focus should be on the identification and evaluation of such limits, or supposed ones, of their possible permeability and the stance of the speaker, that is, of the subject or the group narrating, in relation to the border – be it a wall or a bridge – and the subject or group that represent (as fluid as the relation may be) the otherness beyond the borders. If the group is composed by migrants, the geographical border is concretely crossed, even though the civil and legal profile often long remains unclear, whereas the sharing of a cultural "space" is obviously much slower and more complex, and the same goes for the linguistic adaptation and the reference system in a process of mutual contamination.

In general, every narrative act is affected by the intentions and purposes of the speaker, consciously or not. However, in the specific case of literature about migration in our country, it is vital to acknowledge that there is a strong ideological and rhetorical component that often, and unfortunately, tends to divide and therefore restore a strong concept of border, at least on a metaphorical and symbolic level. On the one hand, there is the story of the people either welcoming such migrants and/or, to use a common expression, the people "subjected to the invasion" and on the other hand, there is the story of the migrants, who react in different ways to the disorientation and to the phases of learning and adaptation. These two types of narration and their subcategories also follow variable patterns of mutual influence, with possible compensatory phenomena. Finally, in this complex tangle of stories, possibly extreme positions emerge (together with a range of moderate stances), especially when considering the perspectives of the people welcoming migrants "affected by the invasion", already implicit in their choice of labels. [13] Such stories go through the media, adapting the paradigmatic and technical features of each of them from time to time. Each medium has both potential and limitations that can be either functional or dysfunctional, according

[13] In general, in media (re)presentation, the point of view of the target society becomes a *range* between two extremes, pietism (for instance, some exaggerated aspects of the "media circus" after the death of Aylan Kurdi) and aggression. The latter extreme provides the input for all the debate and rhetoric of meanness and do-goodery: see *Narrability Journal*, 2(1), March 2018; Nicolosi 2016.

to the content and type of recipient, whether presumed or ideal. [14]

For the sake of brevity, this chapter mainly analyses examples taken from two macro sectors of the media, narrative and social media. The reasons for this choice will be explained from time to time together with related examples. In contemporary media (Costa 1999), [15] social media are extremely dynamic and, almost emblematically, represent the tendency toward speed, typical of new technology, as opposed to more traditional media and, in general, to those disciplines that prefer conservation and memory. Furthermore, the speed at which discussions and interactions occur turn social media into a sort of podium (fiction/reality) where people can discuss various topics, including current events. However, communicating at a level that does not belong to everyday life may lead to misunderstanding, (lower awareness) on the basis of which such communication seems less subject to the concept of individual liability, also in a legal sense. As is well known, it is a place for a heated, and often highly aggressive, debate, which leads to divisions, also resorting to medieval labels ("Guelphs" and "Ghibellines") posed alongside new ones ("bleeding hearts" and "villains"). [16] While some more traditional media, like television and newspapers, functions to the mediation between subjects, filtering communications and transmitting official and/or institutional communications with a certain authority, the structure and the rules of social media allow for more direct conversation and higher interaction from all types of users. Considering that the subject is topical and that there is widespread interest in it, stimulated by ideological and political trends, especially thanks to media overexposure, the

[14] Each *medium* has its own peculiarities and meets certain needs, according to criteria that are not comparable with those of other individuals. It is vital that each form of communication is mediated by a channel, and is therefore subject to the rules of the channel chosen, be it the voice, in case of oral communication, or the lens of a video camera or any other filter, whether technological or not (Bolter and Grusin 2002). According to the double logical *remediation*, contemporary culture aims at combining "immediacy" (transparency) and "hypermediation" (opacity) in the various media environments. According to Bolter and Grusin, *remediation* characterizes not only contemporary digital new technologies, but most ways of communicating of old and modern western cultures. Therefore, there is not a significant discontinuity between digital and old media. New media reshape old ones and, at the same time, old media must be turned into new versions (Jakobson 1957, 1963; Sebeok 1991). The same *fabula* can be tackled by different communication means, but it will undergo changes and adjustments in different ways according to the *medium* chosen, which depends on, among other things, the choice of the codes and the nature of the desired effect on the user. The types of use and relation with the recipient are fundamental to develop the content. The *medium*, as is widely known, modifies the principles of communication and the types of messages. The adaptations that texts must undergo are frequent, with most disparate results, to be adapted for media other than the ones they were written for. A case in point in this field are the studies by McLuhan.

[15] While mass communication chooses channels such as television, cinema, newspapers and, on an experimental basis, the web, what arouses is the suspicion that the availability of information is not ascertainable according to satisfying parameters, on the one hand, and that, on the other, it is not structured according to criteria that are aesthetically remarkable. The information contents generally identified as a message are adjusted according to the means of transmission and, in this sense, it can be interesting to evaluate the terms and methods of transposition, which are, at the same time, a conversion and a translation.

[16] *Narrability Journal*, op. cit.

topics somehow related to migration, reception and various possible, desired or deplorable levels of interaction are a recurring centre piece of discussions and debates of various purposes. The migrant becomes a "virtual space for debate" or "virtual battlefield", with tones ranging from pietism to satire, in ways that range from an analytical and scientific approach to self-serving accusations, lacking in empirical basis. Even though in this context several different voices can be heard, thus making it possible to understand the migrant's point of view, as well as that of the destination society, the voice of the latter seems to be more represented, also because of higher and undiversified availability of means and access channels. A detailed and systematic analysis of the events reported in such media could therefore allow a clear picture of the migrant through the eyes and the voice of the receiving society. Furthermore, these polyphonic means, and the great amount of linguistic codes involved, could also lead to a system as synaesthetic as it is fluid, precisely given the speed and the related lack of memory.

Not taking into account the variables of "volume" and "noise," harsher and more intense by nature, affecting the numerous cases in which confrontation on social media degenerates into aggression and attack, such communication can give an extremely varied picture of the migration phenomenon and of the figure of the migrant, which reflects strong fragmentation from the point of view of the receiving society. In this context, the narration of the figure of the migrant is still mainly structured according to conventional binary patterns, on the model of the fundamental identity/alterity dichotomy, even though the evaluation, whether implicit or not, develops in different levels, ranging from the acceptance and the enhancement of differences as a source of value and, as a consequence, of human, cultural, linguistic enrichment of a new collective heritage or opportunities, which would be otherwise neither recognizable nor accessible, to the denial of anyone different, labelled as invaders, usurpers or even apostates wanting to erase the customs and traditions of the country of destination to impose their own.

In the virtual reality of social media, the phenomenon of the "fake" is at the same time typical, widespread and very interesting, and is a sort of further separate virtual world, with borders that are not easily discernible, especially by a naïve user, or one not used to accurate verification of source reliability (Fontana 2017, 2018). Different rules and reasons underlie the spread of the phenomenon, from economic interests to propaganda, conspiracy, divertissement, and satire or mocking. Whatever the reason(s), which would require more research, the result is an overlapping of levels and spaces, from the real world to the virtual one, and even up to the fake one, each with its own rules, its own function in relationships between people and, particularly relevant for our analysis, each with its own narrative structure and specific narrating typologies and formulas. Ironically, this is how the Ebola epidemic, for example, only exists (hopefully) on the web. [17]

---

[17] https://www.ilfattoquotidiano.it/2014/10/28/ebola-allarmismo-lepidemia-nel-web/1175445/ (Pollicino and Quintarelli 2017; Perucchietti 2018)

In this sense, also narration has its own space, different from that of the physical world, which has specific characteristics of its own. For each medium, spatial considerations as such are superimposed on literary, meta-literary or meta-textual observations and the ones related to paradigms of genres and means (Costa 1999; Bigliazzi 2002).[18] The diegetic space and the mimetic space both become words in narrative,[19] whereas they are separated in theatre plays.[20] In this context, it is not necessary to define a concept such as that of space with its physical and substantial characteristics, since the subject of cultural studies is more the perception and the interpretation humans have and narrate of themselves, of their environment, of their culture and finally of the world rather than the arrangement of and the interaction between humans and objects in a world led by constant, empirical rules. Each culture can make complete sense if found in its own context and evaluated based on its territory, on the places and habits that it shaped and by which it was itself shaped. In this sense, space is neither boundless nor invariably definite, but shaped and transformed by social and cultural actions, which make it a circumscribed place, continuously adjusting itself to the needs of its inhabitants. Even space becomes completely malleable when it is entered into discourse and subjected to the aims and purposes of such discourse. In discourse, be it an essay, a description or a work of fiction, space acquires more characteristics filtered by the points of view of the author, which can be subjective or not. In particular, narrative plots interweave spatial and interpersonal relationships on the basis of geographical and toponymic delineations. In this context, meeting another person, be it desired or feared, becomes the chance to discuss and, possibly, re-define culture and spaces.

First, the migrant talks about themselves, their particular condition and usually introduce themselves as a migrant. Just as Saint Augustine wrote to introduce the

---

[18] Considerations about cyberspace are also interesting, which compared with the "Newtonian space": "cyberspace is not a pre-existing void to be filled with moving (and living) particles of matter and thought, subject to the universal laws of science and philosophy. It is rather an entity in the making, an unending surface of intersecting, but not necessarily interacting discourses, each developed according to its own assumptions and rhetoric", in Mihalache 2000.

[19] Also the space on the page can be, in its turn, characterized by particular graphics, as in the famous novel by Laurence Sterne, *Tristram Shandy* or the works by Stephane Mallarmé and the metaphysical poets.

[20] Here the scene symbolizes the space of the other, represented in a sort of symbolic extension (Jacquart 1974). Conversely, the diegetic space is similar to the one of a text that, in the case of the theatre, is performed rather than read. Furthermore, the audience in its turn lives in a particular space, shared with the others and subject to strict, set rules, which are equally meaningful both in the most common case of respect and in the particular case of violation (rule of the fourth wall. In general, spaces can be chosen or endured, individual or collective. In ancient times, a particular value was given to the agora and the theatre, and in most recent times, to cabaret or the cinema). The representation of the space at the theatre is subject to objective difficulties, such as sizes and characteristics of the stage, delimitation of the scene, empirical and technical restrictions and special effects, whereas, for instance, the cinema can resort to potentially unlimited resources that, from a narrative point of view, can be compensated or even enriched by the reader's imagination.

books he wrote in the year 397 AD, initiating the literary genre of confessions with the work of the same name, those who feel the need to fully narrate their life experience are usually moved by an exceptional event that played a vital role in defining their own identity, and that event often becomes the underlying principle of the story. In the case of Saint Augustine this event was conversion, in the case of the migrant this is generally an event, or a series of events, experiences and emotions linked to their migratory experience or to migration itself. Of course, that experience is narrated in various ways, intertwining the needs of the narrator (including "answering" to those who reject them, often in the attempt to break down metaphorical "border walls") with different levels of interest from the recipient, based on the public's inclusion and interaction, the medium used, and the format, in addition to the situation, the purposes and the organizational structure of the performance, in the broadest sense. They are often shared cultural, artistic and/or scientific initiatives,[21] aimed at fostering the psycho-emotional well-being of the migrant and/or mutual acquaintances.

Along these lines, the particular case of narrative, in its various genres and subgenres, represents a very interesting case, as it allows more articulated exposure and, together with it, paints a picture that, thanks to its potential and the typical characters therein, offers compromises and understanding, often on the part of the writer (be it the author – migrant and/or exposed at various levels and for various reasons to a strong level of intercultural contamination – or in the frequent case of co-authorship, already mentioned in this chapter). Often, but not always, such works (here, too, intended in a broad sense) can be brought back to the category of so-called "migrant literature" (with some variations of the name) found in many languages and national literary corpora. Given the significance of the phenomenon, the media exposure and the consequent public interest, in Italy in particular, migrant literature has gained an important position in the field of critical and literary analysis and debate has been opened to understand if it presents opportunities or constitutes the umpteenth ghettoization process (Bhabha 1994). On the one hand, this type of literature undoubtedly meets most of the above mentioned needs for communication, for (self)expression and representation, for definition of the self.[22] On the other, being classified in the category of migration literature meets the epistemological and methodical requirements of scientific disciplines but also those empirically based criteria of uniformity and belonging. Even if the most used label is "migrant literature", its definition and inclusion/exclusion

[21] Consider, for instance, events such as the "Melting Pot", the "International Mother Language Day" or "A Night with Ben", the Series of Dialogues on Migrations, European projects such as "Daraja", which saw the direct involvement of the University of Pavia or, more generally, phenomena such as the Theatre of the Oppressed or various musical or artistic experiences.

[22] Among other things, think about the ways a destabilizing experience is handled, about the need to introduce oneself and one's own experience, to communicate a peculiar and emblematic condition with its opportunities and limits, about the need to narrate and represent one's identity (individual, cultural, transcultural), about the several examples in the odeporic narrative, whose stories usually narrate the encounter/clash between cultures, and so on.

criteria are more fleeting – the foreign origin of the author or the evaluation of the generational level,[23] or the topics tackled, writing methods and much more – and, once again, they imply a deep analysis of, among others, the language issue (due to a generic multilingualism or polyglotism), which goes beyond the chronological borders of modern times, well illustrated by the following example, based on an analysis of writing from one of the most symbolic authors, Igiaba Scego:

> Afro-Italian author, or rather, a citizen of the Italian language, who no longer uses Italian as a means to communicate or share her own story – like the first books of migrant authors released in the Nineties; and neither does she employ Italian as a mainly rhetorical form, a symbol of literature, used as a heterogeneous language ("other language" of "another culture"), as many writers experienced from the Middle Ages onwards [...], trying their hands at Italian as outsiders: among several examples, we can mention Montaigne, Byron, and Pound. Scego instead, like many other contemporary authors, uses Italian as a language within which is her own story and identity. In other words, Italian is no longer a communicative expedient, or a literary choice, but a condition for living.
>
> (Brogi 2011)

Naturally, the chosen language (and its reference culture and literature) becomes subject to adaptation and contamination processes in turn, usually towards more dynamism and liveliness, international openness, relative simplification (Offenheim 1999), higher awareness of needs, uses, difficulties in expressing states of mind and concepts of other cultures. Loan words are very common, and the reason why can easily be linked to the fact that, among other things, such works are provided with glossaries and similar tools.

In light of what has been stated above, migrant literature can indeed be considered a category of national literature, maybe having a special status, although it is necessary to take into account opposing ideas and difficulties in definitions, which are also affected by ideological fears.

> Having to face continuous publications, Italian cultural institutions and academies have reacted and are still reacting mainly with peaceful indifference [...] or critical openness [...], defining the situation with the term "phenomenon of migrant writing" [...]. In the latter case, there have been very significant occasions to elaborate and discuss, which were also brave for various reasons, considering the continuous opposition from the surrounding habitat, composed by an often racist ideological environment and an economic-political context continuously affected by financial cuts in the world of culture. Despite this, it is legitimate to doubt whether both a self-defensive narrow-mindedness and an unconditional open-mindedness can sometimes turn into two separate types of discriminatory logic,

[23] Authors can be included in or excluded from the category (depending on the reference criteria chosen from time to time) according to their belonging to the first or second generation or to the various middle generations (1.25, 1.50, 1.75; see Ceravolo 2016).

confirmed to be hegemonic in the very same moment they lead, due to both explicit rejection and friendly humiliation, to a prejudice of firm non-involvement (which can be mentioned only if contained).

(Brogi 2011)

Generally, geography reproduced in text must take into account such conditions and uncertainties, in line with the stylistic and poetic choices of the author. The chaotic dimension of modern times often generates the needs for a shelter, for a demarcated and separated geography, clearly identifiable and well-established, within which it is possible, among other things, to build or rebuild a world (Archetti 2002) [24] or, at least, investigate, evaluate and criticise aspects of the real world found inside a clear framework and more easily analysed by means of logic, hermeneutics and sometimes satire. Part of the work produced can be assimilated in the new interpretation of the classical topos of hortus conclusus, [25] marked off by definition, drawing a significant part of its meaning from the very fact of being demarcated (Nerozzi 1990): an island whose characteristics are in part similar and in part specific as compared to the garden described in the English novels of the seventeenth century and to some American novels of the eighteenth century. [26] The sea voyage, in particular, becomes the main reference point for any type of travel which, as such, leads from the known to the unknown, from what is familiar to what is foreign. [27] The island becomes, in its turn, a planet (Cattabiani 1998) in many modern (pseudo)science fiction novels. In general, isolation implies reclusion, exclusion, whether suffered or desired, endured or voluntary, as well as estrangement and possibly marginalizsation. [28] From a modern point of view, the island can also be seen as a shelter: [29] the individual clings to the rocks to take refuge from the

[24] This separate environment is often a chance for a utopian or dystopian dissertation, the *elsewhere* is another place, the alternative to what can be found (etymology: aliterubi = elsewhere; utopia = other place, non-place).

[25] M. Cobb, *The enclosed space*: The *Locus conclusus*, or simply *hortus*, as a green world it can be a defined place in which we try to contain, limit, and identify the otherness (often represented by shadows, projections, aliens, robots and monsters of different types in their different incarnations or metamorphosis) with creativity itself created or borrowed from reality or imagination, from the real world or from other worlds, and usually in communication with the real world (Carotenuto 2001; Mussapi 2002).

[26] "To be born and live on an island means being surrounded by the sea but as an external, and especially internal, dimension on the inside. It is not surprising that in the literature and theatre plays of the British Isles the sea is […] not only a constant element, both realistically and metaphorically speaking, but is probably the central element that moves from American literature (and the best example is Moby Dick) slowly towards other types of English literature" (Lombardo 1997: 53). The traditional and conventional image of the Island can be preserved or undermined for different purposes (Palusci and Bertacco 2008).

[27] Metaphors about sea voyage, also in a modern technological context, are common, from navigating on the web to GPS navigation devices.

[28] R. Zemeckis, *Cast Away*, 2001.

[29] "The sky donated the islands to Earth so that they could be used as a shelter", B. de Saint-Pierre.

ocean. If, in classical literature, the island becomes a planet, in the postmodern literature, individuals cling to rocks of their own in the immensity of the sea and the space, in constant movement in an indefinite and limitless dimension, in a dangerous place where one gets lost (Bauman 1999).[30]

> Ever he would wander, self compelled, to the extreme limit of his cometary orbit, beyond the fixed stars and variable suns and telescopic planets, astronomical waifs and strays, to the extreme boundary of space, passing from land to land, among peoples, amid events.
>
> (Joyce 1922)

And in the Italian space, not far from us, at the physical level of the real world, there is Lampedusa, the cliff that often spares lives from the sea (Nicolosi 2016):

> We are all homeless refugees in the tangle of the world. Rejected at the border by an army of words, we look for a story where to take shelter.
>
> (Wu Ming 2 and Mohamed 2012: 77)

Bibliography

Akmajian, A., Demers, R.A. and Harnish, R.M. (1984) *Linguistics. An Introduction to Language and Communication*, Cambridge: MIT Press.

Archetti, M. (2002) *Lo spazio ritrovato. Antropologia della contemporaneità*, Rome: Meltemi.

Athanasopoulos, P. and Bylund, E. (2017) 'The Whorfian time warp: Representing duration through the language hourglass', *Journal of Experimental Psychology: General*, 146(7): 911–916.

Barth, J. (1967) 'The literature of exhaustion', *The Atlantic*, 220(2): 29–34.

Barth, J. (1972) *Chimera*, New York: Random House.

Barth, J. (1984) 'The Literature of Replenishment' in J. Barth, *The Friday Book: Essays and Other Non-Fiction*, London: The John Hopkins University Press, 193–206.

Bauman, Z. (1999) *La società dell'incertezza*, Bologna: Il Mulino.

Bhabha, H.K. (1994) *The Location of Culture*, New York-London: Routledge.

Bigliazzi, S. (2002) *Sull'esecuzione testuale. Dal testo letterario alla performance*, Pisa: ETS.

Bolter, J.D. and Grusin, R. (2002) *Remediation. Competizione e integrazione tra media vecchi e nuovi*, Milan: Guerini e associati.

Brogi, D. (2011) 'Being Different without Fear: On Igiaba Sciego's Oltre Babilonia (and More)' in S. Brancato (ed.) *Afroeuropean Configurations: Readings and Projects*, Cambridge: Cambridge Scholars Publishing, 198–209.

[30] The role that the sky and the stars had in sea voyages is also interesting (Mussapi 2002).

Carotenuto, A. (2001) *L'ultima Medusa. Psicologia della fantascienza*, Rome-Milan: Bompiani.
Cattabiani, A. (1998) *Planetario. Simboli, miti e misteri di astri, pianeti e costellazioni*, Milan: Mondadori.
Ceravolo, F.A. (2016) *Cervelli in transito*, Rome: Carocci.
Chini, M. and Andorno, C. (eds.) (2018) *Repertori e usi linguistici nell'immigrazione. Un'indagine su minori alloglotti, dieci anni dopo*, Milan: FrancoAngeli.
Cosso, A. (2013) *Raccontarsela. Copioni di vita e storie organizzative: l'uso della narrazione per lo sviluppo individuale e d'impresa*, Bologna: Lupetti.
Costa, M. (1999) *Estetica dei media. Avanguardia e tecnologia*, Rome: Castelvecchi.
Damasio, A. (2012) *Il sé viene alla mente. La costruzione del cervello cosciente*, Milan: Adelphi.
Fabietti, U. (1995) L'*identità etnica. Storia e critica di un concetto equivoco*, Rome: La Nuova Italia Scientifica.
Fontana, A. (2017) *Io credo alle sirene: Come vivere (e bene!) in un mare di Fake News*, Milan: Hoepli.
Fontana, A. (2018) 'Il "cattivismo" come scusa. Il ruolo del "Signore Oscuro" e dell'"Evil duo" nell'immaginario pubblico e nell'azione sociale', *Narrability Journal*, 2(1).
Jacquart, E. (1974) *Le théatre de dérision*, Paris: Gallimard.
Jakobson, R. (1957) *On Human Communication*, Cambridge: MIT Press.
Jakobson, R. (1963) *Essais de linguistique générale*, Paris: Editions de Minuit.
Joyce, J. (1922) *Ulysses*, Paris: Shakespeare and Company.
Le Guin, U.K. (1974) *The Dispossessed: An Ambiguous Utopia*, New York: Harper & Row.
Lombardo, A. (1997) 'Shakespeare e il mare' in A. Lombardo (ed.) *Giornale di bordo. Saggi sull'immagine poetica del mare*, Rome: Bulzoni.
Lyotard, J.F. (2008) The Postmodern Condition, Milan: Feltrinelli.
McKay, M., Davis, M. and Fanning, P. (2009) *Messages: The Communication Skills Book*, Oakland: New Harbinger.
Mihalache, A. (2000) *The Postmodernity of Cyberspace*, Charlotte: Spark Online.
Mussapi, R. (2002) *Inferni, mari, isole. Storie di viaggi nella letteratura*, Milan: Mondadori.
Nerozzi, P. (1990) *Virtù e malinconia. Saggi su Clarissa by Samuel Richardson*, Milan: Marcos y Marcos.
Nicolosi, G. (2016) *Lampedusa. Corpi, immagini e narrazioni dell'immigrazione*, Milan: FrancoAngeli.
Offenheim, L. (ed.) (1999) *Samuel Beckett and the Arts: Music, Visual Arts and Non-Print Media*, New York: Garland.
Palusci, O. and Bertacco, S. (2008) *Postcolonial To Multicultural*, Milan: Hoepli.
Perucchietti, E. (2018) *Fake News*, Bologna: Arianna.
Pollicino, O. and Quintarelli, S. (2017) *Parole e potere: Libertà d'espressione, hate speech e fake news*, Milan: Egea.
Randall, W.L. (1995) *The Stories We Are: An Essay on Self-Creation*, Toronto: University of Toronto Press.
Remotti, F. (1996) *Contro l'identità*, Rome-Bari: Laterza.
Sebeok, T.A. (1991) *A Sign is Just a Sign*, Bloomington: Indiana University Press.
Spivak, G.C. (1987) *In Other Worlds: Essays in Cultural Politics*, London: Routledge.
Whitebrook, M. (2001) *Identity, Narrative and Politics*, London: Routledge.

Wu Ming 2 and Mohamed, A. (2012) *Timira. Romanzo meticcio*, Turin: Einaudi.
Wynter, S. (1990) *Out of the Kumbla: Caribbean Women and Literature*, Trenton: Africa World Press.
Zemeckis, R. (2001) *Cast Away*, DreamWorks, 20th Century Fox, Image Movers/Playtone, USA.

Chapter 19

Crossing borders

Genetic mutations

Cesare Danesino and Carla Olivieri

The human genome is composed of more than 3 billion "letters", the nucleotides (base pairs, bp, in the double helix of DNA), which contain the instructions for building an individual. Each person is composed of about 3.72 × 1013 cells (Bianconi et al. 2013) that share the same information.

Currently, we know that these instructions include less than 25,000 genes (1.5% of total DNA) that encode for the production of proteins; but we are only at the beginning of understanding the instructions hidden in the remaining 98.5% of our DNA.

These non protein-coding regions were once called "junk DNA" but nowadays we know that they include fundamental regulatory sequences (Ezkurdia et al. 2014; Consortium 2004; Pennisi 2012).

Moreover, a large variability is present between single individuals: 1 in 800 base pairs are different between one individual and another one (Auton et al. 2015) and most of these differences lie in the so called "non coding regions", whose significance is not at present completely known. This variability may originate from heredity (variants transmitted either by the mother or the father) but can be increased by novel differences arising in the DNA of that individual. Each time a change in DNA sequence is observed we call it a "variant". However, if this change affects a functional characteristic and can lead (at least in part) to a pathological phenotype, it is called a "mutation".

Why does this happen? We know of different mechanisms that can lead to a mutation. An error can occur in copying DNA from one cellular generation to another or when the cell tries to remove/correct damage in DNA caused by physical and chemical agents. But it is also well known that the presence of DNA variants is essential for evolution and adaptation to changes in the environment.

As a variant can be inherited FROM the prior generation, so it can be passed TO the next generation. Therefore, we can follow the human migrations and track the "journey" of some of these variants. This is called "population genetics" and will also be discussed in Chapter 21.

We present the story of a small number of these variants, which we have studied in a rare disease, called Hereditary Hemorrhagic Telangiectasia (HHT). This disease was described for the first time in the latter years of the nineteenth century as a hereditary disorder leading to peculiar skin malformations called telangiectases. Later, it was observed that the patients also have recurrent nosebleeds and finally the advanced imaging technologies led to the discovery of vascular malformations in the internal organs, mostly the lungs, liver and brain. The disease was also called Rendu-Osler-Weber Syndrome (ROW) from the names of the physicians who first described it.

We will use HHT as an example for each of the topics of our section.

19.1. *The disease*

HHT is inherited as an autosomal dominant trait. This means that the disease is present in individuals who have a single copy of a pathogenic variant at a particular locus (heterozygotes); the genes involved in HHT are on one of the 22 pairs of autosomes (non-sex chromosomes). Thus, it has no relevance if the parental transmission of the disease is patri-or matrilineal. Moreover, the manifestation of HHT is not affected by the sex of the patients, even if some differences between males and females can be found at the level of selected clinical symptoms.

HHT is a disorder that affects endothelium, the cell layer that lines the lumen of the vessels. It is characterized by typical vascular malformations called telangiectases (when present in cutis and mucosae) and arteriovenous malformations (AVMs) in internal organs. These malformations arise in typical sites: telangiectases can be found on the face, in the nose, on the lips, in the mouth, on the fingertips and in the gastrointestinal tract. Nasal telangiectases bleed because they are ruptured by the continuous air flux. Epistaxes are the most common symptom of the disease and can be so frequent and copious that they can lead to anemia and require transfusion. Gastrointestinal telangiectases can also bleed and lead to anemia.

Arteriovenous malformations arise in the lungs, liver and brain, and are the major cause of morbidity and mortality of the patients, as they may cause strokes and brain abscesses (pulmonary AVMs), liver and cardiac insufficiency (hepatic AVMs) and brain haemorrhages (cerebral AVMs).

HHT diagnosis is based on the four so called "Curaçao Criteria", which are based on clinical signs. The diagnosis is "definite" when at least three criteria are present; "possible or suspected" when two criteria are present and "unlikely" if only one criterion is present.

In children of affected subjects, the presence of even a single criterion suggests a high index of clinical suspicion, as in HHT clinical signs are age dependent (Shovlin et al. 2000) and penetrance is complete only after the age of 40 (Plauchu et al. 1989). This means that the clinical signs of the disease are worsening and becoming more frequent after the fourth decade of life.

The disease shows a high variability in the phenotype, also within the same family, and there is currently no explanation for this.

19.2. *Genetic heterogeneity*

HHT is a genetic disorder: it is caused by mutations in genes coding for specific proteins. At least four genes, if individually mutated, can lead to HHT or HHT-like disease. The first gene identified is ENG, coding for the protein Endoglin (McAllister et al. 1994). This gene is located on the long arm of Chromosome 9 and mutations in ENG lead to HHT type 1. The second is ACVRL1, on the long arm of Chromosome 12, coding for the ALK1 protein and related to HHT2 (Johnson et al. 1996). Mutations in SMAD4, on the long arm of Chromosome 18, are related to JP-HT Syndrome, which combines clinical signs of both HHT and juvenile polyposis (Gallione et al. 2004). In 2013 mutations in GSF2, coding for BMP9 on the long arm of Chromosome 10, were associated to an HHT-like syndrome (Wooderchak-Donahue et al. 2013).

All these proteins work in the same signalling pathway, called the Transforming Growth Factor β/Bone Morphogenetic Proteins (TGFβ/BMPs) pathway, which is involved in angiogenesis (the formation of novel vessels from pre-existing ones).

19.3. *Families and new mutations*

The genetic bases of HHT and the clinical correlations explain why most of our patients belong to families in which the disease is already present. In fact, we are dealing with an autosomal dominant disorder, not affecting the reproductive fitness, in which morbidity appears often only once an individual reaches older age.

About 83% of index cases have an affected parent. In the remaining 17% of patients the mutation is not present in his/her parents, but probably arose during their gametogenesis as a "de novo" mutation. This patient will be the founder of a novel HHT family.

19.4. *Geographic distribution*

Worldwide

There is a worldwide distribution of HHT but, in some regions, the disease's prevalence, estimated as 1 in 5,000, is unusually higher. This is the case in the Netherlands Antilles, where HHT prevalence is as high as 1/1639, presently the highest of any geographical location in the world.

In this region, only two ENG mutations were found and a "founder effect" was demonstrated for both of them (Gallione et al. 2000). A founder effect was also demonstrated (for different mutations) in the county of Funen in Denmark (Brusgaard et al. 2004) and in the Rhône-Alpes region of France (Lesca et al. 2004).

In Italy

We were the first group to study HHT in Italy, as our work started in 1993 when the first HHT Italian family was identified (Buscarini et al. 1994). In 1998, CO started molecular analyses and we were the first group in Italy to perform mutation analyses in HHT patients (Olivieri et al. 2002).

We have now collected the largest cohort of HHT patients in Italy, and one of the largest in Europe, with more than 500 different families and more than 1,900 DNA samples from affected subjects and their relatives (both affected and non-affected) (Olivieri et al. 2007). We also participated in the establishing of two of the three major HHT clinical reference centres in Italy (in Crema (CR) and in Pavia), which help us to collect patients' clinical data. In collecting information about the patients, we not only register the place of birth but also, when it is possible, the geographical origin of the parents and grandparents. The patients come from all the Italian regions except one (Valle D'Aosta, the smallest Italian region, in the northwestern mountainous area, bordering France). What is the "Italian HHT picture"? An extended collaboration with the colleagues of the other Italian centres studying HHT (Bari et al., manuscript in preparation) allows us to have a good snapshot of the distribution of HHT mutation in Italy.

We can observe different situations:

(a) A specific mutation is found only in Italy: either in a single family (or patient), or in a group of patients (or families) sharing the same geographical origin.
(b) The same mutation is found only in the Italian group of patients, but the geographical origin of carriers is spread nationwide.
(c) The same mutation is found in the Italian cohort and in at least one additional different population.
(d) The same mutation is present in many different populations (we can say "worldwide")

How can we explain these data? The fact that most HHT mutations are "private", that is, different families have their own specific mutation, is a well-known characteristic of many genetic diseases. All patients descending from the same subject, in whom an error in DNA occurred causing the disease, obviously show the same mutation and it can easily explain why we find some "Italian mutations" that are never found in other cohorts of patients (Olivieri et al. 2007). An example of (a) is provided by the ACVRL1 mutation c. 289_294 delCACAAC (p. H97_N98del); we found it in 16 families all coming from the area of Bergamo; this mutation was never found in any other Italian patient and it is not reported outside of Italy in any international database (excluding our report). The mutation causes the in frame deletion of two amino acids (histidine in position 97 and asparagine in position 98) and it is certainly pathogenic for HHT as it co-segregates with the disease in all families studied.

None of the families were aware of being related to each other, but we can confirm that we have "traces" of a common origin of this mutation. We are already studying the families in order to reconstitute the founder haplotype, a set of highly polymorphic genetic markers that identify a specific chromosomal region. The hypothesis tested by these genetic studies is that subjects related to each other from a genetic point of view share at least part of these markers in different genomic regions. Our preliminary unpublished data on the haplotype surrounding the mutation strongly support the hypothesis of a common ancestor who lived at least 250 years ago.

We can also suggest a common ancestor for other mutations we found only in Italy, and only in specific regions. For example, the ACVRL1 c.205_209 dup5 mutation is present only in patients coming from northwest Sardinia (the counties of Sassari and Oristano) and we are trying to obtain more information from the families and to recruit relatives of the patients to search for the common haplotype (these studies requires large families).

The same is of course true for other mutations in different countries. Good examples are the ACVRL1 c.1112dupG mutation, widely distributed in the Haute Savoie region in France (Lesca et al. 2008), the ENG c.360C>A mutation in Denmark (Brusgaard et al. 2004) and the ENG IVS1+1 (g>a) mutation in the Netherlands Antilles (Gallione et al. 2000).

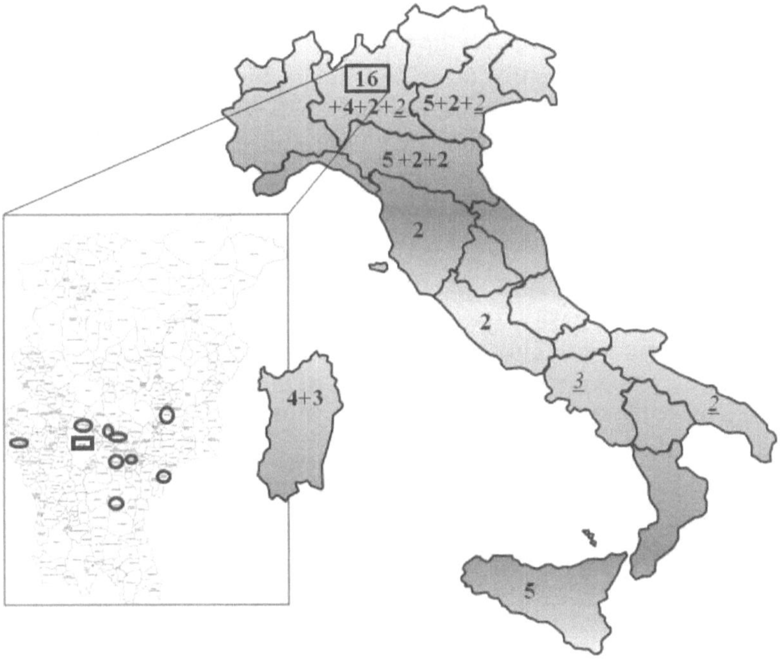

Figure 19.1. Geographic Distribution of Italian HHT families sharing the same disease-causing mutation. In Bold: number of families with the same ACVRL1 mutation. In Italic underlined: number of families with the same ENG mutation. Boxed: the founder effect in the Bergamo province

As for point (b), the origin of this type of mutation can be interpreted as in the case of point (a) but with a larger impact of migration within Italy; the collaboration with the colleagues in Bari allowed us to "join" apparently unrelated families (not sharing any family names and coming from cities located far apart in Italy). For example, we found the same ENG (dup E5_E7) mutation in two apparently unrelated families, the first coming from Liguria, in the north western part of Italy, and the other coming from Puglia, in the south eastern part of Italy. Only after collecting additional family data and enlarging the genealogical tree were we able to connect the two families. This mutation spreading was due to migration from southern to northern Italy in the second part of the twentieth century. We have at least five additional similar observations (ACVRL1: c.68-1 g>c; p.R93X; c.392 del C; c.1134G>A). The relation between genetics and Italian migrations in the past has been extensively studied (Zei et al. 1993; Fiorito et al. 2016; Campanella et al. 2015).

Point (c). There is evidence that part of the mutations found in HHT are shared by populations belonging to different countries. However, at least in some cases, a "geographical" or "historical" relationship can be found between these populations. In 2007 we published a study in collaboration with our French colleagues and we were able to demonstrate that several mutations are shared by the Italian and French cohorts of patients. For these mutations it was possible to demonstrate common haplotypes between the two groups of patients. For example, the ALK1p.Arg374Trp mutation has been reported so far only in France and Italy. One Italian patient shared alleles with three French patients at the level of two markers, D12S296 and D12S1677, flanking the disease-causing gene, ACVRL1. These alleles, allele 5 and 1, are not present in the French control sample, and this support the hypothesis of a common origin of the mutation. We have stronger evidence for a common origin of the patients sharing another ACVRL1 mutation, p.Arg144X. Several patients from both countries shared the ?-6-144X-5-6-7 haplotype, with a very high chance of a common origin. The ESTIAGE program (Genin et al. 2004) helped us to estimate that this mutation arose about 500 years ago. The two countries are neighbours and there is a large amount of historical and demographic data reporting migration from Italy to France; therefore, the most likely hypothesis is that this mutation first appeared in Italy and then moved to France with migrants (Lesca et al. 2008).

Geographical closeness is not mandatory, as demonstrated by the history of the c. 1238G>T mutation in ENG gene. This mutation was found in two apparently unrelated families in the inhabitants, of African origin, in the Netherlands Antilles. The authors reported the finding of the same mutation in a Dutch family. Historical data proved that the region where the family lived was in the past involved in extensive trading and migration with the Netherlands Antilles. Thus, they searched in these two populations for a common haplotype, using genetic markers around the identical mutation, and found it. Available evidence indicates that there is a European origin for this mutation which was introduced into the African slave population by a Dutch colonist (Gallione et al. 2000).

What happened in the past is also true for present times. We reported in 2014 about mutations found in North African and Sub-Saharan HHT patients. One of these patients, born in Senegal, is now living in Italy; he carries the c. 1232 G>A (p.R411Q) mutation in ACVRL1 gene (Canzonieri et al. 2014). The patient belongs to a large family and two affected siblings migrated from Senegal to France. Each of the patients has at least four children and we have clinical records that, as expected, show that 50% of children are similarly affected. We now have the same mutation in Senegal, Italy and France and, as the mutations in either ACVRL1 or ENG do not reduce consistently reproductive fitness, we may expect in the future to observe larger groups of patients sharing this mutation in these countries. Interestingly, we also found this mutation in different Italian families coming from Friuli, Lombardy and Sardinia (see point (d)).

However, in some cases, an identical mutation may arise independently in different subjects (point (d)). If we observe the same mutation in both familial cases and de novo ones, we can obviously exclude a founder or migration effect and have evidence of independent origin of the DNA change.

This may happen just by chance or because the involved DNA region is a mutation hotspot. "Nucleotide positions with an exceptionally high mutation frequency are called hotspots" (Rogozin et al. 2003).

We can also consider that the "weight" of a change in the DNA sequence, and subsequently on the protein structure and function, can be very different. For instance, we demonstrated that almost all mutations in the extracellular domain of ALK1 affecting cysteine, an amino acid involved in disulphide bonds, which are essential for maintaining a correct 3D protein structure, impact on the spatial conformation of this protein region, leading to the loss of its function.

This type of mutation is quite frequently found in our cohort but also in groups of patients from different countries (Scotti et al. 2011). In this case, we can exclude that this large-scale distribution is related to a single founder event or to extensive migration.

Similarly, changes in the histidine residue at position 328 of the ALK1 protein are surely pathogenetic, as they affect the threonine kinase domain of the protein, which is essential for its function.

In the HHT mutation database (http://arup.utah.edu/database/HHT/) we observe three different DNA changes affecting the CAC codon (three-base sequence) coding for that histidine: 1) when the first C is changed to a T, we obtain the codon TAC, which is for tyrosine; 2) the A is changed into C and we obtain CCC, coding for proline; 3) the last C is mutated into an A and we obtain CAA, leading to the insertion of a glutamine instead of the correct amino acid. Whatever amino acid replaces the histidine, the effect on the protein is relevant, causes the disease, and as a consequence, we recognize it at a clinical level.

Sometimes a different process is involved: not a different position at the same codon, as seen before, but the same position in DNA is changed in different ways, leading to different changes. We reported such a change in 2006 in the position 1127 of the coding region of ACVRL1 (Olivieri et al. 2006). The codon is ATG, the amino acid normally present is methionine, but we observed a mutation changing T into an A: the new combination is AAG and the amino acid becomes lysine. A change in the same position was reported by Johnson et al. in 1996, and later by other groups, but in this case the mutation caused the T to G substitution and the inserted amino acid was arginine. Finally, in 2006, Fernandez et al. reported the third possible change: T to C, leading to the amino acid threonine (Fernandez-L et al. 2006). All these changes arose from different mutations, always affect methionine in position 376 and the patients are obviously not related to each other.

On the other hand, it is well known that not all the amino acid changes lead to a disease. This is also true for HHT and we found different changes which can be considered as "benign"; for example ACVRL1 p.Ala482Val; ENG p.Pro131Leu, p.Gly191Asp, p.Gly545Ser are observed in more than 1% of the general population and can be interpreted as polymorphisms.

All the observations we presented here for HHT can obviously also apply for other genetic diseases presenting with a worldwide distribution and not affecting the reproductive rate.

There are some final considerations we wish to add. As a general point on rare disease, we underline the importance of genetic screening, performed in specialized centres, with a demonstrated experience on a specific disease. This allows not only to find the disease-causing mutation, but also to insert these results in a broader research context to better understand the pathogenesis of the disease. Moreover, it is relevant to offer a family, in which a rare disease is present, with a pre-symptomatic screening (when available). We can so identify the subjects at risk to develop the clinical signs of a disease and to program the necessary follow up. An additional advantage of extended testing in the family is the identification of non-carriers of the mutation with their exclusion from useless clinical screening.

In this perspective, both from a clinical and diagnostic point of view (also at the molecular analysis level), knowing the geographic origin of the patient can be relevant.

As we have discussed, we can have regions and countries in which the prevalence of a disease is higher than in the general population and these differences "migrate" with that population. We have such an example in another rare disease, Pompe disease (or glycogen storage disease type II). It is an autosomal recessive disorder, so affected subjects have both parents as carriers of the disease. Frequently a patient is the descendent of consanguineous marriages or there is a higher incidence in geographically isolated populations or in inhabitants of the same region. The disease causes a high level of morbidity, especially in the classic form of infantile-onset. Prevalence of Pompe disease is 1 in 40,000 people in the United States, and is similar in Italy. However, there are differences among ethnic groups. In Taiwan, in example, the national prevalence is 1/57,000, but it is probably higher in the Chinese population living there (Yang et al. 2014; Lin and Shieh 1996). Interestingly, in Chinese and African-Americans common mutations have been described, while in adult-onset disease in

Caucasians about 50% of mutated alleles are represented by a common mutation in the GAA gene (IVS1-13 t>g) (Hirschhorn and Reuser 2001).

In Italy, recent unpublished data on the results of a neonatal screening for Pompe disease in Tuscany (3 years results), led to the identification of eight subjects with two disease-causing mutations (A. Donati, personal communication). One of these newborns is of Chinese ancestry and the mutations observed are the more frequent ones also observed in the Chinese Pompe patients' group (Liu et al. 2014). Recent demographic information reports that Chinese immigrants in Tuscany represent 1.3% of the local population and 12.4% of the foreign population. [1]

However, demographic data on the incidence of mutations are on average insufficient for use in the National Health Service to identify higher risk subpopulations (as demonstrated for the Bergamo region in HHT and Pompe disease in the immigrated Chinese population). Consequently, the role of second level clinical and genetic centres specialized in rare disease becomes more relevant in the management of immigration-related problems. Similarly, the need for international databases grouping genetic and clinical information increases.

Another important topic is the difference in perceiving the disease between different populations, especially after migration events, that has been widely demonstrated (Kim et al. 2012; Napier et al. 2014). This leads to a growing importance for a patient-personalized approach in medicine. The topic is addressed in this book in Chapter 10 by V. Berlincioni et al.

There is another important point to address. When a rare disease is diagnosed in a patient who has immigrated from countries where clinical and molecular diagnoses are unavailable, we observe that there is also an improvement for siblings remaining in the country of origin, who receive information about the disease and the clinical and diagnostic tools. We have different patients from Africa, from Eastern Europe (i.e. Moldavia) and other countries, who surely shared information on diagnosis and therapy of HHT with their families of origin. Furthermore, there is a growing awareness of the importance of offering a diagnosis to subjects living in countries where the National Institute of Health cannot offer this procedure, as demonstrated by the interest shown by various states and institutions towards an innovative law passed in Serbia in 2015, the "Law on Prevention and Diagnostics of Genetic Diseases, Genetically Caused Anomalies and Rare Diseases" (http://ojs.ius.bg.ac.rs/index.php/anali/article/view/100/312). This is popularly known as "Zoja's law" as it was promoted by the parents of a Serbian child, Zoja, who died from a rare genetic disorder that cannot be diagnosed in Serbia.

We can hypothesize that we are in the era of a new phenomenon, which can be called "reverse migration" of diagnostic capacity: patients migrate from their birthplaces to more developed countries and updated clinical and molecular information "migrate" back to countries of origin.

---

[1] http://www.tuttitalia.it/toscana/statistiche/cittadini-stranieri/repubblica-popolare-cinese/ (accessed on March 16th, 2019).

Bibliography

Auton, A., Brooks, L.D., Durbin, R.M., Garrison, E.P., Kang, H.M., Korbel, J.O., Marchini, J.L., McCarthy, S., McVean, G.A., Abecasis, G.R. and Consortium, G.P. (2015) 'A global reference for human genetic variation', *Nature*, 526: 68–74.

Bianconi, E., Piovesan, A., Facchin, F., Beraudi, A., Casadei, R., Frabetti, F., Vitale, L., Pelleri, M.C., Tassani, S., Piva, F., Perez-Amodio, S., Strippoli, P. and Canaider, S. (2013) 'An estimation of the number of cells in the human body', *Ann Hum Biol*, 40: 463–471.

Brusgaard, K., Kjeldsen, A., Poulsen, L., Moss, H., Vase, P., Rasmussen, K., Kruse, T. and Hørder, M. (2004) 'Mutations in endoglin and in activin receptor-like kinase 1 among Danish patients with hereditary haemorrhagic telangiectasia', *Clin Genet*, 66: 556–561.

Buscarini, E., Buscarini, L., Civardi, G., Arruzzoli, S., Bossalini, G. and Piantanida, M. (1994) 'Hepatic vascular malformations in hereditary hemorrhagic telangiectasia: Imaging findings', *AJR Am J Roentgenol*, 163: 1105–1110.

Campanella, G., Polidoro, S., Di Gaetano, C., Fiorito, G., Guarrera, S., Krogh, V., Palli, D., Panico, S., Sacerdote, C., Tumino, R., Elliott, P., Matullo, G., Chadeau-Hyam, M. and Vineis, P. (2015) 'Epigenetic signatures of internal migration in Italy', *Int J Epidemiol*, 44: 1442–1449.

Canzonieri, C., Ornati, F., Matti, E., Chu, F., Manfredi, G., Olivieri, C., Buscarini, E. and Pagella, F. (2014) 'Hereditary haemorrhagic telangiectasia in North African and sub-Saharan patients', *S Afr Med J*, 104: 256–257.

Consortium, I.H.G.S. (2004) 'Finishing the euchromatic sequence of the human genome', *Nature*, 431: 931–945.

Ezkurdia, I., Juan, D., Rodriguez, J.M., Frankish, A., Diekhans, M., Harrow, J., Vazquez, J., Balencia, A. and Tress, M.L. (2014) 'Multiple evidence strands suggest that there may be as few as 19,000 human protein-coding genes', *Hum Mol Genet*, 23: 5866–5878.

Fernandez-L, A., Sanz-Rodriguez, F., Zarrabeitia, R., Perez-Molino, A., Morales, C., Restrepo, C., Ramirez, J., Coto, E., Lenato, G., Bernabeu, C. and Botella, L. (2006) 'Mutation study of Spanish patients with hereditary hemorrhagic telangiectasia and expression analysis of Endoglin and ALK1', *Hum Mutat*, 27: 295.

Fiorito, G., Di Gaetano, C., Guarrera, S., Rosa, F., Feldman, M.W., Piazza, A. and Matullo, G. (2016) 'The Italian genome reflects the history of Europe and the Mediterranean basin', *Eur J Hum Genet*, 24: 1056–1062.

Gallione, C., Scheessele, E., Reinhardt, D., Duits, A., Berg, J., Westermann, C. and Marchuk, D. (2000) 'Two common endoglin mutations in families with hereditary hemorrhagic telangiectasia in the Netherlands Antilles: Evidence for a founder effect', *Hum Genet*, 107, 40–44.

Gallione, C.J., Repetto, G.M., Legius, E., Rustgi, A.K., Schelley, S.L., Tejpar, S., Mitchell, G., Drouin, E., Westermann, C.J. and Marchuk, D.A. (2004) 'A combined syndrome of juvenile polyposis and hereditary haemorrhagic telangiectasia associated with mutations in MADH4 (SMAD4)', *Lancet*, 363: 852–859.

Genin, E., Tullio-Pelet, A., Begeot, F., Lyonnet, S. and Abel, L. (2004) 'Estimating the age of rare disease mutations: The example of Triple-A syndrome', *J Med Genet*, 41: 445–449.

Hirschhorn, R. and Reuser, A.J.J. (2001) 'Glycogen Storage Disease Type II: Acid α-Glucosidase (Acid Maltase) Deficiency' in *The Online Metabolic and Molecular Bases of Inherited Disease*, New York: McGraw-Hill Education.

Johnson, D.W., Berg, J.N., Baldwin, M.A., Gallione, C.J., Marondel, I., Yoon, S.J., Stenzel, T.T., Speer, M., Pericak-Vance, M.A., Diamond, A., Guttmacher, A.E., Jackson, C.E., Attisano, L., Kucherlapati, R., Porteous, M.E. and Marchuk, D.A. (1996) 'Mutations in the activin receptor-like kinase 1 gene in hereditary haemorrhagic telangiectasia type 2', *Nat Genet*, 13: 189–195.

Kim, Y., Evangelista, L.S., Phillips, L.R., Pavlish, C. and Kopple, J.D. (2012) 'Racial/ethnic differences in illness, perceptions in minority patients undergoing maintenance hemodialysis', *Nephrol Nurs J*, 39: 39–48; quiz 49.

Lesca, G., Genin, E., Blachier, C., Olivieri, C., Coulet, F., Brunet, G., Dupuis-Girod, S., Buscarini, E., Soubrier, F., Calender, A., Danesino, C., Giraud, S., Plauchu, H. and Network, F.-I.H. (2008) 'Hereditary hemorrhagic telangiectasia: evidence for regional founder effects of ACVRL1 mutations in French and Italian patients', *Eur J Hum Genet*, 16: 742–749.

Lesca, G., Plauchu, H., Coulet, F., Lefebvre, S., Plessis, G., Odent, S., Rivière, S., Leheup, B., Goizet, C., Carette, M., Cordier, J., Pinson, S., Soubrier, F., Calender, A. and Giraud, S. (2004) 'Molecular screening of ALK1/ACVRL1 and ENG genes in hereditary hemorrhagic telangiectasia in France', *Hum Mutat*, 23: 289–299.

Lin, C.Y. and Shieh, J.J. (1996) 'Molecular study on the infantile form of Pompe disease in Chinese in Taiwan', *Zhonghua Min Guo Xiao Er Ke Yi Xue Hui Za Zhi*, 37: 115–121.

Liu, X., Wang, Z., Jin, W., Lv, H., Zhang, W., Que, C., Huang, Y. and Yuan, Y. (2014) 'Clinical and GAA gene mutation analysis in mainland Chinese Patients with late-onset Pompe disease: Identifying c.2238G > C as the most common mutation', *BMC Med Genet*, 15: 141.

McAllister, K.A., Grogg, K.M., Johnson, D.W., Gallione, C. J., Baldwin, M.A., Jackson, C.E., Helmbold, E.A., Markel, D.S., McKinnon, W.C., Murrell, J et al. (1994) 'Endoglin, a TGF-beta binding protein of endothelial cells, is the gene for hereditary haemorrhagic telangiectasia type 1', *Nat Genet*, 8: 345–351.

Napier, A.D., Ancarno, C., Butler, B., Calabrese, J., Chater, A., Chatterjee, H., Guesnet, F., Horne, R., Jacyna, S., Jadhav, S., MacDonald, A., Neuendorf, U., Parkhurst, A., Reynolds, R., Scambler, G., Shamdasani, S., Smith, S.Z., Stougaard-Nielsen, J., Thomson, L., Tyler, N., Volkmann, A.M., Walker, T., Watson, J., Williams, A.C., Willott, C., Wilson, J. and Woolf, K. (2014) 'Culture and health', *Lancet*, 384: 1607–1639.

Olivieri, C., Lanzarini, L., Pagella, F., Semino, L., Corno, S., Valacca, C., Plauchu, H., Lesca, G., Barthelet, M., Buscarini, E. and Danesino, C. (2006) 'Echocardiographic screening discloses increased values of pulmonary artery systolic pressure in 9 of 68 unselected patients affected with hereditary hemorrhagic telangiectasia', *Genet Med*, 8: 183–190.

Olivieri, C., Mira, E., Delu', G., Pagella, F., Zambelli, A., Malvezzi, L., Buscarini, E. and Danesino, C. (2002) 'Identification of 13 new mutations in the ACVRL1 gene in a group of 52 unselected Italian patients affected by hereditary haemorrhagic telangiectasia', *Journal of Medical Genetics*, 39: E39.

Olivieri, C., Pagella, F., Semino, L., Lanzarini, L., Valacca, C., Pilotto, A., Corno, S., Scappaticci, S., Manfredi, G., Buscarini, E. and Danesino, C. (2007) 'Analysis of ENG and ACVRL1 genes in 137 HHT Italian families identifies 76 different mutations (24 novel). Comparison with other European studies', *J Hum Genet*, 52: 820–829.

Pennisi, E. (2012) 'Genomics. ENCODE project writes eulogy for junk DNA', *Science*, 337: 1159–1161.

Plauchu, H., De Chadarévian, J., Bideau, A. and Robert, J. (1989) 'Age-related clinical profile of hereditary hemorrhagic telangiectasia in an epidemiologically recruited population', *Am J Med Genet*, 32: 291–297.

Rogozin, I.B., Babenko, V.N., Milanesi, L. and Pavlov, Y.I. (2003) 'Computational analysis of mutation spectra', *Brief Bioinform*, 4: 210–227.

Scotti, C., Olivieri, C., Boeri, L., Canzonieri, C., Ornati, F., Buscarini, E., Pagella, F. and Danesino, C. (2011) 'Bioinformatic analysis of pathogenic missense mutations of activin receptor like kinase 1 ectodomain', *PLoS One*, 6: e26431.

Shovlin, C.L., Guttmacher, A.E., Buscarini, E., Faughnan, M.E., Hyland, R.H., Westermann, C.J, Kjeldsen, A.D. and Plauchu, H. (2000) 'Diagnostic criteria for hereditary hemorrhagic telangiectasia (Rendu-Osler-Weber Syndrome)', *Am J Med Genet*, 91: 66–67.

Wooderchak-Donahue, W.L., McDonald, J., O'fallon, B., Upton, P.D., Li, W., Roman, B.L., Young, S., Plant, P., Fülöp, G.T., Langa, C., Morrell, N.W., Botella, L.M., Bernabeu, C., Stevenson, D.A., Runo, J.R. and Bayrak-Toydemir (2013) 'BMP9 mutations cause a vascular-anomaly syndrome with phenotypic overlap with hereditary hemorrhagic telangiectasia', *Am J Hum Genet*, 93: 530–537.

Yang, C.F., Liu, H.C., Hsu, T.R., Tsai, F.C., Chiang, S.F., Chiang, C.C., Ho, H.C., Lai, C.J., Yang, T.F., Chuang, S.Y., Lin, C.Y. and Niu, D.M. (2014) 'A large-scale nationwide newborn screening program for Pompe disease in Taiwan: Towards effective diagnosis and treatment", *Am J Med Genet A*, 164a: 54–61.

Zei, G., Barbujani, G., Lisa, A., Fiorani, O., Menozzi, P., Siri, E. and Cavalli-Sforza, L.L. (1993) 'Barriers to gene flow estimated by surname distribution in Italy', *Ann Hum Genet*, 57: 123–140.

Chapter 20

Borders of identity

Return migration and failure in West Africa

Giulia Casentini

20.1. *Introduction*

In this chapter I will consider life stories of migrants who return back to their country of origin by taking into consideration the specific case of some Ghanaians. In their paths towards Europe, and then back to Ghana, they cross many borders, both physical and immaterial, and they often experience a substantial change of social status, economic condition, and personal aspiration. The ethnographies I analyze talk mainly about a negative, difficult experience, which does not match with the image, quite diffuse in West Africa, of the successful migrant who comes back home after a period in Europe with an improved economic condition and a newly upgraded social situation. The "failure" I will talk about is mainly characterized by a forced return, either due to security issues (especially if migrants found themselves in Libya during or after the crisis in 2011), due to the lack of economic means to continue their trip, or due to traumatic experiences lived during the transit phase.

The chapter will consider both the traumatic aspect of the return and the inherent value of the resiliency of these migrant experiences that, by being considered negative or particularly distressing, can still disclose the power of the individual agency put in place by people who migrate.

I shall discuss the categories of transit, waiting spaces, migrant identities, and I shall consider the border as a physical limit to be trespassed, but also as a threshold that determines a change in social status.

Paraphrasing Spivak (1988), one can ask: "does the migrant have a voice to speak? And when he/she speaks, who listens"? When we reflect on the last part of the question, on "who listens", the question itself becomes larger if we extend our reference context to the country of origin in the setting of return migration. Of course, the migrant can often feel voiceless and absent (Sayad 2002) in the context of emigration, where he/she has to confront himself/herself with different social values, legislation, and power imbalances. We shall see in this chapter that the returnee too can feel voiceless, stranded, oppressed by the power relations embedded in his/her own new relationship with the country of origin. Nevertheless, returnees can represent a powerful critical actor in discussing and re-shaping the idea of migration itself, its idiosyncrasies and the social image behind the "migration-success-remittances" model that is so diffuse in West Africa nowadays.

20.2. *Methodology and the state of the art*

As Cassarino (2004) states, numerous inquiries from a qualitative point of view have illustrated how multifaceted and heterogeneous the phenomenon of return migration is, leading to a hazy understanding of the issue. This chapter aims at shedding more light on the topic through the qualitative analysis of an ethnographic study conducted in Tamale, Northern Ghana (West Africa) in 2014–2015. The results of the research are based on non-structured and semi-structured interviews with men who had diverse paths of migration; the common thread that links their stories is the "failed" character of their experience, as many defined it. Some of them had to come back forcibly from Libya, others were repatriated from EU member states, and others found themselves irregular in Europe and eventually decided to return.

The literature concerning return migrants has developed significantly in the last decade by observing the role of the domestic diaspora as active subjects and a catalyst of socio-economic changes (Mercer et al. 2009). While considering the case of Ghana, and West Africa more generally, the role of return migrants has been widely investigated, especially concerning their positive role in the country of origin in terms of economic development and of the production of social capital. Black and King (2004) highlight the crucial role of economic remittances as inputs to the development process of the country of origin, and others (Ammassari 2004; Tiemoko 2004; Ungruhe 2012) bring about case studies and points for discussion on the topic. Other scholars (Mazzucato 2008; Thomas 2008) reflect upon the fact that return migration is an instrument for contrasting the large-scale emigration of skilled professionals from African countries, and the so-called brain drain.

As I have investigated elsewhere (Casentini 2017), the contribution of the returnees in the political processes of their own countries is also significant. Thanks to their new social status, often connected to the accrued economic position, they can act as catalysts of stagnant political dynamics, or become critical observers of political and social practices. This role is not always perceived as positive, and returnees can themselves be criticized and ostracized. Nevertheless, their agency is well recognized by the community of origin, and their political role becomes relevant thanks to their experience of migration. Having had the opportunity of living abroad, making that specific social experience and sending remittances back home are definitely identified as actions that contribute to the improvement of the social status of the individual (Nieswand 2017).

What I am presenting here is something different that aims at being included in the complex process of migrants' identity construction. This chapter, indeed, reflects on migrant experiences that do not have a positive outcome in the perception of the communities of origin, but rather describe a feeling of exclusion, strangeness, and liminality (see Dünwald 2010; Maher 2013).

20.3. *Border crossing in West Africa: contemporary challenges*

While considering the complexity of the relations between political entities in the trans-Saharan desert area throughout history, Mbembe (2000) observes that these are moving and fluid worlds that have boundaries characterized by a fragmentation into clans and families, and by cycles of alliances and ruptures.

Mobility is a crucial aspect of the life of West African people: trading, seasonal migration, and traveling are central habits in determining the construction of group identities in this region, also in their historical dimension. As De Bruijn notes (2007), being mobile and the plurality of its forms are essential elements in the shaping of African identities and ways of travelling. West Africa has been a crossroads of pre-colonial trade, especially the Hausa commercial network: the region was and still is a crucial hub that provides an organized system of routes and connections to cross the trans-Saharan area. People on the move often followed these historical routes, and still do today: this aspect demonstrates the high level of adaptability of the Hausa trading network, and the existence of hubs and middlemen that can direct, help, and take advantage of the historical mobility network. The contemporary routes used by migrants towards Libya, and eventually Europe, are often overlapping this historical trade network.

It is important to underline, however, that the mobility network followed by people in this area has been undergoing important changes in recent years. Through the policies of externalization of the EU southern border, various European states, Italy above all, are developing a new strategy that intends to move the European frontier southwards, into African territory. One of the first open acts of externalization was the Italian–Libyan agreement signed by the Berlusconi government with Qaddafi in 2008, followed by other accords that intended to control and limit the mobility of African migrants, with the aim of preventing them from reaching Italian shores and, more generally, the European countries. Morone (2015) argues that the rhetoric on the control of migrant fluxes put in place by Qaddafi was actually based on the hiding of real numbers by Libyan authorities: the vast majority of sub-Saharan migrants used to choose Libya instead of Italy as their country of arrival.

The border control strategies put in place by Europe have had an important consequence on migrant routes and on the increase of corruption and exploitation of people on the move across African borders. The Integrated Border Management (IBM) strategy of the European Union, launched in 2006, was strongly directed towards the fight against illegal migration and the establishment of cooperation agreements and links with "third countries", while not in any way mentioning the protection of fundamental rights and freedoms for people on the move (Cross 2009). This was one of the first signals of an openly protectionist policy of the EU borders, a policy that was going to be reinforced by following agreements and treaties with "third countries" that have been demonstrated to have serious implications for the lives of migrants and for their choices.

Even if West Africans can freely move in the region thanks to ECOWAS agreements, police and smugglers could in any case take advantage of the presence of international frontiers. We shall see that borders drew sharp lines between citizens by investing some of them with rights and duties and by declaring others "aliens" or "foreigners". The negotiation between "state" and "people" is especially clear in marginal areas such borderlands (Baud and Van Schendel 1997).

Hajii gave me detailed information about his trip from Northern Ghana to Libya:

> First, I went to Bawku. There I took a car which goes to Niger. Niamey. I paid 15,000 cfa, from Bawku to Niamey. But on the way, you pay some kind of taxes. To go to Niger you have to pass through Ouaga. You know, Ouaga is in Burkina Faso, and Burkina Faso is at the border with Ghana. So, when you cross the border you pay something. [1]

At that point I asked for clarifications, since to me it was strange that a Ghanaian citizen has to pay a visa to cross a border of a country that belongs to ECOWAS. Hajii continued:

> You know, everybody wants to get something in their pocket ... it is corruption. They knew that I needed to reach Libya because they saw my passport and because I was travelling with others that wanted to go there. I asked them to give me an exit visa. They say if you want the stamp, you have to pay. I said no, I have no money. They say no, you have to pay. I asked them how much, and they said 26 GH cedis. So I paid. I needed that stamp, it helps when you are in Libya and you look for a job, they look at your passport to see where you passed through. So I paid 26. And in Burkina, they collected 1,000 cfa. And from Burkina to Niamey, I paid ... the lorry fare was 15,000 cfa. When you reach Niamey there is a barrier, so if you are coming from Ghana, or from Burkina, you pay 10,000 cfa in addition to the rest. When you are entering Niamey everybody pays to have the stamp. In Niamey, I took a car ... It was a bus, a bus from Niamey to Agadez. It was 15,000 cfa. It took me ... it was a 2-day journey. With the bus. A long bus. Once you arrive in Agadez, police come in and collect your passport, they let you get down and they tell you that you have to pay 10,000 cfa if you want your passport back. Then I bargained, I told them take, I can give you 5,000. They accepted. [2]

The presence of migrants travelling with money in their pockets to confront the long trip, together with the militarization of African borders as a consequence of the

[1] Interview with H.B., 12/4/2014, Tamale (Ghana).

[2] *Ibidem.*

externalization of the EU southern frontier, eventually permits the exploitation of the people on the move. Police corruption and smugglers' activities often put migrants' lives in greater danger, and define new internal borders to control people fluxes. Sometimes these new borders match the international borders between different African states, some other times they are re-designed by these agreements. As observed by Lemberg-Pedersen (2017), borders are always under construction and re-construction: they are dynamic, they are sites of intervention of multiple national (e.g. ministries) and non-national (e.g. the EU, NGOs, industrial companies) actors.

20.4. *Identity construction and de-construction: who is the returnee?*

Some Ghanaians on their way to Libya could make it and stayed there for a while to work; the majority stopped in Libya, and some decided to take on the trip by boat to Italy. People who settled in Libya got caught by the Libyan crisis in 2011, and were eventually forced to leave the country because of the conflict and the increased feeling of insecurity. The rhetoric against sub-Saharan migrants as job stealers, terrorists and also mercenaries rapidly worsened (see Morone 2015). Some of them took the difficult way to the sea, with the aim of reaching Italian territory, others decided to go back home. Some of the latter were repatriated by IOM programs; the majority were forced to use the smuggling network through the trans-Saharan route.

The ethnography contained in this chapter has been collected during various fieldwork in 2014 and 2015 in Tamale, in the Northern Region of Ghana. At that time I was essentially interested in the transit experience, the figure of the smuggler and the hubs where the trip can be arranged by following the trans-Saharan network. I am quite familiar with the area and its inhabitants, but at the same time I was aware of the methodological challenge in interviewing people who have been involved in irregular activities. As Ellis and MacGaffey pointed out, it is extremely difficult to persuade them to give details about their activities (Ellis and MacGaffey 1996: 24), and it is very challenging, as a researcher, to know some of these details. As soon as I started my fieldwork, however, I realized that I should also take into consideration other aspects, such as the trauma lived by the people I was talking with.

I discovered very soon indeed that the vast majority of my informants were returnees who failed in their migratory project and were forced to come back. I decided then to focus on the experience of the return itself, which proved to be full of interesting cause for reflection and theoretical analysis.

The "failed returnees" I spoke with were all very isolated, and even if they were back in their home town they seemed to feel stranded, lonely, abandoned by their own social environment. Rashid, one of my friends and research assistants, explained me how a "failed" returnee looks:

> You see from his eyes that he came back from Libya or Europe. You can see it from the way he moves and the way he speaks. He is no more there, nor completely here. If someone had to come back from his migration experience without money, or he was forced to come back, then maybe he does not feel like going back to his family … he feels ashamed. He feels his home is nowhere. Often they come to live here, in the zongo, [3] where all migrants can stay. [4]

All of them were ready to speak with me at first sight about their trip and their traumatic experiences, even if they did not know me personally. They were all men, who belong to a strongly patriarchal society, and I found their openness quite unconventional: as a Western woman I know that I normally need some time to gain confidence and trust in my male interviewees. With the returnees in Tamale the social rules I was used to were completely upside down. They were even looking directly in my eyes while speaking for the first time, which is normally not polite with a stranger, or in general with a person you do not have familiarity with.

I understood that this meant that their own world was completely upside down, and moreover, that I was perceived as one of the few people that could probably understand them. After that experience they were feeling strangers in Tamale. Furthermore, they evidently needed to talk about that trip to someone, since they probably did not feel at ease in expressing themselves about that failure with their own families and their own friends.

As Ibrahim explained to me, it was very difficult for him to feel understood by his fellows, and he felt almost voiceless in trying to talk about his difficult experience as a return migrant.

> I don't feel like talking. I don't feel like sharing. I don't want to talk about my trip, here they cannot understand. If you don't come back from Libya or Europe with money to show off, here they think that you are hiding something. [5]

As noticed also by Dünwald, "Often the family cannot understand why people are returned, they assume that they committed a crime, or returned for other reasons" (Dünwald 2010).

Dünwald's observations on returnees in Mali can be easily compared to what happens to Ghanaians in Tamale. Their status as "failed returnees", their change in status and social belonging, is evident mostly from their body language, but also from the place in which they chose to reside once they returned. Peter comes from a small village

---

[3] The "zongo" is a historical hausa settlement present in almost all the cities of Ghana, built for traders who stop in various towns of West Africa for commercial reasons. Today zongos still exist and host traders, migrants, and generally strangers who can be there for a period, or even who have been settled for generations. For an extensive analysis on the contemporary use and social value of the zongos see Casentini 2018.

[4] Interview with R.A., 20/04/2014, Tamale (Ghana).

[5] Interview with I.W., 22/04/2014, Tamale (Ghana).

in the Gonja region (Northern Ghana), but when he returned he decided to settle in Tamale.

> I cannot live there again. Maybe here I can find another job to make some money. Maybe then I can go back. I don't know … I don't feel like going back to the village." [6]

As Maher (2013) pointed out in her work on failed return to Senegal, exclusion and marginalization of returnees are caused also by the failed expectations of those at home. Relatives can feel upset and show off their disappointment because the returnee wasted the good amount of money they collected on a failed trip. The failure, though, is not only personal, but it becomes collective. Maher interestingly notices that there is quite a burden on youth today in Senegal: the economic need for cash, the social expectations, and the consequent weight of shame when neither of those objectives can be achieved (Maher 2013). Migration of the youth is a collective business back home: families discuss the use of remittances, the impact of restrictions on migration, and the effects of EU member states' Ghana visa arrangements (Cross 2009/10).

The re-integration in their area of origin can be difficult and challenging. As Abdullah told me, he left to find a remunerative job in Libya, with the aim of fostering his business back home and financing his organization that supported local artists. He had to flee Libya after the crisis in 2011, he spent all his money in trying to cross the desert to go back to Ghana, and when he arrived in Tamale he was broke.

> I left many things. Without your presence, your things can't go on well. You yourself must be there and manage it, nobody else can manage it for you, so … coming back home, I lost most of the things. I lost the shop … the shop became empty, my brothers have spent everything, they just sold things and spent everything. I lost my car, somebody who was taking care of my car used it for himself, to help himself. The organization … lost the funders. I was not only an employee, I was one of the funders. I then lost the organization. So, I came back and I had to restart my life." [7]

20.5. *The experience in Europe: expectations and failures*

Some of the people I interviewed actually made it, and spent some years in Europe (some of my informants lived in Spain, Italy, Germany, Holland). Their decision to come back to Ghana was eventually characterized by the "failure", as it was perceived by them, of their experience in Europe. Difficulties in accessing regular documents, complications in finding a sufficiently well-paid job to send remittances back home,

---

[6] Interview with P.D., 13/05/2014, Tamale (Ghana).

[7] Interview with A.A., 11/05/2014, Tamale (Ghana).

and enormous efforts in adjusting to a condition of stagnation and uncertainty, eventually led them to decide to return.

Following Dünwald's analysis on experiences of failed migration in Mali, one can find some fruitful points of reflection and comparison. Dünwald states that the effects of increasingly strict visa and asylum policies can be multiple and tricky: circular migratory chains can be cut, the divide between the upper and middle classes become deeper, and former transit countries can suddenly become countries of destination, changing deeply the migratory project of many young Africans (Dünwald 2014). Abdullah expressed a clear point in his decision:

> Hemm ... it was a hard decision for me ... but ... I didn't see myself useful in that society, because I have never had a job ... so I didn't see myself useful. So, I just took the decision and came back. [8]

So, what does being "forced" to return mean? As we see from Abdullah's statement, it is not a condition necessarily linked to expulsion, but to the restrictive access to regularization. Abdullah waited, entered into the process of asylum seeking, but eventually the procedures continued for so long that he could not cope with that condition of uncertainty. As Mezzadra points out, these mechanisms of production of illegality for migrants are actually fracturing spaces of access to citizenship rights in Europe. The flexibility of markets, and the transformation of capitalism, are strongly connected to the process of "illegalization" of migrants, who become indeed useful for the maintenance of precariousness in the job market (Mezzadra 2013).

I find interesting to reflect on Abbas's story, who managed to arrive in Europe for the first time through a regular visa, granted by his Dutch girlfriend at that time. Then a Ghanaian friend of his, who was working in Spain, suggested to overstay the visa and try to make some money to send back home to his family, with the aim at becoming a "successful migrant".

As Abbas told me:

> He thought I should have stayed much longer, to overstay my visa, to find a job. I was never given a permit to work, so he thought I should come over to Spain and then stay longer, and then I could work. So, I got convinced by his decision, his idea. I went to Spain, my visa was due. I overstayed my visa, and it became harder. I couldn't do anything but work in the farms, and that was even illegally. So I worked in the farms for some time, I didn't like it, but I had to do it anyway because I needed to make money, so I could help my problems back home. At that time, I was working under someone else's name ... usually this happens if you are hungry for a job, you got no options ... Even if it is illegal ... You cannot do it in any other ways. You have to survive. They do say, that you can survive without money, but it is very hard, you can't survive without money, especially in Europe. Money is everything, from transport to food ... everything is money. And also the

[8] *Ibidem.*

> expectations of the family back home … you are there and maybe you have spent one year, two years, three years … and the family don't see anything, a reason for your travel … so, you want to make a reason for your travel. I think that migration, for myself… it has always be there, and it is still there. You cannot stop it. Nobody can stop it. That is the way the world is created. We would always need each other.[9]

The tension between the dream of making an experience through migration and the need to demonstrate to your family, your friends and your social environment you have become "successful" is well explained by Abbas. Once you get "there", to Europe, it is almost a waste of energy not to try to make money and explore any possibilities; not only for yourself, but also for your family and for the larger community to which you belong, that is expecting something. This "something" is not just resolved by receiving money, but also by receiving back a fulfilled dream, the idea that someone could eventually make it, the pride of a community towards the success of one of its sons.

As Dünwald observes, "failed return does not only mean the failure of a difficult adventure, but also the failure to trespass the threshold of becoming an adult […]. A rejection of a returnee by his family often comes close to social death, cutting off a returnee from all social links within his home society […]. In many cases returnees do not stay with the family but with friends, sometimes people who were equally expulsed" (Dünwald 2014).

20.6. *Conclusion: a way forward*

The ethnographies analyzed in this chapter are made by border trespassing, both in geographical and in imaginative terms. Borders can be re-defined and used by state and non-state powers to control and exploit migration; migrants continuously cross these borders, and while crossing them they change their status, travel conditions, and aspirations.

The concept and the practice of failed return can be interesting and challenging points of analysis to provide a more complex and complete discourse on return migration. The contemporary condition of those migrants who had to cross borders to go back home highlights the contradictions that exist in between expectations and reality, shedding light on the construction of new social borders inside the society of origin.

Nevertheless, as observed by Maher (2013), failure might be re-conceptualized as a productive space wherein novel models of self-creation are tested and produced. Here Maher argues that the so-called failed migrants are not completely stranded and immobile, but they are actually moving forward and creating new forms of social relations and strategies to accommodate their futures. The stories that I have collected can

[9] Interview with A.M., 12/05/2014, Tamale (Ghana).

confirm this statement, even if I think that there are still many critical aspects about the real inclusion of returnees in their home societies.

When Abbas was explaining to me how much he lost in his migratory experience, he also stated that he had to re-invent himself:

> I am an artist, so I said, let's now use my art skills to build my life. Before I travelled I was not really doing art work, I was purchasing them and putting in my shop. But now I don't buy anymore, I thought ok now I produce my own things. And that is what I have been doing since I came back home. [10]

At the same time, when I was talking with Abdullah about his path and his opinion about his new social and economic position in his town of origin he built up an argument about the meaning of migrating today through the desert and the need to educate the youth:

> I think it is not the best. And I think that it is out of ignorance that people are doing it. People travelling by road to the desert, by sea, to get to Europe … it is sad. When I was in Spain, I was looking the TV and see my brothers and sisters dying … there was no way that they can come in a flight. […] But people should see the reality, documentaries and all these things. To know what is happening. One time I bought a CD about that, how people are crossing … in Melilla, how people cross that fence and what happens to them they die through the wire … and it is sad. So one time some people that were close to me … I show it to them. They were quietly watching it. Surprised, and shocked. I thought about doing it again, for the youth, but it means a lot of things … it means a lot of money. And even if is not a lot, it means money, because you don't only need the CD, you need the screen, you need the stage. You need the projector. I can't do it now. [11]

The agency, and the desire to contribute to the social improvement of their place of origin through the experiences they have gone through, even if ruinous, is well explained here. The great absentee is the state of Ghana, which is not taking into full consideration the presence of these returnees and their potential role in Ghanaian society. Ghana is granting a lot of voice and attention to successful migrants who come back from Europe or the United States with capital for investments and/or provide constant remittances that constitute an enormous source of revenue. The World Bank has declared that diaspora remittances in 2015 alone for sub-Saharan Africa amounted to 35.2 billion dollars, a sum larger than the EU trust fund for Africa (World Bank 2016).

The IOM has taken care of a limited number of repatriated Ghanaians from Libya, making available a fund to open a small business activity. These actions are very helpful, but are not sufficient in terms of inclusion of the failed returnees, who feel expelled from the society and abandoned by the state.

---

[10] *Ibidem.*

[11] Interview with A.A., 11/05/2014, Tamale (Ghana).

I want to underline that in 2016 Ghana launched a National Migration Policy (NMP) plan which aims at working on return, readmission and integration of migrants in the national territory. This action could represent a positive way forward for Ghanaians who come back home without a successful story, but who still want to be included and want to contribute to the production of knowledge and to the development of their own place of origin.

Bibliography

Ammassari, S. (2004) 'From nation building to entrepreneurship: The impact of elite return migrants in Cote d'Ivoire and Ghana', *Population Space and Place*, 10(2): 133–154.

Baud, M. and Van Schendel, W. (1997) 'Toward a comparative history of borderlands', *Journal of World History*, 8(2): 211–222.

Black, R. and King, R. (2004) 'Special Issue: Transnational migration, return and development', *West Africa. Population, Space and Place*, 10(2).

Casentini, G. (2017) 'Migrazioni di ritorno e modelli di rappresentanza nel Ghana contemporaneo' in S. Marabello and U. Pellecchia (eds.) *Capitali migratori e forme del potere. Sei studi sulle migrazioni ghanesi contemporanee*, Rome: CISU.

Casentini, G. (2018) 'Migration networks and narratives in Ghana: A case study from the Zongo', *Africa*, 88(3): 452–468.

Cassarino, J.P. (2004) 'Theorizing return migration: The conceptual approach to return migrants revisited', *International Journal on Multicultural Societies*, 6(2): 253–279.

Cross, A. (2009) 'The EU migration regime and West African clandestine migrants', *Journal of Contemporary European Research*, 5(2): 171–187.

Cross, A. (2009/10) 'Migration, mobility and borders: The EU and West African migrant communities', *African Studies Bulletin*, 71: 46–51.

De Bruijn, M. (2007) 'Mobility and society in the Sahel: An exploration of mobile margins and global governance' in H.P. Hahn and G. Klute (eds.) *Cultures of Migration. African Perspectives*, Berlin: LIT Verlag.

Dünwald, S. (2010) 'The tough way back: Failed migration in Mali', *International Conference on Deportation and the Development of Citizenship*, Oxford: Centre for Migration Studies.

Dünwald, S. (2011) 'On migration and security: Europe managing migration from Sub-Saharan Africa', *Cadernos de Estudos Africanos*, 22.

Ellis, S. and MacGaffey, J. (1996) 'Research on Sub-Saharan Africa's unrecorded international trade: Some methodological and conceptual problems', *African Studies Review*, 39(2): 19–41.

Fabietti, U. (2000) *L'identità etnica. Storia e critica di un concetto ambiguo*, Rome: Carocci.

Flahaux, M.L. and de Haas H. (2016) 'African migration. Trends, patterns, drivers', *Comparative Migration Studies*, 4(1): 1–25.

Korf, B. and Raeymaekers, T. (eds.) (2013) *Violence on the Margins. State, Conflict and Borderlands*, London: Palgrave MacMillan.

Lemberg-Pedersen, M. (2017) 'Effective protection or effective combat? EU border control and North Africa' in P. Gaibazzi, A. Bellagamba and S. Dünwald (eds.) *EuroAfrican Borders and Migration Management. Political Cultures, Contested Spaces and Ordinary Lives*, London: Palgrave Macmillan.
Maher, S. (2013) 'Ambiguities of return: Failed clandestine migration out of Senegal', ASA Baltimore, unpublished paper.
Maher, S. (2017) 'Historicizing "irregular" migration from Senegal to Europe', *Anti-trafficking Review*, 9: 77–91.
Mazzucato, V. (2008) 'The double engagement: Transnationalism and integration – Ghanaian migrants' lives between Ghana and The Netherlands', *Journal of Ethnic and Migration Studies*, 34(2): 199–216.
Mbembe, A. (2000) 'At the edge of the world: Boundaries, territoriality and sovereignty in Africa', *Public Culture*, 12(1): 259–284.
Mercer, C., Page, B. and Evans, M. (2009) 'Unsettling connections: Transnational networks, development and African home associations', *Global Networks*, 9(2): 141–161.
Mezzadra, S. (2013) 'Moltiplicazione dei confini e pratiche di mobilità', *Ragion Pratica*, 41: 413–431.
Morone, A.M. (2015) 'Sub-Saharan migrants in post-Qadhafy Libya: Human mobility and international politics', in M. Zaccaria and B. Airò (eds.) *Asia Major: I confine della cittadinanza nel nuovo Medio Oriente*, Rome: Viella.
Nieswand, B. (2017) 'Il capitale di infrazione e disuguaglianza globale nel Ghana meridionale" in S. Marabello and U. Pellecchia (eds.), *Capitali migratori e forme del potere. Sei studi sulle migrazioni ghanesi contemporanee*, Rome: CISU.
Quiminal, C. (2002) 'Retour contraints, retour construits des émigrées maliens', *Hommes et Migrations*, 1236: 35–43.
Sayad, A. (2002) *La doppia assenza. Dalle illusioni dell'emigrato alle sofferenze dell'immigrato*, Milana: Cortina.
Scott, J.C. (2009) *The Art of Not Being Governed: An Anarchist History of Upland South-East Asia*, New Haven: Yale University Press.
Spivak, G.C. (1988) 'Can the subaltern speak?', in C. Nelson and L. Grossberg (eds.) *Marxism and the Interpretation of Culture*, Basingstoke: Macmillan.
Tiemoko, R. (2004) 'Migration, return and socio-economic change in West Africa: The role of the family', *Population Space and Place*, 10(2): 155–174.
Thomas, K.S.A. (2008) 'Return migration in Africa and relationship between education attainment and labour market success: Evidences from Uganda', *International Migration Review*, 42(3): 652–674.
Ungruhe, C. (2012) 'Symbol of success: Youth, peer pressure and the role of adulthood among juvenile male return migrants in Ghana', *Childhood*, 19(2): 259–271.
World Bank (2016) *Migration and Remittances Factbook 2016. Third Edition*, Washington: World Bank Group.

Part III

Deleting the borders?

Chapter 21
Genetic identities beyond conventional boundaries

Alessandro Achilli and Ugo Perego

21.1. *Introduction*

Traditionally, humans have relied on records that they have themselves created to reconstruct their past. At the individual level, such histories are called genealogies and, among other things, they include names, places, and dates of birth of our ancestors. Of course, the greatest limitation of this work is accessing available sources where this information has been preserved. As we move back in time, such documents become increasingly scarce until they are completely missing. Additionally, in modern times, unrecorded family events, such as adoptions and illegitimacies, destruction of archives due to floods, fires, wars, and similar causes, or simply because such records were never kept in the first place, are all serious obstacles in compiling personal genealogies. This is also true about all histories: local, national, or for the whole human species. Among the tools that allow for a deeper look into the human past is DNA, with genetic genealogy as its application to expand individual ancestry, and population genetics as the discipline to trace ancient and modern human migrations.

DNA data found in our cells is a type of record that is inherited generation after generation and can be utilized to shed light on temporal and spatial events related to human history. This genetic material is grouped in 23 pairs of chromosomes found in the nucleus of nearly all cells. Chromosomes 1 to 22 are known as autosomes and the twenty-third set is referred to as the sex-chromosomes (XX in females and XY in males). Additionally, extra-nuclear organelles known as mitochondria carry relatively small genomes (when compared to nuclear DNA) called mitochondrial DNA (mtDNA). Humans receive one set of their chromosomes from their father and the other set from their mother. Therefore, DNA is a connecting link between generations and discloses previously unknown details regarding individuals and populations. Moreover, the study of genetic histories reveals how all humans are more closely related than is generally expected and how "no man is an island entire of itself". Such an approach demonstrates the complex networks, contributions, and overlapping of our ancestries, thus knocking down conventional boundaries and the erroneous, preconceived notion regarding human races. The purpose of this chapter is to describe the use of these genetic markers (autosomes, the male-inherited Y chromosome and female-transmitted mitochondrial

DNA) as they relate to migratory events in ancient times (the peopling of the planet), in modern times (such as recent influxes from Africa and the Middle East to Western Europe), and with regard to one's personal ancestry.

21.2. *Genetic markers*

The study of human populations using genetic markers is more than a century old. Many people believe that these studies were possible only with the discovery of DNA in the 1950s (Watson and Crick 1953), but they can be traced back to the detection of different blood groups from 1900 (Bodmer 2015). Based on the frequencies of blood types A, B, and 0 (and eventually AB), scientists began for the first time to use inherited markers to explore the possible existence of biological "boundaries" between populations. Obviously, the greatest limitation with these early approaches was to draw conclusions based on the use of single genetic variants to define entire ethnic groups. It was apparent that additional polymorphisms and sophisticated techniques were necessary to provide more accurate demographic and geographic subdivisions. Scientists detected additional blood markers, such as the Rhesus (Rh) factors, which were the basis of Luca Cavalli-Sforza's landmark works in population genetics in the 1960s (Cavalli-Sforza et al. 1993). With the advent of computer technology and the discovery and application of HLA types first, and molecular markers later, the history and migrations of populations from a genetic viewpoint was becoming increasingly clearer. Nowadays, data from the mitochondrial DNA, the non-recombining portion of the Y chromosome (Y-DNA), and even from a screening of the 3.2 billion nucleotides comprising the whole nuclear DNA (nDNA), are the standard for such studies. The uniparental characteristics of both mtDNA and Y-DNA have been employed to reconstruct the first detailed phylogenetic trees able to describe the genetic histories of individuals and populations from a female and male standpoint, respectively. Based on single nucleotide polymorphisms (SNPs, genetic variants higher than 1% in the general population), phylogenetic trees have been built and are continually updated, showing precise temporal and spatial distributions of their branches, also known as lineages or haplogroups.[1] Among other things, this information has provided insights into the ancient expansions of our early ancestors, including the out-of-Africa theory, and the timings and routes they followed as they colonized the entire planet (Achilli and Perego 2010). In more recent years, thanks to the latest technological and scientific advances, the picture of world migrations and the relationship among all humans already depicted by uniparental markers has been corroborated by sequencing the entire genome (Nielsen et al. 2017).

---

[1] A group of molecules that share genetic variants acquired by descent from a common ancestor. See Phylotree for mtDNA variation (http://www.phylotree.org accessed on November 6th, 2017), and the International Society of Genetic Genealogy Y-DNA Haplogroup Tree (https://isogg.org/tree accessed on November 6th, 2017).

21.3. *Migrations in ancient times*

Researchers from various disciplines have studied migrations of past human populations in every corner of the planet. Most recently, genomics and palaeogenomics have taken off and thousands of nuclear and mitochondrial genomes have become available (obtained from modern and ancient samples) providing crucial insights concerning the anatomically modern humans' past and leading to a novel research field called archaeogenetics: the use of molecular genetic techniques to study the history of human populations and to track down ancient migrations (Andrews and Luikart 2014; Pagani et al. 2016; Richards et al. 2016).

Genetic studies support anthropological and archeological theories that the anatomically modern humans originated in sub-Saharan Africa circa 200,000 years ago (200 kya), where the deepest splits between human populations lie (Auton et al. 2015; Beltrame et al. 2016; Campbell and Tishkoff 2010; Reyes-Centeno 2016; Tishkoff et al. 2009; Torroni et al. 2006). The rapid climate fluctuations between mild and severe climate conditions, particularly in the past, had major effects on the spread of ancestral populations, starting from the out-of-Africa dispersal, which occurred at around 50–70 kya and left a strong signature on human evolutionary history (Macaulay et al. 2005; Olivieri et al. 2006; Rasmussen et al. 2011; Soares et al. 2010). After leaving Africa, modern humans followed two dispersal routes: one along the southern coast of Asia all the way to Australasia and New Guinea; the other route, towards the Eurasian mainland, contributed to the ancestry of present-day western Eurasian populations (Nielsen et al. 2017).

This type of research has a major scientific and social impact because it allows a leap forward in the description and comprehension of the genetic landscape of our species, also in the specific case of a number of prehistoric and historic events that played an important role in shaping the peopling of different regions. Achievements in this field have been pursued for decades, and the knowledge base has grown in parallel with theoretical and technological advancements.

As an example of the intricacy of human history, a summary of the reconstructed ancestry of European populations through DNA is provided. The prevailing conclusion about the origin of modern Europeans is that Paleolithic hunter-gatherers, particularly from Central Europe, differed genetically from early farmers (Brandt et al. 2014), as well as from modern populations (Haak et al. 2005). This implies that there was a major replacement due to Neolithic migrations (starting ~8–7 kya) from the Near East associated with the onset of farming (Lazaridis et al. 2014; Omrak et al. 2016; Pinhasi et al. 2012). An additional and more recent (early Bronze Age, ~5 kya) contribution has been linked to the Late Neolithic expansion of Steppe pastoralists from southern Russia, considered by many scholars as the source for the Indo-European languages (Brandt et al. 2014; Haak et al. 2015). Recent studies have also revaluated a possible late Paleolithic genetic component related to modern Near Easterners during the first significant postglacial warming period (Bølling-Allerød interstadial,

~14 kya) (Fu et al. 2016; Posth et al. 2016; Richards et al. 2016). In particular, the (extra-nuclear) mitochondrial genome variation suggests that some modern European lineages were already present in late Paleolithic Europe, particularly in the Mediterranean area (Achilli et al. 2005; Achilli et al. 2004; Gandini et al. 2016; Hofmanová et al. 2016; Olivieri et al. 2013; Olivieri et al. 2017; Pala et al. 2012). Certainly, the Mediterranean Sea has facilitated maritime mobility across the diverse societies and economies that have sprung up around the littorals, leading to dense communications and exchange networks, especially during the warmth and stability of the last 11.5 kya (the Holocene epoch). For instance, mitogenome analyses have revealed some recent and direct events of gene flows across the Mediterranean Sea into Europe: i) from the Levant about 3.0 kya, in agreement with the classical historical scenario of a possible Near Eastern origin of Etruscans (Achilli et al. 2007), and ii) from sub-Saharan Africa, which mostly (~65%) took place in rather recent historical times, including the Romanization period, the Arab conquest of the Iberian Peninsula and Sicily, and during the period of the trans-Atlantic slave trade (Cerezo et al. 2012). This is also evident in the present day in the ongoing humanitarian crisis of the Mediterranean Sea, as described hereafter.

21.4. *Migration in modern times*

Since 2000, the global population has increased at a pace of about 1% per year and is currently 7.4 billion people, most of whom (6.2 billion) live in the less developed countries (PRB 2016).[2] In 2016, the highest fertility rates were registered in sub-Saharan Africa (e.g. Niger, with 7.6 children born/woman), where the consequences of the rapid population growth remain a burning issue. Another significant consideration is that more than 3% of the world population is made up by international migrants (244 million people; 15% of whom are below 20 years of age), meaning people living temporarily or permanently outside their country of birth (UN-DESA 2015). Ongoing conflict and violence in many parts of the world have forced approximately 65.3 million people from their homes; one in every 113 people is either an asylum seeker, internally displaced or a refugee (21.3 million). Even a special issue of the journal Nature underlines the urgency of novel approaches at the intersection between science and the humanities to understand a world on the move (Nature 2017).

A tragic example of the current mass migrations is represented by the ongoing humanitarian crisis in the Mediterranean Sea. The lack of legal pathways leaves many individuals escaping persecution with few choices. The UNHCR[3] reports that "increasing numbers of refugees (mostly from sub-Saharan Africa) take their chances

[2] Population Reference Bureau (http://www.prb.org/ accessed on February 14th, 2017).

[3] United Nations High Commissioner for Refugees (http://www.unhcr.org/, accessed on February 14, 2017).

aboard unseaworthy boats and dinghies in a desperate bid to reach Europe" and "many have become victims of smuggling and trafficking and often been subjected to rights abuse en route". In the past two years, more than 1.3 million refugees and migrants reached European shores, mostly landing in Greece and Italy. These two arrival countries reveal important differences and an opposite trend. Migrants landing on the Greek shores come mostly from the Middle East and their number is experiencing a rapid decrease (up to ~80% less) due to the deal signed between the European Union and Turkey to tackle the migrant crisis. On the contrary, the total number of sea arrivals in Italy is increasing (up to ~18%) and the individuals arriving to Italy by sea mainly originate from sub-Saharan Africa, with the following percentages in 2016: Nigeria (21%), Eritrea (11%), Ivory Coast, Guinea, Gambia (7% each), Senegal, Mali (6% each), Sudan, (5%), Bangladesh and Somalia (4% each), other countries (22%). In spite of their various geographic origins, the alleles migrating across the Mediterranean Sea will have a "genetic impact" on the "future gene pool" of European populations.

21.5. *Individual ancestral migrations*

During the last decade, do-it-yourself DNA testing for genealogical purposes has become extremely popular. There are several companies nowadays that are offering these services to the general public.[4] The popularity of these products is such that on the traditional "Black Friday" after Thanksgiving Day in November 2017, one of these companies alone sold 1.7 million autosomal DNA kits in just a few hours.[5] Although these DNA tests are part of a commercial business, the technology used to produce the hundreds of thousands of autosomal SNPs for each client is the same as that which is employed by government and academic institutions. What may cause disputation is the level of accuracy from the interpretation of the results provided by each company, which is based on customized reference population databases. However, when determining the genetic origin of the four major population groups (African, European, Asian and Native American) these tests are reliable and the ancestral painting from these data reflects each individual's dynamic history. As part of this essay, we will use the DNA results of the two authors to demonstrate this concept.

The first case presented is based on genomic data generated by Ancestry.com. The ancestors from the available genealogical records are all from Central Italy, and more precisely from the Marche region on the Adriatic Sea. The ethnicity painting provided by this service is based on Ancestry.com's unique reference dataset and is shown in Figure 21.1.

---

[4] See International Society of Genetic Genealogy WIKI (https://isogg.org/wiki/Autosomal_DNA_testing_comparison_chart).

[5] Ancestry.com, https://www.ancestry.com/corporate/newsroom/press-releases/ancestrydna-breaks-holiday-sales-record-black-friday-cyber-monday-more

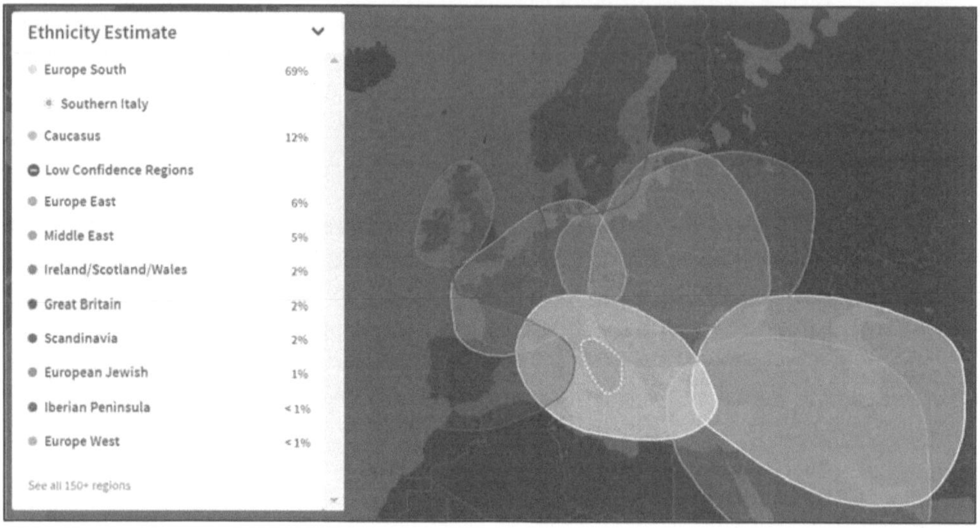

Figure 21.1. Ancestry.com ethnicity estimates for one of the authors based on ca. 640k autosomal SNPs

The first impression coming from this genetic painting is the great ancestral diversity that each individual person carries. However, a few considerations are needed. First, ethnicity estimates at 5% or lower (called low confidence regions in Figure 21.1) are often the result of some sort of genetic background noise. It is only in cases where documents are available to support these small percentages that they become reliable in depicting one's past. Otherwise, there is often a certain percentage of genetic markers that could not be confidently associated with a specific geographic region, either because of the limitations of the reference database used by each lab to generate this type of output, or because some SNPs are not (yet) very discriminating between ethnic groups. On the same lines and as mentioned earlier, there exists an incredible level of admixture observed in the human population, as having DNA associated with a specific region does not necessarily mean that our ancestors came from that area. There could have been a common, now extinct, source population from which different migrations originated, thus resulting in modern, separate genetic pools that are "cousins" rather than ancestral in nature.

In the case of these results produced by Ancestry.com, the available genealogical data of one of the authors is reflected by only 69% of his DNA, showing a strong genetic signal from Central and Southern Italy, as expected from his pedigree chart. However, a significant 12% of this individual's DNA is shared with people from the Caucasus region and no genealogical data is currently available to confirm this ancestry. Other regions represented in the DNA of this person include, among others, 6% from East Europe and 5% from the Middle East. Therefore, it is safe to conclude that notwithstanding an individual would culturally identify him- or herself as belonging to one country or ethnic group, our DNA instead is not limited by conventional boundaries.

The interesting diversity just described was limited to the analysis of the autosomes of a single individual. Another way to approach the richness found in a person's genome is to compare the genetic history depicted by different markers. In this second case, DNA testing produced by the California-based 23andMe company provides an example of how Y chromosome, mitochondrial DNA and autosomal DNA from the same individual show three distinct origins.

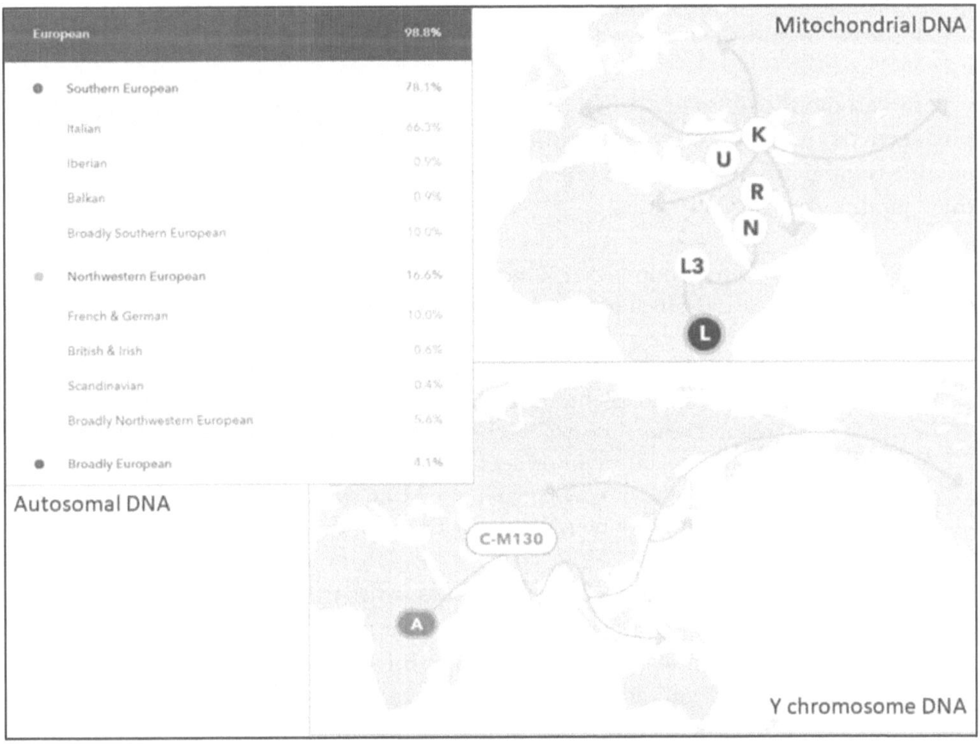

Figure 21.2. 23andMe ancestry reports for one of the authors indicating the distinct ethnic origins based on autosomal DNA, Y chromosome and mitochondrial DNA

As with the other author's Ancestry.com autosomal analysis, there is an expected predominant Southern European legacy that has survived in this individual's genome, as well as other minor ethnicity representations. However, the interesting part comes from the observed uniparental markers: Y Chromosome and mitochondrial DNA.

The second author has a mitochondrial genome with the set of basal mutations belonging to the phylogenetic branch known as haplogroup K, and more specifically to its sub-lineage K1a4a1. From the 23andMe website, here is the migratory description of this specific sub-haplogroup, which is also closely related to maternal lineages found among Ashkenazi Jews:

> Your maternal line stems from a branch of haplogroup K called K1a4a1. Haplogroup K1a4a1 is predominantly European today, and traces back to a woman who lived approximately 10,000 years ago. Europe was at the start of an age of transformation. To the east in the Fertile Crescent, people were successfully domesticating crops and transitioning to a more settled lifestyle. This new technology supported a boom in human populations, and over thousands of years migrations of these new farmers moved gradually westward across the European continent, leading to additional population growth and great cultural changes. K1a4a1 expanded along with these population changes, giving rise to additional branches throughout Europe. Today, members of K1a4a1 can be found at low levels within Europe, including in Eastern Europe and the Caucasus. Though not typically found outside of Europe, one lineage has been identified as far south as Anatolia.

Similarly to the mitochondrial DNA, Y chromosome haplotypes are organized in a phylogenetic tree based on their specific mutations. However, the history of the paternal line is quite different for the same individual, as he belongs to haplogroup C. From the 23andme website, we read:

> The branches of haplogroup C-M130 all trace back to the first major migration of our ancestors out of Africa, which occurred between 50,000 and 60,000 years ago. A relatively small group of people, probably in the range of hundreds to thousands, crossed the Red Sea from the horn of Africa to the Arabian Peninsula. From there these people, already well adapted to the coastal environment, made their way along the shore of the Indian Ocean. Within a few thousand years they had reached Australia, which was more accessible to the Asian mainland at the time due to lower sea levels. Even so, people would have had to make an ocean passage of at least 60 miles to inhabit the island continent. Archaeological evidence suggests they made the trip by about 45,000 years ago at the latest.

As we see with this second example, even if autosomes might seem ethnically homogeneous, multiple migration stories could still have survived in the genes of a single individual when uniparental markers are brought into the equation. Both authors were born and raised in Italy and all their known ancestors are Italian. Culturally and linguistically that is the only identity they would feel they are confined to if DNA was to be left out of the picture. However, when autosomes and uniparental markers are analyzed, the genetic identity of each individual seems to know no borders, as shown by the two examples provided.

21.6. *Beyond the concept of biological race and conventional boundaries*

The previously mentioned out-of-Africa theory implies that all living people trace their ancestry back to a single sub-Saharan origin (Culotta and Gibbons 2016). In other words, although we are all leaves from branches, at the end we belong to the same biological tree, sharing a common African root. Every two humans when compared at the genetic level share more than 99.9% of their DNA. For example, the genome differences between a Pygmy and an individual from Scandinavia would be less than 0.1%. We have too much DNA in common to differentiate humans into different biological racial groups. Therefore, race is obviously only a social/cultural construct. We would find the same genes A, B, C, etc. in any population or ethnic group, but with different variants (alleles). It is the observed variants, and particularly the frequencies, of such alleles that would be different among groups. It is like reading the same book in different languages: the words might look different but the meaning is the same. The color of our skin, the susceptibility to certain diseases, disorders, allergies, etc. are more common in some ethnic or population groups and less in others, but at the end, we might observe more genotypic variation within a population than between populations. Additionally, the genes responsible for phenotypic characteristics that are so evident to the naked eye, such as color of skin, shape of eyes and nose, height, etc. are very small in number (1.5%) when compared to the total amount of coding DNA in our genome. In other words, only a minute amount of our DNA is responsible for the different way we look.

Politically speaking we might come from a specific country, and in cultural terms we might belong to a specific ethnic group, but it is clearly written in our entire DNA that we are all the product of ancient, and often undocumented migrations that our ancestors experienced as they willingly or forcibly moved from place to place. For this reason, although in today's society we can create boundaries to separate specific countries having requirements to control or minimize migrations between them, our DNA shows a very lively gene flow and profound connections between all human beings.

Bibliography

Achilli, A. and Perego, U. (2010) 'Mitochondrial DNA: A female perspective in recent human origin and evolution' in P. Spinozzi and A. Zironi A (eds.) *Origins as a Paradigm in the Sciences and in the Humanities*, Gottingen: V & R Unipress.

Achilli, A., Olivieri, A., Pala, M., Metspalu, E., Fornarino, S., Battaglia, V., Accetturo, M., Kutuev, I., Khusnutdinova. E., Pennarun, E. et al. (2007) 'Mitochondrial DNA variation of modern Tuscans supports the near eastern origin of Etruscans', *American Journal of Human Genetics*, 80(4): 759–768.

Achilli, A., Rengo, C., Battaglia, V., Pala, M., Olivieri, A., Fornarino, S., Magri, C., Scozzari, R., Babudri, N., Santachiara-Benerecetti, A.S. et al. (2005) 'Saami and Berbers – An unexpected mitochondrial DNA link', *American Journal of Human Genetics*, 76(5): 883–886.

Achilli, A., Rengo, C., Magri, C., Battaglia, V., Olivieri, A., Scozzari, R., Cruciani, F., Zeviani, M., Briem, E., Carelli, V. et al. (2004) 'The molecular dissection of mtDNA haplogroup H confirms that the Franco-Cantabrian glacial refuge was a major source for the European gene pool', *American Journal of Human Genetics*, 75(5): 910–918.

Andrews, K.R. and Luikart, G. (2014) 'Recent novel approaches for population genomics data analysis', *Mol Ecol*, 23(7): 1661–1667.
Auton, A., Brooks, L.D., Durbin, R.M., Garrison, E.P., Kang, H.M., Korbel, J.O., Marchini, J.L., McCarthy, S., McVean, G.A., Abecasis, G.R. et al. (2015) 'A global reference for human genetic variation', *Nature*, 526(7571): 68–74.
Beltrame, M.H., Rubel, M.A. and Tishkoff, S.A. (2016) 'Inferences of African evolutionary history from genomic data', *Curr Opin Genet Dev*, 41: 159–166.
Bodmer, W. (2015) 'Genetic characterization of human populations: From ABO to a genetic map of the British people', *Genetics*, 199(2): 267–279.
Brandt, G., Szecsenyi-Nagy, A., Roth, C., Alt, K.W. and Haak, W. (2014) 'Human paleogenetics of Europe – the known knowns and the known unknowns', *J Hum Evol*, 79: 73–92.
Campbell, M.C. and Tishkoff, S.A. (2010) 'The evolution of human genetic and phenotypic variation in Africa', *Curr Biol*, 20(4): R166–173.
Cavalli-Sforza, L.L., Menozzi, P. and Piazza, A. (1993) 'Demic expansions and human evolution', *Science*, 259(5095): 639–646.
Cerezo, M., Achilli, A., Olivieri, A., Perego, U.A., Gomez-Carballa, A., Brisighelli, F., Lancioni, H., Woodward, S.R., Lopez-Soto, M., Carracedo, A. et al. (2012) 'Reconstructing ancient mitochondrial DNA links between Africa and Europe', *Genome Research*, 22(5): 821–826.
Culotta, E. and Gibbons, A. (2016) 'Almost all living people outside of Africa trace back to a single migration more than 50,000 years ago', *Science*. Doi: 10.1126/science.aah7329.
Fu, Q., Posth, C., Hajdinjak, M., Petr, M., Mallick, S., Fernandes, D., Furtwängler, A., Haak, W., Meyer, M., Mittnik, A. et al. (2016) 'The genetic history of Ice Age Europe', *Nature*, 534(7606): 200–205.
Gandini, F., Achilli, A., Pala, M., Bodner, M., Brandini, S., Huber, G., Egyed, B., Ferretti, L., Gómez-Carballa, A., Salas, A. et al. (2016) 'Mapping human dispersals into the Horn of Africa from Arabian Ice Age refugia using mitogenomes', *Sci Rep*, 6: 25472.
Haak, W., Forster, P., Bramanti, B., Matsumura, S., Brandt, G., Tanzer, M., Villems, R., Renfrew, C., Gronenborn, D., Alt, K.W. et al. (2005) 'Ancient DNA from the first European farmers in 7500-year-old Neolithic sites', *Science*, 310: 1016–1018.
Haak, W., Lazaridis, I., Patterson, N., Rohland, N., Mallick, S., Llamas, B., Brandt, G., Nordenfelt, S., Harney, E., Stewardson, K. et al. (2015) 'Massive migration from the steppe is a source for Indo-European languages in Europe', *Nature*, 522: 207–211.
Hofmanová, Z., Kreutzer, S., Hellenthal, G., Sell, C., Diekmann, Y., Díez-Del-Molino, D., van Dorp, L., López, S., Kousathanas, A., Link, V. et al. (2016) 'Early farmers from across Europe directly descended from Neolithic Aegeans', *Proc Natl Acad Sci USA*, 113(25): 6886–6891.
Lazaridis, I., Patterson, N., Mittnik, A., Renaud, G., Mallick, S., Kirsanow, K., Sudmant, P.H., Schraiber, J.G., Castellano, S., Lipson, M. et al. (2014) 'Ancient human genomes suggest three ancestral populations for present-day Europeans', *Nature*, 513(7518): 409–413.
Macaulay, V., Hill, C., Achilli, A., Rengo, C., Clarke, D., Meehan, W., Blackburn, J., Semino, O., Scozzari, R., Cruciani, F. et al. (2005) 'Single, rapid coastal settlement of Asia revealed by analysis of complete mitochondrial genomes', *Science*, 308(5724): 1034–1036.

Nature (2017) 'Human migration', Nature, 543(7643): 21.

Nielsen, R., Akey, J.M., Jakobsson, M., Pritchard, J.K., Tishkoff, S. and Willerslev, E. (2017) 'Tracing the peopling of the world through genomics', *Nature*, 541(7637): 302–310.

Olivieri, A., Achilli, A., Pala, M., Battaglia, V., Fornarino, S., Al-Zahery, N., Scozzari, R., Cruciani, F., Behar, D.M., Dugoujon, J.M. et al. (2006) 'The mtDNA legacy of the Levantine early Upper Palaeolithic in Africa', *Science*, 314(5806): 1767–1770.

Olivieri, A., Pala, M., Gandini, F., Kashani, B.H., Perego, U.A., Woodward, S.R., Grugni, V., Battaglia, V., Semino, O., Achilli, A. et al. (2013) 'Mitogenomes from two uncommon haplogroups mark late glacial/postglacial expansions from the Near East and Neolithic dispersals within Europe', *Plos One*, 8(7).

Olivieri, A., Sidore, C., Achilli, A., Angius, A., Posth, C., Furtwängler, A., Brandini, S., Capodiferro, M.R., Gandini, F., Zoledziewska, M. et al. (2017) 'Mitogenome diversity in Sardinians: A genetic window onto an island's past', *Mol Biol Evol*, 34(5): 1230–1239.

Omrak, A., Günther, T., Valdiosera, C., Svensson, E.M., Malmström, H., Kiesewetter, H., Aylward, W., Storå, J., Jakobsson, M. and Götherström, A. (2016) 'Genomic evidence establishes Anatolia as the source of the European neolithic gene pool', *Curr Biol*, 26(2): 270–275.

Pagani, L., Lawson, D.J., Jagoda, E., Mörseburg, A., Eriksson, A., Mitt, M., Clemente, F., Hudjashov, G., DeGiorgio, M., Saag, L. et al. (2016) 'Genomic analyses inform on migration events during the peopling of Eurasia', *Nature*, 538(7624): 238–242.

Pala, M., Olivieri, A., Achilli, A., Accetturo, M., Metspalu, E., Reidla, M., Tamm, E., Karmin, M., Reisberg, T., Hooshiar Kashani, B. et al. (2012) 'Mitochondrial DNA signals of late glacial recolonization of Europe from Near Eastern refugia', *Am J Hum Genet*, 90(5): 915–924.

Pinhasi, R., Thomas, M.G., Hofreiter, M., Currat, M. and Burger, J. (2012) 'The genetic history of Europeans', *Trends Genet*, 28(10): 496–505.

Posth, C., Renaud, G., Mittnik, A., Drucker, D.G., Rougier, H., Cupillard, C., Valentin, F., Thevenet, C., Furtwängler, A., Wißing, C. et al. (2016) 'Pleistocene mitochondrial genomes suggest a single major dispersal of non-Africans and a late glacial population turnover in Europe', *Curr Biol*, 26(6): 827–833.

PRB (2016) 2016 World Population Data Sheet. Washington, DC: http://www.prb.org/pdf16/prb-wpds2016-web-2016.pdf.

Rasmussen, M., Guo, X., Wang, Y., Lohmueller, K.E., Rasmussen, S., Albrechtsen, A., Skotte, L., Lindgreen, S., Metspalu, M., Jombart, T. et al. (2011) 'An Aboriginal Australian genome reveals separate human dispersals into Asia', *Science*, 334(6052): 94–98.

Reyes-Centeno, H. (2016) 'Out of Africa and into Asia: Fossil and genetic evidence on modern human origins and dispersals', Special issue: Southeast Asia: Human evolution, dispersals and adaptation, *Quaternary International*, 416: 249–262.

Richards, M.B., Soares, P. and Torroni, A. (2016) 'Palaeogenomics: Mitogenomes and migrations in Europe's past', *Curr Biol*, 26(6): R243–246.

Soares, P., Achilli, A., Semino, O., Davies, W., Macaulay, V., Bandelt, H.-J., Torroni, A. and Richards, M.B. (2010) 'The archaeogenetics of Europe', *Curr Biol*, 20(4): R174–183.

Tishkoff, S.A., Reed, F.A., Friedlaender, F.R., Ehret, C., Ranciaro, A., Froment, A.,

Hirbo, J.B., Awomoyi, A.A., Bodo, J.M., Doumbo, O. et al. (2009) 'The genetic structure and history of Africans and African Americans', *Science*, 324(5930): 1035–1044.
Torroni, A., Achilli, A., Macaulay, V., Richards, M. and Bandelt, H.J. (2006) 'Harvesting the fruit of the human mtDNA tree', *Trends in Genetics*, 22(6): 339–345.
UN-DESA (2015) United Nations, Population Division, Department of Economic and Social Affairs (UN DESA) – *Trends in International Migrants Stock: The 2015 Revision*, (POP/DB/MIG/Stock/Rev.2015.
Watson, J. and Crick, F. (1953) 'Molecular structure of nucleic acids: A structure for deoxyribose nucleic acid', *Nature*, 171(4356): 737.

Chapter 22

Migrat.In.G. "Migrations: towards an interdisciplinary governance model"

Some considerations on the contribution of legal scholars to the Strategic Project of the University of Pavia

Ernesto Bettinelli

The "genuine" and rigorous perception of facts and their actual dimension is, generally speaking, an inevitable and essential methodological precondition for any legal scholar, until the moment he identifies and/or elaborates a legal category capable of describing them in all their (legally relevant) different aspects.

In opposition to the actual perception of facts, there is actually, another, conflicting option which is often pursued for reasons of "political realism": under this second perspective, the "fact" is construed or re-construed on the basis of legal resources (definitions, prescriptions, balance of interests taken into account in different ways by the legal system or systems) which are intended to be applied, in order to safeguard the normative categories which are believed to be definitely established in areas that are considered sufficiently similarly precise or hardly amendable.

The term "migrations" (erroneously) interpreted as a phenomenon with an indeterminate and infinitely complex content, which is made up of the sum of different events and situations, that can be deconstructed and categorized in different ways, may be classified and challenged alternatively under one of the two aforementioned perspectives with very different results, both with respect to the legal characterization, on the one side, and to the subsequent policy determinations, on the other.

The most comprehensive and neutral definition of "migrant" refers to an individual "fleeing from its country of origin for a non-predetermined period of time". If the question is posed under the standpoint of the effective and free will of such a flee or exodus, two different figures of migrants can be depicted in their main following characters:

1. *The expatriate*: someone who resolves to move to another State on the basis of an individual "existential" interest, which is usually recognized both by the law of the home country and of the State of arrival. The legal tool ("title") giving legitimacy to such a relocation is the "passport", or equivalent document, whose validity and

efficacy depend on the rules in force in both States. For "liberal-minded" legal orders, the issuance of a passport is usually a "right", while the attribution of validity-effectiveness to passports issued by the authorities of another State is qualified as an interest of the foreign citizen which can be (discretionally) satisfied, through the so-called *visa* procedure, only when the interests at stake are not opposed to those of the granting State. In any case, the process for an expatriate is usually regulated through pre-established (legal) procedures having a prominent contractual nature with an economic added-value.

Such a state of affairs emerges from the sufficiently limited "catalogue" of the reasons to expatriate: work, study/education, tourism (in the case of long-term expatriation), provision of healthcare services, family reunification... Expatriation may be valued under a "give-and-take" perspective. The economic contribution by the expatriate to the host State is normally compensated by the recognition of safeguarding arrangements that are adopted both unilaterally and by means of international conventions. The classic example of such an approach is provided by the Magna Carta Libertatum (art. 41):

> Omnes mercatores habeant salvum et securum exire de Anglia, et venire in Angliam, et morari, et ire per Angliam, tam per terram quam per aquam, ad emendum et vendendum, sine omnibus malistoltis, per antiquas et rectas consuetudines, preterquam in tempore gwerre, et si sint de terra contra nos gwerring; et si tales inventiantur in terra nostra in principio gwerre, attachientur sine damno corporum et rerum, donec sciatur a nobis vel capitali justiciario nostro quomodo mercatores terre nostre tractentur, qui tunc invenientur in terra contra nos gwerrina; et si nostri salvi sint ibi, alii salvi sint in terra nostra. [1]

2. The "forced" migrant: anyone leaving (or fleeing from) the home country for reasons of survival and/or impossible living conditions because of catastrophic events, such as: wars, violations of human rights by totalitarian regimes, famines, natural disasters. The prominent features of those migrations are "desperation" (individual, but often represented or perceived in a massive dimension) and mass-exoduses also for migrants' self-protection or self-identification. This dramatic scenario, indeed tragic, is likely to overshadow the voluntary and individual aspect which nevertheless characterizes also this kind of exodus. Paradoxically, to such a "forced will" is often recognized a lower relevance with respect to the "free will" of the expatriate

[1] A translation into English of clause XVI of the 1215 Magna Carta can be found at the official website of *The Magna Carta Project* (http://magnacarta.cmp.uea.ac.uk/read/magna_carta_1215/Clause_41, accessed on August 1st, 2018), where it reads as follows: "All merchants are to be safe and secure in departing from and coming to England, and in their residing and movements in England, by both land and water, for buying and selling, without any evil exactions but only paying the ancient and rightful customs, except in time of war and if they come from the land against us in war. And if the latter are found in our land at the outbreak of war, they are to be attached without harm to their bodies and goods, until we or our chief justiciar know how merchants of our own land, who are then found in the land against us in war; are being treated, and if ours are safe there, the others are to be safe in our land."

who succeeds in creating an autonomous social space. The objective conditions of the forced migrant easily annihilate any subjectivity. As a consequence, reference is made to law in order to give answers to a phenomenon (an undifferentiated human aggregation) more than to individual situations, each of them linked to individual "existential" interests.

The first theoretical (and practical) issue to be considered concerns the importance that the different legal systems attach to these two types of will (the "free" will of the expatriate and the "constrained" will of the forced migrant). It is indeed evident the discriminatory treatment reserved to the second category, mirrored by a substantial underestimation thereof, since practical attention is mainly devoted to counter the cumulative phenomenon of individual wills. In short, the will to relocate elsewhere as a consequence of misery and the desperate need to survive generally holds, both de jure and de facto, a minor importance with respect to the intention to expatriate in order to satisfy less vital interests.

A review of those areas of legal research (at the supranational, international, European and national level) that look at such two figures seems to be a particularly significant standpoint when assessing the legitimacy of discriminatory policies. Legal scholarship shall, therefore, identify all those legal sources allowing at various levels to positively adhere to the conclusion that the freedom of movement (and of establishment elsewhere) shall be accepted as an absolute and universal right of any individual. The definitely ambitious aim is in fact to define a corpus juris humanitatis, intended as a superior system of rules for all human beings.

Such a roadmap deserves to be explored, even considering the prevailing opinion on the "programmatic" character of such a reconstruction and/or legal rearrangement. In fact, even those universal programmatic norms may constitute a parameter for the decisions of the competent Courts, having jurisdiction at the national or international level, when adjudicating on the status of a natural person.

In this respect, a first consideration regards the incompatibility of the condition of statelessness with such a status, since the "eradicated" individual (which is not able to prove the possession of any citizenship) is deprived of an indispensable connotation of juridical identity. Beyond the international treaties and conventions offering remedies to overcome the condition of statelessness, it should be useful to enquire, by means of a systematic and evolutionary interpretation, if it is possible to derive from a general "principles of humanity" a saving clause allowing, in case of inaction by individual States, the automatic conferral upon the individual of a universal status of "itinerant citizen" enjoying the fundamental rights and freedoms.

The catalogue of the rights and duties that are inherent to such a "global" status may work as a starting point in order to critically re-consider the multidimensional and mutable decomposition of the concept of foreigner citizen (forced migrant) in various categories or sub-groups based on the (apodictic and arbitrary) evaluation of the degree of intensity and quality of sufferings determining the relocation from the country of origin. The most common normative classifications are, in this sense, "political refugee" (asylum seeker), "economic refugee", "environmental refugee". A comprehensive expression that is commonly used is, then, "displaced person". There are differentiated and individual regulations-safeguards for each of those different "categories" of forced migrants (stemming out from national or international sources) with significantly weak criteria of reasonableness that need to be subject to a coherence scrutiny aimed at their desirable homogenization.

Those foreigners that are not falling under one of the above-mentioned protected categories are included in other negative and residual categories, that are far from rigorous and yet very powerful and "stigmatizing", such as those of irregular or illegal migrants determining an actual humiliation of their legal identity of persons.

The "sanction" of the expulsion of illegal migrants from the territory of arrival entails, under a juridical standpoint, the even formal denial of their identity of identifiable person. It would be interesting to proceed to an inventory of the reasons underlying each particular administrative and jurisdictional expulsion measure so to verify how it fails a priori to consider and qualify the histories and wills of such migrants (forced and sans papier).

The practical reason for this approximate practice (that does not recognize the absolute individual right to move elsewhere on the grounds of an objective impossibility to reside and live in the places of origin) is the quantitative reduction of protections awarded to forced migrants by each State of arrival for domestic reasons of economic, social and political viability. Certainly, this is a question that cannot be easily neglected but, at the same time, it cannot be disguised by means of incoherent definitions and through the denial of subjective universal rights founding the corpus juris humanitatis.

In order to avoid any possible drift caused by an unreasonable selection of safeguards, a negative method of analysis should be adopted so to previously identify – on the basis of the already known practices and situations – the actions and inactions (worst practices) that represent under any circumstance unbearable violations of the rights of the person-forced migrant under many treaties, conventions and case-law by supranational courts' rulings.

A very controversial issue relates to the effective recognition of essential social rights (health, housing, education…) when, because of a lack of resources, they are insufficiently granted even to non-foreigners, i.e. citizens in need. This is one of the most insidious causes of social conflict and "racial" intolerance that may be faced, above all, through wealth redistribution policies both at the global and domestic level. From a legal standpoint, it is possible to identify two general principles in order to ensure the formal and substantial equality of individuals living in the same territorial community:

I. The principle expanding the most favorable treatment to individuals irrespective of their status, however obtained.
II. The principle of equal supportive co-participation to those activities of social and work commitment required to the beneficiaries of welfare measures also with a view

to social inclusion (e.g. in consideration of the effectiveness and reasonableness of provisions regarding works of public utility in relation to standard contractual regimes in force for the different categories of domestic workers).

Forced migrations impose their presence to the public opinion and in international politics because of their mass dimensions as a plague disrupting not only foreign populations, forced to flee their countries of origin, but the whole international community as well. Such an impact, sometimes impressionistically depicted as an invasion of locusts, seems to leave little room for normative reasoning by legal scholars, precisely because the categories of the extra-ordinary nature of events and emergency of situations produce attitudes that overcome the legal standards, that are perhaps called for a posteriori to rationalize and justify non-codified or differently codified actions.

In a similar context, the individual conceived as holder of a personal – yet forced – will disappears to be absorbed (by acceding to an organicist interpretation) in a collective and collective body ("migrants") assuming a specific and prevalent subjectivity as a fleeing "people". As a consequence, the effectiveness and appropriateness of any assistance intervention, as well as its quality, are not assessed against the essential rights of the individual, but in a predominantly economic-statistical perspective aiming for the reduction of damages deriving from migratory "waves" (how many people have been rescued, how many meals have been distributed, how many accommodation places have been granted …).

It is indeed difficult also for jurists to escape this realistic and catastrophist interpretation, opposing actual facts to the inadequateness of abstract hypotheses. Therefore, in order not to be inconclusive, the reasoning must move to a different and wider horizon: namely to the organization of the reaction of the international community – through its capacities-possibilities – to the facts causing emigrations-immigrations with disruptive effects under the political, economic and social aspects for single States or even for groups of States. It can be reasonably held that the object of the above-mentioned reactions by the international community (moreover when expressed by means of the use of force) should primarily be the triggering events and not the migrations caused by such original facts.

Migration flows, in their arduous development, should and must be handled on the basis of that duty to rescue that certainly is a supreme cogent principle of the corpus juris humanitatis and that indiscriminately concerns all those situations of danger for humankind.

A good observatory to develop such an approach and to gain an objective awareness about the facts to whom the "principle of humanity" has to be applied may be the periodic and full reports by UNHCR, [2] that not only relates the adventurous and not rarely fatal voyages (in the Mediterranean), but also extensively describes the

[2] see http://unhcr.org/ accessed on July 31st, 2018.

unbearable living conditions of the places of origin and departure of migrants.

As an example, the Report of 18 June 2015 may suggest the opportunity to theoretically re-think the 'nature' and composition of the same 'international community': the main acceleration has started in the first months of 2011, when war in Syria broke out, becoming the main cause of forced migration at the global level. In 2014, in average 42,500 persons per day have become refugees, asylum seekers or internally displaced persons; such a figure corresponds to a four-fold increase in the span of four years. All over the world, a person in 122 is currently a refugee, an internally displaced person or an asylum seeker. If the 59,5 million forced migrants in the world constituted a State, it would be the 24th country in the world in terms of population.

Faced with those blatant figures, the same formal and traditional notion of 'sovereign State', intended as an entity made up of a territory, a population and a governmental authority – either legitimated or self-legitimated – should be reconsidered. According to a conventional idea of international relations, in order to acknowledge the existence of a State, it should be enough to consider the capacity by a 'government' to manage the borders within which it purports to exercise its sovereignty.

It is precisely the theme of the relationships existing between sovereignty and States, as well as the interdependence between those two concepts, to be at the centre of disputes and reconsiderations also by the most recent political philosophy scholars. When getting away from realistic (and conservative) cages and doctrines, it becomes possible to call into question, even from a philological standpoint, the legitimacy of the (self)attribution in the definition of 'State' to those situations in which the governmental authority fails to ensure minimal living conditions to its citizens in territorial areas originally recognized at the international level as constituting a 'State' entity. In fact, the exodus of a considerable quota of population from a territory-State reveals the incapability to exercise an effective State sovereignty by the self-proclaimed governmental authorities that may, at best, demonstrate to possess apparatuses able to establish – and sufficient to ensure – simply their self-preservation. In such a way, in these cases the existence of a State entity should (could) be called into question also by international law, and be substituted by the more appropriate notion of geographically characterized 'factual power".

The fundamental question is, thus, whether the international community should include in its (even legal) organization only the States (as redefined in relation to the adequate standards of living to be granted to the population) or also those de facto authorities territorially characterized.

Forced migrations encourage further analyses when not considered as if they were irreversible catastrophic natural disasters, against which there is no remedy but to wait and take precautions for future possible scenarios.

The removal of unbearable living conditions in the places of origin of migrations is universally and abstractly recognized as the most effective and structural solution; it is also common to admit that this is a typical and imperative mission for the international community. Positions diverge on the subjects allowed to take the consequent actions that may frequently require the use of force against those territorial powers defined as "terrorist" or however "criminal".

Probably, the concept that better helps in addressing the question is "humanitarian interference". Such a qualification is particularly meaningful and suggestive since, besides recalling the corpus juris humanitatis, it also implies that any armed intervention should have as its exclusive goal the restoration of appropriate living conditions in those places that have been coactively left. Certainly, the use of force is one of the most controversial and dangerous tools (that has to be closely tied to criteria of proportionality and adequateness), but it cannot be aprioristically dropped out from the list of reactions in the hands of the international community. Sometimes, those situations are called "international policing activities", and correctly so. This is a line of enquiry that deserves to be explored, as in this dimension the notion of force (also in a military and organized sense) is conceptually different from the notion of war, that can only arise between States. Vice-versa, force has to be used against territorial criminal powers that, as already stated, cannot claim to be a part of the international community because of their inadequacy in ensuring a minimum level of adequate standards of living conditions that – as already stated – should be recognized as one of the objective requirements for the existence of a State.

Humanitarian interference can also take other forms: "rescue" (holding an episodic character) and "international cooperation" (with more lasting and structural characteristics). Differently from force, monopoly by sovereign States or groups of sovereign States, rescue and international cooperation can be exercised (also) at a more diffuse level by subjects not directly connected to State responsibility. Some actors already established themselves in the international community which has in turn recognized their legitimacy to interfere on the basis of the principles of autonomy and neutrality (i.e. the exemplary case – in a certain sense, a model – of the International Organization of the Red Cross and the conventions granting its immunity internationally); other cases are an expression of a global humanitarian governance (such as NGOs, large non-profit foundations for the achievement of human civil, political and social rights) able to manage significant private resources and to influence the strategy of official sectorial agencies revolving around the United Nations organization. It would be very indicative to list (at least above a certain level of budget allocation) those private global organizations and to assess their actual ability of general influence and economic impact on humanitarian policies in the various fields of health, culture and in the eradication of poverty. Furthermore, from the analysis of the by-laws of those private organizations and of their inspiring principles-methods it would be possible to verify their adherence to the norms of the corpus juris humanitatis. The comparison between the programmatic enunciations made by these ever more numerous and active organizations and the declarations contained in the different international conventions, both general and specific, on human rights, could give an idea on the level of humanitarian legal culture in the global civil society (Habermas).

A really problematic aspect regards the legitimization of actions of humanitarian interference, above all those with a military character intended as "international law enforcement" operations. Their goal (i.e. to re-create adequate living conditions in territories where a criminal power has been exercised) without an international entrustment is not considered, in general, to be sufficient and reassuring. Two extreme opinions have essentially been expressed: the necessity of a unanimous deliberation (or, as appropriate, of a qualified majority) of States represented in the international bodies of the United Nations or the unilateral decision even of a single State that, on the basis of the exceptional nature of the emergency, assume unilaterally a substitutive power with a universal value for the protection of human rights.

History shows the weakness of each of those positions: the first easily leads to inaction with even more disrupting effects for those populations suffering from criminal de facto powers; the second may favor interventions other than "international law enforcing" operations with exclusively humanitarian aims, but rather driven by converging economic and/or geopolitical interests.

It is necessary, therefore, to find an intermediate solution rooted in those principles derived from the sources of a corpus juris humanitatis whose re-construction is difficult but not impossible when persecuted with coherency and consistency. Some interesting inputs come from the case of assistance provided in the event of major natural disasters following a unilateral decision of single States. This is a commonly accepted case of humanitarian interference, (possibly) stemming from an international customary law rule demonstrating that the sovereignty principle can surrender before the prevailing right to life-adequate living conditions of individuals, communities, peoples.

There is room for another suggestion within the open lines of research for a consistent juridical answer to the comprehensive question of forced migrations: the idea of a "universal jurisdiction" based on the awareness that forced migrations may be construed as crimes against humanity not only because of the brutality of behaviors against those individuals forced to flee from their places of origin, but also because such conducts may cause victims and damages all along the route of their complex development. Attempts to attribute an extraterritorial jurisdiction to judges and magistrates within national legal orders to initiate investigations on crimes qualified as "international crimes" committed abroad also by foreign citizens have not been crowned by success (e.g. in Spain or Belgium), as the criterion of jurisdiction linked to sovereignty eventually prevailed.

A possible opening comes from Art. 8 of the Italian criminal code, where it affirms that "the foreign citizen committing a political crime abroad is sanctioned according to Italian law upon request by the Ministry of Justice", while also detailing that "it is a political crime any crime offending a political interest of the State".

The vagueness of this particular provision may at least spark an actualized and prospective debate on the possibility for forced migrations to be included within "political" crimes, up to represent actual genocide attempts. Nor it would seem doubtful the offence to the political interest of the State not to suffer from the tragic internal consequences of incontrollable migratory fluxes caused by external illicit conducts.

A limited diffuse jurisdiction, at least at the investigative level, would recall the need and urgency to establish an ad hoc international Criminal Court whose declaratory judgments could legitimize the use of force by the international community as a whole or, in case, by groups of States implementing the above-mentioned principle of "humanitarian intervention".

The views expressed in this chapter (a sort of pro-memoria) are certainly oriented. They suggest that before a crucial theme for global coexistence legal scholars cannot limit themselves to certify the fragmentation and – at times – the contradictory nature of the rules governing at different levels, both national and international, single aspects of migrations isolating them from the phenomenon taken as a whole. Jurists shall take a predictive role: they should systematize and bring coherency to the corpus juris humanitatis which is scattered and forgotten in a chaotic succession of sources still detached from criteria of hierarchy and competence. The identification, magis ut valeant, of the fundamental and non-negotiable principles on the freedom-will of movement in the world and, at the same time, on the minimal living conditions in territories where the "sovereignty" (in its sense as considered above) is not exercised, must not be understood as surreptitiously claiming a substitution with the legitimate public decision-makers in tragic or dramatic choices. Rather, this means, less pretentiously, to identify with sufficient clarity the universally legitimate or universally illegitimate value of actions or inactions upon which the future of mankind depends.

Chapter 23

Freedom of movement and new immigration rights

Carolina Simoncini

23.1. *A cosmopolitan theory between philosophy and law*

In the course of history, moments of political or economic crisis have stimulated critical thinking to establish new rules for a peaceful coexistence: in fact, the internal conflicts of a community generate progressive social fragmentation which philosophy often tasks itself with recreating with the prospect of a new, more balanced structure. We can thus recall Immanuel Kant's work "Perpetual Peace", written in 1795, where the author welcomed the Peace of Basel [1] with relief, wherein Revolutionary France and Prussia ended a conflict that had lasted nearly three years. The philosopher also grasped the ideological rift between Enlightenment philosophy, with which he identified, and the Prussian Empire legacy. Therefore, the signing of the peace treaty constituted, for him, the occasion to theorise the overriding of particularism and the attempt to establish a new coexistence.

Today, a similar perspective finds relevance in the speculation of the philosopher Jurgen Habermas in several dedicated works, with the evocative titles of The Postnational Constellation (2002) and The Inclusion of the Other (1998), to present remedies for widespread forms of social isolation present in contemporary society. Although, in this case, the emergency is not visibly represented by an armed conflict, but by a growing social disparity caused by an uneven distribution of resources and rights, [2] and there remains the problem of rethinking new structures that will unite the communities "of Earth" under more equal rules.

Beyond the different periods the two philosophers belong to, they suggest similar solutions: in their reasoning the adjective "cosmopolitan" recurs associated with, in Kant's case, the noun "right" and, in Habermas's case, with "democracy". In its etymology, we can find the Greek word "kosmos" which not only means "world" but also "organisation", so that both invoke a system constituted, not by a casual set of natural elements, but by an organised architecture that supports a "polis" which is a "state".

In order to realise "perpetual peace", Kant claims the necessity of creating a

[1] The Peace of Basel was signed on April 5th, 1795.

[2] See also Camerlengo 2007: 6.

"republican federation of peoples"[3] based on the principles of freedom, equality and representation, in which the partners accept being subject to common rules "giving reciprocally [...] limitation for convenient scopes" (Lemonnier 1883: 14).

From Habermas's point of view, he wishes for the transposition of such principles on "supranational" mechanisms (Habermas 2002: 45) that would constitute an "alternative to the Nation-state" (ibidem). According to him, it is necessary to found a "political community" that includes people "of any class origin" (ibidem: 49), in whom "a multicultural citizenship" (ibidem: 47) is recognised, that is to say a "political status of citizen of the world, so that they will not belong to the world organization simply through their states, but also represented by a world parliament elected by them" (ibidem: 94). According to the French jurist Delruelle, it is necessary for this scope to redefine the idea of "us" in a more inclusive way, to overcome the perspective which opposes those who belong in history and those who are excluded, those in the centre and those on the outskirts, those visible and those invisible (Delruelle 2010: 121). "We" observes Delruelle, are those inhabitants of the same Earth and those members of the same world community (ibidem: 117). This way, cosmopolitanism should become the new juridical outline of a society, contemporary and globalised, "trans-étatique et trans-nationale" (ibidem) given that because of migration flows, the geographical borders of the States do not anymore represent a singular national and cultural identity, but open up (or have to open up) to new horizons and influences.

A more recent branch of international constitutional law has tasked itself with elaborating a juridical architecture able to support this ambitious project and, for this, it has become necessary to individuate a nucleus of common rules, universally applicable to the community of the Earth. According to the consolidated theory,[4] the most useful instrument in this sense is the transformation of the international law into cosmopolitan law, that is to say the application of the first, not only to the participating States, but to an actual world federation of States, which would accept renouncing to a significant share of their sovereignty, in the name of "a universal citizenship congenial to the practical affirmation of human rights" (Camerlengo 2007: 219).

Another part of the doctrine affirms instead the necessity for a new cosmopolitan law, originating from the constant confrontation between internal institutions of a State and different States that decide to compose the "federation",[5] so that the

---

3 Kant remembers that "A state of peace among men [...] is not the same as the state of nature, which is rather a state of war. For even if it does not involve active hostilities, it involves a constant threat of their breaking out. Thus the state of peace must be formally instituted, for a suspension of hostilities is not in itself a guarantee of peace. And unless one neighbour gives a guarantee to the other at his request (which can happen only in a lawful state), the latter may treat him as an enemy". 'Toward Perpetual Peace', in Reiss 1991.

4 See also Sawodogo 2003; De Frouville 2013: 95; Falk 1995; Franceschet 2000: 277.

5 Consider Camerlengo 2007: 221, which refers to the "constant interaction between the effective national dimension (the 'place' where legislative and interpretive practices are developed following the constitutional principles included within the essential common nucleus) and a new idea of supranational ideal projection (the 'place' which *receives* the legislative and interpretive practices accepted by the individual systems)".

common nucleus of regulations is the result of a continuous dialogue between the stakeholders of the world community.

Whatever the chosen solution will be to reach the creation of universal rules of coexistence, the theories presented agree on one aspect: cosmopolitanism assumes that the Earth becomes a universal space of equality, not fragmented by the sovereignty of the States, that is to say a place in which people can freely exchange experiences to establish a shared set of rules. Following this, the aptitude for individual mobility is essential: the comparison of "differences" presumes the interaction between people coming from different parts of the world. In fact, already the civitas gentium theorised by Kant would have been based on the principle of hospitality, that is to say on the "right [...] [of not] be[ing] treated with hostility when he arrives on someone else's territory". [6] All people, in fact, "present themselves in the society of others by virtue of their right to communal possession of the earth's surface" since no one has "a greater right than anyone else to occupy any particular portion of the Earth". [7]

This thesis has been re-elaborated by Habermas with a more modern vision. He observed that migrants, as "pioneers" of movement, should not be discouraged by defence policies of nations but, on the contrary, should be "listened to". By leaving their countries with the hope of settling into another, they clearly express what the actual needs of people who move around in the world are, which the creation of cosmopolitan regulation should revolve around.

In this chapter, the content of the latter will not be covered, as many studies have already been dedicated to the topic, [8] but it will instead examine the topic of circulation laws in the world territory as a preliminary instrument to spot the needs of people aspiring to become a citizen of the world and, subsequently on this basis, to establish the cosmopolitan right.

23.2. *International humanitarian law as a starting point for a juridical cosmopolitan theory*

To investigate the nature of freedom of movement, it is first necessary to consider the international humanitarian law [9] which, like Kant's cosmopolitanism on the philosophical level, is concerned with granting peaceful coexistence through juridical

[6] 'Toward Perpetual Peace', in Reiss 1991.

[7] *Ibidem.*

[8] Please refer to the many contributions on the topic such as: Camerlengo 2007; Delruelle 2010; Taraborrelli 2004; Bettinelli 2006: 959.

[9] See also Nascimbene 2006: 369 ff.

protection of human rights. [10] They are undergoing a process of "democratisation" [11] which is bringing a universal perspective [12] to the discussion, granting the gradual expansion of human rights across borders.

The juridical starting point of the cosmopolitan theory is certainly the Universal Declaration of Human Rights: [13] their protection constitutes "the ground for freedom, justice and peace in the world" (Pocar 1989: 31). It is "essential to avoid that the individual is forced to revolt against tyranny and oppression, and it contributes to the development of friendly relationships between people" (ibidem). Like the philosophical idea previously mentioned, the Declaration was also conceived in order to mend social and political fractures, prompted by the plight of the Second World War. [14] For this reason, a catalogue of fundamental rights was composed which assumes a universal value, since it assumes its validity through public consent: [15] the majority of the world's inhabitants have, in this way, freely and explicitly accepted sharing a peaceful modus vivendi.

The fulcrum of this protective, universal "contract" is mankind: art. 6 recognises for each individual the right to juridical personhood "anywhere", establishing the foundation for "equality space" which allows anyone to move around in the territory of the world without ever losing his or her identity. All the other essential recognitions are built upon this cornerstone, [16] assembled into four pillars which are personal rights (including the right to equality and the right to life); recognised rights of the individuals in their social relations (including the right to privacy, the right to marry and the right to own property); political rights (including freedom of thought and freedom of assembly); economic and social rights (such as, for example, the right to work and the right to equal remuneration). [17]

Even if, in itself, the Universal Declaration of Human Rights does not have binding

[10] Refer to Nascimbene 2006 and Bobbio 1997: VII.

[11] This term was created by Bobbio 1997: VIII.

[12] As correctly underlined by Cassese (1988: 143) international humanitarian law offers "the emergence of the individual inside a space previously reserved exclusively to sovereign States". On the universal nature of fundamental rights as a premise for the foundation of a cosmopolitan constitutional structure, refer to Camerlengo 2007.

[13] The Declaration has been signed in Paris, on December 10th, 1948, at the General Assembly of the United Nations with 48 votes in favour by Member States, no contrary vote and abstention of Saudi Arabia, South Africa and the six States of the communist countries (Soviet Union, Poland, Czechoslovakia, Yugoslavia, Ukraine, Belarus).

[14] It is significant, in this sense, the fact that in the preface it is specified that "the nonrecognition and the disdain of human rights have brought to barbaric acts which offend the conscience of humanity".

[15] See Bobbio 1997: 18, in which he observes that "*consensus omnium gentium*" is concentrated in the Universal Declaration of Human Rights.

[16] Right to juridical personhood has been described by Nowak 2005: 152 as a "*pre-condition*" and by Detrick 1999: 13 as a "*conditio sine qua non*" for the exercise of every other right.

[17] Regarding this partition, consider Nascimbene 2006: 370.

validity, it represents the juridical and political basis [18] of the following acts or "contracts" of international human rights, such as the International Bill of Human Rights [19] and the International Covenant on Economic, Social and Cultural Rights. [20] The corpus of these recognitions constitutes a kind of fundamental charter of human rights (Nascimbene 2006: 386) which aims to ensure formal equality between individuals.

Yet, the fact that people are not born into and do not live in the same conditions does not elude international law, so that the need for a substantial equality dictates to specifically safeguard some categories of "under-protected" people (Bettinelli 2012: 129). Therefore, the pursuit of universal peace is improved by assisting those with weak status due to gender, age, origin, and political discrimination with the goal, as stated by Bobbio, to expand protection for people, not based on an abstract idea anymore as in the Universal Declaration of Human Rights, but based on a pragmatic one (Bobbio 1997: 11). This way, the safeguarded rights become gradually more specific depending on the discrimination to overcome and the gap to bridge for effective equality. [21]

In this sense, we can think of the Convention of the Rights of the Child [22] which aims to protect an ontologically weak category: the children's rights to rest, to free time, to play and to recreational activities [23] are safeguarded with the awareness, as specified in the Preamble, that "childhood is entitled to special care and assistance".

In the same way, the signatory States of the International Convention on the Elimination of All Forms of Discrimination Against Women [24] have admitted being "concerned [...] [that] extensive discrimination against women continues to exist" [25] and have consequently decided to commit to the elimination of sexual abuse, uxoricide, subjugation, domestic violence, exploitation of prostitution and genital mutilation.

Foreign migrants looking for new possibilities in a country different from that of their origin cannot be disregarded as a weak category. There are numerous Conventions which safeguard different aspects and moments of their itinerant life; it suffices considering the Declaration on the Human Rights of Individuals Who Are Not Nationals of the Country in Which They Live, [26] already from the moment of their entrance into the country. The International Convention on the Protection of the Rights of All Migrant Workers and Members of Their Families [27] is dedicated to the

---

[18] See Nascimbene 2006: 377.

[19] New York, 1966.

[20] New York, 1967.

[21] See Cassese 1988: 74.

[22] New York, 1989.

[23] Art. 31 of the Convention.

[24] New York, 1979.

[25] Preamble of the Convention.

[26] New York, 1985.

[27] New York, 1990.

integration of foreigners in the working world, binding the signatory State to the application of a principle of non-discrimination towards citizens concerning working conditions, social security, freedom of association and the safeguard of individual cultural identity.

If such an international system of protection is articulated, evidently, around a general safeguard of people, integrated with specific protection for some categories of "weaker" individuals, it could be possible anyway to find some cross-freedom present in more or less all of the International Conventions. Those are the rights that constitute the fundamental core of human identity and, as such, they sustain more specific safeguards that would otherwise be lacking the supporting pillars, remaining mere declarations of principles.

Within these supporting rights, we can find also freedom of movement and residency that, as mentioned above, assumes a central importance since it is the only recognition that could actually allow humans to move to different parts of the Earth to share experiences, and in this way to also become "co-inhabitants" [28] of a space of common equality.

In the field of international humanitarian law, such freedom is mainly safeguarded by art. 13 of the Universal Declaration of Human Rights [29] and by art. 12 of the International Covenant on Civil and Political Rights. [30] It constitutes an essential component of the fundamental charter of mankind [31] in its dynamic (circulation) and its static (residency) relationship with the territory of the States. [32] The United Nations

---

[28] 'Toward Perpetual Peace', in Reiss 1991. See also Gozzi 2001: 69, where it is affirmed that "it is the duty to hospitality, imminent from Kant's idea of cosmopolitan rights, that pushes a complex system towards the adoption of corrective initiatives. Actually, direct contact with experiences from those in other countries, which takes place also in the case in which the citizen of another State enters national territory, vigorously urging for a critical verification of their institutes and of their normative practices. The duty to hospitality, if honestly perceived, should promote a qualitative increase of safeguard levels of rights, moreover benefitting also the citizens".

[29] Art. 13: Everyone has the right to freedom of movement and residence within the borders of each State. Everyone has the right to leave any country, including his own, and to return to his country.

[30] Art. 12: Everyone lawfully within the territory of a State shall, within that territory, have the right to liberty of movement and freedom to choose his residence.

2. Everyone shall be free to leave any country, including his own.

3. The above-mentioned rights shall not be subject to any restrictions except those which are provided by law, are necessary to protect national security, public order (ordre public), public health or morals or the rights and freedoms of others, and are consistent with the other rights recognised in the present Covenant.

4. No one shall be arbitrarily deprived of the right to enter his own country.

[31] This is in fact recognised for every man: article 13 of the Universal Declaration of Human Rights uses the term "everyone".

[32] See also Grahl-Madsen et al. 1999: 267, where they state "the provisions of article 13 concern the basic relationship between the State and the individual. Where serfdom or bondage exist (as in Prussia and Imperial Russia into the 19th century or in Denmark in the 18th century) there is no freedom of movement or of residence, not to mention any right to leave the country altogether for those persons who are under the yoke".

Commission on Human Rights has, in this sense, observed that the other rights contemplated by the Declaration can be protected only if this extremely fundamental recognition is preliminarily safeguarded. [33] It is also peculiar in its formulation: the two dimensions are, in fact, expressed not only jointly, but also in the same order, that is to say firstly movement and then residence. [34] This is expressed first of all under a chronological criterion: the individual is protected while their journey is in progress: in the first phase, when they circulate and therefore move, leaving the place where they are and, in the second phase, when they find the need to stay somewhere, settling in a new space. A second criterion is "causal": as underlined by the prevalent doctrine, freedom of movement has a "primary" nature because, in its absence, the person would not even try to "satisfy their very diverse needs in their own or in another state where they intend to or need to go or where there may be stability" (Nascimbene 1984: 223); in this perspective, residence shapes itself as a mere consequence, that is to say a necessary moment that takes place only later, giving meaning to the decision of moving.

This reading, which identifies circulation as the cause and residence as an effect, emerges also from art. 12 of the International Covenant on Civil and Political Rights which does not refer to "liberty of movement and residence", but more precisely, like in a hendiadys, "liberty of movement and freedom to choose his residence". [35] This information stems from the idea that circulation is the "engine" of a general project which will entail the choice of stopping and "putting roots down".

This perspective is welcomed also by specific levels of protection under international humanitarian law. In fact, amongst "regional" Conventions (Nascimbene 2006: 386), article 2 Protocol 4 of the European Convention on Human Rights recognises that everyone lawfully in the territory of a State "[has] the right to liberty of movement

---

[33] Commission of human rights, Sub-commission on prevention of discrimination and protection of minorities E/CN.4/Sub. 2/1997/22, 29th July, 1997. In the report it is observed that movement and residence freedom constitutes an "integral part" of article 3 of the Declaration, which safeguards the right to life, freedom and safety of people; in the same way, the right to look and find, in other countries, asylum from persecution, protected by article 14 of the Declaration, which is defined as a "very important component of freedom of movement" and, in this sense, also article 4, which prohibits slavery which would be "inconceivable in the context of the right of everyone to freedom of movement".

[34] See how art. 2 of Protocol No. 4 of the European Convention on Human Rights which recognises for everyone "lawfully within the territory of a State [...] the right to [move freely] and freedom to choose his residence" and in addition art. 45 of the Charter of Fundamental Rights of the European Union which states "every citizen of the Union has the right to move and reside freely within the territory of the Member States". Also art. 16 of the Italian Constitution states "every citizen has the right to reside and travel freely in any part of the country".

[35] In order to safeguard this specific freedom of choice, the UN Commission on Human Rights, when examining the political situation in Israel in 1998, judged the directive of the Israeli Minister of Internal Affairs, which imposed on the Palestinian citizens who wanted to reside in the east area of Jerusalem the obligation to demonstrate that such area represented for them "the centre of life" in the past seven years, against article 12 of the Covenant. See also the document "Concluding Observations on Israel", (1998) UN doc.CCPR/C/79/Add.93.

and freedom to choose his residence".[36] In the same way, art. 12 of the African Charter on Human and Peoples' Rights[37] recognises for everyone "the right to freedom of movement and residence within the borders of a State".[38]

This cause/effect criterion which links circulation to residency has been confirmed, on the contrary, also by regulations that limit the entry of foreigners. The abovementioned international sources indeed recognise the right of movement and residency of citizens in their home country, but not of foreigners that may leave their country but not enter into another, without authorisation.[39] In other words and, ironically, the universal freedom of emigrating does not correspond to the effective freedom of immigrating.[40] The same contradiction can also be found in the Declaration on the Human Rights of Individuals Who Are Not Nationals of the Country in Which They Live which, even though it is intended to safeguard migrants, it points out in art. 2 that no regulation in the Declaration shall prejudice the enjoyment of the rights accorded by domestic law regarding the entry of foreigners.[41]

The European Court of Human Rights maintains a consolidated position: in the

---

[36] See Bartole et al. 2001: 882, where the authors highlight how the two rights "are in a way complementary. If the individual should be able to circulate, that is to say move freely on the territory of the State, it is obvious that he should also be able to decide to settle in any area, be it a short stay or long enough to cover the concept of 'residency'".

[37] Nairobi, 1981.

[38] Because of its transversal nature, freedom of movement and residence is safeguarded also by conventions which safeguard the individual weak statuses. Art. 15 par. 4 of the Convention on the Elimination of All Forms of Discrimination against Women states that all States Parties "shall accord to men and women the same rights with regard to the law relating to the movement of persons and the freedom to choose their residence and domicile".

[39] For a long time, the international doctrine has been questioning the existence of an immigration right, generating contrasting opinions: on one side the supporters of a right to free movement within States and on the other the supporters of a right of discretional exclusion. Yet, international sources do not consider the unlimited right to immigrate in a country different from the one of origin. Please refer to Quadri 2006: 81 "The analysis of the international practice on the topic has highlighted that each State has always tried to satisfy two needs: on the one hand, the defence of their sovereignty and safety; on the other hand, the concession to foreigners to a minimal equalitarian treatment, in order to avoid retaliation upon their citizens who had to move abroad". This position reflects the doctrine debate of the first half of the 19th century which saw the opposition of the natural law theory, affirming the existence of a right of immigration, opposed to Positivism, according to which the recognition of rights to foreigners succumbs in front of the absolute power of sovereignty of the State on its territory. See also Nascimbene 2013: 45, 1984: 223; Flauss 2010: 47, which affirms "selon une opinion dominante en droit international, la souveraineté de l'Etat s'analyse comme une compétence certes non plus arbitraire, mais néanmoins encore discrétionnaire. En d'autres termes, l'Etat est libre, sous réserve d'engagements ou d'obligations internationaux s'imposant à lui, de règlementer l'admission des étrangers sur son territoire".

[40] See Favilli 2012: 675.

[41] Resolution No. 47/144 of December 13th, 1985, article 2 of the French text: "rien dans la présente Déclaration ne doit s'entendre [...] comme restreignant le droit de tout Etat d'édicter des lois et règlements concernant l'entrée des étrangers". In the same position we can find the Asian–African Legal Consultative Organization which recognises the full right of the States to limit the entry of foreigners. See Charpentier 1997: 56.

case Vilvarajah and Others, [42] for example, the judges dealt with some citizens from Sri Lanka who were denied the recognition of their right to asylum by the United Kingdom. According to the British Government, the abuses they had endured in their country of origin were not demonstrated to be as inhumane and degrading as necessary to be in accordance with art. 3 of the ECHR, justifying the protection besought. The Court confirmed that, in this case, there was a lack of "motifs sérieux et avérés de croire que l'intéressé courra, dans le pays de destination, un risque réel d'être soumis à la torture ou à des peines ou traitements inhumains ou dégradants". [43] To support their arguments, the judges later added that, if the right of asylum had been recognised in any case where a generic risk of abuse in the country of origin is outlined, the entry "of a potentially very large class of people with the attendant serious social and economic consequences" [44] would be authorised.

Therefore, the reason clearly emerges as to why the power to deny entry to foreigners is given to the States: receiving them would mean making arrangements for their stay, evidently leading to a cost that would burden the States' government budget. So, also from this point of view, circulation is naturally a priority: it is sufficient to deny it (namely deny the right to entry) to prevent the exercise of the right to residence which gets downgraded to a mere avoidable consequence.

Freedom of movement and residence become abstract in this criterion of cause/effect. It assumes a "negative" value from the point of view of those States receiving migration flows (preventing entry in order to prevent residence) as opposed to the "active" value from the point of view of those who insist on fully exercising their fundamental right (since they circulate and move, they should have the right to stop and settle down).

These "active" subjects can be included in different categories based on the reason behind their decision to move. On the one hand, we have those who freely decide to move and settle temporarily somewhere else, and on the other hand, we have migrants for whom moving and settling is not an option, but an unavoidable and definite need, since the economic and political conditions of their countries of origin do not allow them to carry on a respectable existence. Recognition under examination is not "just" a fundamental right for them, but a vital right which pertains inherently to their status. Therefore, as previously mentioned, a cosmopolitan right that aims to make the Earth an egalitarian space of welcome should be constructed around the needs of those particular "pioneers" of movement. For this purpose, it is necessary to understand how migrants actually perceive freedom of movement and residence, and verify if the current formulations of this recognition are compatible with their essential needs.

---

[42] European Court of Human Rights, judgement of October 30th, 1991, *Vilvarajah and Others v. the United Kingdom*, series A, No. 215.

[43] Paragraph 90 of the Judgement. In a similar position is the Judgement of February 19th, 1996, *Gul v. Switzerland*, Recueil 1996-1, p. 174.

[44] Paragraph 105 of the Judgement.

23.3. *Freedom of movement and residence for migrants*

The most traditional doctrine defines freedom of movement and residence as "the transfer of a person in a State in which they are not nationals with the aim of residing there" (Mazziotti 1960: 14). Such a notion seems to address mainly the migrants, because it seems to exclude the temporary circulation from one State to the other if there is no the aim of residing.

However, as we have previously observed, international law introduces limitations that reduce the exercise of this freedom by migrants. The States' fear of offering indiscriminate reception of foreigners leaves migrants' circulation and residence with an active and unfinished status because of its uncertain outcome.

On the other hand, international humanitarian law is concerned with defining the status of foreigners who have entered into the host country legally, for whom a wide range of civil and social rights are recognised.

For this purpose, UN Resolution No. 0/144[45] safeguards the rights of individuals who are not nationals in the country they reside in. It is stated, in art. 5 par. 3, that "aliens lawfully in the territory of a State shall enjoy the right to liberty of movement and freedom to choose their residence within the borders of the State". The Resolution, because it is specifically dedicated to migrants, considers freedom of movement and of residence as the central point around which all the rights revolve. The latter constitute specific needs that have to be satisfied to ensure that the life choices of migrants is safeguarded in a dignified and safe manner.

For this purpose, the conditions for adequate reception of immigrants are set: the rights to legal and linguistic assistance to understand, for example, the regulations that govern entry into a host country, are granted. In addition to this, the right to found a family (art. 5, 1, d), the right to retain their own language, culture and tradition (art. 5, 1, f), the right to fair wages (art. 8, 1, a), and the right to health protection (art. 8, 1, c) are granted. Finally, the Resolution is conscious of the difficulties, including economic ones, presented by the uprooting of people from their countries of origin: art. 5, 1, g safeguards the right to "transfer earnings, savings or other personal monetary assets [abroad]".

Moreover, international humanitarian law deals with specifically protecting migrants from different situations which may distinguish the migrant's stay in a new country. The consideration of "integration" as an essential condition of a protected stay in a State is present firstly in the International Convention on the Protection of the Rights of All Migrant Workers and Members of Their Families.[46] In order to give the most inclusive definition, art. 2 broadly designates "Migrant Workers" as those who "[are] to be engaged, [are] engaged or [have] been engaged in a remunerated activity in a State of which he or she is not a national". Despite the definition of

---

[45] Resolution adopted by the General Assembly of the United Nations on December 13th, 1985.

[46] New York, 1990.

"migrants", who are explicitly defined by their need to move to look for new possibilities in life, the prediction is concentrated on inclusive working conditions in the receiving countries. The migrants neglect the dynamic aspect of circulation, which determines the whole existential path of the migrant until a moderately stable "landing" is achieved. Only the migrants' "not belonging" to the State makes the flows of migration apparent, which is here observed at its end stage. This way the Convention concentrates on social rights essential for integration, such as the right to work, to adequate remuneration,[47] to take part in meetings and activities of trade unions,[48] to enjoy the same treatment granted to nationals with respect to social security,[49] to receive any medical care that is urgently required "for the preservation of their life or the avoidance of irreparable harm to their health on the basis of equality of treatment with nationals of the State concerned".[50]

In the same vein, article 6 of the ILO Convention No. 97 of 1949 underlines that every State undertakes to apply to immigrants lawfully within its territory, equivalent treatment to that which it applies to its own nationals in the matter of job and social rights. Similarly, article 10 of the ILO Convention No. 43 of 1975[51] forces each State to "declare and pursue a national policy designed to promote and to guarantee, by methods appropriate to national conditions and practice, equality of opportunity and treatment in respect of employment and occupation, of social security, of trade union and cultural rights and of individual and collective freedoms for persons who as migrant workers or as members of their families are lawfully within its territory".

Such a principle has been received also by the European Court of Human Rights which, with a prominent body of laws, has interpreted article 1 of Protocol 1, safeguarding the right to peaceful enjoyment of property, in union with art. 14 of the ECHR, which ratifies the principle of non-discrimination in the enjoyment of the right safeguarded by the Convention. In accordance, judges have affirmed the discriminatory nature of the imbalanced treatment, applied in some States, between citizens and foreigners when benefitting from welfare.[52] In the case Gaygusuz v. Austria,[53] for example, a Turkish citizen, who had worked in Austria for 11 years, requested Linz's employment agency to recognize his right to an accrued pension, which he was denied because he failed the criterion of Austrian nationality. The Court, pleading the combined provision of the aforementioned regulations, declared that the discrimination

---

[47] Article 25.

[48] Article 26.

[49] Article 27.

[50] Article 28.

[51] Geneva, 1975. The Convention was dedicated to migrations in abusive conditions and to the promotion of equal opportunities and treatment of migrant workers.

[52] Refer to, among others, the Judgement of October 25th, 2005, *Willis v. United Kingdom*, Recueil, 2008.

[53] Judgement of September 16th, 1996, Recueil 1996-IV.

"has no objective and reasonable justification" because "it does not pursue a legitimate aim" and because there is no "reasonable relationship of proportionality between the means employed and the aim sought to be realised". [54]

Similarly, in the judgement of Koua Poirrez v. France [55] the Court recognised an Ivorian citizen's right to a welfare check, considering the French regulations discriminatory, which recognised such services only for its citizens and to those with which France finalised reciprocal agreements.

Moreover, international humanitarian law deals with safeguarding the migrants' health: article 5 of the ILO Convention No. 97 of 1949 bounds the member states to maintain appropriate medical services in order to ascertain "both at the time of departure and on arrival, that migrants for employment and the members of their families [...] are in reasonable health" and "ensure that migrants for employment and members of their families enjoy adequate medical attention and good hygienic conditions at the time of departure, during the journey and on arrival in the territory of destination". Similarly, in the European Convention on the Legal Status of Migrants [56] article 19 states that Each Contracting Party undertakes to grant to migrant workers and members of their families, social and medical assistance on the same basis as nationals.

Right to education is equally relevant and safeguarded by article 14 of the European Convention on the Legal Status of Migrants, according to which migrant workers and members of their families officially admitted to the territory of a Contracting Party shall be entitled to general education, vocational training and retraining, and shall be granted access to higher education, on the same basis and under the same conditions as national workers. Moreover, article 2 of Protocol No. 1 of the European Convention on Human Rights qualifies education as a right that "shall [not] be denied" to anyone. The European Court of Human Rights understood this principle: in the case of Ponomaryovi v. Bulgaria, [57] the Court has considered the obligation to pay taxes to enrol in high school discriminatory, as it was imposed on non-Europeans, and not expected from Bulgarian citizens, therefore violating the combined provision of article 14 of the ECHR and article 2 Protocol 1 of the Convention.

International conventions also oversee safeguarding the right of the migrants to a family, as an essential factor for successful integration. In line with this, article 29 of the Convention on the Protection of the Rights of All Migrant Workers and Members of Their Families acknowledges that "each child of a migrant worker shall have the right to a name, to registration of birth and to a nationality". Article 30 safeguards the right to "education on the basis of equality of treatment with [regard to] nationals of the State". Naturally, protection of the right to a family is tightly bound to the right to adequate accommodation, protected in article 6 of the ILO Convention No. 97 of

---

[54] Paragraph 42 of the Judgement.

[55] Judgement of September 30th, 2003, Recueil 2003-X.

[56] Strasbourg 1977.

[57] Judgement of November 28th, 2011, Recueil 2011.

1949[58] and in article 8 of the European Convention of Human Rights which establishes that "everyone has the right to respect for his private and family life, his home and his correspondence". So, the European Court of Human Rights, in the case Moldvan and Others v. Romania,[59] acknowledged the violation of this last provision when some Romani citizens lived for several years in mixed-use accommodation and unhealthy conditions in an environment that caused damage to their health and physical and mental balance.

Therefore, even if they handle the safeguarding of migrants (those who, by definition, have to move to look elsewhere for new opportunities in life) the examined conventions focus mainly on the safeguard of residency situations, neglecting protecting, in a way as detailed, the phases of circulation, perceived as a state of affairs and seemingly as a secondary issue. In fact, foreigners who benefit from the "human rights" reconstructed in their essential traits, have been able to reach their country of destination. For this reason, residency can be considered the reason for the migration path.

This interpretation seems to be confirmed by provisions which recognise some of the social rights also for illegal aliens present in the state territory. International humanitarian law evidently considers residence in a state as a core phase which should be safeguarded regardless of the way with which migrants attained it. Article 10 of the ILO Convention No. 143 of 1975 is significant in that it guarantees to irregular migrants equality of opportunity and treatment in regard to employment and occupation, social security, trade union and cultural rights. It is moreover stated that the Members commit to respect fundamental rights of migrant workers regardless of the existence of legal status. Article 9 adds that illegal migrant workers shall enjoy equality of treatment for themselves and their families in regards to rights arising out of past employment pertaining to remuneration, social security and other benefits. Paragraph 2 points out that "in case of dispute about the rights referred to in the preceding paragraph, the worker shall have the possibility of presenting his case to a competent body, either himself or through a representative". Also, article 24 of the Convention on the Rights of the Child establishes that no child should be deprived of his or her rights because of their legal status. Article 30 of the Convention on the Protection of the Rights of All Migrant Workers and Members of Their Families deals with recognising the right of every child of a migrant worker to have access to education on the basis of equality of treatment with nationals of the State, specifying that access to public educational institutions shall not be refused or limited by reason of the legal status with respect to stay or employment of either parent or by reason of the legal status of the child's stay in the State of employment.

The body of laws of the European Court of Human Rights has also demonstrated a certain attention towards migrants' residence, even if illegal: it has, in fact, spotted a

---

58 Each Member State undertakes to apply, with treatment no less favourable than that which it applies to its own nationals in respect of accommodation.

59 Judgement of July 12th, 2005, Recueil 2005.

violation of article 3 of the Convention[60] in the case of the expulsion of a non-EU citizen, illegally residing in the United Kingdom, since this measure meant the interruption of medical care with dramatic repercussions on the individual's life.[61]

23.4. *The conditions for a cosmopolitan theory*

The examination of the international conventions dedicated to migrants shows that the "good" they mainly look for is "belonging to the community" (Biondi Dal Monte 2013: 3) with the consequent enjoyment of social rights. In fact, as correctly highlighted by the French jurist Ripert, social rights have the goal of "ensur[ing] equality of living situations despite the differences in wealth" (Ripert 1936). Therefore, to construct cosmopolitan rights, based on the needs of migrants, we will have to understand that integration is a necessary condition of fulfilment. This involves an inversion of the "cause/effect" dynamic which connects freedom of movement to that of residence in general international conventions. For migrants, residence is not just a consequence of movement, but it is the main objective which justifies uprooting and abandoning their country of origin. Circulation assumes, in this way, the form of an instrument, essential for reaching the final goal.

This configuration, which considers the dynamic dimension as functional to the main static dimension, can find, in addition, its theoretical basis in the thoughts of those jurists who, reinterpreting Kant's ideas in a contemporary way, invoke the recognition of a new right to hospitality,[62] that is to say, the right "de tout homme venant d'ailleurs (avec sa culture, sa langue, sa religion, son mode de vie) d'être accueilli et respecté dans sa singularité et dans son alterité" (Delruelle 2010: 121). This seems coherent with the progressive process "d'humanisation du droit international" (Flauss 2010: 47) which, according to the French legal expert Flauss, leads to a reinterpretation of the concept of State "sovereignty" interpreted, not as a "compétence" anymore, but as a "responsabilité de protection" (ibidem) towards migrants.

If international humanitarian law tends to favour the pursuit of "desirable things", as Bobbio (1997: 18) stated, it should be clear that the real "protection" invoked by migrants consists in the recognition not of the right of movement and residence, but of the right to free circulation to find residence.

---

[60] The article states that "No one shall be subjected to torture or to inhuman or degrading treatment or punishment".

[61] We refer to Judgement *D-v. United Kingdom* of May 2nd, 1997, Recueil 1997-III.

[62] Refer also to this work of Colletta's inspiration edited by Carlier 2010, and, especially, the contributions of Delruelle and Flauss.

Bibliography

Bartole, S., Conforti, B. and Raimondi, G. (2001) *Commentario alla Convenzione europea per la tutela dei diritti dell'uomo e delle libertà fondamentali*, Padua: Cedam.

Bettinelli, E. (2006) 'Verso il cosmopolitismo universale?' in S. Staiano (ed.) *Giurisprudenza costituzionale e principi fondamentali*, Turin: Giappichelli, 959–968.

Bettinelli, E. (2012) 'Il clandestino: persona senza status?' in M. D'Amico and B. Randazzo (eds.) *Alle frontiere del diritto costituzionale. Scritti in onore di Valerio Onida*, Milan: Giuffrè, 127–146.

Biondi Dal Monte, F. (2013) *Dai diritti sociali alla cittadinanza. La condizione giuridica dello straniero tra ordinamento italiano e prospettive internazionali*, Turin: Giappichelli.

Bobbio, N. (1997) *L'età dei diritti*, Turin: Einaudi.

Camerlengo, Q. (2007) *Contributo ad una teoria del diritto costituzionale cosmopolitico*, Milan: Giuffré.

Carlier, J. (ed.) (2010) *L'étranger face au droit: XXes journées d'études juridiques Jean Dabin*, Bruxelles: Bruylant.

Cassese, A. (1988) *I diritti umani nel mondo contemporaneo*, Bari: Laterza.

Charpentier, J. (1997) *L'étranger en droit international, Institut des hautes études internationales*, Université de Paris, cours 1996/1997.

De Frouville, O. (2013) 'Perspectives du droit cosmopolitique sur la responsabilité de protéger', *Droits*, 57: 95–118.

Delruelle, E. (2010) 'Démocratie, cosmopolitisme et hospitalité', in J. Carlier (ed.) op. cit., 113–124.

Detrick, S. (1999) *A Commentary on the United Nations Convention on the Rights of the Child*, The Hague: Martinus Nijhoff.

Falk, R. (1995) *On Human Governance*, Cambridge: Pennsylvania State University Press.

Favilli, C. (2012) 'Immigrazione' in *Enciclopedia del diritto*, Milan: Giuffrè, 675.

Flauss, J.F. (2010) 'L'étranger, entre souveraineté nationale et droits de l'homme. Les principes en droit international' in J.-Y. Carlier (ed.) *L'étranger face au droit*, Bruxelles: Bruylant, 45–74.

Franceschet, A. (2000) 'Popular sovereignty or cosmopolitan democracy? Liberalism, Kant and international reform', *European Journal of International Relations*, 6(2): 277–302.

Gozzi, G. (2001) 'Diritti dell'uomo e diritto cosmopolitico. Radici kantiane nell'odierno dibattito sui diritti' in G. Cavallari (ed.) *Comunità, individuo e globalizzazione*, Rome: Carocci, 69–93.

Grahl-Madsen, A., Melander, G. and Ring, R. (1999) 'Article 13' in G. Alfreddson and A. Eide (eds.) *The Universal Declaration of Human Rights*, The Hague: Martinus Nijhoff, 265–278.

Habermas, J. (1998) *The Inclusion of the Other: Studies in Political Theory, Italian edition*, Milan: Feltrinelli.

Habermas, J. (2002) *The Postnational Constellation: Political Essays*, Italian edition, Milan: Feltrinelli.

Lemonnier, C. (1883) 'Un giudizio sulla pace perpetua' in I. Kant, *Perpetual Peace: A Philosophical Sketch*, Italian edition, Milan: Sonzogno.

Mazziotti, M. (1960) 'Circolazione e soggiorno (libertà di)' in *Enciclopedia del diritto*, VII, Milan: Giuffrè, 14–18.

Nascimbene, B. (1984) *Il trattamento dello straniero nel diritto internazionale ed europeo*, Milan: Giuffrè.

Nascimbene, B. (2006) 'L'individuo e la tutela internazionale dei diritti umani' in S.M. Carbone, R. Luzzatto, A. Santamaria (eds.) *Istituzioni di diritto internazionale*, Turin: Giappichelli.

Nascimbene, B. (2013) *Lo straniero nel diritto internazionale*, Milan: Giuffrè.

Nowak, M. (2005) *United Nation Covenant on Civil and Political Rights*, Kehl: Engel.

Pocar, F. (1989) 'La dichiarazione universale dei diritti dell'uomo, fonte di un nuovo diritto internazionale' in Vv.Aa. *I diritti umani a 40 anni dalla Dichiarazione universale*, Padua: Cedam.

Quadri, S. (2006) *Le migrazioni internazionali. Da una disciplina statale dell'immigrazione al diritto internazionale delle migrazioni*, Naples: Editoriale Scientifica.

Reiss, H. (1991) *Kant: Political Writings*, 2nd edition, Cambridge: Cambridge University Press.

Ripert, G. (1936) *Le régime démocratique et le droit civil moderne*, Paris: Librairie générale de droit et de jurisprudence.

Sawodogo, K.D. (2003) *De l'universalité de droit et la particularité des états: le cosmopolitisme juridique kantien comme horizon de salut pour la philosophie politique et la philosophie du droit international*, Villeneuve-d'Ascq: ANRT.

Taraborrelli, A. (2004) *Cosmopolitismo, Dal cittadino del mondo al mondo dei cittadini*, Trieste: Asterios.

Chapter 24

International law as limit to States' discretion on migration and the urge for alternative legal pathways

Humanitarian corridors opened by private sponsors in Italy

Cristina Campiglio and Carola Ricci [1]

24.1. *Introduction*

Whilst little doubt exists on the subsistence of general international law rules relating to the treatment of aliens [2] settled in the territory of a State, [3] it is still difficult to define an international legal regime on migrations binding upon all States. In fact, the issue is, in principle, a matter of exclusive competence (reserved domain or "domestic jurisdiction") of a State: territorial sovereignty implies the exclusive right for each State to protect its borders from uncontrolled fluxes of migrants, [4] and therefore to regulate in absolute freedom the entrance – as well as the residence, expulsion and extradition, and mass expulsion (refoulement) – of aliens on its territory (Nascimbene 1984: 220 ff, 2005: 71 ff). This right is counterbalanced by the obligation to respect relevant legal frameworks in force in other States, and to act with a minimum standard of diligence

[1] To Cristina Campiglio must be referred the first four paragraphs, and to Carola Ricci the remaining paragraphs.

[2] The definition of alien may be inferred from that of citizen, intended as an individual holding the nationality of a given State. In the past, in the framework of the Council of Europe, the following definition had been proposed: aliens are those who "have no actual right to nationality in a State, whether they are merely passing through a country or reside or are domiciled in it, whether they are refugees or entered the country on their own initiative, or whether they are stateless or possess another nationality" (Doc. DH/Exo/Misc. (62) 11, 9 March 1962, 505).

[3] At present, two principles in the international legal order regulate the treatment of aliens: the proportionality in the exercise of State authority on the basis of the "attachment" of an individual to a territorial community, and the obligation to protect such an individual by taking all the necessary preventive and protective measures in case of offenses against him/her. In case of violation by the territorial State, and provided that all internal remedies have been exhausted, the foreign State of origin has the right to act in protection of its citizen (so-called diplomatic protection). See, *inter alia*, Conforti 2018: 248 ff.

[4] In general, a migrant can be defined as someone fleeing his/her home State, towards a foreign State with the intention to get established there for a given period of time.

in order to avoid any violation of their rules. Thus, a State is responsible for violating the territorial sovereignty of another State whenever it fails to fulfill such an obligation stemming out from general international law (e.g. by not adopting the necessary measures to prevent or take action against the use of both vessels flying their own flag, and ports located in its territory, for the illegal trafficking of migrants). A further obligation pending upon all States is to allow their emigrated nationals to re-enter the country.

Exception made for these two obligations, States are completely free to adopt all the policy and legal measures they deem to be adequate. This does not exclude, however, that in the field of migration States could voluntarily – i.e. by means of international agreements, either bilateral or multilateral – decide to take more compelling obligations *vis-à-vis* individual States while at the same time retaining absolute discretion with regard to the management of migrants coming from other States.

24.2. *Entrance, residence and expulsion: universal rules*

The international debate on the existence of an individual right to migrate traces back its origin to the claims made by Europeans to settle in the freshly-conquered territories of the New World, and it is deeply rooted in the doctrines of natural law. [5]

Nowadays, it is not possible to affirm the existence of a general international rule entitling an individual to enter or reside in a State other than their national State, and it is exclusively from voluntary treaty basis that legal obligations can arise for States on the matter. It comes as no surprise, indeed, that the legal framework is actually inconsistent and fragmented.

First and foremost, States have not yet agreed on the adoption of a general treaty on migrations, and the only norms that bind a considerable number of States – since they have been adopted in the framework of the United Nations – pertain to treaties concluded in another sector (which was also included in the domestic jurisdiction of the States until a few years ago): the protection of fundamental human rights.

On the one hand, the rights provided for in the 1966 International Covenants on Civil and Political Rights and on Economic, Social and Cultural Rights have to be granted in principle to all individuals finding themselves on the territory of any State Party without distinction of race, color, language or nationality, [6] and therefore also to

---

[5] See, *inter alia*, De Vitoria (1557); Grotius 1625; de Vattel 1758, where the only exception refers to the state of necessity, according to which any State shall recognize the right of the alien to enter its territory; Politis 1925: 5 ff; Verdross 1931: 327 ff and 343; Cavaglieri 1934: 335; Romano 1939: 203; Hall 1924: 26; Hershey 1927: 257. Further on the limits of domestic jurisdiction, see, *inter alia*, Conforti 2005: 135 ff. For a more detailed reconstruction of natural law doctrines on the right to migrate, see Campiglio 2010: 28–29.

[6] With reference to the concept of equality, see also the 1965 UN Convention on the Elimination of all Forms of Racial Discrimination and the 1958 ILO Convention No. 111 concerning Discrimination in Respect of Employment and Occupation.

migrants (even if illegally present in the territory of the State).

On the other hand, some specific aspects of the migratory phenomenon have been regulated. On the basis of a specific rule included in the 1948 Universal Declaration of Human Rights (i.e. Art. 13) (Grahl-Madsen *et al.* 1999: 265 ff), the International Covenant on Civil and Political Rights states – in its Art. 12 – the right to the freedom of movement and residence for "everyone lawfully within the territory of a State" as well as the right "to leave any country, including his own" (where, furthermore, the individual has, in principle, always the right of return). These individual rights may, however, be subject to restrictions that "are provided by law, are necessary to protect national security, public order (*ordre public*), public health or morals or the rights and freedoms of others, and are consistent with the other rights". Once again, then, State sovereignty or, rather, the collective interest, prevails over the individual right: however, the intervention by the State shall ensure that the individual may exert his/her right to reside, emigrate or be readmitted. This means, in particular, that while managing migratory fluxes the State shall respect some standards of equity that – not having been defined at the international level – fully pertain to its own discretion.[7] It is also useful to add that the State, while free to ban single individuals on the grounds of their harmfulness, should however be obliged to host all those aliens forced to migrate for reason of necessity: this is the case of refugees who, according to general (customary) international law, shall not be rejected at the border.[8]

The same Covenant on Civil and Political Rights also regulates the procedure for the expulsion of an "alien lawfully in the territory of a State" (Art. 13). The expulsion may occur only "in pursuance of a decision reached in accordance with law": the alien shall also "except where compelling reasons of national security otherwise require, be allowed to submit the reasons against his expulsion and to have his case reviewed by" the competent authority (Nowak 2005: 290 ff; Kälin 2003).[9]

Finally, there is another aspect of the migratory phenomenon deserving some attention: the (right to) family reunification, as a corollary to the more general right to respect for the right to family life, as protected by all international acts in the sector of human rights (*inter alia* by Art. 12 of the 1948 Universal Declaration of Human Rights; Art. 17 of the 1966 Covenant on Civil and Political Rights; Arts. 7 *et seq.* of the 1989 Convention on the Rights of the Child). In particular, the Convention on

---

[7] Namely, admitting only a certain amount of migrants, in proportion with the population of the State and to the availability of jobs, it fulfils the principle of equity. Obviously, in case of short-term difficulties (e.g. civil war, epidemics, famines, etc.) the State may temporarily close its borders. On Art. 12 of the Covenant, see *inter alia* Nowak 2005: 259 ff.

[8] Sometimes, national authorities foster the mass exodus of individuals towards other States, with clear consequences on the economic and social order of the latter. In legal scholarship there is a gradually emerging widespread consensus on the international responsibility of the State of nationality for internationally wrongful acts, alongside the corresponding obligation to compensate economic damages suffered from the States of destination.

[9] More in general: Favilli 1988; Stenberg 1989.

the Rights of the Child expressly states (Art. 10) that "applications by a child or his or her parents to enter or leave a State Party for the purpose of family reunification shall be dealt with by State Parties in a positive, human and expeditious manner". States are also called to ensure that "the submission of such a request shall entail no adverse consequences for the applicants and for the members of their family". In case the parents reside in different States, the child has the right to maintain personal relations and direct contact with both parents: as a consequence, "the right of the child and his or her parents to leave any country, including their own, and to enter their own country". Conclusively, it is stressed that the right to leave a country "shall be subject to such restrictions as are prescribed by law and which are necessary to protect the national security, public order, public health or morals or the rights and freedoms of others" (Detrick 1999: 183 ff).

24.3. *The legal status of migrants*

Differently from the question of the entrance, residence and expulsion of aliens, the legal status of migrants is the object of a general treaty, though characterized by a limited concrete impact. In 1990, the General Assembly of the United Nations adopted the International Convention on the Protection of the Rights of All Migrant Workers and Members of their Families: as a result of difficult negotiations (started in 1979), the Convention aims at safeguarding the individual both as a worker and, above all, as a person. This is substantially a human rights perspective, as evidenced by the provision of indispensable and contractually inescapable rights for migrants (Art. 82), on the one hand, and, on the other, by the will to tackle the illegal trafficking of migrant workers (Art. 68). The scope of application is very wide, as it includes many categories of workers (precisely eight, pursuant to Art. 2) but also encompasses the whole migratory cycle, defined as comprising the preparation for migration, the departure, transit and the entire period of stay and remunerated activity in the State of employment, as well as return to the State of nationality or the State of habitual residence (Art. 1.2). Besides the rights ensured exclusively to lawfully resident migrants (Part IV: Art. 36–56), the Convention also provides for other rights that – because of their fundamental nature – must be ensured also to irregular or clandestine migrants (Part III: Art. 8–35): the safeguard of migrants "non-documented or in an irregular situation" aims at discouraging their employment, precisely because they should be entitled to working conditions that are in line with minimum standards.[10] Particularly noteworthy is Art. 8

[10] The Italian Consolidated Immigration Act (Consolidated act of provisions concerning regulations on immigration and rules about the conditions of aliens, legislative decree 286 of 25 July 1998) recognizes to the alien "anyway present at the border or within the territory of the State … the fundamental human rights provided for by the rules of domestic laws, by international conventions in force and by the principles of international law generally recognised" (Art. 2.1).

which – along the lines of the abovementioned Art. 12 of the International Covenant on Civil and Political Rights – recognizes the right to freely leave a State, including the State of nationality, to all migrant workers (irrespective of the regularity of their situations) and to their families. This right could be restricted in exceptional circumstances in case this limitation is provided by law or is necessary to the protection of national security, public order, public health or morals, or to the protection of rights and freedoms of others and is compatible with the other rights recognized in that same Convention. Finally, the right to re-enter and remain in the State of nationality is recognized to migrant workers and their families as well.

To ensure the respect of conventional provisions a monitoring mechanism has been established with a Committee within the United Nations that is competent to receive from States Parties periodic reports on the implementation of the Convention (Part VII: Arts. 72–75); on an optional basis, States may also accept the competence of that same Committee to receive – from other State Parties or individuals – communications on alleged violations of the protected rights. This is a merely political control, as it can never result in a formal "conviction": the non-compliant State will have, at the most, to "justify" its conduct in public.

The provision of a safeguard for irregular workers and the fact that the protected rights shall be ensured by States Parties to all workers within their territory, and therefore also to citizens of third countries (i.e. States that are not a party to the same Convention), also explains why the Convention has met limited participation to the point that to reach the minimum number of ratifications (twenty) for its entry into force it took thirteen years. Notwithstanding the invitation issued in 2003 by the UN Commission on Human Rights to all States "to consider seriously signing and ratifying or acceding to the Convention as a matter of priority", as of today there are only around fifty States Parties, the majority of which are States of emigration or transit (so-called *major senders*).

States of immigration (so-called major receivers) are reluctant to assume such challenging obligations (Baratta 2003). It is also useful to clarify that those obligations are already provided for in other conventions widely ratified by States, such as the repeatedly recalled 1966 UN Covenant on Civil and Political Rights, and in some Conventions adopted in the framework of the International Labor Organization (inter alia the Convention No. 143 of 1975 concerning the rights of migrant workers) (Battaglia 1984). New obligations are limited (e.g. some fiscal benefits, the participation in local elections in the receiving State, the extension of the concept of family to non-matrimonial situations) and could nonetheless be excluded from the conventional constraints through the deposit of reservations. Above all, the Convention does not imply any obligation relating to the entrance of foreign migrants or the regularization of migrants unlawfully present in the territory of the State. The Convention states that it does not affect the right of each State to set admission standards for the admission of migrants and their families (Art. 79) and it cannot be interpreted as implying the regularization of migrants or their family members who are non-documented or in an irregular situation (Art. 35), while at the same time suggesting that, in case State Parties consider the possibility of regularizing the situation of such persons, appropriate account shall be taken of the duration of their stay and of the situation of their families (Art. 69.2). On the other hand, the Convention also includes obligations pending upon the States of provenance (either States of nationality or transit) of the migrants, which at least in part shall balance the obligations taken by the States of destination: among others, it is possible to recall the obligation to allow the re-entry and the resettlement (Art. 67), the obligation to cooperate in the contrast to illegal immigration (Art. 68), and the obligation to provide for adequate consular services (Art. 65.2).

The difficulty to regulate this aspect of the migratory phenomenon is witnessed by the limited success that similar initiatives – taken since the 1970s – have obtained in Europe, i.e. between a more restricted (and homogenous) number of States.

In 1977 the Council of Europe adopted the Convention on the Legal Status of Migrant Workers. This treaty has a significantly more limited scope if compared to the 1990 UN Convention, as it exclusively deals with some categories of workers, provided that they are in a regular situation and they are citizens of States Parties. Nonetheless, the European Convention has also obtained a scarce number of ratifications, and particularly limited to the countries of emigration. In 1992, under the aegis of that same Council of Europe, negotiations brought about the adoption of the Convention concerning the Participation of Foreigners in Public Life at the Local Level. This Convention, only applicable to foreigners lawfully resident in a State Party, also provides for the establishment at the local level of consultative bodies representing foreign residents, as well as the attribution of active and passive voting rights (at the local level) to those aliens residing for at least five years in the territory of the receiving State. Besides, when adhering to the Convention, States have exercised their right to limit their commitments with regard to such an attribution of active and passive voting rights in local elections through the deposit of a declaration thereon.

24.4. *The status of refugee*

A particular category of migrants is represented by those who are forced to flee their country for political or humanitarian reasons: refugees (Plender 2005: 89 ff; Zaniboni 2005: 291 ff; Goodwin-Gill and McAdam 2007). This category of migrants is protected by the 1951 Geneva Convention relating to the status of refugees. The Convention shall apply to any person that "owing to well-founded fear of persecution for reasons of race, religion, nationality, membership of a particular social group or political opinion, is outside the country of his nationality and is unable or, owing to such fear, is unwilling to avail himself (herself) of the protection of that country; or who, not having a nationality and being outside the country of his (her) former habitual residence as a result of such events, is unable or, owing to such fear, is unwilling to return to it" (Art. 1A No. 2). It does not find application, in turn, when it is reasonable to believe that the person has committed an international crime (war crimes, crimes against peace or humanity) or a major criminal offence. In addition, there is a time limit: the situation of danger for the individual has to derive from "events occurred before 1 January 1951", with the further possibility for States to add – at the moment of their adhesion – another (geographical) limitation, i.e. "in Europe" (Art. 1B No. 1: Italy has attached this geographical reservation). However, it must be pointed out that the 1967 New York Protocol (also ratified by Italy), erased both the time and geographical limitations.

The Geneva Convention regards both the legal status of refugees [11] and the administrative measures connected to the entry/presence and expulsion. As for the legal status, the Convention provides for the subjection of the personal status to the law of the country of domicile or residence and the obligation upon the State to ensure to the refugee the most favorable treatment possible, and in any case no less favorable than that accorded – in the same circumstances – to aliens in general. As for the entry/residence, the Convention requires the States not to implement criminal sanctions in case of irregularities where the concerned individuals, "coming directly from a territory where their life or freedom was threatened [...], enter or are present in their territory without authorization, provided they present themselves without delay to the authorities" (Art. 31.1). Precisely because of their particular situation, refugees lawfully in the territory of a State shall not be expelled, save on grounds of national security or public order: in that case, they should be given the possibility to put forward their arguments "except where compelling reasons of national security otherwise require" (Art. 32).

Particularly significant is the prohibition of expulsion and return at the border (*refoulement*) provided for by Art. 33. According to this provision, States shall not expel or return a refugee towards a country "where his life or freedom would be threatened on account of his race, religion", etc.: the prohibition can be limited only where the refugee can be "regarded as a danger to the security of the country in which he is or [...], having been convicted by a final judgment of a particularly serious crime or offence, constitutes a danger to the community of that country". This exception, which looks at safeguarding States from the risk of abusive misuse of the right to asylum by dangerous individuals, could constitute at present an important tool in the fight against terrorism: the Security Council of the United Nations – in a 2001 Resolution [12] – has warned States to be cautious in awarding the status of refugee, inviting them to make sure that "the asylum seeker has not planned, facilitated or participated in the commission of terrorist acts" and that "the refugee status is not abused by perpetrators, organizers or facilitators of terrorist acts" (Carella 2005).

The actual framework emerging from the brief analysis of the States' practice shows

[11] As for minor migrants, see Art. 22 of the 1989 Convention on the Rights of the Child.

[12] Resolution No. 1373, 28 September 2001.

that the latter are still very jealous of their sovereignty and are hardly willing to limit their discretionary power to control their national borders. Nonetheless, limitations to national regimes on entry, residence and expulsion of aliens derive from human rights protection rules, elaborated within the United Nations and regional organizations (as the Council of Europe). Further constraints come from international rules on judicial and border control cooperation in the fights against illegal trafficking. With regard to the status of migrants present in the territory, States refrain from the respect of the obligations stemming out from international conventions: the efforts made by international organizations to grant migrants an adequate standard of protection of their civil, political and economic rights have encountered averseness, especially from the "major receivers".

24.5. *The international commitment to look for alternative legal pathways*

The general "security exception" admitted to justify the non-application of human rights standards set in the abovementioned international treaties has been frequently used in recent practice as an "escape clause" by the same receiver States to justify the mass expulsion or non-admission of persons asking for international protection, even if they had omitted the due scrutiny of each single request of protection, as imposed by the already mentioned customary law rule of non-refoulement. Moreover, the request to grant a visa for humanitarian reasons (also differing from the "persecution for reasons of race, religion, nationality, membership of a particular social group or political opinion" required by Art. 1A of the 1951 Geneva Convention) received in the diplomatic premises of the State parties to said conventions in the territories of third States where the person in need had found a temporary refuge, has been lately often denied by European States. The assertion by the requested State party has been that abroad it could not exercise over the claimant its direct and effective control (i.e. jurisdiction). As a consequence, since the jurisdiction is the prerequisite for the application of the standards of protection set in the same human rights instruments, as in the European Convention of Human Rights (Art. 1 ECHR), the denying States have affirmed to be free not to apply them. [13]

As a result, with specific reference to the European continent, international protection is in principle guaranteed only to those individuals who succeed in reaching the *territory* of a State party to such a Convention. This implies the unacceptable consequence that, as of

---

[13] On the practice of "obstruction asylum" see Goodwin-Gill and McAdam 2007: 371–380, and also further in text, *infra*, at para. 8, dealing as well with the violations of the principle of *non-refoulement* by States Parties of the ECHR, in respect of which it is important to mention, *ex multis*, the decision of the European Court of Human Rights, *Hirsi Jamaa et al. v. Italy*, App. No. 27765/09 (Feb. 23, 2012) and the first comments by Zanghì 2011: 815; Lenzerini 2012; Napoletano 2012; Giuffrè 2012.

today, perilous boat-trips (managed by ruthless traffickers and smugglers) constitute the most feasible option to achieve forms of protection that are complementary to those offered by the 1951 Geneva Convention (Moreno Lax 2017a: 81–116).

Against this background, the development of alternative legal pathways for refugees to access safely the territory of a Member State, also in cooperation with the civil society and the private sector, is a specific commitment, solemnly declared in the UN New York Declaration of September 2016 for refugees and migrants and expressly reaffirmed recently as a specific objective (no. 5) within the Global Compact for Safe, Orderly and Regular Migration, adopted during the intergovernmental Conference held in Marrakech on 10 December 2018 and formally endorsed some days later by the General Assembly on its seventy-third session. [14] The Global Compact is based on a set of "cross-cutting and interdependent guiding principles", including the respect of human rights (litt. *f*) and the promotion of "whole-of-society" approach (litt. *j*) in order to aim at developing or building on "existing national and regional practices for admission and stay of appropriate duration based on compassionate, humanitarian or other considerations for migrants compelled to leave their countries ... such as by providing humanitarian visas, private sponsorships".

Having identified the limits posed by international law to States' discretion in the first part of the present contribution, the further scope of this chapter is to understand to what extent a recent and fruitful private initiative sponsoring a safe alternative pathway spread from Italy, called "humanitarian corridors", may in future become a *general and uniform alternative model* for other European Union States. In fact, such a best practice, which represents currently an *exceptional* legal pathway to enter the country securely, is nowadays restricted to a relatively small number of beneficiaries, but could potentially be extended to other States.

Best practice of private sponsorship comes to Italy: aims and formal legal basis

Among the good practices adopted to allow persons requiring international protection

---

[14] G.A. Res. 71/1, *New York Declaration for Refugees and Migrants* (Sept. 19, 2016), at para. 15 states: "We invite the private sector and civil society, including refugee and migrant organizations, to participate in multi-stakeholder alliances to support efforts to implement the commitments we are making today", and in point 61 it adds: "we encourage deeper interaction between Governments and civil society to find responses to the challenges and the opportunities posed by international migration". Similarly, see also at para. 85 and, within Annex II, para. 15; see Guild 2018. On 13 July 2018 UN Member States finalized the text for the Global Compact for Safe, Orderly and Regular Migration which was adopted in Marrakech last December (text available in all official languages at http://www.un.org/en/conf/migration/), recalling as the fifth of the twenty-three main objectives the enhancement of "availability and flexibility of pathways for regular migration". On the 19 December 2019 the General Assembly began the meeting by taking up a draft resolution titled "Global Compact for Safe, Orderly and Regular Migration" (document A/73/L.66), on which https://www.un.org/press/en/2018/ga12113.doc.htm (accessed on January 15, 2019).

to reach the country of destination in full legality and safety, the well-established Canadian model of private sponsorships [15] has inspired in Italy a rather sui generis initiative and has enabled the entrance of at least 2,000 refugees over a period of two and a half years. For the most part the beneficiaries are Syrian citizens, coming from Lebanon, that have been recently joined by other vulnerable people arriving from Ethiopian camps, fleeing from the neighboring countries of the Horn of Africa (Eritrea, South Sudan, Somalia).

These legal alternative pathways, referred to by the sponsors as "humanitarian corridors", [16] have been opened on the basis of three hybrid Memoranda of Understanding (hereinafter referred to as MoU).

The first Memorandum was concluded on 15 December 2015 by the Italian Ministries for Foreign and Internal Affairs, on the institutional side, and the Federation of Protestant Churches in Italy, the Waldesian Board and the Community of Sant'Egidio, [17] on the private side.

As for the second Memorandum, it was adopted on 12 January 2017 by the Italian Ministries of Foreign and Internal Affairs, on the one hand, and the Italian Bishops' Conference (CEI – acting through the Caritas and the Migrantes Foundation) and the same Community of Sant'Egidio, [18] on the sponsors' side.

All the involved associations are bearing all the costs connected with these laudable and courageous initiatives, which was followed recently by a third one.

---

[15] The Canadian model of private sponsorship, still offering a complementary tool for State reception and resettlement policies, was initially elaborated in order to give a prompt response to the emergency situation resulting from two waves of refugees caused by the Indo–Chinese crisis in the 1970s and 1980s and originally codified in the *1978 Immigration Act*. See Noll and Fagerlund 2002; Courtland Robinson 1998: 138–142; Yahyaoui Krivenko 2012; Ineli-Ciger 2016: 412.

[16] On the definition of "humanitarian corridors" used by the sponsors of the initiative, the absence of any reference to the formal and technical expression generally utilized by international organizations dealing with asylum and migrations has been noted by Morozzo della Rocca 2017: 10. For further comments on the first MoU, see also: Impagliazzo 2016; Sossai 2017; Colmayer and Signorini 2017; Mutti 2017.

[17] According to data released by the Community of Sant'Egidio and by the news agency of the Federation of Protestant Churches in Italy, in the first two years 1,000 Syrian refugees have arrived from Lebanon through this legal and safe way. The first Memorandum also provided for an expansion to Morocco that apparently did not occur (see http://www.santegidio.org, http://www.nev.it, and also https://www.chiesavaldese.org, last visited June 15, 2018). Most of the funds for the project come from the "Otto per Mille" system of the Waldensian Church (through the Diaconal Commission of the Waldensian Church), the Community of Sant'Egidio and the Federation of Protestant Churches, as well as other fundraising initiatives, such as the one launched by the Community of Sant'Egidio. The Community of Sant'Egidio, Federation of Protestant Churches (as part of its Mediterranean Hope project) and the Waldensian Board (see https://www.mediterraneanhope.com/wp-content/uploads/2018/03/Executive-Summary-Humanitarian-Corridors.pdf, last visited June 15, 2018).

[18] The second Memorandum of Understanding, signed in Rome on 12 January 2017 (and financed by funds derived from the "Otto per Mille" free contribution by CEI and the Community of Sant'Egidio), provides for the transfer within 18 months of 500 Eritrean, Somali and South-Sudanese citizens from refugee camps in Ethiopia, chosen both for its role as a "transition country" and for the presence in its territory of NGOs and churches already committed to supporting refugees.

In fact, some days after the arrival of the sixteenth refugees' flight which reached the first 1,000 beneficiaries, the commitment to double the efforts has been confirmed by the same ecumenical associations that have promoted the first project. On 7 November 2017 the Foreign and Internal Ministries, the Community of Sant'Egidio, the Waldesian Board and the FCEI signed a new Memorandum of Understanding based on the model offered by the first two, which will bring to Italy in the next two years another 1,000 people in a condition of "vulnerability" coming for the most part from Lebanese and Ethiopian camps.[19]

At the moment, the Italian projects involve relatively small numbers, if compared to the overall needs. Nonetheless, on the one hand, the 2,000 safe entries already made possible "par avion" are even now comparable to the resettlement quotas registered in other Member States; on the other hand, the model offers remarkable potentialities of expansion and represents "a challenge for Governments and the EU to go further" (Morozzo della Rocca 2017: 10). The example of Canada may be relevant in this regard as well: despite its different critical aspects and the still pending demand for reform,[20] between November 2015 and July 2017 such a system has allowed almost 19,000 Syrian citizens to join the country through private sponsorships,[21] activated both by associations and individuals answering to basic requirements identified by the State in a clear, transparent and easily accessible way.[22]

The Italian agreements have set up highly peculiar procedures for the protected entry of refugees and migrants,[23] as already evident from the definition of the main

---

[19] The third initiative has been supported also by the German Protestant Churches through the fundraising initiative of the traditional "Kirchentag" held in May 2017 (see http://www.mediterranean-hope.com/corridoi-umanitari/la-colletta-del-kirchentag-a-mediterranean-hope-e-sos-mediterranee-2128, last visited June 15, 2018). The "vulnerability" of the new Memorandum of Understanding is defined, similarly to the second agreement, in a wider and more inclusive way (Art. 3). The temporary humanitarian visa is, furthermore, granted "within the limits provided for by the legislation in force" pursuant to Art. 4, even if a reference to Art. 25 of the Visa Code is nevertheless made in the Preamble, point 10, letter *c* (see http://www.santegidio.org, last visited June 15, 2018).

[20] The Canadian Council for Refugees has recommended a revision of the Programme which would allow, *inter alia*, the elimination of the existing restrictions on the regions of provenance of the beneficiaries and the yearly maximum threshold; the re-integration of the Federal Healthcare Programme to pay the basic medical expenses of non-Syrian refugees which, since 2012, are not subsidized anymore. See *Renewing Canada's Private Sponsorship of Refugees Program* (January 2016) and *Private Sponsorship of Refugees in 2017* (January 2017) by the Canadian Council for Refugees/Conseil Canadien pour les Réfugiés, available at http://ccrweb.ca and www.rstp.ca, respectively.

[21] More precisely, this regards 18,865 of a total of 47,735, with another 24,420 directly assisted by the Government and 4,445 arrived through mixed programs. For a detailed overview, see data released by the Department of Immigration, Refugees and Citizenship, *Canada – Admissions of Syrian Refugees by Province/Territory and Census Metropolitan Area (CMA) of Intended Destination and Immigration Category, November 4th, 2015 – July 31st, 2017*, available at http://www.cic.gc.ca.

[22] Minimum instructions on how to propose as a sponsor and/or beneficiary in the Canadian system are presented in the *Private Sponsorship of Refugees Toolkit*, published online at: http://ccrweb.ca/en/private-sponsorship-refugees.

[23] For a definition of protected entry procedures, see *inter alia*: EXCOM Standing Committee,

intended goals. The first common objective is, indeed, to ensure (*i*) the arrival in Italy of "*potential* beneficiaries of international protection, and more specifically of the most vulnerable subjects" in a *legal* and *safe* manner from third countries where they are located, at the expense of the abovementioned religious communities (Art. 2 of the first and second MoU). In addition, these memoranda also ensure (*ii*) the first reception, by these same communities, in a way that may effectively support the process of "socio-cultural integration for an adequate length of time" (Art. 4, second paragraph of both MoU).

A further aim of the two agreements is to (*iii*) "stabilize in Italy" the beneficiaries, who also can profit from the legal assistance from *sponsors* necessary to request international protection once arrived in the country (Art. 4, letter *d* of the first MoU and point 11*c* of the initial recitals of the second MoU). The project, as such, looks at "*excluding* or limiting any secondary and voluntary movement" towards other countries,[24] since – as detailed below – potential beneficiaries are required to express a clear and univocal intention to that effect already in the selection phase.

Once selected, their dossiers are transmitted to the Italian delegation in the country of first asylum (Lebanon or Ethiopia) and then subjected to security checks by the Italian Ministries of Foreign and Internal Affairs. In the absence of any ground for rejection, the Italian authorities may issue a temporary visa and allow beneficiaries to fly safely to Italy. Once arrived in the country, NGOs shall launch the reception and integration phase that they have granted for at least one year at their total expense, while at the same time commencing the formal procedure for requesting international protection to Italian authorities.

As for the legal basis allowing the issuance of the visa, all three memoranda make reference to Article 25 of the Regulation (EC) no. 810/2009, the so-called Visa Code.[25] This provision derogates from the principle of fulfillment of the conditions of the Schengen Borders Code,[26] thus allowing each Member State to issue a visa where national authorities deem it necessary "for humanitarian reasons or national interest reasons or by virtue of international obligations". Such a visa has a "limited territorial validity" (LTV) within national borders for no more than 90 days (over a total period

Complementary Forms of Protection: Their Nature and Relationship to the International Refugee Protection Regime - 18th Meeting, UNdoc.EC/50/SC/CRP.18, 9 June 2000, 4–5; Noll and Fagerlund 2002: 14–21; McAdam 2007: 19–51; Goodwin-Gill and McAdam 2007: 285–345.

[24] This goal is explicitly stated in Art. 3, last paragraph of the second Memorandum.

[25] Regulation (EC) No. 810/2009 of the European Parliament and the Council of 13 July 2009 establishing a Community code on visa (Visa Code); *ex multis*: Peers *et al.* 2015: 251.

[26] Reference is made here to the conditions laid out in Art. 5, par.1, letters *a, c, d, e* of the Schenghen Borders Code, first adopted on 15 March 2006 with Regulation (EC) No. 562/2006 of the European Parliament and the Council establishing a Community Code on the rules governing the movement of persons across borders and recently transposed in Art. 6 of the consolidated version of Regulation (EU) 2016/399 of the European Parliament and the Council of 9 March 2016 on a Union Code on the rules governing the movement of persons across borders.

of 180 days), with exception made in cases where other Member States have accepted to extend its validity in their territories. [27]

In particular, following the judgment *X and X v. Belgium*, rendered by the EU Court of Justice on 7 March 2017,[28] it seems at present difficult to formally maintain the same legal basis recalled by the Italian Memoranda for reasons that will be clarified below.

The beneficiaries of a sui generis protection

The selection of the potential beneficiaries is left by the Memoranda to the NGOs themselves, that shall autonomously prepare for each applicant an individual dossier by collecting the necessary information directly on the ground, particularly in the Lebanese and Eritrean camps where the refugees have found shelter. Therefore, the sponsors – present in the camps and fully aware of the context in which they are operating – have the responsibility to examine the potential beneficiaries and restrict to a list of candidates in accordance with the criteria set out in the Memoranda (Art. 3 of the MoUs).

Beneficiaries may not only be those "persons considered by the UNHCR as deserving, at least *prima facie*, the recognition of the *status* of refugee" pursuant to the 1951 Geneva Convention (and of its 1967 implementing Protocol), but also those persons potentially seeking protection because of their conditions of *objective vulnerability*.

Indeed, the project falls within the already known scheme of Protected Entry Procedures (PEPs) that are supplementary to the system set out by the 1951 Geneva Convention, in order to ensure an alternative legal pathway also to persons in need and objectively vulnerable that are not falling within the definition of "refugees" or lack the recognition of such a status. This may happen not only in the manifold cases connected to situations of humanitarian emergency different from persecution as intended in the Convention, but also, for example, as a consequence of restrictive policies introduced by the shelter State. A similar situation has occurred in Lebanon (a State that is not a Party to the Convention) in 2015, when the government asked to "de-register" the refugees arrived in the country after 5 January 2015, as well as to suspend new registrations. [29]

[27] On that debated provision, see the detailed study commissioned by the Civil Liberties, Justice and Home Affairs of the European Parliament: Ibsen Jensen 2014.

[28] Cf. Case C-638/16, X e X v État belge (Mar. 7, 2017), ECLI:EU:C:2017:173, which, in contrast to widespread expectations, did not confirm the Opinion of Advocate General Mengozzi (Feb. 7, 2017), ECLI:EU:C:2017:93. Among the first comments, see: Moreno-Lax 2017b; Carlier and Leboef 2017; Zoetewij-Turhan and Progin-Theuerkauf 2017a, 2017b; Brouwer 2017; Spinelli 2017; De Vylder 2017; Raimondo 2017; Del Guercio 2017; Favilli 2017.

[29] See *Vulnerability Assessment of Syrian Refugees in Lebanon 2016, conducted jointly by the United Nations*

Compared to similar practices, the Italian Memoranda expand the categories of hypothetically "vulnerable" beneficiaries. With reference to this concept, however, it is possible to find some differences between the two agreements.

The first Memorandum provides for an extension of the protection to two different groups of people: first, those persons for whom "there are reasonable grounds to believe that, in case of return to their countries of origin, they would suffer significant damage also as a consequence of a situation of armed conflict, endemic violence or systemic violation of human rights" (Art. 3 point *b*). This provision recalls and combines the definitions of beneficiaries of subsidiary and temporary protection laid down in the EU legislation, respectively in the so-called "Qualification" and "Temporary Protection" Directives.[30] Secondly, it is possible to select all those migrants that, even where not included in the abovementioned categories, "lie in a situation of particular vulnerability for their personal situation, age or health conditions" including, *inter alia*, "single women with children, women victims of human trafficking, unaccompanied minors, elderly people", disabled or traumatized persons, and people with serious medical needs (Art. 3 point *c*).

Conversely, the second and third Memoranda provide for the extension to other categories of migrants not otherwise covered by the Geneva Convention. Different from the first MoU, the second and the third generically deal with all those persons finding themselves in conditions of serious "vulnerability determined by their personal situation, age or state of health", without any indication (not even by way of illustration) on the causes determining those conditions or on the specific underprivileged categories (Art. 3 point *b*).

Notwithstanding these differences that may further expand the subjective scope of application of the second and third Memorandum and make the selection by the *sponsor* even more flexible, all the Memoranda specify that the identification of the beneficiaries has to take into account "in a *complementary* yet not substitutive manner" also

---

Children's Fund (UNICEF), the United Nations High Commissioner for Refugees (UNHCR) and the United Nations World Food Programme (WFP), 16 December 2016, para. 13 (http://documents.wfp.org/stellent/groups/public/documents/ena/wfp289533.pdf, last visited 15 June 2018).

[30] See respectively, with regards to the beneficiaries of subsidiary protection, Art. 15, letter *c* of Directive 2011/95/EU, recasting Directive 2004/83/EC of 13 December 2011 on minimum standards for the qualification and status of third country nationals or stateless persons as refugees or as persons who otherwise need international protection and the content of the protection granted. Vice-versa, as for the wider subjective scope of Directive 2001/55/EC of the Council of 20 July 2001 on minimum standards for giving temporary protection in the event of a mass influx of displaced persons and on measures promoting a balance of efforts between Member States in receiving such persons and bearing the consequences thereof, see in particular Art. 2 letter *c*. There is a partial overlapping of the categories protected through the two acts but, anyway, as already known, in this moment the second Directive has not yet been "activated", lacking the required (qualified) majority within the Council to approve the proposal by the Commission on the "establishment" of the same pre-requisite of the "existence of a mass influx of displaced persons" (Art. 5.1), notwithstanding the requests made by the most interested Member States. See Goodwin-Gill and McAdam 2007: 325–334, 340–342; Peers *et al.* 2015: 571–615; Munari 2015: 48–54, 60–61; Del Guercio 2016: 297–401; Cherubini 2012: 216–223.

other factors. In doing so it is possible to include in the program persons who can benefit in Italy of the hospitality offered (formally) by *individuals, churches or associations* to provide the conditions for their first reception (Art. 3 point *d*) and/or have *relatives or social communities able to host them* in Italy and for this reason have declared the will to establish and integrate themselves in the country (Art. 3 point *e*). The ultimate aim of this provision is to *facilitate the identification of pathways to integration* (Art. 3 last paragraph of all MoU).[31]

As a consequence, the peculiar nature of humanitarian corridors as a Protected Entry Procedure stands out. They represent, indeed, a laudable initiative by private associations with recognized expertise in the field to provide for an alternative, legal, and safe pathway for single and well-identified individuals and not for multitudes or groups, such as in the case of *resettlement*. The sponsors *select* the beneficiaries of protection directly, with *no delegation* to other organisms or international organizations. In addition, those procedures attribute a special *relevance to the own will of refugees and migrants* – as expressed well before the departure and directly shared with the promoting and "future hosts" – to be steadily and permanently integrated in the country where they will present their request for protection. Another aim is the exclusion of secondary and voluntary movements from the country of reception where pathways of integration already exist and/or there are members of the family or other hosted communities with a lasting presence on the territory.

The *sui generis* nature of the project is evident, not only because it represents an uncommon "model of public mobilization of the civil society in synergy with the State" (Morozzo della Rocca 2017: 10), but also because it is rather different from other protected entry procedures (*ibidem*: 14–18, for a detailed comparison with other *protected entry procedures*).

24.6. *The compatibility of the model with Art. 25 of the Visa Code after the judgment* X and X v. Belgium

Almost three years since the conclusion of the first Memorandum, it is possible to define it as a success story. More than 1,500 persons in need of protection arrived in Italy through safe flights and have been hosted by the participating communities, which have taken care of the inclusion of the beneficiaries, for the most part represented by families with children and persons needing medical care. Even though it is probably too early to predict the overall outcomes, as of today the project has been functioning with respect to its initial objectives. Both the legal and safe arrival, on the one hand, and the first inclusion in communities spread all over the Italian territory and not confined to isolated areas, on the other, have been realized, even if on a small

[31] Emphasis added.

scale. Against this background, the aim of this study, as already mentioned, is to verify, first, if the model may be exported on a larger scale in other States of the Schengen area and, secondly, if the paradigm needs to be adapted to reach this goal.

With regard to the first issue, the Italian best practice has already spread to France. On 14 March 2017 the Ministries of Foreign and Internal Affairs, on the institutional side, and the Community of Sant'Egidio (as a promoter), the *Fédération protestante de France*, the *Fédération de l'Entraide protestante*, the *Conférence des évêques de France et le Secours catholique – Caritas*, on the ecumenical side, have signed a Memorandum. This agreement is bringing to the French territory Syrian and Iraqi families who have fled to Lebanon, with 500 arrivals foreseen in the span of 18 months. [32] Other Member States (namely, Germany and Spain) have also devoted their attention to the project; finally, the Republic of San Marino has already hosted some Syrian families, while the Polish Bishops' Conference has manifested its interest in participating (Sossai 2017: 89).

On the other hand, with regard to the possibility to adjust the model for a uniform European *format*, it seems doubtful that it will be appropriate to maintain its actual legal basis, Art. 25 Visa Code, after the interpretation given to this provision by the European Court of Justice in March 2017 in the case *X and X v. Belgium* where the judges excluded its application to a situation potentially falling within the scope of the Italian Memoranda that are explicitly based on that provision.

In fact, the judges in Luxembourg in the abovementioned decision have established that a Member State (in the case at hand, Belgium), may refuse – without even providing a justification – a request for an LTV visa presented for humanitarian reasons to the Belgian diplomatic premise in Lebanon by a family of Syrian Orthodox-Christian refugees (including three minors), subject to persecution in Aleppo, in case from that request may be inferred, as expressly admitted by the applicants, the further intention to ask for international protection once arrived in Belgium.

According to the Court, a similar request would imply the will to remain on the Belgian territory well over the 90 days permitted by the Visa Code. Consequently, not only the Code itself but also European Union law would be inapplicable, not to mention the standards of protection provided for in the Charter of Fundamental Rights, and particularly in Articles 4 and 18, respectively recognizing the prohibition of torture and inhuman and degrading treatments, as well as the right to asylum.

The Court comes to this (indeed much questionable) conclusion following a rather intricate and non-linear reasoning. The express intention to request international protection formally incorporated in an LTV application is interpreted as a case for non-application of the Visa Code but not as a possible reason of rejection of the same application, pursuant to Art. 32(1) letter *b* of that same Code, as contrary argued by the

[32] In implementing the project called "Opération d'accueil solidaire de réfugiés en provenance du Liban (couloirs humanitaires)", the first beneficiaries arrived in France on 15 July 2017 (http://www.fep.asso.fr, accessed on June 15th, 2018).

Advocate-General. Having a different scope with respect to a short-duration visa, according to the judges in Luxembourg, the request should be re-qualified as a long-term visa. [33] Based on these assumptions, considering that the competence in the field of defining uniform criteria for the issuance of a visa or long-term residence permits provided for in Art. 79, par. 2 point *a* TFEU has not yet been exercised by the Union, the Court finds that the competence is still falling within the Member States' discretion, [34] leaving them free to grant or refuse the visa.

The Court thus affirms the inapplicability of EU law with reference to temporary visas for humanitarian reasons and therefore the unfeasibility to base on EU law and, particularly, on Articles 4 and 18 of the Charter, the obligation for a Member State to grant a LTV to persons that, in case of refusal, would find themselves exposed to a clear danger of persecution and inhuman and degrading treatments in a third country.

This is an inadmissible outcome that openly contradicts the scope of the Visa Code, as declared in its preamble, "aimed at facilitating legitimate travel and tackling illegal immigration through further harmonisation of national legislation and handling practices at local consular missions" (recital no. 3) and at respecting "fundamental rights and observes the principles recognized in particular by the Council of Europe's Convention for the Protection of Human Rights and Fundamental Freedoms and by the Charter of Fundamental Rights of the European Union" (recital no. 29). Such interpretation seems to run counter to previous extensive and significant jurisprudence of the Court in Luxembourg on the interpretative canons to be followed in the exegesis of secondary Union law [35] and contradict also the 1969 Vienna Convention on the law of treaties (Articles 31–32).

24.7. *Which other legal basis under international law?*

The decision to grant States a wide margin of discretion when granting humanitarian visas in circumstances similar to those under analysis – which would have conversely required, according to AG Mengozzi, an obligation to grant the visa on the basis of the Visa Code, as well as of the Charter [36] – shall not imply the prohibition for Member States to conclude agreements with private sponsors for the opening of humanitarian corridors. Nonetheless, at least until either the European legislator will take action to rethink Art. 25 of the Visa Code (Del Guercio 2017: 287–288) [37] or the

[33] See paragraphs 43, 46–47 of the judgment under comment.

[34] *Ibidem*, par. 44.

[35] See the opinion of Advocate General Mengozzi, *supra* No. 36, at paras. 6 and 103; Moreno-Lax 2017b: part I–II; Del Guercio 2017: 291.

[36] See the opinion of Advocate General Mengozzi, *supra* No. 36, at paras 80–88.

[37] See the in-depth evaluation of the added legal value of a future common EU legislation on

Court will adopt a different interpretation, it should be more appropriate not to quote this provision in the forthcoming Memoranda of Understanding, also in consideration of the essential role played in these agreements by the express will of the beneficiary to indefinitely settle and remain in the territory of the State to apply for international protection.

In this sense, it is indicative that the recent Memorandum of Understanding concluded in France some days after the judgment rendered by the Court of Justice does not mention Art. 25 of the Visa Code (Art. 3) as its legal foundation.

The substantial concern that should refrain from embracing the ECJ interpretation, is that humanitarian visas should not be a matter of discretion for the States once the conditions exist to grant temporary protection from serious risk of persecution, of torture or cruel and inhuman treatments, if not death. The legal basis thereof can be found under international law, both general and conventional. In particular, reference has to be made to the principle of *non-refoulement* (and therefore, *in primis*, to Art. 33 of the 1951 Geneva Convention combined with Art. 31 of that same Convention). Despite practices of "obstructing asylum" (Goodwin-Gill and McAdam 2007: 371–380) followed by many States and aimed at factually impeding the access on the territory to exclude *ex ante* the possibility to request international protection, some authors have held that the prohibition of *non-refoulement* shall conversely imply an obligation of admission and temporary stay. Admission and temporary stay have to be intended as *instrumental* to the protection of the applicant, until the State has verified for each request the alleged circumstances as ensured by the Convention or, also, as long as the State has ascertained that the person would not be exposed "in any manner whatsoever" to the risk of persecution, in the country towards which the person in question would be "refouled". [38]

That same principle is recalled by the European Convention on Human Rights as interpreted and applied under the lenses of a large body of case-law of the Court in Strasbourg (Moreno-Lax 2017a: 266–280; Lang 2015; Del Guercio 2016: 120–226), primarily relating to the prohibition of torture and inhuman and degrading treatments and to its extra-territorial effects as enshrined in its Art. 3 (as affirmed clearly in the *Hirsi* case) [39] as well as in Art. 4 of Protocol no. 4 to the ECHR, expressly devoted to the principle of *non-refoulement.* Under the ECHR system, conventional standards

humanitarian visas (introducing an "automatic link between the admissibility declaration and the need to issue an LTV") proposed for the adoption of the European Parliament, by Moreno-Lax 2018.

[38] In this sense, see Hathaway 2005: 278–302. Similarly, see: Coleman 2003:2 40 ff; Lauterpracht and Bethlehem 2003: 113–117; Goodwin-Gill and McAdam 2007: 206–208, 211–13, 290; Lenzerini 2009: 404–414; Hurwitz 2009: 176; Wouters 2009: 148–151, 569–579; Cherubini 2012: 43–48; Lambert 2017: 727; Moreno-Lax 2017a: 247–335. The same approach has been followed, for many years, by the High Commissioner for Refugees, as evident in several acts, *inter alia*: UNHCR, *Advisory Opinion on the Extraterritorial Application of Non-Refoulement Obligations under the 1951 Convention relating to the Status of Refugees and its 1967 Protocol*, 26 January 2007, particularly par. 8, available online at www.unhcr.org.

[39] ECHR, *Hirsi Jamaa et al. v. Italy*, App. No. 27765/09, see No. 2 for bibliographic references.

shall be applicable to those individuals that are subject to the jurisdiction of the State Party (Art. 1), i.e. to those who are under its direct and effective control (Milanovic 2018). Subjection to such a kind of control have been affirmed by the Strasbourg Court in analogous cases where it was held: as in *Markovic*, that "there indisputably exists a 'jurisdictional link' for the purpose of Article 1 ECHR" in bringing a civil action to a court of a State (which just receives it and takes no other active steps); [40] and, as in *Assanidze*, that "in certain exceptional cases, jurisdiction is assumed on the basis of non-territorial factors such as the activities performed by diplomatic and consular representatives of State". [41]

Against this background, the ECJ did not make any parallel reference to this jurisprudence, while – quite the opposite – *implicitly* excluded the jurisdiction of a Member State over people that were present in the consular premises of a Member State abroad at the moment of the submission of the request for an LTV.

Moreover, the same Court did not decide on the specific issue, raised by the referring judge, of the other "international obligations" – as detailed in Art. 25 of the Visa Code. Pursuant to such obligations it should have been affirmed the necessity for an EU Member State to grant a visa permit requested to the consular representation abroad by a family (including underage children) already persecuted for reason of their religious beliefs, whenever there are substantial grounds for believing that they would be in danger of being subjected again to persecution or even torture, directly or indirectly.

This extensive interpretation of the principle of *non-refoulement* (and its extraterritorial effect) is strongly supported by different general rules of international law (customs and principles), as well as by treaty provisions on human rights (Benvenuti 2006: 207; Wouters 2009: 359–520; Salerno 2011: 3; Del Guercio 2016: 54–111). Reference is made, just to mention the most evident, to the *right to life*, as codified in Art. 6 of the 1966 Covenant on Civil and Political Rights (Shelton 2014: 74–90, 149–155), [42] which in its subsequent Art. 7 provides for the *prohibition of torture* and other cruel, inhuman or degrading treatment.

With regard to the first provision, in the recent General Comment No. 36 the Human Rights Committee expressly specifies that "the duty to protect the right to life requires the Member States to take special measures towards persons in situation of vulnerability ... [such as] unaccompanied migrant minors ... asylum seekers, refugees". [43] The Committee upholds a broad interpretation of "the obligation not to

---

[40] ECHR, *Markovic v Italy*, App. No. 1398/03, para. 12 (Oct. 20, 2005). See Moreno-Lax 2017a: 309–311, quoting similarly, *Haydaire v. The Netherlands*, App. No. 876/04 (Oct. 20, 2005), a case of request for reunification of a family, where the Court upheld the existence of the jurisdiction of The Netherlands pursuant to Art. 1 ECHR over the three minor children living in Pakistan while the mother was residing in the requested State.

[41] ECHR, *Assanidze v. Georgia*, App. No. 1503/01, para. 137 (Apr. 08, 2004).

[42] On the expansion of the notion of jurisdiction of State Parties to the Covenant on Civil and Political Rights and the ECHR, see, *inter alia*, De Sena 2002.

[43] General Comment No. 36 (2018) on article 6 of the International Covenant on Civil and Political

extradite, deport or otherwise transfer pursuant to article 6 of the Covenant", postulating that it "may be *broader* than the scope of the principle of *non-refoulement* under international refugee law, since it may also require the protection of *aliens not entitled to refugee status*".

With specific reference to the interconnected prohibition of torture, it has become a rule of such a fundamental character for the entire international community to be afforded an absolute, imperative and non-derogable nature, binding upon all States, including those who did not ratify the 1984 Convention on the Prohibition of Torture and Cruel, Inhuman or Degrading Treatments or Punishment. [44] The same Convention besides includes as well the *refoulement* within the conducts expressly prohibited in Art. 3, to which the brand new General Comment No. 4 adopted by the CAT Committee has been devoted. The latter confirms that the principle of *non-refoulement* "is similarly absolute" and must be applied by any State party "in any territory under its jurisdiction or any area under its control and authority" to citizen or non-citizen "without discrimination subject to the *de jure* or *de facto* control". [45]

Another important obligation for the States relates to the *right to respect for family life*, as well as to the principle of the *best interest of the child*, upon which the 1989 New York Convention has been built (Arts 7 *et seq.*). [46]

All the above-mentioned principles and provisions could have justified the necessity

---

Rights, on the right to life, adopted by the Committee at its 124th session (8 October to 2 November 2018) at paras 23 and 31 (CCPR/C/GC/36).

[44] In the judgment on *Questions Relating to the Obligation to Prosecute or Extradite (Belgium v. Senegal)*, at para. 90 (July 20, 2012), the International Court of Justice held that "the prohibition of torture is part of customary international law and it has become a peremptory norm (*jus cogens*). That prohibition is grounded in a widespread international practice and on the *opinio juris* of States. It appears in numerous international instruments of universal application (in particular the Universal Declaration of Human Rights of 1948, the 1949 Geneva Conventions for the protection of war victims; the International Covenant on Civil and Political Rights of 1966; General Assembly resolution 3452/30 of 9 December 1975 on the Protection of All Persons from Being Subjected to Torture and Other Cruel, Inhuman or Degrading Treatment or Punishment), and it has been introduced into the domestic law of almost all States; finally, acts of torture are regularly denounced within national and international fora". See *ex multis*: Carreau and Marrella 2018: 74–88; Conforti 2018; Cassese and Frulli 2017: 253–255; Scovazzi 2015; Frowein 2013; Scovazzi and Citroni 2013: 126–144, 219–222, 324–340.

[45] CAT, General Comment No. 4 (2017) on the implementation of article 3 of the convention in the context of article 22, CAT-C-GC-4 paras 9-10 and (Feb. 9, 2018), recalling previous CAT communications No. 39/1996, Tapia Paez v. Sweden, views adopted on 28 April 1997, para. 14.5; No. 110/1998, Núñez Chipana v. Venezuela, views adopted on 10 November 1998, para. 5.6; No. 233/2003, Agiza v. Sweden, decision adopted on 20 May 2005, para. 13.8; No. 297/2006, Singh Sogi v. Canada, decision adopted on 16 November 2007, para. 10.2; No. 444/2010, Abdussamatov et al. v. Kazakhstan, decision adopted on 1 June 2012, para. 13.7; and No. 475/2011, Nasirov v. Kazakhstan, decision adopted on 14 May 2014, para. 11.6. See for a comment: Zorzi Giustiniani 2018. As the Committee noted in its General Comment No. 2, "the concept of 'any territory under its jurisdiction' … includes any territory or facilities and must be applied to protect any person" [para. 7.4].

[46] See Campiglio 2010: 28–29 and *supra* para. 2; Del Guercio 2016: 113–118, also recalling relevant provisions in the 1990 Convention on the Protection of the Rights of All Migrant Workers and Members of their Families, as well as the 2000 Protocol on trafficking annexed to the Palermo Convention.

to grant an LTV in the context of the case *X and X v. Belgium*. Even if there has been no *dictum* by the Court on the specific issue, the margin of discretion by Member States cannot be any way exercised without respect for the limits posed by obligations arising from international law. By holding to a formalistic interpretation of European law, judges in Luxembourg preferred to support an overly fragile reading, particularly if measured on the basis of "humanitarian values and of the respect of human rights on the basis of which the European construction is built ... as affirmed in Articles 2 and 3 of the Treaty on the European Union, respectively".[47]

Finally, even where a more restrictive interpretation of those international obligations were admitted, namely affirming that: (*i*) the prohibition of *refoulement* may apply only in those cases where refugees get actual access into the territories of the State Parties, and that (*ii*) for the application of the ECHR standards migrants shall be subjected to the jurisdiction of Member States (and such a jurisdiction is not exercised by a diplomatic representation abroad), the refusal of a visa for humanitarian reasons undoubtedly implies *consequences* for European common asylum policies and for their implementation. This may lead to considering the issue as falling within the competences of the Union precisely owing to the jurisprudence developed by the Court in relation to the '*effet utile*', therefore causing the application of the Charter (and its Art. 18), which would not be subordinated to State discretion.[48]

In any case, the Belgian State should have provided, as a minimum, the reasons for refusing the issuing of an LTV. This constitutes a violation of the right of any individual to an effective remedy, which represents a basic principle not only pursuant to the Charter, but also to the ECHR and is common to the domestic legal orders of Member States (Carlier and Leboef 2017).

24.8. *Open issues for the spread of a virtuous practice in Europe*

It is highly disappointing that in the judgment under analysis the Court has moved away from the long and passionate opinion rendered by the Advocate General Mengozzi, who stood for the application of Art. 25 of the Visa Code and of the Charter of Fundamental Rights. In doing so, the Court has deluded expectations for a courageous and consistent stance that the Union did not uphold on the prevalence of human rights of migrants in conditions of extreme vulnerability and in urgent need of protection over the opposite security and protectionist approaches maintained by the States, rejecting the predominant framing of "humanitarian visas" as matters of diplomatic asylum.

The reasons hindering the application of Art. 25 of the Visa Code seem concealed

---

[47] See the judgment under comment, *supra* No. 6, at para. 6.

[48] *Ibidem*, at paras 49, 70, 76, 80, 88, 90, 97.

in the final paragraphs of the judgment rendered by the Court.[49] Both the judges in Luxembourg and Member States were concerned that, on the one hand, diplomatic representations of Member States in third countries would have immediately become a fast track for the request of LTVs. In addition, the Court did not want to favor the phenomenon of so-called *asylum shopping*, i.e. the possibility for potential beneficiaries of protection to "pick and choose" the Member State from which they would request international protection.

An opposite decision – admits the Court – would have probably caused the collapse of the (already shaky) Dublin system that Member States are stubbornly persisting to keep alive.

Certainly, the Court has lost a chance to use an already existing normative tool in order to harmonize very fragmented national practices, since at present Member States govern the grant of visas for humanitarian reasons, whether of short or long term, in a discretional and non-univocal way (Ibsen Jensen 2014: 28–34). These same practices, where well managed, would conversely ensure to the host State the remarkable advantage to monitor (and select) *in advance* those subjects who have been *already identified* and registered by the public authority as granting greater chances to become fully integrated in the same State. Precisely, a specific warranty comes from their explicit will to establish in the national community (even before the selection process starts) and the further requirement of the already existing links with the host communities. Moreover, in some cases, together with the sponsors they can prove the presence in the territory of already established members of their families, to whom they would nevertheless have the right to be reunited, as a "corollary of the more general right to respect of familiar life".[50]

Nevertheless, some questions are still open with a view to extend the scope of application of the already adopted Memoranda of Understanding. Particularly, a first issue connected to the successful outcome of those virtuous projects is the identification of "safe" States, be they transit or host States.

Under a second perspective, the definition of the concretely applicable selection criteria and procedures should not be completely delegated to private parties in case of generalized extension of the project to a larger number of sponsors that may be interested to explore the possibility to open humanitarian corridors,[51] even when lacking the same expertise in the field as the first sponsors had.

To reach this goal, the latter should encourage a new lexicon on migrations through

---

[49] See the judgment under comment, *supra* No. 6, at paras 48–49.

[50] In this sense, see Campiglio 2010: 28–29, and *supra* para. 2.

[51] The first agreement, as an example, has been a driving force for the launch of a subsequent, unusual project called "Adottiamo il futuro" (*i.e.*, Let's adopt the future) between the FCEI and the Federazione nazionale lavoratori agroindustriali (FLAI-CGIL): this trade union, since 1 May 2017, has committed itself to implementing "mentoring support" for a year, and therefore also to pay the expenses deriving from the reception of one of the families of Syrian refugees arrived in Italy via the humanitarian corridors from Lebanon (see http://www.nev.it).

the diffusion and sharing of the successful methods currently used for integration. This would also allow a better harmonization of arrangements for the admission of refugees by pursuing their integration according to an "adoption-like" method, not intended as a direct intervention by the State, but rather with supporting guidance by public authorities [52] – a direction possibly established at different levels, both national and European, according to the paradigm suggested by the General Assembly of the United Nations of a "multi-stakeholder alliance". [53] It would be, indeed, desirable to direct the *recast* of the relevant EU law, still (difficultly) under way, to this end (Del Guercio 2017: 287–290; Ibsen Jensen 2014: 18–27, 36–37).

Pending a structural reform, [54] the involvement of the third sector may have a decisive role to solve the *impasse* that European governments are currently unable to overcome jointly, even though single countries are showing a greater commitment. As such, humanitarian corridors represent a possibility within the wider framework of intermediary options between an unconditional opening and the closure of all channels for a regular entry – a channel that should be possibly reinforced with the supporting role of the State, the subject that is *primarily* obliged to respect international law and protect fundamental human rights, in order to provide "means to travel to access protection rights (already recognised) under EU law" (Moreno-Lax 2018: 79).

It is thus crucial to immediately start a serious reflection on the reopening of all the existing legal channels of entry in order to rescue today those who cannot wait till an indefinite tomorrow (Favilli 2017b), in full respect of the principle of solidarity among Member States, called to share responsibilities and resources pursuant to Art. 80 TFEU (Munari 2015: 63; Del Guercio 2016: 398 ff; Adinolfi 2014: 497; Morgese 2018: 63–120, 174–88), particularly when the protection of rights which are not theoretical or illusory, but real and effective, is at stake. [55]

---

[52] See Morozzo della Rocca 2017: 30, recalling the effective definition laid down for humanitarian corridors by Impagliazzo 2016: 127 and Riccardi 2013: 103 ff. A model of coexistence "inspired to the values of the Constitution" is at the basis of the *Primo piano nazionale di integrazione*, presented on 27 September 2017 at the Ministry of Internal Affairs. This Ministerial framework aims at striking a balance between the rights and duties of those who are received and of the receivers: the first commit themselves to learning the Italian language, share the values of the Italian Constitution, respect the laws, and participate in the social, economic and cultural life of the territory where they live, while the latter take the commitment to ensure equality of treatment and dignity, freedom of religion, access to education and training, as well as all those interventions aiming at facilitating inclusion in the receiving society, respecting at the same time its non-negotiable values. See: http://www.interno.gov.it (accessed on June 15th, 2018).

[53] See New York Declaration for Refugees and Migrant, supra No. 1, point 15.

[54] The present debate is opened also to the adoption of an EU instrument on humanitarian visas which, in the opinion of Moreno-Lax 2018: 76–79, could find the most suitable legal basis on Articles 77(2)(a) TFEU on common visas, and 77(2)(b) TFEU on controls on persons crossing the EU external borders, and 78(2)(g) TFEU "calling on the EU legislator to adopt measures, as part of the CEAS, aimed at 'managing the inflows of people applying for (international) protection'".

[55] Those are the words used in his Opinion by Advocate General Mengozzi, *supra* No. 6, at para 158.

Bibliography

Adinolfi, A. (2014) 'Art. 80' in F. Pocar and M.C. Baruffi (eds.) *Commentario breve ai Trattati dell'Unione Europea*, Padua: Cedam.

Baratta, R. (2003) 'La Convenzione delle Nazioni Unite sulla protezione dei lavoratori migranti: quali ostacoli all'adesione dei Paesi di ricezione dei flussi migratori?', *Rivista di diritto internazionale*, 86(3): 764–771.

Battaglia, R.M. (1984) 'Le migrazioni abusive e l'occupazione illegale secondo la Convenzione No. 143 del OIL' in G. Gaja (ed.) *I lavoratori stranieri in Italia*, Bologna: il Mulino, 101 ff.

Benvenuti, P. (2006) 'La Convenzione di Ginevra sullo status dei rifugiati' in L. Pineschi (ed.) *La tutela internazionale dei diritti umani*, Milan: Giuffrè.

Brouwer, E. (2017) 'The European Court of Justice on humanitarian visas: Legal integrity vs. political opportunism?', *CEPS Paper*, 9.

Campiglio, C. (2010) 'Disciplina delle migrazioni: limiti internazionali' in V. Gasparini-Casari (ed.) *Il diritto dell'immigrazione. Profili di Diritto italiano, comunitario e internazionale, vol. 1*, Modena: Mcchi, 23–44.

Carella, G. (2005) 'Lotta al terrorismo e protezione dei rifugiati' in U. Leanza (ed.) *Le migrazioni. Una sfida per il diritto internazionale, comunitario e interno: IX Convegno*, Roma, 17–18 giugno 2004, Naples: Editoriale Scientifica.

Carlier, J.-Y. and Leboef, L. (2017) 'The X. and X. case: Humanitarian visas and the genuine enjoyment of the substance of the rights, towards a middle way?', *EU Immigration and Asylum Law and Policy* http://eumigrationlawblog.eu.

Carreau, D. and Marrella, F. (2018) *Diritto internazionale*, Milan: Giuffrè.

Cassese, A. and Frulli, M. (eds.) (2017) *Diritto internazionale*, Bologna: il Mulino.

Cavaglieri, A. (1934) *Corso di diritto internazionale*, Naples: Rondinella.

Cherubini, F. (2012) L'asilo dalla Convenzione di Ginevra al diritto dell'Unione Europea, Bari: Cacucci.

Coleman, N. (2003) '*Non-Refoulement* Revised. Renewed Review of the Status of *Non-Refoulement* as Customary International Law', *European Journal of Migration and Law*, 5(1): 23–68.

Colmayer, L. and Signorini, M. (2017) 'I corridoi umanitari, possibili alternative di ingresso legale in Italia', *Immigrazione.it*, 281.

Conforti, B. (2005) *Le Nazioni Unite*, 7th edn., Padua: Cedam.

Conforti, B. (2018) *Diritto internazionale*, 11th edn., Naples: Editoriale Scientifica.

Courtland Robinson, W. (1998) Terms of Refuge: The Indochinese Exodus and the International Response, London: Zed Books.

De Sena, P. (2002) La nozione di giurisdizione statale nei trattati sui diritti dell'uomo, Turin: Giappichelli.

De Vattel, E. (1758) Le droit des gens ou principes de la loi naturelle appliqués à la conduite et aux affaires des nations et des souverains, London.

De Vitoria, F. (1557) *De Indis (Relactiones morale)*, Lyon.

De Vylder, H. (2017) 'X and X v. Belgium: A missed opportunity for the CJEU to rule on the State's obligations to issue humanitarian visa for those in need of protection', *Strasbourg Observers* http://strasbourgobservers.com

Del Guercio, A. (2016) La protezione dei richiedenti asilo nel diritto internazionale ed europeo, Naples: Editoriale Scientifica.
Del Guercio, A. (2017) 'La sentenza X. e X. della Corte di Giustizia sul rilascio del visto umanitario: analisi critica di un'occasione persa', *European Papers*, 2(1): 271–291.
Detrick, S. (1999) A Commentary on the United Nations Convention on the Rights of the Child, Article 10, The Hague: Brill.
Favilli, C. (1988) I limiti derivanti dal diritto internazionale all'espulsione dello straniero, Viterbo: Union Printing.
Favilli, C. (2017a) 'Visti umanitari e protezione internazionale: così vicini così lontani, *Diritti umani e diritto internazionale*, 11(2): 553–561.
Favilli, C. (2017b) 'L'urgenza di un'azione umanitaria', *il Mulino*, 19 October.
Frowein, J.A. (2013) 'Ius Cogens', in *Max Planck Encycolpedia of Public International Law*, Oxford: Oxford University Press.
Giuffrè, M. (2012) 'Watered-down Rights on the High Seas: Hirsi Jamaa and Others v Italy', *International & Comparative Law Quarterly*, 61(3): 728–750.
Goodwin-Gill, G. and McAdam, J. (2007) *The Refugee in International Law*, 3rd edn., Oxford: Oxford University Press.
Grahl-Madsen, A., Melander, G. and Ring, R. (1999) 'Art. 13' in G. Alfredsson and A. Eide (eds.) *The Universal Declaration of Human Rights*, The Hague/Boston/London: Nijhoff, 265–278.
Grotius, H. (1625) De jure belli ac pacis libri tres, Lausannae.
Guild, E. (2018) 'The UN's search for a Global Compact on Safe, Orderly and Regular Migration', *German Law Journal*, 18(7): 1779–1795.
Hall, W.E. and Higgins, A.P. (eds.) (1924) *International Law*, Oxford: Oxford University Press.
Hathaway, J.C. (2005) *The Rights of Refugees under International Law*, Cambridge: Cambridge University Press.
Hershey, A.S. (1927) The Essentials of International Public Law and Organization, New York: Macmillan.
Hurwitz, A. (2009) The Collective Responsibility of States to Protect Refugees, Oxford: Oxford University Press.
Ibsen Jensen, U. (2014) 'Humanitarian Visas: Option or Obligation? Study for the LIBE Committee, *CEPS Paper in Liberty and Security in Europe*, 68.
Impagliazzo, M. (2016) 'Le vie dell'integrazione 'latina', *Limes*, 7: 127–129.
Ineli-Ciger, M. (2016) 'An examination of the comprehensive plan of action as a response to mass influx of "boat people": Lessons learnt for a comprehensive approach to migration by sea' in V. Moreno-Lax and E. Papastavridis (eds.) *Boat Refugees and Migrants at Sea: A Comprehensive Approach, Integrating Maritime Security and Human Rights*, Leiden: Nijhoff, 408–437.
Kälin, W. (2003) 'Limits to expulsion under International Covenant on Civil and Political Rights' in F. Salerno (ed.) *Diritti dell'uomo, estradizione ed espulsione*, Padua: Cedam, 143 ff.
Lambert, H. (2017) 'Temporary Refuge from War: Customary International Law and the Syrian Conflict', *International & Comparative Law Quarterly*, 66(3): 723–745.
Lang, A. (2015) 'Il divieto di refoulement tra CEDU e Carta dei diritti fondamentali dell'Unione europea' in S. Amadeo and F. Spitaleri (eds.) *Le garanzie fondamentali dell'immigrazione in Europa*, Turin: Giappichelli, 209–244.

Lauterpracht, E. and Bethlehem, D. (2003) 'The scope and content of non-refoulement: Opinion' in E. Feller, V. Turk and F. Nicholson (eds.) *Refugee Protection in International Law. UNHCR's Global Consultations on International Protection*, Cambridge: Cambridge University Press, 87–177.

Lenzerini, F. (2009) Asilo e diritti umani: l'evoluzione del diritto d'asilo nel diritto internazionale, Milan: Giuffrè.

Lenzerini, F. (2012) 'Il principio del *non-refoulement* dopo la sentenza Hirsi della Corte europea dei diritti dell'uomo', *Rivista di diritto internazionale*, 95(3): 721–761.

McAdam, J. (2007) Complementary Protection in International Refugee Law, Oxford: Oxford University Press.

Milanovic, M. (2018) 'Jurisdiction and Responsibility. Trends in the Jurisprudence of the Strasbourg Court', in A. van Aaken and I. Motc (eds.) *The European Convention on Human Rights and General International Law*, Oxford: Oxford University Press.

Moreno-Lax, V. (2017a) Accessing Asylum in Europe. Extraterritorial Border Controls and Refugee Rights under EU Law, Oxford: Oxford University Press.

Moreno-Lax, V. (2017b) 'Asylum Visas as an Obligation under EU Law: Case PPU C-638/16 X, X v Belge (Part I and II)', *EU Immigration and Asylum Law and Policy* http://eumigrationlawblog.eu.

Moreno-Lax, V. (2018) 'The Added-Value of EU Legislation on Humanitarian Visas – Legal Aspects' in W. van Ballegooij and C. Navarra (eds.) *Humanitarian Visas. European Added Value Assessment Accompanying the European Parliament's Legislative Own-initiative Report. Study for the EP*, Brussels: European Parliament Research Service, 23–124.

Morgese, G. (2018) La solidarietà degli Stati membri dell'Unione europea in materia di immigrazione e asilo, Bari: Cacucci.

Morozzo della Rocca, P. (2017) 'I due protocolli d'intesa sui "corridoi umanitari" tra alcuni enti di ispirazione religiosa ed il governo ed il loro possible impatto sulle politiche di asilo e immigrazione', *Diritto, immigrazione e cittadinanza*, 1: 1–31.

Munari, F. (2015) 'Lo status di rifugiato e di richiedente protezione temporanea. La visione Europea del "diritto di Ginevra"' in S. Amadeo and F. Spitaleri (eds.) *op. cit.*, 47–69.

Mutti, A. (2017) 'L'importanza dei corridoi umanitari', *il Mulino*, February 14th.

Napoletano, N. (2012) 'La condanna dei "respingimenti' operati dall'Italia verso la Libia da parte della Corte Europea dei diritti umani: molte luci e qualche ombra', *Diritti umani e diritto internazionale*, 6(2): 436–447.

Nascimbene, B. (1984) Il trattamento dello straniero nel diritto internazionale ed europeo, Milan: Giuffrè.

Nascimbene, B. (2005) 'Flussi migratori tra sovranità statale e cooperazione internazionale' in U. Leanza (ed.) *op. cit.*

Noll, G. and Fagerlund, J. (2002) *Safe Avenues to Asylum? The Actual and Potential Role of EU Diplomatic Representations in Processing Asylum Requests*, Copenhagen: Danish Centre for Human Rights.

Nowak, M. (2005) U.N. Covenant on Civil and Political Rights. CCPR Commentary, 2nd edn. rev., Arlington: Engel.

Peers, S., Moreno-Lax, V., Garlick, M. and Guild, E. (eds.) (2015) *EU Immigration and Asylum Law (Text and Commentary) Volume 3: Asylum Law*, Leiden: Brill.

Plender, R. (2005) 'Forced Migrations Ground and Limits to States' Action' in U. Leanza (ed.) *op. cit.*

Politis, N. (1925) 'Le problème des limitations de la souveraineté et la théorie de l'abus des droits dans les rapports internationaux', *Recueil des Cours de l'Académie de droit international*, 1(6): 5 ff.

Raimondo, G. (2017) 'Visti umanitari: il caso X e X contro Belgio, C-638/16PPU', *SIDIblog*, http://www.sidiblog.org.

Riccardi, A. (2013) 'L'Europa dei migranti. Modelli di integrazione' in M. Impagliazzo (ed.) *Integrazione*, Milan: Guerini e associati.

Romano, S. (1939) *Corso di diritto internazionale*, Padua: Cedam.

Salerno, F. (2011) 'L'obbligo internazionale di non-refoulement dei richiedenti asilo' in C. Favilli (ed.) *Procedure e garanzie del diritto di asilo*, Padua: Cedam.

Scovazzi, T. (2015) 'Le norme generali e le altre categorie di norme' in T. Scovazzi (ed.) *Corso di diritto internazionale. Parte II*, Milan: Giuffrè.

Scovazzi, T. and Citroni, G. (2013) 'La tutela internazionale dei diritti umani' in T. Scovazzi (ed.) *Corso di diritto internazionale. Parte III*, Milan: Giuffrè.

Shelton, L. (2014) Advanced Introduction to International Human Rights Law, Cheltenham: Edward Elgar.

Sossai, M. (2017) 'Canali di ingresso legale sicuro dei migranti in Europa: il modello dei "corridoi umanitari"', in U. Curi (ed.) *Vergogna ed esclusione. L'Europa di fronte alla sfida dell'emigrazione*, Rome: Castelvecchi, 75–89.

Spinelli, F. (2017) 'Sui visti umanitari per i profughi la battaglia è ancora aperta', *Internazionale*, 24 March.

Stenberg, G. (1989) *Non-expulsion and Non-refoulement*, Uppsala: Iustus Forlag.

Verdross, A. (1931) 'Les règles internationales concernant le traitement des étrangers', *Recueil des Cours de l'Académie de droit international*, 3(37).

Wouters, C.W. (2009) International Legal Standards for the Protection from Refoulement: A Legal Analysis of the Prohibitions of Refoulement Contained in the Refugee Convention, the European Convention of Human Rights, the International Covenant on Civil and Political Rights and the Convention against Torture, Cambridge: Intersentia.

Yahyaoui Krivenko, E. (2012) 'Hospitality and Sovereignty: What Can We Learn from the Canadian Private Sponsorship of Refugees Program?', *International Journal of Refugee Law*, 24(3): 579–602.

Zanghì, C. (2011) 'L'intervento in alto mare tra "*non refoulement*", diritti umani e contrasto all'immigrazione clandestina' in N. Parisi, M. Fumagalli Meraviglia, A. Santini and D.G. Rinoldi (eds.) *Scritti in onore di Ugo Draetta*, Naples: Editoriale Scientifica.

Zaniboni, E. (2005) 'Verso l'erosione dell'elemento territoriale dell'istituto dell'asilo nel diritto internazionale?' in U. Leanza (ed.) *op. cit.*

Zoetewij-Turhan, M. and Progin-Theuerkauf, S. (2017a) 'AG Mengozzi's Opinion On Granting Visas to Syrians From Aleppo: Wishful Thinking?', *European Law Blog* http://europeanlawblog.eu.

Zoetewij-Turhan, M. and Progin-Theuerkauf, S. (2017b) 'CJEU Case C-638/16 PP, X and X – Dashed Hopes for a Legal Pathway to Europe', *European Law Blog* http://europeanlawblog.eu.

Zorzi Giustiniani, F. (2018) 'Divieto di non-refoulement e tortura. Osservazioni in margine al General Comment No. 4 alla Convenzione ONU contro la tortura e altre pene o trattamenti crudeli, inumani o degradanti', *Federalismi.it*, 2.

Chapter 25

Emigrations and immigrations in South America

Legal aspects

Giovanni Cordini and Andrea Iurato [1]

25.1. *Italy and Latin America in Giulio Cesare Buzzati's opening speech of the Academic Year at the University of Pavia (1906)*

I would like to start with a reference to the inaugural speech given by the distinguished Professor of International Law Giulio Cesare Buzzati at the University of Pavia during the opening ceremony on 5th November 1906. [2] Buzzati's speech, entitled "Italy and Latin America" ("L'Italia e l'America Latina"), offered an acute and broad overview regarding the Italian emigration and the legislations on the granting of citizenship in different countries of the Latin American continent. Cases regarding numerous states are mentioned: Argentina, Bolivia, Brazil, Colombia, Costa Rica, Ecuador, Mexico, Paraguay, Peru, Uruguay, and Venezuela. The topic chosen for this speech was surely inspired by the verification, not only statistical but also historical, that the Italian emigration to South America remarkably increased between the end of the 1800s and the beginning of the 1900s. Therefore, it was important to underline some legal aspects strictly connected to this phenomenon. The topic is interesting even today, although in from different perspective: in fact, our country, Italy, and Europe in general, are nowadays the favourite destination of a consistent number of migrants. Consequently, we must face problems that the author has already pointed out, with different perspectives and conditions, for Latin American countries. The theme of citizenship is still fundamental when it comes to analysing the problems posed by migratory flows.

---

[1] Giovanni Cordini wrote paragraphs 1 and 2; Andrea Iurato wrote paragraphs 3, 4, 5, 6, 7 and 8.

[2] The opening speech of Giulio Cesare Buzzati, titled "Italy and Southern America" (*"L'Italia e l'America Latina"*) was pronounced on 5th November 1906 and later published by the Tip. Successori Bizzoni, Pavia 1907. I am grateful to the colleague Marco Mugnaini, who gave me the possibility to retrieve the text of this lecture (*"Discorso"*) at the National Library of Florence. It is possible to find significant bibliographic information regarding Professor Giulio Cesare Buzzati (Venice, 26th April 1862 – Milan, 19th November 1920), father of the famous writer Dino Buzzati and eminent Internationalist at the University of Pavia, in the obituary dedicated to him by the "*Rivista di Diritto Internazionale*", a. XIV, Series III, Vol. I, (1921–22), pp. 381–395. Moreover, this obituary contains a long list of the juridical works of Buzzati.

The European Union, at the beginning of the hard and incomplete path towards integration, posed the free movement of persons and the rights of establishment as essential conditions to start this historical process. Considering immigration, the theme of legal integration and the issue of recognition of rights, in relation to the territory where the migrant settles, is still relevant and only partially resolved. In the sharp analysis made by Buzzati, the examination of the legal conditions is forerun by the statistical data and a presentation of the conditions of life of the Italian migrants in different countries of South America, with more specific references to the two countries where this process was particularly relevant. These states are Argentina and Brazil: in these two countries, in fact, broad national Italian communities were being established. Buzzati highlighted the development of "natural communities" ("comunità spontanee") which did not benefit, until that moment, from a coordinated and convergent action by the Italian state. Rightly, the eminent author reminded us that this emigration had, as its main motivation, the search of better socio-economic conditions. This was a sort of "new colonization"; however, this one did not have any of the massacres, raids, and slaveries which characterized the events following the discovery of the Latin American continent and its progressive conquest by the European powers. It is easy to notice similarities with what is happening today in Europe, a continent to which many migrants – forced to leave their territory of origin because of war, famine, degradation of environmental conditions and whatever may endanger life conditions and offend human dignity – look at in the hope of a better future. It is well known that immigration is a phenomenon deeply rooted in the history of different populations, and concerns both individuals and families. The reasons that lead many men and women to migrate are various; however, the seemingly most recurring in history are of economic and social nature. This also emerges from the comparison between different Latin American countries analysed by Buzzati. Regardless of the conditions which determined this phenomenon and which can be precisely classified when analysing the different countries in which the migratory flow is relevant (for this I rely on the supplementary paragraphs of Iurato, PhD) it is possible to notice a common element in the Italian migration in South America: the search of a "new homeland" ("Nuova Patria") in which migrants could build a future for themselves and their families. It was not only a condition of "temporary" residence in a country which was different from the one of citizenship. This consideration involves, first, the political dimension, which had to regulate and discipline the migratory flows; second, the subjective aspect of the relation between migrants and administrations – both on a national and local level – of the various states of Latin America; and third, the relations, never interrupted, between individual migrants, their associations and representations and original communities. The migratory flows analysed by Buzzati allow us to highlight both the constant search of better life and work conditions in a foreign country, as well as some differences. These can be found in every state when analysing historical data which allow the observation of the causes and consequences of every migratory phenomenon and the characteristics of the connected policies. It seems to me that the most evident of these differences depends on the observation that current migratory flows in Latin America must be studied while considering also internal flows and the legislations in force in every single Latin American state.

25.2. *Citizenship and immigration in Latin America: the prevalence of jus soli*

A topic that is discussed extensively in the text is the citizenship, observing how in Latin American states the granting of citizenship by jus soli prevailed. The children of Italian migrants born in the territories of Latin American states, therefore, were considered citizens of the country in which they were born, regardless of the legal condition of their parents. While in almost all the European legislations the granting of citizenship was "surrounded by the strictest regulations and solemn commitments" ("circondata dalle più rigorose disposizioni e da forme solenni"), Buzzati observed that in Latin American countries, for aliens who lived there, a simple declaration in front of the administrative or judicial authorities was sufficient, normally after a brief stay (three years for Chile, two for Argentina, Brazil, Paraguay and Mexico, and one year only for Bolivia, Colombia, Costa Rica, Ecuador, and San Salvador). It is a common opinion in the doctrine that the legal basis of citizenship must be found in the domestic law of every sovereign state (Quadri 1967; Biscottini 1960). The status of citizen is concretely determined by the national law of the community of belonging: a) for what concerns the definition of the ways of acquisition, loss and re-acquisition; b) for cases of stateless status and double or multiple citizenship; c) in relation to the contents of the legal qualification expressed by the status civitatis, that is the determination of the dense twine of rights, duties, obligations and powers which derive from the status of citizen; d) for the definition of the administrative procedures and judicial guarantees concerning the ways of acquisition, loss and re-acquisition of the status civitatis (Cordini 1998). Consequently, the states of Latin America considered autonomously the necessity to integrate immediately the newborns on their territories in their national communities by granting them their citizenship, regardless of their condition of origin. This situation created doubts in Buzzati; in fact, he believed it was detrimental for our migrants to have a division between nationality and citizenship. For this reason, he advocated support measures by the Italian state for our communities abroad. Even in a dated vision which still considered the European states as exporters of civility and progress for other peoples, in continuity with typical conceptions of the colonialism, Buzzati's proposal of "studying the legal and political possibility of the coexistence of the two citizenships" – with the appropriate modifications of this historical legal institution – appears reasonable and well-explained. Illustrating his thoughts on the evolution of the institution of citizenship, the illustrious author indeed referred to the inviolable human rights which were establishing themselves as the cornerstone of the liberal and democratic constitutionalism. In fact, he observed: "man is treated in the same way in all the civil Countries, this means that regarding civil and public rights the alien is more and more assimilated to the national, except for some diversities imposed by the social interest of every State, diversities that tend to decrease more and more every day". Given these circumstances, Buzzati believed it was possible and commendable to leave to migrants in America the rights and duties connected to their original Italian citizenship. These capacities would remain even in case migrants were not able to exercise them concretely because of the circumstances, not for legal reasons. The recent debate on the vote of Italian people abroad, which brought about the constitutional reform for an effective recognition and a concrete and possible exercise of this fundamental political right, seems to confirm the modernity of the topic of the erudite inaugural speech by Buzzati.

25.3. *New migrations and migratory policies in Latin America*

The last fifteen years have represented a season of great openness in the field of human migrations; some scholars affirm that today Latin America has the most liberal attitude in the world towards migratory processes and towards the recognition of migrants' rights (Acosta Arcarazo and Feline Freier 2015a, 2015b).

The change in the characteristics of the migratory flows in the region is one of the main reasons behind this new approach. In the last decade, the flow of Latin American emigrants has overtaken that of immigrants, with an increase in emigration towards Europe. As far as regional flows are concerned, the number of immigrants in traditionally receiving countries such as Argentina, Brazil and Venezuela has decreased, whereas countries of historical emigration, like Ecuador and Chile, have become emerging destinations (Feline Freier 2013).[3]

As for the legal aspects, the fact that the season of Latin American constitutionalism was initiated in the aftermath of the fall of the dictatorial regimes must be considered in the first instance; in fact, it has led to a preeminent role of the protection of human rights.[4] With the recognition in almost all the constitutional charts of the supremacy of the international law and the ratification of numerous treaties regarding human rights, not signed until the last fifteen years or not ratified, most of the countries of the region have overcome their past legislations, full of illiberal and discriminatory principles, typical examples of their past authoritarian governments. In this sense, the "International Convention on the Protection of the Rights of All Migrant Workers and Members of Their Families",[5] ratified by almost all the States of the area during the

[3] Other useful and richer statistics are provided in Ortíz 2013.

[4] For a systematic comparative analysis of the present Latin American constitutions, please refer to Acuña 2012.

[5] Adopted by the General Assembly of the United Nations in Resolution 45/158 of 18.12.1990; entered into force on 01.07.2003.

last decade,[6] has had, among the others, a particularly important role.

The preeminent role of the development, albeit not always linear, of the different processes of regional integration, the MERCOSUR and the Comunidad Andina (Andean Community) above all, must be recognized.[7] Although these processes were initially intended to realize merely economic objectives and the liberalization of exchanges, the pursuit of these goals has required governments to progressively create a space of free movement of persons, or at least of workers. This has brought us to the elaboration of a genuine common policy on migration. For the sake of brevity, only the Agreement on the Regularization of Internal Migration of MERCOSUR Citizens[8] and the Agreement on Residency for Nationals of the MERCOSUR States, Bolivia and Chile, both signed in 2002,[9] can be mentioned. Less developed, but older, is the cooperation on migration within the CAN (Andean Community of Nations): for example, the decision No. 116 of 1977,[10] which aspires to give a uniform discipline to all the aspects of the management of regional migratory flows, and the decision No. 113 of the same year, on the equal treatment in social security for citizens of the Community who moved to another State, member of the Community, for work purposes.[11]

25.4. *Origins and establishment of the right to migrate in recent reforms*

The Argentine Republic

The new season of Ibero-American migratory policies has concerned, to different degrees, the legislations of the countries of the region; among them, Argentina, Ecuador, Uruguay and Bolivia stand out because of their expressed recognition of a human right to migrate.

Argentina was the first nation in the world to recognize by law a "right to migrate" in 2003, identified in Article 4 of the ley de migraciones (migrations act) No. 25.871[12]

---

[6] With the significant exceptions of Brazil and Venezuela: the latter has signed the Convention, but has never ratified it.

[7] Acosta Arcarazo and Geddes 2014; Ceriani Cernadas 2011; Nicolao 2011: 114–116; Novick (ed.) 2010; Romano 2009; Stang 2009; Santestevan 2007; Torales *et al.* 2003.

[8] Acuerdo sobre regularización migratoria interna de ciudadanos del MERCOSUR, Bolivia y Chile, Decisión MERCOSUR 5 de diciembre de 2002.

[9] Acuerdo sobre residencia para nacionales de los Estados partes del MERCOSUR, Bolivia y Chile, Decisión MERCOSUR 06.12.2002.

[10] Decisión No. 16, 17.02.1977, Instrumento Andino de Migración Laboral.

[11] Decisión No. 13, 17.02.1977, Instrumento Andino de Seguridad Social.

[12] Ley 25.871, 17.12.2003, *politica migratoria argentina*, in *Boletin Oficial* 21.01.2004. The law was not the result of a spontaneous political initiative, but rather an imposition: in fact, it was a mediation

as an "essential and inalienable right of a person [...] guaranteed on the basis of the principles of equality and universality". The right is defined as fundamental and universal, but the text of the law does not define its contents and limits. The law does not introduce any liberalization of the entry and residence in the Argentinian territory, but establishes a deep discontinuity with the previous law, the ley Videla, introduced in 1981 during the dictatorship.[13] This law not only required very strict conditions of entry and permanence on the Argentinian territory, but also did not include any protection for irregular immigrants. The reform, entered into force in 2004, shows its innovation from its objectives: guaranteeing the right to family reunification, promoting the integration of regular immigrants, and avoiding any form of discrimination (Art. 3).

Article 5 establishes the obligation of the state to guarantee the effective equality of treatment for aliens and citizens in the enjoyment of their rights, although it immediately adds that it is valid "as long as the conditions established by the law for the entry and the residence are fulfilled". In favour of regular immigrants, the access to social services, public health, public education, justice and social security is provided for them under the same conditions as citizens, with the clarification that the rights to education, also to an academic level, to healthcare services and social assistance are guaranteed to everyone, not representing the possible irregular migratory condition an impediment.

The law goes on to list (Art. 29) a series of personal conditions which preclude the entry to or residence on the Argentinian territory. These are mostly previous police records for particularly serious crimes[14] or crimes connected to immigration; there are also impediments directly linked to the violation of the migration law, such as having presented false documents to the competent authorities in order to have the entry or residence on the Argentinian territory granted, or having entered the territory of the state illegally.

As far as the procedural aspects are concerned, of particular note is the disposition (Art. 61) which compels the DNM (Direción nacional de migraciones, National Directory of Migration), whenever it has ascertained the irregular presence of an alien on the national territory, not to expel him or her immediately, but rather to grant to the person involved a deadline not exceeding thirty days[15] to regulate his or her position.

---

solution to avoid a conviction by the Inter-American Commission of Human Rights (Case *J.C. De la Torre c. Argentina*, Solución amistosa de 21.07.2011, Informe num. 85/11) on account of the fact that the laws in force at that time in the country did not provide any judicial control in deportation procedures of aliens. See Rodríguez Miglio and Toledo 2012: 337 ff.; San Juan 2004.

[13] Ley 22.439, 23.03.1981, ley general de migraciones y fomento de la inmigración, in Boletin Oficial 27.03.1981.

[14] The law includes all the crimes for which a penalty of imprisonment of at least three years is provided for, as well as certain specific types of claims, such as: trafficking of weapons, human beings or drugs, money-laundering, genocide, war crimes, terrorism, crimes against humanity, other crimes within the jurisdiction of the International Criminal Court, facilitation and exploitation of illegal immigration, facilitation and exploitation of prostitution.

[15] The deadline is set by Art. 61 of the Implementing Regulation of the Law (decreto nacional

Having this term expired without the alien having his or her status legalized, the DNM would decree the expulsion but – another disposition worthy of attention – the order must be automatically suspended and forwarded to the judicial authority, which would have to judge its lawfulness. The recipient of any decision of the administrative authority has the right to appeal for a review, going through official channels or challenging before the judicial authority.

The Republic of Ecuador

Argentina was the first country to recognize the right to migrate, but Ecuador was the first country to recognize the same right in its constitution.

Article 3 of the new Charter of 2008 [16] appoints to the state some "primary duties", among which is to guarantee "without any discrimination the effective enjoyment" of the constitutional rights for "its inhabitants". First, referring to all the inhabitants, instead of the citizens only, significantly defines the approach of the Constitutional Assembly towards the matter of the different legal condition of the citizen and the alien.

As regards the dispositions directly regarding migrations, Article 11 lists – among the forbidden reasons of discrimination – also the "migratory condition", which should impede any form of unreasonable inequality not only towards aliens, but also towards those among them who are illegally on the Ecuadorian territory. A section of the Title devoted to the rights is specifically dedicated to "human mobility" and it opens with the recognition, for all men and women, of "the right to migrate" (Art. 40), specifying that "no human being will be identified or considered illegal because of his or her migratory condition". However, it must be taken into account that the second paragraph of the same article applies only to Ecuadorians who have emigrated abroad; this paragraph casts a doubt as to whether the favourite beneficiaries of the recognition of this right are the foreign immigrants or the Ecuadorian emigrants.

Until 2016, the ordinary legislator had not provided for an adaptation of the ordinary legislation to the constitutional parameters. The ley de migracion, in force until the beginning of 2017, [17] represented a mere codification of previous texts, modified various times but never entirely reformed. The text of the law did not mention the rights of the aliens, it only regulated the conditions necessary for entry, residence and expulsion, with emphasis on the latter two.

The legal framework drastically changed with the approval, in January 2017, of the

---

616/2010, decreto reglamentario de la ley 25.871 sobre politica migratoria argentina, in *Boletin Oficial* 06.05.2010).

[16] Constitución de la Republica del Ecuador, in *Registro Oficial* 449, 20.10.2008. For studies on the new Ecuadorian constitution of 2008: Martinez Dalmau 2016; Bagni 2013; Santamaría 2011; Santamaría *et al.* 2008.

[17] Ley de migración, codificación 6, in *Registro Oficial* 563, 12.04.2005.

ley orgánica de moviliad humana (organic law on human mobility), [18] based on a draft law kept inactive for almost two years and approved by the Parliament only a few days before the end of the third and last term of President Correa.

From its very heading, the law explicitly declares its innovative purpose of creating a comprehensive discipline for all the aspects of human migrations, considering all the different conditions of persons in mobility, as specified in Article 1. This article, in fact, defines the objective of the provision as: "regulating the exercise of rights and obligations, the institutional aspects and the procedures related to persons in human mobility, which include emigrants, immigrants, persons in transit, emigrants returned to the Country, applicants for international protection, victims of human trafficking and smuggling of migrants and their families". Therefore, the legislator did not want a mere consolidated law to gather various disciplines, all different and independent, but it rather wanted to compile them under a common frame of principles, definitions and objectives, which impede to the interpreter to consider every category as a separate sector. In fact, they must be considered as part of an organic system, with all that this entails in terms of systematic interpretation of the individual provisions.

Article 2 offers a catalogue of principles which sustains and inspires the whole text, whatever the specific category of the migrant. It states the principle of universal citizenship, defined as "the recognition of the power of every human being to move freely around the world" and "it implies the portability of one's own rights regardless of the migratory condition, nationality and place of origin, which should lead – in the perspective of the legislator – to the progressive disappearance of the status of alien": the appeal of the legal development proposed does not impede one to observe how, in concrete, the disposition does not refer to the conservation, in case of migration, of all the rights, but only to the "human rights". The recognition of the "power" of every human being to move from one territory to another appears more interesting, because it implies the imposition of a stricter limit to the imperium of the State in the matter of entry and residence of aliens.

On one hand, it contains a prohibition to the state to limit the human rights to persons in mobility, and on the other the new doctrine on human mobility, proposed in the discussed law and exposed in the paragraph dedicated to the "free human mobility", contains a positive obligation to the state to protect (amparo) any person, family or other group who is in mobility "with the intention of circulating and staying in the territory of destination temporarily or definitively". A short description must be given of the pro-persona in mobility principle – which prescribes the most favourable interpretation of the provisions imposed by law and secondary acts for the person in mobility – and the reference to the regional integration and to the development and creation of a regional citizenship as future perspectives which entail, as an immediate consequence, a more favourable treatment for regional migrants. The latter, in fact, are exempt from the visa obligation and benefit from a more favourable discipline

[18] Ley 31.01.2017, ley orgànica de movilidad humana, in Registro Oficial, Supl., No. 38, 06.02.2017.

regarding the granting of a residence permit, both temporary and permanent.

The discipline of the expulsion from the territory of the state still does not include the involvement of a judge, although in this matter all the typical due process rights are guaranteed to the alien concerned, even the possible right to have access to legal aid and the right to the free assistance of an interpreter. More interesting is the prohibition to adopt precautionary measures apt to guarantee to execution of the expulsion which imply "the deprivation or restriction of the right to personal freedom". This entails an insurmountable prohibition of adopting detention measures to the alien caught in an irregular condition.

Finally, the law designs the institutional setting based on two principles: the first one is the principle of separation – through the attribution to different authorities – between the programmatic functions and the guarantee ones; the second one is the imposition of the principles of human mobility as a cross-cutting approach to all public policies and to the action of all the administrations, also at the local level.

The Oriental Republic of Uruguay and the Plurinational State of Bolivia

Uruguay is the third state that recognized the "derecho a la migración" (right to migrate) with law No. 18.250, approved in 2008. [19] The framework of the law clearly has its roots in the act approved five years before in Argentina, with an exception made for secondary aspects. Bolivia has recently joined the group of countries that have recognized a "right to migrate"; in fact, it approved the ley de migración No. 370 in 2013, [20] which stands out as the first legislative text in the world to recognize and discipline migrations due to climate changes. [21]

The reform process has concerned other countries; although the reforms which have recently concerned these states have not likewise expressly declared a right to migrate, they have made important progress towards the recognition of the preeminent value of the human rights of migrants. [22]

25.5. *The discursive gap*

These laws, amended in an openly liberal way in favour of migrations, have been

---

[19] Ley No. 8250, *migración*, in *Diario Oficial* 27407, 17.01.2008, art. 1.

[20] Ley No. 70, *ley de migración*, in *Gazeta Oficial* 523NEC, 08.05.2013. Il *derecho a la migración* è enunciato all'art. 12, par. II.1.

[21] Ivi, art. 65.

[22] In particular, about the reforms carried out in Mexico, Costa Rica and Nicaragua see Pizzarro 2011.

criticized by different scholars, political analysts and sociologists in primis, who have stated its instrumentality to propaganda purposes and the consequent ineffectiveness in changing the real conditions of migrants. In these studies, it is common to refer to a "discursive gap" (Acosta Arcarazo and Feline Freier 2015c),[23] which would characterize the migratory policies adopted by the countries of the area in the last fifteen years. It would be constituted by the gap between the solemn declarations made by the heads of state or government on free human mobility, universal citizenship and protection of the rights of aliens and the actual concretization of the new principles in terms of reforms and measures suitable to produce a concrete change in the administrative and judiciary practices on the condition of migrants.

Looking at the instruments of regional integration, the new approach – especially through the MERCOSUR[24] – has induced the governments to place alongside the traditional economic and market goals a growing attention to the social dimension of the processes of integration, in which common policies on human migrations have acquired a preponderant role. This, however, would have created a contradiction: the liberalization policies on international migrations, in fact, would actually mainly be directed towards labour migrants and regional movements, affecting very little or not at all the condition of irregular and overseas migrants. However, the juridical experience shows how the mere statements of principles sometimes can produce relevant legal consequences over time, thanks to the administrative practice and, above all, the jurisprudence.[25]

25.6. *Hesitations and developmental perspectives in the Argentinian jurisprudence*

Looking at Argentina, it can be considered surprising how even several years before the approval of the law of 2004, the jurisprudence of the Supreme Court made impressive steps forward in the field of access for aliens to the same social and civil rights enjoyed by citizens.[26] The Court laid down the principle of total equality between citizens and

---

[23] The concept is repeatedly explained in some contributions by Acosta Arcarazo and Feline Freier, who highlight, about human migration in Latin America, the presence of "a range of smaller and larger gaps between discursive liberalisation and legislative change" that does not differ too much, while in opposite terms, from the situation in the United States and the EU "where similar tensions between liberalism and restrictiveness persist – albeit against the background of restrictive discourse", in Acosta Arcarazo and Feline Freier 2015c: 34; the same opinion is expressed in Acosta Arcarazo and Feline Freier 2015b: 174; Acosta Arcarazo and Feline Freier 2015a: 666 ff.

[24] Romano 2009: 274 ff., even with regard to the CAN, on which please refer also to Stang 2009.

[25] García argues that in Argentina, with regard to the possibility to obtain a residence permit, the right to migrate did not produce any substantial improvement for migrants who are not citizens of MERCOSUR countries: García 2013.

[26] Basing his arguments on both the evolution in the law and in meta-juridical factors, Olmos

(regularly residents) aliens in 1988 in the Repetto case,[27] grounding the judgement on Articles 14 and 20 of the Constitution, which establish equal access to work and professions for citizens and aliens. The Repetto doctrine has influenced the subsequent jurisprudence,[28] leading to the declaration of unconstitutionality of those norms which limited the access to the judicial career only to people born in Argentina or with Argentinian parents,[29] and to the recognition of the right of aliens to have access to the medical profession[30] or contracts in schools.[31]

However, the few law reviews that do exist are unanimous in considering disappointing the practical effects of the new law of 2004 and in pointing out how the administrative and judicial practices are parts of a continuous thread, instead of being discontinuous, with the past. The approval of the new law, in fact, did not lead to a bloom of judgements recalling the new principles, in particular to the right to migrate.[32] Only one of the courts appointed to analyse the merit of a case, the Cámara Federal of the State of Paraná, immediately applied the new legislative framework in the aftermath of its entry into force.[33]

Giupponi suggests a temporal partition, from 1890 to the present, of the Argentine Supreme Court's jurisprudence: Olmos Giupponi 2011.

[27] Corte Suprema de Justicia de la Nación Argentina (CSJN), *Repetto Maria Inés c. Provincia de Buenos Aires*, 08.11.1988, Fallos 311:2272. The case concerned the suspected unconstitutionality of an act approved by the Province of Buenos Aires, in which Argentinean citizenship was required as a prerequisite to obtain a teaching position in a pre-scholar public institute. Please refer to: Rodríguez Miglio and Toledo 2012: 338; Treacy 2011: 191.

[28] The *Repetto* case represents a milestone in the Argentinean constitutional jurisprudence because of the inauguration, by the Supreme Court of the doctrine of the so-called "*categorias sospechosas de constitucionalidad*" and the related test aimed at judging the legitimacy of any act introducing a discrimination in the enjoyment of constitutional rights. According to the Court's judgment: "ante los categóricos términos del art. 20 de la Constitución Nacional (...) toda distinción entre nacionales y extranjeros, en lo que respecta al goce de los derechos reconocidos en la Ley Fundamental, se halla afectada por una presunción de inconstitucionalidad ... aquél que sostenga la legitimidad de la citada distinción debe acreditar la existencia de un 'interés estatal urgente' para justificar aquélla, y no es suficiente, a tal efecto, que la medida adoptada sea 'razonable' (considerando No.)".

[29] CSJN, *Pedro Cornelio Federico Hooft c. Provincia de Buenos Aires*, 16.09.2003, Fallos: 318:1256.

[30] Cámara de Apelaciones en lo Contencioso Administrativo de la Ciúdad Autónoma de Buenos Aires, *Álvaro Guzmán Aguirre c. GCBA*, Expediente 16341.00.

[31] Juzgado en lo Criminal y Correcional de Transición nro. 1 de Mar del Plata, *Sandra Edith Méndez Correa*, 29.05.2002, Causa 3/53.344; Juzgado en lo Criminal y Correcional de Transición nro. 1 de Mar del Plata, *Franca Posteraro c. Dirección General de Cultura y Educación de la Provincia de Buenos Aires*, 12.6.2003, LNL 30.05.2004. For some opposite judgements, refer to: Tribunal Superior de Justicia de la Ciúdad Autónoma de Buenos Aires, *Asociación por los Derechos Civiles c. GCBA*, 09.08.2006. The notary career is still not accessible by aliens or citizens naturalized for less than ten years: Tribunal Superior de Justicia de la Ciúdad Autónoma de Buenos Aires, *Asociación por los Derechos Civiles c. GCBA*, 31.05.2005.

[32] In the aftermath of the entry into force of the new migration act a debate started among Argentinean courts concerning the immediate applicability of the act, considering that no implementing regulation was approved until 2010. Please refer to Rodríguez Miglio and Toledo 2012: 381.

[33] The Court affirmed that: "legality or illegality are referred only to conducts (not to people, 'no

As far as the Supreme Court is concerned, the first references to the new, innovative principles were made only three years after the reform (Zhang Hang 2007[34]).

In these years, the Argentinian courts, especially the local courts, have proved themselves inadequate in the role of guarantor of the rights of immigrants. However, it is significant to refer to an important judgement of the Supreme Court, the I-Hsing Ni case of 2009 on naturalization.[35] The case concerned a Chinese citizen who, after entering the country in 1995, obtained temporary permits, renewed from time to time, but had his request to legalize his position rejected in 2001 because of his insufficient income. The application for citizenship was rejected by the administrative authority, and by the local judges as well, on the basis of a too obvious argument: the period of continuous residence, necessary to apply for citizenship, must be considered as regular citizenship and not mere domicile. The decision and the reasoning of the Supreme Court are surprising: starting from the assumption that the legislation regulating the migratory condition of aliens confines its effects for the sole purpose of discipling the entry and residence of aliens on the Argentinian territory, and that the rule that requires the continuous permanence on the Argentinian territory for two years does not specify the regular nature of this permanence, the Court concluded that the regularity or not of the migratory condition of the alien for naturalization purposes is irrelevant.

25.7. *Minimal role of judges and applicative expectations of the Ecuadorian reform*

Looking at Ecuador, the havens reached by jurisprudence on this topic are directly influenced by the minimal role of guarantor given to the judicial authority on entry, residence and expulsion of aliens, both in the legislation in force until 2017 and in that which has just entered into force. The constitutional reform of 2008 and the recent innovations on international protection, in fact, have given rise to a situation where the most interesting innovations on this subject come from the jurisprudence of the Constitutional Court.

Particularly interesting is the reasoning of the judgement No. 90 of 2015,[36] a proceeding in which the Court of Quito was called upon to verify the violation of the constitutional right to refuge against a foreigner, whose application for the recognition of the refugee status was rejected on the sole ground of not having respected the time limit of fifteen days. In the reasoning, the Court warns the judges having jurisdiction on the substance. It is written that the specific personal situation of the asylum seeker

---

human being is illegal') violating criminal rules, not also administrative ones": Cámara Federal de Apelaciones Paraná, *Azeng Xiankai*, 22.06.2004, quoted and annotated in García 2013: 232.

[34] CSJN, Zhang Hang c. EN-Ministerio de RREE y Culto, 23.10.2007, Fallos 330:4554.

[35] CSJN, *I-Hsing Ni*, 23.06.2009, Fallos 332:1466.

[36] Corte Constitucional, sentencia 090-15-SEP-CC, caso 0056-12-IN, 25.03.2015.

"obliged the judicial and administrative authorities [...] to act as efficient guardians of the constitutional right to a refuge"; the judges, the Court criticises, "have ignored their juridical obligation to protect the constitutional principles" and have resorted "to legal formalities which limit" the constitutional right to a refuge and make the judgement under appeal "lacking a constitutional analysis". "The modern constitutionalism requires the judges to apply the principles and constitutional values through effective juridical reasonings", because "the constitutional justice implies an overcoming of the principle of legality in favour of the lawfulness and constitutionality ones". The judges, therefore, must take into prime consideration the fact that "the Ecuadorian State, as integral part of the international community, has assumed many obligations, including the protection and guarantee of human rights [...] of the persons who have obtained or applied for the status of refugee".

Regarding the new organic law on human mobility, the reform promises to mitigate – and possibly resolve – many of the contradictions which used to characterize the coexistence of the new constitutional principles with the dictatorial legislation. Although there are gaps and equivocal dispositions and the implementing provisions have not yet been published at the time of writing, the more innovative and characterizing aspect of this law is, without any doubt, the integrated approach to human mobility. It will be interesting to see how, in the immediate future, the responsibility assumed by Ecuador as the first legislation in the world to recognize a principle of universal citizenship will be translated into an effective change of the administrative and judicial practices on the legal condition of aliens. Another interesting aspect to analyse will be the concrete form given to the recognition of a higher level of protection of migrants in the decisions of administrative authorities and courts.

However, the Ecuadorian discipline on migrations is still characterized by a persistent gap (although today attenuated) between the innovative impetus of the constitutional principles and a hesitant transposition in the discipline of enforcement. This characteristic is particularly evident when comparing the Ecuadorian legislation with the reforms recently adopted in other legislations of the region. The Ecuadorian experience is comparable, although more mature, to the almost contemporary Bolivian constitutional and legislative reform. On the basis of this, a basic – and necessarily summary – distinction of two models of human mobility can be identified: an "Andean" model and an "Argentinian" one, borrowed from Uruguay. The latter, although more hesitant on the innovation on principles, is characterized by a more solid pragmatism, especially in the procedural guarantees; these two aspects make this model close to the European one.

Analysing the procedural aspects, the significant progresses made by the legislator must be appreciated. Although it is hard to understand the choice to exclude the necessary intervention of the judicial authority in proceedings on expulsion, in contrast with the traditional Argentinian position, these procedures – like others laid down by law – have acquired the standards and guarantees of the due process, whilst maintaining an essentially administrative nature. The choice to exclude a priori the detention from the precautionary measures, to guarantee the execution of repatriations, is particularly significant. For the first time, in fact, the principle of inviolability of personal freedom in proceedings on migrations, laid down by the same law, is applied.

Lastly, the new institutional competences framework, necessary to apply the discipline of human mobility, deserves attention. The imposed cross consideration of the migratory issue on all the administrations at every level of government promises the flourishing of laboratories of public policies, especially at the local level. Moreover, the choice to separate the decision-making and guarantee competences from the controlling and sanctioning ones is particularly significant, especially considering the previous discipline, which is characterized by a securitarian and repressive approach.

25.8. *Content and perspectives of the right to migrate*

Before drawing conclusions on the effectiveness of the right to migrate in the cited legislations, it should be specified what "right to migrate" means. As already discussed, the only legislations in the world that have recognized it, with the name of "right to migrate" or "right to migration", have not defined its content. Moreover, the right to migrate lacks an international recognition and a doctrinal tradition; it must therefore be concluded that the same rules that recognize the right define its content, avoiding ideological or subjective contaminations and limiting themselves to a logical reconstruction of the available legal data.

First, a common misunderstanding must be clarified: the right to migrate is not equated to the freedom of movement. While the freedom of movement is the simple "right to move" from one territory to another, the right to migrate is the right to move in and out a territorial community, and in this sense appears as a right with a political connotation, as Itzcovich (2013) writes. The freedom of movement is historically characterized by its instrumentality to a juridically protected interest, often – but not only – of economical nature: for example, the ius peregrinandi, granted in the Middle Ages to merchants, pilgrims, students and academics. [37] This freedom has been maintained in an economical sense, and is at the basis of regional processes of integration and establishment of free market areas. Therefore, the freedom of movement entails by definition a precarious and temporary relationship between the person and the territory, because it is linked to the persistence of the interest that justifies it: work, study, etc.

Looking at South America, the reported instrumentality of the new migratory policies has brought the lack of normative reforms in some countries, whereas in others it has produced positive, concrete effects only for the benefit of the regional qualified migrants; thus, they must be considered policies of free movement and not measures to implement a right to migrate.

[37] For a past-present comparison in the contest between sovereignty and human migrations, please refer to: M. Meccarelli *et al.* (2012).

However, an in-depth study of the jurisprudence – which here, for the sake of brevity, is only mentioned relatively briefly – allows one to note how the instrumentality of the statements on the right to migrate have been able to produce concrete, also relevant, juridical effects.

Of the two legislations that have been analysed in greater detail, the Argentinian legislation was the first one in the region to realize an organic and coherent approach, thanks to a modern legislation that has abandoned an exclusively police-oriented and controlling approach, preceding the rules on the requirements for the entry and residence of aliens with a catalogue of principles and giving to the persons concerned the means of protection of their rights. Although the administrative and judicial practices show a substantial continuity with the past under different aspects, the jurisprudence of the Supreme Court has reached innovative havens on access to civil and social rights and naturalization. The reasons behind what could appear as a paradox are both historical and juridical. The centuries-old favour that Argentina has reserved to immigration as a factor of demographic and economic development has made the Constitution extraordinarily favourable for immigrants, traditionally Europeans, considered "useful" for the country. Although the policies in favour of European immigration have been superseded, the Constitution has kept this spirit, with norms useful to the courts to overcome laws and practices unfairly disadvantageous for migrants; this did not happen, however, with the rules on entry and residence, which offer, at best, interpretative criteria of the law, not parameters of legality of the law itself (Olmos Giupponi 2011: 136).[38]

Up until recently, the situation in Ecuador was oddly symmetrical: the new regional tendencies influenced only the Constitution, without leading to an organic reform of the legislation. The Ecuadorian courts could easily appeal to the constitutional principles on the irrelevance of the irregular condition of migrants, or on the recognition of the right to migrate, in order to disengage themselves from the wording of the relevant laws. This, however, occurred when an intervention of normative elimination and manipulation by the Constitutional Court was still possible; in fact, until now the persisting existence of a legislation with little or no substantial jurisdictional controlling powers and still inspired to a police-oriented approach impeded a sufficient and widespread implementation of the new constitutional principles.

In conclusion, if, on the one hand, the measures adopted on the basis of regional agreements on free movement of persons are a model comparable (although in an embryonic stage) to the origin and development of the common policy on migration of the European Union (Lages 2013), on the other hand the caution, which is necessary to accept the express recognition of the right to migrate, does not justify a definitive

---

[38] Olmos Giupponi highlights as a new concept of substantive citizenship is affirming in the Argentinean law, based on the adoption of more flexible requirements needed to access naturalization and also on the strengthening of migrants' rights. However, the author's analysis is grounded only in the Argentinean Supreme Court's jurisprudence, while the prevalence of shadows in the judicial and the administrative praxis is not considered.

judgement of mere instrumentality and scarce effectiveness. The recognition of the right to migrate in the legislations of Argentina, Ecuador, Uruguay and Bolivia does not entail opening borders or waiving control on entry and residence of aliens;[39] however, it has produced significant legal consequences, like the establishment of the interpretative criteria of the most favourable norm to migrants and the protection of rights, as well as the definitive recognition of the migrant as a subject of law, entitled to make claims towards the state, regardless of his or her immigration status.

To scholars, the Latin American legislations appear as a vibrant laboratory, where new hypotheses on the evolution of concepts wrongly considered as definitively acquired are tested: borders, citizenship, rights, aliens, etc. In particular, the most interesting aspects for future studies are: 1) the theorization of a right "to escape" or right "to migrate" that reduces the gap of protection between refugees and economic migrants; 2) the increasing strengthening of the old theory of social citizenship, which is prevailing over the traditional one; 3) the experimentation of an effective, coordinated approach between the regional policies on free movement of goods and services and those on free movement of persons.

Bibliography

Acosta Arcarazo, D. and Feline Freier, L. (2015a) 'Turning the Immigration Policy Paradox Upside Down? Populist liberalism and discursive gaps in South America', *International Migration Review*, 49(3): 659–696.

Acosta Arcarazo, D. and Feline Freier, L. (2015b) 'Discursos y políticas de inmigración en Sudamérica: ¿Hacía un nuevo paradigma o la confirmación de una retórica sin contenido?', *Revista Interdisciplinar de Movilidad Humana*, 44: 171–189.

Acosta Arcarazo, D. and Feline Freier, L. (2015c) 'Beyond smoke and mirrors? Discursive gaps in the liberalisation of South American immigration laws' in D.J. Cantor et al. (eds.) *A liberal tide: towards a paradigm shift in Latin American migration and asylum policy-making?*, London: Institute of Latin American Studies, 33–56.

Acosta Arcarazo, D. and Geddes, A. (2014) 'Trasnational diffusion or different models? Regional approaches to migration governance in the European Union and Mercosur', *European Journal of Migration and Law*, 16: 19–44.

Acuña, E.R. (2012) *Il costituzionalismo in vigore nei Paesi dell'America Latina*, Turin: Giappichelli.

Bagni, S. (ed.) (2013) *Dallo Stato del bienestar allo Stato del buen vivir. Innovazione e tradizione nel costituzionalismo latinoamericano*, Bologna: Filodiritto.

Biscottini G. (1960), 'Cittadinanza' in *Enciclopedia del diritto*, Milano: Giuffrè, 140 ff.

---

[39] This is the reason why it's not shareable the opinion affirming that the right to migrate in Latin America led to the upturning of the historical principle according to which the State maintains the power to decide if and at what conditions aliens can enter and live within its borders, therefore nowadays "las personas y los grupos humanos tienen en principio el derecho a decidir en qué organización política quieren vivir y ejercer la todalidad de sus derechos": Vior and Bonilla 2008.

Ceriani Cernadas, P. (2011) 'Luces y sombras en la legislación migratoria latinoamericana', *Nueva Sociedad*, 233: 84–86.

Cholewinski, R. et al. (eds.) (2007) *International migration law: Developing paradigms and key challenges*, The Hague: Asser Press.

Cordini, G. (1998) *Elementi per una teoria giuridica della cittadinanza: profili di diritto pubblico comparato*, Padova: Cedam.

Domenech, E.E. (eds.) (2009) *Migración e política: el Estado interrogado. Procesos actuales en Argentina y Sudamérica*, Córdoba: Universidad Nacional de Córdoba.

Feline Freier, L. (ed.) (2013) 'Migrantes extracontinentales en América del Sur: estudio de casos', *OIM Cuadernos Migratorios*, 5.

García, L. (2013) *Nueva política migratoria argentina y derechos de la movilidad. Implementación y desafiós de una política basada en derechos humanos a través de las acciones ante el Poder Judicial (2004-2010)*, PhD Thesis, Universidad de Buenos Aires.

Itzcovich, G. (2013) 'Migrazioni e sovranità. Alcune osservazioni su concetto, fonti e storia del diritto a migrare', *Ragion Pratica*, 41: 433–450.

Lages, R. (2013) 'Breves notas sobre la libre circulación de personas y la política comunitaria de inmigración en los procesos regionales de integración económica. Una visión comparada de las experiencias europea y sudamericana', *Escenarios Actuales*, 3: 11–24.

Martinez Dalmau, R. (2016) 'Democratic constitucionalism and constitucional innovation in Ecuador. The 2008 Constitucion', *Latin American Perspectives*, 43(206): 158–174.

Meccarelli, M., Palchetti, P. and Sotis, C. (eds.) (2012) *Ius peregrinandi: il fenomeno migratorio tra diritti fondamentali, esercizio della sovranità e dinamiche di esclusione*, Macerata: Edizioni Università di Macerata.

Nicolao, J. (2011) 'La integración regional en la política migratoria argentina', *Ánfora*, 18(31): 101–121.

Novick, S. (ed.) (2010) *Migraciones y MERCOSUR: una relación inconclusa*, Buenos Aires: Editorial Catálogos.

Olmos Giupponi, M.B. (2011), 'Citizenship, migration and regional integration: Re-shaping citizenship conceptions in the Southern Cone', *European Journal of Legal Studies*, 4(2): 122–123.

Ortíz, P.A. (2013) 'Características y desafíos de la migración para la seguridad social en la región latinoamericana', *Revista Chilena de Derecho y Ciencia Política*, 4(1): 15–42.

Pizzarro, J.M. (2011) *Migración internacional en América Latina y el Caribe. Nueva tendencias, nuevos enfoques*, Santiago de Chile: CEPAL.

Quadri, R. (1967) 'Cittadinanza' in *Novissimo Digesto Italiano*, vol. III, Turin: Utet: 310 ff.

Rodríguez Miglio, E. and Toledo, L. (2012) 'Jurisprudencia argentina en materia de derechos de migrantes' in P. Ceriani Cernadas and R. Fava (eds.) *Políticas migratorias y derechos humanos. Remedios de Escalada*, Buenos Aires: Ediciones de la Universidad Nacional de Lanús.

Romano, S. (2009) 'Integración económica, desarrollo y migraciones en el Mercosur. Una aproximación crítica' in E.E. Domenech (ed.) *Migración e política: el Estado interrogado. Procesos actuales en Argentina y Sudamérica*, Córdoba: Universidad Nacional de Córdoba: 257–300.

San Juan, C. (2004) 'Control migratorio y derechos humanos', *Revista Argentina de Derechos Humanos*, 1: 267–324.

Santamaría, R.Á. (2011) *El neoconstituctionalismo trasnformador: El Estado y el Derecho en la Constitución de 2008*, Quito: Rosa Luxemburg Foundation.

Santamaría, R.Á., Jimenéz, A.G. and Dalmau, R.M. (2008) *Desafíos constitucionales. La constitución ecuatoriana del 2008 en perspectiva*, Quito: Ministerio de Justicia y Derechos Humanos.

Santestevan, A.M. (2007), 'Free movement regimes in South America: the experience of the MERCOSUR and the Andean community' in R.I. Cholewinski, R. Perruchoud, and E. MacDonald (eds.) *International migration law: developing paradigms and key challenges*, The Hague: T.M.C. Asser Press.

Stang, F. (2009) 'El migrante unidimensional. El dispositivo jurídico migratorio en la Comunidad Andina de Naciones' in E.E. Domenech (ed.) *Migración e política: el Estado interrogado. Procesos actuales en Argentina y Sudamérica*, Córdoba: Universidad Nacional de Córdoba: 301–353.

Torales P., González, M.E. and Vichich, N.P. (2003) 'Migraciones laborales en Sudamérica: la Comunidad Andina', *Estudios Sobre Migraciones Internacionales*, 60.

Treacy, G.F. (2011) 'Categoria sospechosas y control de consistitucionalidad', *Lecciones y Ensayos*, 89: 181–216.

Vior, E.J. and Bonilla, B.A. (2008) 'El derecho humano a la migración y las ciudadanías interculturales emergentes: el caso de la minoría de origen boliviano en la Ciudad de Buenos Aires', IX Congreso Argentino de Antropología Social, Universidad Nacional de Misiones, Posadas.

Chapter 26

Experiencing and crossing borders through music

Fulvia Caruso

Asylum seekers, refugees, forced migrants, and economic irregular migrants are definitions that technically differ but stand for the same conditions: displaced persons in motion that arrive traumatized in Europe in search of a better life, and remain traumatized during all of the procedures for regularization or expulsion.

The conditions of irregular migration in Europe today bring about situations in which people from many different countries are forced to live together for years in centres for extraordinary acceptance (C.A.S.), forced into new forms of community (or a total lack of it).

Going to visit some of the C.A.S. in and around Cremona, wondering what I could do to develop an action research project in these structures to avoid the growing intolerance of the citizens, I could see these young boys from different nations of the Middle East and Africa listening to their music with smartphones and earphones throughout the day, isolated from each other, unable to reconstruct relationships except with the few that had the same national or ethnic belonging.

I could not help wondering about the role music has in their lives, and which kinds of music they where listening to, and why. Was it from their homeland or from the places they passed through during their route to asylum? Was it popular or traditional? Local or global? How could I research their musical listenings and practices while helping them to find their place in society? Can music really help in having a voice, a place, and a space in society? Can music have a role in bridging the borders between "us" and "them", Italians and foreigners?

Any kind of musical commitment can help people to model and reflect on their own cultural, social and religious belonging. Music is a powerful tool not only to model a new understanding of a transnational cultural identity, but also to creatively intervene in the creation of public opinion about cultural, ethnic and religious diversity that more and more characterize the Italian ethnoscape. The problem was: which kind of music, and how?

I have imagined an action research project in reception centres that both gathers information on musical listenings of the asylum seekers, and finds a way to use music to improve their life conditions, starting from their own listenings and knowledge about music and the sharing of our musical competences. [1]

While the literature about music and migration is quite large, few studies exist about asylum seekers in Europe. [2] Most of those that do exist concern musicians or music making at the professional or semi-professional level [3] and/or were conducted in refugee camps outside Europe. [4] Settings that differ from the ones we are dealing with, at least insofar as they are organized by nationality and/or ethnicity on a large scale, can be immense and last for years; in more or less improvised villages, people there escape to survive and become stateless, perhaps forever, and can pass their whole lives there. What exists in common with the Italian situation are the psychological and emotional conditions of the persons involved.

26.1. *Conditions experienced by irregular foreigners in Italy*

In Italy illegal entry is permitted only if there are the conditions for obtaining the status of refugee, a residence permit for subsidiary protection or a residence permit for humanitarian reasons. When irregular migrants enter Italian soil, they are forced into a reception organization that has a three-level structure. The first level is that of the Centres of first aid and reception (CPSA) which gives medical aid, photo-signals everyone and collects requests for the International Protection and Identification and Expulsion Centres (CIE). The second level is that of the Centres of Reception (CDA), which exist only for the period needed for the identification procedure, and the Processing Centres only for asylum seeker identification (CARA). The third level is that of the Protection System for Asylum Seekers and Refugees (SPRAR), processing centres mostly managed by municipalities, with government financial help, that should host asylum seekers who have applied for asylum until they receive the decisions on their applications. These structures should provide a way for integration offering Italian language classes, vocational education, guidance

---

[1] Part of a larger research study on music and migration in Cremona. See Caruso, in Macchiarella, forthcoming.

[2] See Calais Writers 2017; Emery 2017; Pettan 2010; Quinn 2014; Sweers 2015.

[3] Many multi-ethnic orchestras and choirs are growing around Europe (see Riiser 2010). Oliver Potratz founded the German-Afghan *Safar Project* at the University of Music Franz Liszt in Weimar. Also *Musicians Without Borders* conducts several initiatives for migrant integration. Several projects are on the web: *Music in Exile* (http://musicinexile.org/); *A Restless Art*; the Music for Global Human Development of the Canadian Centre for Ethnomusicology (http://m4ghd.org and Frishkopf 2017), the Sauti Zetu Nakivale in Uganda (https://sautizetunakivale.wordpress.com/category/informazioni/); *Sounds beyond the border* (https://sinirinotesindensesler.org), *ArteMigrante nel mondo* (http://artemigrante.eu), *MusicFund* (http://www.musicfund.eu/index.html), *Social Impact of Music Making* (http://www.musicfund.eu/simm/index.html). The SEM created a web repository *Music and Social Justice Resources Projects*.

[4] Among many, for example Reyes Shramm 1999. For a review of the literature see Lidskog 2017. We have been inspired by: Croom 2015; Frishkopf 2017; Järviluoma and Leppänen 2012; Lenette and Sunderland 2016; Lenette and Procopis 2016; Storsve et al., 2010; Swijghuisen Reigersberg 2017.

and legal assistance, and a stable presence of linguistic and cultural mediators. [5]

Due to the large amount of irregular migrants these structures are not sufficient, and Public Prosecutor's Offices individuate structures managed by civilians – normally non-profit community organizations and NGOs, dioceses or municipalities – that have to follow specific rules indicated by the Public Prosecutor's Offices in the announcements for the creation of these structures. [6] These are the Centres for Extraordinary Acceptance (CAS).

CAS were designed to overcome the lack of beds within the ordinary reception facilities. The length of stay in these places should have been limited to the length of time it takes for transfer to SPRAR. Nevertheless, since the number of foreigners arriving[7] is too high, in the last two years SPRAR are only for those who have already been accepted as refugees, and CAS are the only places where asylum seekers are hosted. They live there for one to two years or more, waiting for the decision on their status. Seen as an answer to an emergency, these centres have few rules to follow as regards services for the asylum seekers, and are mostly outside the control of the state.

Although the Public Prosecutor's Offices try to aggregate persons who came from the same geographical areas, in the various CAS there are persons who come from very different situations. They differ in nationality, ethnicity, language, religion, social background, level of schooling and life story. All of them had to experience years of deprivation and trouble to get to Italy, and at the same time have been exposed to diverse cultural inputs. This condition of continuous contact with different traditions and cultures continues following their arrival, when they are forced to live with unknown people from different nations.

> In anthropological terms, refugees are people who have undergone a violent 'rite' of separation and unless or until they are 'incorporated' as citizens into their host state (or returned to their state of origin) find themselves in 'transition', or in a state of 'liminality'. This 'betwixt and between' (Turner 1969) status may not only be legal and psychological, but social and economic as well. Moreover, encoded in the label 'refugee' are the images of dependency, helplessness and misery, e.g. 'The presence of floating groups of oppressed and miserable persons presents the international community today with one of its greatest challenges' (Lillich 1984). 'As Zia Rizvi noted: "Once an individual, a human being becomes a refugee, it is as though he has become a member of another race, some subhuman group" (Dunbar-Ortiz and Harrell-Bond 1987).
>
> (Harrell-Bond and Voutira 1992: 7)

---

[5] For more information see www.sprar.it/english.

[6] In 2016 the Italian Ministry of Internal Affairs published the "Carta della buona accoglienza" (Chart of good acceptance) to give (non-mandatory) indications to the CAS. See http://www.interno.gov.it/it/notizie/carta-buona-accoglienza-nuovo-modello-integrazione.

[7] Mostly male. Women make up only 13% of the irregular foreigners and are hosted only in SPRAR, in secure structures, or in apartments with their family. Unaccompanied minors follow a different protocol, as they are immediately accepted due to the 1989 New York Convention on children rights.

As already mentioned, one of the things that seems to guide their days are the media and social media and, most of all, listening to music. A must for every CAS is the Internet connection. It is a way of re-orienting oneself, keeping ties with their own past, and distracting them from their current state of precariousness and traumatic memories. But it is also a way to avoid creating bonds with one another.

That is why I decided to do something with music in the CAS of Cremona. I asked some students and former students to imagine together where and how to intervene, and the result has been two completely different projects: one in the Cremona diocese CAS, the other in a CAS in Vigolzone, outside Piacenza. [8]

26.2. *The action research*

I decided we could structure musical activities only after having listened to the musical stories of the people hosted in the CAS. That "listening perspective" I then found in Pilzer: listen to these persons without any prejudice, avoiding the classical informant-researcher relationship, and being open minded about the kind of music we would have met.

> Learning and singing new songs is a way for profoundly marginalized people of whatever age to remain contemporary, and to maintain contact with mainstreams, real or imagined. Learning manifestly popular songs, or engaging in decidedly "mainstream" musical practices, is another way of participating in societies to which one has not been granted full membership. So, in the study of survivors' music, we must be ever willing to relinquish such prejudices against new music, against popular music, and so on.
>
> (Pilzer 2015: 488)

We wanted to get in touch with them and use their music as a tool to rethink their future, moving from the music of their past and their present to then create a new present. In both cases it has been a hard task. At the beginning they were highly diffident with us due to the marginalization experiences they witness everyday. Most of

---

[8] The Cremona diocese CAS hosts about 300 irregular migrants coming from Bangladesh, Afghanistan, Pakistan, Palestine, Syria and from several African countries (Cameroun, Ethiopia, Ghana, Guinea Conakry, Libya, Mali, Mauritania, Niger, Nigeria, Senegal, Somalia, Sudan, Togo and Tunisia). It is structured so as to offer several services, including courses in Italian literacy. *C'era una volta* is a small agro-tourism business (holiday farm) in Vigolzone, in the countryside outside Piacenza, which was converted to a CAS in 2015. It hosts 15 to 20 men between 18 and 31 years of age from Guinea, Guinea Bissau, Ivory Coast, Mali, Senegal, and Togo. When we started to operate there, they only had a place to stay, food, inappropriate clothing and three Moroccan cultural-linguistic mediators for practical needs such as to deliver food or to bring someone to the lawyer or to the doctor, and received Italian lessons once a week. From 2016 they have had an Internet connection and Italian lessons by a professional teacher three days a week.

them have no attitude in telling about themselves. We tried with a "sonic diary" but discovered that most of them were illiterate. Listening to their music, sharing our music with them, musiking together, has been our way to understand their musical life and memory. Most importantly, this allowed us to work with almost anyone, even those who have no talent for music (Pilzer, 2015).

This project involved several students and former students. In Cremona the leading person is Gaianè Kevorkian, in Vigolzone Elisa Tartaglia with Rossella Calvia, Clara Fanelli, Mattia Signaroldi and Francesco Brianzi.

In the first case, in September 2015, I started to investigate with the help of Gaianè Kevorkian in the Cremona Dioceses CAS, discovering that the Oghene Damba musical group had already existed for several months. We decided to start following it. In the second case Elisa Tartaglia wrote the project Musical identities in line with my intentions and was invited by the owner of the C'era una volta reception center to realize it in November 2015. Their work gave birth to a musical group: the Viens voir. It is impossible to give an account of both ongoing experiences in detail, but I will try to summarize what we are doing and make some comments on it. [9]

26.3. *Oghene Damba*

The dioceses CAS needed a long period of observation due to the quantity and diversity of asylum seekers. Fortunately, Bawa Salifu, a Ghanaian cultural mediator and musician, had recently created the musical group Oghene Damba Cremona Boys Musical Theatre and we decided to start by following the group by participating in their rehearsals and performances. The group currently consists of 15 young men between 18 and 25 of age, coming from Nigeria, Ghana and Mali. [10] None of them are professional nor semi-professional musicians, but they had all experienced studying and performing music at school or in the village. Bawa teaches the gifted ones how to play percussions, while the singers and dancers experiment with their skills independently.

My students started to go to their rehearsals every week, occasionally dancing or playing a little. It took them a lot of time and energy to be accepted, but after few

[9] For a deep analysis of the Oghene. I use the word as they write it down, even if the correct version should be ogene. Damba performances: see Gaianè Kevorkian, "Oghene Damba: modalità di auto-rappresentazione nelle performance dei richiedenti asilo della Casa dell'Accoglienza", Undergraduate degree Dissertation, Pavia University, 2017. A detailed description of the workshops in Vigolzone can be found in M. Signaroldi (2017) *Musica e migrazione: ricerca di protocolli di musica partecipativa nei centri di accoglienza per migranti*, Masters degree Dissertation, Pavia University, 2017.

[10] In time the group changed participants and still is changing due to the precariousness of the situation. At the time of writing they are Bawa Salifu, Osman Allhassan, Ambrose Ejije, Emeka Nse, Muntari Yussif (Djembe), Zack Sajoro (bottle), Ismail Issah (Shekere), Nelson Amadin and Stephen Emmanuel (soloist singers), Oyi Ogieva, Ikechukwu Okechukwu Kohnson, Aliameka Olochwuckum (vocals), and Chimezie Chimuanja, Ousuman Gassama, Owrasu Mikeb (dance).

months Gaianè and Simone Rude (the more regular attendees) were so confident that the group let them play with them. Nevertheless, we could record only public performances they held in Cremona, and only Gaianè was allowed to take short videos of their rehearsals. The learning process is only by playing, and every attempt where we tried to get explanations of their music or their personal stories was unsuccessful or lightly detailed. Most of the understanding we achieved about their musical project was given during a meeting I organized at our department in April 2016, and thanks to the analysis Gaiané did of their performances. [11]

They play their own songs, Agawu would define "dance mode", often created together on the basis of pop songs the two solo singers knew from home. Texts of the songs are small fragments, mostly in broken English, and deal with love, hope for the future, and gratitude to Cremona for hosting them. Above these repeated melodic lines, often in antiphonal style, the instruments (4 djembe, 1 sangban, and 1 shekeré, sustained by 1 bottle) create progressively a strict polyrhythmic organization of parts, with a strong presence of improvisation. The dancers gather the group with unique dance styles they have processed during 2016 from the different traditions of the dancers. We cannot recognize any specific tradition in their music and dance. As Bawa told us: "We try to form an African music, not Nigerian, Ghanaian or Malian, but a mixture of all". [12]

The Oghene Damba create a multi-dimensional show, composed of single elements (music, dance, dress) that are brought together and adapted to each other with the intention to create a shared cultural "African" belonging to demolish local, regional or ethnic borders. This "Africaness" is also inspired by the Western imagination of African music, to be admired and accepted by the Cremonese public.

26.4. *Viens Voir*

In Zerbione none of the asylum seekers is a musician. Our workshop is optional, and is normally attended by 8 to 10 of them. Over time a quite regular group developed, until August 2016 when most of them had to leave the centre; a second group started in September with the newly arrived.

Elisa Tartaglia started a workshop with the help of cultural-linguistic mediators. We decided that the first step had to be sharing our musical attitudes and tastes: every

---

[11] I continued the study in 2018 and 2019. The results of this are in the forthcoming article "Faire de la musique ensemble: un programme de recherche action avec des migrants à Crémone (Italie)", *Cahiers d'ethnomusicologie*, vol. 32/2019 *Musiques de migrants*, editée par Denis Laborde et Luc Charles-Dominique and in the chapter book "Music and migration in Italian contemporary scenario: challenges and results", in *Music and Minorities*, edited by Marko Kölbl and Hande Saglam, Klanglese 12–13, open access series of the Department of Folk Music Research and Ethnomusicology, University of Vienna.

[12] Interview of March 23 2016.

participant presents himself or herself musically playing or singing or sharing a recorded song. This allows us to create an informal and non-hierarchical setting, and at the same time investigate their musical tastes. The other exercise we did, and still do from time to time, is to choose a word and a song according to the feeling this word expresses. In her second report Elisa wrote that: "This allows us to meet a large variety of repertories. What we proposed was almost always mainly with the purpose to talk about something through music and to tell about us with it." [13] The result of the first sharing [14] could light up their feelings about their situation: homesickness, pride for their homeland, difficulties they are heaving with paperwork, and doubts about having left home. A second important part of our workshops is a group improvisation with body and voice based on different role-plays and interactions (also with self-made instruments) through very simple rhythms, which when combined create intricate polyrhythmic dialogue.

The difficulty, then, is to be able to listen to each other and to relate (musically) to the others. This is the harder task: attitude to relation.

In January 2016 two other students of mine, all musicians and French speaking, joined the group and we could start a new step: to play real instruments and compose new songs. They decided to try with home made percussions, which seemed easier to manage. [15] Soon after, when the owner of the Centre started to give economic help to the workshop, we bought three djembes. After this, Mattia joined the group with his guitar: finally, a man! A bluesman! This helped a lot in the confidence of the group and Bernard – who was very reluctant about the workshop until that moment – started to learn guitar, even if with a strong percussive attitude. [16] In winter 2017 a new student joined the group, Francesco Brianzi, a percussionist who taught them to build and play the cajon.

The last step of the workshop is to compose new songs. It is both a way to learn Italian and to interact not only playing, and a way to (re)gain self-confidence and the ability to imagine creatively and in so doing reimagine their future. That is why adventure was the first word we decided to work on. For us it was positive, linked to explorations, new worlds, the future… But for them it was something linked to their past experience of traveling to Europe. [17] I will not go into detail, but step-by-step the

---

[13] E-mail communication, November 2 2015.

[14] A name that is a manifesto: "Oghene" in Igbo means "Music", "Damba" in *dagbani* means "Dance", they affirm themselves as Cremonese through a complex performance made of music, dance and dressing.

[15] Elisa has some knowledge of African percussions and her master's degree dissertation was on the use of African percussion in inclusion processes in multicultural, disability and disease settings.

[16] This does not mean that guitar is a good choice in CAS situations. In the Cremona diocese CAS, for example, a first attempt at guitar lessons made by an Amnesty International volunteer failed miserably.

[17] The songs chosen by the participants for the theme were: Ismael Isaac, Lampedusa; Van Baxy, Tounka; Americo Gomes, Bissau; Amaral, Konata; Bibi-Reine, Inyama. The two songs they composed, and the various texts composed and not used for songs, were all about their experiences of crossing the Mediterranean.

group found a sort of balance in expressing their past through songs, and even more their present and their future.

In a "bottom-up approach" we start from a word and listen to songs related to it, first in Italian, explaining their meaning (also to help them to learn Italian), then they propose songs they know on similar topics and finally we split into two or three groups and work on our own words around the topic. Composing starts by the creation of the text, but often is immediately accompanied by a melody. To compose in Italian is still too hard for them, so they use some French and mostly their own family languages, which are more effective for expressing feelings. After the distribution between vocal soloist (normally the one who invented the text) and choir is decided, they arrange the music so as to reflect the meaning of the words. We always try to give them something to prepare during the week, such as to improve the accompanying rhythms or the lyrics. We realized it was very useful for that purpose to record parts of the workshops with their mobile phones. They also started to write down the words, helping each other. This improved their skills, and recently they started to imagine text and melody during the week.

Musically, they mix African popular music genres such as rap, reggae and mbalax, which they normally listen to, with traditional African melodic and rhythmic elements. I suppose this happens because they have understood that Italians are interested in traditional African music and because the improvisation exercise we continue to practice at every workshop is more about traditional patterns.

They composed some new songs and memorized other African popular songs chosen during the workshops, and had two concerts: one in Piacenza in June 2016 with the first formation, and in Cremona in March 2017 with the second. [18] They decided to call themselves Viens voire, the song by Tiken Jah Fakoly they shared with us at the beginning of our experience. It means so much for them because it magnifies the beauties of Africa and invites Italians to see them with new eyes.

They understood that through songs they can express efficaciously their opinions and start a process of agency and self-confidence.

Over these two years they have composed very meaningful songs, such as Siou Toumala Meta (Patience is hard), whose text was written in Mandinka by Ismaila Drame Moro to denounce the oppressive conditions of staying in the reception center and repeating the same things everyday, waiting for documents that never arrive. The group decided that the arrangement had to mirror the meaning of the words, creating an ostinato of homorhythmical pulse, as in the transcription (by Mattia Signaroldi) of the first melodic phrase:

---

[18] First formation: Elisa Tartaglia clarinet; Awali Bagnah voice and double guiro; Rossella Calvia, Clara Fanelli, rattles and voice; Mohamed Bah, Malang Danfa, Diaby Lacine, djembe; Bernard Malou, Mattia Signaroldi, guitar; Fode Noba voice. Second formation: Elisa Tartaglia clarinet; Aliou Balde cajón; Francesco Brianzi, percussions; Rossella Calvia, Clara Fanelli, rattles and voice; Ismaila Drame Moro, voice; Malang Danfa, Doudou Danfakha, Abdourahim Djitte, Diaby Lacine, djembe; Bernard Malou, Mattia Signaroldi, guitar; Fode Noba voice.

Figure 26.1. Siou Toumala Meta, first melodic phrase

26.5. *To create harmonies from differences*

Despite experiencing daily contact, the asylum seekers know very little about each other and often do not cooperate with one another. In the CAS there is an almost total lack of help and mutual teaching.

The traumatic experiences they have lived and the difficult situation that Italy offers are highly challenging. Musical workshops bring some positivity into their lives. More importantly, this task required them to organize their time and to listen to everyone's opinions, learning to work together for a common purpose.

It is still a work in progress, but we can affirm that through the development of musical and compositional competences, and moreover through the creation of a shared musical language, they have learnt something that goes beyond music: a progressive move from a passive situation to one of social activity; growth of confidence with the others and the self; development of listening skills, group spirit and ability to work together; and development of communicative and linguistic competences.

The bottom-up setting is fundamental in order to develop the right relational skills; even so, there is a great need for improvised interactions and musical role plays to develop the group, in particular their listening attitude and concentration. We realized that public performances are crucial to bringing people to change their minds towards asylum seekers. Often they are challenging for the asylum seekers on one hand because they have poor musical skills, and on the other hand because they create an expectation of gain. But it is an important result that we do not want to miss. Each concert ends with moments of social interaction that are vital for asylum seekers. As an Oghene Damba boy told us, even one single smile is a precious result.

In the future we would like to explore the possibility of realizing workshops with less homogeneous groups. The challenge is to find a musical common ground. Despite the too widely spread opinion that globalization means homogenization, we are finding very differentiated musical tastes and listenings, even if mostly in the huge field of popular music. Only ethnomusicology can catch this challenge.

Our intention is to "create harmonies from differences" (Schiller and Meinhof 2011: 32) and to bridge as many borders as we can. Recently, thanks to an idea put forward by Gaianè, we started a new project in the diocese CAS: a radio transmission where asylum seekers have to present the music they listen to and to explain to listeners the reasons for their choices. In this way we can collect information about their musical attitudes and at the same time help them to communicate with Italians and be motivated to learn Italian. We realized in Zerbione that the exercise of participatory listening allows migrants to win against the tendency of isolating themselves as an individual. The radio program is intended as amplified participatory listening, at least in the preparation of each episode, which is prepared all together in a bottom-up setting. These relational bridges can be the beginnings of new processes of personal agency and self-determination, and establish new social worlds. We started the pilot experience with six sub-Saharan African people in July, but intend to involve other migrants from a wider range of national backgrounds in the near future. We will see how many borders we are able to overcome.

Bibliography

Calais Writers (2017) *Voices from the 'Jungle': Stories from the Calais Refugee Camp*, London: Pluto Press.

Caruso, F. [forthcoming] 'How do we go about singing a new song about migration?' in I. Macchiarella (ed.) *Travelling Musics/Musicians/Musicologists*, Udine: Nota.

Croom, A.M. (2015) 'Music practice and participation for psychological well-being: A review of how music influences positive emotion, engagement, relationships, meaning, and accomplishment', *Musicae Scientiae*, 19(1): 44–64.

Emery, E. (2017) 'Radical ethnomusicology: Towards a politics of 'No Borders' and 'insurgent musical citizenship' – Calais, Dunkerque and Kurdistan', *Ethnomusicology Ireland*, 5: 48–74.

Frishkopf, M. (2017) 'Popular music as public health technology: Music for global human development and 'Giving Voice to Health' in Liberia', *Journal of Folklore Research*, 54(1(2)): 41–86.

Glick, S. and Meinhof, U.H. (2011) 'Singing a new song? Transnational migration, methodological nationalism and cosmopolitan perspectives', *Music and Arts in Action*, 3: 21–39.

Harrell-Bond, B.E. and Voutira, E. (1992) 'Anthropology and the study of refugees', *Anthropology Today*, 8(4): 6–10.

Järviluoma, H. and Leppänen, T. (2012) 'Becoming audible! Asylum seekers, participatory action research and cultural encounters', Situating popular musics: IASPM 16th International Conference Proceedings on-line, 297–306.

Lenette, C. and Procopis, B. (2016) 'They Change Us: The social and emotional impacts on music facilitators of engaging in music and singing with asylum seekers', *Music and Arts in Action*, 5(2): 55–68.

Lenette, C. and Sunderland, N. (2016) '"Will there be music for us?" Mapping the health and well-being potential of participatory music practice with asylum seekers and refugees across contexts of conflict and refugee', *Arts & Health*, 8(1): 32–49.

Lidskog, R. (2017) 'The role of music in ethnic identity formation in diaspora: A research review', *International Social Science Journal*, 66(219-220): 23-38.
Pettan, S. (2010) 'Music in War, Music for Peace: Experiences in Applied Ethnomusicology', in J. Morgan O'Connell and S. el Shawan Castelo Branco (eds.) *Music and Conflict*, Champaign: University of Illinois Press, 177–192.
Pilzer, J.D. (2015) 'The Study of Survivors' Music', in S. Pettan and J.T. Titon (eds.) *The Oxford Handbook of Applied Ethnomusicology*, Oxford: Oxford University Press, 481–510.
Quinn, N. (2014) 'Participatory action research with asylum seekers and refugees experiencing stigma and discrimination: The experience from Scotland', *Disability and Society*, 29(1): 58–70.
Reyes Shramm, A. (1999) *Songs of the Caged, Songs of the Free: Music and the Vietnamese Refugee Experience*, Philadelphia: Temple University Press.
Riiser, S. (2010), 'National identity and the West-Eastern Divan Orchestra', *Music and Arts in Action*, 2: 19–37.
Schiller, N.G. and Meinhof, U.H. (2011) Singing a New Song? Transnational Migration, Methodological Nationalism and Cosmopolitan Perspectives, *Music & Arts in Action*, (3)3: 32.
Storsve, V., Westbye, I.A. and Ruud, E. (2010) 'Hope and recognition. A music project among youth in a Palestinian refugee camp', *Voices: A World Forum for Music Therapy*, 10(1).
Sweers, B. (2015) 'Music and Conflict Resolution. The Public Display of Migrants in National(ist) Conflict Situations in Europe: An Analytical Reflection on University-Based Ethnomusicological Activism' in S. Pettan and J.T. Titon (eds.) *The Oxford Handbook of Applied Ethnomusicology*, Oxford: Oxford University press, 511–550.
Swijghuisen Reigersberg, M.E. (2017) 'Collaborative music, health, and wellbeing research globally: Some perspectives on challenges faced and how to engage with them', *Journal of Folklore Research*, 54(1): 133–159.

Chapter 27

Free voices beyond the borders

The experience of the Italian exiles in Radio Londra (1940-1945)

Francesca Fiorani

27.1. *The 'war of words' and the role of the BBC*

If it is true that the strength of words is not enough to win a war by itself, it is not improper to state that between 1939 and 1945 a real 'war of words' [1] burst out all over Europe, in which propaganda became a weapon to weaken enemies. The BBC played a vital role in this context, becoming the reference broadcasting label for both the Allies and those tuning into its frequencies in the occupied countries, thus eluding censure and reticence by the government radios.

At the beginning of the war, the BBC did not yet have organized propaganda, all the more so when compared to the impressive consensus-generating machine orchestrated by Goebbels's Ministry in Hitler's Germany. The policy for the use of the radio put in place by the two countries was based on completely different and, in the eyes of English people, almost irreconcilable views.

The main idea of the BBC was a sheer and symmetric replication of the German model, which implied a total falsification of the truth, which would be not only impossible to carry out, but also counter-productive in a country that wanted to introduce itself to Europe as a democracy forerunner, adopting a strict principle of truth and consistency (Briggs 1970: 9) as a guideline for its broadcasting of information.

The style of the BBC was therefore still anchored to transparency ethics, as it decided that any event – whether a landslide victory or a devastating defeat – had to be communicated transparently.

It was in the years when the United Kingdom was most vulnerable, with heavy air raids raging throughout the country, that most of the programmes broadcast were on the air, with a schedule that was slowly widened and refined.

A turning point in the management of the propaganda was the creation, between

---

[1] For the term, see Briggs 1970: 3 ff.; for the BBC and the *Italian Service* during the war see Piccialuti Caprioli 1976 vol. 1–2; Lo Biundo 2014; Pizzaroso Quinteiro 1989.

1941 and 1942 of the Political Warfare Executive, which should have worked together with the Ministry of Information, enhancing the results obtained until that moment.[2] The operational centre of the PWE was headquartered in the same building as the BBC, thus allowing a very strict collaboration and, sometimes, a direct supervision on the contents and the formats of the broadcasts. Nevertheless, the broadcaster remained considerably autonomous, also because the PWE mainly interfered about the so-called black broadcasting, which were for military communications only (Briggs 1970: 13).

In winter 1939, a European Service was set up, aimed at coordinating all the 'regional' sections broadcasting in different countries of the continent. This authority was under the direct control of the BBC and was managed by the broadcaster itself, though in conjunction with the government and the PWE. A Monitoring Service was born in parallel, whose task was to write down and address to the other members the information broadcasted by the radio and the foreign press, following a rising number of newscasts.[3]

To carry out the programmes of the different Regional Services, the broadcaster wanted numerous mother tongue staff, relying on collaboration with many exiles, who, fleeing from political and racial persecutions, found refuge in Great Britain.

Studying how the BBC worked during the war, alongside its activities, is therefore a privileged standpoint on a particular context of intellectual migration in the 1900s. In these years, prominent antifascist and anti-Nazi personalities became authors of the texts and speakers of the broadcasts, with the radio having turned into an ideal loudspeaker for their ideas and fight against dictatorships.

Despite having to adapt to the general guidelines that the British government provided to the BBC, such individuals, uprooted from their original environment and unable to express themselves freely in their country, found a way to raise their voices again, overcoming the boundaries of those nations that they were forced to leave.

Such possibility was also given to the exiles who, in the same period, were labelled as enemy aliens by the British authorities and public opinion, that is Italian, German and Austrian people actively involved and protected by the BBC, which tried to defend their dignity as opponents and workers even in a time of heightened nationalism.

In the following pages, the ways in which the broadcaster managed the foreign staff are examined, with a focus on, among the different Regional Services, the Italian Service. This became, from 1940 to 1945, a vital centre of antifascist propaganda, around which a group of prominent intellectuals, who were against fascism, gravitated. They had been forced into exile because of their Jewish origins and were called upon to channel their skills into the creation of heterogeneous programmes. The broadcasts of Radio Londra became very popular in Italy and were able to win over a wide audience from different social and political classes thanks to different ways of communication, which conveyed clear messages and topics, suitable for crossing that boundary which

---

[2] For the Political Warfare Service see Briggs 1970: 32 ff.

[3] See Piccialuti Caprioli 1976, vol. 1: XIV.

dictatorship and war had made impenetrable by air; a geographical, military but most of all ideological and political boundary, which separated fascist Italy from Great Britain.

27.2. *Enemy aliens or resources? The management of the foreign staff*

As the war broke out, the British government started a massive operation of detentions and confinements in prison camps, which hit individuals and communities of 'enemy nationalities'. For the Italian people, the measures came into effect right after the declaration of war of 10th June 1940, addressing men between 16 and 70 who had been living in the United Kingdom for less than 20 years. [4]

When the tension was really high, such as in the first months of the war, the massive employment of foreign staff by the BBC was causing several problems. Since the beginning of 1939, a series of internal memoranda show how the BBC started to work on the management of its enemy employees during the war, drawing up lists of people involved, trying to confirm work permits and, in certain cases, showing interest in the applications for naturalization of non-British collaborators. [5]

In April 1939, the broadcaster forwarded one of these lists to the Undersecretary of the Home Office, highlighting not only the necessity of keeping the existing staff, but also considering hiring new people as the possibility of a war was approaching. [6] The request was reiterated several times and, in December of the same year, the management of the broadcaster reported a highly difficult situation, complaining about the tardiness of the Ministry in handling the permit applications and insisting on the need to hire staff able to work on the foreign broadcasts in a fast and not excessively restrictive way. It was added: 'British subjects have been tested for many of the foreign broadcasts, but in some way they make slips in phrase or pronunciation, which can be detected by the country to which the broadcast is directed'. [7]

As for Italy, the issue became decisive in 1940. In that year, summer was marked by detentions and confinements, indiscriminate operations that also involved those overtly against the regime. Many of the people hired by the Italian Service, even though classified as antifascist, underwent such measures, sharing their fate with the collaborators of the German-speaking sections.

---

[4] For the process that led to detention and confinements measures see Cesarano and Kushner 1993; Sponza 2000: 75–77. For a focus on the experience of Italian people in prison camps, see Bernabei 1997, 2000.

[5] See the various *memoranda* and the communications inside the British Broadcasting Corporation, Written Archives Centre (henceforth BBC, WAC), Staff policy – Aliens, 1937 – June 1939.

[6] BBC note, not reading, to the Undersecretary of State for the Ministry for Internal Affairs, 11th April 1939, BBC, WAC, Staff policy – Aliens, 1937 – June 1939.

[7] *BBC and wartime procedures for dealing with aliens*, circular of 12th December 1939, BBC, WAC, Staff policy – Aliens, July – January 1939.

The British broadcaster disclosed the name of its collaborators, committing to recover those who had not been arrested and offering to act as a medium to help members of staff who had a relative in confinement. [8]

Also, in the following years, the desire to lessen restrictions imposed by the legislation for foreign staff was constant. There were continuous requests for curfew exemptions [9] and attempts to introduce special terms, such as the possibility of staying in structures partnered with the broadcaster after night shifts. [10]

Applications of naturalization were still encouraged, also in the light of the difficulties faced in replacing highly qualified journalists and speakers. [11]

The voices that rose in defence of the alleged enemy aliens, actually collaborators of proved professionalism, were many. In June 1941, John Armitage, an official, wrote:

> I have avoided as possible the words enemy aliens as it is possible to be a German or an Italian and a friendly alien [...] Germans, Austrian and Italians working for the BBC and broadcasting to their own countries risk a great deal for our cause. They have the full confidence of the BBC in their work and we naturally wish to extend them every possible facility provided by the Corporation for rest and recreation. [12]

Still, at the beginning of 1943, Robert Burns, Monitoring Service Director, piled it on:

> At the stage of war most of the alien population in this country has been absorbed, really good candidates are extremely rare and it is vitally important for us, particularly in dealing with the language of the enemy, that we should have first rate monitors. [13]

The broadcaster was anything but predictable in tackling the issue. The much-feared risk of the 'fifth column' was relentlessly feeding the fears of the public, unsettled by the presence of enemies in such delicate positions, sometimes even handling confidential information.

Protecting its employees often meant defying prejudices, which were very common, especially in conservative environments. Particularly annoyed by the fact of having to

---

[8] BBC Internal Memo: internment of enemy aliens, 20th July 1940, BBC, WAC, Staff policy – Aliens, January – October 1940.

[9] See the correspondence among the BBC, Home Office and Scotland Yard of October 1940, with repeated requests for allowing foreign people to move freely during the curfew (see BBC, WAC, Staff Policy – Aliens, January–October 1940).

[10] Several examples of requests in this sense are founded in all Staff Policy dossiers – Aliens by BBC WAC.

[11] BBC internal note on the naturalisation of *enemy aliens*, 17th December 1940, BBC, WAC, Staff Policy – Aliens, November 1940–1941).

[12] John Armitage's letter to the Chief of Buckingham Police, 12th June 1941, BBC, WAC, Staff Policy – Aliens, 1940–1941.

[13] Note by Robert Burns, 25th February 1943, BBC, WAC, Staff-Policy, 1942–1943.

justify its external policies, the BBC stated on several occasions that nationality alone was not sufficient to discredit an individual, confirming the vital role of the emigrants in propaganda activity.

27.3. *The Italian Service: organization and staff*

The first broadcasting of what would later turn into the Italian Service of the BBC dates back to 22nd December 1939. The service, which was initially limited to a short and simple newscast, was enriched with contents and staff, who, at the beginning of 1941, was already a large group. In its first months of activity, the Italian Service was managed by Cecil Sprigge, journalist and former Italian correspondent for the Manchester Guardian, a long-time supporter of antifascism in England. In January 1941, Sprigge was replaced by another reporter, who worked in Rome for the Reuters Agency, C.F. Whittall. Both heads of the service were professionals with a great knowledge of the Italian language and political environment.

The idea at the base of the Italian Service was to reach 'the soft underbelly of Fascism', [14] getting the attention of those social classes that were starting to impatiently perceive the conceited and pretentious rhetoric of the regime, no longer able to hide its failures, and the burden, both moral and economical, of a disastrous war.

There was awareness in Britain of the possibility of relying on a considerable margin of action and on a wider audience, compared to Nazi Germany: [15] British people considered the German public opinion as a solid monolith, difficult to shatter, meanwhile the distance between Mussolini and a part of the Italian population was a very useful factor to prove the effectiveness of the propaganda system.

To that end, the hiring of Italian staff for the writing and hosting of the broadcasts was incentivized, leaving more space to the exiles than usual, for instance, in the case of the German Service. Anyone striving for this job had to face a scrupulous interview in which, besides professional skills, also political positions, especially in relation to fascism, were verified.

Running one's eyes over the names of the staff, we can find many members of the Free Italy Movement, the Italian antifascist organization founded in September 1940 by Carlo Petrone, from Salerno. [16]

Some protagonists of the movement's second phase of activity started working for the BBC, in the first instance the brothers Paolo and Piero Treves who were the sons of the socialist executive Claudio Treves. Taught to have values of democracy and antifascism, they both suffered living far from their father, who died in exile in Paris in

---

[14] See Isola (1996: 481).

[15] For a broader overview on the activity of the BBC German Service, see Briggs 1970: 386–394 and Pronay and Taylor 1984.

[16] For information about him see Oddati 1980.

1933, and they had long been watched over by the fascist authority. [17] They were hired together with their cousin, Uberto Limentani, [18] Livio Zeno Zencovich, a journalist from Trieste, and Ruggero Orlando, who had worked with EIAR until 1938, when he moved to London and started to distance himself from fascism. [19] In 1942 Umberto Calosso became part of the staff. He was member of the Socialist Party since 1918, and he had been an exile in Malta, where he took part in the clandestine movement and established the first contact with the Allies. [20]

The typical collaborator of the Italian Service was therefore an avowed and already known antifascist, who had had to leave Italy for political or racial reasons, with a high level of education and a good knowledge of the language. Usually, the Italian emigrants started working as translators or writers and finally, once they proved that their voice sounded pleasant on the microphone, could become speakers.

Despite the important presence of Italian hosts, the undisputed star of the Italian Service was Colonel Harold Stevens, who became famous in Italy under the affectionate nickname of 'Colonnello Buonasera'. The British officer looked to Italy 'as a monarchic conservative', (Piccialuti Caprioli 1976: XVI), giving his radio speeches a British stamp.

27.4. *Speaking to Italy beyond the border: the topics of the radio broadcasts*

The programme schedule of Radio Londra was varied. Besides the traditional newscasts, an important role was played by the talks, comments to the main events of the day or thoughts about more general topics. Among the most popular programmes, the one previously mentioned hosted by Colonel Stevens and 'Sul fronte e dietro il fronte italiano' (Italian Correspondent), hosted by Paolo Treves and dedicated to the Italian political situation after the armistice. [21]

Alongside the talks, the radio dramas were particularly relevant in the programme schedule. They were short and had recurring or occasional characters. The BBC chose to experiment such forms of propaganda to go beyond the middle class, the preferential listeners of the broadcasts, and to engage a wider audience. Think about 'Sottovoce' (Undertone), where three characters used to have a dialogue: Paolo, who had been

---

[17] About Paolo Treves, see his autobiography (Treves 1996). Also see the anthology edited by Fiorani (2017). About Piero Treves, see Pertici 1999: 199–257, 259–264; Cavaglion 2006.

[18] About Limentani, who after the war taught Italian Literature at the University of Cambridge see Boyde 1990.

[19] About Orlando, see Forno 2013.

[20] For information about Calosso, see Cavallari 1973 and Brunazzi 1981.

[21] A selection of texts of this broadcast was published in the post-war period. See Treves 1945.

against fascism since it came to power, Leo, who usually disapproved of the regime too, and Vittorio Rossi, dazzled by the propaganda and the myths of the dictatorship. The sketches of 'Politica in Pantofole' (Politics in Slippers – an informal political broadcast) in which a young man, Mario, officer of the Ministry of Popular Culture, always on the verge of a nervous breakdown due to the difficulties in having to justify the lies of the government, was contradicted by the sharp comments of his uncle.

The gags in 'Conversazioni sull'Asse' (Axis Conversation) aimed at debunking the alliance with Hitler's Germany. These saw Bacher, a German, and an Italian man as the main character and from the dialogues, the air of superiority with which the alleged ally looked to Italy emerged, with continuous clichés ranging from the poor organizational skills, discipline and work attitude, hypothesizing a clear cultural backwardness.

A typical example of a popular programme was undoubtedly 'All'Osteria del Buonumore' (At the Tavern of the Good Mood), a setting populated by histrionic caricatures from different parts of Italy – Rome, Veneto, Naples and Sicily – each one having a heavy regional accent. The osteria was the perfect place to speak freely, without fearing censorship or repercussions. The favourite target of the customers was clearly the Duce, depicted as a weak little man almost completely subdued to Hitler. The episodes always ended with a song, in rhyme, sung by the customers, sometimes with famous tunes as a backing track. Thus, as an example, on 6th September 1941, accompanied by the popular tune La bela Gigogin the patrons chanted: 'Hitler chiama Mussolin/ al Quartiere Generale/ corre il fido cagnolin/ alla voce del Padron.'[22] (Hitler calls Mussolini/ before the Headquarters/ and the loyal little dog starts rushing/ to the voice of his Owner).

A comic touch was also to be found in 'Il nostro segretario federale' (Our Federal Secretary), where a fascist harangued the 'camicie nere di Vattelapesca' (the Blackshirts of Whatever-his-name-is) and the even more famous 'Monologo dell'Omo qualunque' (Monologue of the Ordinary Man), hosted by Elio Nissim, from Florence, who gave voice to a lower-middle class Italian, with no experience in politics and hostile towards fascism mainly because he was exasperated by the bombings and the hardships caused by the war.

Besides the series described so far, there were also broadcasts created according to the circumstances, such as single war episodes, particular celebrations or adaptations of works written by antifascists. In 1941, for instance, Paolo Treves worked on a programme that reconstructed the main events in the murder of Giacomo Matteotti on its anniversary, dramatizing them.[23] Also noteworthy is the adaptation of the novel Fontamara by Ignazio Silone,[24] published in German in Switzerland in 1933 but

---

[22] *'All'Osteria del Buonumore'*, 6th September 1941, BBC, WAC, *Italian Service* Scripts (henceforth ISS), 1st August – 27th September.

[23] See *Il delitto Matteotti*, April 1941, Fondazione di Studi Storici Filippo Turati, Florence, Fondo Paolo Treves, (henceforth FT, FPT), Radiotrasmissioni, b. 12.

[24] The five episodes were broadcasted between July and August 1941. See BBC, WAC, ISS, 1st August – 27th September.

censored in Italy: the painful experiences of some peasants living in Marsica oppressed by the fascist violence described to the listeners the class politics of the regime, which affected the poorest classes too, projected just in words, introducing a valuable novel that had been inaccessible up to that moment to the Italian audience.

All the programmes clearly showed the main message that the voices in London wanted to be sent, which was in contrast to the official propaganda of the regime: fascism was neither independent nor had a significant political and cultural structure.

The debunking attempt of the BBC was in line with the directives of the Foreign Office and the PWE, which were given to the broadcaster every week and suggested the topics to highlight in the programme schedule. Alongside the weekly guidelines, related to particular moments of the war, there were the Standing Directives, which were a summa of instructions for the broadcasts addressed to the Italian audience.

From 1940, one of them stressed the importance of insisting on the difference between fascism and the Italian population, stating that: 'Majority of Italians are anti-Fascist. Propaganda should be therefore more anti-Fascist than anti-Italians'.[25] This continued to be a vital thought, which was later revived by the PWE throughout the war and accurately followed by the BBC. The broadcasts, indeed, did not feature direct attacks against Italian people and the only critics towards them came from the Bacher, the German character of 'Axis Conversation', thus bearing witness to the poor loyalty of the Nazi ally. The British propaganda did not hesitate to ridicule Mussolini and the Fascist Party officials as much as they could, blaming them as the only ones responsible for the ruinous war in which the country was engaged. Indeed, the Duce was the favourite target of all the programmes of Radio Londra, mocked in the songs of Osteria del Buonumore due to his submission to Hitler, and accused of murders and cruelty in the most serious ones.

In 1941, the PWE, noticing that there was still consensus towards the Italian leader, suggested avoiding attacks that would appear as too vulgar and focusing more on his collaborators, who were easier to debunk in the eyes of the public.[26] In reality, it did not change the aim of the propaganda that much, which continued to be against Mussolini, focused on depicting the dictator as a 'Quisling', a collaborationist without his own identity completely subdued to the German power.

At the same time, the directives suggested to foster the hostility towards Nazism, urging listeners not to trust the alleged ally, praising instead the superiority of the British civilization, which was more effective both in war and politics.[27]

---

[25] Directives on British propaganda to Italy, 20th September 1940, The National Archives, London, Foreign Office (henceforth NA, FO), 898/161. In May 1942, it was also specified that: "*Our attitude to the Fascist regime is one of unqualified dislike and contempt, but our attitude to Italians as a whole is one of sympathy and regret for the blend of folly and misfortune which brought them where they are*". See Directives on British propaganda to Italy, May 1942, NA, FO 898/163.

[26] Directives on British propaganda to Italy, 15th July 1941, NA, FO 898/162.

[27] About *Radio Londra* and its making of the myth of the 'bad German man' opposed to the 'good Italian man' see Focardi 2013: 3–11.

The PWE also suggested avoiding invectives towards the institutions, with which the British establishment wanted to preserve a dialogue: the King and his family, the Catholic Church and the Army. Such suggestions were generally followed by the BBC and, indeed, the monarchy, as well as the fact that the Church is almost absent from the programmes. This is an interesting factor to consider, as it shows the general adaptation of the broadcaster to the personal directives proposed by the Foreign Office, which were sometimes in contrast to the ideas of several Italian members of staff, who aimed to discredit all the accomplices in the rise of fascism. [28]

Finally, the PWE recommended the BBC not to indulge in too many specific promises or hypotheses about the future of Italy, particularly after the armistice, since the issue was still complex and the historical phase quite delicate.

The analysis of the broadcasts following the fall of fascism provides significant insights also into the way Italian people were depicted. Up until that moment, in line with the above-mentioned directions by the PWE, all the main characters of the dramas and talks were not, all things considered, committed fascists. Think about Mr. Rossi in 'Sottovoce', who was superficially charmed by the promises of the propaganda, or the young employee of the Ministry of Popular Culture in 'Politica in Pantofole', who often acknowledged, exhausted, the fake news spread by the propaganda. What stood out was that just a few people adhered to the dictates of fascism and that therefore no one could have been thought of having full responsibility for the crimes committed.

The first attempts to tackle the issue of consensus in a more critical way, though without taking a hard or accusatory line, are to be found in the programme 'Lettere a un italiano' (Letters to an Italian) by Paolo Treves, broadcasted the day following 25th July 1943.

In each episode, the speaker read a letter addressed to two fictional recipients. The first, Carlo, was a young and educated man in his twenties/thirties, the embodiment of the 'Littorio generation'. Carlo joined fascism motivated by a firm belief:

> Dear Carlo, you are not one of those people pretending having forgotten their badge at home. However, I also know that nowadays that is not such a safe symbol anymore. [...] Not too long ago, you trustingly believed in the party, in the value of the party as keeper and guard of the Revolution. [29]

Once the failure of the fascist project was acknowledged, young people had to openly face the crossroads they were at, with a chance, even for those who had believed in the

[28] See the review by Paolo Treves about the responsibilities of the monarchy, the Church and the Army, which appeared in the newspaper 'The Left News' in 1941, now published in Fiorani 2017: 71–76. The topics of the article were later tackled in Treves 1942: 105–119.

[29] *Letter to an Italian*, 19th August 1943, FT, FPT, Radio broadcasts, b. 12. Copies of the typescripts are also present in the BBC, WAC, ISS, 1st June – 30th August 1943 e BBC, WAC, ISS, 1st September – 31st January 1943.

regime and identified themselves with it, to redeem themselves, and to take part in the democratic restoration of the nation.

The latter addressee was generically called 'the lawyer': member of the liberal pre-fascist ruling class, he came to terms with the regime, describing it as the 'lesser evil' of the country, was now praising the government led by Badoglio, which, however, the British propaganda pointed towards as another form of dictatorship.

Treves openly accused those who did not want to oppose fascism, probably due to the fear of a possible Bolshevik threat:

> Dear lawyer, you are a bit scared of Italian people. [...] Back in 1922, you and the other so-called conformists had already lost yourselves and the country for the fear of the population and therefore you have associated yourselves with its enemies, historically failing your mission. Today, I am writing you just to report the problem [...] for the sake of Italy, what happened in 1922 shall not be repeated. [30]

It is probably one of the most interesting interpretations in the programmes of this period, in which the frequency of the 'Omo Qualunque' column increased, which depicted the average Italian man, who now was keeping his distance from fascism, eager for the quietness of life before the war.

27.5. *Radio Londra, an experience of democracy*

Gianni Isola defined Radio Londra as a 'myth' of unified Italy (Isola 1996: 479–486), a phenomenon able to deeply mark the social national tissue. Its programmes were interested in and engaged nationwide with different social classes. Tuning in to the BBC spread like wildfire during the war, turning from an occasional episode into a regular appointment, a daily challenge to the sanctions imposed by the regime. Even though 'the clandestine listening was not always a sign of a consistent anti-Fascism, but rather of the raising impatience towards the war and the dictatorship that spread over the Country' (Isola 1996: 482); however, there were fully aware and organized forms of participation with the phenomenon.

At the beginning of their job at the Italian Service, the radio, for many exiles, was almost a completely unknown tool, if compared to the press, with which most of them were more familiar. The collaboration with the BBC developed their skills in that field, making them fully aware of its great potential.

Working with the prestigious broadcaster offered them a further chance to settle in the British society, helping them to feel less as strangers and lonely, which were common feelings among the exiles.

---

[30] *Letter to an Italian*, 9th August 1943, FT, FPT, Radio broadcasts, b. 12.

Those against fascism also saw the radio as an effective means of propaganda, which allowed them to reach a much wider audience when compared to readers of foreign press or antifascist leaflets. In Italy, the development and the spreading of the radio coincided with the beginning of fascism and, therefore, the contents and the style of the broadcast had to be in line with its precepts, thus making it a 'single disc-gramophone', to the detriment of its natural pluralism. [31] The model of Radio Londra led to a higher awareness of having to give back the radio medium its original dignity once restoring democracy in Italy, making it a concrete symbol of freedom and defence of civil rights.

Bibliography

Bernabei, A. (1997) *Esuli ed emigrati italiani nel Regno Unito 1920-1940*, Milan: Mursia.

Bernabei, A. (2000) 'The Interment of Italians in Britain' in F. Iacovetta, R. Perin and A. Prencipe (eds.) *Enemies Within. Italian and Other Internees in Canada and Abroad*, Toronto: University of Toronto Press, 256–279.

Boyde, P. (1990) 'Uberto Limentani', *Italian Studies*, 45: 1–5.

Briggs, A. (1970) *The History of Broadcasting in The United Kingdom*, vol. 3. The War Of Words, Oxford: Oxford University Press.

Brunazzi, M. (ed.) (1981) *Umberto Calosso antifascista e socialista. Atti del convegno storico commemorative di Asti 13-14 Ottobre 1979*, Venezia: Marsilio.

Cavaglion, A. (2006) 'Prefazione' in P. Treves (author), A. Cavaglion and S. Gerbi (eds.) *Scritti novecenteschi*, Bologna: Il Mulino, VII–XXIII.

Cavallari, G. (1973) 'Calosso Umberto' in *Dizionario Biografico degli Italiani*, vol. 16, ad vocem.

Cesarano, D. and Kushner, F. (1993) *The Internment of Aliens in Twentieth Century Britain*, London: Frank Cass.

Fiorani, F. (2017) *"In un paese schiavo con sensi liberi". Antologia degli scritti di Paolo Treves*, Milan: Biblion.

Focardi, F. (2013) *Il cattivo tedesco e il bravo italiano. La rimozione delle colpe della seconda guerra mondiale*, Bari: Laterza.

Forno, M. (2013) 'Orlando Ruggero' in *Dizionario Biografico degli Italiani*, vol. 79, ad vocem.

Isola, G. (1996) 'Radio Londra' in M. Isnenghi (ed.) *I luoghi della memoria. Simboli e miti dell'Italia unita*, Rom-Bari: Laterza.

Lo Biundo, E. (2014) *London Calling Italy. La propaganda italiana di Radio Londra nel 1943*, Milan: Unicopli.

Oddati, N. (1980) *Carlo Petrone. Un cattolico in esilio. 1939-1944*, Rome: Edizioni Cinque Lune.

Pertici, R. (1999) *Storici italiani del Novecento. III Storiografia*, Pisa-Rome: Istituti Editoriali e Poligrafici Internazionali New Line.

[31] The expression is used by Paolo Treves in one of his thoughts about broadcasting communication in the post-war era. See Treves 1948, now in Fiorani 2017: 163–167.

Piccialuti Caprioli, M. (1976) *Radio Londra 1940-1945. Inventario delle trasmissioni per l'Italia, vol. 1–2*, Rome: Ministry of Cultural and Environmental Heritage.
Pizzaroso Quinteiro, A. (1989) *Stampa. Radio, propaganda degli Alleati in Italia 1943–1946*, Milan: FrancoAngeli.
Pronay, N. and Taylor, P.M. (1984) '"An Improper Use of Broadcasting…". The British Government and Clandestine Radio Propaganda Operations in Germany during the Munich Crisis and after', *Journal of Contemporary History*, 19(3): 357–384.
Sponza, L. (2000) *Divided Loyalties. Italians in Great Britain during the Second World War*, New York: Peter Lang.
Treves, P. (1942) *Italy. Yesterday, Today, Tomorrow*, London: Gollancz.
Treves, P. (1945) *Sul fronte e dietro il fronte italiano*, Rome: Sandron.
Treves, P. (1948) 'La radio in democrazia', *Idea*: 657–659.
Treves, P. (1996) *Quello che ci ha fatto Mussolini*, Manduria: Lacaita.

Chapter 28

The great migration game

Who wins and who loses?

Flavio Antonio Ceravolo

Despite having assumed new and ever-changing meanings, human migration is an ancient phenomenon which has characterized the unfolding of human history. Yet, today, a debate has been ignited about the worldwide displacement of people, assuming serious tones both in public and institutional sectors. What are the reasons for such passion, such fear? Do the data support the protective measures that some governments have launched? Who bears the social costs of migration? Who, conversely, benefits from the state of alarm that is created? These and many other questions should motivate our critical spirit to pursue a better understanding of a complex and multi-faceted phenomenon. One must address both the requests of the migrants themselves and also the concerns that, more or less fairly and rationally, assail the citizens of host countries. Furthermore, it seems legitimate to ask what happens in the countries that see so many of their citizens leave to seek their fortune abroad. These citizens are often the most promising potential human resource. Indeed, we could say that truly the best talents have the scarcest probability of returning to the country of origin because they have many opportunities to well establish themselves in the host country. Migration thus assumes a powerful role in the redistribution of opportunities for development and growth across different countries. One can, in fact, come to believe that migration is a process of reproducing inequality across the central and peripheral countries.

28.1. *Introduction*

Every day we read articles that recount stories about migration. Some have become, all things considered, mundane and do not shock us, others explore a new aspect of the phenomenon which we hadn't considered. Moreover, all of the stories can be seen and recounted from different angles and perspectives. The unquestionable value of this volume is exactly in its unorthodox push towards multidisciplinarity that obliges the reader to engage in the beneficial exercise of learning languages and analytical models that pertain to (almost) all fields of human knowledge. This approach is the result of a long mediation project among scientists who have accepted the challenge of working together to reassemble an elaborate puzzle. It is not my task to ensure the experiment succeeds, it will be the reader who evaluates that, but I am certain the undertaking is utterly worthy and provides the reader with many tools for original interpretations of the migration phenomenon. After the comparison with the contributors of this volume many questions remain unanswered. Questions that perhaps readers had not before posed to themselves. I have been studying human migration for many years, but reading the work of many colleagues who participated in this common initiative has been an extraordinary adventure of critical awareness and education for me, and has raised new questions I had never considered.

Moreover, it presents a rather original challenge. Specialist literature on migration is often not very osmotic and only recently have disciplinary fences been lowered enough to allow the exchange of knowledge. This is evident within the domain which is traditionally labelled as human and social sciences. Up until fairly recently, compared to similar phenomena, there was a coexistence of not only different linguistic labels in different disciplines, but also conflicting theoretical traditions that were often not in dialogue with each other. Only in the last decade the debate has opened up to a more systematic transdisciplinarity. The hard sciences, however, have entered this debate which has recently become much wider. This volume, by explicit choice of the authors, was created with the intention of overcoming these fences and is the result of the common tension caused by reflection and confrontation with oneself. It is therefore about a process that adds further complexity because it multiplies the points of view.

For exactly this reason, summarizing this volume is very difficult. What have we learnt from reading synopses of legal, sociological and political analyses, that we have not gained from discoveries about the genetic roots of our biodiversity? It seems to me that one can say we have learnt not to confuse the complexity of the migration phenomenon itself with the complexity of the effects that the migration phenomenon triggers in the global human society. Furthermore, we have learnt to distinguish the different causes that trigger the phenomenon of migration and to read them in contrast with the more general trends that characterize this period of human history to which all of us are direct witnesses.

The working hypothesis with which I would like to conclude this collective work is that it is necessary to shift part of our reflection from migrants to those who are not migrants, but are involved with migration for many reasons. In particular, I would like to propose taking up Collier's (2013) suggestion and reflecting on migration, detouring from the beaten tracks, in order to venture into discussing socio-political trends on an eminently macrostructural level. For this reason, I will concentrate on three aspects in particular: the consequences for the societies of departure, the social and economic consequences for the host societies, and finally the errors (more or less voluntary) in government politics implemented in Western countries with respect to the question of migration.

28.2. *The consequences for the societies of departure*

First we must clarify, if there were still the need, that migration can have very different causes. A huge array of personal motivations is usually hiding behind the customary labels of economic migration or forced migration. These motivations are related to the social, economic and political conditions of the migrant's country of departure. Every simplification – as clarified several times in the numerous contributions to this volume – is a rather intense exercise in reduction of the complexity, even if it is necessary. Some aspects are nevertheless truly unifying. For example, the motive that pushes an individual to set out on a migratory journey, takes the shape of a potential loss of human capital for the country of origin (Collier 2013).

Much has been written and said on the concept of human capital, I will not in any way refer to the debate on this topic here; I limit myself to considering the concept in terms functional to my argument. It is therefore enough to define the human capital of an individual rather uncouthly in terms of a sum of competencies and capacities that may translate into advantages for oneself or for the community in which one lives (Foray 2016). In this sense, we could conclude that every time a person decides (or is compelled) to leave their own country of origin, the consequence is a loss in terms of a reduction in the sum of human capital resources that will affect many different aspects of life in that country (Batista and Vicente 2011).

According to economic literature on development, the data have shown with a certain clarity that human capital is, still today, in the era of automation and robotization. This is an essential factor for economic growth and social development. It therefore seems rather automatic to close the argument maintaining that migration is nevertheless clear impoverishment for the country of origin in terms of potential for development (Collier 2013). In reality, the process is more complex than it may seem, for at least two reasons.

First, indeed, we may observe that migratory plans might not be permanent and could acknowledge a possibility of a return in time. At least in terms of a principle, we must accept the possibility that some migrants acquire resources during part of their life that then they transfer to the country of origin on their return. Furthermore, it is not unusual that migrants (above all economic migrants), once settled in the host country, share a part of their income with people in the country of origin, giving rise to the phenomenon of so-called "remittances" (Ambrosini 2011). Some authors in the literature have clarified that there are also non-financial "remittances" that are potentially as useful for the country of origin. Migrants, indeed, form a network of potential contacts that can be utilized in a developed country and that could presumably benefit economic entities in the host country. In short, on the one hand, the country of departure would lose human capital and, on the other, it would gain indirect income and useful contacts in countries with developed economies. The overall result could even be positive. Usually, however, the data recount very different stories.

The depletion of human resources for countries of origin almost always affects the indirect advantages connected to migratory fluxes. There are at least three reasons for this impoverishment, following Collier's argument. The first reason, as it is or should be known, is that it is the individuals with the most talents and abilities who migrate – above all in the case of economic migration, but also often in the case of forced migration (Zanfrini 2007). However, it is certainly the individuals with the highest personal human capital who have the best opportunities for settling in the host country and as a consequence are the least inclined to return to their homeland (Ambrosini 2011). In other words, we could say that the human resource depletion is more severe because it is the individuals who have a greater strategic value for economic development that leave their country of origin and this can only bring about a reduction in the capacity for internal production of value and wealth. This process gives shape to genuine processes of talent brain drain that intensify and reproduce disparities between core and surrounding countries. Reconsidering brain drain as a systemic phenomenon that not only assails scientists and the best brains, but also the human capital of the middle class, is also useful to highlight the pervasiveness of these phenomena by provoking further inequalities between countries of origin and host countries (Beltrame 2008). What one loses, another gains, but it is not a matter of exchange between those involved. The fluxes always originate from the same area and precisely due to the effect of the inequalities that these fluxes trigger, this movement is further reinforced.

The second effect is connected more generally with the relational aspects this impoverishment produces. A depletion of human resources is also, for obvious reasons, an impoverishment of the very fabric of society in terms of a relational network (Collier 2013). Each migrant represents a network node that is missing in the society of origin. To express this idea in a rather concise manner, we can maintain that a reduction of the total social capital of a given local society always corresponds to a reduction of the aggregate amount of human capital. On one hand, as we have already mentioned and as many authors in specialist literature demonstrate (see the excellent revision by Ambrosini 2011), it is true that migrants can represent a relational bridge between the society of origin and the host society and that this can have positive effects for the social and economic development of the country of departure. In the same way, it is indisputable that the absence of someone who was first present in a social context creates that which Burt defines as a structural hole, that is, an absent node in the relational network. This reduced relational quality can have numerous effects, but once again for reasons of economy of thought, we will concentrate on those of a socio-political nature. Reduced relational density decreases the probability of idea pluralism and therefore weakens the public debate of a country. If the individuals with the highest human capital who can play an opinion leading role are missing, the level of deprivation becomes more grave.

The third aspect of the matter refers to a question that is discussed less in mainstream literature, but from my point of view, is not less important. One often worries about the fact that migrants bring their own cultures to the host societies and that this creates possible problems of integration. Indeed, as Portes and Rumbaut (2011) maintain in their theory on segmented assimilation, migrants can create authentic cultural identities resistant to integration. An important part of literature, on the other hand, refers to the idea that cultural hybridization is a natural tendency for general human development in our globalized society, which is difficult to dispute (Massey 1998). Migratory processes can, therefore, give rise to crossbred, ambivalent identities, or oppositional radicalized identities. But what happens to the original country's cultural identity? Is he who remains capable of defending their cultural heritage and of establishing constructive relational dynamics with the increasingly aggressive demands of globalization, or is there a risk of falling back into a colonizing hybridization that ends up only depleting the cultural biodiversity of our planet?

Finally, we could push ourselves to maintain that the countries of origin run the risk of putting a process of multidimensional impoverishment to the test. This process triggers spirals of further marginalization, ultimately further tearing apart countries that constitute the world's centre of balance and countries condemned to find themselves in the increasingly economically, socially and culturally distant periphery (Collier 2013). These dynamics, if not controlled, could cause deflagration processes, fed over time by the feeling of exclusion and inequality which, with all probability, are largely responsible for the increase in violent events which have occurred in recent years.

In this way, there are many processes for possible development models which could be employed on an international level. In particular, for some time the specialist scientific community has contemplated the politics of international cooperation. It has been brilliantly highlighted that project structures need to overcome the typical philanthropic attitude that has permeated a whole season of humanitarian aid and move decisively towards the idea of a respectful integrated development of the role that local decision-makers and beneficiaries should have when establishing intervention priorities and determining their development plan (Collier 2013). Among the most virtuous of examples in this sense have been provided by decentralized cooperation projects that have been implemented in local community networks in Western countries with emerging countries' communities. These projects have encouraging results in the construction of channels to exchange resources, knowledge and above all in the promotion of a culture of mutual recognition. We could push ourselves to say that, in principle, this type of approach truly constitutes a knowledge, culture and human capital circulation model – beyond the circulation of goods and services – towards which one could move, with greater conviction, creating integrated development and not developed centres and marginal peripheries.

28.3. *Effects on host countries*

If, until now, we have maintained that the loss of human capital for the countries of origin constitutes an impoverishment, it is logical now to maintain that the arrival of new human resources must be considered an enrichment for the host countries. Therefore, in the beginning, the countries that welcome migrants should primarily reap the benefits from this process. Immigrants are then largely a desirable resource (Benhabib 2006). The news in the papers, however, seems to follow a completely different narrative which tends to emphasize the explosive social role of migratory processes. It clearly highlights, and accentuates each negative event, mostly those which provoke clamour and controversy in public opinion. It seems to demonstrate on a daily basis that the reality that we observe and experience every day has little in common with the theories of the advantages from effective immigrant integration, which instead constitutes a long reflection on vague and do-good ideals (Pogliano 2014). What are the social and economic reasons that make immigrants problematic? Who should be most afraid of the immigrants and why? Does someone have interests in fuelling this narrative? In order to respond to these questions, we begin from the opposing thought: immigrants can be a competitive resource.

Despite that which we can think from reading newspapers, migration, perhaps more evidently in some European countries, is truly a resource. The data, from multiple independent sources, demonstrate that immigrants significantly and systematically contribute to the growth of the gross domestic product of host countries more than they economically cost. Above all for some Western countries, their contribution to the creation of wealth is crucial and the economic system of these countries require this army of human capital (Collier 2013). It is no longer unusual to hear about entrepreneurs calling on governments to be careful in limiting the amount of immigrants, using scaremongering tactics about delocalized production caused by the lack of the necessary (cheap) workforce required to keep production in their country. Even in our country, despite the rising anti-immigration tensions, we must recognize that, for some sectors of the economy and in other areas, the contribution that these immigrants offer in terms of workforce is undeniable (Fullin 2011).

Once again, however, as we can see, the issue is very complicated. Immigrants are useful because they are ready to offer themselves to cover – regardless of their starting qualifications – the least desirable sectors of the employment market. Numerous studies have demonstrated (for a critical discussion on the topic see Fullin 2011; Pastore et al. 2013) that there is a higher concentration of immigrants in the least secure, lowest paid and most dangerous sectors of the employment markets throughout Europe, including Italy. Furthermore, immigrants are considerably more exposed to the phenomenon of over-education, often giving up on finding an occupation consistent with their educational qualifications (Dell'Aringa and Pagani 2011). Moreover, such educational credentials are often not even recognized in the host countries so the legal system itself ends up fuelling situations of status inconsistency. Consequently, it is impossible to access an occupation in line with the actual educational and human capital they possess.

Immigrants are therefore useful, but are they also dangerous competitors? For whom? Certainly not for those entrepreneurs who require an available workforce to offer itself at a lower cost. They are not even dangerous competitors for those who practice liberal professions because the access to these professions is controlled by formalized recognition mechanisms (often managed by the same professional bodies). They are dangerous competitors for those who populate the most exposed sectors in our employment market: self-employed workers in the first instance and employed manual labourers in the second. Immigrants are dangerous competitors in these professional spheres; they contribute to the decline in wages and therefore make it more difficult to obtain an acceptable income. In times of economic crisis, like those we have experienced in recent years, this dynamic becomes even more critical and inevitably causes a cycle of tension that leads to an escalation of social tension.

Social tension that is further fuelled by the state of exclusion that characterizes the immigrants' situation. They are always suspended between precarious substantive citizenship rights and barely recognized legal rights, and an effective participation in constructing social and economic balances within the host country's society. Social tension that becomes, for natives, feelings of generalized fear, stigmatization, labelling, xenophobia and, ultimately, fertile terrain for fundamentalism on the one hand and for populism on the other. Social tension that, for immigrants, becomes anger and frustration due to the lack of recognition of their citizenship rights. From here, fake news only raises narratives about migration as a problem, and tends to depict all immigrants in the same way: dangerous (Pogliano 2014). These narratives have succeeded because they span the individual fears of a large part of the native population, which is more exposed to precarious living conditions and less capable of looking at the phenomenon with a critical eye. These very narratives, then, fuel the feeling of exclusion experienced by the same immigrants, never truly Italian even when they are born in our country. Furthermore, there are no counter-narratives that emphasize the other aspects of the phenomenon, the positive ones, the stories of integration. In any case, these have less media success because they do not benefit from the wave of sensationalism, they are stories of ordinary lives and for this reason are less interesting. Recounting migration through these rather partial lenses cannot help having political effects.

The eruption of migratory dynamics, indeed, has constituted a logical supposition for a genuine political revolution that has involved most Western countries. Today, we are witnessing the continual erosion of the traditionally progressive electoral base and support of the least privileged classes shifting towards populist and conservative political groups. The mainstay of a significant portion of the political policies of these groups is made up of generalized social fears linked to migration. Fuelling the tension, even with alarmist mechanisms based on fake news (or at least debatable interpretations of the data) has become an effective model of political communication for stimulating widespread agreement. From this comes the promise (that is unfortunately increasingly carried out) to construct walls, set up barbed-wire fences and implement emergency policies to deal with arrivals. Initiatives that appear rather debatable from an ethical point of view. Lined up on the distinctly opposite side of this political role reversal are many big entrepreneurs, requesting greater rationality in the regulation of fluxes of arrivals, in order to secure a workforce as well as new talent pools. Major high-tech entrepreneurs were among the most bitter opponents of the anti-immigration movement desired by former President Trump in the United States. They traditionally absorb the best international talent in the most advanced technological sectors, causing extremely significant fluxes of brain drain in the least developed countries.

The social representation of the tension linked to migratory pressure is rather varied in public discourse within host countries, especially in Europe. Furthermore, some countries have been able to enjoy a strategic position which is less exposed to the direct arrival of large fluxes of economic migration and, more importantly, have been less permeated by large arrivals of forced migration experienced by other countries on the frontline. As some of the evidence in this text has shown, the border between the Mediterranean and the Balkan Routes have exposed Italy, for example, to an onerous process of initial reception (Dal Zotto 2014). Our country was, like the rest of Europe, completely unprepared to accomplish this task, but – despite the rather on-the-fence position of the EU – knew to quickly implement management policies that have had substantial success. However, these management policies must not be considered in terms of a governance model for the phenomenon of migration, but as a government's response to an emergency situation that is fundamentally still unresolved. In fact, we could maintain that following some in-depth analyses performed on the basis of a vast amount of empirical data (for example, see Dal Zotto 2014), that prolonging the absence of systematic policies produces a persisting emergency framework that authorizes governance with special measures that would probably not be in any way politically justified in a non-emergency situation and so would not be able to be upheld (Collier, 2013).

28.4. *Managing the phenomenon of migration: errors and omissions*

Fundamentally, Western countries' policies regarding migration are still prisoners to a misunderstanding that needs to be resolved. Governing the migration phenomenon and managing the emergency of migratory fluxes are two completely different things. Government policies on the phenomenon are by definition long-term policies that should aim to intervene in the causes of the migration phenomena. They should establish a difference between the phenomena of the people movement – which are in some ways desirable from the point of view of globalizing the right to planetary citizenship – and the phenomena of forced one-way displacement from the global peripheries to the major centres of economic aggregation that can conversely cause chronic tension. The emergency management policies are, by definition, reactive measures and so should be characterized by their temporary and exceptional nature. This difference is rather expected and I have certainly adopted, once again, a rather extreme simplification, but the public debate about migration often seems to systematically confuse these two ideas.

On the basis of substantial semantic overlapping of these two public policy ideas, there has been a historical evolution of public representation of the issue of migration. Since when did migration become a pressing topic of public debate? Once again it seems to me to be useful to gather the information with which Collier concludes his book on the subject. As I have maintained above, Western countries, above all those that found themselves in a position of greater exposure, have been caught more or less unawares of the explosion of consistent fluxes as a result of epochal changes of the socio-political structures in a significant part of the global peripheries. The processes of economic and financial globalization have in fact already accelerated dynamics that were primed by the growing situation of inequality between developed and developing countries (Collier 2013). Over time, the increasingly frequent political instabilities resolved by armed conflicts and the following humanitarian diasporas are added to these processes. In short, over the last two decades, there has been an ever-increasing number of people crowded at the borders of Western countries who bring with them a need for reception and integration. Rather similar phenomena – even if in peculiar moments and ways – have even involved the entire American continent, but let us focus our attention for the time being on Europe.

The response of Western governments and, in particular, European governments, has been fragmented and rash in what has been defined in the literature as an emergency framework. The exceptional cases continue to provide occasions for the construction of tools contingent on regulation that eventually assume stability through statutes. At the same time, the public representation of the emergency lends itself to exploitation that impedes the development of a long-term political debate (Dal Zotto 2014). Everything is becoming an emergency and there is no more space to reflect on the historic changes that are being addressed. The emergency response produces cyclical policies that fuel new emergencies and end up absorbing all the available resources instead of using medium-term policies to avoid contingent traumatic situations.

Western countries, and particularly European countries, have fallen into the trap of continual emergency and have confronted the phenomenon of migration in a completely unseemly manner. It is devoid of a common line of action resulting from political reflection that pays close attention to the consequences that are being triggered on a global level. In other words, the weight of the phenomenon that has interested the whole European continent was, for a long time, left to the political good will of some countries, those that are the most exposed. Still today, faced with an increasingly animated debate within the EU, the policies of migrant reception and integration are still disappointing (see the contributions from Confalonieri in this volume). Italy, in this convulsive context, has understood how to produce significant new measures, designing a veritable cutting-edge reception system over time. The development of integration policies, that are insufficient and still vague, has not been as efficient (Dal Zotto 2014).

On the other hand, by re-employing the distinction first proposed between the two levels of governance, it seems reasonable to place reception within the confines of emergency policies. The additional processes require long-term reflection that cannot exclude a more articulated evaluation of the economic, political and social effects that migration, in all its forms, can produce on the host society. A reflection that cannot belong to only one country, in spite of what happens in neighbouring countries, otherwise one is condemned to experience further circumstances of inequality. Economically powerful countries end up attracting and integrating more qualified human capital, acquiring a strategic advantage to the detriment of their neighbours who find themselves having to integrate a workforce less capable of maintaining internal competition. In short, once again, what one loses, another gains, even between European countries. On this front, based on the recognition of this unequal game between member countries, important anti-Europeanist arguments are founded, which have permeated the evolution of the political setting in which we live.

Finally, one can reasonably maintain that an international community that is fundamentally incapable of negotiating shared solutions and a Europe operating at too many different speeds impedes the planning of regulatory solutions that avoid the emergency level and instead offer solutions of a systematic nature. However, it is the very absence of systematic solutions that fuels the divisive tensions both on an international and intranational level. Emergency provokes social tension, that in turn provokes reactive dynamics that escalate the tension and make the emergency situation more serious. In this way an inflationary spiral of emergency is triggered, potentially producing catastrophic consequences in both economic and international security terms (Collier 2013).

28.5. *The great game and its consequences*

How do we overcome this impasse? Very realistically, still following Collier's analyses, as well as others' (Heckmann 2005), the path to follow is complex and passes through a gradual introduction of countercyclical management measures for migration into the political agenda. In other words, defusing the many timebombs caused by the emergency is not an operation that can be suddenly achieved. We cannot imagine taking away more resources than necessary from emergency management processes and in the same sense, it is reasonable that Western governments should dedicate some of their attention to policies that guarantee internal security. At the same time, we need to start working at an inter- and intranational level to construct a framework of systematic governance of the migration phenomenon, planning policies that intervene in possible causes of chronic conditions and encourage the evolution of the conditions of people's natural movement all over the world. It is a very ambitious objective that seems unrealistic today, but with all probability just by going in this direction – at least aiming in this direction – those destructive tendencies that we see continuously growing around us can be averted.

Choosing this process of activating systematic migration governance policies could seem, in the first instance, the fairest choice in terms of equity, but this is not the motive that should move the institutions of national and international management to decisively turn down this road. The apparent unsustainability of the emergency framework over time should convince the institutions of the need to implement this type of policy. The walls and barbed-wire fence policy requires constant surveillance and in the long term there is no barrier that resists the pressures of history. Some ethical principles are important not so much because they are fair, but because there are inevitable consequences that are produced if they are ignored. Even cartoon characters teach our children that with great power comes great responsibility. Let us hope that those who hold great political and economic power in their hands remember this.

Bibliography

Ambrosini, M. (2011) *Sociologia delle migrazioni*, Bologna: Il Mulino.

Batista, C. and Vicente, P.C. (2011) 'Do migrants improve governance at home? Evidence from a voting experiment', *The World Bank Economic Review*, 25(1): 77–104.

Beltrame, L. (2008) 'Globalizzazione e fuga dei cervelli', *Rassegna Italiana di Sociologia*, 49(2): 277–295.

Benhabib, S. (2006) *I diritti degli altri. Stranieri, residenti, cittadini*, Turin: Cortina.

Castles, S. (2004) 'The factors that make and unmake migration policies', *International Migration Review*, 8(3): 852–884.

Collier, P. (2013) *Exodus. How Migration is Changing Our World*, Oxford: Oxford University Press.

Dal Zotto, E. (2014) 'Frame dell'emergenza e migrazioni forzate. Il caso dell''Emergenza Nord Africa', in P. Musaro and P. Parmiggiani (eds.) *Media e migrazioni. Etica, estetica e politica del discorso umanitario*, Milan: FrancoAngeli.

Dell'Aringa, C. and Pagani, L. (2011) 'Labour market assimilation and over-education: The case of immigrant workers in Italy', *Economia Politica*, 28(2): 219–240.

Foray, D. (2016) *L'economia della conoscenza*, Bologna: Il Mulino.

Fullin, G. (2011) 'Tra disoccupazione e declassamento professionale. La condizione degli stranieri nel mercato del lavoro italiano', *Mondi Migranti*, 1.

Heckmann, F. (2005) *Integration and Integration Policies: IMISCOE Network Feasibility Study*, Bamberg: European Forum for Migration Studies.

Massey, D.S. (1998) *Worlds in Motion. Understanding International Migration at the End of the Millennium*, Oxford: Clarendon Press.

Pastore, F., Salis, E., Villosio, C. (2013) 'L'Italia e l'immigrazione low cost: fine di un ciclo', *Mondi Migranti*, 1.

Pogliano, A. (2014) 'Immigrazione, media, opinione pubblica: crisi dell'umanitario?' in P. Musaro, P. Parmiggiani (eds.) *Media e migrazioni. Etica, estetica e politica del discorso umanitario*, Milano: Franco Angeli.

Portes, A. and Rumbaut, R.G. (2011) 'Immigration, diversity and social capital', presented at the Norface Conference, University College, London.

Zanfrini, L. (2007) *Cittadinanze. Appartenenze e diritti nella società dell'immigrazione*, Rome-Bari: Laterza.

Index

A

H

I

N

O

P

Q

R

S

V

W

Contributors

Editor

Anna Rita Calabrò is Associate Professor at the University of Pavia, where she teaches Sociology and Sociology of Migrations. She is Director of the Inter-Department Centre for Gender Studies of the University of Pavia, manager of the Strategic University Theme 'Migrat.In.G.' and coordinator of the Master course in Immigration, Gender, Family Models and Integration Strategies. Her research activities focused on many different realities: youth gangs, detained minors, Roma people. Her theoretical reflection is mainly about three themes: time, identity, ambivalence. Her most recent research activities include studies on the role of women in the political and institutional arena, and on the gender disequalities in local administrations.

Contributing authors

Francesca Acerbi is Medical Doctor specializing in Psychiatry at University of Pavia; she actively participates in researching and clinical activities of Department of Brain and Behavioral Sciences, section of Eating Disorders and laboratory of Psychiatry, Culture and Environment.

Alessandro Achilli is Associate Professor of Genetics at the University of Pavia and Visiting Scientist at the University of Huddersfield. Author and co-author of 93 articles in international ISI journals, he analyzes the DNA sequence variation for defining origins, evolution and migrations of human (and animal) populations. Dr. Achilli recently received the national scientific qualification of Full Professor in Genetics and in Anthropology and he is ranked among the "Top Italian Scientists".

Alessia Arossa is first-level Medical Director at the Complex Structure Obstetrics-Ginaecology at the San Matteo General Hospital in Pavia. The main research lines in her activity are: the role of ultrasound in the first trimester in short-term neonatal prognosis in high risky pregnancies; the CMV infection during pregnancy.

Zuzanna Brocka is an Italian qualified lawyer (avvocato), LL.M (EUI), Ph.D. candidate in Law in co-tutelle at the Faculty of Law and Administration of the University of Łódź in Poland and at the Faculty of Law of the University of Pavia. Brocka is author of articles in the field of European law. Her current research focuses on European integration and judicial lawmaking.

Vanna Berlincioni is a Medical Doctor, psychiatric specialist, with a Phd in Psychiatry and Relational Science. Researcher in the Department of Brain and Behavioural Science at the University of Pavia. Full Member of the Italian Psychoanalytical Society, President of the Italian Society of Medical Psychotherapy. Member of the editor´s office of Polaris – Psychoanalysis and contemporary world review.

Barbara Berri is Ph.D. in English and American Studies, and Honorary Fellow in English and American Literature, that she teaches at the University of Pavia, where she works in the Strategic Theme 'Migrat.In.G.'. Among her research interests are: the problems related to the translation and transcodification of the message; the opportunities and emergencies intrinsic to intercultural communication.

Ernesto Bettinelli has been Professor of Constitutional Law mainly at University of Pavia until 2016. During his academic career he has published scientific works on political and civil liberties, human rights, political parties, electoral systems, direct democracy, political system and constitutional organization, constitutional reforms. He held public positions of national importance. Currently, he is President of a Not Governmental Organization ("Agency n. 1 of Pavia for Ayamé") committed to support a rural community in Ivory Coast.

Cristina Campiglio is Full Professor of International Law at the University of Pavia. Her main research interests concern private international law, particularly family issues; the fundamental human rights, and more specifically the respect of private and family life; the so-called international biolaw, with particular attention to the methods of medically assisted procreation and genetics.

Fulvia Caruso is Associate Professor of Ethnomusicology in the Department of Musicology and Cultural Heritage at the University of Pavia (Cremona). She also teaches Ethnomusicology in the School for Advanced Studies for Ethno-Anthropological Heritage at Rome's "La Sapienza" University since 2012. Her fields of research are: music and migration; intangible heritage; music and ritual; oral poetry and narrative styles; and visual ethnomusicology.

Cristina Catania is Medical Doctor specializing in Psychiatry at University of Pavia; she actively participates in researching and clinical activities of Department of Brain and Behavioral Sciences, section of Eating Disorders and laboratory of Psychiatry, Culture and Environment.

Giulia Casentini obtained a Ph.D. in Anthropology, Ethnology and Cultural Studies at the University of Siena in 2011. She is Research Fellow in History of Africa at the University of Pavia since 2011. She has been conducting fields of anthropologic and archive research in Western Africa, mainly Ghana and Togo, since 2005.

Flavio Ceravolo is Researcher in Sociology at the Department of Political and Social Sciences of the University of Pavia. His research interests are: social mobiliy; the youth condition; the evaluation of public policies and local development; the regulatory mechanisms of international cooperation for development; the university system. Author of several publications, his last book is 'Cervelli in transito' (Carocci, 2017).

Maria Antonietta Confalonieri has been Associate Professor at the Department of Political and Social Sciences of the University of Pavia, where she taught European Political Organization, Analysis of Public Policies, Gender Studies. She has been Representative of the Dean for international student mobility, President of the council of the degree's course on Political Sciences and International Relations, member of the council of the Inter-Department Centre for Gender Studies. Her most recent research interests included Eurosceptic parties and the europeanization of public policies.

Giovanni Cordini is Full Professor of Compared Public Law and Environment and Territory Law at the University of Pavia, where he has been Director of the Department of Political and Social Sciences. Among his research interests are: citizenship, immigration, asylum.

Fiammetta Corradi teaches Sociology and Economics and Society at the Department of Economics and Management Sciences of the University of Pavia. Her scientific interests focus on cultural and communicative processes, with special reference to financial markets. One of her latest publications is "The Disenchantment of Bitcoin: Unveiling the Myth of a Digital Currency" (with P. Höfner, 2018).

Emanuela Dal Zotto is Research Fellow in Sociology at the Department of Political and Social Sciences of the University of Pavia, as part of the Strategic Theme of the University 'Migrat.In.G', and member of the scientific committee of the Coordinated Research Center "ESCAPES - Laboratory of Critical Studies on Forced Migration" of the University of Milan. Since 2011 she conducts research activities on migrations by sea and reception system in Italy.

Cesare Danesino is Full Professor of Medical Genetics at the Department of Molecular Medicine of the University of Pavia. He is responsible of projects on Rare Diseases as Hereditary Hemorrhagic Telangiectasia, Shwachman-Diamond Syndrome and Glycogen storage disease Type II. His clinical activity is about the diagnosis of genetically determined disorders, with a specific interest in Genetic Counselling. He acts as referee for several international Journals. He published over 200 papers on peer reviewed journals.

Federica Di Pietro specialized in International Private Law with a particular focus on migration law. She holds a Phd in "International and Criminal Justice" from the University of Pavia (Italy) and Cordoba (Spain) with a doctoral thesis on "The application of Islamic family law in France, Spain and Italy".

Edoardo Errichiello is currently Assistant Professor of Medical Genetics at the Department of Molecular Medicine, University of Pavia. His main research topics concern the use of Next gerenation sequencing (NGS) techiniques in different fields of human genetics, such as neurodevelopmental diseases, with a particular focus on prenatal inherited pathological conditions.

Silvia Favalli is a post-doc research fellow at the Department of Political and Social Sciences of the University of Pavia (Italy). She has also the professional qualification to practice as an Attorney at law (Avvocato) in Italy. Her research interests include International law, EU law, human rights law, disability law, migration and refugee law.

Francesca Fiorani is a PhD student in Contemporary History at the University of Pavia. Her research focuses on the history of political and intellectual exile in the Twentieth Century, and particularly on the figure of Paolo Treves, of whom she edited the collected work "In un paese schiavo con sensi liberi" (2017).

Luisa Frigeni is lawyer, and obtained his Ph.D in Criminal Law at the University of Pavia with a dissertation on irregular migration and criminal law. She collaborated with the Strategic Theme of University 'Migrat.In.G.'.

Valentina Fusari holds a PhD in Geopolitics (University of Pisa). She has been assistant professor at the Adi Keih College of Arts and Social Sciences (Eritrea), and currently she is adjunct professor of Population, Migration and Development at the University of Pavia. Her research interests focus on population dynamics in Eritrea, historical demography in colonial populations, hidden populations.

Katarzyna Gromek-Broc has been Associate Professor at the University of Pavia in the Department of Political and Social Sciences since 2013, after working in Europe, Asia, Australia and South America. She set up York Law Journal in 2013. Her research interests include European law, Comparative Law, Labour Law, Bioethics, and Human Rights.

Gianluca Gualdi is psychologist and psychotherapist with a systemic-relational approach, lecturer CPG "Emotional and relational aspects of development" and of the Psychology module at the Master "Immigration, Gender, Family Models and Integration Strategies" at the University of Pavia, where he is an expert in the subject in Psychology. Psychologist at minor and mother-child communities, he deals with projects in schools, teacher training and the Erasmus + ENRETE project "Promoting Resilience through teacher training".

Andrea Iurato is a Lawyer expert in Immigration Law and PhD in Public Law at the University of Pavia. In Pavia he was also post-doc researcher and contract professor of the "Migration and the Law" course, dealing with Immigration Law in Europe and Latin America.

Nehir Edibe Kurtas graduated in Molecular Biology and Genetics at the Institute of Technology of Izmir (Turkey), and is a Ph.D student in Genetics and Molecular and Cellular Biology at the Department of Molecular Medicine of the University of Pavia

Antonio M. Morone is Assistant Professor of Contemporary African History at the Department of Political and Social Sciences, Pavia University (Italy). His research interests are dealing with colonial and postcolonial society in Somalia and Libya.

Carla Olivieri is Associate Professor in Applied Biology at Department of Molecular Medicine of the University of Pavia, Italy. During her PhD in Human Pathology she became responsible for the molecular analysis in Hereditary Hemorrhagic Telangiectasia, establishing the first Italian database for the pathology and the first reference center for molecular analysis. In recent years, molecular analysis has been flanked by cellular function studies and analysis of circulating miRNAs. She has been chosen as a referee by international journals and has more than 40 publications published in peer reviewed journals.

Ugo A. Perego received a BS and a MS in Health Sciences from Brigham Young University (Utah, USA) and a PhD in Genetics and Biomolecular Sciences from the University of Pavia (Italy). He is currently the Director of the LDS Rome Institute Campus and a Visiting Scientist at the University of Pavia. He has given nearly 200 international lectures and published extensively on DNA topics related to population migrations, ancestry, forensics, and history. Dr. Perego recently received the national scientific ranking of Associate Professor in Genetics.

Carola Ricci is Associate Professor at the University of Pavia, where she teaches International Law and Human Rights and International Justice. She is member of the group of legal experts of the Committee on Civil Liberties, Justice and Home

Affairs of the European Parliament. She has participated to several Italian and international research projects, mainly on judicial cooperation in civil matters.

Arianna Arisi Rota (PhD in History of European Society) is Associate Professor of Contemporary History in the Department of Political and Social Sciences, University of Pavia, where she teaches courses of Contemporary History, 19th-20th-Century, and History of Diplomacy. Her research focuses on Long 19th-Century political mobilization and on the history of the diplomatic machinery, 18th-21st-Century.

Angelo Scotto is a PhD in Political Science; he currently collaborates with the Department of Political and Social Sciences at the University of Pavia. His research focuses on local migration policies and political participation. His last book is "Emergenza permanente" (Epoké 2017).

Elisa Signori is actually full professor of Contemporary History at University of Pavia (Department of Humanities) and since 2013 she is professor of Contemporary History at Università della Svizzera Italiana (USI) in Lugano Switzerland too. Research topics: Italian antifascist exile in France, Switzerland, USA. Fascist Italy. History of Italian University. Academic migrations and Elites' Formation in Europe. Switzerland and Italy. History of contemporary Lombardy.

Carolina Simoncini got a PhD in Italian constitutional law at the University of Pavia. At the moment, she is Attaché temporaire d'enseignement et de recherche (ATER) at Université Lyon 3 – Jean Moulin. Her research fields are the freedom of mouvement and residence of migrants in European Union and the connections between law and politics in the Italian contemporary history.

Arsenio Spinillo is Director of the Complex Structure Obstetrics-Ginaecology at the San Matteo General Hospital in Pavia. Previously, he has been Associate Professor of Obstetrics and Ginaecology at the University of Pavia. He authored more than 100 articles on indexed journals.

Salvatore Tuccari has completed his Degree in Law from Bocconi University in Milan in 2013. He has then a Postgraduate in Legal Studies from Pavia School of Law in 2015. Since 2016, he is an Instructor of Public Law at the Political Science school of Pavia. He has officially got the qualification as a lawyer since 2016.

Maria Assunta Zanetti is Associate Professor at the Department of Brain and Behavioral Sciences at the University of Pavia. She currently teaches Psychology of Language Development and Educational Psychology. Her main research interests include socio-emotional development and resilience, youth risk behaviours, language development, bullying and cyberbullying, vocational guidance, decision-making processes and early achievement and gifted children development.

Orsetta Zuffardi has been full Professor of Medical Genetics at the Department of Molecular Medicin of the University of Pavia until October 2017. She has been involved for more than 30 years in clarifing the molecular basis of fetal malformations and the following counseling. She has collaborated and still collaborates with several European Centers of Genetics in order to highlight the genetic cause for rare diseases, including those extremely rare in consanguineous people in order to provide better genotype-phenotype correlation and proper counseling to the couples.